Childbirth and Authoritative Knowledge

Childbirth and Authoritative Knowledge

Cross-Cultural Perspectives

EDITED BY

Robbie E. Davis-Floyd
Carolyn F. Sargent

WITH A FOREWORD BY

Rayna Rapp

UNIVERSITY OF CALIFORNIA PRESS

Berkeley   Los Angeles   London

University of California Press
Berkeley and Los Angeles, California

University of California Press
London, England

Several chapters have been previously published in slightly different versions:
Chap. 5 appeared in *Medical Anthropology Quarterly* 8:1, March 1994. Chaps. 3, 4, 6, 7, 12,
15, and 16 appeared in *Medical Anthropology Quarterly* 10:2, June 1996. All reprinted by
permission of the American Anthropological Association. Not for further reproduction.
Chap. 9 appeared in *Social Science and Medicine* vol. 41, no. 1, 1995, pp. 47–68. Reprinted
by permission of Elsevier Science Ltd, Oxford, England.
Chap. 17 appeared in *Voix féministes/Feminist Voices*, May 1997. Reprinted by permission of
the Canadian Research Institute for the Advancement of Women.

Library of Congress Cataloging-in-Publication Data

Childbirth and authoritative knowledge : cross-cultural perspectives /
edited by Robbie E. Davis-Floyd, Carolyn F. Sargent.
    p.   cm.
    Includes bibliographical references and index.
    ISBN 0-520-20625-8 (cloth : alk. paper).—ISBN 0-520-20785-8
(pbk. : alk. paper)
    1. Birth customs.   2. Childbirth—Cross-cultural studies.
3. Knowledge, Sociology of.   I. Davis-Floyd, Robbie.   II. Sargent,
Carolyn Fishel, 1947–   .
GT2460.C37   1997
392.1'2—dc21   96-48263

Printed in the United States of America

1 2 3 4 5 6 7 8 9

The paper used in this publication meets the minimum requirements of American
National Standard for Information Sciences—Permanence of Paper for Printed Library
Materials, ANSI Z39.48-1984.

To Brigitte Jordan, midwife to the Anthropology of Birth

CONTENTS

vii

FOREWORD

Rayna Rapp

Perhaps because it was considered a "woman's subject," reproduction long remained on the margins of anthropological theory and research. Ancestral status can, of course, be claimed for Margaret Mead and Niles Newton's 1967 "The Cultural Patterning of Perinatal Behavior"; and for Lucille Newman's series of provocative, brave, and lonely articles on reproductive topics as diverse as abortion, childbirth, and the impact of having a first baby, which she first began writing in the mid-1970s. A decade ago, we were lucky to be able to get our hands on Brigitte Jordan's award-winning *Birth in Four Cultures,* published in 1978 by Eden Press, perennially out of print, and now (thankfully!) in its fourth edition. Jordan's insistence that childbirth had an ecology, and could therefore be studied behaviorally, social structurally, and historically as well as normatively, dramatically widened the range of tools, personnel, and social relations worthy of anthropological attention and analysis. Collectively, those of us who have worked in the anthropology of birth or the politics of reproduction owe her a great debt: she helped us to imagine a range of questions that could be subjected to empirical and theoretical investigation.

The important work begun in *Birth in Four Cultures* is clearly continued and transformed in *Childbirth and Authoritative Knowledge: Cross-Cultural Perspectives.* Robbie Davis-Floyd and Carolyn Sargent have brought together a rich array of essays that take their inspiration from Jordan, offering thoughtful and detailed case studies of what she calls "authoritative knowledge." This concept is elaborated in an opening essay by Brigitte Jordan in which she provides a closely grounded ethnographic account of how medical authority is socially constructed and maintained throughout the messiness of birth in a North American hospital. Jordan offers delicious descriptions based on the "thereness" of participant observation: nurses force patients into eye contact with the powers of their incantations; second stages of labor are recorded in compliance with ritual exigencies, not rational measurements; doctors' entrances are staged in a manner as grand as the entrada of Aida. Jordan uses her exquisite sense of description to birth a theoretical framework that both grows from and reflects back on the data: authoritative knowledge isn't produced simply by access to complex technology, or an abstract will to hierarchy. It is a way of organizing power relations in a room that makes them seem literally unthinkable in any other way. Antonio Gramsci would, I think, have approved of Jordan's method, for it makes visible the enormous work required to impose a consensual reality across power differences.

And it is this work of constructing and maintaining authoritative knowledge in childbirth that is the focus of all the essays in this volume. In settings as diverse as war-torn Sierra Leone, where medically trained personnel have no choice but to work with indigenous birth specialists; Nepal, where WHO creates a uniform TBA (traditional birth attendant) out of a congeries of local practices and practitioners to the exclusion of the very embedded expertise it hopes to preserve and foster; Oaxaca, Mexico, where indigenous notions of physiology are constantly discredited by government training courses for local midwives; high-tech North America, where active suppression of whatever it is that women might know, think, or imagine about themselves in the birth process occurs. Reporting on the ebbs and flows of authoritative knowledge in childbirth across sixteen societies, the essays in the volume suggest a remarkable range of hegemonic, shared, and contested knowledge formations.

Collectively, such work opens up possibilities for both relativizing the status of Western biomedicine and insisting that its powers be open to sharing and revision in specific local contexts. Moving beyond Brigitte Jordan's insight that the authoritative knowledge of obstetricians and gynecologists should be an object of comparative social investigation rather than unreflective veneration, the work included in *Childbirth and Authoritative Knowledge* will surely inspire the next wave of anthropological investigations. Its rich and diverse ethnographic contributions are at once a testimony to the vivid work now being produced about birth cross-culturally and a force for moving the study of reproductive politics to the center of social analysis.

Introduction

The Anthropology of Birth

Robbie E. Davis-Floyd and Carolyn F. Sargent

CROSS-CULTURAL APPROACHES TO THE STUDY OF CHILDBIRTH I: IN HONOR OF BRIGITTE JORDAN

It has been fifteen years since the first edition of Birth in Four Cultures *appeared, published by Eden Press in Montreal. The book was, in many ways, a sleeper. It was hardly advertised, never reviewed in major journals, and always difficult to obtain. Nevertheless, it slowly gathered a following. Libraries began to complain that it regularly got lifted off their shelves. Upset professors called because they couldn't get copies for their courses. After some years I began to get letters from places like Mongolia and Lesotho. An Italian translation appeared. It seemed that in spite of its underground status the book had some amount of impact in the uses it found in the ongoing enterprise of changing the American way of birth, as well as in defining the study of childbirth as a legitimate area of anthropological inquiry.*

—BRIGITTE JORDAN,
Preface to the 4th edition of Birth in Four Cultures *(1993:xi)*

The birth process is a universal part of human female physiology and biology, but in recent decades anthropologists have come to understand that birth is almost never simply a biological act; on the contrary, as Brigitte Jordan has written, "birth is everywhere socially marked and shaped" (1993:1). During anthropology's first century, most anthropological fieldwork was carried out by men, who in general either were not interested in or were denied access to the birth experience in the various cultures they studied (McClain 1982). Those who did write about parturition tended toward providing long lists of seemingly irrational food taboos and folk beliefs (see, e.g., Ford [1945] 1964) or toward examining childbirth not for its own sake but as a means for studying ritual and its practitioners (Lévi-Strauss 1967; Paul 1975; Paul and Paul 1975; Schultze Jena 1933). As early as 1950 it was pointed out that "there are practically no good, direct, personal observations of childbirth among primitives by competent observers" (Freedman and Ferguson 1950:365)—a statement that remained largely true[1] into the 1970s, when women entering the field began to explore indigenous birth customs from the inside and to understand them as integrated systems of knowledge and praxis.

In our initial attempts at writing the history of the field, we tried to sort out who was first, second, and so on; in other words, we sought to establish a hierarchy of primacy. But we quickly became aware that this sort of top-down schema was inappropriate to describe what has emerged as a sometimes individualistic but often profoundly cooperative endeavor[2] undertaken almost simultaneously during the 1960s and 1970s by a number of pioneering women who can be said to be the mothers and grandmothers of the field. These include Margaret Mead and Niles Newton (1967); Sheila Kitzinger (1962, 1978a, 1978b, 1979a, 1980a, 1980b, 1980c, 1982a); Lucille Newman (1965, 1976, 1980, 1981); Nancy Stoller Shaw (1974); Dana Raphael (1975); Carol McClain (1975); Sheila Cosminsky (1977); and Brigitte Jordan (1977, [1978] 1993). Each of these women made a significant contribution to the birth of this field. For example, Mead and Newton's 1967 survey of the little that was then known about cross-cultural childbirth pointed to the integrity and systematicity of the childbirth practices of traditional cultures and highlighted the enormous need for good birth ethnography. Niles Newton's own work (1972, 1973, [1955] 1977; Newton and Newton 1972) on the sexuality of birth and breastfeeding and the interplay between Western culture and women's physiology was groundbreaking at the time, and is still on the cutting edge of biocultural research. Lucille Newman wrote a number of original, courageous, and provocative articles on diverse reproductive topics including abortion, childbirth, and the impact of having a first baby. And Carol McClain explored cognition and behavior regarding pregnancy and birth in Ajijic, Mexico. Her research represented one of the earliest efforts to analyze this domain as a relevant cultural system in dynamic flux—a system that she coined the term "ethno-obstetrics" (McClain 1975) to describe.

Nevertheless, it was the 1978 publication of Jordan's *Birth in Four Cultures*—a small book that was at once accessible, comprehensive, and groundbreaking—that most saliently served to focus anthropological attention on childbirth as a subject worthy of in-depth ethnographic fieldwork and cross-cultural comparison, and that inspired many others to enter the field. As Faye Ginsburg and Rayna Rapp pointed out in their recent review, "Jordan's empirically based comparative study of birth in its full sociocultural context gave new legitimacy to the grounded study of human reproduction in anthropology" (1991:320–321). Robert Hahn (pers. com.) adds, "Jordan's work is not only a landmark cross-cultural study of childbearing but also an insightful analysis of methodological issues in anthropology"; he calls Jordan "midwife to the anthropology of childbirth."

We cannot blame the lack of early interest in childbirth solely on male ethnographers. It is noteworthy that even the handful of well-known female ethnographers of the first half of the twentieth century paid little or no attention to birth. This omission reflected not only gender bias in anthropology but also the general bias of earlier generations of American anthropologists toward social and cultural phenomena and away from biology. Jordan's "biosocial" approach worked to rectify this imbalance in anthropology, as well as to counterbalance the medical bias toward "the physiological, and often pathological, aspects of childbearing" (1978:i). She provided detailed ethnographic accounts of childbirth in a Mayan community in Yucatan, contrasting this woman-centered communal style of birthing with the highly technologized birthways of the United States and the midwife-attended births of Holland and Sweden. Her biosocial perspective, with its emphasis on the "mutual feedback" between biology and culture, gave her a comparative framework for integrating "the local view and meaning of the event, its associated biobehaviors, and its relevance to cross-system issues regarding the conduct of birth" (1978:8). In other words, she analyzed each culture's birthways as a system that made internal sense and could be compared with all other systems—a holistic conceptualization that enabled her to avoid reifying any one system, including American biomedicine. Jordan made it clear that the wholesale exportation of the American system of birth to the Third World was having extremely detrimental effects on indigenous systems, reminding us that these systemic effects were also individual and personal—felt by women in their bodies. Recognizing the need for strong policy recommendations, Jordan presented an alternative model for the "fruitful accommodation" of the biomedical and indigenous systems—a model that would allow "not only an analysis of Maya practices according to the criteria of medical obstetrics, but also an analysis of medical obstetric practices according to the criteria of the indigenous system" ([1978] 1993:136). Such a dialogic approach would, for example, show that from an American point of view, the Maya women encourage pushing much too early in labor, often resulting in a swollen cervix and a more painful and difficult labor than necessary. Likewise, from a Maya point of view, the medical practitioners in the clinics would be seen to be acting inappropriately when they forbid women to be accompanied by other women for support—a primary criterion of indigenous Maya birth—as well as when they demand unnecessary genital exposure, which the Maya perceive as shameful. Such dialogue would lead to mutual accommodation of both systems (see Jambai and MacCormack, Daviss, this volume), rather than to the top-down imposition of Western birthways that has typified most development programs to date (see Sesia, Pigg, this volume).

Jordan's contributions to the anthropology of birth did not end with the 1978 publication of *Birth in Four Cultures,* for which she won the 1980 Margaret Mead Award, or with its 1980 or 1983 reissues. She continued to pioneer advances in the field with the disturbing analysis of court-ordered cesarean sections that she and Susan Irwin (1987) jointly carried out, which illuminated the intensifying hegemony of the biomedical mode of birth; with her innovative and often-cited study of the training workshops given for Yucatecan midwives by physicians and nurses (1989); with her appraisal of the spread of what she terms "cosmopolitical obstetrics" and its effect on indigenous midwifery systems (1990); and most recently with the 1993 publication of a revised and expanded edition of *Birth in Four Cultures,* which includes an extensive new section on "authoritative knowledge" in childbirth—the knowledge that counts, on the basis of which decisions are made and actions taken. Jordan has given many talks at conferences around the world in the interests of understanding and improving maternal-child health, continues to serve as a member of the World Health Organization (WHO) Task Force on Human Resources for Safe Motherhood based in Geneva, and has provided guidance and inspiration not only to a new generation of scholars in the fields of the anthropology of birth and reproduction—many of whom are represented in this book— but also to many birth practitioners who have drawn extensively on her work to illuminate and facilitate their own.[3] In particular, her cogent analysis of the differences between the apprenticeship and didactic modes of learning in midwifery training (1989) serves today as an increasingly important resource for the independent midwifery community in the United States. As its members struggle with issues of certification and licensing, they are turning to Jordan's work to help them understand the essence of the apprenticeship system they are fighting so hard to honor and preserve (see Davis-Floyd and Davis, this volume).

For these reasons, we have dedicated this collection—based as it is on her fundamentally rich and useful concept of authoritative knowledge (see below)—to Brigitte Jordan, and it is in her honor that these chapters, most of which were written especially for this collection, are presented.

CROSS-CULTURAL APPROACHES TO THE STUDY OF CHILDBIRTH II: GROWTH OF A FIELD

Women's health care in every society is a reflection of the total culture. . . . It is important for those who provide women's health care to be aware not only of cultural diversity in birth practices, but also of the social roots of the variation.
—MARGARITA KAY,
Anthropology of Human Birth *(1982:viii)*

The concepts of "natural fertility" and "natural childbirth" are cultural constructs. Our lives are lived in socially interdependent groups guided by cultural rules. . . . Therefore, the profound human reality is a synthesis of biological function, cultural definitions and rules, and social action. That synthesis is the focus of this book.

—CAROL MACCORMACK,
Ethnography of Fertility and Birth *([1982] 1994:2)*

The first two edited collections to focus on pregnancy and birth from a cross-cultural perspective were Margarita Kay's *Anthropology of Human Birth* (1982) and Carol MacCormack's *Ethnography of Fertility and Birth* (1982); both collections built on Jordan's *Birth in Four Cultures*. Subsequently, the 1980s saw an explosion of anthropological interest in childbirth, in part as a consequence of the women's movement. In-depth ethnographic studies of birth were conducted in Guatemala by Sheila Cosminsky (1977, 1982); in Jamaica and Great Britain by Sheila Kitzinger (1978a,b, 1982a); among the Bariba of Benin by Carolyn Sargent (1982, 1989b, 1990); among Egyptian villagers by Soheir Morsy (1982); in Sierra Leone by Carol MacCormack (1982); in Malaysia by Carol Laderman (1983); in Colombia and Mexico by Carole Browner (1983, 1985, 1986, 1989); in India by Patricia Jeffery, Roger Jeffery, and Andrew Lyon (1984, 1989); among the !Kung of the Kalahari (Konner and Shostak 1987); among the Efe (Tronick, Winn, and Morelli 1985; Tronick, Morelli, and Winn 1987); among the Inuit (O'Neil and Kaufert 1990); and among Greek women (Lefkarites 1992; Georges, this volume).[4] In general, such studies paint a picture of viable, healthy, and culturally embedded indigenous systems that have been or are in danger of being severely disrupted by the importation of a technomedical system that grants them no validity, and seeks to replace them with a type of birth "management" that relies heavily on machines that are poorly understood, difficult or impossible to fix in rural areas, too costly to be widely offered, and that, even in the West, have not been shown to improve birth outcome in a variety of large-scale studies.[5] Because of biomedical practitioners' general disregard for, and lack of knowledge of, the specifics of indigenous systems, the areas in which biomedical information might be useful to those systems are usually not identified. Thus countless potentially fruitful opportunities for complementarity and cooperation between the indigenous health care system and biomedicine are too often lost. It is incumbent on anthropologists interested in the study of childbirth to actively seek ways to enhance this potential for complementarity (see, e.g., Jordan [1978] 1993:chaps. 5, 8).

In recent years anthropologists and other social scientists have expanded their focus beyond birth to many related areas. These include women's experiences of miscarriage and stillbirth (Layne 1990); adolescent and teen pregnancy (Lancaster and Hamburg 1986; Ward 1990); the relationship of mother-infant sleeping patterns to SIDS (McKenna 1990); the highly politicized domains of family planning (Ward 1986, 1991; Georges 1996); abortion (Ginsburg 1989; Rylko-Bauer 1996; Rylko-Bauer and Antoniello 1996); population control (Foucault 1977, 1978; McLaren 1984); the cultural construction of new social members (Aijmer 1992); and the socioeconomic, ecological, and political factors influencing infant and child survival (Polgar 1971, 1975; Miller 1981, 1986, 1987; Handwerker 1986, 1989; Nations and Rebhun 1988; Hern 1992a, 1992b; Scheper-Hughes 1987, 1989, 1992; Laughlin 1994). Another new focus of anthropological research is the increasing technological permeation of the reproductive experience in the United States and abroad. Key works have investigated the politics of reproduction (Paige and Paige 1981; Handwerker 1990) and the history of birth-technologization (Litoff 1978; Oakley 1984; Leavitt 1986; Wertz and Wertz 1989; Kunisch 1989); such groundbreaking research has made it clear that the cultural arena of birth serves as a microcosm in which the relationships between rapid technological progress and cultural values, normative behaviors, social organization, gender relations, and the political economy can be clearly viewed.

The above writers and others have also applied such perspectives to the recent emergence and wildfire spread of the new reproductive technologies (Arditti, Klein, and Minden 1985; Corea et al. 1987; Rothman 1987; Stolcke 1986; Whiteford and Poland 1989; Martin 1991), including infertility treatments (Lorber 1987; Spallone and Steinberg 1987; Gerson 1989; Klein 1989; Modell 1989; Franklin 1990; Sandelowski 1990, 1991, 1993); surrogacy (Charo 1987; Doane and Hodges 1988; Rothman 1989; Sault 1994; Ragone 1994); prenatal diagnostic testing (Rapp 1984–1987; Rothman 1986; Press and Browner 1994; Rothenberg and Thompson 1994; Browner and Press 1995); the repercussions for notions of kinship and social relatedness of all of the above (Strathern 1992; Edwards et al. 1993); and the handling of newborns in the NICU (Newman 1980, 1986, 1988; Guillemin and Holmstrom 1986; Levin 1988, 1989; Anspach 1989). Again, reproduction serves as a microcosm of broader trends: the massive application of technology worldwide to the harnessing and control of nature is encapsulated in the increasingly sophisticated efforts of researchers and technicians in all of the above fields to take cultural control of human perpetuation. As with the damming of rivers, such efforts create massive ripple effects that change more than the water's flow. Amniocentesis, for example, is a diagnostic technology that is widely used by American couples to identify, and often abort, defective fetuses, and to obtain information about the sex of their child before birth. Exported to India and massively applied, its ripple effects become manifest in eugenic misuse: in some areas, selective abortion of female fetuses is already altering the male/female population ratio (Jeffery, Jeffery, and Lyon 1984, 1989;

Miller 1986; Patel 1989; see also Laughlin 1994). Concomitantly, Rayna Rapp's (1987–1997) major studies of genetic counseling clearly show its ripple effects: the "neutral" medicalized discourse that counselors use to present options such as amniocentesis to expectant parents often limits their choices, stills their individual voices, and further medicalizes their perceptions and future experiences of pregnancy and birth.

As the field has expanded, efforts have been made at comprehensive review. Charles Laughlin (1989, 1992, 1994) defines and reviews the field of "pre- and perinatal anthropology." Carole Browner and Carolyn F. Sargent's (1990) assessment of anthropological studies of human reproduction generally focuses on the articulation between a society's core values and organizational principles and the ways in which it structures human reproductive behavior. Faye Ginsburg and Rayna Rapp (1991) address the politics of reproduction; their wide-ranging and succinct review is the most comprehensive to date. Forward-looking edited collections that are giving focus to the emergent field of the anthropology of reproduction include Ginsburg and Rapp's *Conceiving the New World Order: The Global Politics of Reproduction* (1995); Sarah Franklin and Helena Ragone's *Reproducing Reproduction* (1997), and Robbie Davis-Floyd and Joseph Dumit's *Cyborg Babies: From Techno-Sex to Techno-Tots* (1997).

THE ANTHROPOLOGY OF WESTERN CHILDBIRTH

In achieving the depersonalization of childbirth and at the same time solving the problem of pain, our society may have lost more than it has gained. We are left with the physical husk; the transcending significance has been drained away. In doing so, we have reached the goal which is perhaps implicit in all highly developed technological cultures, mechanized control of the human body and the complete obliteration of all disturbing sensations.
— SHEILA KITZINGER,
Women as Mothers *(1978b:133)*

Although Jordan's work has long been a focal point for social scientists and birth professionals, it is the work of anthropologist and childbirth educator Sheila Kitzinger that has done the most to bring anthropological awareness of the cultural variability of birth practices into the popular consciousness. Her 1978 publication of *Women as Mothers: How They See Themselves in Different Cultures* gave new legitimacy to the natural childbirth movement then gaining adherents in Europe and the United States by demonstrating the arbitrary and culture-bound aspects of Western technological birth (see also Kitzinger 1989d, 1994a).[6] During the 1980s, Kitzinger was joined in this endeavor by a number of anthropologists who focused their critical gaze on Western birthways. They included Shelly Romalis (1981); Robbie Davis-Floyd (1983, 1987a, 1987b); Pamela Eakins

(1986); Emily Martin (1987); Robert Hahn (1987); Laura O'Banion (1987); and Karen Michaelson (1988); as well as noted sociologists Ann Oakley (1977, 1980, 1984) and Barbara Katz Rothman (1981, 1982, 1985, 1986, 1987, 1989), and Italian researchers Grazia Colombo, Franca Pizzini, and Anita Regalia (1987; Pizzini 1990). Such researchers unanimously agree on the narrow and intensely ethnocentric bias in Western, and especially American, technomedicine—a system of health care that objectifies the patient, mechanizes the body, and exalts practitioner over patient in a status hierarchy that attributes authoritative knowledge only to those who know how to manipulate the technology and decode the information it provides. In the United States, the early and provocative in-hospital fieldwork of Nancy Stoller Shaw (1974), in combination with Diana Scully's (1980) ethnographic observations of obstetricians-in-training, sheds new light on what Scully termed "the miseducation of obstetrician/ gynecologists," a process that Davis-Floyd later analyzed as ritual initiation into the medical technocracy (1987a, 1992: chap. 7; see also Konner 1987).

Nancy Shaw's *Forced Labor* (1974) was the first anthropological work to note the assembly-line aspects of American childbirth. Emily Martin (1987) expanded this theme into a full-fledged analysis of the medical application of mechanistic metaphors of production and dysfunction to menstruation, childbirth, and menopause, based on 165 interviews with middle- and working-class women. Martin found that their responses to the medicalization of their body functions varied according to race and social class: working-class women tended to resist this medicalization, while middle-class women more or less accepted it. Complementing Martin's analysis, Davis-Floyd's (1992) study of the responses of 100 white middle-class women to their pregnancy and birth experiences showed a high degree of acceptance of and satisfaction with what she termed "the technocratic model of birth," as did similar studies by Carol McClain (1983, 1985, 1987a, 1987b), Margaret Nelson (1983), and Carolyn Sargent and Nancy Stark (1989; see also Kitzinger 1987b).

In contrast, Ellen Lazarus's rich ethnographic studies of the medical treatment of poor and working-class Puerto Rican and white women in clinics reveal universal resentment of their rushed, impersonal, and often indifferent treatment (1988, 1990, this volume; see also Johnson and Snow 1982; McClain 1987b; Boone 1988; Poland 1988, 1989). The systematic discrediting and elimination of black midwives in the American South has been well documented by Molly Dougherty (1978, 1982), Debra Susie (1988), and Gertrude Fraser (1988, 1992); Fraser's work also reveals the often tragically cruel treatment of poor black women by hospital personnel. The above studies are complemented by Robert Hahn and Marjorie Muecke's (1987) comparative overview of birth in five American subgroups—middle-class whites, lower-class blacks, Mexican-Americans, traditional Chinese, and Hmong. To date, there have been almost no studies focusing on the experiences of middle-class minority women (but see Glenn, Chung, and Forcey 1994).[7]

Unique in the anthropology of birth is the work of physical anthropologist Wenda Trevathan (1987; see also Trevathan, this volume). Trevathan's *Human Birth: An Evolutionary Perspective* (1987) begins with an analysis of primate labor and birth and continues through the archaeological record to reconstruct the birthways of early humans and the dawn of midwifery. She supplements this perspective with ethnographic fieldwork in a midwife-run El Paso birth center, in which most birthing women receive one-on-one labor support and little or no technological intervention. Trevathan's research clearly shows the benefits to mother and child of continuous woman-to-woman contact, of safeguarding—rather than regulating—the process of birth as it unfolds, of providing a supportive environment, and of allowing uninterrupted time after birth for the formation of a strong mother-infant bond.

Choice and Change

Before the advent of hospital birth in the United States, women had no choice about whether or not to be "awake and aware" during childbirth. Most women gave birth at home attended by midwives, although physicians began to enter the birth arena in large numbers by the mid-1800s. By the turn of the century, obstetricians began an organized campaign to systematically eliminate the competition from midwives (a campaign that came close to achieving total success, even in rural areas, by the 1960s) (Litoff 1978; Leavitt 1986; James-Chetelat 1989). Many women, especially the "delicate" ladies of the upper classes, lived in fear of the natural biological process of birth, dreading the pain, the danger, and the loss of modesty and control. When scopolamine—the drug that causes "twilight sleep"—was introduced in Germany in the 1930s, it seemed to offer the possibility of relief from many of these fears. Wealthy American women began to go to Europe to have their babies, eventually forming societies that actively sought to induce physicians to offer scopolamine in the United States. By the 1940s, such groups, in alliance with physicians, began to convince the general public that the progressive, "modern" way of giving birth was to divorce oneself from outdated servitude to biology by giving birth in the hospital under total anesthesia (Leavitt 1986; O'Banion 1987; Wertz and Wertz 1989). Likewise, the progressive parenting of infants became defined by the bottle and the scheduled feeding instead of the breast (Millard 1990).

The increasing use of scopolamine in American hospitals gave rise to rampant abuse. Scopolamine did not actually render a woman unconscious, it merely made her lose memory. Physicians and nurses felt justified in slapping, gagging, and strapping down the women who, under the influence of scopolamine, screamed, bit, ran, and generally acted like wild animals (Harrison 1982:87). By the early 1950s, horrific tales of such abuse began to fill the columns of popular women's magazines. The Lamaze movement, which encouraged women to be awake and aware, was in large part an effort to end the abuses of the scopolamine era. By the late 1960s, the progressive, "modern" way of giving birth was the "natural childbirth" of Dick-Read and the training for childbirth advocated by Lamaze— a movement that initially presented a radical and heretical challenge to the dominant orthodoxy of total medical control. Throughout the 1970s and early 1980s, the rhetoric of "natural" or "prepared" childbirth defined the "modern" birth.

In the wider society, the "modern" era of postwar America—in the standard popular view—was at first characterized by the often-monotonous uniformity of the industrial products of modernization. In the 1940s and 1950s, for one simple example, all telephones had dials, sat upright, and were black. The 1960s saw the introduction of several different styles and colors, and by the 1970s the number of options began to increase exponentially—a trend paralleled in many arenas of American economic, architectural, social, ethnic, and sexual life. By the 1980s, the term "postmodern" was being employed in many fields in recognition of the multiplicity and diversity that seemed to distinguish contemporary society from the greater uni- and conformity of the "modern" era that preceded it. Parallel trends are visible in childbirth. In this postmodern era, we have gone beyond the unconscious anesthetized births of the 1940s and 1950s, the systematic elimination of lay midwifery, the demise of breastfeeding (Raphael 1973; Jelliffe and Jelliffe 1975; Millard 1990), and even "natural childbirth" to an enormous range of options and historical shifts. These include the presence and active involvement of fathers during pregnancy and at birth (Trevathan 1987:112–115);[8] the renaissance of midwifery (Kobrin 1966; Newman 1981; Rothman 1982, 1983; Dye 1986; Reid 1989; Kitzinger 1991) and of breastfeeding (Gussler and Mock 1983; Raphael 1973, 1976; Raphael and Davis 1985; Trevathan 1987; Dettwyler 1988; Kitzinger 1989c, 1995b);[9] the spread of freestanding birth centers such as the one in which Trevathan worked (see also Rooks et al. 1989); the rising popularity of home birth (Kitzinger 1980b, 1991) and water birth (Odent 1984; Harper 1994); and even "unassisted childbirth" (Moran 1981; Shanley 1994).

But as with so many generalizations, the distinction between a univariate "modern" era and a multivariate "postmodern" era fails to hold on closer examination. The apparent conformity of the 1950s was in truth replete with diversities and resistances both in the wider society and in birth. Many women giving birth in that era managed to have intervention-free births in supportive environments—often small country hospitals, hospitals run by religious institutions, or clinics staffed by nurse-midwives. A number of "old-fashioned" general practitioners attended women at home; lay midwives still flourished in rural areas and sometimes in cities; nurse-midwifery was on the rise; and a few scattered practitioners even experimented with water birth. These birthing diversities of the scopolamine era have been little examined in the literature; they are ripe for scholarly research.

And today's apparent diversity of choice, which at first glance seems wide open, may only be superficial. As Alma Gottlieb has pointed out (pers. com.), we tend to romanticize the scope of "choice" in contemporary American society. Americans are generally proud of their individuality, their freedom of choice, but recent anthropological research demonstrates that race, religion, and socioeconomic class still circumscribe most choices in overwhelming ways (see especially Ortner 1991; Newman 1993). And in the marketplace, as consumers we find the array of products to choose among impressive—but could we really make a choice not to use them at all (see Rothman 1985:32)? And so it is with birth. In spite of the apparently vast range of options for childbirth in the 1990s, technobirth remains hegemonic: 98 percent of American women give birth in hospitals; in many hospitals, 80 percent receive epidural anesthesia. Around half of all labors are augmented with pitocin, episiotomies are performed in over 90 percent of first-time births, almost everyone is hooked up to electronic fetal monitors, and the cesarean rate stands at 21 percent. The most heretical contestations of this hegemony—independent midwifery and home birth—remain confined to less than 2 percent of the birthing population. This continued, even intensified medical hegemony both reflects and displays the power still vested in the patriarchal capitalist system (Rothman 1989); women's complicity in the establishment and maintenance of that system (Arney 1982; Sargent and Stark 1987); the transformation of American medicine into a megabusiness (Starr 1982); and American society's profound fear of nature and wistful, uneasy confidence in the technological products of culture (Davis-Floyd 1992, 1994b).[10]

A CALL FOR NEW DIRECTIONS IN BIRTH RESEARCH

A multiplicity of knowledge forms currently lays deconstructive claim to the monopoly created by the Western biomedical system. . . . The next moves in the study of reproduction will be made from inside a critique of the study of science. Our work

is exciting, for it opens up the possibility of both revitalizing the power of Western biomedicine and insisting that power be open to sharing and revision.
— RAYNA RAPP,
commentary on "Birth in Twelve Cultures: Papers in Honor of Brigitte Jordan," a symposium at the annual meeting of the American Anthropological Association, San Francisco, December 1992

As women's fight for control of reproduction takes on increasingly global dimensions, information on cross-cultural birth is in great demand. In this section, we seek to further the growth of this field by highlighting areas in need of anthropological research. For example, the contestations of tech-nomedical hegemony in childbirth are as varied as its manifestations and are played out in local, national, and global domains. Local contestations by childbirth activists, in the United States and elsewhere in the developed world, challenge standard hospital practice and are often effective at making change (see Szurek, Wagner, this volume). Such activists, who include midwives, childbirth educators, parents, and the occasional physician (see, e.g., Northrup 1994; Hays 1996), are engaged in a serious struggle to "reclaim" childbirth from its technomedical takeover, to redefine it as normal, and to combine the best scientific research on the physiology of birth with an attitude of honor and respect for women and their bodies, in order to create and popularize a gentler, more helpful, and less harmful system of birth. The methods and values of these activists, their language and discourse, beliefs and practices, successes and failures, have much to teach about intentional culture change; they deserve anthropological attention as surely as does the technomedical system they resist.[11] To date, almost no such research has been done, with the exception of Jenny Kitzinger's (1990) study of the development of the childbirth reform movement in Britain and Jane Szurek's study of childbirth activists in Tuscany (this volume; see also Edwards and Waldorf 1984). Much more is needed, as national policy makers are beginning to confront these contestations: obstetric technologies constitute a disproportionately large portion of medical costs worldwide, and any serious efforts toward health care reform must address this problem (see Lazarus, this volume).

In the Third and Fourth worlds, "modernization" has generally been defined as a movement toward the Western supervaluation of high technology and away from preindustrial lifeways. Almost everywhere one looks, indigenous systems of birth knowledge are being replaced by, competing with, or acceding to second-tier status under technomedical imports (see Sesia, Sargent and Bascope, Pigg, this volume)—a process that needs anthropological analysis and could be greatly ameliorated by anthropological input. In rare cases, viable accommodations between indigenous and imported systems are being worked out (see MacCormack, Daviss, this volume); these need in-depth attention, as they represent a potential that could take root elsewhere.[12] Attention should also be paid to the fractures and fissures within technomedicine itself. This obstetrical system, even as it enjoys massive exportation to other countries, is contested by nurses, midwives, holistic physicians, and other dissenters inside its ranks; these contestations and their effects are ripe for ethnographic investigation.[13]

In Eastern Europe, the dissolution of the Soviet Union and its repercussions have thrown domains of authoritative knowledge in childbirth into contestation and flux: technobirth triumphs in some countries and hospitals, while others cautiously eye natural childbirth and midwifery models or maintain rigid and outdated medical systems (see Chalmers, this volume). Little literature as yet exists on contemporary transformations of childbirth in the former Soviet Union and its neighbors; this is an area that cries out for anthropological research.

In the United States, low standards of prenatal care and high infant mortality in inner cities are juxtaposed against the near-wholesale exportation of the American technocratic model of birth to the Third World. Medical claims for the superiority of technocratic birth fail to take into account the demonstrated safety of planned, midwife-attended home birth in many countries (Kitzinger 1991; Davis-Floyd 1992; Jordan [1978] 1993; Goer 1995; Rooks 1997), or the enormous health problems generated for mothers and babies by such basic unmet needs as clean water, sanitary living conditions, and adequate nutrition. This situation is as endemic in U.S. urban ghettos as in the cities and villages of the Third World, and is unrelieved by the worldwide channeling of finite health care funds into sophisticated diagnostic technologies of limited practical value (Jordan [1978] 1993: chap. 8). To better understand the pervasiveness of this global phenomenon of neglecting low-cost, large-scale public health initiatives in favor of expensive technologies available to the few, new and extensive anthropological studies of the political economy of childbirth are needed (see Szurek, this volume). Questions to be addressed here include, for example, What is the relationship of the type of obstetric care mandated by governments and hospital administrators to the economy and the political priorities of a given nation-state? In the United States, a political economic approach would perforce address the reasons for the advent of managed care and capitation and their implications for obstetrics. These implications are serious, and need investigation. In the Third World, such an investigation would address, perhaps, the relationships between a governmental decision to eliminate midwife-attended home birth in favor of birth in the hospital, the political pressures influencing that decision, and the local and global market forces driving that nation's developing economy.

One obvious and viable solution to the problems and limitations of high-tech birth lies in midwifery. Midwives still attend the births of the majority of the world's babies, although their autonomy, reputation, and viability are seriously compromised by national governments in many areas (see Kitzinger 1990; Sargent 1989b; Sargent and Bascope, this volume). In North America, where midwifery was all but eradicated during the first two-thirds of the twentieth century, it has undergone a renaissance (Schlinger 1990; Burst 1979, 1980; Chester 1997; Rooks 1997). In Canada, direct-entry midwifery is being legalized, legitimized, and given government support in several provinces; this success is the result of a decade of intensive effort by birth activists, which deserves extensive research and documentation.[14] In the United States, independent midwives and nurse-midwives are becoming political activists and are enjoying considerable success in promoting their profession (see Davis-Floyd and Davis, this volume). Offering safe, effective, and responsive care, midwives are increasingly sought by middle-class women both in and out of the hospital; they have long offered nurturant and low-cost care to indigent women underserved by the obstetrical profession. Many midwives are becoming full-scale primary health care practitioners, filling a vital need for such services in rural and inner-city communities. Nevertheless, both independent midwives and nurse-midwives remain under attack from physicians all over the United States, even as the World Health Organization actively seeks to promote and enhance midwifery worldwide (see Wagner, this volume).[15] In Europe, where the midwifery tradition has remained unbroken, midwives are now losing their autonomy and much of their ability to offer truly woman-centered care to the tightening hegemony of techno-obstetrics—a phenomenon that is also heavily affecting nurse-midwives in the United States and that deserves intensive anthropological analysis.[16]

At the other end of the spectrum, an evolving anthropology of midwifery will do well to take careful note of the extreme cross-cultural variation in the kinds of care available to pregnant and birthing women, most especially in regard to the effects of cultural notions about women's bodies. For example, in Polynesia, where women's bodily functions are accepted and valued, pregnant women have high status, are treated with great consideration, and enjoy the care of respected expert midwives and the benefits of a sophisticated and elaborate system of authoritative knowledge about birth (Ward 1989). In dramatic contrast, in Bangladesh and rural North India, where menstruation and birth are regarded as disgusting and intensely polluting, few women are willing to regularly attend other women in childbirth, as when they do, the pollution of birth adheres to them as well (Blanchet 1984; Jeffery and Jeffery 1993). This profound cultural devaluation of birth and birth attendants affects millions of women in countries such as India and Bangladesh, presenting strong challenges to efforts at improvement in maternal health care.

Much anthropological research and specific policy guidance for development planners is needed in all the areas discussed above. The phenomena of pregnancy and birth are essential aspects of biological and cultural reality. Every day, they constitute the beginning of life for thousands of new global citizens, the end of life for some, and the stuff of lived experience for women as mothers. How women live those experiences—their own choices plus the treatment they receive from others—will influence their own lives and those of their families, for better or for worse. Those who would help from the outside cannot know what the inside experience is like, cannot offer assistance that is truly useful, without good ethnography.

The anthropology of birth is still a relatively new field with a primary need for basic ethnographic research. We need detailed ethnographies of the diverse ethno-obstetrical systems of the world. What is their relationship to cultural notions of the body, to women's status, to the culture's history, to its present situation? What can each system learn from the other? We need to understand these systems both from the anthropologist's perspective and from the mother's. What is the experience of childbirth like for individual women embedded in their larger cultural systems? We must let women's voices be heard: a primary focus of anthropological research should be women's birth narratives. We must also pay attention to the somatic aspects of birth (Alma Gottlieb, pers. com.), as experienced and described by women and as studiable by researchers. What can women's bodies tell us about childbirth? How can we learn to listen? Now that the connection between hormones and emotions has been made clearer, can we return to biology to uncover the physical effects on labor and birth of cultural expectations and individual dreams and fears? Can we develop a language that expresses the deep physiology of birth as well as its cultural overlay? What would it be like to speak in the language of the birthing body?[17]

And what effect does language itself have on women's perceptions of their biological experiences? Language is the filter through which experiences are interpreted and expressed. Some contemporary theorists insist that it is the medium through which social life is constructed. In the United States, that medium is hegemonically technomedical; the richly organic alternative discourse of homebirthers is beginning to be studied as well (Coslett 1994; Davis-Floyd 1994b; Miller 1994, 1996). But multiple folk discourses on birth and the body remain unrecorded. How do women talk about birth and their birthing bodies in other ethnic groups and cultures? Our field would benefit from finely textured discourse analyses of women's reproductive speech.

While anthropological attention to discourse is, of course, long-standing, in recent years discourse analysis has become one of the focal points of postmodernism in anthropology. For the past ten years, postmodernism as a critical perspective has given us strong conceptual tools for moving our discipline past the objectifying Self/Other distinction and the Western/ indigenous hierarchy of values that were formerly so entrenched in the language of anthropology, and toward the direction Jordan advocated when she argued for a mutual accommodation of indigenous and biomedical systems of birth, based on respect for women's bodies and women's biosocial needs. Postmodernism at its best entails reflexivity, a refusal to oversimplify multiplicities into misleading dichotomies, and a willingness to turn the critical gaze onto oneself even as one strives to interpret the beliefs and behaviors of others (Marcus and Fischer 1986; Clifford and Marcus 1986). Yet the postmodern approach to ethnography sometimes suffers from hyperreflexivity, paralyzing degrees of abstraction, and overattention to a textual analysis detached from embodied experience. The useful and grounded work of women in birth deserves equally useful and grounded anthropological attention. Such grounded analysis is and has been provided in anthropology for the past twenty years by feminist theory. Long before postmodernism was articulated in anthropology, feminist scholars were actively calling attention to the Self/Other distinction and were bringing a high degree of reflexivity to the scholarly study of gender relations in society, including close attention to the limitations of patriarchal Western language—and indeed, of its uncritical acceptance at various times by feminist theorists themselves (Mascia-Lees, Sharpe, and Cohen 1989). In recent years, the convergence of these two strong theoretical perspectives has resulted in a deep, continuously emergent, and highly productive alliance between postmodernism and feminism (e.g., Butler 1990, 1993; Hirsch and Keller 1990; Nicholson 1990; di Leonardo 1991; Barrett and Phillips 1992; Butler and Scott 1992). This alliance often offers rich possibilities for deeper linguistic, somatic, and theoretical explorations of birth.

The phenomena of pregnancy and birth as women experience them are very real, and are massively affected by the constant technological, political, and social changes of the postmodern world. We suggest that the effects of these changes can be fruitfully addressed through a combination of postmodern and feminist anthropological perspectives that can be applied to the anthropological analysis of reproduction in a focused and systematic way. The linguistic, literary-deconstructive, and reflexive turns that are both controversial and central to the present moment in anthropology suggest a certain fluidity of boundaries between the sciences and the humanities. The best of these tendencies can be merged with the hard-edged activism implicit and explicit in much feminist analysis to address the profound questions generated by the interface between the female body and contemporary societies.

Inspired by the interactions of postmodernism and feminism, we suggest the need for special attention to (1) conflicts and tensions in systems of authoritative knowledge (Davis-Floyd and Sargent 1996); (2) the language of birth (see, e.g., Rabuzzi 1994; Kahn 1995; Coslett 1994) and the affective flow between the public discourse about birth and women's private experience (see Rapp 1984, 1988a, 1988b; Duden 1993); (3) the intense subjectivity and reflexivity of studying a process that so directly concerns women as a gender, and is, for many of us, so profoundly experience-near (see Rapp 1987; Davis-Floyd 1989; Aijmer 1992; Kahn 1995); (4) the multiple voices and divisive agendas within feminism concerning issues of the female body and the non/primacy of its reproductive role (Treichler 1990; for the beginnings of this debate, see Ortner 1974; Mathieu 1978); (5) the agency and self-conscious choices of birthing women and birth practitioners (see Sargent and Stark 1989; Browner and Press, Georges, this volume); (6) the multiplicities of discourse, ideology, and treatment with which birthing women in many cultures must now cope (see Pigg, Szurek, this volume); (7) the ideological and cultural factors that work to channel women's choices along hegemonically approved routes (see Rothman 1989); (8) the politics of birth as cultural representation and expression (see Aijmer 1992; Davis-Floyd 1994b; Daviss, this volume). In this endeavor, the present volume constitutes but a beginning. It is our hope that this book will act both as a useful source of information about birth across cultures and as a charter for future research and further growth of the field.

SYNOPSIS AND ORGANIZATION OF THIS VOLUME

I think that what we need to think about is how we can move from a situation in which authoritative knowledge is hierarchically distributed into a situation where it is, by consensus, horizontally distributed—that is, where all participants in the labor and birth contribute to the store of knowledge on the basis of which decisions are made. In our technocratized systems we need to ask: What would have to happen for the woman to truly become a part of the decision-making process? What if her knowledge, both bodily and intellectual, were to be accorded legitimate status? What if she had a place in the professional participation structures set up around the birth? Could there be a translation process between what the woman knows and what the staff understands to be the situation? Could there be a mutual accommodation of these divergent ways of knowing such that one single authoritative knowledge structure emerges? This, I believe, is the challenge for the future of childbirth in the technologized Western world as well as in the developing countries of the Third World.

—BRIGITTE JORDAN,
*introductory remarks to "Birth in Twelve Cultures: Papers in Honor
of Brigitte Jordan," a symposium at the annual meeting of the American
Anthropological Association, San Francisco, December 1992*

This book brings together under one cover research on birth in sixteen different cultures. It contains fourteen chapters authored or coauthored by anthropologists who have conducted ethnographic research on birth (nonanthropologist coauthors include midwife Elizabeth Davis and physician Amara Jambai), supplemented by four chapters presenting interdisciplinary perspectives from a social psychologist (Chalmers), an epidemiologist (Johnson), a former staff member of the World Health Organization (Wagner), and a community midwife (Daviss). All the chapters are theoretically linked through the medium of Jordan's concept of authoritative knowledge (occasionally glossed throughout the book as "AK")—the interactionally displayed knowledge on the basis of which decisions are made and actions taken—which Jordan herself describes in detail in chapter 1. These works by diverse authors investigate the constitution of authoritative knowledge about birth as an ongoing social process that builds and reflects contested power relationships and cultural values in a wide range of communities, both local and global.

The chapters are grouped into five parts. In Part I, "The Social Construction of Authoritative Knowledge in Childbirth," Brigitte Jordan (chapter 1) explicates and delineates the notion that is addressed by every chapter in this book, giving the concept life and immediacy through a microanalysis of the production of authoritative knowledge in a videotaped hospital birth. In chapter 2, Wenda Trevathan searches for the evolutionary seeds of midwifery and a social childbirth based on an accumulated body of authoritative knowledge extending beyond the mother's own body wisdom. The four chapters in Part II, "Intracultural Variations in Authoritative Knowledge about Birth: Biomedical Hegemony and Women's Choices," explore the dynamic interplay between biomedical hegemony and the choices women make. Through analyses of prenatal care and childbirth in Greece, the United States, and Japan, these chapters make it clear that women must construct their choices in relation to and often in terms of the hegemonic ideology and ethos of Western biomedicine, which leaves little cultural space for alternative conceptions, thus calling into question the notion of "choice" in relation to culture. In chapter 3, Eugenia Georges describes the role of the multiple ultrasound scans routinely performed in Greece—which obstetricians promote and women actively demand—in the production of authoritative knowledge about pregnancy. Carole Browner and Nancy Press (chapter 4) describe how a multiethnic group of pregnant women in the United States balanced prenatal biomedical advice against their own embodied knowledge, challenging biomedical authority when it was based solely on clinicians' judgments and acquiescing to it when it was backed by the power of technology. Asking, "What do women want?" in chapter 5, Ellen Lazarus illustrates the limitations on choice and control stemming from differential access to authoritative biomedical knowledge about birth among lay middle-class women, health professionals, and poor women. Taking a different tack, Deborah Cordero Fiedler (chapter 6) compares midwifery and obstetrical systems of authoritative knowledge in Japan, showing how territory and technology work to consolidate the authoritative status of the obstetrician; nevertheless, as Fiedler illustrates, Japanese midwives continue to play a key role in maintaining the cultural definition of birth as a healthy and natural, not a pathological, event both in the hospital and in independent midwifery clinics, thereby extending the range of women's choices.

The four chapters in Part III, "Intercultural Variations in Authoritative Knowledge about Birth: Hierarchy, Community, and the Local Social Ground," address the tensions—first described by Jordan ([1978] 1993)—between hierarchical and communitarian systems of authoritative knowledge as they are lived out on the local social ground by women, birth practitioners, and development planners. Carolyn Sargent and Grace Bascope's comparison of ways of knowing about birth in Texas, Jamaica, and the Yucatan (chapter 7) reveals the startling contrasts between top-down systems in which the woman herself is granted no authority of knowing and a lateral system in which AK is communally shared between the woman and her female attendants—a theme that is elegantly developed in Sheila Kitzinger's cross-cultural typology of authoritative touch (chapter 8). In chapter 9, Stacey Leigh Pigg deconstructs the globalized vision of "traditional medicine" that development planners draw on in their attempts to link development goals to local realities. A student of the diversity of birthways in the various cultures and subcultures of Nepal, Pigg approaches this question from the bottom up; from this perspective, it becomes clear that the univariate approach of the development planners marginalizes local sources of knowledge even while ostensibly working with them. In the subsequent chapter, Beverley Chalmers, herself a development consultant, presents a top-down overview of current childbirth practices in Eastern Europe, asking painful questions about exactly what models of AK development planners should rely on in their efforts to reform the outdated and still-totalitarian birthing systems of the members of the former Soviet Union. The dialectic between these two chapters makes salient the politics, the paradoxes, and the unconscious cultural biases that complicate cross-cultural efforts at childbirth reform.

The four chapters in Part IV, "Fighting the System: Creating and Maintaining Alternative Models of Authoritative Knowledge," present countercultural contestations of biomedical hegemony. Jane Szurek (chapter 11) examines the political and strategic discourse and practices of birth activists in Tuscany as they work to construct and offer to Italian women an alternative and woman-centered system of AK—one that fundamentally challenges the hegemonic biomedical system and its embeddedness in Italy's political economy. In chapter 12, Robbie Davis-Floyd, an anthropologist, and Elizabeth Davis, a midwife, explore independent midwives' willingness to rely on intuition as a form of both spiritual [18] and embodied authoritative knowledge in home birth. In chapter 13, epidemiologist Kenneth C. Johnson discusses the scientific support for woman-centered low-intervention midwifery care provided in recent years by the randomized controlled trial (RCT); at the same time, Johnson demonstrates the limitations of the RCT for evaluating midwifery care and describes a large non-RCT epidemiologic research project on the outcomes of several thousand midwife-attended home births in North America. Johnson's emphasis on the value of "evidence-based care" echoes over fifteen years of effort by the World Health Organization to develop a core of scientific studies that objectively assess the efficacy—or lack thereof—of the intensifying Western trend toward high-tech birth. As a result, supporters of traditional birthing systems and of alternative birth in the West have looked to WHO for over a decade for authoritative validation. Nevertheless, WHO's construction of itself as a source of alternative AK for childbirth was and is a highly contested phenomenon. Although this phenomenon has been the work of many, it is possible to point to one man, Marsden Wagner, as the catalyst for this ground swell of effort. Chapter 14, "Confessions of a Dissident," chronicles Wagner's personal struggles, during his tenure as a staff member of WHO, to generate and disseminate objective evaluations of biomedical procedures, the results of those studies (which demonstrated the unnecessary nature of many medical procedures and the viability of midwife-attended home birth), and the resulting alienation and ostracism he suffered at the hands of the European medical community.

Part V, "Viable Indigenous Systems of Authoritative Knowledge: Continuity in the Face of Change," describes the remarkable resilience, tenacity, and creativity of four indigenous birthing systems that are holding their own in the face of an increasingly biomedical birthing world. In chapter 15, Paola Sesia extends Brigitte Jordan's ([1978] 1993, 1987) analyses of midwifery training, describing how Oaxacan ethno-obstetrics, although profoundly disregarded in biomedical training courses, nevertheless remains vital and authoritative through the consensual demands of women. Sesia's focus on prenatal care includes a detailed description of the *sobada* (prenatal massage) given by midwives and its multiple hands-on functions during pregnancy, which biomedical prenatal care has no potential to dislodge or replace. In chapter 16, physician Amara Jambai and anthropologist Carol MacCormack describe a native system of authoritative knowledge in the Pujehun district of Sierra Leone that has remained astonishingly vital even through the near-total disruption caused by repeated invasions and war; in this culture, even in the refugee camps, biomedical and traditional systems of AK coexist in a complementary relationship that has its roots in the women's secret society of Sande. In chapter 17, community midwife Betty-Anne Daviss tells the story of Povungnituk, an Inuit community that is actively reclaiming birth through the training of Inuit midwives and the construction of a community birthing center to eliminate the forced evacuation of women to high-tech hospitals in southern Canada. The final chapter, by Megan Biesele, describes childbirth among the Ju-/'hoan (!Kung) of the Kalahari—one of the few cultures in the world in which women, past and present, go off into the bush to pursue an ideal of solitary birth, a cultural practice that Biesele analyzes in terms of Ju/'hoan privileging of self-control and ritual circumspection during initiatory rites of passage.

Authoritative Knowledge: Extending the Scope

The utility and power of the concept of authoritative knowledge are evident throughout this collection.[19] Taken as a whole, these chapters show how authoritative knowledge is produced, displayed, resisted, and challenged in social, clinical, and political interactions. They illuminate the links between control of technology and the hierarchy of relations between specialists and patients, and clarify the articulation between the production of authoritative knowledge and the distribution of power in societal institutions. The inherent authority of Western technomedicine, which is increasingly taken for granted on a global scale, is not assumed in this book; rather, case studies from North America, Europe, and societies in Asia, Africa, and Latin America illustrate the global spread of obstetrical orthodoxy and its dynamic (and sometimes suffocating) relations to local ideas and practices. While serving to remind us that orthodox "ways of knowing" increasingly dominate obstetrics worldwide, these studies also demonstrate the continued and/or renewed viability of indigenous and midwifery models of authoritative knowledge, the resilience of low-technology birth systems, and the possibility for interactional cooperation and accommodation between biomedicine and other ethno-obstetrical systems.

In so doing, these studies expand and enrich the concept of authoritative knowledge itself. Trevathan's work extends the notion of authoritative knowledge about childbirth backward in evolutionary time. Her emphasis on the survival value of other women's assistance at childbirth suggests the evolutionary basis for the rich birthing cultures that have developed in countless human societies, and points to the strong evolutionary advantages of the systems of authoritative knowledge so developed. Trevathan's insistence on the value of social birth poses the question of when, if ever, anatomically modern human females were the sole possessors of authoritative knowledge in childbirth.

Systems of AK that define solitary birth as the norm or the ideal, like that of the Ju/'hoan as described by Biesele, are salient in their rarity.[20] Independent midwives in the United States as discussed by Davis-Floyd and Davis honor women's own authoritative knowledge about birth in a lateral way that makes the woman and the midwife equal collaborators in the birthing enterprise. The traditional midwives of Oaxaca (Sesia) and of the Yucatan (Sargent and Bascope) hold positions of cultural authority but share their birth knowledge with other experienced women; thus experienced birth-givers are honored for their own accumulated authoritative knowledge, whereas first-time mothers are expected to defer to the collaborative wisdom of the elders. This sort of collaborative construction of authoritative knowledge about birth reinforces Jordan's emphasis on the potential for consensual and interactive systems of AK.

Fiedler's study of Japanese birth supports Jordan's point that authoritative knowledge is usually possessed by those who control the artifacts necessary to produce the work, whereas the chapter by Sargent and Bascope shows that even when those artifacts are absent, as in Jamaican hospitals, it is possible for medical personnel to maintain a monopoly on AK about birth. These authors thus extend Jordan's work to suggest that "the constitution of authoritative knowledge also reflects the distribution of power within a social group" and that AK is not only re-created through discourse but can be embedded in status and social position.

The chapters by Georges, Browner and Press, and Lazarus all describe women's choices; they show that even when a certain type of AK seems at first glance to be entirely top-down, closer scrutiny often reveals that those who appear to be its victims in fact are consensual participants who both derive benefit from the cognitive and procedural status quo and actively participate in its construction. Those who resist that status quo must work to develop alternative systems of AK that are strongly cohesive and clearly articulated enough to withstand tremendous pressure from the orthodox establishment (Szurek, Davis-Floyd and Davis, Johnson, Wagner, Daviss). In so doing, such resisters, like their orthodox counterparts, will rely on science for legitimation of their efforts; it is of anthropological interest that neither they nor their orthodox counterparts contest science as the final arbiter of truth.[21] Equally fascinating are the profound differences in relation to the birthing body between the biomedical and the alternative approaches: the chapters in Part IV illustrate the valuation, indeed, the privileging, of women's bodily knowing in alternative birthing systems, while the chapters by Jordan, Georges, Lazarus, and Sargent and Bascope reveal the near-complete devaluation of women's bodily knowing in medicalized birth.

Wagner's "Confessions of a Dissident" describes the tremendous effort it takes to go against the grain of orthodox obstetrical AK, even when science supports the new direction. One result of Wagner's efforts to constitute WHO as an authoritative source of alternative knowledge about birth on a global scale was official WHO support for midwifery and for the training and upgrading of "traditional birth attendants." While on the surface such efforts seem laudable, their implementation by development planners can lead to such twists as identifying and training "traditional birth attendants" in cultures that have none; Pigg's chapter, "Authority in Translation," documents the cultural problematics of even well-intentioned efforts to "upgrade" indigenous birth traditions. Pigg's work suggests the possibility that truly integrated and successful systems of AK can derive some benefit from top-down teaching but must also grow grassroots-style, from the bottom up, if they are to be flexible enough to meet the changing needs of a given population. Jambai and MacCormack's chapter on Sierra Leone indeed demonstrates the adaptablity and resilience, even in the face of war, of just such a grassroots system—one that benefited from a fruitful accommodation of local and biomedical ways of knowing about women's health care. Studies by Sesia on Oaxacan prenatal care and Daviss on Inuit reclamations of birth also demonstrate the resilience of grassroots systems of AK in the face of tremendous pressures from biomedicine.

The chapters on Inuit, Oaxacan, and Ju/'hoan birthways hint that the continued viability of an indigenous culture may be directly related to its ability to maintain its own authoritative status in relation to birth. Indeed, in these cultures as in Sierra Leone, control of authoritative knowledge related to reproduction and birth becomes visible as a potent site of cultural preservation and renewal, reinforcing Ginsburg and Rapp's (1995) emphasis on reproduction as a site of defense of cultural identity. Additionally, Daviss's chapter demonstrates the beneficial results of combining indigenous values and traditions with the AK of North American independent midwifery (rather than of technomedicine). There is a difference between indigenous systems of AK that have grown out of a community or a culture's collective experiences of birth and systems like those described in Part IV that have been consciously constructed in direct opposition to the biomedical system-as-hegemony; Daviss's chapter shows how completely that difference is blurred when indigenous and alternative systems of AK join forces to resist further biomedical intrusion and to create new models of birth—a type of alliance that holds rich potential for the future.[22]

In honor of Brigitte Jordan, and with great pride, we present the following chapters. The mere existence of this collection is a tribute to the vitality of the broader field of women's studies, as well as to the burgeoning anthropological interest in issues involving women's bodies, women's lives, and women's births.

NOTES

We wish to thank Rayna Rapp, Sarah Franklin, Alma Gottlieb, Carole Browner, Carol McClain, Ellen Lazarus, Lynn Morgan, Eugenia Georges, Wenda Trevathan,

Sheila Kitzinger, and Brigitte Jordan for their helpful comments and suggestions on this introduction.

Seven chapters from this volume (Sesia, Georges, Browner and Press, Fiedler, Jambai and MacCormack, Sargent and Bascope, Davis-Floyd and Davis) appear in a special issue of *Medical Anthropology Quarterly*, "The Social Production of Authoritative Knowledge in Childbirth" (10, no. 2 [1996]); we gratefully acknowledge the enormous benefit these articles received from the contributions of Gay Becker, *MAQ* editor, Norman Fineman, copy editor par excellence, and numerous anonymous reviewers; another chapter (Lazarus) appeared in an earlier issue (8, no. 1 [1994]) of *MAQ*. One chapter (Pigg) appeared first in *Social Science and Medicine* (41, no. 1 [1995]) and is reprinted (with revisions) by permission of Elsevier Science Ltd, Oxford, England. And one chapter (Daviss) appeared first in *Voix Féministes/Feminist Voices*, May 1997, and is reprinted by permission of the Canadian Research Institute for the Advancement of Women. We are also grateful for the helpful recommendations on the entire collection made by Rayna Rapp, Sarah Franklin, and Virginia Olesen, and for the unflagging support and encouragement we received from our UC Press editor, Stanley Holwitz.

1. A notable exception is the physician George Engelmann, who traveled widely observing childbirth and in 1882 wrote *Labor among Primitive Peoples* (reprint 1977). For a valuable summary of his work, including excellent reproductions of his drawings of the positions women in the societies he visited adopted for birth, see Ashford 1988.

2. For example, Sheila Kitzinger (pers. com. 1995) notes,

> In the sixties, those of us who were entering this field were working alone. I was very much influenced by Margaret Mead, who came to the Institute of Social Anthropology at Oxford where I was [in graduate school]. She encouraged me when I was feeling very isolated and unsure of myself. . . . I first met Niles Newton at the Paris Conference on Psychosomatic Medicine in Obstetrics and Gynecology in 1962. She and I were both focusing on birth and breastfeeding as a part of women's sexuality. I was approaching it from an experiential point of view, and [later she began work] on the hormonal aspects. We were both also deeply concerned about the practice of episiotomy. For many years we kept in regular touch.

3. In recent years, a career shift has taken Brigitte Jordan (Gitti) from direct work with birth to industrial research. These days she divides her time between the Xerox Palo Alto Research Center and the Institute for Research on Learning (IRL), where she specializes in adapting anthropological field methods to research in complex, high-technology work settings. She has not forsaken birth: one of her recent IRL publications is an exciting and progressive comparison of the hierarchical distribution of authoritative knowledge (AK) in hospital birth (see chapter 1) with the egalitarian and shared access to AK in the high-tech work environment of air traffic controllers (Jordan 1992).

4. For an outstanding review of all available literature relevant to the broader field of the anthropology of reproduction, see Ginsburg and Rapp 1991.

5. The medical literature on these subjects is too vast to cite here. For summaries of much of this literature, see Davis-Floyd 1992:chap. 3; Goer 1995; and Rooks 1997. Researchers, practitioners, social scientists, and others around the world refer to the authoritative 1,500-page work *Effective Care in Pregnancy and Childbirth*, 2 vols. (Chalmers, Enkin, and Keirse 1989). (An abridged version, entitled *A Guide*

to Effective Care in Pregnancy and Childbirth [Enkin, Keirse, and Chalmers 1989], was also produced.) Since the publication of these invaluable reference works, which review all the available scientific research on childbirth up to 1989, new information is published electronically through the Cochrane Pregnancy and Childbirth Database (available through British Medical Journal Publications, London). See Johnson, this volume, for a more in-depth discussion of *Effective Care* and complete information on obtaining access to the Cochrane Database.

6. Sheila Kitzinger's careful research into myriad aspects of contemporary childbirth has served as an important stimulus in both the anthropology of birth and the international field of childbirth education. Kitzinger is perhaps the most prolific author in both fields. Her publications, of which there are dozens, have been translated into nineteen languages. They include studies of birth and sexuality (1985a–c), of women's experiences of episiotomy (Kitzinger and Simkin 1984), of breastfeeding (1980a, 1989c), childbirth (1962, 1989a, 1989b), crying babies (1990), unhappiness after childbirth (1992), home birth (Kitzinger and Davis 1978; Kitzinger 1980b, 1991), and the year after childbirth (1994c). Kitzinger has also published a number of influential, informative, and woman-centered guidebooks for pregnant women, including *Your Baby, Your Way* (1987), *The Complete Book of Pregnancy and Childbirth* (1989), and *Giving Birth: How It Really Feels* (1989). All of these books contain the results of countless interviews Kitzinger has conducted with childbearing women and birth practitioners; she is meticulous about allowing women's voices to be heard. She began focusing on women's experiences of obstetric and technological intervention in the U.K. during the 1960s, producing a series published by the National Childbirth Trust. *Some Mothers' Experiences of Induced Labour* (1975), written at a time when around half of all births in the U.K. were induced, was followed by *Some Women's Experiences of Episiotomy* (1981a) and *Some Women's Experiences of Epidurals* (1987b). Widely publicized in the national media, these pioneeering studies, which recorded women's experiences in women's own words, raised awkward questions, challenged the medical system, and stimulated further research by obstetricians. As a result of their publication, women began to say no to labor induction and episiotomy and obstetricians reduced their rates of administration. Kitzinger's *Good Birth* guides (1979c, 1983) also had a dramatic effect in the U.K. These were consumer guides to some 300 maternity hospitals in Britain; each reported on the birth experiences of over 1,500 women. For the first time, these books opened up maternity hospitals to consumer scrutiny and evaluation. The guides achieved wide publicity, helped to give women a voice, and stimulated improvements in obstetric care. In all her work, Kitzinger seeks "to show how research can be equated to political action" (pers. com. 1995); for her, that is the critical equation.

7. We are concerned about possible unfortunate results of this dearth of information. For example, in a recently published guide to cultural diversity for genetic counselors and geneticists (Fisher 1996), the chapter on African-Americans points out that "health care providers tend not to make class distinctions among African Americans, the result being erroneous assumptions about clients' backgrounds and health care experiences that perpetuate stereotypes, miscommunication, and conflicts between practitioner and client" (Telfair and Nash 1996:5).

8. Trevathan's thorough discussion of the available studies on the roles of fathers at birth indicates the need for more research. Earlier studies focused on the

couvade as the father's symbolic participation in the birth process (Munroe, Munroe, and Whiting 1973; Riviere 1974; Browner 1983); but Trevathan describes rich engagement and "engrossment" of fathers with infants at birth. Fathering in general is drastically understudied in anthropology; one of the few exceptions examines the intimate, affectionate, and active role of fathers among Aka pygmies (Hewlett 1991).

9. Recent excellent studies on breastfeeding include work by Valerie Fildes (1986); Ann Millard (1990; Millard and Graham 1984, 1985a, 1985b); and three edited collections: Penny Van Esterik's *Beyond the Breast-Bottle Controversy* (1989); Vanessa Maher's *The Anthropology of Breastfeeding: Natural Law or Social Construct?* (1994); and *Breastfeeding: Biocultural Perspectives* (Stuart-Macadam and Dettwyler 1995).

10. When questioned about their increasing reliance on technology, physicians point to the "malpractice crisis" in obstetrics. Fear of lawsuits leads them to take the legally safe road: because the technomedical model of birth is hegemonic, careful adherence to its supervaluation of aggressive intervention will be the physician's best protection in court. It is important not to accept such assertions at face value. In recent interviews with physicians who are holistically inclined, Davis-Floyd has found their attitude toward lawsuits to be entirely different from that of more mainstream physicians. Anthropologists to date have not undertaken either large-scale or case study investigations of actual malpractice lawsuits and their outcomes. We recommend this area as one ripe for investigation.

11. Biographical anthropology could play a role here: for example, Sheila Kitzinger, Marsden Wagner, and Michel Odent are among the most famous and influential of contemporary heroes in the international alternative birth movement; their lifework and their ongoing efforts at global reform are worthy of serious scholarly study, as are the lifeworks of many other childbirth reformers around the world.

12. Many indigenous cultures are maintaining viable and healthy traditional birth systems (e.g., Maiden and Farwell 1995; Jambai and MacCormack, Daviss, this volume). An outstanding film, *Nyamakuta—The One Who Receives: An African Midwife* documents this process among the Shona of Zimbabwe. Made in 1989, the film is 34 minutes long, was produced by Chris Steppard, and is available from Filmmakers Library, Inc., 124 E. 40th St., New York, NY 10016. Another excellent ethnographic film is *Birth and Belief in the Ecuadorian Andes,* Lauris McKee, California Media Extension Services, University of California, 1994 (27 minutes, VHS).

Birthing in Peace, a 32-minute video filmed in northeastern Brazil by midwife Peggy Olsthoorn, documents a successful fusion of traditional and biomedical obstetrical systems. A Brazilian obstetrician, Dr. Galba Araujo, organized the building of maternity clinics throughout northeastern Brazil, staffing them with local midwives who were given biomedical training but were strongly encouraged to continue with their traditional style of birth: the mother labors while walking or resting in a hammock and gives birth upright on a birthing stool with little or no insertion of hands into the vagina; after birth, the baby stays with the mother. Such practices, continued in the clinics, kept infection and mortality low, and were incorporated by Dr. Galba as far as possible into hospital practice in Fortaleza, Ceara, where he was director of obstetrics. The video is available in VHS, PAL, and SECAM from Special Journeys, Box 8705, Victoria, B.C., Canada, V8W 3S3 (604-478-2341).

13. For one brief example, in October 1992 a group of nurses at St. Vincent Hospital in Santa Fe declared themselves conscientious objectors to infant circumcision and refused to participate in its performance. In January 1995 their status as conscientious objectors was secured by a legally binding hospital document, the "Memorandum of Understanding for Circumcision Procedure." They have created a video about circumcision and their reasons for opposing it, and are in the process of forming a national organization, Nurses for the Rights of the Child, to fight routine circumcision. Information about the nurses of St. Vincent can be obtained from Mary Conant and Betty Katz Sperlich, 369 Montezuma, #354, Santa Fe, NM 87501 (505-989-7377).

14. After a long history of alegal midwifery in Canada (James-Chetelat 1989), in 1992, Ontario became the first province to legalize direct-entry midwifery. Other provinces are considering following the "Ontario model" for direct-entry midwifery training, which was set up in the form of university baccalaureate midwifery degree programs. Problems arose from the issue of which of the approximately 100 midwives already practicing in Ontario prior to legislation would be licensed. The tensions generated by the way in which many of their applications for licensure and evaluations were handled are problems that other Canadian provinces are trying to avoid. The process of midwifery legalization and the establishment of midwifery training programs in Canada and elsewhere would benefit tremendously from an anthropological investigation (Bourgeault 1996). (The term "direct-entry midwife" is used by different groups of midwives to mean different things. In its broadest usage, it simply means a midwife who entered midwifery directly—without passing through nursing; in this meaning, the term is used by independent midwives to distinguish themselves from certified nurse-midwives. In its narrowest usage, it means midwives who received their training through a formal university-based degree-granting program. In the United States, the American College of Nurse-Midwives—which is beginning to certify "direct-entry" midwives—would prefer to restrict the term to this narrower meaning; nevertheless, independent midwives continue to use the term in its broader sense. [See Davis-Floyd n.d.; Davis-Floyd and Davis, this volume.])

15. According to a recent article in *Science* (August 1995), in spite of a strong international focus on the part of WHO and other health agencies on primary health care and on the training of traditional birth attendants (TBAs) to provide prenatal care and cleanliness at birth and to transport women with complications, the rate of maternal mortality in the developing world has not improved in the past fifty years. International campaigns to improve child health that began in the 1960s have reduced the death rate of children under five by half, but made no dent in maternal deaths. A woman in Africa has a 1 in 21 lifetime risk of dying from birth complications; in Asia, 1 in 54; in northern Europe, 1 in 10,000. "The discrepancy between rich and poor countries is up to 10 times higher for maternal mortality than for infant mortality" (*Science* 1995:780). Obstetric emergencies account for up to 75 percent of all deaths; these include hemorrhage, septic abortion, eclampsia (convulsions and coma triggered by high blood pressure), infection, and

obstructed labor. When midwives or TBAs transport a woman to a heal[?] facility for treatment of these conditions, the essential equipment and s[?] often lacking. WHO is responding by making "emergency obstetric care" a[?] ponent of "essential obstetric care" a high priority, with varying respon[?] the governments of developing countries. This new initiative, along with [?] "Mother-Baby Package" unveiled at WHO's 1995 conference in Geneva, is r[?] possibilities for anthropological research.

16. East Germany would provide an excellent case study here: up until th[?] Berlin Wall fell, midwives attended many hospital births with minimal technology; they relied instead on a wide repertoire of herbs and homeopathic remedies and traditional midwifery techniques. As East German hospitals have been Westernized, this midwifery birth knowledge has been discounted and swept away in favor of shiny new machines. Good ethnography on the Western transformations of East German birth is greatly needed, as is research on the extent to which European midwives and nurse-midwives in the United States are themselves coming to rely on the high technologies of birth.

17. See Robbie Pfeufer Kahn, *Bearing Meaning: The Language of Birth* (1995), for an extraordinary and passionate writing of the birthing body. At the same time, we must keep in mind that in some cultures, less significance is attributed to biological than to social birth—the culturally important event that marks the infant's acceptance as a full member of society (Morgan 1990:94–95). Thus the questions arise for investigation: "Why is biological birth so important in this society? What is the social context within which American social scientists are analyzing birth? This social context would include the abortion controversy, the advent of reproductive imaging technologies, the revitalization of midwifery, our society's eagerness to attribute social significance to biological events" (Lynn Morgan, pers. corres.)—and, we might add, biological meaning to social events.

18. The role of religion and spirituality in women's birth choices and in midwifery deserve more scholarly attention (Klassen 1995). Of interest here is the work of Jacqueline Vincent-Priya, a physician who has conducted extensive research on midwives in Thailand, Indonesia, and Malaysia (see Vincent-Priya 1991). She observes that midwives in these countries attend women in labor while working under a spiritual mandate that gives them both "access to more knowledge, through dreams, and the confidence of having a spirit always on hand to show them how to deal with emergencies and other problems to which they do not know the answer" (Vincent-Priya 1991:10). This spiritual mandate serves as a locally embedded form of authoritative knowledge for midwifery practitioners. Jacqueline Vincent-Priya is founder of the Birth Traditions Survival Bank, a multifaceted collection of information from all over the world about traditions associated with conception, pregnancy, birth, and the neonatal period. The collection consists of a computerized database of relevant articles and books, a photographic and artistic library, and empirical data from research. The purpose of the bank involves preserving these birth traditions and making them accessible to all interested parties. The bank publishes a monthly newsletter; for subscription and membership information, write to Halldora Lazlo, Dept. of Midwifery Studies, University of Central Lancashire, Preston PR1 2HE, Lancashire, U.K.

19. Please note that none of the studies reported on in this volume, with the

exception of Jordan's analysis in chapter 1, was initially undertaken with the idea of authoritative knowledge in mind. Rather, this concept was employed as an analytical tool after the ethnographic research was complete. We suggest that an exciting direction for future research would be to set out from the beginning to investigate the production, articulation, and (perhaps) the contestations of authoritative knowledge in specific areas of praxis, within specific communities, during specific events and interactions.

20. Carolyn Sargent's (1989b) work showed similar honor invested in Benin women who birth alone—a phenomenon now confined only to the rural areas of that country. In the United States, Laura Kaplan Shanley (1994), Jeannine Parvati Baker (1986a, 1986b, 1991, 1992), and Marilyn Moran (1981) serve as national spokespersons for women who choose to birth unassisted, or with their husbands only; this "radical fringe" of the natural childbirth movement has a philosophy and discourse worthy of anthropological investigation.

21. Social scientists have long recognized the culturally and individually malleable aspects of the scientific enterprise (see Rubinstein, Laughlin, and McManus 1984).

22. For example, independent midwives in North America who have created and implemented an international direct-entry midwifery certification process for the Certified Professional Midwife (CPM) (see Davis-Floyd and Davis, this volume) are currently investigating the possibility of offering that certification to Hispanic *parteras* (traditional midwives) in the southwestern United States and Mexico. The certification process involves documentation of births, a challenging written exam, and a skills evaluation; offering it to traditional midwives would necessitate alterations that are presently being explored. These might include (1) identifying appropriate standards of care for specific communities; (2) adapting the certification process to reflect these standards and to respect the values and AK of the parteras—which can differ from community to community; (3) developing and offering skills-sharing workshops to give the parteras fluency in the AK of North American home birth midwifery (which is the standard used to develop CPM certification) and the ability to utilize those home birth technologies (see Davis-Floyd and Davis, this volume, note 11) that the parteras would consider to be both appropriate and helpful; (3) working in cooperation with the parteras to facilitate their integration of these technologies into their practices, and to help them gain access to the proper supplies on an ongoing basis. (For more information, contact the North American Registry of Midwives, c/o Sandra Morningstar, Wild Rose Lane, HCR 79, Box 14B, Kaiser, MO 65047-9711.)

REFERENCES

Aijmer, Goran, ed.
   1992   *Coming into Existence: Birth and Metaphors of Birth.* Gothenburg, Sweden: Institute for Advanced Studies in Social Anthropology.
Anspach, Renée
   1989   "Life and Death Decisions and the Sociology of Knowledge: The Case of Neonatal Intensive Care." In *New Approaches to Human Reproduction: Social and*

Ethical Dimensions, ed. L. M. Whiteford and M. L. Poland, 53–69. Boulder, Colo.: Westview Press.

Arditti, Rita, Renate Duelli Klein, and Shelley Minden, eds.
    1985   *Test-Tube Women.* Boston: Pandora Press.

Arms, Suzanne
    [1975] 1981   *Immaculate Deception.* New York: Bantam Books.

Arney, William Ray
    1982   *Power and the Profession of Obstetrics.* Chicago: University of Chicago Press.

Ashford, Janet Isaacs, ed.
    1984   *Birth Stories: The Experience Remembered.* Trumansburg, N.Y.: Crossing Press.
    1988   *George Engelmann and "Primitive" Birth.* Solana Beach, Calif.: Janet Isaacs Ashford.

Baker, Jeannine Parvati
    1978   *Hygeia: A Woman's Herbal.* Monroe, Utah: Freestone Publishing.
    1986a   *Conscious Conception: Elemental Journey through the Labyrinth of Sexuality.* Monroe, Utah: Freestone Publishing.
    1986b   *Prenatal Yoga and Natural Birth.* Rev. ed. Monroe, Utah: Freestone Publishing.
    1991   "The Deep Ecology of Birth: Healing Birth Is Healing Our Earth." Monroe, Utah: Freestone Publishing.
    1992   "The Shamanic Dimension of Childbirth." *Pre- and Perinatal Psychology Journal* 7(1):5–20.

Barrett, Michelle, and Anne Phillips
    1992   *Destabilizing Theory: Contemporary Feminist Debates.* Cambridge: Polity Press.

Berman, Morris
    1989   *Coming to Our Senses: Body and Spirit in the Hidden History of the West.* New York: Simon and Schuster.

Blanchet, Therese
    1984   *Meanings and Rituals of Birth in Rural Bangladesh.* Dhaka, Bangladesh: University Press Ltd.

Boone, Margaret
    1988   "Social Support for Pregnancy and Childbearing among Disadvantaged Blacks in an American Inner City." In *Childbirth in America: Anthropological Perspectives,* ed. Karen Michaelson, 66–79. South Hadley, Mass.: Bergin and Garvey.

Bourgeault, Ivy
    1996   "Delivering Midwifery: An Examination of the Process and Outcome of the Incorporation of Midwifery in Ontario." Ph.D. dissertation, Graduate Department of Community Health, University of Toronto.

Brackbill, Yvonne, Karen McManus, and Lynn Woodward
    1988   *Medication in Maternity: Infant Exposure and Maternal Information.* Ann Arbor: University of Michigan Press.

Brackbill, Yvonne, June Rice, and Diony Young
    1984   *Birth Trap: The Legal Low-Down on High-Tech Obstetrics.* St. Louis: C. V. Mosby.

Browner, Carole

1983   "Male Pregnancy Symptoms in Urban Colombia." *American Ethnologist* 13(3):494–510.

1985   "Traditional Techniques for Diagnosis, Treatment, and Control of Pregnancy in Cali, Colombia." In *Women's Medicine: A Cross-Cultural Study of Fertility Regulation,* ed. Lucille F. Newman, 99–124. New Brunswick: Rutgers University Press.

1986   "The Politics of Reproduction in a Mexican Village." *Signs* 11:710–724.

1989   "The Management of Reproduction in an Egalitarian Society." In *Women as Healers: Cross-Cultural Perspectives,* ed. Carol S. McClain, 58–71. New Brunswick: Rutgers University Press.

Browner, Carole H., and Nancy A. Press

1995   "The Normalization of Prenatal Diagnostic Testing." In *Conceiving the New World Order: The Global Politics of Reproduction,* ed. Faye Ginsburg and Rayna Rapp, 307–322. Berkeley: University of California Press.

Browner, Carole, and Carolyn Sargent

1990   "Anthropology and Studies of Human Reproduction." In *Medical Anthropology: Contemporary Theory and Method,* ed. Thomas M. Johnson and Carolyn F. Sargent, 215–229. New York: Praeger.

Burst, Helen Varney

1979   "On the Essentiality of Professional Midwives in Any Good Maternity Plan." In *Compulsory Hospitalization or Freedom of Choice in Childbirth?* ed. David Stewart and Lee Stewart, 2:371–378. Marble Hill, Mo.: NAPSAC Reproductions.

1980   "The American College of Nurse-Midwives: A Professional Organization." *Journal of Nurse-Midwifery* 25(1):4–6.

Butler, Judith

1990   *Gender Trouble: Feminism and the Subversion of Identity.* New York: Routledge.

1993   *Bodies that Matter: On the Discursive Limits of "Sex."* New York: Routledge.

Butler, Judith, and Joan W. Scott, eds.

1992   *Feminists Theorize the Political.* New York: Routledge.

Chalmers, Beverley

1990   *African Birth: Childbirth in Cultural Transition.* River Club, South Africa: Berev Publications.

Chalmers, Iain, Murray Enkin, and Marc Keirse, eds.

1989   *Effective Care in Pregnancy and Childbirth.* 2 vols. New York: Oxford University Press.

Charo, R. A.

1987   "Problems in Commercialized Surrogate Mothering." *Women and Health* 13(1-2):195–201.

Chester, Penfield

1997   *Sisters on a Journey: Portraits of North American Midwives.* New Brunswick: Rutgers University Press.

Clifford, James, and George E. Marcus, eds.

1986   *Writing Culture: The Poetics and Politics of Ethnography.* Berkeley: University of California Press.

Colombo, Grazia, Franca Pizzini, and Anita Regalia
1987   *Mettere al mondo: La produzione sociale del parto.* 2d ed. Milan: Franco Angeli Libri.
Corea, Gena
1985a   *The Hidden Malpractice.* New York: Harper and Row.
1985b   *The Mother Machine: Reproductive Technologies from Artificial Insemination to Artificial Wombs.* New York: Harper and Row.
Corea, Gena, et al.
1987   *Man-Made Women: How the New Reproductive Technologies Affect Women.* Bloomington: Indiana University Press.
Coslett, Teresa
1994   *Women Writing Childbirth: Modern Discourses of Motherhood.* Manchester: Manchester University Press.
Cosminsky, Sheila
1977   "Childbirth and Midwifery on a Guatemalan Finca." *Medical Anthropology* 6(3):69–104.
1982   "Childbirth and Change: A Guatemalan Study." In *Ethnography of Fertility and Birth,* ed. Carol MacCormack, 205–230. New York: Academic Press.
Cunningham, F. Gary, Paul C. MacDonald, and Norman F. Gant
1989   *Williams Obstetrics.* 18th ed. Norwalk, Conn.: Appleton & Lange.
Davis-Floyd, Robbie E.
1983   "Pregnancy and Cultural Confusion: Contradictions in Socialization." In *Cultural Constructions of Woman,* ed. Pauline Kolenda, 9–71. Prospect Heights, Ill.: Waveland Press.
1987a   "Obstetric Training as a Rite of Passage." *Medical Anthropology Quarterly* 1(3):288–318.
1987b   "The Technological Model of Birth." *Journal of American Folklore* 100(398):93–109.
1988   "Birth as an American Rite of Passage." In *Childbirth in America: Anthropological Perspectives,* ed. Karen Michaelson, 153–172. Beacon Hill, Mass.: Bergin and Garvey.
1989   "Knowing: A Story of Two Births." Unpublished manuscript.
1990   "The Role of American Obstetrics in the Resolution of Cultural Anomaly." *Social Science and Medicine* 31(2):175–189.
1992   *Birth as an American Rite of Passage.* Berkeley: University of California Press.
1993   "The Technocratic Model of Birth." In *Feminist Theory in the Study of Folklore,* ed. Susan Tower Hollis, Linda Pershing, and M. Jane Young, 297–326. Urbana: University of Illinois Press.
1994a   "Mind Over Body: The Pregnant Professional." In *Many Mirrors: Body Image and Social Relations in Anthropological Perspective,* ed. Nicole Sault, 204–233. New Brunswick: Rutgers University Press.
1994b   "The Technocratic Body: American Childbirth as Cultural Expression." *Social Science and Medicine* 38(8):1125–1140.
n.d.   "The Development of Direct-Entry Midwifery in North America: Implications for Health Care Policy." Unpublished manuscript.
Davis-Floyd, Robbie E., and Joseph Dumit, eds.

1997   *Cyborg Babies: From Techno-Sex to Techno-Tots.* New York: Routledge. In press.
Davis-Floyd, Robbie E., and Carolyn F. Sargent, eds.
    1996   "The Social Production of Authoritative Knowledge in Childbirth." Special issue, *Medical Anthropology Quarterly* 10(2).
Dettwyler, Katherine
    1988   "More than Nutrition: Breastfeeding in Urban Mali." *Medical Anthropology Quarterly* 2(2):172–183.
di Leonardo, Micaela, ed.
    1991   *Gender at the Crossroads of Knowledge: Feminist Anthropology in the Postmodern Era.* Berkeley: University of California Press.
Doane, J., and D. Hodges
    1988   "Risky Business: Familial Ideology and the Case of 'Baby M.' " *Differences* 1(1):67–82.
Dougherty, Molly C.
    1978   "Southern Lay Midwives as Ritual Specialists." In *Women in Ritual and Symbolic Roles,* ed. Judith Hoch-Smith and Anita Spring, 151–164. New York: Plenum.
    1982   "Southern Midwifery and Organized Health Care: Systems in Conflict," *Medical Anthropology* 6(2):113–116.
Duden, Barbara
    1991   *The Woman Beneath the Skin: A Doctor's Patients in Eighteenth-Century Germany.* Translated by Thomas Dunlop. Cambridge, Mass.: Harvard University Press.
    1993   *Disembodying Women: Perspectives on Pregnancy and the Unborn.* Translated by Lee Hoinacki. Cambridge, Mass.: Harvard University Press.
Dye, N. S.
    1986   "The Medicalization of Birth." In *The American Way of Birth,* ed. Pamela Eakins, 21–46. Philadelphia: Temple University Press.
Eakins, Pamela, ed.
    1986   *The American Way of Birth.* Philadelphia: Temple University Press.
Edwards, Jeannette, Sarah Franklin, Eric Hirsch, Frances Price, and Marilyn Strathern
    1993   *Kinship in the Age of Assisted Conception.* Manchester: Manchester University Press.
Edwards, Margot, and Mary Waldorf
    1984   *Reclaiming Birth: History and Heroines of American Childbirth Reform.* Trumansburg, N.Y.: Crossing Press.
Ehrenreich, Barbara, and Deirdre English
    1973a   *Complaints and Disorders: The Sexual Politics of Sickness.* Old Westbury, N.Y.: Feminist Press.
    1973b   *Witches, Midwives, and Nurses: A History of Women Healers.* Old Westbury, N.Y.: Feminist Press.
Engelmann, George
    [1882] 1977   *Labor among Primitive Peoples.* New York: AMS Press.
Enkin, Murray, Marc Keirse, and Iain Chalmers
    1989   *A Guide to Effective Care in Pregnancy and Childbirth.* Oxford: Oxford University Press.

Faust, Betty B.
    1988   "When Is a Midwife a Witch? A Case Study from a Modernizing Maya Village." In *Women and Health: Cross-Cultural Perspectives,* ed. Patricia Whelehan, 21–39. South Hadley, Mass.: Bergin and Garvey.

Fildes, Valerie
    1986   *Breasts, Bottles, and Babies: A History of Infant Feeding.* Edinburgh: Edinburgh University Press.

Fisher, Nancy, ed.
    1996   *Cultural and Ethnic Diversity: A Guide for Genetics Professionals.* Baltimore: Johns Hopkins University Press.

Ford, Clellan Stearns
    [1945] 1964   *A Comparative Study of Human Reproduction.* Reissue. New Haven, Conn.: Human Relations Area Files Press.

Foucault, Michel
    1977   *Discipline and Punish: Birth of the Prison.* Translated by A. Sheridan. New York: Pantheon.
    1978   *History of Sexuality.* Vol. 1 Translated by R. Hurley. New York: Pantheon.

Frankenberg, Ronald
    1988   "Gramsci, Culture, and Medical Anthropology: Kundry and Parsifal? or Rat's Tail to Sea Serpent?" *Medical Anthropology Quarterly* 2(4):324–337.

Franklin, Sarah
    1990   " 'Deconstructing Desperateness': The Social Construction of Infertility in Popular Representations of New Reproductive Technologies." In *The New Reproductive Technologies,* ed. M. McNeil, I. Varcoe, and S. Yearly, 200–229. New York: St. Martin's Press.

Franklin, Sarah, and Helena Ragoné, eds.
    1997   *Reproducing Reproduction.* Philadelphia: University of Pennsylvania Press.

Fraser, Gertrude
    1988   "Afro-American Midwives, Biomedicine, and the State: An Ethnohistorical Account of Birth and Its Transformation in Rural Virginia." Ph.D. dissertation, Department of Anthropology, Johns Hopkins University.
    1992   *Afro-American Midwives, Biomedicine, and the State.* Cambridge, Mass.: Harvard University Press.

Freedman, Lawrence Z., and Verna Masius Ferguson
    1950   "The Question of Painless Childbirth in Primitive Cultures." *American Journal of Orthopsychiatry* 20(2):363–372.

Friedl, Ernestine
    1990   "Society and Sex Roles." In *Anthropology: Contemporary Perspectives,* ed. Phillip Whitten and David Hunter, 215–219. Glenview, Ill.: Scott Foresman.

Fuller, Nancy, and Brigitte Jordan
    1981   "Maya Women and the End of the Birthing Period: Postpartum Massage and Binding in Yucatan, Mexico" *Medical Anthropology* 5(1):35–50.

Gaskin, Ina May
    1989   *Spiritual Midwifery.* 3d ed. Summertown, Tenn.: Book Publishing Company.

Georges, Eugenia
1996   "Abortion Politics and Practice in Greece." *Social Science and Medicine* 42(4):509–519.
Gerson, D.
1989   "Infertility and the Construction of Desperation." *Socialist Revolution* 89(3):45–66.
Ginsburg, Faye D.
1989   *Contested Lives: The Abortion Debate in an American Community*. Berkeley: University of California Press.
Ginsburg, Faye, and Rayna Rapp
1991   "The Politics of Reproduction." *Annual Review of Anthropology* 20:311–343.
1995   "Conceiving the New World Order: The Global Stratification of Reproduction." Introduction to *Conceiving the New World Order: The Global Stratification of Reproduction,* ed. Faye Ginsburg and Rayna Rapp, 1–18. Berkeley: University of California Press.
Ginsburg, Faye, and Rayna Rapp, eds.
1995   *Conceiving the New World Order: The Global Politics of Reproduction*. Berkeley: University of California Press.
Glenn, Evelyn Nakato, Grace Chung, and Linda Rennie Forcey
1994   *Mothering: Ideal, Experience, and Agency*. New York: Routledge.
Goer, Henci
1995   *Obstetric Myths versus Research Realities*. Westport, Conn.: Bergin and Garvey.
Golding, J., M. Paterson, and L. J. Kimlen
1990   "Factors Associated with Childhood Cancer in a National Cohort Study." *British Journal of Cancer* 62:304–308.
Gray, Brenda
1982   "Enga Birth, Maturation, and Survival." In *Ethnography of Fertility and Birth,* ed. Carol MacCormack, 75–113. New York: Academic Press.
Guillemin, Jean, and L. L. Holmstrom
1986   *Mixed Blessings: Intensive Care for the Newborn*. New York: Oxford University Press.
Gussler, J. D., and N. Mock
1983   "A Comparative Description of Feeding Practices in Zaire, the Philippines, and St. Kitts-Nevis." *Ecology of Food and Nutrition* 13:75–85.
Hahn, Robert A.
1986   "Perinatal Ethics in Anthropological Perspective." In *Contemporary Issues in Fetal and Neonatal Medicine,* ed. William B. Weil and Martin Benjamin, 213–238. Boston: Blackwell Scientific Publications.
1987   "Divisions of Labor: Obstetrician, Woman and Society in *Williams Obstetrics,* 1903–1985." *Medical Anthropology Quarterly* 1(3):256–282.
Hahn, Robert A., and Marjorie A. Muecke
1987   "The Anthropology of Birth in Five U.S. Ethnic Populations: Implications for Obstetrical Practice." *Current Problems in Obstetrics, Gynecology, and Fertility* 4:134–171.

Handwerker, W. Penn
  1989   *Women's Power and Social Revolution: Fertility Transition in the West Indies.* Newbury Park, Calif.: Sage.
  1990   "Politics and Reproduction: A Window on Social Change." In *Births and Power: Social Change and the Politics of Reproduction,* ed. W. Penn Handwerker, 1–38. Boulder, Colo.: Westview Press.
Handwerker, W. Penn, ed.
  1986   *Culture and Reproduction: An Anthropological Critique of Demographic Transition Theory.* Boulder, Colo.: Westview Press.
  1990   *Births and Power: Social Change and the Politics of Reproduction.* Boulder, Colo.: Westview Press.
Harper, Barbara
  1994   *Gentle Birth Choices.* Rochester, Vt.: Healing Arts Press.
Harrison, Michelle
  1982   *A Woman in Residence.* New York: Random House.
Hays, Bethany
  1996   Commentary on *The Social Production of Authoritative Knowledge in Childbirth,* ed. Robbie Davis-Floyd and Carolyn Sargent. Special Issue, *Medical Anthropology Quarterly* 10(2).
Heriot, Jean
  1996   "Fetal Rights vs. the Female Body: Contested Domains." *The Social Production of Authoritative Knowledge in Childbirth,* ed. Robbie Davis-Floyd and Carolyn Sargent. Special Issue, *Medical Anthropology Quarterly* 10(2):176–195.
Hern, Warren
  1992a   "Shipibo Polygyny and Patrilocality." *American Ethnologist* 19(3):501–522.
  1992b   "Family Planning, Amazon Style." *Natural History* 101(12):31–37.
Hewlett, Barry
  1991   *Intimate Fathers: The Nature and Context of Aka Pygmy Paternal Infant Care.* Ann Arbor: University of Michigan Press.
Hirsch, Marianne, and Evelyn Fox Keller, eds.
  1990   *Conflicts in Feminism.* New York: Routledge.
Hunte, Pamela A.
  1981   "The Role of the *Dai* in Urban Afghanistan." *Medical Anthropology* 5(1):17–26.
Huxley, Laura, and Pierro Ferrucci
  1992   *The Child of Your Dreams: Approaching Conception and Pregnancy with Inner Peace.* Rochester, Vt.: Destiny Books.
Jacobson, B., G. Eklund, L. Hamberger, D. Linarsson, G. Sedvall, and M. Valvereius
  1987   "Perinatal Origin of Adult Self-Destructive Behavior." *Acta Psychiatrica Scandinavica* 76:364–371.
Jacobson, Bertil, Karin Nyberg, Gunnar Eklund, Marc Bygdeman, and Ulf Rydberg
  1988   "Obstetric Pain Medication and Eventual Adult Amphetamine Addiction in Offspring." *Acta Obstetrica et Gynecologica Scandinavica* 67:677–682.
Jacobson, Bertil, Karin Nyberg, and L. Grondlabh et al.

1990 "Opiate Addiction in Adult Offspring through Possible Imprinting after Obstetric Treatment." *British Medical Journal* 301:1067–1070.

James-Chetelat, Lois

1989 "Reclaiming the Birthing Experience: An Analysis of Midwifery in Canada from 1788 to 1987." Ph.D. dissertation, Department of Sociology and Anthropology, Carleton University, Ottawa.

1990 "The Cultural Roots of the Canadian Birthing System." *Pre- and Perinatal Psychology Journal* 4(4):301–318.

Jeffery, Patricia M., Roger Jeffery, and Andrew Lyon

1984 "Female Infanticide and Amniocentesis." *Social Science and Medicine* 19:1207–1212.

1985 *Contaminating States and Women's Status*. New Delhi: Indian Social Institute.

1989 *Labour Pains and Labour Power: Women and Childbearing in India*. London: Zed Press.

Jeffery, Roger, and Patricia M. Jeffery

1993 "Traditional Birth Attendants in Rural North India: The Social Organization of Childbearing." In *Knowledge, Power, and Practice: The Anthropology of Medicine in Everyday Life*, ed. Shirley Lindenbaum and Margaret Lock, 7–31. Berkeley: University of California Press.

Jelliffe, D. B., and E. F. P. Jelliffe

1975 "Human Milk, Nutrition, and the World Resource Crisis." *Science* 188:557.

Johnson, Shirley M., and Loudell F. Snow

1982 "Assessment of Reproductive Knowledge in an Inner City Clinic." *Social Science and Medicine* 16:1657–1662.

Jones, Carl

1987 *From Parent to Child: The Psychic Link*. New York: Warner Books.

Jordan, Brigitte

1977 "The Self-Diagnosis of Early Pregnancy: An Investigation of Lay Competence." *Medical Anthropology* 1(2):1–38.

[1978] 1993 *Birth in Four Cultures: A Cross-Cultural Investigation of Childbirth in Yucatan, Holland, Sweden and the United States*. 4th ed. Prospect Heights, Ill.: Waveland Press.

1984 "External Cephalic Version as an Alternative to Breech Delivery and Cesarean Section." *Social Science and Medicine* 18(8):637–651.

1987 "The Hut and the Hospital: Information, Power and Symbolism in the Artifacts of Birth." *Birth* 14(1):36–40.

1989 "Cosmopolitical Obstetrics: Some Insights from the Training of Traditional Midwives." *Social Science and Medicine* 28(9):925–944.

1990 "Technology and the Social Distribution of Knowledge." In *Anthropology and Primary Health Care*, ed. Jeannine Coreil and J. Dennis Mull, 328–342. Boulder, Colo.: Westview Press.

1992 "Technology and Social Interaction: Notes on the Achievement of Authoritative Knowledge in Complex Settings." IRL Technical Report, IRL 92-0027. Palo Alto, Calif.: Institute for Research on Learning.

Jordan, Brigitte, and Susan Irwin

1987 "A Close Encounter with a Court-Ordered Cesarean Section: A Case of Differing Realities." In *Case Studies in Medical Anthropology: A Teaching and Reference Source,* ed. Hans Baer, 185–199. New York: Gordon and Breach.

1989 "The Ultimate Failure: Court-Ordered Cesarean Section." In *New Approaches to Human Reproduction,* ed. Linda Whiteford and Marilyn Poland, 13–24. Boulder, Colo.: Westview Press.

Kahn, Robbie Pfeufer

1995 *Bearing Meaning: The Language of Birth.* Urbana: University of Illinois Press.

Kaminski, H. M., A. Stafl, and J. Aiman

1987 "The Effect of Epidural Analgesia on the Frequency of Instrumental Obstetric Delivery." *Obstetrics and Gynecology* 69:770.

Kay, Margarita, ed.

1982 *Anthropology of Human Birth.* Philadelphia: F. A. Davis.

Kitzinger, Jenny

1990 "Strategy of the Early Childbirth Movement: A Case Study of the National Childbirth Trust." In *The Politics of Maternity Care,* ed. Jo Garcia, Robert Kilpatrick, and Martin Richards, 154–168. London: Oxford University Press.

Kitzinger, Sheila

1962 *The Experience of Childbirth.* London: Gollancz Press. (Reissued in the U.S. by Penguin, New York, in 1967, with subsequent editions in 1972, 1978, 1981, 1984.)

1975 *Some Mothers' Experiences of Induced Labour.* London: National Childbirth Trust.

1978a *Giving Birth: The Parents' Emotions in Childbirth.* New York: Schocken Books.

1978b *Women as Mothers: How They See Themselves in Different Cultures.* New York: Random House.

1979a *Education and Counselling for Childbirth.* New York: Schocken Books.

1979b *The Good Birth Guide.* London: Fontana Press.

1980a *The Experience of Breastfeeding.* New York: Penguin.

1980b *Birth at Home.* New York: Viking Penguin Books.

1980c *Pregnancy and Childbirth.* London: Michael Joseph.

1981a *Some Women's Experiences of Episiotomy* (with Rhiannon Walters). London: National Childbirth Trust.

1981b *Sheila Kitzinger's Birth Book.* New York: Grosset and Dunlap.

1982a "The Social Context of Birth: Some Comparisons Between Childbirth in Jamaica and Britain." In *Ethnography of Fertility and Birth,* ed. Carol P. MacCormack, 181–204. New York: Academic Press. (Reissued in 1994 by Waveland Press, Prospect Heights, Ill.)

1982b *Birth Over Thirty.* London: Sheldon Press.

1983 *The New Good Birth Guide.* London: Penguin.

1985a *Birth Over Thirty.* New York: Viking Penguin.

1985b *Women's Experience of Sex.* New York: Penguin.

1985c   "The Sexuality of Birth." In *Women's Experience of Sex,* by Sheila Kitzinger, 209–218. New York: Penguin.

1987a   *Your Baby, Your Way.* New York: Pantheon.

1987b   *Some Women's Experiences of Epidurals.* London: National Childbirth Trust.

1989a   *The Complete Book of Pregnancy and Childbirth.* New York: Alfred A. Knopf.

1989b   *Giving Birth: How It Really Feels.* New York: Farrar, Straus, Giroux.

1989c   *Breastfeeding Your Baby.* New York: Alfred A. Knopf.

1989d   "Childbirth and Society." In *Effective Care in Pregnancy and Childbirth,* ed. Iain Chalmers, Murray Enkin, and Marc Keirse, 99–109. New York. Oxford University Press.

1990   *The Crying Baby.* New York: Penguin.

1991   *Home Birth and Other Alternatives to Hospital.* New York: Doring Kindersley.

1992   "Birth and Violence Against Women: Generating Hypotheses from Women's Accounts of Unhappiness after Childbirth." In *Women's Health Matters,* ed. Helen Roberts, 63–80. New York: Routledge.

1994a   *Ourselves as Mothers.* New York: Addison-Wesley.

1994b   *Birth Over Thirty-Five.* New York: Viking Penguin.

1994c   *The Year After Childbirth.* New York: Scribner's.

1995   "Commentary." In *Breastfeeding: Biocultural Perspectives,* ed. Patricia Stuart-Macadam and Katherine A. Dettwyler, 385–393. New York: Aldine de Gruyter.

Kitzinger, Sheila, ed.

1981   *Episiotomy: Physical and Emotional Aspects.* London: National Childbirth Trust.

1991   *The Midwife Challenge.* 2d ed. London: Pandora Press.

Kitzinger, Sheila, and John Davis, eds.

1978   *The Place of Birth.* London: Oxford University Press.

Kitzinger, Sheila, and Penny Simkin, eds.

1984   *Episiotomy and the Second Stage of Labor.* Minneapolis: ICEA Publications.

Klassen, Pamela E.

1995   "Religion and Spirituality in Home Births." Dissertation prospectus, Department of Religion and Society, Drew University.

Klein, Renate Duelli, ed.

1989   *Infertility.* Winchester, Mass.: Unwin Hyman/Pandora.

Kobrin, F.

1966   "The American Midwife Controversy." *Bulletin of the History of Medicine* 40:350–363.

Konner, Melvin

1987   *Becoming a Doctor: A Journey of Initiation in Medical School.* New York: Viking.

Konner, Melvin, and Marjorie Shostak

1987   "Timing and Management of Birth among the !Kung: Biocultural Interaction in Reproductive Adaptation." *Cultural Anthropology* 2(1):11–28.

Kopytoff, Igor

1990   "Women's Roles and Existential Identities." In *Beyond the Second Sex: New*

Directions in the Anthropology of Gender, ed. Peggy Reeves Sanday and Ruth Gallagher Goodenough, 75–98. Philadelphia: University of Pennsylvania Press.

Kunisch, Judith
  1989   "Electronic Fetal Monitors: Marketing Forces and the Resulting Controversy." In *Healing Technology: Feminist Perspectives,* ed. Kathryn Strother Ratcliff, 41–60. Ann Arbor: University of Michigan Press.

Laderman, Carol
  1983   *Wives and Midwives: Childbirth and Nutrition in Rural Malaysia.* Berkeley: University of California Press.

Lancaster, Jane, and Beatrice Hamburg, eds.
  1986   *School-Age Pregnancy and Parenthood: Biosocial Dimensions.* Hawthorne, N.Y.: Aldine de Gruyter.

Laughlin, Charles D.
  1989   "Pre- and Perinatal Anthropology: A Selective Review." *Pre- and Perinatal Psychology Journal* 3(4):261–296.
  1990   "The Evolution of Helplessness in the Human Infant and Its Significance for Pre- and Perinatal Psychology." *Pre- and Perinatal Psychology Journal* 4(4):267–280.
  1992   "Pre- and Perinatal Anthropology II: The Puerperium in Cross-Cultural Perspective." *Pre- and Perinatal Psychology Journal* 7(1):23–60.
  1994   "Pre- and Perinatal Anthropology III: Birth Control, Infanticide, and Abortion in Cross-Cultural Perspective." *Pre- and Perinatal Psychology Journal* 9(1):85–102.

Layne, Linda
  1990   "Motherhood Lost: Cultural Dimensions of Miscarriage and Stillbirth in America." *Women and Health* 16(3):69–98.

Lazarus, Ellen
  1988   "Poor Women, Poor Outcomes: Social Class and Reproductive Health." In *Childbirth in America: Anthropological Perspectives,* ed. Karen Michaelson, 39–54. South Hadley, Mass.: Bergin and Garvey.
  1990   "Falling through the Cracks: Contradictions and Barriers to Care in a Prenatal Clinic." *Medical Anthropology* 12(3):269–288.

Lazarus, Ellen, and Elliott H. Phillipson
  1990   "A Longitudinal Study Comparing the Prenatal Care of Puerto Rican and White Women." *Birth* 17(1):6–11.

Leavitt, Judith
  1986   *Brought to Bed: Childbearing in America 1750–1950.* New York: Oxford University Press.

Lefkarites, Mary P.
  1992   "The Sociocultural Implications of Modernizing Childbirth among Greek Women on the Island of Rhodes." *Medical Anthropology* 13(4):385–412.

Levin, Betty
  1988   "The Cultural Context of Decision-Making for Catastrophically Ill Newborns." In *Childbirth in America: Anthropological Perspectives,* ed. Karen Michaelson, 84–97. South Hadley, Mass.: Bergin and Garvey.

1989   "Decision-Making about the Care of Catastrophically Ill Newborns." In *New Approaches to Human Reproduction: Social and Ethical Dimensions,* ed. L. M. Whiteford and M. L. Poland, 84–97. Boulder, Colo.: Westview Press.

Lévi-Strauss, Claude
1967   "The Effectiveness of Symbols." In *Structural Anthropology,* by Claude Lévi-Strauss, 186–205. Garden City, N.Y.: Doubleday.

Life
1989   "Birth Without Women." February: 54.

Litoff, Judy Barrett
1978   *American Midwives: 1860 to the Present.* Westport, Conn.: Greenwood Press.
1986   *The American Midwife Debate: A Sourcebook on Its Modern Origins.* New York: Greenwood Press.

Lorber, J.
1987   "In Vitro Fertilization and Gender Politics." *Women and Health* 13(1-2):117–133.

MacCormack, Carol P.
1982   "Health, Fertility, and Birth in Moyamba District, Sierra Leone." In *Ethnography of Fertility and Birth,* ed. Carol P. MacCormak, 115–141. New York: Academic Press.

MacCormack, Carol P., ed.
[1982] 1994   *Ethnography of Fertility and Birth.* 2d ed. Prospect Heights, Ill.: Waveland Press.

Maher, Vanessa, ed.
1992   *The Anthropology of Breastfeeding: Natural Law or Social Construct?* Providence, R.I., and Oxford: Berg.

Maiden, Anne, and Edie Farwell
1995   "Even the Baby Knows: Birth in Tibetan Cultures." Unpublished manuscript.

Marcus, George E., and Michael M. J. Fischer
1986   *Anthropology as Cultural Critique: An Experimental Moment in the Human Sciences.* Chicago: University of Chicago Press.

Marnie, Eve
1988   *LoveStart: Prenatal Bonding.* Santa Monica, Calif.: Hay House.

Martin, Emily
1987   *The Woman in the Body.* Boston: Beacon Press.
1991a   "The Ideology of Reproduction: The Reproduction of Ideology." In *Uncertain Terms: Negotiating Gender in American Society,* ed. Faye Ginsburg and Anna Lowenhaupt Tsing, 300–314. Boston: Beacon Press.
1991b   "The Egg and the Sperm." *Signs* 16(3):485–501.

Mascia-Lees, Frances, Patricia Sharpe, and Colleen Cohen
1989   "The Postmodern Turn in Anthropology: Questions from a Feminist Perspective." *Signs* 15(1):7–33.

Mathews, Holly
1990   "Killing the Medical Self-Help Tradition among Afro-Americans: The Case of Midwifery in North Carolina, 1917–1983." Unpublished manuscript.

Mathieu, Nicole-Claude
  1978   "Man-Culture and Woman-Nature?" *Women's Studies International Quarterly* 1:55–65.
McArthur, C., M. Lewis, and E. G. Know
  1992   "Investigation of Long-Term Problems after Obstetric Epidural Anesthesia." *British Medical Journal* 304:1279–1282.
McClain, Carol Shepherd
  1975   "Ethno-Obstetrics in Ajijic." *Anthropological Quarterly* 40(1):38–56.
  1982   "Toward a Comparative Framework for the Study of Childbirth: A Review of the Literature." In *Anthropology of Human Birth*, ed. Margarita Kay, 25–60. Philadelphia: F. A. Davis.
  1983   "Perceived Risk and Choice of Childbirth Service." *Social Science and Medicine* 17(23):1857–1865.
  1985   "Why Women Choose Trial of Labor or Repeat Cesarean Section." *Journal of Family Practice* 21(3):210–216.
  1987a   "Some Social Network Differences Between Women Choosing Home and Hospital Birth." *Human Organization* 46(2):146–152.
  1987b   "Patient Decision-Making: The Case of Delivery Method after a Previous Cesarean Section." *Culture, Medicine, and Psychiatry* 11:495–508.
McClain, Carol, ed.
  1989   *Women as Healers: Cross-Cultural Perspectives.* New Brunswick: Rutgers University Press.
McKenna, James
  1990   "Evolution and Sudden Infant Death Syndrome." Pts. 1–3. *Human Nature* 1(2):145–303.
McLaren, A.
  1984   *Reproductive Rituals: The Perception of Fertility in England from the Sixteenth Century to the Nineteenth Century.* London: Methuen.
Mead, Margaret, and Niles Newton
  1967   "Cultural Patterning of Perinatal Behavior." In *Childbearing: Its Social and Psychological Aspects*, ed. S. Richardson and A. F. Guttmacher, 142–244. Baltimore: Williams and Wilkins.
Michaelson, Karen
  1988   *Childbirth in America: Anthropological Perspectives.* South Hadley, Mass.: Bergin and Garvey.
Millard, Ann V.
  1983   "Perceptions of a Family Planning Campaign in Rural Mexico." In *Women, Health, and International Development*, ed. Margaret I. Aquwa, 59–67. East Lansing: Office of Women in International Development, Michigan State University.
  1985   "Child Mortality and Economic Variation among Rural Mexican Households." *Social Science and Medicine* 20(6):589–599.
  1990   "The Place of the Clock in Pediatric Advice: Rationales, Cultural Themes, and Impediments to Breastfeeding." *Social Science and Medicine* 31(2):211–221.
Millard, Ann V., and Margaret A. Graham
  1984   "Principles that Guide Weaning in Rural Mexico." *Ecology of Food and Nutrition* 16:171–188.

1985a "Breastfeeding in Two Mexican Villages: Social and Demographic Perspectives." In *Breastfeeding, Child Health, and Child Spacing,* ed. Valerie Hull and Mayling Simpson, 55–77. London: Croom Helm.

1985b "Abrupt Weaning Reconsidered: Evidence from Central Mexico." *Journal of Tropical Pediatrics* 31:229–234.

Miller, Barbara

1981 *The Endangered Sex: Neglect of Female Children in Rural North India.* Ithaca: Cornell University Press.

1986 "Prenatal and Postnatal Sex Selection in India." Women in International Development Publication Series, no. 107. East Lansing: Michigan State University.

1987 "Female Infanticide and Child Neglect in Rural North India." In *Child Survival: Anthropological Perspectives on the Treatment and Maltreatment of Children,* ed. Nancy Scheper-Hughes, 135–144. Dordrecht: D. Reidel.

Miller, Janneli

1994 "Of Midwives, Commands, and Birth: A Commentary on the Efficacy and Performance of Magical Words." Paper presented at the 23d annual meeting of the American Anthropological Association, Atlanta.

1997 "Whole Births, Whole Selves: Identity and Resistance in Homebirth Narratives." In *Cyborg Babies: From Techno-Sex to Techno-Tots,* ed. Robbie Davis-Floyd and Joseph Dumit. New York: Routledge. In press.

Modell, Judith

1989 "Last Chance Babies: Interpretations of Parenthood in an In-Vitro Fertilization Program." *Medical Anthropology Quarterly* 3(2):124–138.

Moran, Marilyn A.

1981 *Birth and the Dialogue of Love.* Leawood, Kan.: New Nativity Press.

Morgan, Lynn

1990 "When Does Life Begin? A Cross-Cultural Perspective on the Personhood of Fetuses and Young Children." In *Abortion Rights and Fetal "Personhood,"* 2d ed., ed. Edd Doerr and James W. Prescott, 94–114. Long Beach, Calif.: Centerline.

Morse, Janice M., and Carolyn Park

1988 "Differences in Cultural Expectations of the Perceived Painfulness of Childbirth." In *Childbirth in America: Anthropological Perspectives,* ed. Karen L. Michaelson, 121–129. South Hadley, Mass.: Bergin and Garvey.

Morsy, Soheir

1982 "Childbirth in an Egyptian Village." In *Anthropology of Human Birth,* ed. Margarita Kay, 147–174. Philadelphia: F. A. Davis.

Munroe, R. L., R. H. Munroe, and J. W. M. Whiting

1973 "The Couvade: A Psychological Analysis." *Ethos* 1:30–74.

Nations, Marilyn, and L. A. Rebhun

1988 "Angels with Wet Wings Won't Fly: Maternal Sentiment in Brazil and the Image of Maternal Neglect." *Culture, Medicine, and Psychiatry* 12:141–200.

Nelson, Margaret K.

1982 "The Effect of Childbirth Preparation on Women of Different Social Classes." *Journal of Health and Social Behavior* 23(4):339–352.

1983   "Working-Class Women, Middle-Class Women, and Models of Child-
        birth." *Social Problems* 30(3):284–297.
Newman, Katherine
1993   *Falling from Grace*. New York: Random House.
Newman, Lucille F.
1965   "Culture and Perinatal Environment in American Society." Ph.D. disser-
        tation, University of California, Berkeley.
1976   "Unwanted Pregnancy in California: Some Cultural Considerations." In
        Culture, Natality, and Family Planning, ed. J. F. Marshall and S. Polgar, 156–
        166. Chapel Hill: University of North Carolina Press.
1980   "Parents' Perceptions of Their Low Birth Weight Infants." *Pediatrician*
        9:182–190.
1981   "Midwives and Modernization." *Medical Anthropology* 5(1):1–12.
1986   "Premature Infant Behavior: An Ethological Study in a Special Care
        Nursery." *Human Organization* 45(4):327–333.
1988   "The Artificial Womb: Social and Sensory Environments of Low
        Birthweight Infants." In *Childbirth in America: Anthropological Perspectives*, ed.
        Karen Michaelson, 204–210. South Hadley, Mass.: Bergin and Garvey.
Newton, Niles
[1955] 1977   *Maternal Emotions: A Study of Women's Feelings toward Menstruation,
        Pregnancy, Childbirth, Breastfeeding, Infant Care and Other Aspects of Their Femi-
        ninity*. N.p.: Paul B. Hoeber.
1972   "Childbearing in Broad Perspective." In *Pregnancy, Birth, and the Newborn
        Baby*. Boston: Delacorte Press.
1973   "The Interrelationships between Sexual Responsiveness, Birth, and
        Breastfeeding." In *Contemporary Sexual Behavior: Critical Issues in the 1970s*,
        ed. Joseph Zubin and John Money. Baltimore: Johns Hopkins University
        Press.
Newton, Niles, and Michael Newton
1972   "Childbirth in Crosscultural Perspective." In *Modern Perspectives in Psycho-
        Obstetrics*, ed. J. Howells, 150–172 Edinburgh: Oliver and Boyd.
Newton, Niles, Michael Newton, and Jeanine Broach
1988   "Psychologic, Physical, Nutritional, and Technologic Aspects of Intrave-
        nous Infusion During Labor." *Birth* 15(2):67–72.
Newton, Niles, D. Peeler, and Michael Newton
1968   "Effect of Disturbance on Labor: An Experiment Using 100 Mice with
        Dated Pregnancies." *American Journal of Obstetrics and Gynecology* 101:1096–
        1102.
Nicholson, Linda J., ed.
1990   *Feminism/Postmodernism*. New York: Routledge.
Northrup, Christiane
1994   *Women's Bodies, Women's Wisdom: Creating Physical and Emotional Health
        and Healing*. New York: Bantam Books.
Oakley, Ann
1977   *Becoming a Mother*. New York: Schocken Books.
1980   *Women Confined: Towards a Sociology of Childbirth*. New York: Schocken
        Books.

1984   *The Captured Womb: A History of the Medical Care of Pregnant Women.* New York and Oxford: Basil Blackwell.

O'Banion, Laura

1987   "Delivering Labor in the 20th Century." Paper in lieu of master's thesis, Department of Anthropology, University of Illinois at Urbana-Champaign.

Odent, Michel

1984   *Birth Reborn.* New York: Pantheon Books.

1986   *Primal Health: A Blueprint for Our Survival.* London: Century.

1992   *The Nature of Birth and Breastfeeding.* Westport, Conn.: Bergin and Garvey.

Olsthoorn, Peggy

1993   *Birthing in Peace* (Nascendo em Paz). VHS video, 32 minutes. Special Journeys, Box 8705, Victoria, B.C., Canada V8W 3S3 (604-478-2341).

O'Neil, John, and Patricia A. Kaufert

1990   "The Politics of Obstetric Care: The Inuit Experience." In *Births and Power: Social Change and the Politics of Reproduction,* ed. W. Penn Handwerker, 53–68. Boulder, Colo.: Westview Press.

Ortner, Sherry

1974   "Is Female to Male as Nature Is to Culture?" In *Woman, Culture and Society,* ed. Michelle Zimbalist Rosaldo and Louise Lamphere, 67–88. Stanford: Stanford University Press.

1991   "Reading America: Preliminary Notes on Class and Culture." In *Recapturing Anthropology,* ed. Richard Fox, 163–189. Santa Fe: School of American Research.

Paige, Karen E., and Jeffrey Paige

1981   *The Politics of Reproductive Ritual.* Berkeley: University of California Press.

Patel, V.

1989   "Sex Determination and Sex Pre-selection Tests in India: Modern Techniques for Femicide. *Bulletin of Concerned Asian Scholars* 21(1):2–10.

Paul, Lois

1975   "Recruitment to a Ritual Role: The Midwife in a Maya Community." *Ethos* 3:449–467.

1978   "Careers of Midwives in a Mayan Community." In *Women in Ritual and Symbolic Roles,* ed. Judith Hoch-Smith and Anita Spring, 129–150. New York: Plenum.

Paul, Lois, and Benjamin D. Paul

1975   "The Maya Midwife as Sacred Specialist: A Guatemalan Case." *American Ethnologist* 2(4):707–725.

Peterson, Gayle

1981   *Birthing Normally: A Personal Growth Approach to Childbirth.* Berkeley: Mindbody Press.

Peterson, Gayle, and Lewis Mehl

1984   *Pregnancy as Healing: A Holistic Philosophy for Pre-Natal Care.* 2 vols. Berkeley: Mindbody Press.

Pizzini, Franca

1990   *From the Hands of Women into the Hands of Men: Images from the History of the Medicalization of Childbirth, 18th–20th Centuries.* Video, 22 minutes (NTSG and PAL). Department of Sociology, Group for Research into the Condition of Women, University of Milan, Via Conservatorio 7, Milano 20122, Italy.

Poland, Marilyn L.

1988   "Adequate Prenatal Care and Reproductive Outcome." In *Childbirth in America: Anthropological Perspectives,* ed. Karen Michaelson, 55–65. South Hadley, Mass.: Bergin and Garvey.

1989   "Ethical Issues in the Delivery of Quality Care to Pregnant Indigent Women." In *New Approaches to Human Reproduction: Social and Ethical Dimensions,* ed. Linda M. Whiteford and Marilyn L. Poland, 42–50. Boulder, Colo.: Westview Press.

Polgar, Stephen, ed.

1971   *Culture and Population.* New York: Schenkman.

1975   *Population, Ecology, and Social Evolution.* The Hague: Mouton.

Press, Nancy A., and Carole H. Browner

1994   "Collective Silences, Collective Fictions: How Prenatal Diagnostic Testing Became Part of Routine Prenatal Care." In *Women and Prenatal Testing: Facing the Challenges of Genetic Technology,* ed. Karen H. Rothenberg and Elizabeth J. Thomson, 201–218. Columbus: Ohio State University Press.

Rabuzzi, Kathryn

1994   *Mother with Child: Interpretations of Childbirth.* Bloomington: Indiana University Press.

Ragoné, Helena

1994   *Surrogate Motherhood: Conception in the Heart.* Boulder, Colo.: Westview Press.

Raphael, Dana

1973   "The Role of Breastfeeding in a Bottle-Oriented World." *Ecology and Food Nutrition* 2:121–126.

1976   *The Tender Gift: Breastfeeding.* New York: Schocken Books.

Raphael, Dana, ed.

1975   *Women and Reproduction.* The Hague: Mouton.

Raphael, Dana, and Flora Davis

1985   *Only Mothers Know: Patterns of Infant Feeding in Traditional Cultures.* Westport, Conn.: Greenwood Press.

Rapp, Rayna

1984   "XYLO: A True Story." In *Test-Tube Women,* ed. R. Arditti, R. Klein, and S. Minden, 313–328. Boston: Pandora Press.

1987   "Moral Pioneers: Women, Men, and Fetuses on a Frontier of Reproductive Technology." *Women and Health* 13(1-2):101–116. (Reprinted in *Gender at the Crossroads of Knowledge: Feminist Anthropology in the Postmodern Era,* ed. Micaela di Leonardo. Berkeley: University of California Press, 1991.)

1988a   "Chromosomes and Communication: The Discourse of Genetic Counseling." *Medical Anthropology Quarterly* 2(2):143–157.

1988b   "The Power of Positive Discourse: Medical and Maternal Discourses on Amniocentesis." In *Childbirth in America: Anthropological Perspectives,* ed. Karen Michaelson, 103–116. South Hadley, Mass.: Bergin and Garvey.

1990   "Constructing Amniocentesis: Maternal and Medical Discourses." In *Un-*

certain Terms: Negotiating Gender in American Culture, ed. Faye Ginsburg and Anna L. Tsing, 28–42. Boston: Beacon Press.

1993a   "Reproduction and Gender Hierarchy: Amniocentesis in Contemporary America." In *Sex and Gender Hierarchies: The Anthropological Approach,* ed. Barbara D. Miller, 108–126. Cambridge: Cambridge University Press.

1993b   "Accounting for Amniocentesis." In *Knowledge, Power, and Practice: The Anthropology of Medicine in Everyday Life,* ed. Shirley Lindenbaum and Margaret Lock, 55–76. Berkeley: University of California Press.

1994a   "Commentary on AAA Panel on 'Reproducing Reproduction,' " *Newsletter of the Council on Anthropology and Reproduction* 2(1):1–3.

1994b   "Women's Responses to Prenatal Diagnosis: A Sociocultural Perspective on Diversity." In *Women and Prenatal Testing: Facing the Challenges of Genetic Technology,* ed. Karen H. Rothenburg and Elizabeth J. Thompson, 219–233. Columbus: Ohio State University Press.

1995a   "Heredity, or Revising the Facts of Life." In *Naturalizing Power: Feminist Cultural Studies,* ed. Carol Delaney and Sylvia Yanagisako, 69–86. New York: Routledge.

1995b   "Risky Business: Genetic Counseling in a Shifting World." In *Articulating Hidden Histories,* ed. Jane Schneider and Rayna Rapp, 75–189. Berkeley: University of California Press.

1997a   "Real Time Fetus: The Role of the Sonogram in the Age of Monitored Reproduction." In *Cyborgs and Citadels: Anthropological Interventions into Techno-Humanism,* ed. Gary Lee Downey, Joseph Dumit, and Sharon Traweek. Seattle: SAR/University of Washington Press. In press.

1997b   "Refusing Prenatal Diagnosis: The Uneven Meanings of Bioscience in a Multicultural World." *Science, Technology and Human Values.* In press.

1997c   *Moral Pioneers: Fetuses, Families, and Amniocentesis.* New York: Routledge. In press.

Reid, Margaret

1989   "Sisterhood and Professionalization: A Case Study of the American Lay Midwife." In *Women as Healers: Cross-Cultural Perspectives,* ed. Carol McClain, 219–238. New Brunswick: Rutgers University Press.

Riviere, P. G.

1974   "The Couvade: A Problem Reborn." *Man* 9:423–435.

Romalis, Coleman

1981   "Taking Care of the Little Woman: Father-Physician Relations during Pregnancy and Childbirth. In *Childbirth: Alternatives to Medical Control,* ed. Shelly Romalis, 92–121. Austin: University of Texas Press.

Romalis, Shelly, ed.

1981   *Childbirth: Alternatives to Medical Control.* Austin: University of Texas Press.

Rooks, Judith Pence

1997   *Childbirth in America: The Past, Present, and Potential Role of Midwives.* Philadelphia: Temple University Press.

Rooks, Judith P., Norman L. Weatherby, Eunice K. M. Ernst, Susan Stapleton, David Rosen, and Allan Rosenfield

1989   "Outcomes of Care in Birth Centers: The National Birth Center Study." *New England Journal of Medicine* 321:1804–1811.

Rothenburg, Karen H., and Elizabeth J. Thompson, eds.

1994   *Women and Prenatal Testing: Facing the Challenges of Genetic Technology.* Columbus: Ohio State University Press.

Rothman, Barbara Katz

1981   "Awake and Aware, or False Consciousness? The Co-option of Childbirth Reform in America" In *Childbirth: Alternatives to Medical Control,* ed. Shelly Romalis, 150–180. Austin: University of Texas Press.

1982   *In Labor: Women and Power in the Birthplace.* New York: W. W. Norton. (Reprinted in paperback under the title *Giving Birth: Alternatives in Childbirth.* New York: Penguin, 1985.)

1983   "Midwives in Transition: The Structure of a Clinical Revolution." *Social Problems* 30(3):262–271.

1985   "The Meanings of Choice in Reproductive Technology." In *Test-Tube Women,* ed. Rita Arditti, Renate Duelli Klein, and Shelley Minden, 23–34. London: Pandora Press.

1986   *Tentative Pregnancy: Prenatal Diagnosis and the Future of Motherhood.* New York: Viking.

1987   "Reproductive Technology and the Commodification of Life." *Women and Health* 13(1-2):95–100.

1989   *Recreating Motherhood: Ideology and Technology in Patriarchal Society.* New York: W. W. Norton.

Rubinstein, Robert, Charles Laughlin, and John McManus

1984   *Science as Cognitive Process.* Philadelphia: University of Pennsylvania Press.

Rylko-Bauer, Barbara

1996   "Abortion from a Cross-Cultural Perspective: An Introduction." *Social Science and Medicine* 42(4):479–482.

Rylko-Bauer, Barbara, and Patricia Antoniello, eds.

1996   "Symposium: Abortion from a Cross-Cultural Perspective." *Social Science and Medicine* 42(4):479–560.

Sandelowski, Margaret

1990   "Fault Lines: Infertility and Imperiled Sisterhood." *Feminist Studies* 16(1):33–52.

1991   "Compelled to Try: The Never-Enough Quality of Conceptive Technology." *Medical Anthropology Quarterly* 5(1):29–47.

1993   *With Child in Mind: Studies of the Personal Encounter with Infertility.* Philadelphia: University of Pennsylvania Press.

Sargent, Carolyn

1982   *The Cultural Context for Therapeutic Choice.* Dordrecht: D. Reidel.

1985   "Witches, Merchants, and Midwives: Domains of Power among Bariba Women." In *African Healing Strategies,* ed. Brian du Toit and Ismail H. Abdallas, 96–108. New York Trado-Medic Books.

1989a   "Women's Roles and Women Healers in Contemporary Rural and Urban Benin." In *Women as Healers: Cross-Cultural Perspectives,* ed. Carol S. McClain, 204–219. New Brunswick: Rutgers University Press.

1989b   *Maternity, Medicine, and Power: Reproductive Decisions in Urban Benin.* Berkeley: University of California Press.

1990   "The Politics of Birth: Cultural Dimensions of Pain, Virtue, and Control among the Bariba of Benin." In *Births and Power: Social Change and the Politics of Reproduction,* ed. W. Penn Handwerker, 69–80. Boulder, Colo.: Westview Press.

Sargent, Carolyn, and Nancy Stark
   1987   "Surgical Birth: Interpretations of Cesarean Deliveries among Private Hospital Patients and Nursing Staff." *Social Science and Medicine* 25(12):1269–1276.
   1989   "Childbirth Education and Childbirth Models: Parental Perspectives on Control, Anesthesia, and Technological Intervention in the Birth Process." *Medical Anthropology Quarterly* 3(1):36–51.

Sault, Nicole
   1994   "How the Body Shapes Parenthood: 'Surrogate' Mothers in the U.S. and Godmothers in Mexico." In *Many Mirrors: Body Image and Social Relations in Anthropological Perspective,* ed. Nicole Sault, 292–318. New Brunswick: Rutgers University Press.

Scheper-Hughes, Nancy
   1989   "Lifeboat Ethics: Mother Love and Child Death in Brazil." *Natural History* (October): 142–147.
   1992   *Death Without Weeping: The Violence of Everyday Life in Brazil.* Berkeley: University of California Press.

Scheper-Hughes, Nancy, ed.
   1987   *Child Survival: Anthropological Perspectives on the Treatment and Maltreatment of Children.* Dordrecht: D. Reidel.

Schlinger, Hilary
   1990   *Circle of Midwives: Organized Midwifery in North America.* Independently published by Hilary Schlinger.

Schultze Jena, Leonhard
   1933   *Indiana 1: Leben, Glaube, and Sprache der Quiche von Guatemala.* Jena: Verlag von Gustav Fischer.

Scully, Diana
   1980   *Men Who Control Women's Health: The Miseducation of Obstetrician-Gynecologists.* Boston: Houghton Mifflin.

Sepkoski, C., T. B. Brazelton, et al.
   1992   "The Effects of Maternal Epidural Anesthesia on Neonatal Behavior during the First Month." *Developmental Medicine and Child Neurology* 34:1072–1080.

Shanley, Laura Kaplan
   1994   *Unassisted Childbirth.* Westport, Conn.: Bergin and Garvey.

Shaw, Nancy Stoller
   1974   *Forced Labor: Maternity Care in the United States.* New York: Pergamon Press.

Shearer, Beth
   1989   "Forced Cesareans: The Case of the Disappearing Mother." *International Journal of Childbirth Education* 4(1):7–10.

Spallone, Patricia
   1989   *Beyond Conception: The New Politics of Reproduction.* Granby, Mass.: Bergin and Garvey.

Spallone, Patricia, and D. L. Steinberg, eds.
  1987   *Made to Order: The Myth of Reproductive and Genetic Progress.* New York: Pergamon Press.

Star, Rima Beth
  1986   *The Healing Power of Birth.* Austin: Star Publishing.

Starr, Paul
  1982   *The Social Transformation of American Medicine.* New York: Basic Books.

Steppard, Chris
  1989   *Nyamakuta—The One Who Receives: An African Midwife.* VHS video documentary, 34 minutes. Filmmakers Library, Inc., 124 E. 40th St., New York, NY 10016.

Stolcke, V.
  1986   "New Reproductive Technologies: Same Old Fatherhood." *Critical Anthropology* 6(3):5–31.

Strathern, Marilyn
  1992   *Reproducing the Future: Essays on Anthropology, Kinship, and the New Reproductive Technologies.* New York: Routledge.

Stuart-Macadam, Patricia, and Katherine A. Dettwyler, eds.
  1995   *Breastfeeding: Biocultural Perspectives.* New York: Aldine de Gruyter.

Sukkary, Soheir
  1981   "She Is No Stranger: The Traditional Midwife in Egypt." *Medical Anthropology* 5(1):27–34.

Sullivan, Deborah, and Rose Weitz
  1988   *Labor Pains: Modern Midwives and Home Birth.* New Haven: Yale University Press.

Susie, Debra Ann
  1988   *In the Way of Our Grandmothers: A Cultural View of Twentieth-Century Midwifery in Florida.* Athens: University of Georgia Press.

Telfair, Joseph, and Kermit B. Nash
  1996   "African Americans." In *Cultural and Ethnic Diversity: A Guide for Genetics Professionals,* ed. Nancy Fisher, 36–59. Baltimore: Johns Hopkins University Press.

Thorp, James A., V. M. Parisi, P. C. Boylan, and D. A. Johnston
  1989   "The Effect of Continuous Epidural Analgesia on Cesarean Section for Dystocia in Nulliparous Women" *American Journal of Obstetrics and Gynecology* 161(3):670–675.
  1993   "The Effect of Intrapartum Epidural Analgesia on Nulliparous Labor." *American Journal of Obstetrics and Gynecology* 169(4):851–858.

Treichler, Paula
  1990   "Feminism, Medicine, and the Meaning of Childbirth." In *Body/Politics: Women and the Discourses of Science,* ed. M. Jacobus, Evelyn Fox Keller, and Sally Shuttleworth, 132–156. New York: Routledge.

Trevathan, Wenda R.
  1987   *Human Birth: An Evolutionary Perspective.* Hawthorne, N.Y.: Aldine de Gruyter.

Tronick, E. Z., G. A. Morelli, and S. Winn
    1987   "Multiple Caretaking of Efe (Pygmy) Infants." *American Anthropologist* 89:96–106.
Tronick, E. Z., S. Winn, and G. A. Morelli
    1985   "Multiple Caretaking in the Context of Human Evolution: Why Don't the Efe Know the Western Prescription for Child Care?" In *The Psychobiology of Attachment and Separation,* ed. M. Reite and T. Field, 191–206. New York: Academic Press.
Van Esterick, Penny, ed.
    1989   *Beyond the Breast-Bottle Controversy.* New Brunswick: Rutgers University Press.
Varney, Helen (Burst)
    [1980] 1987   *Nurse-Midwifery.* 2d ed. Boston: Blackwell Scientific Publications.
Verny, Thomas, and Pamela Weintraub
    1991   *Nurturing the Unborn Child: A Nine-Month Program for Soothing, Stimulating, and Communicating with Your Baby.* New York: Delacorte.
Vincent-Priya, Jacqueline
    1991   *Birth Without Doctors: Conversations with Traditional Midwives.* London: Earthscan Publications.
Ward, Martha C.
    1986   *Poor Women, Powerful Men: America's Great Experiment in Family Planning.* Boulder, Colo.: Westview Press.
    1989   *Nest in the Wind: Adventures in Anthropology on a Tropical Island.* Prospect Heights, Ill.: Waveland Press.
    1990   "The Politics of Adolescent Pregnancy: Turf and Teens in Louisiana." In *Births and Power: Social Change and the Politics of Reproduction,* ed. W. Penn Handwerker, 101–113. Boulder, Colo.: Westview Press.
    1991   "Cupid's Touch: The Lessons of the Family Planning Movement for the AIDS Epidemic." *Journal of Sex Research* 28(2):298–305.
Wertz, Richard W., and Dorothy C. Wertz
    1989   *Lying-In: A History of Childbirth in America.* 2d ed. New Haven: Yale University Press.
Whiteford, Linda M., and Marilyn L. Poland, eds.
    1989   *New Approaches to Human Reproduction: Social and Ethical Dimensions.* Boulder, Colo.: Westview Press.
Woodward, L., et al.
    1982   "Exposure to Drugs with Possible Adverse Effects During Pregnancy and Childbirth." *Birth* 9:165.

PART ONE

The Social Construction of
Authoritative Knowledge in Childbirth

ONE

Authoritative Knowledge
and Its Construction

Brigitte Jordan

Jordan uses her exquisite sense of description to birth a theoretical framework which both grows from, and reflects back on, the data: authoritative knowledge isn't produced by access to complex technology, or some will to hierarchy in the abstract. It is a way of organizing power relations in a room which makes them seem literally unthinkable in any other way. In childbirth, authoritative knowledge in high-tech America takes the form of active suppression of whatever it is that women might know, think, or imagine about themselves in the birth process.

—RAYNA RAPP,
commentary on "Birth in Twelve Cultures: Papers in Honor of Brigitte Jordan," a symposium at the annual meeting of the American Anthropological Association, San Francisco, December 1992

Twenty years ago when I began investigating obstetrics and midwifery in Yucatan, there were few anthropologists who had even *considered* these topics in any systematic way. There was a groundbreaking survey article by Margaret Mead and Niles Newton that mostly bemoaned the fact that there were no good ethnographic data on childbirth, and there were some cross-cultural comparisons pulled out of the Human Relations Area Files (see introduction). But there were few anthropologists who thought of this as a legitimate topic in anthropology—and even that is saying too much. It wasn't that people argued about its legitimacy; it simply wasn't there. Childbirth did not exist in anthropology. There was no notion of birth as a cultural system; the idea of ethno-obstetrics—a term coined by Carol McClain (1975)—had not seen the light of day; and the notion that Western cosmopolitan obstetrics could be studied in a comparative anthropological manner as just another ethno-obstetric system—an idea for which Robert Hahn (1987) is responsible—had not been considered. For a struggling graduate student, those were intellectually lonely days indeed.

So I am tremendously pleased to see how far we have come. The anthropology of birth is now a lively and vital field, and if I have contributed to its growth, I take great pleasure in that. In my current life I am trying to understand, together with my colleagues at Xerox Palo Alto Research

Center and the Institute for Research on Learning, how people organize themselves to work together, play together, and live together—and what we as anthropologists and social scientists can do to contribute to the design of better working and learning environments. In recent years, I have been less directly concerned with childbirth and have focused more on the underlying question of cultural change, in particular, the role new kinds of artifacts and technologies play in that change. But while the shift from medical anthropology to the anthropology of work may seem fairly radical, there are also some themes that have remained constant, and that actually have deepened in significance for me in my exposure to industrial work settings. One of these is the notion of authoritative knowledge.

AUTHORITATIVE KNOWLEDGE

One of the aims of this chapter is to elaborate the notion of authoritative knowledge that I introduced in a series of earlier publications (Jordan 1977, 1983, 1987a, 1987b, 1988, 1989; Jordan and Irwin 1987, 1989; Irwin and Jordan 1987; Suchman and Jordan 1991). The central observation is that for any particular domain several knowledge systems exist, some of which, by consensus, come to carry more weight than others, either because they explain the state of the world better for the purposes at hand (efficacy) or because they are associated with a stronger power base (structural superiority), and usually both.

In many situations, equally legitimate parallel knowledge systems exist and people move easily between them, using them sequentially or in parallel fashion for particular purposes. But frequently, one kind of knowledge gains ascendance and legitimacy. A consequence of the legitimation of one kind of knowing as authoritative is the devaluation, often the dismissal, of all other kinds of knowing. Those who espouse alternative knowledge systems then tend to be seen as backward, ignorant, and naive, or worse, simply as troublemakers. Whatever they might think they have to say about the issues up for negotiation is judged irrelevant, unfounded, and not to the point (Jordan 1989). The constitution of authoritative knowledge is an ongoing social process that both builds and reflects power relationships within a community of practice (Lave and Wenger 1991; Wenger 1990). It does this in such a way that all participants come to see the current social order as a natural order, that is, the way things (obviously) are.

The devaluation of nonauthoritative knowledge systems is a general mechanism by which hierarchical knowledge structures are generated and displayed. Regarding its role in education, the French anthropologist Pierre Bourdieu comments on the role that formal education may play in the devaluation of folk knowledge in a class-structured society. He says,

[Formal schooling] succeeds in obtaining from the dominated classes a recognition of legitimate knowledge and know-how (e.g. in law, medicine, technology, entertainment, or art), entailing the devaluation of the knowledge
and know-how they effectively command (e.g. customary law, home medicine, craft techniques, folk art and language, and all the lore handed on in
the hedge-school of the witch and the shepherd . . .) and so providing a
market for material and especially symbolic products of which the means of
production are virtually monopolized by the dominant classes (e.g. clinical
diagnosis, legal advice, the culture industry, etc.). (Bourdieu and Passeron
1977:42)

In the medical field, Paul Starr gives a compelling account of the historical transformation of authoritative knowledge in America. He points out
that well into the twentieth century, medical care was provided by a multi-
stranded, pluralistic medical system within which the knowledge held by
barber surgeons, homeopaths, folk healers of various kinds, midwives, and
other empirically based practitioners was considered authoritative by different parts of the population. A series of events culminating in the Flexner Report of 1910[1] resulted in establishing allopathic professional knowledge as the dominant form—a transformation that quickly delegitimized
all other kinds of healing knowledge, putting the newly defined medical
profession in a position of cultural authority, economic power, and political influence. Starr introduces the idea of "cultural authority," which refers
to "the probability that particular definitions of reality and judgments of
meaning and value will prevail as valid and true." He argues that the acquisition of cultural authority had the consequence that doctors came to be
in charge of "the facts," that is, to have the authority to define when somebody is dead or alive, sick or well, competent or not (Starr 1982:13–15).

The process whereby the authority of any particular knowledge system
and the power relations supporting it and benefiting from it come to be
perceived not as socially constructed, relative, and often coercive but as
natural, legitimate, and in the best interest of all parties is termed "misrecognition" by Bourdieu and Passeron (1977). Others as well have pointed
out that this process makes the achieved order of the world appear to be a
fact of nature, with the consequence that the dominant positions in that
order are also a fact of nature, and hence cannot be changed. In other
words, the best way to avoid change or revolution is to make change or
revolution unthinkable (Linde 1988).

Authoritative knowledge is persuasive because it seems natural, reasonable, and consensually constructed. For the same reason it also carries the
possibility of powerful sanctions, ranging from exclusions from the social
group to physical coerciveness (Jordan and Irwin 1989). Generally, however, people not only accept authoritative knowledge (which is thereby

validated and reinforced) but also are actively and unselfconsciously engaged in its routine production and reproduction.

It is important to realize that to identify a body of knowledge as authoritative speaks, for us as analysts, in no way to the *correctness* of that knowledge. Rather, the label "authoritative" is intended to draw attention to its
status within a particular social group and to the work it does in maintaining the group's definition of morality and rationality. *The power of authoritative knowledge is not that it is correct but that it counts.*

I want to further point out that when we, as analysts, say that somebody
"has" knowledge, authoritative or otherwise, this constitutes a commitment
to try to come to an understanding of how participants in a social setting
make that fact visible to each other, ratify it, enforce it, elaborate it, and so
on, since we see knowledge not as a substance that is possessed by individuals but as a state that is collaboratively achieved within a community of
practice (Lave and Wenger 1991; Wenger 1990). By authoritative knowledge I mean, then, the knowledge that participants agree counts in a particular situation, that *they* see as consequential, on the basis of which *they*
make decisions and provide justifications for courses of action. It is the
knowledge that within a community is considered legitimate, consequential, official, worthy of discussion, and appropriate for justifying particular
actions by people engaged in accomplishing the tasks at hand.

In order for people to work together, there must be a publicly available
set of practices and reasonings that is developed and warranted within a
particular setting and that systematically informs the work and interaction
of participants (Heath and Luff 1991). In all social groups people provide
justification for what they do, reasons for why they do what they do in this
way and not another, or, when trouble arises, why things should have been
done in a particular way. Authoritative knowledge is about accountability
in a community of practice—a community that produces and reproduces
itself even as it produces and reproduces its version of authoritative knowledge. By authoritative knowledge I specifically do *not* mean the knowledge
of people in authority positions (though others have used the concept that
way). To the extent that persons in positions of authority are members of
a community of practice, they will share the local version of authoritative
knowledge with other members, but it is the local production and display
that I want to focus on in the present analysis. Authoritative knowledge is
an interactionally grounded notion. What I am specifically interested in is
how participants in particular environments make visible to themselves
and to each other what the grounds are for their proceedings. I thus forgo
theoretically derived notions of authority and knowledge in favor of investigating how participants deal with such issues in actual situations.

Let me explain how I came to develop this notion. One issue that arose
for me very early on in my work came from the observation that in some

situations, some kinds of knowledge count and others don't, regardless of "truth value." This first became apparent when I was investigating women's competence in the early self-diagnosis of pregnancy in a feminist health clinic where some women kept insisting that they knew they were pregnant before a medical pregnancy test was conclusive. This conflicted, at the time, with my own opinion that only a pregnancy test could "really" tell. But when I conducted a study with women who later had abortions (so that it was clear whether they were in fact pregnant or not), it turned out that these women were always right (Jordan 1977). (The single exception was a woman who was getting hormone injections for weight control from her doctor—a popular medical fad at the time.) But I also had every reason to believe the physicians who told me that the women in their offices didn't know if they were pregnant or not, and that doctors would be doing "countless needless abortions" if they took what women said at face value. It was then that I seriously began to question the idea that knowledge is in people's heads and that you either have it or you don't. What I observed couldn't be accounted for in those terms, with that particular conceptualization, since it looked like women "knew" in one setting, and didn't in another. And I felt that this ignorance was not a question of being modest, or intimidated by doctors, but rather that the social interaction was such that in one case such knowledge could be produced and displayed and in the other it was not allowed and didn't emerge.

I faced a similar set of issues when, years later, I began to investigate cases of court-ordered cesarean sections in the United States (Jordan and Irwin 1987, 1989; Irwin and Jordan 1987). Here too it turned out that some women were adamant that they didn't need a section. Some of these women had sections against their will, others had babies at home or in hiding. But what struck me is that among all the cases in which a section occurred and in which an outcome assessment could be made, there was not a single one in which the section, in retrospect, appeared necessary. I began to think seriously about why and how it was the case that women's knowledge didn't count while medical knowledge carried the day. Which kind of knowledge was "correct" obviously wasn't the decisive factor.

From the court-ordered section cases I learned that women who escaped sections had powerful social networks within which their version of reality was upheld and supported. They also usually were able to remove themselves physically from the hospital. The ones who got the sections were the ones who did battle with the prevailing view alone or as an isolated couple on alien territory. They were often the women who were poor, foreign, and illiterate.

And then in my work with village midwives and the medical personnel who attempted to train them, again, it became apparent that the midwives, who in the environment of hospital-based training courses often appeared stupid, illiterate, and inarticulate, showed a completely different face when engaged in doing their own work in their own communities, where their skills were acknowledged and respected. And so, in the course of the years, I began to realize that in any particular social situation a multitude of ways of knowing exist, but some carry more weight than others. Some kinds of knowledge become socially sanctioned, consequential, even "official," and are accepted as grounds for legitimate inference and action. In some groups, differing kinds of knowledge come into conflict; in others, they become a resource for constructing a joint way of seeing the world, a way of defining what shall count as authoritative knowledge.

This is the case, for example, in childbirth in Yucatan, where women in the rural communities draw on a large body of wisdom that is assembled in each particular birth from a shared history and from the experience of those present, that is, the woman's immediate family, the village midwife, and other experienced women in the community. In such situations, all participants lend a hand to give aid—physical, emotional, ritual, spiritual—and if the labor is drawn out and difficult, they build a shared store of knowledge through stories, demonstrations, and remedies. In this manner, a joint view of what is going on in *this* labor, with *this* woman-plus-baby, is constructed in which everybody involved in the birth participates. In contrast to Western medicalized births, there is no one in charge here. There is no single decision maker. It is certainly not the midwife (which was initially a surprise for me, as I expected her to act as some sort of doctor equivalent); it is not the woman, either (which is something that I, as a feminist graduate student, would have loved to see). Rather, the store of knowledge required for conducting a birth is created and re-created by all participants jointly as they do the work of birthing.

What may be interesting is that my colleagues and I have also found this horizontal distribution of authoritative knowledge in our more recent work in high-technology workplaces. For example, when we studied the control center for an airline's ground operations (Jordan 1992), we found that the people who work there are also constantly engaged in informing each other about the state of *their* world, where the "world" at issue is the world of planes in the air, on the ground, and at the gates and their state of readiness in regard to passengers, baggage, fuel, food, and crews. In this situation, information coming into the operations room through any of a number of channels (such as printers, radios, telephones, computer screens, video monitors) is potentially relevant to everybody in the room; it is not treated as privileged. People do not withhold information, they constantly give and solicit help, and they develop shared work practices and technologies that support the joint updating of the common stock of knowledge on the basis of which decisions are made in the room.

To be sure, there are supervisors in the ops room. But for the routine work of getting planes in and out, they function not so much as controllers of information and decision makers but as an extra pair of hands, an extra set of vigilant eyes, somebody who can keep watch over a particular problem as it develops and possibly link to outside resources if they are required. The routine decisions are all made by the working team.

In contrast to the ops room, there are other situations in which multiple kinds of knowledge do not come together, in which one kind of knowledge wins out and carries the day. This is typical for American hospital births, in which medical knowledge supersedes and delegitimizes other potentially relevant sources of knowledge such as the woman's prior experience and the knowledge she has of the state of her body. Nonmedical knowledge is devalued by all participants, usually including the woman herself, who comes to believe that the course charted on the basis of professional medical knowledge is the best for her. In the rare case that she does not acquiesce and decides to actively resist, we get, as we have seen, the phenomenon of the court-ordered cesarean section—that is, the legal enforcement of one particular kind of knowledge.

THE ACHIEVEMENT OF AUTHORITATIVE KNOWLEDGE IN AN AMERICAN HOSPITAL BIRTH

In the rest of this chapter, I explore the role of technology and social interaction in the constitution and display of authoritative knowledge by drawing on videotaped data from a high-technology birth setting. I argue that obstetric technology and technical procedures are central in this environment and that the "ownership" of the artifacts necessary to manage the labor simultaneously defines and displays who should be seen as possessing authoritative knowledge, and consequently as holding legitimate decision-making power.

I have chosen this particular birth because it provides a particularly telling example of the situation that is of interest to me here: work settings where the business at hand is collaboratively accomplished and technologically mediated. I am using *this* case because I have especially good video data on it, which is required for doing the kind of close analysis that I hope will make my point. Some will object that the birth I describe is not typical; that theirs was different; that births in their community are not carried out like this. However, my argument here does not hinge on whether American births generally look like the one I describe. The conclusions I draw apply to American hospital births only to whatever extent particular births partake of the social and material features outlined below. Where there is a different social organization and different distribution of technological resources, different characteristics will prevail. Conversely, this analysis is at least suggestive for work settings that share the technological, social-interactional, spatial, and organizational characteristics of the case described here.

On the videotape, we see a woman laboring in a high-technology hospital ready to push her baby out. However, what her body tells her, what she knows (and displays) by virtue of her bodily experience, has no status in this setting. What counts is the technologically and procedurally based knowledge of the physician that is inaccessible to the woman, but without which the birth is not allowed to proceed. Competing kinds of knowledge held by the woman and other participants in the scene are jointly suppressed and managed. In this case and others like it, authoritative knowledge and attendant decision making are hierarchically distributed compared to midwife-supported birth.

The Data

The data come from a large research project on the dynamics of care during the second stage of labor that was carried out in a perinatal center of a western city in the United States between 1986 and 1989.[2] The protocol for the project included videotaping of women's labors from about an hour before the birth of the baby through an hour afterward. In addition to these videotapes, I had access to a summary of the medical record and the transcript of an interview conducted with the women about four weeks postpartum. While the birth I will be analyzing was not atypical for births in that particular hospital, its typicality or lack thereof is not what matters for my analysis. Rather, I use this birth as a means to illustrate the mechanisms by which, in high-technology settings, authoritative knowledge comes to be distributed in particular ways. I do intend to claim that my argument holds for settings that are like this one in regard to hierarchically organized ownership of the salient technologies, be they labor rooms or not. What I am specifically not claiming is that births in American hospitals are always or typically conducted in this way. The point here is not to indict American birthing practices but rather to show what happens when technology-dependent knowledge becomes hierarchically distributed. (For a transcript of this labor, see Jordan 1992.)

The Setting

The people present in the labor room with the woman are, initially, her husband and a nurse-technician who has been taking care of her throughout the labor. The husband appears intimidated by the scene. He comes to the woman's bedside when she calls him but gets out of the way when the medical team moves in. The nurse is in a delicate position. She is the liaison (not to say interface) between the woman and the physician who will perform the delivery. As such, she needs to assess the woman's state within a small range of error to be able to call the physician in time to be there for the crucial stages of labor and delivery that require his presence, but not so early as to waste his valuable time. Throughout the labor, she is very much preoccupied with the electronic fetal monitor (EFM), a machine that plots the strength of uterine contractions against the fetal heartbeat. The EFM is widely believed to give early warning of intrauterine difficulties, even though it has never been shown that routine EFM treatment improves birth outcome (Leveno et al. 1986; Prentice and Lind 1987). It is positioned at the bedside in such a way that the nurse can consult it in the same glance with which she looks at the patient. Since the woman's medical chart has been placed on top of the fetal monitor, the activity of making periodic entries in the chart also involves turning to the machine.

The Story of This Birth.   The woman on the tape has been in labor for about ten hours. She is twenty-five years old and this is her second child. She is in bed, flat on her back, attached to an intravenous (IV) pole through a line that goes into her left hand; she is connected to the electronic fetal monitor through wires coming out of her vagina. The videotape is started about half an hour before the baby is born. In the preceding hours, during the first stage of labor, the woman's cervix has slowly opened up so that the baby's head can pass through. She is now in the second stage of labor. During this stage, women experience increasingly powerful urges to push that become progressively more irresistible until the baby is finally pushed out.

In this particular case, however, the woman is not allowed to push. Every effort is made to keep her from giving in to the overpowering impulse to bear down. She is asked to suppress the urge long enough for the physician to come in and pronounce her ready. The physician is paged several times but does not appear. Meanwhile, the woman is doing Lamaze breathing, a learned type of breathing intended to help her last through the contractions without pushing. The pattern sounds something like "he he he hoo, he he he hoo." The visible and audible breathing pattern women are taught provides a convenient standardized metric by which the degree to which they are in or out of control can be assessed by themselves and by their attendants. The nurse makes every attempt to help the woman remain within acceptable behavioral norms by breathing with her in the Lamaze pattern. As time goes on, the woman's distress and pain become more and more pronounced.

The nurse leaves for a short while to see about paging the doctor herself. A nursing student (who has been running the camera) takes her place until she returns. A woman medical student comes in. She and the nurse agree that the woman should be checked. The medical student performs a vaginal examination without asking the woman's permission or explaining what she is doing. The examination is inconclusive both in the sense that the medical student cannot feel what the state of the woman's cervix is and in the sense that even if she knew, it wouldn't matter because she cannot give the official permission to push.

The physician finally arrives, together with a male medical student. He examines the woman and declares that she is ready to push. The staff prepare her for the delivery. They put her feet in stirrups and swab her down with antiseptic solution. The husband is told to take his place at her head. The woman medical student puts on gloves to deliver the baby. The physician stands ready with a suctioning tube. As the head emerges, he suctions the baby's nose and mouth. The child is delivered by the medical student, who announces that it's a boy. She immediately gives the baby to a pediatrician, who dries him, suctions him, and gives him an Apgar score, out of the mother's line of sight. The camera remains mostly on the baby being processed. Quick cuts to the mother show her in pain. Presumably the placenta is delivered. Finally, several minutes after the baby is born, he is given to his mother to hold. She touches his cheeks gingerly, with one finger. After a while mother and father slowly peel away the layers of clothing to take a peek at their baby. The mother begins to smile. Her face is transformed.

Access to Technology and the Hierarchical Distribution of Knowledge. What is massively evident on the tape is that throughout the labor participants work hard to maintain the definition of the situation as one in which the woman's knowledge counts for nothing. They all know that she "cannot" push until the doctor gives the official go-ahead. Within this particular knowledge system, it is believed that only the doctor can tell when a woman is ready to push—information he gains from checking the dilation of the cervix during a vaginal examination. This fiction is maintained collaboratively, by agency of the woman herself, her husband, the nurse, the medical student—in the face of the fact that anybody who cares to look or listen can see that this woman's body is ready to push the baby out.[3]

What the woman knows and displays, by virtue of her bodily experience, has no status in this setting. Within the official scheme of things, she has nothing to say that matters in the actual management of her birth. Worse, her knowledge is nothing but a problem for her and the staff. What she knows emerges not as a contribution to the store of data relevant for making decisions but as something to be cognitively suppressed and behaviorally managed. In the labor room authoritative knowledge is privileged,[4] the prerogative of the physician, without whose official certification of the woman's state the birth cannot proceed.

How is it, then, that the participants in the labor room display to each other and to themselves that authoritative knowledge is held by the physician and that the woman's knowledge does not count? If technology is seen not only as a collection of complex gadgets and machinery but also as the methods and techniques developed in the communities of practice that use these technologies,[5] then we see that technologies create particular kinds of social spaces within which certain activities are more or less possible and more or less likely. In the present context, I am particularly interested in the ways in which technologies are socially situated, that is to say, are given meaning in and through social interaction, are appreciated for their symbolic value as well as their use value, are owned and displayed by different segments of a community of practice, and are used to express power, expert status, and other socially meaningful relationships between people.

Women who have their babies in the hospital are likely to know a great deal about obstetric technologies. Especially if they have gone through pre-natal medical care, they have become familiar with a great deal of it during their pregnancies. They know about screening and stress tests, ultrasound examinations, electronic fetal monitoring, and the like. They also know that just beyond the doors of the labor room is an operating room where C-sections can be performed.

In spite of such exposure to obstetric technology, it appears that this particular woman is inert with respect to the technologies salient in the setting. None of them are ordered, operated, or interpreted by her. She apparently understands little about the role of the intravenous drip of oxytocin that has been increasing the strength of her contractions, nor does she know how and why such an increase was ordered. Similarly, there is no evidence that she actively processes the output of the fetal monitor, in spite of the fact that it is right next to her bed and that there are times when it contradicts her experience. One might say that the artifacts and procedures that make up professional obstetric practice are arcane to her. She doesn't look, she doesn't touch. She is passively tethered to the IV pole on one side of her bed and to the fetal monitor on the other.

The nurse, in contrast, is very much involved with the machinery. It provides for her a level of reality that her unmediated observations, her direct experience of the woman's state, do not. Throughout the labor, she looks to the EFM for information about the course of the contractions. We see her eyes glancing at the machine, often just when the woman is in greatest distress. In this setting, checking with the machine is not an occasional event but an ever-present phenomenon.[6]

The Medical Staff as Gatekeepers. As a member of the medical team, the nurse is an expert reader, interpreter, and user of the information the EFM machine provides. The laboring woman is not, and no attempt is made to explicate the role of EFM information in decision making about the conduct of her labor. Other artifacts and procedures important for the conduct of birth are even less transparent and at the same time more restricted as to who can legitimately and consequentially employ them. For example, only the physician can do the vaginal examination on the basis of which the woman will be "allowed" to push the baby out. It is interesting that there are others in the room who are known to be competent to do that examination, such as a nurse standing off camera. But she says she doesn't want to do it because the physician would have to repeat it anyway. Insofar as her knowledge is not, cannot be, consequential in this setting at this time, it has no status. In other words, it is not so much the information that the woman is ready to push which is necessary here (that information, as we have seen, is amply available), but rather, this information has to be produced by the right person to become authoritative knowledge. Though everybody knows that the woman (whom one *might* consider the central actor) is ready to give birth, this information counts for nothing until it is legitimized by the physician. Within this system, only the physician can give the go-ahead. It is this gatekeeping function that is acknowledged by the participants when they agree that it would be futile for any one of them to do a vaginal examination now.

One might ask, why are nurses allowed to perform dilation checks at other times during labor? It appears that progress checking is one of the functions of the auxiliary staff that contributes to the proper staging of the main event. By reserving the certification to the physician, however, the system also assures that the birth does not proceed without him, which is, after all, an ever-present threat.

The requirement that it be the physician who decides when the woman can push has a further consequence. The nurse notes the time of the pronouncement, and it is this time that officially determines the beginning of second stage. In this particular case, the baby is born six minutes later, which makes the official duration of the second stage, as noted in the medical record, six minutes. One can judge from all the behavioral signs that the second stage, in fact, began quite a bit earlier, at a time when the physician who is required for certification was simply not present. This artificial punctuation of the labor process produces prejudiced statistics that enter into computations of average length of second stage and thereby become normative for the management of labor. Birth attendants practicing in home settings argue that hospital-based data are skewed in the direction of shortening the normal stages of labor.

Status of the Woman's Knowledge.   In this labor room, there coexist two versions of reality, two alternative claims to relevant knowledge. The woman presents hers verbally and bodily. She knows she has to push and says so clearly.[7] She also expresses it in the visible, almost superhuman effort she marshals to suppress the urge to push. But every time she tries to get her desire—her expressed knowledge about the state of her body—acknowledged and made the basis for proceeding with the birth, her version of reality is overridden, is ignored, is denied, or, most frequently, is sidetracked, deflected, and replaced with some other definition of reality. Something else is offered up as being more relevant, as might happen to an obstinate child whose parent opts for distraction rather than confrontation. This phenomenon is massively present, as an inspection of any part of the transcript will reveal. For example:

Woman: I gotta push *now.*	*Nurse:* You can pretty soon.
Woman: I can't.	*Nurse:* Look at me.
Woman: I can't.	*Nurse:* All you can do is try.
Woman: HOO. . . . H (pain sound).	*Nurse:* It's almost gone.
Woman: I can't.	*Nurse:* Take a cleansing breath.
Woman: I can't.	*Nurse:* Let's just say you can.
Woman: I just wanna push.	*Nurse:* I know . . . it'll feel better for you to push, but in the meantime I don't want you to.[8]

The woman is instructed to override what her body tells her and to act and feel otherwise. How is that "misrecognition" of her own interests accomplished? More specifically, how can a person be enlisted in the incredibly difficult enterprise of resisting such powerful bodily impulses?

One strategy is to encourage her to do the patterned Lamaze breathing. When the woman cries out that she cannot control the pushing urge anymore, the nurse bends over her with direct eye contact and makes the official "he he he hoo" sounds, forcefully suggesting that that is the way to control the painful urge. The woman, in desperation, pours her wrenching bodily experience into the making of the permitted sounds, the officially sanctioned language of distress in this situation. As long as she produces the magic incantation "he he he hoo," no matter how desperate—insofar as these are the officially sanctioned sounds and not an idiosyncratic outcry—she is seen by herself and those around her as "not out of control," "collaborating," "a good patient."[9] And by holding on to those sounds and not giving in to uncontrolled breathing, writhing, and screaming, the woman expresses her desire to be a good patient while, in the modulating of the "he he he hoo" through clenched teeth or with sobbing outbreath, she can nevertheless express her pain and misery without being censured for losing control.[10]

So it is the case here that the nurse and the other bystanders in the room (i.e., the woman's husband, the medical student, the nursing student who operates the camera, and a second nurse who had been paging the doctor) understand clearly that this woman is ready to push. Yet this knowledge counts for nought. It has no status and no consequences. The woman is spoken to consolingly, encouragingly, soothingly, or firmly, as her behavior requires, often in a kind of singsong voice that is close to the inflection familiar from kindergarten and grade school teachers. The attendants' pseudointimate voices emphasize the childlike status of the woman. The staff are nice to her because she cannot help it if she lapses into unapproved behavior. As with small children, they may even have to physically restrain her on occasion, but they do it for her benefit.

Another way of controlling the woman's behavior is by straightforwardly giving orders:

Husband: You want some ice?	[woman pats her face rhythmically with washcloth, indicates "no"]
Woman: I just wanna push.	
Nurse: I know it won't be long— it'll feel better for you to push	[speaks to woman without looking at her while writing in chart]
but in the meantime I don't want you to	[leans toward woman and whispers]
okay?	[emphatic]

As things become more difficult, the nurse uses a large number of unmitigated imperatives, such as: "look at me"; "come on"; "breathe with your mouth"; "take a cleansing breath"; "take a deep sigh." The nurse also indicates correct behavior with such praise as "good," "perfect," a clear indication of who in this situation holds the knowledge that counts. These evaluations, again, are similar to those used by teachers in schools (Mehan 1979) and reinforce the woman's childlike position.

Information derived from the machine serves as a resource and a justification for negating and redefining the woman's experience. For example, at one point the nurse, consulting the monitor, tells the woman what she should be feeling:

Nurse: [The contraction] is at the peak . . .
　　　　it's going down . . .
　　　　it's a smaller contraction . . .
　　　　almost gone . . .

But the nurse's characterization contradicts the rising, not decreasing, pain visible in the woman. So we have in this scene simultaneous but conflicting claims about what the woman's body is up to. The nurse's knowledge is machine-based; she can see the contraction fading away. But the woman is falling apart because her experience is quite otherwise. What we get here is a negation of what the woman's body tells her by what the machine tells the nurse.

STAGING THE PHYSICIAN'S PERFORMANCE

The physician's unquestioned status and authority rest, in the last analysis, on a social contract that accords him that authority. What I am interested in here is how, for participants in this delivery (the woman, her husband, and the medical staff), this authority is not only displayed, but in its implementation is interactionally achieved. It becomes visible in the ritual deference paid to the superior status of medical knowledge. It is also displayed in the way activities in the labor room are orchestrated, unfolding in the manner of a dramatic theatrical metaphor. As the labor progresses, there is a palpable buildup of tension, not, as one might expect, foreshadowing the moment the woman gives birth, but rather leading up to the entrance of the physician without whom the delivery literally cannot proceed. His entry is eagerly awaited. He is paged, with increasing urgency, at least four times in twelve minutes before he finally appears.

Then he sweeps in with his entourage, a male medical student holding his white coat. Without a glance at the woman he walks over to the fetal monitor, cursorily checks the output and then confers briefly with the nurse and the female medical student. The team members take their positions as if on a stage or in the battlefield, around the lower end of the woman's body, essentially dividing her into two parts: the "interaction end" at her head, to which the husband is delegated, and the "business end," where the important work of getting the baby delivered takes place.[11]

The physician performs the long-awaited examination standing up, looking away over the woman, with the nurse gazing up at him. This is an achieved arrangement. One can do a vaginal examination standing up or one can get down to the woman's level as midwives are wont to do, looking at her, talking to her as they do the exam. This doctor's attitude and stance, and the framing that is done by the team, are meaningfully produced; it is not that the world is that way "naturally." Nor is this kind of framing of the physician restricted to this labor room or labor rooms in general. It is common in medical interactions that have staff of various ranks present (as, for example, attending physicians, nurses, residents, and medical students during walking rounds). Mavis Kirkham (1988), observing labors in hierarchical hospital settings, notes the staff "waiting on" the doctors in what she calls a pattern of "dancing attendance." She also notes that such actions inevitably reinforce the situation that led to them.[12]

The team not only frames him physically but also shadows him verbally. They explain, highlight, and interpret his actions to the woman with whom he does not communicate directly. The medical student explains: "He is checking to see if you can push, okay?"

The team takes up what the physician says, repeating his words, translating them, pointing out their significance:

Doctor:	Yeah she can push.	[to nurse]
Nurse:	Can she? plus one?	[looking up at doctor getting ready to write]
Doctor:	Yeah plus two.	[nurse writes in chart]
Woman:	Oh NO.	[in pain]
Nurse:	You can push, it'll feel good.	[to woman, with relief, like a good news announcement]

The repetition of the physician's words by the staff highlights, like a theater chorus, what is to be considered important. The physician's professionalism is expressed in his totally impersonal attitude toward the woman. He treats her as an object, a performance that is made possible by the fact that others isolate and shield him. He never has to deal with this woman as a person. The only time he addresses her before the birth is when he says, "Let me check you before you get another contraction." The woman, in that she makes no interactional demands on him, collaborates in this construction.

PARTICIPATION STRUCTURES IN THE LABOR ROOM

Students of interaction (e.g., Goffman 1963, 1981; Erickson 1981, 1982, 1991; Heath 1986; Kendon 1985, 1990; Goodwin and Goodwin 1992; Goodwin 1990; Suchman 1996) have noted that important social "work" is done through participation frameworks—fluid structures of mutual engagement and disengagement characterized by bodily alignment (usually face-to-face), patterned eye contact, situation-appropriate tone of voice, and other resources the situation may afford.

What is striking in the labor room is that the laboring woman, who might be seen as the focal participant, has only limited access to the various participation structures we observe. She is primarily engaged in dyadic interaction with the nurse, or, occasionally, with her husband. But these sometimes intense interactions are always in the service of the business at hand: dedicated to maintaining the current definition of reality by preventing her from letting her bodily experience gain ascendance. These dyadic interactions appear to be the only legitimate type of interaction for her. She does not enter into other kinds of participation frames. As soon as other people enter the room, such as the woman medical student or later on the physician with his entourage, the laboring woman is virtually excluded from any sort of engagement in talk or activity. Neither the physician nor the students introduce themselves to her. The physician never looks at her, doesn't address her until he stands ready to perform the vaginal examination, and then simply announces what he is going to do—a type of statement to which the most appropriate response is silent compliance.

The nurse is involved in a number of different participation frameworks, shifts that are indicated by changes in body posture (e.g., straightening up, turning away from the woman and toward the door) and, maybe most significant, by voice quality. There is a reciprocated, bantering tone in her interaction with the medical student, an enthusiastic, dramatic inflection when she asks the physician "Can she [push]?" even as she speaks to the woman in a multimodulated parental voice.

In this setting, social interaction (beyond that required to maintain control) is done without the woman. Business gets done with her as an object but not as an actor. At the height of the drama when she is in great pain and barely able to control the pushing urge, the nurse and the medical student have a little chat, engage in a little private chuckle. The woman's head comes up from her pillow as if trying to see, as if trying to make a bid for inclusion or at least for acknowledgment of her plight, but to no avail. Her physical position is such that even eye contact is not easily initiated and, at any rate, there is no opening for her in the participation structure that is already set up.

Once the doctor enters, the staff interact as a team of which the physician is the focal member and from which the woman is specifically excluded. No input is solicited from her; talk is not produced for her overhearing or participation. No explanations are given. They do the business of examining her and preparing for the delivery among themselves. The woman is the object to be prepared and to be delivered.

The result of this systematic objectification of the woman is that there are two different enterprises going on in the room. The woman is desperately struggling against the sensations of her body, cajoled and parented by the nurse, who, in turn, has one eye on the medical team. The second, quite separate enterprise is to deliver the baby, which is the business of the staff. For all practical purposes, the woman has nothing to do with that, nor has she anything to say about it. She is not giving birth, she is delivered.

When the doctor finally announces that she can push, the announcement is directed to the medical team and not to the woman. The doctor says "She can push," and the nurse relays the message, "He says you can push," as if doctor and woman were not in the same room. In the ways in which participation structures are set up in the labor room, her exclusion is ratified, executed, and displayed over and over again. This is one of the mechanisms by which she is denied any say in the conduct of her labor, by which she is given the message that she doesn't count.

We have seen, then, that in the labor room several different kinds of knowledge are actually present, but the only kind that counts is the knowledge delivered by the physician. This knowledge is communicated downward along a hierarchical structure of which the woman is the most distal member. All major decisions are reserved to the physician who is in charge of "the facts," the knowledge on which rational decision making is to be based.

SOME THOUGHTS ABOUT THE DESIGN OF LABOR ECOLOGIES

The structure of interaction described above contrasts with other types of arrangements that one could *imagine* for the conduct of birth, as well as some that are in place in other settings. In the particular labor room I analyzed, ownership of authoritative knowledge was limited to the authorized staff and distributed differentially and hierarchically among them while the central participant, the woman in labor, was excluded. In that context, medical knowledge is not only privileged, but supersedes and delegitimizes other potentially relevant information sources such as the woman's prior experience and the knowledge she has of the state of her body. This kind of knowledge is suppressed and delegitimized by all participants, including the woman herself. Professional medical knowledge, in contrast, is displayed as based on privileged technical procedures, machine outputs, and test results interpreted by nurse and physician specialists. It is this kind of knowledge that provides legitimation for the management of labor and delivery.

Maybe the question we want to ask at this point is, Does this kind of analysis—that is, an analysis in terms of authoritative knowledge—give us any leverage for restructuring the shape of birth in our own society? I believe it does. What we need to think about is how we can move from a situation in which authoritative knowledge is hierarchically distributed into a situation in which it is, by consensus, horizontally distributed—that is, in which all the participants in the labor and birth contribute to the store of knowledge on the basis of which decisions are made.

For our technocratized birthing systems, we would need to ask questions such as, What would have to happen for the woman to truly become a part of the decision-making process? What if her knowledge, both bodily and intellectual, were to be accorded legitimate status? What if she had a place in the professional participation structures set up around the birth? Could there *be* a translation process between what the woman knows and what the staff understands to be the situation? Could there be a mutual accommodation of divergent ways of knowing such that one single authoritative knowledge structure emerges? This, I believe, is the challenge for the future of childbirth in the technologized Western world, as well as in the developing countries of the Third World.

Given the crucial role and status of technologies in such potential accommodation, one way in which we could see this happen is if the process of birthing is accomplished with low rather than high technology. This is a path taken consciously by midwives attending home births in those areas of the world where high-technology births are not easily available to the majority of people. In such situations typically, though with exceptions, the process is collaboratively achieved, on the basis of a shared view of what is, or might be, right or wrong with the labor, and what can be done about it.

As we realize, however, that most of the technologized modern world is unlikely to go back to simpler technologies, we might also speculate whether there are other ways of coming to an accommodation of the woman's knowledge with the biomedical basis for decision making. One might ask, What if machine outputs and test results were to be made available and comprehensible to the woman and her nonspecialist attendants? What if labor rooms built in the possibility of transforming papered walls into large interactive information displays that could show, in graphic and comparative form, what is known about the state of the labor on the basis of physical examinations, monitor outputs, and test results? What if such displays were routinely used for generating conversations between the woman, the medical staff, and the woman's attendants—that is, the people concerned with making this birth successful? It would be during such conversations that agreement could be established about the meaning of patterns observed, alignment could be sought between what the woman experiences and what the machines show, and joint decisions could be made based on the best available evidence from all sources.

My prediction is that just as airplane seats will be equipped in the future with information displays that tell us what we want to know about the flight we are on (e.g., location, sights below, technical data, poetry about flying) so also will we eventually have labor information displays that are accessible and understandable to all participants, that can provide suggestions about relaxation and positive imagery as well as allow the exploration of what-if scenarios. For example, one could imagine that during a dystocic labor the group gathered around the laboring woman might want to understand what could happen to the baby if the mother changed positions, and compare that to the effects of an oxytocin infusion.

What is more important than any technology, however, is that new communities of practice arise, in which pregnant (and nonpregnant) women (and men) can begin to explore the space of labor events and what they mean, what kinds of consequences different actions and interventions might have, for what kinds of procedures consensus exists and where it is shaky, so that in the long run the physician and medical staff would become expert consultants, guides through the maze of specialized information, rather than function as privileged decision makers about the management of birth. In contrast to the labor room described here, where much energy has to be expended on suppressing the rival knowledge that is constantly threatening to seep in, there would be no competing knowledge. Rather, management decisions would be based on taking maximal advantage of the different perspectives contributed by team members toward the shared understanding of the labor and the situation of the woman-cum-baby.

A redesign of the ecology of labor would also affect the social structure of birth participation. In the labor room I described there is a clear hierarchy. Checking the woman's cervix and deciding whether she can push are duties reserved only for the physician. He does not participate in the earlier stages of the labor. He is awaited. He is paged a number of times, and when he is not found, every attempt is made to stifle the woman's real need to push the baby out until the doctor can perform the examination and authorize the next stage of the delivery. The woman's body's natural responses are systematically erased and then reconstructed under the disinterested tutelage and coaching of the medical staff. This has the effect of taking away any notion of achievement from the woman, so that, indeed, as the nurse says, the medical staff will "finish this up and have that baby." In the ways in which the woman is led to collaborate in the violation of her body, the abnegation of her self, the misrecognition (in Bourdieu's sense) of her own interest, in all these ways "the way power circulates in the world" (to use Foucault's words) is displayed.

By contrast, in an alternative birth ecology participants would not focus on the technical expert in the way they do on the physician; there would be neither anticipation nor grossly deferential orienting. The expert is not framed in the central position but rather moves in and out of the interactional frameworks of the labor room as the situation requires. While he or she may take charge in touchy situations, the ordinary decisions of normal birth management emerge out of what is known by everybody about the current state of the labor. In such a setting, authoritative knowledge would be horizontally rather than hierarchically distributed, and its production and use would be shared by all participants.

At this time, such integrated alternative birth ecologies do not exist, though pieces are in evidence in a variety of settings. As we ponder the impact of new technologies on the course of labor and birth, it might be worth our while to give serious attention to the possibility of designing labor ecologies that legitimize at the same time the knowledge of the medical staff, the woman's participation in their knowledge system, and her own bodily knowing.

NOTES

The analysis presented in this chapter has been published as part of a larger study that compares the organization of work and the production of authoritative knowledge in two high-technology settings: this particular labor room and an airlines operations room in a western metropolitan airport (Jordan 1992). It also appears in slightly different form as chapter 6 of the fourth edition of *Birth in Four Cultures* (Jordan [1978] 1993).

I thank my colleagues from the Interaction Analysis Laboratory at Xerox Palo Alto Research Center and the Institute for Research on Learning for shaping my thinking about the issues discussed here. I am particularly indebted to Bracha Alpert, who was an early collaborator on these data. The current version of this document has benefited from critical readings and substantive contributions by Phil Agre, Liam Bannon, Carole Browner, Debra Cash, Terry Craig, Sr. Mary Christine Cremin, Robbie Davis-Floyd, Martha Feldman, Wendy Freed, Jim Greeno, Robert Hahn, Chuch Kukla, Joyce Roberts, Barbara Rylko-Bauer, Ron Simons, Lucy Suchman, and Valerie Wheeler, and from the editorial sleight-of-hand of Paul Duguid. I am deeply indebted to Robbie Davis-Floyd not only for her editing competence and cheerfulness in the face of multiple revisions but also for her unflagging enthusiasm and dedication.

1. The Flexner Report of 1910 was a Carnegie-sponsored study of the state of the medical profession in the United States that revealed a wide array of unregulated and competing schools of medicine. The report led to the enforcement of much higher standards, coupled with substantial funding, for allopathic medical schools and physicians and to the closing of homeopathic and other "irregular" medical schools, many of which had admitted blacks and women. Thus the Flexner Report was instrumental in cementing the cultural dominance of "regular" (allopathic) medicine and in ensuring that the vast majority of American physicians would be white, middle- and upper-class, and male (Ehrenreich and English 1973; Wertz and Wertz [1977] 1989).

2. The project, "A Comparison of Supported versus Directed Care during the Second Stage of Labor," was supported by grant no. 1-RO1 NR 01500-03 NCNR, NIH,DHHS, and directed by Joyce Roberts. I thank her and her team for sharing their data and insights.

3. It is worth mentioning here that in less hierarchically organized obstetric systems, such official certification is not necessary. In Holland, a country that has vastly better outcome statistics than the United States, it is a combination of what the woman says and observations of her state by her midwife that determine when it is time to push (see Jordan [1978] 1993:chap. 3).

4. By "privileged" I mean to suggest that access is restricted.

5. This definition is an elaboration of the one adopted by the World Health Organization conference on primary health care at Alma Ata, Mongolia (WHO 1978).

6. For example, during an arbitrarily selected five-minute segment of the tape we see the nurse look at the EFM nineteen times. It would be well to keep in mind that there are alternative sources of information on the state of the labor, typically used in less technologized and less hierarchically organized settings. For example, Dutch midwives monitor the woman's experience by observing her breathing and the rising and ebbing tensions in various parts of her body. With a hand on the woman's abdomen they gauge the strength of her contractions directly, while a simple fetal stethoscope provides information on the fetal heartbeat.

7. Within seventeen minutes of the birth of the baby, the woman explicitly states on eight occasions that she has to push. On another sixteen occasions during that time, she indicates her inability to resist the urge to push with pleas like: "I can't, I can't."

8. There is much evidence that nonanswers of various sorts are a common strategy for dealing with women in obstetric settings. For example, Kirkham, who observed 113 labors, describes similar responses in labor wards in the U.K. She cites the following as a typical pattern: Woman: "How long?" Nurse: "Not long." Woman: "How long is that?" Nurse: Silence. End of conversation. Or changes subject (Kirkham 1988).

9. We can speak of the woman as "losing control" and see her as "losing control" only if we subscribe to the view that she should shape her behavior according to what the medical staff requires of her at this time. Within another framework, for example, one that sees pushing as precisely what her body *should* be doing at this stage, she would simply be doing what she is supposed to be doing. I find it personally disturbing that I myself did not see the absurdity of this formulation of "losing control" until it was pointed out to me. This is just one of the ways in which, to use Harvey Sack's expression, culture has us by the throat.

10. Subscribing to the "he he he hoo" generates a double bind for the woman. If the pain gets so intense that she cannot maintain the pattern, her abandoning it tells her and her attendants not only that she is now "out of control" but also that *she* did it, that by abandoning the Lamaze breathing she made herself lose control. The common reprimand "If you had done your Lamaze, you wouldn't have lost control" is true by definition.

11. I first drew attention to the operational bifurcation of the woman's body in hospital deliveries in Jordan 1987a.

12. Kirkham contrasts "waiting on doctors" with "waiting on the labor," which, she says, good midwives do when they are in charge of birth. They take their cues from the laboring woman, whereas for the vast majority of women whose labors she observed, the cues they gave and indeed their specific requests were ignored. Midwives and occasional doctors who waited on the labor, by contrast, actively listened to the woman. Such listening is rare in most hospital settings because the staff's primary responsibility appears to be listening to and waiting on the doctor.

REFERENCES

Bourdieu, Pierre, and Jean-Claude Passeron
   1977 *Reproduction in Education, Society, and Culture.* Sage Studies in Social and Educational Change, vol. 5. London and Beverly Hills: Sage.

Ehrenreich, Barbara, and Deirdre English
   1973 *Witches, Midwives, and Nurses: A History of Women Healers.* Old Westbury, N.Y.: Feminist Press.

Erikson, Frederick
   1981 "Classroom Discourse as Improvisation: Relationships between Academic Task Structure and Social Participation in Lessons." In *Communicating in the Classroom,* ed. Louise Cherry Wilkinson, 158–182. New York: Academic Press.
   1982 "Money Tree, Lasagna Bush, Salt and Pepper: Social Construction of Topical Cohesion in a Conversation among Italian-Americans." In *Analyzing Discourse: Text and Talk,* ed. Deborah Tannen, 43–70. Georgetown University Roundtable on Languages and Linguistics 1981. Washington, D.C.: Georgetown University Press.
   1991 " 'They Know all the Lines': Rhythmic Organization and Contextualization in a Conversational Listening Routine." Arbeitspapier Nr. 18, KontRI (Kontextualisierung durch Rhythmus und Intonation), Fachgruppe Sprachwissenschaft, Universität Konstanz.

Goffman, Erving
   1963 *Behavior in Public Places: Notes on the Social Organization of Gathering.* New York: Free Press.
   1981 *Forms of Talk.* Philadelphia: University of Pennsylvania Press.

Goodwin, Charles, and Marjorie Harness Goodwin
   1993 "Context, Activity, and Participation." In *The Contextualization of Language,* ed. Peter Auer and Aldo di Luzio, 77–99. Amsterdam: Benjamins.

Goodwin, Marjorie Harness
   1990 *He-Said-She-Said: Talk as Social Organization among Black Children.* Bloomington: Indiana University Press.

Hahn, Robert
   1987 "Divisions of Labor: Obstetrician, Woman and Society in *Williams Obstetrics,* 1903–1985." *Medical Anthropology Quarterly* 1(3):256–282.

Heath, Christian
   1986 *Body Movement and Speech in Medical Interaction.* Cambridge: Cambridge University Press.

Heath, Christian, and Paul Luff
   1991 "Collaborative Activity and Technological Design: Task Coordination in London Underground Control Rooms." Proceedings of the 2d European Conference on Computer-supported Cooperative Work, Amsterdam.

Irwin, Susan, and Brigitte Jordan
   1987 "Knowledge, Practice and Power: Court-Ordered Cesarean Sections." In *The Anthropology of American Obstetrics,* ed. Robert Hahn. Special Issue of *Medical Anthropology Quarterly* 1(3):319–334.

Jordan, Brigitte
  1977   "The Self-Diagnosis of Early Pregnancy: An Investigation of Lay Competence." *Medical Anthropology* 1(2):1–38.
  [1978] 1993   *Birth in Four Cultures: A Cross-Cultural Investigation of Childbirth in Yucatan, Holland, Sweden and the United States.* 4th ed., revised and expanded by Robbie Davis-Floyd. Prospect Heights, Ill.: Waveland Press.
  1983   *Birth in Four Cultures: A Cross-Cultural Investigation of Childbirth in Yucatan, Holland, Sweden and the United States,* 2d ed. Montreal: Eden Press.
  1984   "External Cephalic Version as an Alternative to Breech Delivery and Cesarean Section." *Social Science and Medicine* 18(8):637–651.
  1987a   "The Hut and the Hospital: Information, Power and Symbolism in the Artifacts of Birth." *Birth* 14(1):36–40.
  1987b   "High Technology: The Case of Obstetrics." *World Health Forum* 8(3):312–319.
  1988   "Embodied Knowledge, Authoritative Knowledge." Paper presented at the 87th annual meeting of the American Anthropological Association, Invited Session on Embodied Knowledge, Phoenix, November.
  1989   "Cosmopolitical Obstetrics: Some Insights from the Training of Traditional Midwives." *Social Science and Medicine* 28(9):925–944.
  1990   "Technology and the Social Distribution of Knowledge." In *Anthropology and Primary Health Care,* ed. J. Coreil and D. Mull, 98–120. Boulder, Colo.: Westview Press.
  1992   "Technology and Social Interaction: Notes on the Achievement of Authoritative Knowledge in Complex Settings." IRL Technical Report, IRL92-0027. Palo Alto, Calif.: Institute for Research on Learning.
Jordan, Brigitte, and Susan Irwin
  1987   "A Close Encounter with a Court-Ordered Cesarean Section: A Case of Differing Realities." In *Encounters with Biomedicine: Case Studies in Medical Anthropology,* ed. Hans Baer, 185–199. New York: Gordon and Breach.
  1989   "The Ultimate Failure: Court-Ordered Cesarean Section." In *New Approaches to Human Reproduction,* ed. Linda Whiteford and Marilyn Poland, 13–24. Boulder, Colo.: Westview Press.
Kendon, Adam
  1985   "Behavioral Foundations for the Process of Frame Attunement in Face-to-Face Interaction." In *Discovery Strategies in the Psychology of Action,* ed. G. Ginsburg, M. Brenner, and M. von Cranach, 229–253. London: Academic Press.
  1990   *Conducting Interaction: Patterns of Behavior in Focused Encounters.* Cambridge: Cambridge University Press.
Kirkham, Mavis
  1988   "Midwives and Information-giving During Labor." In *Midwives, Research, and Childbirth,* 1, ed. Sarah Robinson and Ann M. Thomson, 117–138. London: Chapman and Hall.
Lave, Jean, and Etienne Wenger
  1991   *Situated Learning: Legitimate Peripheral Participation.* New York: Cambridge University Press.

Leveno, K. J., F. G. Cunningham, S. Nelson, M. Roark, M. L. Williams, D. Guzick, S. Dowling, C. R. Rosenfeld, and A. Buckley
    1986   "A Prospective Comparison of Selective and Universal Electronic Fetal Monitoring in 34,995 Pregnancies." *New England Journal of Medicine* 315:615.

Linde, Charlotte
    1988   "Common Sense and Its History: The Study of Cognitive Macrostructures." Paper presented at the 87th annual meeting of the American Anthropological Association, Phoenix, November.

McClain, Carol Shepherd
    1975   "Ethno-Obstetrics in Ajijic." *Anthropological Quarterly* 40(1):38–56.

Mehan, Hugh
    1979   *Learning Lessons: Social Organization in the Classroom.* Cambridge: Cambridge University Press.

Prentice, A., and T. Lind
    1987   "Fetal Heart Rate Monitoring During Labor—Too Frequent Intervention, Too Little Benefit." *Lancet* 2:1375–1377.

Starr, Paul
    1982   *The Social Transformation of American Medicine.* New York: Basic Books.

Suchman, Lucy
    1996   "Constituting Shared Workspaces." In *Communication and Cognition at Work,* ed. David Middleton and Yrjo Engestrom, 35–60. New York: Cambridge University Press.

Suchman, Lucy, and Brigitte Jordan
    1991   "Validity and the Collaborative Construction of Meaning." In *Questions about Questions: Inquiries into the Cognitive Bases of Surveys,* ed. Judith Tanur, 160–178. New York: Russell Sage.

Wenger, Etienne
    1990   "Toward a Theory of Cultural Transparency: Elements of a Social Discourse of the Visible and Invisible." Ph.D. dissertation, Department of Information and Computer Science, University of California, Irvine.

Wertz, Richard W., and Dorothy C. Wertz
    [1977] 1989   *Lying-In: A History of Childbirth in America,* rev. ed. New Haven: Yale University Press.

World Health Organization (WHO)
    1978   "Primary Health Care." International Conference on Primary Health Care, Alma Ata, USSR, September 6–12.

TWO

An Evolutionary Perspective on Authoritative Knowledge about Birth

Wenda R. Trevathan

My goal in this chapter is to persuade the reader that the evolutionary perspective on birth is one that adds to our understanding of how birth today is constructed and experienced. I also hope to persuade that seeing ourselves as resulting from evolutionary forces does not inevitably lead to assuming that we are passive victims of our evolved bodies. Rather, in Andrea Wiley's words, "we embody our past and make it an object of study in order to learn from it" (1992:232). I now turn to the subject at hand, an evolutionary perspective on authoritative knowledge about birth.

Review of the cross-cultural literature on childbirth reveals that the concept of isolated birth is either virtually unknown or a rarely achieved ideal (Konner and Shostak 1987; Trevathan 1987; for exceptions to this pattern, see Sargent 1989; Biesele, this volume). In almost every known routine circumstance, a birthing woman alerts someone else to her state and is attended by a close female relative, a friend, or a midwife. She may communicate her needs and physical experiences to her attendant, but it is often that other person who makes most of the decisions about the birthing process. The larger historically rooted social group may have already made decisions about where birth is to take place, what position the woman will be in when she delivers, what "artifacts" will be used during delivery (Jordan 1987), who receives her newborn infant, and how she may or may not behave during labor and delivery. Only in rare instances can a woman act and behave exactly as she wishes during the birth process. But has this always been so? Most scholars would agree that historical circumstances are crucial for understanding our present conditions, but I want to push that domain back five million years, before birth was social, before anyone except the individual birthing female herself had power over birth.

I suggest that it was the evolutionary process itself that first transformed birth from an individual to a social enterprise. This initial transformation having been made, it was then a simple process by which control over birth was also transferred from the individual to the person in attendance. Initially this person in whom authoritative knowledge was vested was probably a nearby companion, most likely another female, whose experience with birth and life was similar to that of the parturient herself. In other words, they were each embedded in and products of the same social milieu. Their lived experiences were similar and so the attendant could more likely be empathetic with the birthing female.

My argument is that selection for bipedalism was what set hominids on the trajectory toward social and cultural interventions in birth. But it was not simply due to a narrowing of the pelvis in conjunction with an increase in brain size as many have believed (Washburn 1960). Birth is a challenge for most primate species (Schultz 1949). One of the hallmarks of this mammalian order is a large ratio of brain or head size to body size. This means that the passage of the fetal head through the maternal pelvis is generally a tight squeeze. Because of this, mortality from cephalopelvic disproportion is not insignificant in primate species such as marmosets, squirrel monkeys, baboons, and macaques (Leutenegger 1981). Although the passageway is not so narrow in modern chimpanzees, gorillas, and orangutans (Leutenegger 1972), it is likely that the last common ancestor of humans and great apes had a pelvis/neonatal head ratio similar to that of modern gibbons. (Selection for increased body size in great apes occurred after the divergence of the ape and human lines.) But modern primates still accomplish birth without assistance, so it is probable that human ancestors before five million years ago did so as well.

I speculate that ancestral females of the Miocene epoch (24 million to 5 million years ago), before the origin of the family Hominidae, probably decided where to deliver their infants, what position to be in for delivery, and perhaps even when to deliver. There is evidence from anecdotal accounts that female monkeys and apes can stop contractions when they are uncomfortable with their surroundings or otherwise feel it is unsafe to deliver. (This has been particularly vexing to primatologists who, anxious to observe deliveries, have waited hours for the event, only to find that it occurs as soon as they go home for the evening or leave their observation post for a few minutes.)

Approximately five million years ago selection began to favor the anatomical and behavioral changes that led to bipedal walking in hominids (Lovejoy 1988). Whatever the "cause" of this new mode of locomotion (unlike that of any other animal species) or the benefits, it resulted in fundamental changes in the way birth occurred.

In quadrupedal species like monkeys, the infant emerges from the birth canal facing in the same direction as the mother (see, e.g., Graham-Jones

1962; Doyle, Pelletier, and Bekker 1967; Hopf 1967; Rothe 1974; Stevenson 1976; Kadam and Swayamprabha 1980; Kemps and Timmermans 1982). This means that the mother can reach down with her hands and guide it from the birth canal, or it can crawl up toward her nipples, unassisted. With the evolution of bipedalism, the birth canal was reoriented so that the inlet was broadest in the transverse dimension, the outlet in the sagittal or front-to-back dimension. The relevant fetal dimensions are also perpendicular: the head is broadest in the sagittal dimension, the shoulders in the transverse dimension. This means that the human infant must undergo a series of rotations to pass through the birth canal without hindrance (Berge, Orban-Segebarch, and Schmid 1984).

The anatomical change more important to my argument here requires that the human infant emerge from the birth canal facing *away* from the mother. This hinders her ability to reach down and clear a breathing passageway for the infant and to remove the cord from around the neck if it interferes with breathing or continued emergence. If she attempts to guide the infant from the birth canal, she risks pulling it against the body's angle of flexion, perhaps damaging nerves and muscles in the process (Trevathan 1988).

I have argued that with the origin of bipedalism, risks of mortality from unattended birth became greater than whatever risks were associated with having others in the vicinity of the birthing woman (Trevathan 1987). I conjecture that ancestral females who sought assistance at the time of delivery simply had more surviving and healthier offspring than those who continued the ancient mammalian pattern of delivering alone. Thus the transfer of authoritative knowledge from the birthing woman to her attendants may have begun as long ago as five million years. At that time the trade-off was probably "worth it," however, in that having assistance at birth probably made the difference between life and death for a significant number of hominid mothers and infants. (It should be emphasized that communication about birth at this time was not language-based, so it is likely that accumulation of knowledge about birth was limited.)

With encephalization in the genus *Homo* (about 2 million years ago), the already-tight fit became even tighter, although one of the compromises to the conflict between selection for large brains and narrow birth canals may have been to delay most of brain growth to the postnatal period (Montagu 1961; Gould 1977). The generalized mammalian pattern is to give birth to infants with about half of the adult brain size. The earliest members of the genus *Homo,* with adult brain size of about 700 cubic centimeters (cm^3), may have had a pelvis adequate for delivering an infant with a brain size of 350 cm^3, half the adult size. I speculate that infants of the earliest *Homo* species may not have been any larger than ours today, but their brains were much more advanced and they were far less helpless at birth than are our infants, who have the same brain size of 350 cm^3 but representing only 25 percent of modern adult brain size. Giving birth to more helpless infants, unable to assist themselves during delivery, very likely posed more challenges to ancestral females. I argue that this infant helplessness further added to the advantages of having another person present at delivery.

As many have pointed out, the most important service provided by birth attendants in most world cultures is emotional support for the birthing woman. It is more difficult to guess when in human evolutionary history this need became manifest than it is to assess the beginnings of the physical dependence on assistance, but I would propose that it was a product of encephalization, which began with the genus *Homo*. I speculate that some-time between the origin of our genus (2 million years ago) and our species (200,000 to 40,000 years ago) women became conscious of the vulnerability of themselves and their infants at the time of birth and began to seek out others for more than physical support. And with this hypothesized consciousness would have come the fear, doubt, and uncertainty that may eventually have led most women to abandon their faith in their own authority and turn it over to someone deemed by themselves or their culture to have legitimate knowledge concerning childbirth.

Most likely birth was initially accomplished by joint communication and coordinated action between the parturient and her attendant, so the birthing woman's knowledge was just as or even more important than that of her attendant (Sargent [1989] reports this to be true for most normal births among the Bariba women whose births she observed). Only recently in some industrialized nations have we reached the extreme at which her knowledge is regarded as irrelevant. For millions of years the birthing female was the most important member of the "obstetrical team," but today her knowledge about her body is often suppressed and "managed." In many contemporary birthing settings it is assumed that the woman has nothing useful to tell about her body or the birth and that only the machines and medical gatekeepers have the knowledge necessary to produce a healthy baby (see Jordan, this volume). Even worse, in some settings, she "misrecognizes" (Bourdieu and Passeron 1977) these sources of knowledge and mistrusts her own thoughts and feelings, even if she were allowed to express them.

I have suggested that maternal and infant mortality are far lower today than they would have been had the practice of seeking assistance at birth never been taken up. Thus if we place value on reducing mortality, then we can say it is "better" for individual women and the human species as a whole for attendance at birth to be a human norm. The primary currency valued in evolution is reduced mortality and higher reproductive success, which is why we have birth attendants in the first place. It was not likely initially a conscious phenomenon: those who sought assistance simply had more surviving offspring than those who did not. Rather, if my argument about heightened awareness of vulnerability at birth is true, our ancestors may have sought support to reduce fear of death or complications.

I suggest that the proximate determinant of birthing behavior was probably emotional and based on the need for a supportive companion. Perhaps one reason that birth is such a powerful emotional as well as physical experience for all women is that it is these emotions (e.g., fear, anxiety, uncertainty) that lead them to seek assistance, whereby mortality is reduced. This is a behavior remarkably different from that of most other mammals, who seek solitude at the time of birth. I would argue, therefore, that just as selection has operated to reorient the pelvis for bipedalism, it has operated on the emotions associated with birth so that successful delivery could more easily occur. In other words, I suggest that emotions of childbirth that lead women to seek companionship are the human adaptation to obstetrical complications resulting from bipedalism.

Like aspects of the evolutionary process itself, "better" is measured today by statistics showing reduced mortality. Studies in the United States and other industrialized nations revealing women's dissatisfactions with their childbirth experiences, statistics showing higher rates of postpartum depression following cesarean sections, and other evidence of negative sequelae from high-tech obstetrics mean little compared with mortality and morbidity data. "Well, my birth experience was terrible, but at least I have a healthy child" is a frequently heard comment today in some settings. I would not try to argue that the flip side of that phrase would be better ("I had a wonderful birth experience, but the baby is not healthy"), but I certainly do not believe it is an either/or situation. There is no reason that we cannot have both a wonderful birth experience and a healthy baby, as millions of women who give birth under conditions wherein they have more control can attest.

Recent work by John Kennell, Marshall Klaus, and their colleagues suggests that not only does emotional and social support contribute to more positive feelings about birth, it also serves to improve the biomedical outcome of birth. A review of studies of social support in several different settings revealed that having a support person or "doula" present at delivery served to reduce cesarean section rate, the length of labor, and the use of forceps (Klaus et al. 1992). Six weeks after birth, the effects were still apparent, as seen in increased breastfeeding success, less anxiety and depression, and higher self-esteem.

The gist of my argument is that we have behind us a heritage of 225 million years of mammalian evolution during which time control of birth lay entirely within the laboring female herself. Beginning with the origins of bipedalism approximately five million years ago, having someone present to help during the final stages of delivery, especially with aspects of neonatal respiration, probably made the difference between life and death for many hominid mothers and infants. With encephalization and the origins of consciousness, which accompanied the origin of the genus *Homo* some two million years ago, awareness of vulnerability may have heightened the emotional impact of birth, which probably led the normally gregarious human female to seek companionship at this time. Through its effect on mortality and morbidity, natural selection has brought about this pattern of behavior, but the proximate factor is emotional. In other words, women experience heightened emotion at birth, which leads them to seek companionship, which, in turn, leads to the ultimate outcome of lowered mortality and greater reproductive success for the women who behave in this manner.

The Cartesian dualism between mind and body has come under close scrutiny with important and justified criticism by medical anthropologists who note that modern medicine has been primarily concerned about the body at the expense of the mind or the soul. Certainly, the mind/soul or "mindful body" (Scheper-Hughes and Lock 1987) recedes into the background in biomedicine. But, from my perspective as a biological anthropologist, critical medical anthropology has pushed the body itself too far into the background.

Nancy Scheper-Hughes and Margaret Lock (1987) proposed the study of the emotions as a promising area of inquiry for studying the human body as embedded in nature, society, and culture, including the sociopolitical enterprise or "body politic." They begin with the assumption that the body is the result of both physical and symbolic forces, that it is both "naturally and culturally produced." They talk of three bodies: the mindful body, the social body, and the body politic. At the risk of adding to the "proliferation of bodies," I want to add the evolved body to these discussions, both as it relates to health and illness and, in the present case, as it relates to birth. To understand more fully human be-ing, we must be aware that we are, as individuals, products of evolution, history, culture, society, biosocial development, and learning.

Clifford Geertz (1980), Scheper-Hughes and Lock (1987), and others have argued that without culture, we would not have emotions, or at least, we would not know how to interpret them. Perhaps this is true for many of the more complex emotions like ennui, despair, passion, and love. But I have little doubt that many animals feel pain and social animals know how to interpret aloneness (see Cheney and Seyfarth 1990:235–255 and Goodall 1986:114–145 for discussions of emotions in nonhuman primates). Both sensations or emotions have been critical to their survival, and I would argue that they have evolved because they enhanced survival in the past. Feelings of pain led to avoidance of stimuli that caused the pain, and feelings of aloneness led to seeking others in whose company there was greater security. These feelings were present in our primate ancestors long before human culture gave them meaning at the level of consciousness.

The evolutionary perspective argues that we are not dependent on external sources of ascorbic acid or susceptible to certain pathogens because of sociopolitical forces but because of evolutionary forces. Whether or not we *develop* scurvy or measles is largely dependent on sociopolitical circumstances, but that is not why they are challenges for our species in the first place. By the same reasoning, we are not dependent on others at birth because of sociopolitical concerns but because of our evolutionary history. The shape and nature of that dependence is, of course, clearly rooted in sociopolitical circumstances, as is clearly demonstrated in much of this volume (see especially Jordan, Szurek, Sargent and Bascope, Daviss).

The relatively new field of Darwinian or evolutionary medicine has as its goal the linking of knowledge of human evolutionary history and synchronic cultural studies with recent developments in biomedical and clinical research. Those of us who adopt this perspective argue that only by understanding the human condition in its evolutionary and historical context and in the myriad ways in which it is represented across cultures and in individual women's lived experiences can we begin to bring about changes in contemporary medical practice that positively influence not only morbidity and mortality but human be-ing as well. It is a pragmatic approach that I hope will itself evolve to bridge the gap between critical medical anthropology and Western biomedicine.

REFERENCES

Berge, C., R. Orban-Segebarch, and P. Schmid
    1984 "Obstetrical Interpretation of the Australopithecine Pelvic Cavity." *Journal of Human Evolution* 13:573–587.
Bourdieu, Pierre, and Jean-Claude Passeron
    1977 *Reproduction in Education, Society, and Culture.* London: Sage.
Cheney, Dorothy L., and Robert M. Seyfarth
    1990 *How Monkeys See the World: Inside the Mind of Another Species.* Chicago: University of Chicago Press.
Doyle, G. A., A. Pelletier, and T. Bekker
    1967 "Courtship, Mating, and Parturition in the Lesser Bushbaby (*Galago senegalensis moholi*) under Semi-natural Conditions." *Folia Primatologica* 7:169–197.
Geertz, Clifford
    1980 *Negara: The Theatre-State in Nineteenth-Century Bali.* Princeton: Princeton University Press.

Ginsburg, Faye, and Rayna Rapp
  1991   "The Politics of Reproduction." *Annual Reviews of Anthropology* 20:311–343.
Goodall, Jane
  1986   *The Chimpanzees of Gombe.* Cambridge, Mass.: Belknap Press.
Gould, Stephen Jay
  1977   *Ontogeny and Phylogeny.* Cambridge, Mass.: Harvard University Press.
Graham-Jones, O., and W. C. O. Hill
  1962   "Pregnancy and Parturition in a Bornean Orangutan." *Proceedings of the Zoological Society of London* 139:503–510.
Hopf, S.
  1967   "Notes on Pregnancy, Delivery and Infant Survival in Captive Squirrel Monkeys." *Primates* 8:323–332.
Jordan, Brigitte
  1987   "The Hut and the Hospital: Information, Power, and Symbolism in the Artifacts of Birth." *Birth* 14(1):36–40.
Kadam, K. M., and M. S. Swayamprabha
  1980   "Parturition in the Slender Loris (*Loris tardigradus lydekkerianus*)." *Primates* 21:567–571.
Kemps, A., and P. Timmermans
  1982   "Parturition Behavior in Pluriparous Java Macaques (*Macaca fascicularis*)." *Primates* 23:75–88.
Klaus, Marshall, John Kennell, Gale Berkowitz, and Phyllis Klaus
  1992   "Maternal Assistance and Support in Labor: Father, Nurse, Midwife, or Doula?" *Clinical Consultations in Obstetrics and Gynecology* 4:211–217.
Konner, Melvin, and Marjorie Shostak
  1987   "Timing and Management of Birth among the !Kung: Biocultural Interaction in Reproductive Adaptation." *Cultural Anthropology* 2(1):11–28.
Leutenegger, W.
  1972   "Functional Aspects of Pelvis Morphology of Simian Primates." *Journal of Human Evolution* 3:201–222.
  1981   "Encephalization and Obstetrics in Primates with Particular Reference to Human Evolution." In *Primate Brain Evolution: Methods and Concepts,* ed. E. Armstrong and D. Falk, 85–92. New York: Plenum.
Lovejoy, Owen
  1988   "Evolution of Human Walking." *Scientific American* 259:118–125.
Montagu, Ashley
  1961   "Neonatal and Infant Immaturity in Man." *Journal of the American Medical Association* 178:56–57.
Rothe, H.
  1974   "Further Observations on the Delivery Behavior of the Common Marmoset (*Callithrix jacchus*)." *Zeitschrift für Säugetierkund* 39:135–142.
Sargent, Carolyn
  1989   *Maternity, Medicine, and Power: Reproductive Decisions in Urban Benin.* Berkeley: University of California Press.

Scheper-Hughes, Nancy, and Margaret M. Lock
  1987   "The Mindful Body: A Prolegomenon to Future Work in Medical Anthro-
      pology." *Medical Anthropology Quarterly* 1(1):6–41.
Schultz, A. H.
  1949   "Sex Differences in the Pelves of Primates." *American Journal of Physical
      Anthropology* 7:401–424.
Stevenson, M. F.
  1976   "Birth and Perinatal Behaviour in Family Groups of the Common Mar-
      moset (*Callithrix jacchus*), Compared to Other Primates." *International Zoo
      Yearbook* 16:110–116.
Trevathan, Wenda R.
  1987   *Human Birth: An Evolutionary Perspective.* Hawthorne, N.Y.: Aldine de
      Gruyter.
  1988   "Fetal Emergence Patterns in Evolutionary Perspective." *American An-
      thropologist* 90:19–26.
Washburn, Sherwood L.
  1960   "Tools and Human Evolution." *Scientific American* 203:3–15.
Wiley, Andrea S.
  1992   "Adaptation and the Biocultural Paradigm in Medical Anthropology: A
      Critical Review." *Medical Anthropology Quarterly* 6:216–236.

PART TWO

Intracultural Variations in Authoritative Knowledge about Birth

Biomedical Hegemony and Women's Choices

THREE

Fetal Ultrasound Imaging and the Production of Authoritative Knowledge in Greece

Eugenia Georges

First used in the 1960s to monitor high-risk pregnancies, fetal ultrasonography is today a routine aspect of prenatal care in most industrialized countries. Though its use has become routine, women and practitioners alike recognize that ultrasound is not just another diagnostic tool used in pregnancy (Spitz 1990). Part of the historical transformation of medicine brought about by "visualizing" technologies (Barley 1988; Kassirer 1992; Reiser 1978), its impact on the practice of obstetrics is deemed "profound" (Cunningham, MacDonald, and Grant 1985). With the rapid diffusion of the technology, this impact is becoming increasingly global. In Greece, where high-technology obstetrics has almost completely replaced local models of pregnancy and birth in a span of one or two generations, repetitive and intensive fetal scanning is now a universal feature of prenatal care.

This chapter examines some of the ways in which pregnant women and obstetricians experience the intensive use of fetal ultrasound in a small city in eastern Greece. To date, little is known of the diffusion of this technology outside the North American and Western European contexts, and still less is known of the culturally inflected experiences of women and obstetricians as they interact with it.[1] Ethnographic material from Greece offers an opportunity to examine comparatively the role of ultrasonography in the ongoing medicalization of pregnancy and to explore the ways in which this reproductive technology helps generate power and meaning, as well as diagnoses and measurements.

In keeping with the theme of this volume, I focus specifically on the ways in which fetal imaging collaborates in the production of authoritative medical knowledge within Greek clinical discourse and obstetrical practice. Authoritative knowledge, as Jordan ([1978] 1993:154) has argued, is knowledge that counts as legitimate and consequential. As authoritative knowledge is continually reinforced and reproduced through hierarchical social interactions, such as clinical encounters, other ways of knowing are delegitimized (Jordan [1978] 1993:152). Like the process of hegemony in general, authoritative knowledge involves the ongoing construction of consensus regarding what is thinkable and unthinkable (Williams 1980). As Jordan has observed, technologies of many sorts play an important role in the performance and display of authoritative knowledge because of their symbolic (as well as practical) value, their association with experts, and their expression of power and other significant relationships among persons engaged in a community of practice (Jordan [1978] 1993:158).

Among the biomedical technologies deployed in the Greek context, I argue that fetal ultrasound plays a privileged role in the process of generating authoritative knowledge in prenatal care for pregnant women and doctors alike. To grasp this role more fully, it is necessary to put aside common-sense understandings of efficacy (efficacy, in any case, remains unproven for the routine use of ultrasound in normal pregnancies) [2] and look instead to how the apparatus embodies and helps to construct specific kinds of social, cognitive, and expressive order in the world (Pfaffenberger 1992; Winner 1985). From this perspective, technology, as a consequence of its formulation in specific political and cultural contexts, is charged with what Corlann Bush (1983:155) has called a "valence": a bias or tendency "to seek out or fit in with certain norms and to ignore or disturb others." The valence embodied in a technology may "pull" actors toward specific patterns of use, as Margarete Sandelowski (1991) has demonstrated in her study of the "never enough" quality of conceptive technologies that compels couples to repeated treatment. As she points out (Sandelowski 1991:31), such an approach complements a perspective from "outside" that focuses instead on how social forces "push" technology use in directions that reinforce broader cultural values and political agendas (e.g., patriarchy, pronatalism).

I contend that the particular valence of fetal ultrasound and much of its impact and authority have to do with its unique positioning at the intersection of popular and scientific technologies of the visual and with the codes and conventions for representing the "real" that are embedded in these technologies (see Duden 1993; Fiske 1987; Petchesky 1987; Sontag 1989). In ultrasonography, the visual and the scientific—two highly significant components of the modern in Western culture—are deliberately joined together. Indeed, in the history of the development and design of medical ultrasound, the production of recognizable visual images emerges as a central goal, a goal that seems "to have been as important as an appreciation of what the electronic equipment could and could not do" in diagnostic terms (Yoxen 1987:301).

A focus on ultrasonography's valence, I argue, makes it possible to extend Jordan's insights regarding authoritative knowledge in a new direction: In addition to analyzing how the ultrasound apparatus is deployed in the hierarchical social interactions that produce authoritative knowledge, I also examine how ultrasound's inbuilt capacity for visualization of the fetus has the powerful potential to merge natural and technological processes, and in doing so, how it has the potential to produce a novel cognitive and bodily experience of pregnancy. By reconfiguring the way women first sensually apprehend the "reality" of their pregnancies, I argue that ultrasonography can act as an especially potent facilitator in the production and enactment of authoritative knowledge. Because doctors, as well as women, are enmeshed in the nontechnical, discursive aspects of medical technology and its scientific rationality, I also describe their subjective experiences with ultrasonography, a topic that has received little attention. Finally, I examine the unusually intensive use of this technology in the context of the political economy of Greek health care delivery.

SETTING: A PUBLIC HOSPITAL IN EASTERN GREECE

This research was conducted over ten months as part of an ongoing study begun in 1990 of Greek women's changing reproductive experiences. Most of the research described in this chapter took place in a public hospital in a small city in eastern Greece. This city, like Greece generally, is heavily dependent on massive seasonal tourism from northern Europe. With its comparatively prosperous economy, this cosmopolitan city attracts migrants from other parts of Greece and provides many amenities to its surrounding communities, including specialized medical services.

The public hospital I studied is part of the National Health System (ESY) established in 1983 by the socialist government that held power through most of the 1980s. The great majority of Greek doctors are employed at relatively modest salaries in publicly subsidized health care, with only about 15 percent in the private sector (Colombotos and Fakiolas 1993; Philalithis 1986). Most physicians employed by the ESY are not permitted to see private patients.

Generally speaking, Greek families who can afford them prefer private maternity clinics to the public hospitals, which often have low prestige and mainly serve poor women (Arnold 1985; Lefkarites 1992; Tzoumaka-Bakoula 1990). Indeed, the ultimate sign of "distinction" (in Pierre Bourdieu's [1984] sense) is to give birth in a private clinic in Athens, where the best "machines" and doctors can be found. In this context, the public hospital I studied is unusual in that it is commonly perceived, as pregnant women and their husbands often explained, to be superior to the sole private clinic, as much for its stock of "machines" (*mihanimata, mihanes*) as for the high quality of its doctors. An additional attraction is that prenatal care is informally structured in such a way as to allow women to avoid the most common source of dissatisfaction with public hospitals: the lack of continuity in care (Dragona 1987). For reasons to be explained below, women attending the public hospital are able to see the same obstetrician throughout their pregnancies. As a consequence of these circumstances, the hospital draws a large number of women not only from the city itself but from the surrounding region as well, including many middle-class women who could afford to pay for private care. Annually, some nine hundred births take place in the public hospital (out of a national total of about 100,000).

METHODS

In the public hospital, I was allowed to observe and record the daily stream of prenatal consultations, ultrasound scans, and births and was given access to records of birth outcomes for the 1980s. In addition to observation and informal interviews both with doctors and with women before and after ultrasound scans, I conducted structured interviews in Greek with nine obstetricians (all male), seven nurse-midwives (all female), and twenty-six postpartum women within one to three days of giving birth. These were young (average age 24.5 years), married women in almost equal proportions of "working-class" and "middle-class" backgrounds.[3] All but three had just given birth to their first or second child. For comparative purposes, I also visited the sole private clinic in the city. Interviews with its obstetricians revealed no notable differences in procedures and technologies from the public hospital.

Two months were also spent in Athens, the center of Greek medical education and the principal point of diffusion of new techniques and forms of knowledge. In Athens, I observed the training of obstetrical residents in ultrasound techniques in a major teaching hospital and interviewed professors of obstetrics on such topics as their views of ultrasonography and the content of their lectures to medical students.

PREGNANCY AND BIRTH IN GREECE: MODERN MEDICAL HEGEMONY

The redefinition of pregnancy and birth as technology-intensive medical events is one manifestation of the widespread modernization that has occurred in Greece since World War II. Throughout the country, the modernizing process has produced an epistemological rupture in which old explanations and practices, local knowledge of the pregnant body among them, are being displaced by technological discourses, including the discourse of biomedicine (see Stewart 1991:117). Although part of a global process, this medicalization is far from universal and homogeneous. It proceeds rapidly but unevenly. Some areas of knowledge (such as fertility control) remain relatively unmedicalized (Georges 1996). Furthermore, the medicalization of pregnancy and birth has taken place in a seemingly paradoxical cultural context of pervasive suspicion of the doctors themselves (Arnold 1985:231; Velogiannis-Moutsopoulos and Bartsocas 1989:214). The prevailing attitude in Greece has been succinctly summarized as "trust science, but be suspicious of physicians" (Arnold 1985:210).

Today, lay midwives are all but extinct, and alternative discourses of non-medicalized birth have yet to appear. Birthing at home has become unthinkable (young women sometimes laughed at the suggestion), and a technomedical model of pregnancy and birth is firmly in place (Bréart et al. 1992; Dragona 1987; Tzoumaka-Bakoula 1990). Hospital birth includes the routine use of pubic shaving, enemas, intravenous drips, pitocin to augment labor, electronic fetal monitors, episiotomies, the lithotomy position with arms and legs strapped to the delivery table, and, in the public hospital I studied, birth by cesarean section for about one-third of women.

Pregnancy is intensively monitored through monthly prenatal visits with obstetricians, in which fetal ultrasound scanning plays a prominent role. The public hospital got its hand-me-down scanner from Athens in the mid-1980s, and soon thereafter, fetal scanning became a routine procedure. By the 1990s, no pregnancy went unscanned, and women typically had three to five scans over the course of a normal pregnancy. The modal number in my sample was four, but a few women had had up to seven. Normal pregnancies are scanned with ultrasound for a large variety of reasons, including confirming a suspected pregnancy, charting fetal growth, establishing due dates, ascertaining presentation of the fetus, and, surprisingly often, responding to a woman's request to "see the baby."

Such intensive monitoring of pregnancy is not a regional aberration, but reflects Greek obstetrical practice generally. Medical students in Athens are taught to do three scans per normal pregnancy, one in each trimester, and a recent survey of more than five hundred normal pregnancies in Athens found that, in fact, nearly all women (93 percent) had had at least one fetal ultrasound scan, with about one-fourth experiencing two or more scans in the third trimester alone (Bréart et al. 1992).[4]

The technomedical redefinition of pregnancy and birth has permeated women's everyday consciousness through a variety of routes. Universally accessible prenatal care probably provides the most direct exposure. In addition to intensive surveillance of pregnancy via batteries of tests, clinical examination, and ultrasound, monthly prenatal visits provide the occasion for monitoring women's behavior and for providing biomedical lessons. As one doctor described it, the obstetrician's role was "to explain to the woman what it means to be pregnant, what's happening inside of her."

Much of the discourse in the prenatal visits I observed centered on questions of risk and maternal responsibility for the outcome of pregnancy. Women, and often their husbands, routinely asked doctors to advise them about a variety of behaviors (sexual relations, diet, taking medications and supplements, bathing in the sea)[5] that were regarded as potentially risky for the pregnancy.

Technomedical definitions of pregnancy and birth also permeate women's everyday consciousness indirectly through such popular sources as magazines, television, videos, state-sponsored as well as private childbirth classes, and, in particular, the pregnancy guides read by more than half (54 percent) of the women. Often seen on the bedside tables of postpartum women in the hospital, these guides offer readable, step-by-step descriptions of the technomedical model of pregnancy and birth. The most popular of these is *Birth Is Love,* written by an Athenian nurse-midwife (Sikaki-Douka n.d.). Despite its sentimental title, *Birth Is Love* is largely devoted to educating women about how to become modern pregnant subjects, urging them, for example, to be prompt for appointments and precise and concrete in their reports to the doctor. It begins with several pages of reprints of Lennart Nilsson's widely known fetal photographs, which "reveal" to women the contents of their pregnant bodies, and devotes an entire section to fetal ultrasound entitled "Camera in the Uterus: Boy or Girl?" Thus, both directly through repeated clinical encounters and indirectly through popular forms that translate expert knowledge, women's everyday consciousness is exposed to a model of pregnancy as biomedical event.

THE PROCEDURE: "PUTTING THE BABY ON TELEVISION"

The congruence of fetal imaging and popular visual technologies is explicitly acknowledged in Greek everyday usage. Ultrasound is most commonly referred to as "television" (*tileorasi*), and doing an ultrasound is referred to as "putting the baby on television" (*na valoume to moro stin tileorasi*).[6] Television is an apt metaphor for fetal ultrasound imaging in Greece. It is ubiquitous and provides a major vehicle for the dissemination of images of modernity, the West, and "modern" behavior throughout Greece (Handman 1983; McNeill 1978).[7] The women I interviewed were nearly all born around the time television was first introduced in Greece (1966), and have thus grown up with its discursive conventions, not least of which is its "ability to carry a socially convincing sense of the real" (Fiske 1987:21).

The ultrasound scan as performed in the public hospital is a formulaic procedure that resonates with ritual overtones (see Davis-Floyd 1992). The description that follows, which is based on my repeated observations, is of a typical session, which usually lasts about five minutes. For most women, it is replicated several times over the course of their pregnancies, with little variation and in near-silence.

Toward the conclusion of the routine prenatal examination, the doctor (or the woman) may suggest "putting the baby on television." The woman then follows the doctor down the hospital corridor to a small room, lit dimly only by the shadowy gray light emanating from the ultrasound monitor. No other medical personnel are present during the session, but the woman may be accompanied by family members, usually her husband and possibly a small child. The woman lies on the examining bed next to the apparatus and, generally without being instructed to do so (since she has usually done this before), wordlessly pulls her skirt or slacks and underwear down below her abdomen. The doctor squirts her exposed abdomen with a coupling gel and begins to probe its surface with the transducer.

The screen is generally turned toward the doctor. The woman can view it by craning her neck, but her eyes are often directed toward the doctor's face. Quickly and silently, the doctor scans the entire fetal image, then focuses on the genital area for a while. At this point, he may break his silence to announce "girl" or "boy"—unless the woman has already jumped in to tell him she doesn't want to know the sex. (This rarely happened, however.) Or he may tell the woman that the position or age of the fetus doesn't permit him to see the sex this time and that he will look again next month. Finally, the doctor scans to the skull and freezes the image to measure the biparietal diameter (skull width). He checks a chart over the bed on which the woman is lying and announces the age of the fetus, in weeks and days. If the doctor himself does not tell the woman at this point that "the baby is all right" (no anomaly was ever detected in the more than eighty sessions I observed), she will ask him. Most often, this is the only time she speaks. Finally, the doctor wipes the gel from the woman's abdomen with a paper towel, and leaves. After pulling up her clothes, the woman follows the doctor back to the office. If her husband is with her, as was the case with about one-third of the women, they may exchange a few quick comments in the corridor, usually about the fetus's announced sex.

FETAL ULTRASOUND AND WOMEN'S CHANGING EXPERIENCES OF PREGNANCY

The women I spoke with almost uniformly regarded ultrasound in a positive light. As enthusiastic "consumers," they exerted a strong demand for fetal imaging that was, in part, a product of the machine's status as a metonym for the structural and symbolic superiority of modern medical science and technology. As noted earlier, this was reflected in many women's expressed preference for the hospital because of its "machines."

When women specifically discussed their subjective experiences with ul-trasound, several themes repeatedly emerged. Contrary to my expecta-tions, these themes did not vary by social class. First, women depended on the technology to assuage feelings of uncertainty associated with the unpredictability of pregnancy. Although awareness of certain kinds of "risks" to fetal health has been heightened by women's exposure to bio-medical discourse, both physical and mental disabilities have historically been highly stigmatized in Greek culture (Arnold 1985:257; Blue 1993; Blum and Blum 1965:63; Velogiannis-Moutsopoulos and Bartsocas 1989:230). They are dreaded not only for their direct consequences for the affected individual but also for the stigma they may bring to the entire family. Since disabilities are often believed to be hereditary, they may affect the marriage prospects of other family members.

Women commonly described feelings of "anxiety" (*anhos*), "anguish" (*agonia*), and "nervousness" (*trak*) just before the scan, which were put to rest once the doctor announced, "The baby is all right." This statement by Maria, a twenty-five-year-old hairdresser, was typical: "I had a lot of anxiety before my first ultrasound, because you can't know what's inside you. Until then, you only see your stomach. After, I felt more sure. You see that all is well." All of the women I spoke with took the doctor's assurance that "the baby is all right" to mean that the fetus was physically integral, or, to use the women's words, that the "baby had its hands and feet," "all its organs," and was "whole" or *artimeles* (entirely limbed). What it could not reveal, the women generally agreed, was how these organs, including the brain, functioned. Despite this widely acknowledged limitation, the ultrasound scan nonetheless provided considerable reassurance of fetal "health" to the great majority of women.

Women also often depended on doctor and machine to mediate their contact with the fetus and to establish its reality. Of special note was the primacy of visualization over other forms of bodily experience in making the fetus "real," as heard in many women's statements. For instance, Popi, twenty-four, a working-class housewife, said,

> I didn't believe I had a baby inside me. When you don't feel it or see it, it's hard to believe, it's something that you can't imagine—how the baby is, how it's growing, how it's moving. . . . After I saw it on the screen, I did believe it. I felt it was more alive in me. . . . I had also seen it [a fetus] on television but it's different to see your own.

And Stavroula, twenty-five, a middle-class housewife:

> [With ultrasound] you have an idea of what you have inside you. I became conscious that it was a person. I hadn't felt it as much before, I had to see it first. At that moment, you feel that it's yours, the only thing that's yours.

For these women (quite different in terms of their education and class), as for many others, the murky ultrasonographic image furnishes readily recognizable "evidence" of fetal reality. Because the resolution of the image produced by the hospital's hand-me-down scanner is rather poor, women appear to actively interpret fetal images according to the codes of objectivity and realism that underwrite modern visual technologies (television, videos, and photography) in general (see Duden 1993; Fiske 1987; Petchesky 1987; Sontag 1989). Furthermore, exposure to television from an early age may have socialized this generation of Greek women (like Western European and North American women) to be "relatively flexible readers of images" (Condit 1990:85), and thus prepared them to metaphorize the shadows that appear on the screen into "my baby." The "truthfulness" and authority of the image are further reinforced through the dramatic ability of the cameralike apparatus to compensate for the deficiencies of the human eye—both the doctor's and the woman's (see Crary 1990). In this regard, women's use of metaphors of other visualizing machines (television, camera, microscope) to refer to the ultrasound apparatus is revealing. In any case, with ultrasound, a new commonsense mode of apprehending the "reality" of the fetus is established and positively valued early in the pregnancy.

Historical change in the sensory experience of this reality was reflected in an exchange that occurred between Stavroula and her mother, who was present at this point in the interview. Stavroula's mother interjected that she had felt what her daughter was describing when she first sensed her baby move inside her. To which Stavroula replied, "You feel it more intensely when you see it." For most women, because of the intensive use of fetal imaging, seeing, or rather, being shown, the fetus now usually precedes feeling it inside them. Besides this temporal precedence, these women's comments further suggest that doctor- and machine-mediated "seeing" demotes bodily experience to a secondary order of significance.

Yet many women's comments revealed greater complexity and hint at how ultrasonography might work to reconfigure women's senses by giving a tactile quality to the pregnancy through the visualization of what is, without the technology, impossible to see. As in Stavroula's case, many women explained that the fetus is *felt* as more alive, more present, when it's *seen*. The ability of modern visual technologies to impart a material and tactile quality to what is seen, especially if this is something that was previously unseen or hidden, was noted by Walter Benjamin (Taussig 1992:144), and several of the women interviewed seem to be making a similar point. By adding a tactile modality to the visual, the authority of ultrasound to represent fetal reality is further enhanced, particularly early in the pregnancy when women's sensual apprehensions of the fetus are to a large extent a product of interactions with the machine and the information it creates.

A final theme to emerge from women's descriptions of ultrasonography that I wish to discuss is the strong pleasure that many of them derived from seeing the fetal image. For instance, Katerina, twenty, a middle-class housewife, explained, "The first time I saw the baby, I was crazy with happiness. It was a contact with the child. Every time I went to the doctor, I wanted to see the child again." Litsa, a twenty-eight-year-old shopkeeper, said, "After my first ultrasound I felt like I did when I saw it after giving birth—that much happiness." And Zambeta, eighteen, a clerk in a bakery, exclaimed,

> I had four ultrasounds and that wasn't enough! When the doctor first suggested it, I couldn't wait to see it. I was so impatient, the minutes-long wait seemed like eons. . . . I thought it would be like on television, that I would see the little hands, like under a microscope. But I wasn't disappointed: I saw it move, I saw that it was healthy.

The pleasure many women enthusiastically express can be traced to multiple aspects of the scan. There is, first, pleasure in the assurance of fetal health, as Zambeta mentions ("I saw that it was healthy"). Other pleasures appear to derive their impact and poignancy from the influence of television's realist conventions on women's reception of ultrasound images (see Fiske 1987). Thus the ecstatic sensation of contact that Katerina describes is enabled, or at least enhanced, by ultrasonography's ability to reveal fetal movements in "real time." Real-time ultrasonography, like "live" television, imparts a feeling of nowness that is symmetrical with the "lived time" of the pregnant woman, and in the process, promotes a sense of immediate contact with the fetus ("I saw it move"). There is also pleasure from the privileged ability to be "all-seeing" and "all-knowing" about the fetus ("you see how it is"). Knowledge of the sex of the fetus further reinforces this ability, and appears to be especially valued because the ideal gender composition of families is often quite specific: one boy and one girl.[8] Although women share this "spectatorial privilege" (Fiske 1987:25) with the doctors, they move beyond the doctors' terse declarations of fetal age, sex, and "health" and actively appropriate the fetal images for themselves, endowing the fetuses with qualities and attributes that are meaningful to them alone ("you feel that it's yours, the only thing that's yours"; "I felt it was more alive").

Nonetheless, as Foucault (e.g., 1982) has famously cautioned, the connections between pleasure and power, the "positive" forms of power, must not be overlooked: to mediate this visual connection to the fetus, women had to depend on doctor and machine. In the process, they exposed themselves to the possibility of the manipulation of their desire, as I discuss below.

ULTRASOUND AND THE DOCTORS

By the early 1990s, most Greek obstetricians had an ultrasound scanner in their offices. As Dr. M., a clinical professor of obstetrics in Athens, commented, "Every obstetrician-gynecologist who gets a degree inevitably buys an ultrasound machine, or sends [his patients] to someone who has one. It's like a stethoscope—that's what ultrasound has become for every obstetrician."

As is the case in the United States, ultrasonography is not recognized as a separate specialty in Greece. The scanning technique appears deceptively simple, although in fact, ultrasound is the most operator-dependent of all medical imaging technologies. Greek obstetricians learn to use ultrasound on rotation as part of their basic medical education, but few receive additional training. As Dr. M. went on to lament, "Many do ultrasound, but they don't know what they're seeing." (It should be noted that the situation in the United States is not substantially different, prompting a leading ultrasonographer to a similar lament: "One would think that the number of incompetent or poorly trained practitioners would decline [with time]. This has not been the case" [Craig 1990:561].)

Whereas women almost uniformly regarded ultrasound in a positive light, a clear generational divide marked the views of the obstetricians in the public hospital. Doctors under forty saw the machine as indispensable, enabling them to practice "modern" obstetrics. To quote Dr. A., in his midthirties: "Obstetrics has made great progress in recent years because of fetal ultrasound. It provides information that just could not be gotten by other means. . . . Ultrasound is the single most important diagnostic tool we have." Similar perceptions were held by nearly all younger obstetricians, despite the fact that hospital records revealed little or no change in outcome statistics since the introduction of routine imaging. The sole exception was the cesarean section rate, which had nearly doubled in four years: from 18 percent in 1985 (the year before the scanner was acquired) to 35 percent by the end of the decade.[9]

In contrast to the younger generation of obstetricians, the oldest obstetricians in the hospital were often critical of the ways in which the machine was routinely used. Arguing against what he considered to be a false sense of precision generated by ultrasonography, a senior obstetrician (in his late fifties) flatly asserted that "obstetrics is an art, not a science." Dr. N. criticized what he called the "overuse" of ultrasound and complained that it can "distance the doctor from the patient." Dr. L., another senior obstetrician, expressed annoyance and regret at the loss of value of his physical senses that had occurred as older hands-on methods, such as dating the pregnancy by measuring the height of the uterine fundus, have been completely replaced by ultrasound.

> There are few things my hands can't find that the ultrasound can. My hands
> are my eyes . . . but patients think it's more modern to use a machine. They
> themselves wouldn't trust just a manual exam. The doctor needs to show that
> he's modern too. That is, some will do an exam with a machine just because
> a woman will trust him more if he does. . . . Now, machines are used as a way
> for doctors to advertise themselves.

The above quote suggests something of how obstetricians perceive the
role of ultrasound in countering the pervasive mistrust of physicians mentioned above. The last sentence is also significant, and requires some explanation. Throughout Greece, the relatively low salaries paid to ESY doctors
are often supplemented by the gratuities given by patients as tokens of
appreciation for the care they have received. This practice is an integral
aspect of the informal culture of the public health care system. Gift-giving,
which includes flower arrangements and assortments of pastries and choc-
olates as well as cash, must be understood within the wider paternalistic
ethos that characterizes doctor-patient relationships in Greece (Velogiannis-Moutsopoulos and Bartsocas 1989). It is also necessary to distinguish
this practice from the institution of the *fakelaki,* or "little envelope," which
is an extra fee demanded in advance by a doctor to expedite hospital care
(Colombotos and Fakiolas 1993). Gift-giving is an (often insistent) gesture
made post facto by patients and their families to demonstrate appreciation
to doctors (and other hospital staff) for their "help." Although individual
sums may be fairly modest, cumulatively they do provide some incentive
for doctors to be responsive to patient demands and thus play a role in
determining the contours of the Greek health care delivery system (Colom-
botas and Fakiolas 1993). For instance, the probability of receiving gratuities after a birth encourages doctors to provide continuity in prenatal care,
something that women highly desire and appreciate.

Informal expressions of gratitude may also have played a role in promoting the intensification of fetal scanning in the hospital. I have already
noted women's enthusiasm and strong demand for fetal ultrasound. The
department's policy *not* to charge for obstetrical scans (in contrast to scans
performed in other departments, for which there is a charge) must be
placed in this context. As one doctor explained, "If we charged, all the
women would leave!" Although a tongue-in-cheek exaggeration, this comment does illustrate the importance attributed to the technology (and its
liberal use) in attracting women to the hospital. Even though often overworked, salaried public sector doctors still want "to advertise themselves,"
that is, attract and keep women, whom they treat as their individual patients, for the extra income they represent. Fetal ultrasound scanning has
thus been fitted into the preexisting informal political economy of health
care, which it helps to reinforce.

Although some critics regard the systemic practice of gift-giving as yet another example of the corruption and clientism endemic to Greek society, it is from the clients' perspective also possible to view it as a form of resistance to the "externally imposed depersonalization of relations" (Tsoukalas 1991:14; see also Gourgouris 1992) represented by the ESY, and more generally as a form of resistance to the state and its labyrinthine regulations. By such informal means, Greek women and their families are able to finesse and personalize an ostensibly rigid public bureaucratic structure.

NORMALIZING PREGNANCY: REAL-TIME DUE DATES

[A] *man whose eye dominates records through which some sort of connections are*
established with millions of others may be said to dominate.
—LATOUR 1986:29;
emphasis in original

In addition to producing the information women want to know, that is, fetal sex and health, each routine scan generates a "precise" dating of the pregnancy in weeks and days. By repeatedly comparing fetal anthropometric measurements taken from the ultrasound image with antenatal growth charts compiled from survey data, the doctor is able to sustain a "constant web of observation around the normal individual" (Armstrong 1983:101). With the aid of this observational web, the fetus becomes temporally normalized and new technological rhythms are superimposed on the pregnancy. In the process, individual pregnancies are synchronized with what might be called "doctor's time," and a "temporal symmetry" is established in which the rhythms of the pregnancy and the doctor's expectations come to coincide (Zerubavel 1981, cited in Barley 1988:126–127).[10] This artifactual synchronicity has significant practical implications: if a woman's pregnancy failed to conform to expectations, the result was usually an attempt to induce labor via amniotomy (artificial rupture of the membrane), pitocin, and/or a cesarean section.

The following interaction illustrates more concretely how doctors used the ultrasound machine to produce authoritative dates, and in the process, delegitimize information provided by women. On her first prenatal visit to Dr. Y., a twenty-year-old pregnant woman was unable to pinpoint precisely the date of her last menstrual period. The more Dr. Y. probed, the more upset and confused the woman appeared and the more exasperated the doctor became.[11] Finally, Dr. Y. told her to follow him to the ultrasound room. After looking at the screen briefly, he informed her that the information she had given him was wrong. When she asked him for the "correct" date of her pregnancy, he didn't reply, but rather commented, "Now that you're going to be a mother, you have to pay more attention and be more responsible." To this, the young woman said nothing. In this instance, the combined use of ultrasound and growth charts not only enabled Dr. Y. to discredit this woman's knowledge and substitute his own, machine-derived, knowledge as authoritative, it also enabled him to reinforce her place in the broader system of patriarchal and hierarchical social relations within which the medical encounter is embedded.

Sometimes, women resisted attempts to normalize their pregnancies. During one scanning session, all went according to routine until the doctor announced the fetal age, "Eight weeks and one day." To this the woman responded forcefully, "Eight weeks and six days—*I know!*" Such resistance was rare, however. To the contrary, the ultrasound machine was usually treated as the ultimate arbiter of due dates. Women, who actively demanded the procedure, were unlikely to challenge dates produced by doctors in interaction with a technology that embodies the authority not only of biomedical science but also of the visual codes for uncovering "reality." [12]

Last, ultrasound also offered doctors an avenue for resolving diagnostic differences among themselves and for asserting authority and control over the management of patients, as another example illustrates. Based on clinical evidence, a young resident disagreed with the due date assigned by Dr. R., his superior, to a woman now late in her ninth month of pregnancy. Believing the woman to be dangerously overdue, he recommended immediate delivery by cesarean section. Dr. R. responded to the resident's challenge by doing an ultrasound scan, even though Dr. R. himself had instructed the residents that scans late in pregnancy are not useful for purposes of dating.[13] Dr. R.'s scan confirmed his original, later due date. In a somewhat unusual outcome, the resident was able to prevail (the woman was a family friend), and the subsequent cesarean revealed meconium staining, a sign of fetal distress.

CONCLUSION

At the most general level, the intensive use of fetal ultrasound imaging in the public hospital is another example of the imperative character of medical technology, that is, of the drive to use technology simply because it exists (Fuchs 1968; Koenig 1988; Tymstra 1989). In this case, the technological imperative to use, and possibly overuse, ultrasonography is inflected as well by specifically Greek cultural meanings and sociopolitical institutions. These include a "modern" trust in science and technology unfettered by oppositional discourses (e.g., no "natural childbirth" movement exists in Greece), coupled with mistrust of physicians and existence of an informal economy within the public hospital system that creates an incentive for doctors to freely offer scans. In still other respects, I have argued in this chapter that the intensive use of fetal ultrasound imaging reflects the "pull" of its particular valence: its tendency to produce a straightforward sense of reality and visual pleasure. Above all, this tendency seems to be enabled and reinforced by the ubiquity of television and the early socialization of this generation of young Greek women into its conventions. It is possible that a common, early experience with television and its realist representational codes may also account for some of the striking similarities found in the responses of North American, Western European, and Greek women to sonographic fetal images (Hyde 1986; Lydon and Dunkel-Schetter 1994; Milne and Rich 1981; Mitchell 1993; Villeneuve et al. 1988; for some differences between Greek and North American women, see Mitchell and Georges 1997), as well as for the lack of notable social-class differences among the women I interviewed.

As I have described it, ultrasound's valence endows the fetal images it generates with the potential to shape the subjective experiences of pregnant women in ways that differ substantially from, say, the printouts of lab results or electronic fetal monitors, which, like most other medical technologies, remain esoteric and opaque to nonexperts. In the Greek context I have described, the apparatus plays a critical role in reconfiguring what can be called "the structure of feeling" of pregnancy, that is, the tangible way women live and experience their pregnancies within a specific technosocial, cultural, and political context (see Probyn 1991; Williams 1961). This reconfiguration has several manifestations. The visually derived pleasures experienced through the display of the fetal image substitute for older, felt ones or conjure a novel merger of visual and tactile sensations. The slower rhythms of nontechnological pregnancy are accelerated, as the emotional milestones (e.g., quickening, learning the sex) are experienced much earlier. Embedded in the prevailing discourse of risk and maternal responsibility, ultrasound also reinforces preexisting anxieties concerning pregnancy; in most instances, it also provides relief by allaying these anxieties. For, as Diane Beeson (1984:164) has observed of prenatal diagnosis generally, just embarking on the process raises questions about the outcome of the pregnancy, despite the fact that "there is a 98–99% chance that no problem will be found in any given pregnancy." Of course, with the birth of a healthy baby, the power of technology and of the medical profession is affirmed (Beeson 1984:177; Hubbard 1990:167).

Although on occasion doctors in the public hospital use ultrasound to silence women (as in the example of Dr. Y.), the apparatus more commonly produces pleasure and knowledge, which women actively seek. Although some feminist critics (e.g., Oakley 1984; Rothman 1986) are certainly correct in pointing to the ways in which fetal imaging extends patriarchal medical authority over pregnancy, the strong demand for and enthusiastic reception of fetal imaging by pregnant women also suggests the emergence of a new consciousness, of their transformation into modern pregnant subjects (Duden 1993:107; Petchesky 1987).

Doctors, particularly those of the younger generation, also associate the technology with the modern practice of obstetrics. Doctors are aware of the ways in which the knowledge produced by ultrasound is dependent on the technology and its inbuilt assumptions, but they too have become "encircled" by the authority of technoscience (Strong 1984). Even though some doctors lament its distancing effects, the loss of value of their own embodied knowledge, and the false sense of precision it creates, ultrasound nonetheless has displaced many hands-on clinical techniques. Furthermore, on occasion, and despite full awareness of its limitations, doctors use the apparatus to achieve such nonmedical ends as bolstering existing authoritative relations with junior doctors and exerting control over the management of pregnant women.

Similarly, even as women actively and enthusiastically demand it, ultrasound provides a context for performing and reinforcing medical authority and in doing so helps consolidate a growing, but still recent and not yet complete, medical hegemony over women's reproductive experiences.

NOTES

Research was funded by the American Council of Learned Societies, the Landes-RISM Foundation, and Rice University Faculty Research Awards. I am very grateful to these institutions for making this project possible. I also wish to thank Deanna Trakas and the Institute for Child Health for initial assistance in Athens and in the public hospital, and for their continuing support. For their helpful suggestions at various stages of the writing, I thank James Faubion, Michael Herzfeld, Dimitra Gefou-Madianou, Ann Millard, Eleni Papagaroufali, Deanna Trakas, and Lida Triantafillidou. I am deeply grateful to Robbie Davis-Floyd for her encouragement and suggestions.

1. For North America, see Lydon and Dunkel-Schetter 1994; Milne and Rich 1981; Mitchell 1993; and Rapp 1991. For Western Europe, see Fellous 1990; Hyde 1986; and Villeneuve et al. 1988.

2. The rapid diffusion and intensive adoption of obstetrical ultrasound has occurred despite important controversies. Although certain serious conditions, for example, abnormal placement of the placenta, can only be diagnosed with ultrasound, its routine use as a screening tool has not been found to improve patient care and fetal outcomes for most women (Craig 1990:552; Ewigman et al. 1993). Additionally, although no short-term adverse effects on the health of infant or mother have been detected, the question of ultrasound's long-term safety remains unresolved (Oakley 1993; Shearer 1984).

3. "Class" designation was based largely on the woman's level of education and, where applicable, her occupation.

4. These figures are based on my analysis of the data in Bréart et al. 1992.

5. Bathing in the sea was considered risky for either of two reasons. A long-standing concern is that cold currents can harm the pregnancy and cause a woman to miscarry. Alternatively, the sea is feared as a medium of infection of the fetus.

6. An arresting example of the institutionalization of this usage came from the official stationery of the director of an ob-gyn clinic in another city, which had printed below the name of the clinic, "Department of Ultrasound-Television."

7. According to a recent European Community (EC) survey, on average Greeks watch more hours of television than any other EC members. An estimated 40 percent of Greek households had VCRs by the end of the 1980s (Zaharopoulos 1991:81).

8. It is a truism that male children are most highly desired in Greece, but no such preference was expressed by the young urban women I interviewed. See also Dubisch 1991:37, which reports a similar preference for balance on the island of Tinos. There was also no evidence of sex-selective abortions in the public hospital. Hospital records revealed roughly unchanged sex ratios at birth before and after the introduction of fetal imaging. In any event, sexing of the fetus occurs relatively late in the pregnancy, and is recognized by most women not to be 100 percent accurate.

9. The relationship between electronic fetal monitoring and increased performance of cesarean sections is well established. See Davis-Floyd 1992:279 for a summary of this research.

10. A dramatic (but cross-culturally not unusual) example of this symmetry was found in a 1983 study of the timing of births in Greece. Studying all births for that year, Tzoumaka-Bakoula (1990:85) found that a disproportionately small number took place on Sundays and between 5:00 and 8:00 P.M.

11. Arnold (1985:224–225) reports a similar encounter in her study of childbirth in rural Crete: "The doctor is shouting at the patient, asking her why she can't remember the exact date of the first day of her last period . . . the woman starts to cry."

12. Rebecca Sarah (1988:68) has described a similar pattern for the United States.

13. The biparietal diameter, usually the sole measure taken during a scan in the public hospital, is subject to variation from the molding that the fetal head undergoes in the uterus, particularly after the thirty-third menstrual week of the pregnancy. Thus, after 29 menstrual weeks, biparietal diameter is considered to be accurate ±2 to 3 weeks (DuBose 1990).

REFERENCES

Armstrong, David
    1983   *The Political Anatomy of the Body.* Cambridge: Cambridge University Press.
Arnold, Marlene S.
    1985   "Childbirth Among Rural Greek Women in Crete: Use of Popular, Folk, and Cosmopolitan Medical Systems." Ph.D. dissertation, University of Pennsylvania, University Microfilms, Philadelphia.
Barley, Stephen R.
    1988   "On Technology, Time and Social Order: Technically Induced Changes in the Temporal Organization of Radiological Work." In *Making Time: Ethnographies of High-Technology Organizations,* ed. F. Dubinskas, 123–169. Philadelphia: Temple University Press.

Beeson, Diane
  1984 "Technological Rhythms in Pregnancy: The Case of Prenatal Diagnosis by Amniocentesis." In *Cultural Perspectives on Biological Knowledge,* ed. T. Duster and K. Garrett, 145–181. Norwood, N.J.: Ablex.
Blue, Amy
  1993 "Greek Psychiatry's Transition from the Hospital to the Community." *Medical Anthropology Quarterly* 7(3):301–318.
Blum, Richard, and Eva Blum
  1965 *Health and Healing in Rural Greece.* Stanford: Stanford University Press.
Bourdieu, Pierre
  1984 *Distinction: A Social Critique of Judgement and Taste.* Cambridge: Cambridge University Press.
Bréart, G., N. Mlika-Cabane, M. Kaminski, S. Alexander, A. Herruzo-Nalda, P. Mandruzzato, J. G. Thornton, and D. Trakas
  1992 "Evaluation of Different Policies for the Management of Labour." *Early Human Development* 29:309–312.
Bush, Corlann
  1983 "Women and the Assessment of Technology: To Think, to Be, to Unthink, to Free." In *Machina Ex Dea: Feminist Perspectives on Technology,* ed. J. Rothschild, 151–170. New York: Pergamon Press.
Colombotos, John, and Nikos Fakiolas
  1993 "The Power of Organized Medicine in Greece." In *The Changing Medical Profession: An International Perspective,* ed. F. Hafferty and J. McKinlay, 138–149. New York: Oxford University Press.
Condit, Celeste M.
  1990 *Decoding Abortion Rhetoric: Communicating Social Change.* Urbana: University of Illinois Press.
Craig, Marveen
  1990 "Controversies in Obstetric and Gynecologic Ultrasound." In *Diagnostic Medical Sonography: A Guide to Clinical Practice,* vol. 1, *Obstetrics and Gynecology,* ed. M. Berman, 551–562. Philadelphia: J. B. Lippincott.
Crary, Jonathan
  1990 *Techniques of the Observer: On Vision and Modernity in the Nineteenth Century.* Cambridge, Mass.: MIT Press.
Cunningham, F. Gary, Paul C. MacDonald, and Norman F. Grant
  1985 *Williams' Obstetrics.* 17th ed. Norwalk, Conn.: Appleton and Lange.
Davis-Floyd, Robbie
  1992 *Birth as an American Rite of Passage.* Berkeley: University of California Press.
Dragona, Thalia
  1987 *Ghenisi: I ghineka brosta se mia kenouria zoi.* Athens: Dodoni Publications.
Dubisch, Jill
  1991 "Gender, Kinship and Religion: 'Reconstructing' the Anthropology of Greece." In *Contested Identities: Gender and Kinship in Modern Greece,* ed. P. Loizos and E. Papataxiarchis, 29–46. Princeton: Princeton University Press.

DuBose, Terry J.
  1990   "Assessment of Fetal Age and Size: Techniques and Criteria." In *Diagnostic Medical Sonography: A Guide to Clinical Practice,* vol. 1., *Obstetrics and Gynecology,* ed. M. Berman, 273–298. Philadelphia: J. B. Lippincott.
Duden, Barbara
  1993   *Disembodying Women: Perspectives on Pregnancy and the Unborn.* Cambridge, Mass.: Harvard University Press.
Ewigman, Bernard, James Crane, Frederic Frigoletto, Michael LeFevre, Raymond Bain, and Donald McNellis
  1993   "Effect of Prenatal Ultrasound Screening on Perinatal Outcome." *New England Journal of Medicine* 329:821–827.
Fellous, Michele
  1990   *Avoir un enfant à voir: Approche socio-anthropologique d'une innovation technique médicale, l'échographie obstétricale.* Paris: IRESCO-CNRS.
Fiske, John
  1987   *Television Culture.* New York: Routledge.
Foucault, Michel
  1982   "The Subject and Power." In *Michel Foucault: Beyond Structuralism and Hermeneutics,* ed. H. L. Dreyfuss and P. Rabinow, 208–226. Chicago: University of Chicago Press.
Fuchs, Victor
  1968   "The Growing Demand for Medical Care." *New England Journal of Medicine* 279:190–195.
Georges, Eugenia
  1996   "Abortion Policy and Practice in Greece." *Social Science and Medicine* 42(4):509–519.
Gourgouris, Stathis
  1992   "Nationalism and Oneirocentrism: Of Modern Hellenes in Europe." *Diaspora* 2:43–71.
Handman, Marie-Elisabeth
  1983   *La Violence et la ruse: Hommes et femmes dans un village grec.* La Calade, Aix-en-Provence: Edisud.
Hubbard, Ruth
  1990   *The Politics of Women's Biology.* New Brunswick: Rutgers University Press.
Hyde, Beverly
  1986   "An Interview Study of Pregnant Women's Attitudes to Ultrasound Scanning." *Social Science and Medicine* 222(5):587–592.
Jordan, Brigitte
  [1978] 1993   *Birth in Four Cultures: A Cross-Cultural Investigation of Childbirth in Yucatan, Holland, Sweden and the United States.* 4th ed. Prospect Heights, Ill.: Waveland Press.
Kassirer, Jerome P.
  1992   "Images in Clinical Medicine." *New England Journal of Medicine* 326:829–830.
Koenig, Barbara
  1988   "The Technological Imperative in Medical Practice: The Social Creation

of a 'Routine' Treatment." In *Biomedicine Examined,* ed. M. Lock and D. R. Gordon, 465–496. Dordrecht: Kluwer Academic Publishers.

Latour, Bruno
1986 "Visualization and Cognition: Thinking with Eyes and Hands." *Knowledge and Society: Studies in the Sociology of Culture Past and Present* 6:1–40.

Lefkarites, Mary
1992 "The Sociocultural Implications of Modernizing Childbirth Among Greek Women on the Island of Rhodes." *Medical Anthropology* 13:385–412.

Lydon, John, and Christine Dunkel-Schetter
1994 "Seeing Is Committing: A Longitudinal Study of Bolstering Commitment in Amniocentesis Patients. *Personality and Social Psychology Bulletin* 20(2):218–227.

McNeill, William H.
1978 *The Metamorphosis of Greece since World War II.* Chicago: University of Chicago Press.

Milne, Lynne, and Olive Rich
1981 "Cognitive and Affective Aspects of the Responses of Pregnant Women to Sonography." *Maternal-Child Nursing* 10:15–39.

Mitchell, Lisa
1993 " 'Seeing the Baby': Women and Fetal Ultrasound Images." Paper presented at the 92d annual meeting of the American Anthropological Association, Washington, D.C.

Mitchell, Lisa, and Eugenia Georges
1997 "Baby's First Picture: The Cyborg Fetus of Ultrasound Imaging." In *Cyborg Babies: From Techno-Sex to Techno-Tots,* ed. R. Davis-Floyd and J. Dumit. New York: Routledge. In press.

Oakley, Ann
1984 *The Captured Womb: A History of the Medical Care of Pregnant Women.* Oxford: Basil Blackwell.
1993 *Essays on Women, Medicine and Health.* Edinburgh: Edinburgh University Press.

Petchesky, Rosalind
1987 "Foetal Images: The Power of Visual Culture in the Politics of Reproduction." In *Reproductive Technologies: Gender, Motherhood and Medicine,* ed. M. Stanworth, 57–80. Minneapolis: University of Minnesota Press.

Pfaffenberger, Bryan
1992 "Social Anthropology of Technology." *Annual Review of Anthropology* 21:491–516.

Philalithis, Anastas
1986 "The Imperative for a National Health System in Greece in a Social and Historical Context." In *Socialism in Greece,* ed. Z. Tzannatos, 145–173. Brookfield, Vt.: Gower.

Probyn, Elspeth
1991 "The Body Which Is Not One: Speaking an Embodied Self." *Hypatia* 6(3):111–124.

Rapp, Rayna
1991 "Constructing Amniocentesis: Maternal and Medical Discourses." In *Un-*

certain Terms: Negotiating Gender in American Culture, ed. F. Ginsburg and A. Lowenhaupt Tsing, 28–42. Boston: Beacon Press.

Reiser, Stanley
  1978   *Medicine in the Reign of Technology.* Cambridge: Cambridge University Press.

Rothman, Barbara Katz
  1986   *The Tentative Pregnancy.* New York: Viking.

Sandelowski, Margarete
  1991   "Compelled to Try: The Never-Enough Quality of Conceptive Technology." *Medical Anthropology Quarterly* 5(1):29–47.

Sarah, Rebecca
  1988   "Power, Uncertainty and the Fear of Death." In *Embryos, Ethics and Women's Rights,* ed. E. H. Baruch et al., 59–71. New York: Harrington Park Press.

Shearer, Madeleine H.
  1984   "Revelations: A Summary and Analysis of the NIH Consensus Development Conference on Ultrasound Imaging in Pregnancy." *Birth* 11(1):23–36.

Sikaki-Douka, Aleka
  n.d.   *O Toketos Ine Aghape,* 4th ed. Athens.

Sontag, Susan
  1989   *On Photography.* New York: Farrar, Straus, Giroux.

Spitz, Jean Lea
  1990   "Sonographer Support of Maternal-Fetal Bonding." In *Diagnostic Medical Sonography: A Guide to Clinical Practice,* vol. 1, *Obstetrics and Gynecology,* ed. M. Berman, 565–571. Philadelphia: J. B. Lippincott.

Stanworth, Michelle, ed.
  1987   *Reproductive Technologies: Gender, Motherhood and Medicine.* Minneapolis: University of Minnesota Press.

Stewart, Charles
  1991   *Demons and the Devil: Moral Imagination in Modern Greek Culture.* Princeton: Princeton University Press.

Strong, P.
  1984   "Viewpoint: The Academic Encirclement of Medicine?" *Sociology of Health and Illness* 6:339–358.

Taussig, Michael
  1992   *The Nervous System.* New York: Routledge.

Tsoukalas, Nikos
  1991   " 'Enlightened' Concepts in the 'Dark': Power and Freedom, Politics and Society." *Journal of Modern Greek Studies* 9:1–22.

Tymstra, Tjeerd
  1989   "The Imperative Character of Medical Technology and the Meaning of 'Anticipated Regret.' " *International Journal of Technology Assessment in Health Care* 5:207–213.

Tzoumaka-Bakoula, Ch.
  1990   "Frondidha Kata ton Toketo." In *Perighenitiki Frondidha stin Ellada,* ed. E. Valassi-Adam, S. Nakou, and D. Trakas, 85–88. Athens: Institute of Child Health.

Velogiannis-Moutsopoulos, L., and C. S. Bartsocas
  1989   "Medical Genetics in Greece." In *Human Genetics: A Cross-Cultural Perspective,* ed. D. Wertz and J. Fletcher, 209–234. Heidelberg: Springer.
Villeneuve, Claude, Catherine Laroche, Abby Lippman, and Myriam Marrache
  1988   "Psychological Aspects of Ultrasound Imaging During Pregnancy." *Canadian Journal of Psychiatry* 33:530–535.
Williams, Raymond
  1961   *The Long Revolution.* London: Penguin.
  1980   "Base and Superstructure in Marxist Critical Theory." In *Problems in Materialism and Culture: Selected Essays.* London: Verso.
Winner, Langdon
  1985   "Do Artifacts Have Politics? In *The Social Shaping of Technology: How the Refrigerator Got Its Hum,* ed. D. MacKenzie and J. Wajcman, 26–38. Philadelphia: Open University Press.
Yoxen, Edward
  1987   "Seeing with Sound: A Study of the Development of Medical Images." In *The Social Construction of Technological Systems,* ed. W. Bijker, T. Hughes, and T. Pinch, 281–303. Cambridge, Mass.: MIT Press.
Zaharopoulos, Thimios
  1991   "Power, Freedom and Broadcasting in Greece." *Modern Greek Studies Yearbook* 7:69–86.

FOUR

The Production of Authoritative Knowledge in American Prenatal Care

Carole H. Browner and Nancy Press

Recent attention has focused on strategies employed by the institution of biomedicine to attain medical hegemony in U.S. society. There has been little research, however, on the role individual patients may play in furthering this process. Drawing on Brigitte Jordan's concept of authoritative knowledge (AK), this account therefore examines the circumstances under which a group of pregnant American women facilitated biomedical expansion by accepting the advice offered by their prenatal care providers. We consider the significance of competing forms of knowledge, particularly "embodied knowledge," in determining which biomedical recommendations the women incorporated into their own pregnancy practices.[1] We also discuss some of the other criteria the women used when deciding whether or not to follow biomedical advice.

We will examine the role of biomedical technology in dislodging women's confidence in embodied knowledge and in consolidating biomedical AK in prenatal care. Embodied knowledge guided many of women's decisions about whether or not to accept specific prenatal recommendations in areas of prenatal care not yet subject to technological surveillance. Women also rejected biomedical recommendations they could not easily incorporate into their ongoing daily life routines. Yet few refused the offer of ultrasound or other forms of prenatal diagnostic screening. We argue that this is because most U.S. women regard information derived from technology as inherently authoritative knowledge (Davis-Floyd 1992; Rapp 1987).

We define embodied knowledge as subjective knowledge derived from a woman's perceptions of her body and its natural processes as these change throughout a pregnancy's course (Belenky et al. 1986). Jordan's (1977) pioneering work documented how a group of California lay women used embodied knowledge to accurately diagnose their own pregnant state prior to biomedical confirmation. The women employed a variety of phenomenological indicators as diagnostic criteria, including breast enlargement or soreness, nipple tenderness, feelings of extreme "heaviness" or bloating, food cravings, and intolerance to particular foods or smells. Other research found that women in the Colombian city of Cali used these same phenomenological indicators as well as other more idiosyncratic ones such as skin discolorations and pubic itching to diagnose their pregnancies (Browner 1980).

Jordan's conceptualization of authoritative knowledge frames our discussion. She defines AK as rules that carry more weight than others "either because they explain the state of the world better for the purposes at hand ('efficacy') or because they are associated with a stronger power base ('structural superiority'), and usually both" (Jordan 1993:152). In nonhierarchical settings, individuals choose from among several equally legitimate sets of rules or forms of knowledge. However, in situations of structural inequality, one set of rules or form of knowledge often gains authority, devaluing and delegitimating others in doing so. Although Jordan argues that the power of AK derives in part from the fact that it is consensually constructed, she does not describe the processes through which consensus is achieved in a previously contested domain. We intend this account to cast light on this issue.

The prenatal period is our focus because it offers a rare glimpse of medicalization processes in action (Thompson, Walsh, and Merkatz 1990). Although American women have, for the most part, accepted the legitimacy of biomedical authority and its associated technologies such as cesarean delivery in childbirth since the early part of this century, they continue to remain uncertain about its importance during the prenatal period (Browner 1990; Reid and Garcia 1989). As indications for "high-risk" pregnancies proliferate and more links are postulated between maternal behavior and negative fetal outcomes, pregnant women find themselves expected to accept intensifying prenatal surveillance (Terry 1989). Yet many are deeply ambivalent about the value of this extensive medical scrutiny (Hubbard 1995). Among patients, then, consensus is still lacking about the nature and extent of the role biomedicine should play in prenatal care.

The prenatal period provides a lens through which to examine the role lay women play in constructing a domain of authoritative knowledge, as they decide which medical advice to incorporate into their own health care practices and which to ignore. Focus on this issue can also illuminate the processes of biomedical expansion, as it reveals how technology designates certain kinds of knowledge as "authoritative" and in doing so helps drive medicalization processes.

METHODS AND CHARACTERISTICS OF THE STUDY POPULATION

The data analyzed here are based on interviews with 158 pregnant women who were enrolled in prenatal care at one of five branches of a health maintenance organization (HMO) located in southern California. Semi-structured, open-ended, tape-recorded interviews of one and a half to four hours' duration were conducted in informants' own homes or at the HMO. Tapes were transcribed, coded with Ethnograph (Seidel 1988), and subjected to content analysis; the Crunch Interactive Statistical Package (CRISP; Bostrom and Stegner 1984) was used to analyze the quantifiable data. We were broadly interested in women's self-care during pregnancy, and in how they incorporated biomedical prenatal advice into their previously existing self-care routines. In gathering data, therefore, particular attention was paid not only to the changes pregnant women made in their lives due to pregnancy but also to the sources of the information on which these changes were based.[2]

Because other research has amply documented the role of ethnicity and social class in shaping attitudes toward prenatal care and women's self-care practices during pregnancy (Kay 1980; Lazarus 1994; Martin 1987; Rapp 1993; Spicer 1977), we expected that this study would produce similar results. This proved not to be the case. No significant differences by ethnicity or social class were found in the women's attitudes toward prenatal care or their pregnancy practices.

Lazarus reported similar results from her research on Puerto Rican and European-American obstetrical patients at a U.S. inner-city hospital. She writes, "The Puerto Rican and white women held similar beliefs about pregnancy and birth, managed these events in a similar fashion, and behaved similarly in their clinical interactions, despite the fact that the Puerto Rican women maintained a strong, separate cultural identity" (Lazarus 1988:36). Lazarus finds that the clinic organization and the exigencies of medical resident training had a more powerful impact on doctor-patient interaction and women's pregnancy practices than did cultural differences among patients. The following discussion will therefore combine the results from subgroups of informants, with the exception of a small number of recent immigrant Mexicans (n = 18) who drew on considerations not taken into account by the other groups when deciding whether or not to accept clinicians' biomedical prenatal recommendations.

The women interviewed ranged in age from eighteen to thirty-five (mean age = 26.8, s.d. = 4.5) and had 0 to 6 children (mean = 1.3, s.d. = 1.1) and 0 to 9 previous pregnancies (mean = 2.1, s.d. = 1.68). One-third had had at least one induced abortion (mean = 0.45, s.d. = 0.74, range 0–3). Sixty-three percent were European-American,[3] 25 percent were Mexican-American (i.e., born in the United States to parents of Mexican ancestry or immigrated to the United States by the age of ten), and 12 percent were Mexican immigrants (i.e., immigrated to the United States after the age of ten). Median household income was $30,000 to $35,000, although 22 percent had incomes below $15,000 and 22 percent had incomes over $50,000. Most had completed high school, although 25 percent had not; only 12 percent had earned a bachelor's degree or more.

THE CULTURE OF PRENATAL CARE IN THE UNITED STATES

In the United States today, prenatal care is fundamentally about getting and giving information.[4] Providers collect data on the state of pregnant women's bodies and the condition of their developing fetuses. At the same time, they want their clients to understand how and why their bodies are changing, in part because they expect this will make them more likely to follow providers' recommendations. In reality, much of prenatal care can be seen as a process of medical socialization, in which providers attempt to teach pregnant women their own interpretations of the signs and symptoms the women will experience as the pregnancy proceeds and the significance that should be attached to them.

Most women's goals when they sought prenatal care dovetailed closely with those of providers: women wanted to give providers access to their bodies for prenatal monitoring, and they wanted to learn how their doctors thought they should care for themselves and act during pregnancy. Typical, then, was Ana Martínez's[5] description of why she enrolled in prenatal care:

> Because . . . [in] your first couple of months you don't know what's going on . . . getting your blood lab [sic], if you are diabetic, [and] to check all the diseases the baby could carry. And well, there's so much information and pamphlets that they're willing to give. . . . [And also] if I'm feeling real weird, like I get a kick and it feels really warm after the kick but only in one spot, . . . to me it's like, is that normal?

Implicit in this comment is also the fact that Ana saw her prenatal care as providing important emotional reassurance. Others were more direct in this regard. As Denise Roberts said, "It comforts me to be told this is how you're going to be feeling." And Helena Suárez explained, "The nurses know me when I walk in. They say, 'Oh, you look really great.' . . . It gives you that extra boost." Other women saw this emotional support more indirectly. Mary Zim, for instance, valued the fact that her providers helped her set limits in her otherwise busy life. She commented, "It [prenatal care] helps me feel good about saying I'm not doing this, that I don't need to be Superwoman all the time." Similarly, Ruthann Almond focused on the prospects for long-term reassurance that prenatal care offered. She said she was scrupulous about keeping all her prenatal appointments: "I don't want to think back and say, oh man, I had this condition, they could have done something about it, and I didn't go to my appointments." Other women liked prenatal care because the technologies used, like the fetal stethoscope and ultrasonography, made them feel closer to the fetus. As Stefany Jones explained, "After I heard the baby's heartbeat, it was different than before. . . . It [prenatal care] just makes it more real."

But for many, the informational function of prenatal care is of primary importance, partly because they see being informed as foremost among the responsibilities conferred by pregnancy. Popular literature and the media insist that pregnant women must attend to their bodies to a degree that others need not. Some women therefore are disappointed when they receive what they consider scant biomedical information. Said Jenifer Lowe, "When I had my last child . . . I was kind of surprised because I had a girlfriend who was pregnant at the same time and she said, 'I don't do this and I don't do that,' and I thought, he didn't tell *me* all that stuff." Alicia Aguilar similarly remarked, "We [society] know more, but I don't think the information is readily available. . . . I want to hear specifically why am I feeling like that. [If the doctor says] 'Oh, that's normal.' O.K., why?" Our informants, then, expected their prenatal providers to offer accurate interpretations of their sensations and bodily experiences while simultaneously providing reassurance that their pregnancies were proceeding as expected.

Despite this emphasis on information, however, the pregnant women in our study did not uncritically accept biomedical authority within the domain of prenatal care. One reason was the frequency with which they discovered that the biomedical information they or others had been given was wrong. Rebeca Cardinas explained, "The first time they thought I was going to have twins, but that turned out to be wrong. This time, they felt my uterus was too small for where I said I was in the pregnancy. But I was right." Said Mara Green, pregnant with her fourth child, "After my first, they said they were sure I would never have children again." Similarly, speaking of her child born with a cleft palate, Jeanie Puck explained, "A couple of the doctors said he's going to be a very underweight child. . . . They said that for the first two years, he won't be more than ten pounds. And he's already eight and a half pounds and he'll be four months old tomorrow! So that's totally blown out what those doctors said already."

Others voiced skepticism about the accuracy of information derived from prenatal testing. Elaine Irwin remarked, "I went to my first prenatal thing and they showed the films about the AFP [alpha-fetoprotein] test . . . and . . . this lady next to me said, 'I took all those tests and nothing told me [that my child would be born with Down's syndrome].' " Marta Jimenez, speaking of friends, reported the opposite experience: "They were told the baby would definitely be born mentally retarded. They prepared themselves and all this other kinds of stuff and she [the baby] was fine."

Women also were skeptical about the validity of biomedical information because of the speed with which biomedical advice to pregnant women has changed. Although most said they believed the advice they themselves were receiving was more correct than that given their mothers, that it was often so different gave some pause. Similarly, some drew on their own or others' personal experiences to question current biomedical wisdom regarding the negative consequences of alcohol and tobacco use during pregnancy. Finally, many multiparous women had received prenatal care from a different physician for each pregnancy, and had received conflicting advice from each, providing further evidence that they could not simply accept what doctors said. Many indicated that they were inclined to accept physicians' advice as authoritative, but they demonstrated a degree of ambivalence while doing so.

PREGNANT WOMEN'S RESPONSES TO BIOMEDICAL ADVICE

For the purposes of this analysis, biomedical authoritative knowledge is defined as recommendations intended to safeguard the health of a pregnant woman or her fetus. It includes information from women's own prenatal care providers, from other biomedical authorities, and from books and other written materials. Advice from lay sources not purportedly backed by biomedical authority will not be considered here.

The women in our study were met with a vast and often confusing array of information, offered either in generic form or as individually tailored recommendations. The HMO offers all pregnant clients a three-hour prenatal education class. The class reviews the physiological and psychological changes associated with pregnancy, describes the nature of the prenatal care the HMO will provide, and gives the HMO's recommendations for diet, exercise, weight gain, and rest. Our informants also had access to a wide array of written materials, both at the HMO and elsewhere. These included a ninety-six-page booklet published by the HMO entitled "Preparing for a HEALTHY BABY," as well as books, especially the very popular *What to Expect When You're Expecting* (Eisenberg, Murkoff, and Hathaway 1991), subscription magazines, and free "throw-away" magazines that are essentially advertising supplements. Of all written materials, these last were probably most widely read by our informants. When medically indicated, the HMO also provided women with individual consultations with a dietician or one or more biomedical specialists.

Having so much information available, however, was not necessarily helpful or reassuring. The following quote offers insight into the range of considerations a woman we call Kristin Robinson took into account when seeking to evaluate and make use of specific prenatal recommendations.

KR: At the very beginning I didn't know I could take Tylenol, I was thinking Tylenol and aspirin was [*sic*] the same thing. . . . So I had a headache . . . [and] I finally called this hot line and they said, "Do you have any Tylenol?" and I'm thinking what an idiot, I've had this headache four hours. . . .

Interviewer: Did you have any qualms about taking Tylenol after that?

KR: Not until I went to my chiropractor . . . because I was saying if I couldn't take Tylenol I would be going crazy because my back was hurting me more with the pregnancy and he said (he doesn't even have any kids, he's just a chiropractor), "Well, you know all those things are going into the little baby and that might not be a good idea." I remember leaving there thinking I'm just not going to [take it], suffer a little more before I take it, even though I would try not to anyway.

Interviewer: Sounds like you were pretty influenced by authority figures.

KR: Yeah, I mean it makes sense. I also had a sister-in-law whose doctor told her NutraSweet was really bad, and my other sister-in-law in the same room said, "Oh, just don't listen to her because my doctor said that and from what I read I thought that was just hogwash." [And] I thought, NutraSweet is in *practically everything* and I've always been kind of a weight watcher so I would use it. . . . I wouldn't use Sweet 'N Low because I've heard that's not good.

Interviewer: So during your pregnancy, what did you do?

KR: At the beginning I would just use sugar, and then I think I read that NutraSweet was okay. And then [when] my sister-in-law said "My doctor said that it's really not good," it was almost after the fact because I had already used some and I thought, I'm not going to panic. I've read that it's okay and heard it's okay.

Interviewer: So you're more likely to trust something you've read than something you hear?

KR: Yeah, even if it was her doctor, but still.

We see Kristin Robinson confronting a lack of consensus among clinicians and her confusion as to how to proceed. Kristin indicates that she misunderstood advice she had initially been given on over-the-counter painkillers, and incorrectly assumed that both aspirin and Tylenol were prohibited. A severe headache led her to seek new advice from a hot line. She was relieved to learn that they considered Tylenol safe during pregnancy. She accepted this as authoritative information until a practitioner she consulted for a different problem questioned her judgment. Although she casts doubt on his authority ("He doesn't even have any kids, he's just a chiropractor"), in the end she accepts it over the medical hot line because his explanation "makes sense."

Kristin finds the situation with artificial sweeteners similarly confusing. Here she must weigh information gleaned from her own reading against what pregnant relatives report having been told by their physicians. In the end she accepts what she has read over what her relatives report, in part because she has already engaged in the purportedly damaging behavior ("It was almost after the fact because I had already used some and I thought . . . I've read that it's okay and heard it's okay"). She supports her position with a relative, who also questions biomedical authority on this subject ("Just don't listen to her because my doctor said that and from what I read I thought that was just hogwash," Kristin indicates the relative replied). In neither instance does Kristin indicate that she asked her prenatal care providers for advice or clarification.

This example illuminates some of the dynamics called into play when pregnant women evaluate information from diverse sources and incorporate some of it into their own self-care. We see such evaluation as an ongoing process, not a discrete event. Below we offer an analysis of the factors that differentiated biomedical prenatal recommendations our informants incorporated from those they did not. For the most part, women accepted recommendations that were confirmed by embodied knowledge and experience and rejected those that ran counter to their preexisting beliefs about how to care for themselves during pregnancy and those they could not easily incorporate into their everyday lives.

Biomedical Recommendations Women Incorporated

Embodied knowledge guided many women's decisions about whether to incorporate specific prenatal recommendations. Women who had already borne children commonly drew on their embodied experiences in this regard. Some, for example, incorporated advice that promised to resolve physiological problems they experienced in previous pregnancies. Lorraine Tann was told to limit physical activities during her current pregnancy because she experienced premature labor the first time. She says she has done so: "I notice I have more contractions when I do too much." Others reported being particularly conscientious about following dietary recommendations because they gained excessive weight during a previous pregnancy and suffered associated physical problems as a result.

As women's pregnancies passed through different stages, some clinical advice that had initially been rejected because it seemed to have no value was ultimately accepted. Embodied knowledge confirmed its value. Donna Kadence explained why she reduced her use of caffeine: "I didn't at first.

. . . Then I started feeling it moving [after drinking coffee]. It made me go, there's a person kickin' on me, saying 'No, no don't do that!' " Similarly, Carol Hughes ultimately agreed with her doctor to stop bike riding: "When I was almost four months I took a good eight-mile bike ride and two days later I had a pain on my side that kept me doubled over all day long. So I've decided to keep my bike riding to not at all."

These examples are important in revealing some of the processes at play when pregnant women eventually incorporated biomedical recommendations they had initially rejected. Early in pregnancy, they are told a great many things about pregnancy management, some of which seem implausible or unnecessary at the time. But that information may subsequently be drawn on to help women interpret unfamiliar experiences and sensations. Whether or not Carol Hughes's bike ride caused the pain she felt two days later, the fact remains that those events became linked in her mind because of what her doctor had said. Biomedical advice provided many women with a framework for interpreting new, unexpected, and sometimes frightening bodily experiences.

Our informants also incorporated biomedical advice that had clear and immediate physiological results. Tricia Moss, for instance, reported walking more during her pregnancy as her doctor had advised. When asked why she was doing so, she replied, "To tell you the truth I don't know. It just makes me feel better." Others eliminated or limited foods they ordinarily loved because they caused gastric distress. Women who, physicians felt, might be miscarrying because they were experiencing vaginal bleeding were told to stay off their feet for a specific period of time ranging from a few days to several months. Many, like Elena Arroyo, reported that the problem was resolved when they complied: "As soon as I did what they told me, that really, really helped a lot."

Some prenatal dietary recommendations were incorporated because they fit women's own preexisting physiological inclinations. Jeanette Simons, for example, found it easy to follow biomedical prohibitions against alcohol use in pregnancy: "Normally I don't drink at all when I'm pregnant, but I don't have any desire to either." Cindi Baker reported a similar experience with coffee: "I just didn't like drinking it anymore."

But embodied knowledge was not the only principle for evaluating biomedical knowledge. Physicians' recommendations consistent with women's own prior understandings about how they should care for themselves during pregnancy were incorporated as well. Priscilla Abbott, for instance, willingly drinks more milk whenever she is pregnant. "I think I need the calcium," she explains. Jenny LaValle drastically cut back on sugar because, she said, "I know sugar can make children hyper, so I'm sure a developing baby can get real hyper too." Like several others, Anne Walse stopped strenuous exercise: "Water skiing I love to do, and jet skiing, but I won't because if I fall off and something happens to me, it also happens to the baby."

Some of the advice adopted by Mexican immigrant informants was incorporated because it was congruent with understandings derived from Mexican ethnomedical systems (Browner 1985). Several ate fewer hot chile peppers, for instance, because they feared their babies would be born red, irritated, and with their faces covered with pimples. Others stopped lifting heavy objects for fear the baby would be born with a hernia. Still others walked more because they feared inactivity would cause the fetus or the placenta to "stick" to their backs, causing protracted labor.

Finally, women regardless of immigration status accepted prenatal biomedical recommendations they could easily incorporate into their ongoing daily lives. For example, Bonnie Brown, who was considered dangerously overweight by her doctors, said, "I don't limit my intake of sugar or fats like I know I should. [But] I do take a prenatal supplement. I think it would be a good thing if I would change [my diet], but it would just be an overall lifestyle change which up to now I've been too undisciplined to make."

In sum, embodied knowledge provided a standard against which biomedical prenatal recommendations were assessed. Those confirmed physiologically were adopted. In addition, advice consistent with ways women believed they should care for themselves during pregnancy, and advice they experienced as benign, were incorporated as well.

Biomedical Recommendations Women Did Not Incorporate

Many women also drew on their own embodied experience when they chose not to incorporate specific prenatal biomedical recommendations. Those who had already borne healthy children were especially likely to act independently, referring back to a prior pregnancy or delivery when giving the rationale for rejecting a clinical recommendation. Kitty Carson, for instance, is one of many informants who was unwilling to give up smoking during pregnancy despite being urged to do so. "I smoked during my first pregnancy and I had a nine-pound baby," she explained. "[And the baby] had a nine on the Apgar,[6] which the highest is ten. So for me it was like okay." What Kitty seems to be saying here is that biomedicine's universalistic claim that smoking during pregnancy is harmful to the fetus simply does not conform to her own embodied experience.

In this regard it is noteworthy that several who scrupulously followed prenatal recommendations in earlier pregnancies and bore healthy children said they were less concerned about doing so during their current pregnancy. As Rachel White explained, "After my first child what came out was, I was born to have babies. . . . So I'm not as rigid as I was before." In cases such as these, women seem to be crediting themselves or their embodied knowledge with the successful outcome rather than the biomedical recommendations they so conscientiously observed.

Biomedical advice that did not bring about the promised physiological changes was also generally rejected. Rosa Rodriquez states, "I was told to do Kegel exercises, but I don't really get around to them because . . . you do them but you don't find no results." Karen Brooks decided not to follow her physician's recommendation that she exercise. She remarked, "The last time I was pregnant, I was told that if I exercise a lot that my labor would be easy. So I was still in labor for seventeen hours. This time I'm not doing anything. Who knows, maybe this baby will just pop out." In such situations, women felt their own embodied experience overrode the promise of medical science.

Biomedical advice that was not consistent with women's own ideas about how to best care for themselves during pregnancy was not incorporated either. Kristin Robinson, for example, explained why she decided not to take prenatal vitamins: "They really say those vitamins are good, but I don't know. I eat pretty good anyways so." Eva Capitans was one of many who did not strictly follow the recommended prenatal dietary regimen because in her view it was excessive. She remarked, "The doctors gave me nutritional papers saying you should be eating so much proteins and poultry, milk and so forth. I don't go by it specifically. . . . I don't like step-by-step, four servings of this, I just eat my regular and know somehow or other." Similarly, Annette Ascew understood that alcohol use was strongly discouraged during pregnancy. Nevertheless, she said, "If I want [a beer] I'm going to have one because I think it's better to make me happy instead of being stressed. That's more important to me than putting a little alcohol in my body."

Most important, perhaps, women turned down biomedical advice that could not be readily incorporated into the existing contexts of their ongoing daily lives. For instance, Lucy Kammer was thirty-three weeks pregnant when she began experiencing frequent premature contractions. "The doctors said lay in bed until you have this baby," she said. "And that would be like two months. How am I supposed to lay in bed with three kids?" During her first trimester of pregnancy, Donna Ooms had morning sickness so severe that it interfered with her ability to work as a beauty technician. She explained, "I was downing like a bottle of [antinausea medication] a day just to be able to go to work. They said taking doses that high wasn't cool . . . but I didn't have a whole lot of choice." The women's frustrations stem from the fact that they feel that biomedical advice is often offered without sufficient regard for the realities of their lives.

Kitty Carson put these other women's views into perspective when she described how she herself incorporated dietary recommendations and other prenatal biomedical advice: "I tend to think you have to take all the medical things and relate 'em to your family, too. The first one I cooked a lot of big meals. Now I have two kids, I don't have the time. You need time just to sit back and kick up your feet—[you can't] worry about having these big family-style dinners every night." Aware, then, that it would be unrealistic and impractical to adopt all prenatal recommendations, Kitty Carson selected those she could incorporate into her life with the least difficulty and to the greatest positive effect.

In this regard it is clear that our informants did not incorporate biomedical recommendations they perceived to be "too costly." Bonnie Brown, for instance, explained why she has not changed her diet during pregnancy: "Everything says that you should limit your fats. But I love to cook, and I just cook the way I've always known how." Carmen Acevedo found it difficult to cut back on physical activities as she was advised: "I like to pick up things and be cleaning [which] is bad for me so sometimes I'll hide and I'll do it." With a history of two prior miscarriages, Chris Knight feared she might be exercising too much because she was experiencing frequent strong premature contractions. Yet she could not bring herself to stop: "I just want to try to not be so overweight after the baby is born." She therefore compromised, modifying the frequent aerobic workouts she would not abandon according to how her body responded at any particular point in time. "Sometimes I just march in place when I have contractions," Chris explained.

Other women also forged compromises they could live with. They rejected biomedical advice they found burdensome, rationalizing their decisions with the belief that their overall prenatal behavior was generally in conformity with biomedical expectations. Although Bonnie Brown, for example, was unwilling to cut back on sugar and fats, she readily gave up drinking, in the belief that alcohol was potentially more damaging to fetal development than sugar or fats. Similarly, Jackie Prince described her pregnancy diet: "More milk, more vegetables. You're not going to get me off my potato chips. Even though they say it's not good for you. But I don't drink or smoke or anything so . . ." Dina Warren's compromise concerned exercise: "My doctor advised me not to go to the gym, . . . but I ride my bike, which she doesn't like either, but, sorry, I have been riding my bike."

Finally, some immigrant Mexican women drew on "social" considerations when they turned down biomedical advice. Although Nancy Ramos, for instance, had been taught in prenatal class to avoid smoky areas, she said she has not been entirely successful. "Sometimes we have visitors who stay with us and they're smokers. But I simply can't do anything about that," she explained. In a similar vein, although Celia Zarate was told by her doctor to strictly control her diet, she found that social considerations sometimes made it difficult to comply. In one instance, after accepting a dinner invitation, she wanted to call her hostess to inquire about what would be served. Her husband flatly rejected her plan, saying, "We can't ask them what they're going to serve when they invite us."

One final example of how social considerations influenced Mexican women's prenatal behavior may make the point best. Susana Ortiz was seven months pregnant when her father suddenly died in Mexico. Susana immediately began to prepare to return home for the funeral. A friend who thought it might be dangerous for Susana to fly suggested that she check with her physician. The doctor said that she absolutely should not fly and discouraged her from even making the trip by car. Susana flew home anyway. Afterward, she explained, "Imagine if I didn't go to the funeral. What would my people think? I'm the only daughter and the only one that lives here [in the U.S.]. I'm the oldest. My place was there." Interestingly we never saw such "social" considerations as the reason either the European-American or Mexican-American women gave for rejecting a biomedical recommendation.

In deciding, then, what to regard as authoritative knowledge in prenatal care, women drew to some extent on embodied knowledge, although other considerations, especially preexisting beliefs about how they should best care for themselves during pregnancy, also played a part. But for many the more important factor was the extent to which the recommendations could be incorporated into the existing contexts of the women's daily lives.

DISCUSSION

These data clearly show that pregnant American women do not consider prenatal recommendations to be authoritative simply because they are issued by physicians. In this account, we have focused on a wide range of prenatal recommendations, from those that might seem discretionary, such as advice about exercise and diet, to interventions of a more serious nature, such as those indicated in the event of a threatened miscarriage. Nonetheless, these women were no more likely to follow biomedical recommendations if the problem was regarded by either doctors or the women themselves as benign or medically serious. In this regard our informants are like other American women and men who seldom uncritically follow biomedical advice (Chrisman and Kleinman 1983; Conrad 1985; Hunt et al. 1989; Hunt, Browner, and Jordan 1990; Stimson and Webb 1975). Rather, they are reflective actors who continually evaluate the clinical recommendations they receive. The extent to which they acknowledge those recommendations to be authoritative is based on the bodily changes they are experiencing, their own prior history and knowledge, and the everyday life situations in which their illnesses are experienced and treatments employed.

In other words, patients are active interpreters of medical information, picking and choosing, using and discarding advice according to internal and external constraints and considerations. In the case of our pregnant informants, embodied knowledge and everyday life exigencies proved pivotal in their selectively designating certain biomedical knowledge as authoritative. The women challenged biomedical authority in prenatal care specifically when they saw it as based solely on clinicians' judgments. In these cases women balanced these judgments against their own embodied knowledge and the extent to which they could accommodate their lives to the recommendations being proposed.

Valuing information derived from embodied knowledge over biomedical knowledge in prenatal care, as these women do, contrasts with the attitudes and behavior characteristic of most American women as they give birth. During labor, American women are highly acquiescent to biomedical authority at the expense of embodied knowledge (Bromberg 1981; Davis-Floyd 1992, 1994; Jordan 1993; McClain 1990; Nelson 1983; Sargent and Stark 1987, 1989). The vast majority readily accede to the biomedical assumption that a range of clinical technology, including fetal monitoring, episiotomy, and cesarean delivery, must be employed. Although we did not collect data on this subject, we have no reason to expect that our informants would feel or act different from most other American women during childbirth.

American women acquiesce to the biomedical assumption that technology is essential for a successful delivery for several reasons. Many believe it is safer for them and their newborns. Others feel that it offers them more "control." On a deeper level, the attraction seems to stem from pregnant women's lack of confidence in their own bodies and their ability to successfully give birth on their own. Their unwillingness to trust embodied knowledge during childbirth contrasts with the importance we have seen it granted in pregnancy by the women in this study.

What, then, differentiates prenatal care from childbirth in the minds of the women in our sample and, quite likely, of many other American women? Why does their faith in embodied knowledge during pregnancy become subordinated to biomedical knowledge when it comes time to give birth? Part of the answer clearly lies in the differential role of biomedical technology in the two domains. While childbirth in America is now primarily a technological endeavor, this is not yet the case for prenatal care.

Studies on the growing importance of prenatal diagnosis provide insight into this distinction (Browner and Press 1995; Lippman 1989; Petchesky 1987; Rapp 1987, 1988, 1990; Rothman 1986; Georges, this volume).

They show that few women refuse the technologies of prenatal testing such as ultrasound or other diagnostic procedures when they are recommended by health care providers, even though the women themselves may see no particular use for the information such testing can provide. Such technologies, which are culturally regarded as both accurate and incontrovertible, help make the pregnancy more real (see Georges, this volume) and allow women to feel they are doing all they should to assure the fetus's health.

Like other Americans, pregnant women are deeply ambivalent about the value of technology (Habermas 1972; Knorr-Cetina and Mulkay 1983; Ziman 1976). Yet few reject it out of hand, for scientific information occupies a uniquely privileged spot in American culture. Information produced by science marshals inherent respect, although it may have no apparent use. We see this clearly with regard to prenatal diagnostic testing, where a physician's recommendation usually carries the force of command and even suggestions by nurses and other medical staff carry heavy weight. For example, in the state of California, alpha-fetoprotein testing (for neural tube defects and Down's syndrome) is both paid for by the state and persistently recommended to pregnant women by biomedical practitioners. In a study we carried out of women's responses to the offer of this test (Browner and Press 1995; Press and Browner n.d.), we found that in spite of the fact that its results are often ambiguous, very few women rejected it. Once it is widely available, prenatal diagnostic technology cannot be refused neutrally, as that can imply lack of responsibility on the mother's part. Adhering to the routines of scientifically based prenatal care, such as AFP testing and ultrasound scans, is women's only culturally approved means of reassuring themselves, and others, that they are doing "all that can be done" to ensure a healthy pregnancy. This contrasts sharply with their attitudes about other prenatal recommendations, which, as we saw, were incorporated only if they met the various criteria for usefulness that the women applied. Authoritative knowledge in the prenatal domain, then, is not a single entity but rather is composed of constituent parts (Sargent and Bascope, this volume): women often rely on their own embodied knowledge more heavily than clinicians' opinions; in contrast, they acquiesce to biomedical authority when it is backed by the power of technology.

While, as we have shown in this chapter, women often take prenatal advice based on clinicians' judgments with the proverbial grain of salt, evaluating its feasibility and checking it against their own bodily knowing, it is also the case that women increasingly defer to biomedical authority in those domains of prenatal care where clinical technologies predominate. The invention and elaboration of such technologies are integral to biomedicine's efforts to legitimize its hegemony. These processes can be examined in the cultural domain of prenatal care, where lay women still feel free to choose among competing views of what is best for them during pregnancy. But as the role of clinical technology grows more predominant, pregnant women may increasingly defer to biomedical authority. In so doing, they help create the consensus that biomedicine holds authoritative knowledge in the domain of prenatal care.

NOTES

The research was supported in part by NICHD grant HD11944 and grants from the University of California, Los Angeles, Chicano Studies Research Center and Academic Senate. Laura Fernea, Ellen Lodge, Kathy Kubarski, Susan Wilhite, Nancy Warwick, and Tina Zenzola helped conduct the interviews. Beatriz Solis and Mabel Preloran provided countless forms of invaluable assistance during the periods of data collection and data analysis. We thank all of them for their flexibility, enthusiasm, and help. We also thank the administration and staff of the HMO for facilitating the project during the long course of data collection and our informants for their willingness to communicate their experiences. Linda Hunt, Ann V. Millard, Mabel Preloran, Arthur J. Rubel, and Nancy Warwick made helpful comments on earlier drafts of this chapter. Robbie Davis-Floyd was an incisive and sensitive editor.

1. Gardner (1995:29) defines these as the everyday measures pregnant women believe they should take to bring about a successful pregnancy.

2. Copies of interview guides are available from the first author.

3. The European-American sample was also stratified by religion (59% Catholic, 41% non-Catholic Christian) because of our interest in the role of religion and religiosity in pregnant women's decisions about prenatal diagnostic testing (see Press and Browner 1994).

4. Although studies consistently find that women who enroll in prenatal care have better birth outcomes than those who do not, the reasons why remain unknown (Chalmers, Enkin, and Keirse 1989). The consensus among researchers at this time is that women who receive prenatal care may be less likely to use substances such as alcohol, tobacco, and narcotics, all of which can affect fetal health and development.

5. All proper names are pseudonyms.

6. A system of scoring an infant's physical condition one minute after birth. The heart rate, respiration, muscle tone, color, and response to stimuli are scored 0, 1, or 2. The maximum total score for a normal baby is 10.

REFERENCES

Belenky, Mary Field, Blythe Clinchy, Nancy Goldberger, and Jill Tarule
1986 *Women's Ways of Knowing: The Development of Self, Voice, and Mind.* New York: Basic Books.

Bostrom, Alan, and Bruce Stegner
    1984   Crunch Interactive Statistical Package (CRISP), Version 84.1. San Francisco.
Bromberg, Joann
    1981   "Having a Baby: A Story Essay." In *Childbirth: Alternatives to Medical Control,* ed. Shelly Romalis, 33–62. Austin: University of Texas Press.
Browner, C. H.
    1980   "The Management of Early Pregnancy: Colombian Folk Concepts of Fertility Control." *Social Science and Medicine* 14B:25–32.
    1985   "Criteria for Selecting Herbal Remedies." *Ethnology* 24:13–32.
    1990   "Cultural Perspectives on Prenatal Care and Birth Outcomes in the Latino Community." Paper presented at the annual meeting of the Southwestern Anthropological Association, Long Beach, Calif.
Browner, C. H., and Nancy Press
    1995   "The Normalization of Prenatal Diagnostic Testing." In *The Politics of Reproduction,* ed. Faye Ginsburg and Rayna Rapp, 307–322. Berkeley: University of California Press.
Chalmers, Iain, Murray Enkin, and Marc J. N. C. Keirse, eds.
    1989   *Effective Care in Pregnancy and Childbirth.* Vol. 1: *Pregnancy.* Oxford: Oxford University Press.
Chrisman, Noel, and Arthur Kleinman
    1983   "Popular Health Care, Social Networks and Cultural Meanings: The Orientation of Medical Anthropology." In *Handbook of Health, Health Care and Health Professions,* ed. David Mechanic, 569–590. New York: Free Press.
Conrad, Peter
    1985   "The Meaning of Medications: Another Look at Compliance." *Social Science and Medicine* 20:29–37.
Davis-Floyd, Robbie E.
    1992   *Birth as an American Rite of Passage.* Berkeley, Los Angeles, and London: University of California Press.
    1994   "The Technocratic Body: American Childbirth as Cultural Expression." *Social Science and Medicine* 38(8):1125–1140.
Eisenberg, Arlene, Heidi E. Murkoff, and Sandee E. Hathaway
    1991   *What to Expect When You're Expecting.* New York: Workman Publishing.
Gardner, Carol Brooks
    1995   "Learning for Two: A Study of the Rhetoric of Pregnancy Practices." *Perspectives on Social Problems* 7:29–51.
Habermas, Jürgen
    1972   *Knowledge and Human Interests.* London: Heinemann.
Hubbard, Ruth
    1995   *Profitable Promises: Essays on Women, Science and Health.* Monroe, Me.: Common Courage Press.
Hunt, Linda M., C. H. Browner, and Brigitte Jordan
    1990   "Hypoglycemia: Portrait of an Illness Construct in Everyday Use." *Medical Anthropology Quarterly,* n.s., 4:191–210.
Hunt, Linda M., Brigitte Jordan, Susan Irwin, and C. H. Browner

1989 "Compliance and the Patient's Perspective: Controlling Symptoms in Everyday Life." *Culture, Medicine, and Psychiatry* 13(3):315–334.

Jordan, Brigitte

1977 "The Self-Diagnosis of Early Pregnancy: An Investigation of Lay Competence." *Medical Anthropology* 1:1–38.

1993 "The Achievement of Authoritative Knowledge in an American Hospital Birth." In Jordan, *Birth in Four Cultures: A Cross-Cultural Investigation of Childbirth in Yucatan, Holland, Sweden and the United States,* 4th ed., 151–168. Prospect Heights, Ill.: Waveland Press.

Kay, Margarita Artschwager

1980 "Mexican, Mexican American, and Chicana Childbirth." In *Twice a Minority: Mexican American Women,* ed. Margarita B. Melville, 52–65. St. Louis: C. V. Mosby.

Knorr-Cetina, Karin D., and Michael Mulkay, eds.

1983 *Science Observed: Perspectives on the Social Study of Science.* London: Sage.

Lazarus, Ellen

1988 "Theoretical Considerations for the Study of the Doctor-Patient Relationship: Implications of a Perinatal Study." *Medical Anthropology Quarterly,* n.s., 2:34–58.

1994 "What Do Women Want? Issues of Choice, Control, and Class in Pregnancy and Childbirth." *Medical Anthropology Quarterly,* n.s., 8:25–46.

Lippman, Abby

1989 "Prenatal Diagnosis: Reproductive Choice? Reproductive Control?" In *The Future of Human Reproduction,* ed. Christine Overall, 182–194. Toronto: Women's Press.

Martin, Emily

1987 *The Woman in the Body.* New York: Beacon.

McClain, Carol Shepherd

1990 "The Making of a Medical Tradition: Vaginal Birth after Cesarean." *Social Science and Medicine* 31:203–210.

Nelson, Margaret K.

1983 "Working-Class Women, Middle-Class Women, and Models of Childbirth." *Social Problems* 30:284–297.

Petchesky, Rosalind Pollack

1987 "Foetal Images: The Power of Visual Culture in the Politics of Reproduction." In *Reproductive Technologies: Gender, Motherhood and Medicine,* ed. Michelle Stanworth, 57–80. Minneapolis: University of Minnesota Press.

Press, Nancy, and C. H. Browner

1993 " 'Collective Fictions': Similarities in Reasons for Accepting Maternal Serum Alpha-Fetoprotein Screening Among Women of Diverse Ethnic and Social Class Backgrounds." *Fetal Diagnosis and Therapy* 8(suppl. 1):97–106.

n.d. "Why Women Say Yes to Prenatal Testing." *Social Science and Medicine.* In press.

Rapp, Rayna

1987 "Moral Pioneers: Women, Men and Fetuses on a Frontier of Reproductive Technology." *Women & Health* 13:101–116.

1988 "The Power of 'Positive' Diagnosis: Medical and Maternal Discourses on

Amniocentesis." In *Childbirth in America: Anthropological Perspectives,* ed. Karen L. Michaelson, 103–116. South Hadley, Mass.: Bergin and Garvey.

1990   "Constructing Amniocentesis: Maternal and Medical Discourses." In *Uncertain Terms: Negotiating Gender in America,* ed. Faye Ginsburg and Anna L. Tsing, 28–42. Boston: Beacon Press.

1993   "Amniocentesis in Sociocultural Perspective." *Journal of Genetic Counseling* 2:183–195.

Reid, Margaret, and Jo Garcia
1989   "Women's Views of Care During Pregnancy and Childbirth." In *Effective Care in Pregnancy and Childbirth.* Vol. 1: *Pregnancy,* pts. 1–5, ed. Iain Chalmers, Murray Enkin, and Marc J. N. C. Keirse, 131–142. Oxford: Oxford University Press.

Rothman, Barbara Katz
1986   *The Tentative Pregnancy: Prenatal Diagnosis and the Future of Motherhood.* New York: Penguin.

Sargent, Carolyn, and Nancy Stark
1987   "Surgical Birth: Interpretations of Cesarean Deliveries among Private Hospital Patients and Nursing Staff." *Social Science and Medicine* 25(12):1269–1276.

1989   "Childbirth Education and Childbirth Models: Parental Perspectives on Control, Anesthesia, and Technological Intervention in the Birth Process." *Medical Anthropology Quarterly* 3(1):36–51.

Seidel, John V.
1988   The Ethnograph. Version 3.0. Littleton, Colo.: Qualis Research Associates.

Spicer, Edward, ed.
1977   *Ethnic Medicine in the Southwest.* Tucson: University of Arizona Press.

Stimson, Gerry, and Barbara Webb
1975   *Going to See the Doctor: The Consultation Process in General Practice.* London: Routledge and Kegan Paul.

Terry, Jennifer
1989   "The Body Invaded: Medical Surveillance of Women as Reproducers." *Socialist Review* 19:13–43.

Thompson, Joyce E., Linda V. Walsh, and Irwin R. Merkatz
1990   "The History of Prenatal Care: Cultural, Social, and Medical Contexts." In *New Perspectives on Prenatal Care,* ed. Joyce E. Thompson, Linda V. Walsh, and Irwin R. Merkatz, 9–30. New York: Elsevier.

Ziman, John
1976   *The Force of Knowledge: The Scientific Dimension of Society.* Cambridge: Cambridge University Press.

FIVE

What Do Women Want?

Issues of Choice, Control, and Class in American Pregnancy and Childbirth

Ellen Lazarus

This chapter analyzes issues of choice and control for women in childbirth. My research on childbirth in the United States over the past twelve years shows that many women feel responsible for the events at birth but they in fact have only limited influence over the medical procedures applied. Biomedicine, with its reliance on technology, is both a forceful practice and a powerful ideology. It has a tremendous influence over how women are thought of and how they themselves think about childbirth. Concentrating solely on the force of technology, however, diverts attention from social relationships of power and dominance (Martin 1987) in which the relationship between doctor and patient and the authority of medical institutions constrain women's choices and, consequently, their control. A focus of this analysis, which draws on my research with poor and middle-class women in the 1980s, is that knowledge about childbirth is inextricably related to medical hegemony and social class.

Knowledge about childbirth embraces more than an awareness of biological processes such as the stages of birth, changes in the pregnant body, or the growth of the fetus. It is about health care. It is also about choosing a doctor and about understanding how the health care system works. Birth knowledge, then, is comprised of both biological knowledge of pregnancy and birth and social knowledge. This social knowledge includes knowledge of medical procedures that occur during pregnancy and birth in addition to institutional knowledge of the hospital as a bureaucracy—who is responsible for what decisions and how a patient can exert pressure to obtain the kind of care she wants. Women are concerned about the personal aspects of such care and about their ability to act on their knowledge to access specific care. There appears to be a connection between a desire for knowledge about birth and control over birth; not all women want birth knowledge to the same extent.

According to my research, choices and control are more limited for poor women, who are overwhelmed with social and economic problems. They are usually unemployed; they have less education and more unplanned births; they start childbearing at earlier ages and are frequently unmarried. In addition, many poor women have no health insurance, leading to fewer choices for perinatal care. Thus many resort to clinics for low-income patients where they often have difficulty communicating with doctors, usually resident physicians with little experience. Poor women are constrained by the conditions under which they have babies and the kinds of care open to them (Lazarus 1988a), and this affects their ability to acquire knowledge about birth and their ability to act on such knowledge.

In this analysis of the issues of medical hegemony, choice and control, and social class and knowledge, I compare three groups of women. The first group consists of women who are mainly patients of physicians in private practice; they have no other ties to the medical system. The second group consists of women who are more familiar with the medical system because they are health professionals or, in a few cases, the spouses of physicians. These two groups are both middle class. I will refer to the first group as lay middle-class women and the second as health professionals. The third group consists of poor women who received prenatal care at a public clinic and gave birth at a large, urban county hospital.

All women in my studies, regardless of social class or ethnicity, wanted what they perceived to be quality medical care. Women spoke about childbirth as a natural process, but at least to some degree, they accepted the medical view of birth: that any number of things could go wrong and that ultimately they had to rely on the authoritative knowledge and concomitant technological expertise of their physician to ensure that they had done everything possible to have a healthy baby.

There were, however, notable differences between lay middle-class women and poor women; the latter were limited by their access to resources, their differing relationships with hospital personnel, particularly physicians, and the effect of receiving care in a public clinic. Their concerns consistently focused on continuity of care rather than on issues of control.

I found a spectrum of opinions among lay middle-class women, from a desire for the most advanced technology to a desire for the least invasive, most "natural" birth possible in a hospital. The views of some middle-class women expressed an ambivalence created by tension between these opposing perspectives. Choosing a doctor who they believed would guide them not only through pregnancy and birth but also through the medical system was a priority that enabled them to deal with these considerations. The health professional group also held diverse views, but their greater knowledge about the health care system enabled them to exercise more control over childbirth.

I conclude with a discussion of the implications of authoritative biomedical knowledge in light of changing management of birth whereby power is shifting from doctors to hospitals and insurance companies. I then suggest some policy considerations.

MEDICAL HEGEMONY

Birth in the United States is a medical event controlled by the medical profession (see Ehrenreich and English 1978; Michaelson 1988; Wertz and Wertz 1977). A significant social science literature documents various aspects of this phenomenon: the growth of the authority of obstetricians over birth (see Arney 1982; Leavitt 1986); the training of obstetric residents as surgeons (Corea 1985; Scully 1980); and the dependence on sophisticated medical technology to distinguish "the normal progression" of pregnancy, labor, and birth from "pathological" variants (Davis-Floyd 1992; Jordan 1980; Rothman 1984, 1989).[1]

This medical view of birth as potential pathology, in which something could go wrong at any time, is a powerful and dominant model. Paula Treichler (1990) forcefully argues that despite the existence of multiple meanings of childbirth in a pluralistic society such as the United States, the monopoly of professional authority over birthing resources defines and also gives official meaning to both the biological dimension and the social context of childbirth. It is this socially sanctioned, legitimized knowledge that Brigitte Jordan refers to as authoritative knowledge. Such knowledge precludes other ways of knowing; what a woman's body tells her has little status in the birth setting.

> What counts is the technologically and procedurally based knowledge of the physician, which is inaccessible to the woman, but without which the birth is not allowed to proceed. Competing kinds of knowledge held by the woman and other participants in the scene are jointly suppressed and managed. In this case and others like it, authoritative knowledge and attendant decision-making are hierarchically distributed. (Jordan [1978] 1993:152)

For example, the director of obstetrics at a major medical center was quoted in the *New York Times* as saying "Natural childbirth is alive and well but it has become a marriage of biology and technology" (Brozan 1988:1,14). The same article points out that doctors have changed the definition of natural childbirth "to include any birth in which the mother is awake and delivers vaginally" (p. 14). This model dictates that birth must be managed by advanced technology, such as electronic fetal monitoring or ultrasonography.

In addition, physicians are fearful of malpractice suits and are, therefore, cautious. Ruth Hubbard (1984) points out that to the medical profession, being cautious means using all birth technology available. In turn, this dominant ideology of medically controlled birth as "normal" birth envelops women's thoughts about their own births and the use of technological interventions.

Women's acceptance of and desire for advanced technology, then, sets the stage for the technological fix providing the perfect birth. It facilitates the medical profession's ability to negotiate the biological behavior of women into similar patterns of social behavior: medical control of gestation, labor, and delivery. If a woman does not do "everything" (and that means availing herself of technological birth), the process is her individual responsibility and ultimately she must be blamed if she does not have the "perfect" birth (Hubbard 1984).

CHOICE AND CONTROL

A combination of social movements over two decades—the feminist movement, a natural childbirth movement, and a health consumer's movement—has changed birth practices and women's views of childbirth in the United States. In particular, the issue of reproductive choice has been central to feminist ideology and activism. Barbara Rothman (1984) writes that many feminists thought that information would give women control over choices, thereby empowering them. Advanced technology has, according to Rothman, opened some choices but closed others.

Fetal monitoring, for example, may inform a woman that her fetus is in distress. She can then choose to have a cesarean section. But how accurate is the information she receives? How can she know that her physician is not overreacting to the machine and is presenting all options? How rational can she be at this time? Recent research demonstrates that routine ultrasound screening does not improve perinatal outcome among low-risk women (Ewigman et al. 1993). Women want assurances, however, that growth and development are normal, and most women accede to a medical evaluation of their condition regardless of how well informed they believe they are. Hubbard remarks that many women believe that pregnancy interventions are increasing the range of positive reproductive choices but that they "find it impossible to imagine how they could live without the technologies that past women lacked, never missed, and often were better off without" (1984:338).

Cesarean section is a good example of the technology boom that has changed childbirth. Cesarean sections have increased drastically in the last three decades. In 1965 the national rate for cesarean sections was 4.5 per 100 deliveries, whereas in 1991 the national rate was 23.5 cesarean sections per 100 deliveries (*Morbidity and Mortality Weekly Report* 1993:285). According to Mortimer Rosen, the former chairman of the Department of Obstetrics and Gynecology at Columbia-Presbyterian Medical Center in New York and co-chairman of the American College of Obstetrics and Gynecologists (ACOG) committee that reviewed obstetric practices, the increase of cesarean sections and the attitude toward them can be attributed to a powerful set of what he calls "myths" subscribed to by both doctors and patients.

> Doctors began to act as if the technology being developed could predict and solve all problems. We were generating false confidence and we were beginning to forget that instruments such as electronic fetal monitors were tools to be used by the doctor, not decision-making machines to replace medical judgment.
>
> On the patient side, there was the development of the expectation of a perfect outcome. Women seem to come in believing that all babies can be born healthy. A dead or damaged baby is no longer simply a tragedy, but an outcome that is someone's fault. People don't seem to think there are things that can go wrong that are simply out of the doctor's control. Perhaps this attitude developed partly because we in the medical community sold our technology and the successes we had too well.... At any rate, the mixture of these changing attitudes was bound to produce more cesareans. Patients expected a good outcome; both patient and doctor believed the cesarean was some sort of guarantee of this; even the doctor who doubted the cesarean was going to make a difference knew that he might be asked in court why he hadn't done everything in his power—i.e., a cesarean—to save the baby. Given the cesarean myths, the explosion in cesarean rates was inevitable. The myths continue to feed the growth in cesarean rates and are always on a collision course with the real world where babies die and no medical miracle can save them. (Rosen and Thomas 1989:xi–xiii)

To these beliefs can be added the more lucrative financial return for a cesarean section delivery (Mitford 1992). Studies show a significant relationship between socioeconomic status of patients and cesarean sections (Gould, Davey, and Stafford 1989). The rate of cesarean sections is much higher in suburban hospitals, where most patients are insured, than in inner-city hospitals, where many patients are uninsured or on Medicaid. This occurs despite the fact that urban hospitals associated with medical schools are tertiary care centers serving high-risk populations. A cesarean birth can cost three times as much as a vaginal birth, and while hospitals and doctors make money on insured patients, they lose money on Medicaid patients and uninsured women. Thus they are under pressure to minimize high-cost procedures for low-income patients. Furthermore, residents, who see public clinic patients and usually train at inner-city hospitals, are paid a flat salary regardless of the kind of delivery.

In addition, many obstetricians, fearful of malpractice suits, practice defensively, preferring to control birth through cesarean sections (Localio et al. 1993). In court proceedings linking malpractice suits to birth, physicians are asked if they did everything possible to assure a healthy birth, and "everything possible" means a cesarean.[2]

The cesarean example can be extended to advanced birth technology in general. Women "buy" the "myths" of technology, understandably confusing medical facts with the medical ideology created and believed by the medical profession. That 99.9 percent of all births occurred in hospitals and 95.3 percent of these hospital deliveries were attended by physicians in 1990 attests to this continued reliance (Monthly Vital Statistics Reports 1993).

SOCIAL CLASS AND KNOWLEDGE

Arguments have been made that the significance given to a feminist vision of taking control of one's life and body is a middle-class perspective. Carol McClain (1981, 1983) found that women's decisions on choices of childbirth services were based on balancing risks and benefits. Women discounted risks and magnified the benefits of chosen options. Linnea Klee (1986) found different ideologies of childbirth among women making choices between conventional hospital births, alternative birth centers, and home births. Nevertheless, those voluntarily seeking care outside of hospitals comprise a minute percentage, and they are usually middle class.

Other studies show a wide range of views among middle-class women. Some women want all the technology made available by biomedicine; others want a more "natural" childbirth. In a study looking at childbirth education and childbirth models, Carolyn Sargent and Nancy Stark (1989) found that their informants, mainly middle class, received "ideologic messages" from both health professionals and relatives but that patients "bought" the medical model. They generally welcomed medical interventions and wanted their pain suppressed. Margaret Nelson (1986) makes the point that the reason a middle-class model of childbirth has dominated much of the literature is that much feminist writing focused on the natural as a contrast to medicalized birth (Oakley 1986; Romalis 1981). She writes, however, that the middle-class model is coming closer to a hospital birth catering to a clientele for which the hospitals compete.

While there is a literature focusing on poor women (Boone 1985; Lazarus 1988b; Poland 1987; Shapiro et al. 1983), there are few comparative studies of women of different social classes. Emily Martin (1987; 155) writes of the "differing treatment of women in labor," concluding that whether the dominant mechanism is race or class "both profoundly affect birthing."

> For a white middle-class woman, the salient issue may be to stall going to the hospital so the clock cannot be started or to organize and demand that all hospitals in the region install birthing rooms; for a white working-class woman, [there] lurks the larger issue of finding a way to pay for prenatal, obstetrical, or infant care; for a black working-class woman, the issues of stalling and paying may be crucial, but even if she contends with them, she still may have to find a way to avoid downright mistreatment or to manage to have matters explained to her at all. (Martin 1987:155)

Nelson (1986), in one of the few studies specifically designed to examine class differences in childbirth, compared middle-class and working-class women. In this study, all the women saw the same group of private doctors in a Vermont teaching hospital. In neither group did women receive the precise treatment they wanted. Middle-class women wanted to participate actively in childbirth and to avoid interventions; working-class women wanted more interventions. Working-class women wanted less pain and reduced labor. In contrast to the findings of Sargent and Stark (1989), the middle-class women in Nelson's study were looking for a pleasurable, often "natural" experience. Nelson writes that another model is needed for "working-class women who have fewer opportunities for making choices; even pregnancy often appears to be outside their control" (1986:171).

Birth models are similar to models of sickness and health in that they are made up of beliefs and expectations that are part of a person's cultural experience and cognitive being. Arthur Kleinman (1980) points out that models of sickness and health are often ambiguous and inconsistent. It may be more useful to focus on knowledge that people bring to an experience and to factor in issues of power and social class.

People know a variety of medical facts, but they do not know all these facts in the same way. People know things from circumstances and experience and from their reactions to symptoms and treatment (Young 1982). In turn, knowledge filters and constructs experiences (Wright and Treacher 1982). Medical knowledge, as with most knowledge, is inseparable from social relationships and social experiences. It is unequally distributed, therefore, and connected to matters of power and control. In biomedicine, control is limited by the power held by the medical profession and more and more by medical institutions. Because the doctor-patient relationship is asymmetrical, power becomes domination; one actor is more autonomous and the other more dependent (Pappas 1989). This power disparity is further widened by social class. Thus there is an interdependence between knowledge, one's ability to act on such knowledge, the social institutions that constrain actions, and one's position in the larger structure of a society. Nevertheless, no matter how little power people have, they do act. As Anthony Giddens says, "human beings reflexively monitor their conduct via the knowledge they have of the circumstances of their activity" (1979:254).

RESEARCH FINDINGS

The influence of technological care over choice and control and its intersection with social relationships have surfaced repeatedly in my own observations and inquiries over the past decade in the obstetrics and gynecology department of a large urban teaching hospital. I interviewed women about their pregnancy and childbirth experiences and obstetricians, midwives, residents, medical students, and nurses about their views on childbirth, and I observed interactions between women and physicians. I found women to have unequal access to knowledge and differing degrees of desire for such knowledge.

In one two-year study conducted during the early 1980s, I followed fifty-three indigent women through their prenatal care to the postpartum period in a large public clinic, examining how they managed their pregnancies and childbirths, what they wanted in terms of health care, and the kind of care they received. I attended clinic appointments and observed interactions with doctors, midwives, and the medical staff, met women's families and friends both at the hospital and in their homes, and sometimes attended their labors and childbirths. Poor women who used the clinic were nineteen years old on average at the birth of their first child. Most had dropped out of school before they became pregnant; only one woman attended school during her pregnancy. The average number of years of schooling was 10.5. They often faced birth alone; of the eighteen teenaged women between sixteen and nineteen years old, only seven were married. Many of those who were married described unstable marriages. Many of the babies' fathers were unemployed, and forty-five of the fifty-three women received Medicaid. Only three women had medical insurance; the rest paid the lowest fees on a sliding scale. Seventy-five percent of the pregnancies were unplanned (Lazarus and Philipson 1990).

Subsequently, in the late 1980s, I conducted a study on the childbirth experiences of middle-class women. In this study, forty-five women who had had babies at seven hospitals were interviewed in their homes or at their jobs after giving birth. Average age of these women at the time of their first pregnancy was thirty. All but one were college graduates, and many had advanced degrees. All were married; most pregnancies were planned; all had at least some medical insurance. Many had postponed marriage or pregnancy until their careers were established. They had far greater access

than the poor women to information on both birth and medical procedures. They read extensively about birth and took birth preparation
courses. Nineteen were doctors, nurses, or doctors' wives and thus had
special access to knowledge about the medical system.

Social class differences were reflected in the different concerns of the
women. For example, whereas poor women described pregnancy and birth
complications of friends, family, or their own previous experiences, lay
middle-class women and middle-class health professionals described concerns about infertility problems, miscarriages, the ticking of the biological
clock. Middle-class health professionals spoke about "high-risk cases" needing to be handled by perinatologists.

Certain patterns emerged that reflected a two-class system in which poor
women and both groups of middle-class women were experiencing pregnancy and childbirth under very different circumstances, both in their
daily lives and in their health care experiences. Those differences affected
their access to information. As Petchesky (1983:223) warns, "By collapsing
class into gender, the notion of sex as class ignores the obvious, piercing
differences—of power, authority, and resources—among and between
women." Poor women using the clinic had less access to birth knowledge
and less desire for that knowledge and for the control that comes with it.
The women who were health professionals used this knowledge in their
decision making, as I will illustrate. It is these differences in access to and
desire for knowledge, particularly social knowledge, that I want to pursue.

Unequal Patient Access to Knowledge

Regardless of social class, all of the women studied wanted medical information to be shared with them. Accepting birth as a medical process,
women wanted information not only about pregnancy care, fetal development, and labor and delivery but also about the medical system: how
people are treated, what medical personnel do, and how the hospital
"worked."

They all wanted to be treated with dignity and respect and to receive
emotional support. In the words of a poor woman, "I want a doctor who
cares about me—who tells me about things." A health professional, when
asked what was most important to her in choosing an obstetrician, replied,
"Warmth." She went on to say, "I want a person who not only handles the
technology, but someone who talks to you—is always available and is non-
judgmental." A poor woman in the clinic said, "I don't want to be treated
like a guinea pig." A lay middle-class woman declared, "I wish residents
could understand how awful it is to be treated like a piece of meat. I don't
mind helping them learn, but I didn't appreciate being treated like a laboratory animal."

Poor Women.   Poor women's choices for obtaining perinatal care were few or nonexistent; they had to use public clinics. Going to a clinic was not pleasant. Speaking with the medical staff could be hard, made even harder after long and wearisome two- to four-hour waits. Inexperienced resident physicians in training also had difficulty communicating during five- to ten-minute office visits with women of another social class, regardless of whether women were black, Hispanic, or white. Twenty-two women classified as low-risk, and assigned to certified nurse-midwives for prenatal care, or whose babies were delivered by midwives, were more satisfied, explaining that they received more personalized care. The remainder of the poor women were shifted among many different people—nurses, aides, clerks, nutritionists, and social workers—over the course of their pregnancies. Such organization hindered developing a relationship mutually satisfying to both the caregiver and the pregnant woman. Since medical personnel continuously shifted, there was no single caregiver to provide support and transmit information. Contradictory explanations led to unnecessary tests. At other times, women were not told why they were having tests, nor were they informed about test results. This kind of treatment frustrated them. Their expectations of both medical and emotional support were not met. The medical record became the chief link from one visit to the next.

At the clinic women were asked to participate in birth-related decisions, a practice that can be traced to the women's health movement. For example, women were asked which delivery method they preferred. However, they often did not have enough information to make such decisions. Some said they did not know and the matter was dropped, ostensibly due to patients' lack of interest. Others said, "Natural, I guess," without having a clear vision of what "natural" meant. Without support, without enough information, choices were difficult to make. When women were asked to make decisions their answers thus reinforced the stereotypical medical view that clinic patients were too ignorant to make meaningful choices. This response reinforces the reproduction of the hierarchical authoritative knowledge and decision making that Brigitte Jordan ([1978] 1993) describes as characteristic of the Western obstetrical system.

Women who sought care in the clinic had limited ways to respond, yet human agency always exists. Some women became noncompliant; they did not take their prenatal vitamins or they missed clinic appointments. Ultimately the women in my study returned to the clinic and accepted impersonal care because they needed to know that everything regarding the baby was as it should be. They came believing the technological level of care was high, as indeed it was in this teaching hospital. Nevertheless, clinic procedures, lack of continuity of care necessitated in part by rotations of residents in and out of the clinic, and long waits affected rapport and, indeed, almost every aspect of the relationship between resident physician and patient.

By contrast, it was not surprising that coordinators of the government-funded, citywide Maternity and Infant Care Outreach Project (known as M&I) said that the major reason women give for not coming for prenatal care is their prior experience with the prenatal health system. These women, often preoccupied with other priorities in their lives, made this choice—and they, of course, did not have a friendly advocate, the anthropologist, sharing their clinic experiences with them. Public clinic care remains one of many expressions of poor women's powerless position in society. Poor women have few choices, they are less assertive than private patients, and their medical knowledge is more fragmented; in a busy clinic it becomes easy for them to fall through the cracks of the system (Lazarus 1990).

Lay Middle-Class Women.   Lay middle-class women wanted an obstetrician who inspired confidence and communicated well. This desire in itself was not different from that of the poor women. The difference was that the women who saw private physicians could choose their obstetricians. After deciding to become pregnant, this was their most important decision. If they had previously seen obstetricians with whom they were dissatisfied, doctors who did not pay attention to them or were condescending, they made new choices based on recommendations from friends who were pleased or who knew of obstetricians with "good reputations" or on recommendations from other physicians they knew and trusted. Several African-American women expressed the importance of seeing "obstetricians of color."

Choices were circumscribed for some private patients because their medical insurance benefit package required them to select an obstetrician from a particular list or, if they were members of an HMO (health maintenance organization), choice was limited to caregivers in a particular obstetrics department. They did, nevertheless, have options. One woman, a college professor, said, "When I found out I was pregnant with my first child after a miscarriage, I went to the head of Ob/Gyn, who I take is a very famous person, and said, 'Who is the best person you've got? You know me. You know what I want.' "

A trusted physician was viewed as one's advocate in the medical structure, someone to protect and guide one through the system. Middle-class women believed that choosing a doctor who shared their views gave them some control over their pregnancy and birth management. Similar to findings by Sargent and Stark (1989), "control" had various meanings. Sargent and Stark found that women interpreted control in terms of personal behavior or as control over the environment. Women in their sample, regardless of education, generally were not concerned with controlling decision making in the hospital. "Rather, they aimed for restricted participation, defined as the ability to remain alert during labor, while reducing or eliminating discomfort" (p. 48). Among the middle-class women in my study, for some, it meant involvement in decision making, asserting oneself, exercising some power over what happened. Some women had definite views about technical interventions such as whether to have epidural anesthesia or an episiotomy. Some women asked doctors for their cesarean section rates and checked to see if they were board certified or where they did their residency. They requested a personal birth plan in their medical record with information about their desire for little or no medication, about diagnostic tests, about monitoring, about supplemental feedings for the baby. They wanted to be able to refuse what they considered to be intrusive technology. Thus control for some meant few or no interventions. For others, it meant a more personal control, not screaming or crying during labor and childbirth. For all, choosing the right caregiver was related to their perception of control.

Choosing a hospital for the delivery was also an important consideration for middle-class women. They based their decisions on past experiences, insurance coverage, and sibling visitation privileges. Several women were concerned about whether a hospital had a neonatal intensive care unit—"just in case." Others wanted a hospital that allowed the baby to room with them.

Middle-Class Health Professionals. The middle-class health professionals were concerned about issues similar to those of lay middle-class women. They held a wider range of views about the kind of health professional they wanted to attend to them. Six of them (a family practitioner, the wives of two family practitioners, a pediatrician, and two nurses) chose midwife-assisted births, whereas only one lay middle-class woman made this choice. They believed this was consistent with their more "natural" view of birth. Under the care of a midwife, they would more likely be treated as if they were low-risk even if there were some risk factors. A family physician commented, "I made the decision [to choose a midwife] . . . then I made sure that the backup physician was someone who wasn't C-section happy."

Significantly, it was important for the health professionals to have some control over the social situation in which childbirth was to take place—the hospital, the maternity floor, and the health personnel with whom they would be involved. This was true regardless of whether individual women in this group wanted a low-technology, more "natural" birth or a high-technology birth. Women who were health professionals tried to anticipate problems and to make arrangements before the birth. For this reason, physicians or nurses often chose to deliver in the hospital where they were employed. They spoke about the lack of quality control in hospitals and how they dealt with the many things that go wrong. The examples below illustrate these attitudes.

> I am an assertive, knowledgeable nurse. I woke up the second night—someone was wheeling the baby out at 2:00 in the morning. The aide said she was taking the baby to be weighed. I said, "That is at six. Bring the baby back!" I mean some women don't know they can keep the baby with them. That is why I wanted a private room—to have more control. . . . I know the head nurse; you have to know people. The overall feeling was that these are the rules and we don't bend them. Someone who is a first-time mom wouldn't have a prayer.

This nurse was a first-time mother herself; she meant a first-time mother not conversant with the system.

A family physician said,

> I felt I could control who was in the [labor] room and my breathing techniques. I had music—Bach to rock. I picked ———— Hospital despite the fact that I think it's a terrible environment for having a baby. It was so familiar, . . . a comfort to me having a baby someplace where I really knew the territory. . . . I think it is the same idea people have when they want to have a home birth.

In contrast, an anesthesiologist wanted to control her experience through technology.

> Basically what I wanted was that as soon as I arrived in Labor & Delivery and was going to be committed to delivery, I wanted an epidural placed because I know the value of an epidural. I know that this would be the best thing for me plus it would keep everything from hurting. I wanted internal monitors placed. A lot of patients say they don't want that thing in them. They don't realize that this is the best way to monitor a baby. I wanted to be sure that everything was being done to make sure that this baby was doing fine. I wanted to be sure that I delivered back in the delivery room instead of in the bed like a lot of private patients who think that they don't want to bother moving over on a cart going back to a sterile-looking operating room. I felt that it was important to deliver in the operating room where the pediatricians can best resuscitate the baby, where the doctor could deliver the baby easily and there would be no problems with shoulder dystocia [difficulty in delivery] or anything like that, so he could see to sew me up the best. So I wanted to optimize it for the baby.
>
> I don't really care about the birth experience like a lot of patients do— into soft lights, soft music garbage. For me it was getting a good baby. I've seen too many times where patients are so concerned about it being a lovely

experience for them that this has overridden the desires for having a good baby and they put themselves and their birth experience in front of having a "good" baby come out and having the best care for that baby. I kept the OB doctors' schedules by my bedside at home, but I also had the anesthesiologists' schedules and pretty much there were a lot of different people that I would not have wanted to give me my anesthetic. It was known that I would not have my residents present.

One obstetrician carefully selected an obstetrician, later to become her professional partner, and she chose the hospital where she worked. But she encountered an unexpected obstacle.

My first experience involved a very aggressive resident, a new first-year intern, who came in and placed an epidural without a consultation from his attending physician, although he knew both my husband and I were physicians and I was on faculty. He just came in and put it in and of course you're in labor, 6 centimeters and crying or screaming. I didn't care who put it in as long as there was someone available. So he put it in, and it turned out it was not placed correctly. I got medication and had an adverse reaction with low blood pressure. The baby's heart rate started to drop and became bradycardiac. . . . I needed to have a cesarean section. . . . They dosed the epidural again. . . . The attending physician came in and whether he [the anesthesiology intern] told her the whole story about my reaction and she really understood what he was talking about or not, they proceeded to give me more of the medication and what ended up happening was totally terrible. Instead of an epidural [I had] a total spinal. I was unable to breathe on my own, unable to see, could not open my eyes, could not lift my hand, and at the same time I was conscious and could hear everything that's being said. And people are saying, "This is a big fuck-up," and by then they are calling in everybody to come and help.

I couldn't move [and] breathe. They were ventilating me. . . . I really thought I was dying. Immediately afterward I had to go for a myelogram where they try to see where the needle was inserted under fluoroscopy and they had to irrigate my spinal canal with fluids and then I came back with meningitis about four days after birth and I had to be on prednisone.

I was really angry that I missed my whole labor experience. I got the epidural because I was in pain. Sure I asked for it, but at the same time I didn't ask for someone to come in who didn't know what he was doing—basically an intern unsupervised. And I felt like I was really cheated out of my whole labor experience with my first pregnancy. . . .

For the second baby I chose the chairman of the department of anesthesiology for my epidural.

At the beginning of her first birth, the woman, who was also a physician, thought she had everything under her control. She wanted a birth with a moderate level of technology, but because of a life-endangering iatrogenic effect, the birth required a higher level of technology. Her solution was to seek more expertise the next time. With all her planning and access to knowledge, she still was not able to cover all contingencies.

Differing Degrees of Desire for Knowledge and Control

Poor women were not concerned with control issues in pregnancy or in childbirth; however, they definitely were concerned with the quality of their health care. In this regard, they stressed that what they wanted most was continuity of care. They believed that if they had a doctor who knew them, that doctor would tell them what they needed to know. They complained when residents gave them contradictory information about due dates, whether they should have a cesarean section, or how their pregnancy was progressing. One woman stated,

> If it was my first baby I wouldn't come—too scary here—never in a million years. I feel more comfortable seeing a woman doctor because I can talk to women better at the visits. Also the exam is embarrassing. For the delivery, it doesn't matter. The doctors spend about five minutes with me [in the clinic]. That's okay if there is nothing wrong, but how would they know when they spend so little time with you? Sometimes I feel like a guinea pig. If I wasn't worried because of my last preemie I wouldn't come back. . . . They didn't take my blood pressure. I had to tell them afterward. I didn't see the nurse. Even if the nurse was around, I wouldn't have wanted to see her at that point. I got out at 4:30. It's hurry up and wait.

Lay middle-class women and middle-class health professionals wanted to believe that they had control over the process as a part of control over their lives. They were motivated to find out what to expect in pregnancy and birth, both emotionally and physically, and what to anticipate in the actual hospital experience. With greater access to information and a wider variety of choices, it was easier for them to attend birth preparation classes, to pay a baby-sitter, to transport themselves to a doctor, and to read about childbirth preparation.

The degree of control, however, remained limited for middle-class women too. In what they intended to be one of the most significant experiences of their lives, all of the women believed there was the possibility that something could go wrong, and therefore birth, in the last analysis, must be a medical event. Even women in private care, who believed that birth was treated too much as an illness by obstetricians and by the hospital, saw it as a medical event. In the words of one lay middle-class woman,

> I would encourage doctors to convey to pregnant women that they are just that—pregnant. Not sick, not dying, not disabled. Pregnant. If doctors act as though it is an illness, then most assuredly women will respond in kind, which contributes to an apprehensive and anxiety-ridden pregnancy.

Although concerned with participating in procedure decisions, the woman was one of several who chose to schedule a repeat cesarean section.[3]

> I had one [a cesarean section] the first time and it was never even considered an option [subsequently] to deliver vaginally. I read plenty . . . because my first section was fairly traumatic and I didn't want to repeat the experience. I thought it was nice to schedule exactly when my baby would be born and [to] know I would not have to endure a hard and long labor.

I have interviewed well-educated professional women who have requested cesarean sections believing that technological control will assure that everything will go well and ensure a healthy baby. (See also Davis-Floyd 1994.) For example, an obstetrician related the following story to me about a member of her family. This relative and her husband were highly educated and considered themselves environmentally concerned; they did not eat foods containing possible carcinogens, nor did they own a microwave oven because they were apprehensive about electromagnetic exposure. The woman had difficulty conceiving, eventually becoming pregnant through artificial insemination. Ten weeks before the expected delivery, her physician informed her that the baby was high and large—perhaps a difficult delivery. (The physician relating the story pointed out that obstetricians have a poor record of predicting fetus size.) Believing that this pregnancy was their only chance to have a baby and fearful that something would go wrong if left to the natural course of events, the couple refused a trial of labor and scheduled a cesarean section. According to my obstetrician informant, "Patients and doctors both see C-sections as no big deal. They don't see C-sections as surgery. Zip her open and take the baby and sew her up. It is not seen as a major operation."

The constraints of personal vulnerability in the face of technical medical complexity, like the constraints of social class, circumscribe the degree of control available to people in general in the medical system. Some lay middle-class women and health professionals believed it was important to be able to refuse intrusive tests or procedures, yet they found themselves unprepared for contingencies unique to their individual pregnancies. They described their dependency during labor and birth or during an unexpected cesarean section when they were unable to make effective decisions about which tests or procedures were in fact intrusive.

These two groups of women had more access to information than poor women, but it was never enough. No matter what they knew, it could not empower them within the medical system. Knowledge itself could not give them authority, nor could they know all the contingencies of the birth process or of institutional care. Despite all their preparations, then, they were cognizant of and even willing to subordinate themselves to medical authority. One lay middle-class woman commented, "As long as I know I am healthy—everything is going okay—I have control, but if I had toxemia, forget it. I am in his hands and he can do anything he wants to do." A second said, "There comes a point where you feel not trusting your doctor is not trusting your own judgment because you put time into selecting him, and should you begin to doubt him, you lose confidence in your own ability to make sound judgments."

This view was expressed by the health professional group as well. The family physician referred to earlier said, "I didn't have the illusion of control. In labor I gave over that control." She did assert herself, however: "The attending physician wanted me to move to the delivery room [my informant had wanted to deliver in the labor room]. We [she, her husband, and the midwife] had to conspire against her [the attending physician]—so we decided to tell the attending [physician] the birth happened too quickly."

Some women assert themselves even more directly. Martin (1987) describes women unstrapping external fetal monitors when doctors and nurses left the labor room, taking showers during labor, or trying to avoid fetal monitoring. She points out that the childbirth activist literature can be viewed as guides to self-defense in the hospital. Women who do assert themselves, however, are often resented by hospital staff. In my research, a middle-class health professional (a physician) commented about people who insist on specific requirements.

> Probably patients who come in with a list of demands end up getting inferior care both medically and probably in other ways [like] support. . . . Their demands compromise what you would ordinarily do for them, which would be to offer them medical care. . . . The support personnel are so annoyed by the demands and are so caught in a trap by the demands because they can't provide the care that really is necessary, that they tend to resent the patients and probably cannot be as supportive.

Another physician who was a new mother stated,

> I get angry because I think [aggressive patients] come with a lot of misconceptions, and they are sort of putting all the things that they've heard about and all their other experiences, they are putting that all on me. . . . They still want an unwritten guarantee that they are going to have a healthy baby with no interventions, and I can't provide that. I tell them that I think monitoring is real important. . . . I think we have the technology, that you can use it in a way that's helpful for mom and baby and also allow families to still be together and experience the kind of birth they'd like to experience but still monitor.

Nevertheless, most women in all three groups did not complain and were generally satisfied with their care. However, on occasions when poor women and lay middle-class women were dissatisfied, they were hesitant to express their feelings or complain. A prevailing attitude expressed by one lay middle-class mother illustrates this perspective:

> Expect the unexpected. If you are too rigid and "planned," you will be unprepared for any abrupt changes, crises, or complications. It is so important to go with the flow.

Furthermore, many women felt uncomfortable questioning authoritative control and chose to remain silent. When I informed an attending physician that women did not like sharing a labor room with another woman, he was surprised and replied that women never said anything about this and that, therefore, he assumed laboring in private was unimportant to them. Perhaps, as Oakley points out, there is "an equation of silence with satisfaction: the woman who does not complain about her antenatal care is assumed to be satisfied with it" (1986:283; see also Lorber 1979).

SUMMARY

My informants' responses were bounded by the medical system in which they, like almost all women in the United States, had babies. Most of the women I came to know believed that a medicalized birth in the hospital was their choice. To varying degrees, they believed in the hegemony of medicine over their childbirth experiences. Women in all three groups were aware that they did not control the circumstances of their baby's birth. Lay middle-class women and middle-class health professionals, acknowledging that they had limited control, felt strongly that it was essential to choose a doctor who they believed would guide them not only through pregnancy and birth but also through the medical system. They recognized, as Jordan ([1978] 1993) describes, the doctor as a gatekeeper with whom the good patient collaborates by willingly demonstrating accepted and approved behavior. The health-professional group, having more knowledge about how the system worked, aggressively arranged their birth situations and their stays in the hospital. Knowledge about the medical system gave them a sense of power and, therefore, some limited control in a situation in which they did not have authoritative control.

By contrast, choices and expectations were limited for poor women. They were young women with multiple social and economic problems that called for support and guidance. They rarely reached a point where they had sufficient knowledge to manipulate the system to obtain more influence over their childbirth. While they would have preferred to have chosen a doctor, their main concern was for care provided by someone who knew them, someone who cared for them during pregnancy and, if possible, delivered their babies. They were much more interested in continuity of care than in making choices that would give them more control.

CONCLUSIONS AND IMPLICATIONS

The consumer and feminist movements have created a consciousness among pregnant middle-class women that they must control their own lives, that they must assert themselves and make choices—in doctors, in hospitals, in treatment options. At the same time, women's decisions are influenced by their acceptance of or ambivalence toward ever-increasing routine use of advanced technology and, most certainly, by compliance with control over birth by physicians and hospital managers. In my studies, women held a range of beliefs about technology, from "as little as possible" to a desire for a "very technological birth." In analyzing what women want, it is important to focus on the hegemony of technology and medical ideology that dominates birth in the United States. Equally important is a focus on the social structure and the relationship between doctor and patient, on how women are treated in public clinics and on women's personal experiences and how they respond (see Sargent and Bascope, this volume). The distribution of power in social relationships, particularly in asymmetrical relationships sometimes involving class and ethnicity, shapes behavior (Baer, Singer, and Johnson 1986; Singer 1989). Women's personal experiences define what they know, what they want, and the choices they truly have.

The Hospital Management of Birth

Human reproduction takes place in socially prescribed ways; in the United States, it is part of medicine. In regard to larger political and economic processes, medicalized birth allocates resources in childbirth and specifies what can be done under what circumstances. It enshrines official power and authority over birth. In recent years, physicians, while reluctant to share power with midwives and other birth attendants, nevertheless have had to relinquish power within the medical system. Decisions concerning procedures that physicians once controlled are now dictated by private insurers, federal programs, and hospital administrations. Medical services are provided by many people who genuinely care, but they are dependent on institutions that control the purse. In U.S. medicine, the priority is profit, as it is in the wider society.

A market orientation has led hospital management to deal with competition with comparable institutions through public relations and image enhancement. Marketing has become a hospital priority, often eclipsing the focus on individual treatment in what has been called the "corporatization" of medicine.[4] With a surplus of doctors and hospital beds in areas that serve the middle class, competition for patients is fierce. For that reason, hospital administrations emphasize the challenge of the competitive

marketplace. They announce through slick mailings and newspaper adver-
tisements how their hospitals use the latest technological marvels in an
atmosphere of compassion and emotional support. (A typical newspaper
pronouncement was headlined "We don't just look at you as a human body,
we look at you as a human being.") Competition is instrumental in providing services. One of my informants who readily took advantage of the marketing plan her hospital offered referred to these options as "unbelievable
yuppie things." She was not atypical of both the lay middle-class women
and many of the health professionals. Women in both groups were well
aware of these offerings designed to lure them to specific hospitals.

In many parts of the country today, a woman contemplating childbirth
can avail herself of a wealth of information. Many of these aids have been
adopted by hospitals from the health consumer and feminist movements
emphasizing choice in childbirth. There are books and magazine articles
on prenatal testing, on health care during pregnancy, on fetal development, on choosing an obstetrician, on the latest birth technology, on labor
and delivery, and on cesarean section. A woman can have preconception
counseling and attend classes on exercise, on breastfeeding, or on sibling
preparation during her pregnancy. She can obtain a written guide to
health care options and services at area hospitals. She can rent a baby
beeper to reach the father when labor begins. She can rent videotapes on
the baby's physical and personality development, on parent relationships,
and on parenting.

The birth of her baby, even by cesarean section, is made more pleasant
by the presence of a "significant other." She can deliver the baby in a "birthing room," which looks like a bedroom decorated with tasteful wallpaper.
She is no longer shaved or given an enema, and her arms are no longer
strapped down. And in some hospitals she and her husband can choose
to cap all this with a gourmet candle-lit dinner in her maternity room,
compliments of the management.

These changes in childbirth make the experience for some women,
mainly urban and suburban middle-class women, more pleasant and enable them to be more informed. Some of these features extend to poor
women in teaching hospitals. For example, poor women may be invited to
attend birth preparation classes (although it may be difficult to do so without a car). They may be encouraged to bring a companion with them to
their child's birth, and many public clinics provide educational information for patients. Women do benefit from these services during the perinatal period. McClain points out, "Many hospitals now recognize that maternal emotional well-being during labor and delivery contributes positively
to a healthy pregnancy outcome" (1981:1033). Contradictory messages
abound, however. The medical establishment "creates" birth as a "natural"
family event, not as a crisis, right in the hospital. At the same time, an

increasing reliance on technological innovations in childbirth continues to keep knowledge of the workings of the system in authoritative hands.

The Changing Role of the Obstetrician

As technology permeates childbirth, there are contradictory discussions in the medical literature about future directions in obstetrics. For many obstetrician-gynecologists, obstetrics is losing its glamour (Willson 1990). Many obstetricians resent decisions over medical procedures being decided by nonmedical personnel, including hospital administrators and insurance company employees. In addition, liability insurance and the emotional effect of being unfairly charged with malpractice have led many obstetricians to accept "only patients with minimal risk of developing complications" (Willson 1990:1137). More and more obstetrician-gynecologists are giving up obstetrics completely and at an early age (Willson 1990).

Key changes must address the training of physicians. There is a negligible emphasis in obstetric-gynecological training on women's health and preventive care or on reproduction as a healthy process. While medical schools are beginning to address issues surrounding the delivery of care, in actuality, little time is spent in residency programs on medical specialties on bioethics, informed consent, professional responsibility, and communicating with patients. Residents are expected to develop these skills on their own. More and more residency programs are staffed by subspecialists with their own research agendas—maternal-fetal medicine (ultrasonography), reproductive endocrinology (infertility), or high-risk conditions such as diabetes.[5] These highly specialized physicians train residents and emphasize high technology and pathology, priorities of the medical board exams.[6] Furthermore, overworked and exhausted, residents cite getting enough sleep as a primary goal while patients' needs in overloaded clinics are often slighted (see Graham 1991).

It has been suggested that the focus of obstetrics and gynecology change to preventive obstetrics and gynecology or that obstetrician-gynecologists refocus as primary care physicians. A survey of obstetric and gynecology department chairpersons concluded, however, that the education of medical students and residents has been enhanced by the development of subspecialties (Zuspan and Sachs 1988).

Policy for the Future

There is a great deal of "consumer" dissatisfaction with medical care in the United States in general. A reorganization of medicine is coming about largely for economic reasons, because of its high cost, not because of its quality of care. The economic genesis of the changes should not prevent reformers from taking an opportunistically patient-oriented view toward the new system. This is a time when birth could become less medicalized and move toward a stronger provision of alternative care such as increased midwife-aided prenatal care and deliveries for normal births and to more freestanding birth centers (see Baruffi, Strobino, and Paine 1990; Rooks et al. 1989). Jordan's thesis that medical knowledge is privileged knowledge that supersedes and delegitimizes other kinds, that of nurses and women giving birth, suggests that a redesign of an "ecology of labor" would change labor from a hierarchy to a horizontal system whereby authoritative knowledge would not be the privilege of the physician but rather shared knowledge. "In the long run the physician and medical staff would become expert consultants, guides through the maze of specialized information, rather than functioning as privileged decision-makers about the management of birth" ([1978] 1993:167).

Ideally, a transformation in health care delivery could be an opportunity for the two-class system of medical care to be abolished. In some tertiary care centers, poor women are seen in examination rooms and wait in waiting rooms different from those used by middle-class women. Under a "managed competition" system, poor women continue to receive care in separate and unequal programs such as health maintenance organizations geared to the poor which provide few choices of doctors and hospitals. In addition, private patients have their choice of doctors and hospitals prescribed by the package purchased by their employers. A single payer system consisting of a single accountable insurance fund would eliminate the insurance bureaucracy that makes up a large part of the health care dollar. This plan, similar to those now followed by most Western European countries and Canada, provides universal and accessible care that addresses the issue of the uninsured and the large numbers of women who receive little care or care in emergency rooms. Under a single payer program, people choose their own doctor and decisions are made by women and their doctors; they are not dictated to or excluded by insurance companies or self-contained hospital corporations. Thus similar opportunities for care could be provided to all women. Poor women would still come to childbirth with different needs, beliefs, and knowledge than middle-class women, but, at least, the barrier of separate and unequal care would be reduced.

NOTES

This work was partially supported by a grant from the Cleveland Foundation. An earlier version of this chapter appeared in *Medical Anthropology Quarterly*, n.s., 8, no. 1 (1994):25–46.

1. See also Browner and Sargent 1990; Eakins 1986; Ginsburg and Rapp 1991; Kay 1982; McClain 1982; Martin 1987; Michaelson 1988; Whiteford and Poland 1989.

2. One obstetrician told me how he protects himself: "Everything I do, I document, document, and document."

3. In 1980–1985 only 4.9 percent of mothers with a previous cesarean had a vaginal birth after cesarean, demonstrating that the "once a cesarean, always a cesarean" norm prevailed (Placek, Taffel, and Moien 1988). "In 1986, 8.5% of women who had a previous cesarean delivered vaginally, compared with 24.2% in 1991" (*Morbidity and Mortality Weekly Report* 1993:287).

4. The phrase "corporatization of medicine" is attributed to Ralph Nader, Shaker Lecture Series, Shaker Heights, Ohio, Spring 1991.

5. Serious epidemiological issues facing the country, such as high infant mortality among the poor and teenage pregnancy, are often cited regarding the necessity of quality care for the indigent and uninsured, but despite estimates that 17 to 20 percent of the next generation will have mothers eleven to eighteen years of age and much evidence linking perinatal problems to poverty, these studies are not a major focus in mainstream obstetric research. Academic obstetrician-gynecologists are attracted to biological studies of pathology and the small percentage of births that are classified as complicated. (See Burrow and Ferris 1988.)

6. Lectures on normal labor and delivery for medical students during their clerkships were given by a nurse-midwife at the time of this study. In her view, "[Residents] are insecure without ultrasound and never experience obstetrical life without monitors."

REFERENCES

Arney, William
    1982   *Power and the Profession of Obstetrics.* Chicago: University of Chicago Press.
Baer, Hans A., Merrill Singer, and John H. Johnson
    1986   "Introduction: Toward a Critical Medical Anthropology." *Social Science and Medicine* 23(2):95–98.
Baruffi, Gigliola, Donna M. Strobino, and Lisa L. Paine
    1990   "Investigation of Institutional Differences in Primary Cesarean Birth Rates." *Journal of Nurse-Midwifery* 35(5):274–281.
Boone, Margaret S.
    1985   "Social and Cultural Factors in the Etiology of Low Birthweight among Disadvantaged Blacks." *Social Science and Medicine* 20(10):1001–1011.
Browner, Carole H., and Carolyn F. Sargent
    1990   "Anthropology and Studies of Human Reproduction." In *Medical Anthropology: Contemporary Theory and Method,* ed. Thomas M. Johnson and Carolyn F. Sargent, 215–219. New York: Praeger.
Brozan, Nadine
    1988   "Women Gain as Technology Becomes Part of Natural Birth." *New York Times,* 13 November, 1, 14.

Burrow, Gerard N., and Thomas F. Ferris
   1988   *Medical Complications During Pregnancy,* 3d ed. Philadelphia: W. B. Saunders.
Corea, Gena
   1985   *The Mother Machine.* New York: Harper and Row.
Davis-Floyd, Robbie E.
   1992   *Birth as an American Rite of Passage.* Berkeley: University of California Press.
   1994   "The Technocratic Body." *Social Science and Medicine* 38(8):1125–1140.
Eakins, Pamela S., ed.
   1986   *The American Way of Birth.* Philadelphia: Temple University Press.
Ehrenreich, Barbara, and Deirdre English
   1978   *For Her Own Good: 150 Years of the Experts' Advice to Women.* New York: Anchor.
Ewigman, Bernard, et al.
   1993   "Effect of Prenatal Ultrasound Screening on Perinatal Outcome." *New England Journal of Medicine* 329 (912):821–827.
Giddens, Anthony
   1979   *Central Problems in Social Theory.* Berkeley: University of California Press.
Ginsburg, Faye, and Rayna Rapp
   1991   "The Politics of Reproduction." *Annual Reviews in Anthropology* 20:311–343.
Gould, Jeffrey B., Becky Davey, and Randall S. Stafford
   1989   "Socioeconomic Differences in Rates of Cesarean Section." *New England Journal of Medicine* 321(4):233–239.
Graham, Susan Brandt
   1991   "When Babies Die: Death and the Education of Obstetrical Residents." *Medical Teacher* 13(2):171–175.
Hubbard, Ruth
   1984   "Personal Courage Is Not Enough: Some Hazards of Childbearing in the 1980's." In *Test-Tube Women: What Future for Motherhood?* ed. Rita Arditti, Renate Duelli Klein, and Shelly Minden, 331–355. Boston: Pandora Press.
Jordan, Brigitte
   [1978] 1993   *Birth in Four Cultures: A Cross-Cultural Investigation of Childbirth in Yucatan, Holland, Sweden and the United States.* 4th ed. Prospect Heights, Ill.: Waveland Press.
   1980   "Margaret Mead Award 1980: Some Thoughts on Birthing Studies, Applied Anthropology and Anthropology." *Practicing Anthropology* 3(1):29–30, 81–83.
Kay, Margarita A., ed.
   1982   *Anthropology of Human Birth.* Philadelphia: F. A. Davis.
Klee, Linnea
   1986   "Home Away from Home: The Alternative Birth Center." *Social Science and Medicine* 23(1):9–16.
Kleinman, Arthur
   1980   *Patients and Healers in the Context of Culture.* Berkeley: University of California Press.

Lazarus, Ellen S.
  1988a   "Theoretical Considerations for the Study of the Doctor-Patient Rela-
          tionship: Implications of a Perinatal Study." *Medical Anthropology Quarterly*,
          n.s., 2:34–59.
  1988b   "Poor Women, Poor Outcomes: Social Class and Reproductive Health."
          In *Childbirth in America: Anthropological Perspectives*, ed. Karen Michaelson,
          39–54. South Hadley, Mass.: Bergin and Garvey.
  1990   "Falling Through the Cracks: Contradictions and Barriers to Care in a
          Prenatal Clinic." *Medical Anthropology* 12:269–287.
Lazarus, Ellen S., and Elliot H. Philipson
  1990   "A Longitudinal Study Comparing the Prenatal Care of Puerto Rican
          and White Women." *Birth* 17(1):6–11.
Leavitt, Judith Walzer
  1986   *Brought to Bed: Childbearing in America 1750–1950*. New York: Oxford
          University Press.
Localio, A. Russel, et al.
  1993   "Relationship Between Malpractice Claims and Cesarean Delivery." *Jour-
          nal of the American Medical Association* 269(3):366–373.
Lorber, Judith
  1979   "Good Patients and Problem Patients: Conformity and Deviance in a
          General Hospital." In *Patients, Physicians and Illness*, 3d ed., ed. E. Gartly Jaco,
          202–217. New York: Free Press.
Martin, Emily
  1987   *The Woman in the Body: A Cultural Analysis of Reproduction*. Boston: Beacon
          Press.
McClain, Carol
  1981   "Women's Choice of Home or Hospital Birth." *Journal of Family Practice*
          2(6):1033–1038.
  1982   "Toward a Comparative Framework for the Study of Childbirth: A Review
          of the Literature." In *Anthropology of Human Birth*, ed. Margarita Artschwager
          Kay, 25–59. Philadelphia: F. A. Davis.
  1983   "Perceived Risk and Choice of Childbirth Service." *Social Science and Med-
          icine* 17(23):1857–1865.
Michaelson, Karen, ed.
  1988   *Childbirth in America: Anthropological Perspectives*. South Hadley, Mass.:
          Bergin and Garvey.
Mitford, Jessica
  1992   *The American Way of Birth*. New York: Dutton.
Monthly Vital Statistics Reports
  1993   *Advance Report of Final Natality Statistics* 41, no. 9, suppl. (25 Febru-
          ary): 7.
Morbidity and Mortality Weekly Report
  1993   "Health Objectives for the Nation." *Morbidity and Mortality Weekly Report*
          42, no. 15 (23 April): 285–289.
Nelson, Margaret
  1986   "Birth and Social Class." In *The American Way of Birth*, ed. Pamela S. Ea-
          kins, 142–174. Philadelphia: Temple University Press.

Oakley, Ann
   1986   *The Captured Womb: A History of the Medical Care of Pregnant Women.* New York: Basil Blackwell.
Pappas, Gregory
   1989   "Some Implications for the Study for the Doctor-Patient Interaction: Power, Structure and Agency in the Works of Howard Waitzkin and Arthur Kleinman." *Social Science and Medicine* 30(2):199–204.
Petchesky, Rosalind
   1983   "Reproduction and Class Divisions among Women." In *Class, Race and Sex: The Dynamics of Control,* ed. Amy Swerdlow and Hannah Lessinger, 221–241. Boston: G. K. Hall.
Placek, P. J., S. M. M. Taffel, and M. Moien
   1988   "1986 C-Sections Rise; VBACs Inch Upward." *American Journal of Public Health* 78:562–563.
Poland, Marilyn
   1987   "Barriers to Receiving Adequate Prenatal Care." *American Journal of Obstetrics and Gynecology* 157(2):297–303.
Romalis, Shelley, ed.
   1981   *Childbirth: Alternatives to Medical Control.* Austin: University of Texas Press.
Rooks, Judith P., et al.
   1989   "Outcomes of Care in Birth Centers." *New England Journal of Medicine* 21(26):1804–1811.
Rosen, Mortimer, and Lillian Thomas
   1989   *The Cesarean Myth: Choosing the Best Way to Have Your Baby.* New York: Penguin.
Rothman, Barbara Katz
   1984   "The Meaning of Choice in Reproductive Technology." In *Test-Tube Women: What Future for Motherhood?* ed. Rita Arditti, Renate Duelli Klein, and Shelly Minden, 23–33. Boston: Pandora Press.
   1989   *Recreating Motherhood.* New York: W. W. Norton.
Sargent, Carolyn, and Nancy Stark
   1989   "Childbirth Education and Childbirth Models: Parental Perspectives on Control, Anesthesia, and Technological Intervention in the Birth Process." *Medical Anthropology Quarterly,* n.s., 3:36–51.
Scully, Diane
   1980   *Men Who Control Women's Health: The Miseducation of Obstetrician-Gynecologists.* Boston: Houghton Mifflin.
Shapiro, M. C., et al.
   1983   "Information Control and the Exercise of Power in the Obstetrical Encounter." *Social Science and Medicine* 17(3):139–146.
Singer, Merrill
   1989   "The Coming of Age of Critical Medical Anthropology." *Social Science and Medicine* 28(11):1193–1203.
Treichler, Paula A.
   1990   "Feminism, Medicine, and the Meaning of Childbirth." In *Body/Politics: Women and the Discourse of Science,* ed. Mary Jacobus, Evelyn Fox Keller, and Sally Shuttleworth, 113–138. New York: Routledge and Kegan Paul.

Wertz, Dorothy, and Richard Wertz
  1977 *Lying In: A History of Childbirth in America.* New York: Free Press.
Whiteford, Linda, and Marilyn Poland, eds.
  1989 *New Approaches to Human Reproduction: Social and Ethical Dimensions.* Boulder, Colo.: Westview Press.
Willson, J. Robert
  1990 "Scientific Advances, Societal Trends, and the Education and Practice of Obstetrician-Gynecologists." *American Journal of Obstetrics and Gynecology* 162(5):1135–1140.
Wright, Peter, and Andrew Treacher
  1982 *The Problem of Medical Knowledge: Examining the Social Construction of Medicine.* Edinburgh: University of Edinburgh.
Young, Allan
  1982 "The Anthropologies of Illness and Sickness." *Annual Reviews in Anthropology* 11:257–286.
Zuspan, Frederick, and Larry Sachs
  1988 "The Impact of Subspecialties on Obstetrics and Gynecology: Presidential Address." *American Journal of Obstetrics and Gynecology* 158(4):747–753.

SIX

Authoritative Knowledge and Birth Territories in Contemporary Japan

Deborah Cordero Fiedler

It is trivial to raise the point that birth takes place somewhere, be it in the bush, in a hut in the jungle, or in a modern hospital. What is not quite so trivial is to consider that birth, by the mere fact that it is located somewhere, inevitably takes place on somebody's territory.

— BRIGITTE JORDAN,
Birth in Four Cultures

In this chapter I address issues of authoritative knowledge and territory in contemporary Japanese childbirth. By territory, I mean both the physical and the social environment of birth. Indeed, a primary focus of this chapter is the ways in which the physical location of birth reflects and creates social territories, which in turn powerfully affect the physical processes of labor and birth and women's experience of those processes.

I consider the relationship between the definition of birth and the territory of the birthing process, which includes both the physical location of birth and the professional paradigms of care associated with different locations. I focus on two contrasting institutional settings: a hospital (the most common health care institution for birth in Japan) and a midwife-operated clinic (the least common one). These two locations illustrate differences and similarities in the social structuring of the experience of birthing according to location and its corresponding paradigm of care. A central difference between each location is that care in each is institutionally structured around different assumptions: in the hospital setting, care is structured to facilitate potential obstetrical intervention; in the midwife-operated clinic, care is structured by the assumption that obstetrical intervention will not be necessary.

In hospital births in Japan the obstetrician's access to and control over certain technological tools and techniques reflect and legitimate his[1] ultimate authoritative status over the midwife who delivers the baby and the woman who is giving birth. This occurs despite the obstetrician's limited direct physical involvement and despite his limited use of obstetrical instruments in most uncomplicated births. Brigitte Jordan has similarly

TABLE 6.1   Live Births by Location and
Attendant, 1950–1991, Total Japan

	1950	1955	1965	1975	1985	1991
Location						
Home	95.4%	82.4%	16.0%	1.2%	0.2%	0.1%
Institution	4.6%	17.6%	84.0%	98.8%	99.8%	99.9%
Primary Attendant						
Midwife	90.1%	79.6%	28.8%	8.9%	3.1%	1.8%
Physician	5.2%	16.2%	70.7%	91.1%	96.9%	98.1%

SOURCE: Adapted from Ministry of Health and Welfare 1992:30.

observed that in births in the United States, it is the control of specialized obstetrical technology, not necessarily the extent to which it is used, that reflects the "hierarchical social position of birth participants in medical settings" (1987:39).

Jordan suggests that a general property of technological systems is a tendency toward the upscaling of technology in response to a problem: "when different levels of technology are available, the solution to problems that arise at one level is almost always sought on the next higher level and rarely on the next lower level" (1987:39). In Japan the prevailing cultural definition of birth is that it is primarily a healthy—albeit potentially dangerous—physiological event. Such an understanding does not obviate the need for obstetrical intervention; rather, the cultural value placed on minimizing such intervention results in the view that obstetrical technology is valued more as a potential than as an actual application. This view, however, does not interfere with the view that the obstetrician is the source of authoritative knowledge.

BACKGROUND

Jordan has asserted that in the United States there is "concomitant change in the location of the event (moving from home to hospital), in personnel (which changes from nonspecialist to specialist attendants), and in the distribution of authoritative knowledge" (1987:39). This pattern is evident in the case of Japan. The Japanese birthing system underwent a rapid and dramatic structural change in the late 1950s and early 1960s (see table 6.1). In the course of ten years, the location of birth shifted from the home to a health care institution, and the obstetrician became the designated holder of authoritative knowledge for birthing. By 1991, in national-level statistics, obstetricians were listed as the primary attendants in 98.1 per-

TABLE 6.2   Live Births by Health Care Institution,
1950–1991, Total Japan

	1950	1955	1965	1975	1985	1991
Institution						
Hospital	2.9%	10.8%	36.8%	47.4%	55.5%	55.7%
Obstetrician-operated clinic	1.1%	4.5%	34.3%	44.2%	42.4%	43.3%
Midwife-operated clinic	0.5%	2.4%	12.9%	7.2%	2.0%	0.9%

SOURCE: Adapted from Ministry of Health and Welfare 1992:31.
NOTE: Percentages do not add up to 100% because the table does not include live births occurring in the home.

cent of all live births (Ministry of Health and Welfare 1992). Yet, despite the fact that they have for the most part ceased to be independent practitioners attending births in the home or their own clinics, midwives continue to play integral roles in hospital births and are the primary managers of births that do not require obstetrical intervention. (The role division of labor between obstetricians and midwives is discussed later in the chapter.)

As the location of birth switched from home to institution, some midwives initially established their own freestanding clinics for birthing (see table 6.2).[2] In 1965, 12.9 percent of all live births occurred in a midwife-operated clinic. Since then, however, the number of births occurring in midwife-operated clinics has steadily declined. By 1991, 99.9 percent of all live births occurred in some type of health care institution. Only 0.9 percent of these births, however, took place in a midwife-centered institution; 99 percent occurred in an obstetrician-centered institution, either a hospital (55.7%) or an obstetrician-operated clinic (43.3%). The reasons for this decline shed light on similar processes in other countries and constitute a rich subject for future research.

METHODS

The data presented in this chapter come from a larger body of field data, which I collected primarily in Tokyo between 1987 and 1990 and during a three-week interval in 1991, for a study on social support for pregnancy and childbirth. The main focus of my research was the examination of the traditional practice of *satogaeri* (homecoming) childbirth in contemporary Japan, the custom of women returning to their natal home for support at the time of their birth. Data presented here are based on observations of care at the time of labor and birth, the videotaping of two births (which I use for an in-depth analysis according to location of the structure of care at the time of birth), and interviews with specialists and nonspecialists about their experiences with birthing.

I observed care at a number of clinical settings to obtain contextual information on maternity health care delivery services. My entry into these various health care settings was facilitated by the fact that I was a registered nurse, with a total of eight years experience in women's health care, five within a labor and delivery unit. This professional identity, more than my identity as a Ph.D. candidate in anthropology, was instrumental in gaining entry to the usually restricted territory of hospital-based obstetrical units. For an eight-month period in 1988 and 1989, I observed for eight-hour intervals, three days a week, the care provided in the obstetrical unit of a large national hospital located in downtown Tokyo. During this period, I was given free access to all areas of the unit, including the prenatal clinic, prenatal classes, the labor and delivery area, the nursery, the communal breastfeeding room, and the postpartum ward. For comparative purposes, I also observed for two- to three-week periods, several days a week, the care provided at a private maternal and child hospital, which was also located in downtown Tokyo, and at a midwife-operated clinic in the neighboring Kanagawa prefecture. At these two locations as well I was allowed to observe all aspects of routine care with relatively few restrictions. In addition, I toured the maternity units of various hospitals and clinics in Tokyo, Iwate prefecture, and Yamagata prefecture.

During a three-week return trip in 1991, I videotaped two births in Tokyo: the first at the aforementioned private maternal and child hospital where I had observed care and the second at a midwife-operated clinic that I had previously toured. Time constraints and the convenience of the clinic staff dictated the days designated for videotaping; although I made no attempt to obtain "representative" births, given my previous observations and interviews I was able to assess that these were fairly typical births. These videotapes provide the data for a major section of this chapter.

While observing care at the above institutions, I had the opportunity to conduct more than twenty-five informal, unstructured interviews with health professionals, patients, and patients' family members. Moreover, during tours of clinics and hospitals, I was able to question the health professionals who served as my guides about the structure of maternity care at their institutions. I draw on these informal interviews for supplementary information.

In addition, I conducted a series of open-ended, semistructured interviews with twelve patients in the prenatal care clinic regarding their past and current pregnancy and childbirth experiences. I subsequently followed these women as much as possible during prenatal health visits, labor and birth, and the postpartum period, which included their adjustment at home after discharge from the hospital.

The data collected from the above interviews formed the basis of a structured interview schedule on ideal sources of social support for pregnancy and childbirth. During 1989 and 1990, I conducted (with the help of a research assistant) structured interviews with a sample of forty-eight women. This was a nonrandom sample that was obtained from various sources, including a public health well-baby clinic and a parenting support group. These interviews elicited women's attitudes about specialist and nonspecialist (i.e., family and friends) social support during pregnancy, labor, and birth. They revealed women's differing attitudes about specialists and nonspecialists as sources of information, emotional support, and physical support. I draw heavily on these interviews for this chapter.

PROFESSIONAL TERRITORIES AND PARADIGMS OF BIRTH CARE IN JAPAN AND THE UNITED STATES

Human cultural definitions of childbirth have regarded it as a normal physiological or social event, an event fraught with danger, and even illness and pathology (Jordan [1978] 1993; Kay 1982; Mead and Newton 1967; Ford 1945). As Jordan has noted,

> For any particular domain a multitude of ways of knowing exist, some of which, by consensus, come to carry more weight than others, either because they explain the state of the world better for the purposes at hand ("efficacy") or because they are associated with a stronger power base ("structural superiority"), and usually both. (1992:2)

Social scientists who study childbirth in the United States have conceptualized two opposing paradigms of birth care: the "medical" model and the "midwifery" model (Lichtman 1988; Rothman 1984); or, as Robbie Davis-Floyd (1992) has thought of them, the "technocratic" model and the "holistic" model—terms that draw attention to the manner in which these paradigms of birth care mirror opposing movements in the wider society. As in the American cultural arena, in Japan the medical or technocratic model of childbirth has assumed dominance and authoritative status.

The two paradigms outlined above represent different "ways of knowing" about the universal physiology of human childbirth. They operate in distinct professional territories, which in turn structure the physical process of birth in opposing ways. In the medical or technocratic model, birth is viewed as inherently pathological, or more precisely, as a problematic mechanical process in danger of constant malfunction. Such a view engenders a high degree of technological monitoring of and intervention in the birth process. Proponents of the midwifery or holistic model, in contrast, perceive birth to be an inherently normal physiological process with powerful emotional and spiritual dimensions—a perception that underlies a nurturant, noninterventive approach to birth care and a belief that birth should most properly take place in alternative birth centers or the home. The medical or technocratic model uses a classifying, separating approach to the process of labor and birth, treating the woman as an object and her body as a machine. Furthermore, this model dichotomizes the mind and the body as well as the mother and the infant. The midwifery or holistic model, in contrast, assumes a holistic, integrating approach that treats the woman as a subject and does not produce a dualistic separation between the woman's body and mind or between the mother and infant (Davis-Floyd 1992; Rothman 1984).

The distinctions drawn by Ronnie Lichtman, Barbara Rothman, and Davis-Floyd between these two approaches to birth provide a useful background to highlight the differences in the Japanese approach. In the United States, the two models differ in the extreme; in Japan, they do not. Thus, in this chapter, I use the terms *obstetrical* model and *midwifery* model to describe approaches to birth in Japan. The obstetrical model denotes a more physiological approach to birth than is practiced under the medical or technocratic model in the United States—in short, rather than assuming that birth is an inherently dysfunctional process, this model assumes that until proven otherwise birth is normal.

Margaret Lock (1993) has observed that female life-cycle transitions are generally less medicalized in Japan than in northern Europe and North America. She attributes this to different representations of the female body. Whereas the discourse on menopause in Japan situates a woman's aging within the family, in the West it is situated within the individual. Similarly, the life-cycle transition of childbirth is viewed as being situated in the family as evidenced by the common occurrence of satogaeri (home-coming) childbirth in contemporary Japan. Nonspecialists and specialists alike acknowledge the importance of a new mother after discharge from a hospital or a clinic being in her natal home and receiving care and support from her own mother in the postnatal period. In an uncomplicated pregnancy and birth, the mother-daughter bond is considered to be stronger than the specific obstetrician-patient bond; and thus most obstetricians do not discourage a woman from returning to her natal home even when the return requires a change in health care providers and health care institutions in the last trimester of pregnancy. Obstetricians only discourage a woman from returning to her natal home when complications are present. This is further evidence of the view of childbirth as a primarily normal physiological event.

Such a view fosters a less interventive approach to birth than is found in U.S. hospitals. For example, it is common for Japanese women to eat and drink during labor and to walk from the labor room to the delivery room; it is uncommon for them to routinely have analgesia, anesthesia, or operative intervention during birth. The cesarean section rates for hospitals and obstetrician-operated clinics in 1990 were 11 percent and 8 percent, respectively (Ministry of Health and Welfare 1992:114); in the same year, the cesarean section rate in U.S. hospitals was 23.5 percent (Taffel et al. 1992:21).

Use of the term *obstetrical* emphasizes the professional territory from which this model is derived and which it represents in contemporary Japan. It also reflects the historical development of obstetrical domination over normal pregnancy and birth in Japan and, in part, the influences of American obstetrical practices exported to Japan during the postwar period. Today, Japanese childbirth practices more closely resemble those of Western Europe and England, where midwives remain an integral part of the maternity care system, albeit with some loss of autonomy and responsibility. (They, like Japanese midwives, primarily practice in the hospital in a role viewed as auxiliary to that of obstetricians.) [3]

In spite of their structural subordination, the continuing involvement of midwives in the Japanese obstetric system has worked to facilitate the definition of birth as normal. In contrast to the pathologizing technocratic approach to birth that is dominant in the United States, the Japanese obstetrical model sees birth as being primarily physiological and only potentially pathological. The obstetrical orientation focuses on the potentiality rather than the actuality of pathology; thus birth is defined as a vulnerable time that requires medical consultation or supervision but not necessarily routine medical intervention. In Japanese hospitals midwives carry out labor support and attend all normal deliveries; obstetricians do not routinely appear during normal labor but are always present in the delivery room to perform any interventions that may be required.

In the United States, insurance coverage of routine technological interventions in uncomplicated births supports a pathological definition of birth. In Japan, the economic infrastructure does not support such a definition. Under the Japanese national health insurance system, until proven otherwise birth is defined as a normal condition rather than an illness. Thus in the absence of documented complications birth is not routinely covered by health insurance. While the presence of the obstetrician at the time of birth is considered essential should a complication develop, in the absence of demonstrable pathology, birth is viewed as best handled with a minimum of obstetrical technological intervention.

Other important factors in maternal and child health in Japan are universal, early, and regular prenatal care. Prenatal care in Japan is promoted through a state-mandated maternal and child health program. The focal point of this program is a maternal and child health handbook (*boshi kenkō techo*) that is issued by local government offices to all expectant mothers in Japan. This handbook contributes to a considerable degree to the standardization of the experience of pregnancy and birth. It is designed to function as a source of health information (e.g., the prescribed frequency of prenatal examinations) and as a detailed health record of the results of those examinations. That the handbook remains in the possession of the pregnant woman is significant. Whether the empowerment of the woman by the Japanese government is intentional or not, the fact remains that Japanese women are entrusted with agentic participation in their prenatal and birth care. In the United States, women are not regarded as competent to possess this information and are denied access to their medical charts, with the result that the obstetrician's authoritative status is enhanced.

The initial, general instructions in the handbook are conveyed under the main title "Becoming a Good Mother to Your Baby." In this section, pregnant women are instructed to "consult a doctor, midwife, public health nurse, or nutritionist for guidance concerning daily life, nutrition and environment to maintain good health during pregnancy and to have a safe delivery" (JOICFP 1988:2). The handbook does not limit options for appropriate care to the obstetrician. Complications of pregnancy, however, are considered to be the exclusive domain of the obstetrician, and women are instructed to notify an obstetrician immediately if they manifest various "warning symptoms" associated with complications of pregnancy.[4]

Although the guidelines provided in the maternal and child health handbook consider a range of health care providers to be appropriate (from independent midwives to hospital-based obstetricians), most women nevertheless receive prenatal care from an obstetrician. In the hospital setting the obstetrician is the primary provider of care for all pregnant women during the prenatal period, regardless of the presence or absence of complications. This is in contrast to the period of labor and delivery, during which the midwife is the primary provider of care for uncomplicated cases; the obstetrician is notified during labor only if a complication had developed during pregnancy or if one arises during labor. For all births, however, an obstetrician is called just prior to delivery in case an obstetrical intervention is necessary.

Most of the women I interviewed selected the obstetrician rather than the midwife as the ideal source of information. To the extent that the obstetrician can verify the presence or absence of pathology, he is considered an invaluable source of information and emotional support. However, many women also perceive that access to this specialist's time is limited. Consequently, they try by consulting with a friend or family member to determine if their specific concerns and questions warrant the obstetrician's input. With the medicalization of pregnancy and birth, however, the distinction between medical and nonmedical concerns has become difficult for women to make.

Japanese women tend to view midwives as ancillary specialists who function as intermediaries, interpreting and explaining the obstetrician's diagnoses and recommendations. Since most obstetricians are male and all midwives are female, midwives are also viewed as good supplementary sources of information and emotional support because of their experiential understanding of birthing.

In popular perception, the midwife in independent practice is more structurally similar to the obstetrician than is the midwife who practices in the hospital setting. This is illustrated by the use of the term *sensei,* a respectful term of address, to refer to obstetricians and midwives in independent practice.[5] Midwives who are dependent employees in a hospital setting are not referred to as sensei. Thus the use of this term marks the birthing authority and the associated body of "knowledge that counts" in each institutional setting.

TERRITORIES OF BIRTH AND PARADIGMS OF CARE IN THE HOSPITAL AND THE MIDWIFE CLINIC

In this section, I draw on data from videotapes of two births to describe how birth is structured differently in a hospital and a midwife-operated clinic.[6] While the midwife is the one who delivers the baby in both locations, she operates under different paradigms of care. In the hospital setting, the obstetrician is the holder of authoritative knowledge and the obstetrical model prevails; in the midwife-operated clinic, the midwife is the holder of authoritative knowledge and the midwifery model of care, which assumes that obstetrical intervention is not necessary for most births, is practiced.

In both locations, videotaping was started after labor had already started (approximately one hour prior to birth) and continued until the end of the initial infant care period and the beginning of the woman's recovery period. Both women were giving birth to their second child. Neither had complications during pregnancy. In the hospital, the woman's labor was artificially induced. In the midwife-operated clinic, labor started spontaneously. Both births were considered to be "normal" in the context of their settings. Below I present a description and a comparative interpretation of the two videotaped births.

The Settings

The videotapes clearly show that the woman assumes a passive patient role in the hospital. During labor she is in bed, wears a hospital gown, and is attached to specialized obstetrical equipment. In the midwife-operated clinic, in contrast, the woman wears her own clothing throughout the labor and birthing process, and she is active and experiences labor in a room without specialized obstetrical equipment. The "labor room" is a Japanese-style "bath room," a room with a deep bathtub. The woman alternates between sitting in the tub or kneeling on all fours on the floor outside of the tub.

In the hospital and the midwife-operated clinic, labor and birth each occur in two different rooms. In the midwife-operated clinic, the delivery room is actually a "multipurpose" room. It serves as an examination room for antepartum, intrapartum, and postpartum examinations and as a delivery room. There is also the option of giving birth in a tatami room (a room with straw floor matting), with a futon (quilted cotton bedding), which gives flexibility in positioning for birth. Thus the birth on the videotape represents the high end of complexity of birth technology in the midwife-operated clinic. The delivery room in the hospital birth, in contrast, is a specialized room that is used for delivery only. In the hospital it represents the low end of technological complexity; the operating room, used for cesarean births, is the high end.

In both locations, the woman walks (rather than being transported by wheelchair or stretcher) to the delivery room. This move occurs at essentially the same point in labor—when the cervix is dilated approximately eight centimeters. In both cases birth occurs on a "delivery table," with the woman lying in a dorsal position; and in both cases a midwife "catches" the baby.

Birthing Technology and Attendants/Support Systems

Birth in the hospital is supported by a great deal of complex technology during labor and birth (e.g., a hospital bed during labor, an IV and a pump to infuse an oxytoxic agent to induce labor contractions, an electronic fetal monitor, and suction equipment to clear secretions and fluids from the baby's airway). The woman's connection to the hospital staff is also mediated through specialized equipment (i.e., an intercom/call bell system).

In the videotaped hospital birth, the woman is alone most of the time during labor. Only specialists are in attendance (husband-attended birth was available, however, at this hospital).[7] The midwife who cares for the woman during labor and who attends her birth comes into the labor room periodically to check on the woman's condition. Because she is not with the woman continuously, the midwife relies on the electronic fetal monitor printout, the woman's report of her bodily sensations, and vaginal examinations to assess the woman's progress in labor. When the midwife enters the room for a periodic check, she looks at the electronic fetal monitor printout first before she asks for the woman's depiction of her bodily experience of labor. In this instance the electronic fetal monitor takes precedence over the woman, revealing technology as a location of authority. When the woman uses the call system to summon the midwife, however, the midwife attends to the woman before the machine.

Although the woman walks to the delivery room in the hospital, she again assumes a passive role after mounting the delivery room table. She is reconnected to the electronic fetal monitor, and the fetal heart sounds are more audible than in the labor room. In the labor room the monitor served as an electronic attendant that provided an ongoing record of labor in the midwife's absence. In the delivery room, however, even though at least one midwife is always present, no one directly attends the woman most of the time. Thus the monitor continues to act as an attendant that provides an auditory alarm of changes in the baby's heart rate and that notifies the health care specialists. Otherwise, preparations are conducted *around* the woman. When the woman has contractions, the midwives often loudly perform the patterned breathing with the woman but without interrupting their activities.

Whereas during labor the woman in the hospital birth is alone for most of the time until she transfers to the delivery room, the woman in the midwife-operated clinic birth is never alone. Specialists *and* nonspecialists are in attendance. Only one type of specialist (midwife) is present in the midwife-operated clinic, whereas in the hospital setting there are two (obstetrician and midwife). The woman is accompanied by her husband during labor and by her husband and her daughter at birth; after birth, for early infant care, a female family member is also present.

Because birth in the midwife-operated clinic is continuously attended by a midwife and the woman's husband, a jointly negotiated, ongoing assessment of the woman's bodily experience and the progression of her labor takes place. The husband times the contractions, and the woman discusses her bodily sensations. When the contractions become closer and stronger, a joint decision is made between the midwife and the woman to go to the examination room to determine cervical dilation.

Structuring of the Birth Process

At the entrance to the delivery suite in the hospital, the midwife and the woman must stop to change from the hospital slippers or shoes into delivery room slippers; no such change of footwear takes place in the midwife-operated clinic.[8] In the hospital setting, delivery room slippers may serve two functions: keeping outside pollution from entering the delivery room and also keeping the pollution associated with birth within the confines of the delivery room area.

In the hospital birth, action on the woman intensifies on her arrival in the delivery room and as the moment of birth approaches (similar to descriptions of hospital births in the United States [Davis-Floyd 1992; Jordan 1987]) in anticipation of the presence of the obstetrician and possible obstetrical intervention. Much of the preparation centers around first spotlighting and then cleaning, shaving, and isolating the woman's perineal area, preparations that ritually separate the upper and lower halves of a woman's body and isolate and demarcate the lower half of the body as the domain of the specialist.

In the midwife-operated clinic setting, demarcation occurs but to a limited degree. Fewer sterile drapes are used; the woman's feet are not strapped into footrests; her perineal area is not shaved; and her bladder is not emptied with a catheter. A bright overhead light is turned on shortly before the birth, but no spotlights are directed on the woman's perineal area.

In the midwife-operated clinic, numerous efforts are made to integrate the woman's upper and lower body and to integrate the physical and social experiences of birth. For example, the midwife repeatedly informs the woman and her family about what is happening to her body (e.g., how far the baby has descended in the birth canal and how much she can see of the baby's head). A mirror is held by one of the assistant midwives so that the woman and her family can watch as the baby's head emerges. The midwife directs the woman to reach and feel the baby after it is almost halfway out and then encourages her to lift the baby up onto her abdomen.

In both births, the specialists direct the women's actions to achieve an optimal birth; their different perspectives on birth, however, lead them to behave in contrasting ways. In the hospital setting, after the lower half of the body is isolated and marked, a mechanistic approach to the management of birth prevails—an approach that is maintained by the midwives themselves, who conform to obstetrical notions of how birth should be conducted. The hospital-based specialists expect the woman to maintain a position that does not impede their actions, and they ensure that she does so by strapping her feet into place. In addition, she is told repeatedly to keep her legs spread open and her buttocks in close range of the midwife's hands. In the hospital birth, the midwife on ten different occasions tells the woman to open her legs wide. But the woman's knees invariably come back together, thus demonstrating that the mechanistic approach is not effective in these instances.

The obstetrician echoes these directives when he enters the room. He dons surgical gloves and loudly instructs the woman, "Slide your buttocks down more to the foot of the table. A little faster. Move down a little more. More, more. Slide down. More, more, more. Slide, slide." As the birthing authority, he also supplies the rationale for his directives. He tells the woman, "The baby is in pain so move down quickly. Spread your legs open. That's it, that's it. You'll be giving birth."

In the midwife-operated clinic birth, the emphasis is on having a slow, controlled birth, rather than on having a speedy one. As in the hospital, the midwife tells the woman to spread her legs. But she also uses various indirect means to achieve this goal, such as encouraging the woman to do a circular, butterflylike motion with her hands, extending them from her chest toward the ceiling and then fluttering them outward toward the walls. This arm movement is synchronous with her patterned breathing and suggests openness and relaxation. The midwife also encourages the woman's husband and young daughter (who are close to the woman at the head of the delivery table) to make motions synchronous with the woman's arm movements.

As in the hospital, the "birthing authority" in the midwife-operated clinic provides the rationale for the model of care in operation. As birth becomes imminent, the midwife tells the woman, "The baby is about to be born. Slower is better. It's a shock for the baby to come out too quickly."

The midwife talks continuously to the woman, using two interwoven "voices." One is the voice of "birthing authority." When one of the assistant midwives uses a fetal doppler (with the volume loudly audible) to check the baby's heart rate, she uses this voice to comment on the condition of the baby, saying such things as "Fine. What an excellent baby!" She also comments on the progression of labor: "I'm starting to see the baby. I can see about two centimeters of the body!" This voice also directs the actions of her two assistants.

The midwife's second voice reflects an "empathetic identification" (Suzuki 1986) with the baby about to be born. She addresses the woman as *okāsan* (mother) or *mama,* the husband as *otōsan* (father) or *papa,* and the couple's daughter as *onēchan* (older sister). These terms of address do not accurately reflect the relationship between the midwife and the woman and the woman's family members but rather include the midwife as if she were a family member. Through this voice, the midwife situates the birth event in the family domain.[9] The midwife's use of an empathetic voice reflects a major difference between the midwifery model and the obstetrical model.

The midwife directs the woman's actions to include her in the act of birthing the baby. Prior to the emergence of the baby's head, the midwife encourages the woman to do the patterned breathing and associated arm movements to achieve a slow, controlled birth. After the baby's head is out, but before the rest of the body emerges, the midwife tells the woman to reach down to feel the top of the baby's head. When the baby's shoulders are out, the midwife encourages the woman to reach out with her hands to pull the baby toward her. The midwife continues to support the baby's body with her hand. The baby's body still has not completely emerged; the feet remain in the woman's vagina. After the baby cries the midwife pulls out the rest of the baby's body from the woman's vagina and places the baby on the woman's abdomen. The midwife emphasizes a slow, controlled birth with the direct participation of the mother by encouraging her to control the speed of the birth herself.

Interpretation

Although the structural features of care differ widely between the two births, the women in both locations are beseeched to comply with the birthing authority's directives and both are told of the negative effects that noncompliance has on the baby rather than on the woman herself. In the hospital setting, the woman is directed to comply with a fast birth because the baby is "in pain"; in the midwife-operated clinic, she is advised to go slowly and that it is "a shock" to the baby to be born quickly. In neither location is the woman given primacy as a woman but instead she is perceived as the producer of a child.

Emily Martin (1987) and Davis-Floyd (1992) have emphasized that in the United States the primary focus during birth is on the production of the new social member, the baby. In the United States, as in Japan, it is not uncommon to suggest implicitly or explicitly that women's lack of compliance with the birth specialists' directives will have a negative impact on the baby. In both places, the woman is perceived to have little authoritative knowledge about the baby's condition or her own.

In the United States (as Davis-Floyd shows in this volume), independent midwives and many nurse-midwives often go to great lengths to show respect for the mother's knowledge about her birth. What constitutes authoritative knowledge in birth can be constructed interactionally between the mother and the midwife during labor, as it is in Yucatan between the midwife and the mother's older female relatives and friends (Jordan 1992). But in Japan, as evidenced by these two videotaped births in differing institutional settings, the midwife who owns and operates her own freestanding clinic, like the obstetrician in the hospital, assumes the role of sensei and does not hesitate to consider herself, at least in relation to the mother and her family, the authority and the authoritative possessor of the knowledge that counts.

"OWNERSHIP" OF THE NECESSARY TOOLS OF THE TRADE AND AUTHORITATIVE KNOWLEDGE

In this section I demonstrate, based on another birth I observed, how the control of obstetrical technology—"tools of the trade"—reflects and legitimates the obstetrician's authoritative knowledge in the delivery room in the hospital setting. Much as Jordan ([1978] 1993) found that "normal" but "difficult" births were instructive for understanding the full extent of the support systems, it was through the observation of a difficult birth that I gained greater insight into the local definition of what constitutes pathology in birth and into the role divisions of midwives and obstetricians in the hospital setting. As illustrated in this section, the definition of pathology as an abnormal condition requiring obstetrical intervention is fluid. The marker of pathology in birth is the use of specialized obstetrical technology.

The case presented here is one I observed shortly after arriving at the obstetrical unit of the large national hospital where I observed care for an eight-month period. I was told by the head nurse to go directly to the delivery room where I observed a patient who had been pushing for a long time. The woman was lying on her back while she pushed during contractions, turning to her right side to rest between contractions. She had an intravenous line, was connected to an external monitor, and had oxygen flowing through a nasal cannula. The baby's head remained high and delivery required that a forceps or vacuum extractor be used (depending on how far the baby had descended in the birth canal). The obstetrician who was responsible for performing the delivery had already been notified.

No family members were in attendance. Because this was considered a difficult birth, the room was filled with specialists, both attendants and observers. In addition to the midwife who had been managing the birth, there were two assistant midwives, a junior staff obstetrician, a pediatrician, two student nurses, and me. The junior staff obstetrician was standing by the main midwife and holding the forceps. Everyone awaited the arrival of the obstetrician.

When the obstetrician arrived, he assumed the position of birth agent; the midwife stepped aside. The obstetrician administered a local anesthetic, cut an episiotomy, and applied the forceps. With the next contraction one of the assistant nurse-midwives applied fundal pressure, and the obstetrician, with relative ease, delivered the baby's head. After the baby's head was out, the obstetrician stepped aside and the midwife resumed her position as direct birth attendant. Replacing one type of specialized equipment with another, the obstetrician placed the forceps on the instrument table and picked up the suction catheter to await the delivery of the rest of the baby's body. The midwife, using her gloved hands, finished the delivery. At birth, the baby was limp and not crying. While the midwife clamped and cut the umbilical cord, the obstetrician suctioned the baby's nose and throat. The midwife rubbed the baby's back and slapped the soles of the feet until the baby gave a slight cry. The baby was then removed from the delivery room and placed in a heated bed in an adjacent room, where the pediatrician and a midwife did the initial infant care.

Interpretation

This was not a "normal" delivery. It was perceived to require the intervention of the obstetrician and the use of specialized equipment. Also, it involved the attendance of additional personnel. (The pediatrician is not summoned to the delivery room except in abnormal cases.) For normal births, usually only one obstetrician and one assistant midwife are present. Furthermore, observers such as myself and the two student nurses were encouraged to attend.

Although this birth was deemed "abnormal" (i.e., requiring the intervention of the obstetrician), this designation was not fixed. After the obstetrician delivered the baby's head with the forceps, he stepped aside instead of delivering the rest of the body. Forceps are used to deliver only the baby's head. Because it is the widest presenting part, once the head is out the rest of the body generally comes out quite easily. Thus when obstetrical equipment was no longer needed, the case was no longer "complicated" and the midwife resumed her position of command, using her hands to deliver the rest of the baby.

Jordan argues that "the 'ownership' of the artifacts necessary to accomplish the work at the same time defines and displays who should be seen as possessing authoritative knowledge and, consequently, as holding legitimate decision-making power" (1992:1). This case demonstrates that in Japan what constitutes a complicated birth requiring obstetrical intervention is a need for the use of tools (i.e., forceps, vacuum extractor, and other surgical instruments, in the case of cesarean sections), which only an obstetrician possesses the authoritative knowledge to command. When these tools are not needed, the obstetrician is not needed as a direct player in the birth. While complicated births involve the use of specialized obstetrical "tools of the trade," difficult births that do not require the use of equipment are often handled by a midwife with an obstetrician's supervision. On other occasions, for example, I observed midwives vaginally delivering a pair of twins and a footling breech presentation baby, with an obstetrician in attendance who provided only verbal guidance during the delivery. In the United States, these would be considered abnormal and risky births that required the physical intervention of an obstetrician. In Japan, however, because the obstetrician's tools were not needed, he did not become physically involved with the birth.

This is typical of hospital births in Japan, where an obstetrician is in attendance but does not directly intervene during most births. The midwife is the direct birth agent until the placenta is expelled. At that point, the midwife steps aside for the obstetrician, who performs an internal examination to check for retained placental pieces and for lacerations, and then does any suturing that is required. The midwife then cleanses the perineal area, applies perineal pads and the abdominal sash (*haraobi*), and begins the postpartum care of the woman. The physician's direct role thus ends when obstetrical tools are no longer needed.

Because of the prevailing physiological definition of birth in Japan, the midwife is the principal player in the minute-to-minute care during labor and birth. However, because potential for pathology is also considered to be significant, the obstetrician and his obstetrical tools are also perceived to be needed.

This case also demonstrates that the definition of normality and abnormality associated with birth in Japan is fluid. Normal births can acquire abnormal features that require the intervention of an obstetrician, such as a prolonged second stage or the slow descent of the presenting part. But a single abnormality does not define the rest of the birth. When the obstetrician's intervention is completed (and presuming that no other intervention by the obstetrician is required), the birth is perceived as being normal and the midwife resumes the position of direct birth agent.

In the Japanese hospital setting, the obstetrical model is the officially sanctioned approach. When a midwife practices in a dependent employee role and ideological conflicts occur between the two models, the obstetrical model takes precedence over the midwifery model, a precedence reflected even in the way that national-level statistics are recorded.[10] Unfortunately, however, national statistics do not reflect the conceptual and logistical importance of the midwife's contribution in contemporary Japan, as these statistics list the obstetrician as the primary attendant for nearly all births, regardless of the fact that the majority of babies are delivered by midwives with varying degrees of intervention by the obstetrician and limited application of obstetrical technology.

CONCLUSION

In hospital births, the obstetrician's ownership and control of the "tools of the trade" demonstrate and validate his ultimate authoritative status over the midwife. In both Japan and the United States, the obstetrician's superior cultural status reflects the supervaluation of sophisticated technologies. In the United States, this supervaluation, combined with devaluation of women's bodies as defective machines (in need of constant manipulation and improvement by other, more perfect machines [Davis-Floyd 1992]), has resulted in technological interventions in nearly all hospital births. In Japan obstetrical technology is more laterally integrated, and there is a tendency to continuously reorient to the lowest level of technological and professional intervention due to two factors: (1) cultural definition of women's bodies and the birth process as primarily normal and healthy and (2) a fluid view of complications during birth. There is a minute-to-minute microlevel propensity to define birth as normal and minimize technological intervention—a propensity much in evidence wherever midwives are the primary birth attendants. This helps to explain the relatively low use of anesthesia and analgesia, forceps, and cesarean sections in Japanese birth.

The coexistence of the midwifery and obstetrical models of care in Japan serves to limit the widespread and routine application of obstetrical technology in hospital births. In contemporary Japan we see "just-in-case obstetricians" rather than "just-in-case obstetrics" (a term used by Suzanne Arms [1977] to refer to the tendency of obstetricians in the United States to use unnecessary interventions in a preventive mode). But even though midwives continue to be integral participants in birthing (even as dependent employees in the hospital setting), the obstetrician's hierarchical position over the midwife remains based on his control of obstetrical technology and the dominance of the obstetrical model over the midwifery model remains the basis of authoritative knowledge.

NOTES

The research presented in this chapter was funded by a Fulbright (IIE) Graduate Research Fellowship, a Japan Foundation Doctoral Dissertation Fellowship, and an Andrew Mellon Pre-Doctoral Fellowship and was facilitated by affiliation with the Health Sociology Department, Faculty of Medicine, University of Tokyo. My thanks go to the women who generously allowed me to interview them and observe their births, to the many health professionals in the various hospitals and clinics where I conducted my research, and to Yayoi Kawamata, who served as my interview assistant. Of the many individuals who supported and encouraged my research in Japan, I would like especially to acknowledge L. Keith Brown, Joseph D. Fiedler, Teruko Fukuoka, Sadao Horiguchi, Shigeko Horiuchi, Shigeki Minoru, Kyoichi Sonoda, and Takashi Wagatsuma. I am grateful to L. Keith Brown, Ellen Madono, Lipika Mazumdar, Susan C. Pearce, Jenn Phillips, Carolyn Sargent, Richard Scaglion, Lila Shaara, John Singleton, Janice A. Slater, Martha Ann Terry, Rubie S. Watson, and the *Medical Anthropology Quarterly* reviewers and editors for their constructive comments on this chapter at various stages. I would especially like to thank Robbie Davis-Floyd for the encouragement, support, and editorial assistance she provided at all stages of this chapter's development.

1. The masculine pronoun is used for obstetricians because most obstetricians are male. In 1986, 11 percent of the physicians practicing gynecology and obstetrics were women (Ministry of Health and Welfare 1993:109).
2. Clinics are inpatient facilities that are smaller than hospitals. A hospital (*byōin*) is defined as an institution with twenty or more inpatient beds. Clinics have

fewer than twenty inpatient beds and are privately owned and administered by a midwife (*josanin*) or an obstetrician (*sanin*).

3. It is noteworthy that in Japan, as well as in Sweden and Holland, the majority of births are midwife attended, and perinatal and infant mortality rates are among the lowest in the world (Jordan 1993; Ministry of Health and Welfare 1992). Factors associated with low infant mortality rates in Japan (e.g., universal access to prenatal care, state support of breastfeeding through monetary incentives, postpartum home visitation programs by maternal and child health workers, and a low rate of cesarean births) are similar to those in Western European countries and distinguish Japan from the United States (Korte 1992).

4. The "warning symptoms" of complications of pregnancy include the following: "edema, genital bleeding, abdominal pain, fever, diarrhea, constipation, unusual vaginal discharge, severe headache, dizziness, nausea, vomiting, fatigue caused by severe morning sickness, or lack of fetal movement" (JOICFP 1988: 2–3).

5. The term "sensei" is often difficult to directly translate into English because it is used to refer to a variety of respected persons, including, but not limited to, professionals such as teachers, doctors, dentists, writers, lawyers, and politicians. Furthermore, it may be used independently or affixed to the family name. In any case, its usage implies respect and deference on the part of the speaker (Miura 1983).

6. The use of a video camera allowed me to be a more detached observer in a setting in which I had been a participant, as an obstetrical nurse. By repeatedly reviewing the videotapes, I was able to gain more insight into the structural aspects of obstetrical care, care with which I was very familiar. Furthermore, since I used a handheld camera, I could better understand both my biases (by viewing what I had selectively recorded) and the biases of the health care professionals (by considering the directions they gave me and the limitations they placed on me).

7. The option of having one's husband present in the delivery room at the time of birth is a recent one in Japanese hospitals, and is not widely and routinely available. At this particular hospital, the option of having a supportive person present for birth is limited to the husband, which in Japan is equivalent to the father since few births occur outside of marriage.

8. Much in the same way that Japanese change from their "outside shoes" to their "inside slippers" on entering a home, it is common to change from one's outside shoes at the main entrance of the hospital or at the entrance to a specific unit. The inside shoes or slippers are changed again on entering the delivery room.

9. The use of family terms of address in extrafamily situations is not uncommon. Within the Japanese family terms of address tend to harmonize with the position of the youngest child. This is also extended to extrafamily situations (Suzuki 1986).

10. The dominance of the obstetrical model over the midwifery model in the hospital setting is exemplified by the omission in a class taught in the hospital by a midwife to new mothers of the diaphragm (*pessari*) as one option for postpartum contraception. The midwife teaching the class told me afterward that she did not include the diaphragm as an option because the head of the obstetrics department felt that it was an old-fashioned means of birth control and did not want it included

in the discharge teaching. This midwife felt differently, acknowledging that it was a method that was promoted in her midwifery training. She felt uncomfortable excluding it but also felt constrained to do so. The midwife in independent practice, however, often actively promotes the diaphragm as a method of contraception, a method she can independently provide and a woman can control. The midwife practicing independently may not only exert more control over the content of practice, she can also establish a professional identity in the community by providing new approaches to birthing. These new methods, such as "active birth," may be adopted from other countries. In these cases, the name of the method is written in *katakana,* the syllabary used primarily for writing words borrowed from foreign languages, and thus appears new and exotic. A midwife may devise her own method and apply her own name to it. One example is a method of breast massage used to facilitate breastfeeding called the *Okeitani* method, named after its originator.

REFERENCES

Arms, Suzanne
    1977   *Immaculate Deception.* New York: Bantam Books.
Davis-Floyd, Robbie
    1992   *Birth as an American Rite of Passage.* Berkeley: University of California Press.
Ford, Clellan Stearns
    1945   *A Comparative Study of Human Reproduction.* New Haven: Yale University Press.
Japanese Organization for International Cooperation in Family Planning, Inc. (JOICFP)
    1988   *Maternal and Child Health Handbook of Japan.* Tokyo: JOICFP.
Jordan, Brigitte
    [1978] 1993   *Birth in Four Cultures: A Cross-Cultural Investigation of Childbirth in Yucatan, Holland, Sweden and the United States.* 4th ed. Prospect Heights, Ill.: Waveland Press.
    1987   "The Hut and the Hospital: Information, Power, and Symbolism in the Artifacts of Birth." *Birth* 14:36–40.
    1992   "Technology and Social Interaction: Notes on the Achievement of Authoritative Knowledge in Complex Settings." IRL Technical Report, IRL92-0027. Palo Alto, Calif.: Institute for Research on Learning.
Kay, Margarita Artschwager
    1982   "Writing an Ethnography of Birth." In *Anthropology of Human Birth,* ed. Margarita Artschwager Kay, 1–24. Philadelphia: F. A. Davis.
Korte, Diana
    1992   "Infant Mortality: Lessons from Japan." *Mothering,* Winter:83–88.
Lichtman, Ronnie
    1988   "Medical Models and Midwifery: The Cultural Experience of Birth." In *Childbirth in America: Anthropological Perspectives,* ed. Karen Michaelson, 130–141. South Hadley, Mass.: Bergin and Garvey.

Lock, Margaret
  1993   "Ideology, Female Midlife, and the Greying of Japan." *Journal of Japanese Studies* (19)1:43–78.
Martin, Emily
  1987   *The Woman in the Body: A Cultural Analysis of Reproduction.* Boston: Beacon Press.
Mead, Margaret, and Niles Newton
  1967   "Cultural Patterning of Prenatal Behavior." In *Childbearing: Its Social and Psychological Aspects,* ed. Stephen A. Richardson and Alan F. Guttmacher, 142–244. Baltimore: Williams and Wilkins.
Ministry of Health and Welfare
  1992   *Maternal and Child Health Statistics of Japan* (Boshieisei no Omonaru Toukei). Tokyo: Mothers' and Children's Health Organization.
  1993   *Health and Welfare Statistics in Japan.* Tokyo: Health and Welfare Statistics Association.
Miura, Akira
  1983   *Japanese Words and Their Uses.* Rutland, Vt.: Charles E. Tuttle.
Rothman, Barbara Katz
  1984   *Giving Birth: Alternatives in Childbirth.* New York: Penguin.
Suzuki, Takao
  1986   "Language and Behavior in Japan: The Conceptualization of Personal Relations." In *Japanese Culture and Behavior,* ed. Takie Sugiyama Lebra and William P. Lebra, 142–157. Honolulu: University of Hawaii Press.
Taffel, Selma M., Paul J. Placek, Mary Moien, and Carol L. Kosary
  1992   "U.S. Cesarean Section Rates 1990: An Update." *Birth* (19)1:21–22.

PART THREE

Intercultural Variations in Authoritative Knowledge about Birth

*Hierarchy, Community, and
the Local Social Ground*

SEVEN

Ways of Knowing
about Birth in Three Cultures

Carolyn F. Sargent and Grace Bascope

In her elaboration of the concept of authoritative knowledge, Brigitte Jordan ([1978] 1993:152) observed that when, for any particular domain, more than one knowledge system exists, one kind of knowledge often gains ascendance. The legitimizing of one way of knowing as authoritative often leads to the devaluation of all other ways of knowing. Thus one system of authoritative knowledge comes to appear natural, reasonable, and shared (Jordan and Irwin 1989). People actively engage in the production and reproduction of authoritative knowledge, thus continually reinforcing its validity. Correspondingly, Paul Starr refers to authority as "the probability that particular definitions of reality and judgments of meaning and value will prevail as valid and true" (1982:13). Cultural authority, such as the authoritative knowledge of physicians, may reside in scholarly or scientific texts. Authority may also entail the control of action; in this sense authority implies the "possession of some status, quality, or claim that compels trust or obedience" (Starr 1982:9). It is in their capacity as cultural authorities that specialists such as physicians, nurses, and midwives make judgments on what constitutes illness, labor complications, or necessary delivery procedures.

Through her well-known analyses of birth in several cultures, Jordan ([1978] 1993) has explored the constitution and display of authoritative knowledge regarding birth in high- and low-technology settings. In this research, she has focused especially on the degree of autonomy allowed to the laboring woman, and the extent to which she may be said to "own" the birth. She notes that at birth, as in other social situations, various "ways of knowing" exist, some of which possess more weight than others. Certain individuals appear to possess knowledge that is authoritative, that "counts"

([1978] 1993:87). Such authoritative knowledge is accepted as legitimate, is socially sanctioned, and serves as grounds for action.

In this chapter, we reexamine the merits of the concept of authoritative knowledge developed by Jordan. We critique selected features of her propositions regarding the constitution and display of authoritative knowledge systems and attendant power relationships by examining the forms that authoritative knowledge takes in birthing systems in Mexico, Texas, and Jamaica. We intend to contribute to the understanding of how authoritative knowledge is displayed at birth by focusing on (1) the relationship between the hierarchical distribution of knowledge about birth and reliance on technological intervention in labor and delivery; (2) the relative valuation of biomedical and alternative ways of knowing about birth in the three systems; and (3) the relationship between the expression of authoritative knowledge and authority positions—in particular, the implications of the distribution of power among pregnant women and those who assist them.

The concept of authoritative knowledge has received attention generally in anthropological research (Clifford 1986; Marcus and Fischer 1986) and, increasingly, from medical anthropologists engaged in the critical examination of the social production of knowledge (Kaufert and O'Neil 1993; Lindenbaum and Lock 1993; Rapp 1993; Young 1982). A central concern among these anthropologists has been the privileging of biomedicine as a realm of knowledge, separate from other cultural or social domains and perceived as objectively valid (Lock and Scheper-Hughes 1990; Rhodes 1990:160). Cultural analyses of biomedicine aim to contextualize biomedicine and reveal its historical, theoretical, and culturally constructed foundations (Martin 1987, 1991; Rhodes 1990). Correspondingly, the production of biomedical knowledge, and the legitimation of such knowledge as scientifically valid and authoritative, is itself a cultural process, appropriate for anthropological investigation (Lindenbaum and Lock 1993; Rhodes 1990).

The production and display of authoritative knowledge regarding birth has recently attracted particular interest, generated initially by Jordan's study of the production of authoritative knowledge in high-technology settings (Jordan [1978] 1993: chap. 6; 1994; see also chapter 1, this volume). In a detailed analysis of a birth occurring in a high-technology hospital, Jordan documents the priority accorded to technologically and procedurally based knowledge of the physician. Competing kinds of knowledge held by the woman or by other participants are judged irrelevant (Jordan [1978] 1993:152). Her focus is on how technology-dependent knowledge becomes hierarchically distributed ([1978] 1993:155), through social interaction among participants at birth. As a consequence of this process of interaction, technological knowledge becomes that knowledge which "counts," and on the basis of which decisions are made. In the United States, for example, most members of society accept a technomedical view of birth, including childbearing women, medical professionals, and lay persons (Jordan and Irwin 1989:19). In this and other high-technology birthing systems, there is a clear lack of priority allocated to the laboring woman's experience of her body as a form of knowledge, and primacy is given to the expertise of obstetricians who manage the technology or artifacts of labor (Jordan [1978] 1993:151).

Recently, Jordan's propositions regarding authoritative knowledge have been further explored, validated, and challenged by numerous researchers engaged in the study of the birth process (Davis-Floyd and Sargent, this volume). For example, research by Carolyn Sargent and Nancy Stark (1989) and Robbie Davis-Floyd (1994) concerning women's perspectives on technological intervention during birth in hospital births in the United States also indicates that women value the medicalization of birth. Indeed, many women prefer more, rather than less, medical intervention during delivery (see also McClain 1985). This research substantiates the conclusion that "most women willingly submit themselves to the authority of the medical view. . . . [T]hey manage to experience the technologies and procedures as reassuring and the delegation of authority to physicians as functioning in their own . . . best interests" (Jordan and Irwin 1989:20).

Jordan's analysis of authoritative knowledge emphasizes the importance of control of the technical procedures necessary to manage labor for defining who should be seen as legitimate decision makers during delivery ([1978] 1993:151). Following her argument, authoritative knowledge distinctly *does not* mean the knowledge of persons in positions of power and authority. Rather, what is of interest is how particular practices and reasonings are legitimized and reproduced within a "community of practice" ([1978] 1993:154) in specific social situations such as birth.

Our reanalysis of Jordan's propositions regarding authoritative knowledge employs three cases, each of which raises important issues concerning the determinants and display of authoritative knowledge. By means of these case studies in differing birthing systems, we examine the significance of control of technology and the relevance of status positions for determining the distribution of power among participants at birth. While Jordan argues that authoritative knowledge is possessed by those who control the artifacts necessary to accomplish the work, we argue that it is also contingent on shared experience and social position. We consider the extent to which authority entails some status or position that, as Starr argues, compels trust or obedience (1982:9). In addition, we debate whether the knowledge that "participants agree counts" is necessarily generated through social interaction (Jordan [1978] 1993:154), and we consider the forms that such social interaction may take. We also explore the variation in acceptable ways of knowing about birth—the validity of women's personal and experiential knowledge about labor in relation to the growing worldwide legitimacy of biomedical constructs of birth.

The settings for our discussion include a Maya village in Yucatan, Mexico; a public general hospital in Texas; and a public maternity hospital in Kingston, Jamaica. The Maya village of Yaxuna in the central Yucatan peninsula has a population of about four hundred and does not have a functioning clinic, resident doctor, or nurse. Most women deliver at home, attended by a lay midwife and family members. In urban Jamaica and Texas, home births are rare and almost all women deliver in hospitals. Most low-income women in these major metropolitan centers deliver in the two hospitals represented in our study. Both Memorial Hospital in Texas (a pseudonym) and Victoria Jubilee Hospital in Kingston target indigent populations and handle approximately fifteen thousand births annually. Details regarding the methodologies employed in each study will be discussed below.

HOME BIRTH IN YUCATAN

We begin with a discussion of childbirth among rural Maya in Mexico because Jordan's initial groundbreaking research was situated in a similar Maya community. We observe significant commonalities as well as some areas of divergence between Jordan's and our observations which warrant attention. Through our exploration of Maya childbirth, we assess the display of authoritative knowledge in a low-technology birthing system. We consider the extent to which those participating in a birth share or monopolize decision-making authority, the implications of technological interventions at birth for the distribution of power among those present, and the links between social status in the community and the right to claim authoritative knowledge.

Fieldwork on Maya childbirth was conducted in the spring of 1991 and 1992 and in the summer of 1994 in the community of Yaxuna. Yaxuna is a village of subsistence cultivators located twenty-nine kilometers from the highway on a dirt road. Village households are close-knit economic units, in which men and women perform complementary tasks. Married women carry significant authority within the home and may have independent control over their own economic endeavors, such as dressmaking or community gardening. Daughters remain in the home until marriage, at which time they enter the homes or spheres of influence of the husband's family.

Research on medical beliefs and practices in this community formed part of a broader baseline ethnographic survey conducted for the Yaxuna Archaeological Project.[1] Data collection included unstructured interviews with government health personnel in the surrounding villages concerning the organization of local health services, as well as interviews with the eighty-four women of reproductive age in the village. Of these women, twenty-four were postpuberty but unmarried. The rest were married, and all except six had children.

Unmarried women were interviewed regarding common health problems, sources of health care, and concepts of well-being. Women with children were interviewed concerning birth concepts and practices. Additional information regarding local health concerns was acquired during participation in medical consultations held by two volunteer physicians (an internist and a pediatrician) from the United States. One author (Bascope) observed eight women through their prenatal visits and deliveries and also attended postpartum consultations between new mothers and local midwives. She observed both village midwives who were then still practicing, in attendance at local births.

There is no doctor or nurse resident in Yaxuna, and the community has formally requested that the government assign a doctor there. Members of the community built a clinic with federal aid and communal labor, hoping to attract a permanent physician. However, the new clinic remains unstaffed, as the village population is held to be insufficient to warrant resident staff. Correspondingly, the primary birth attendants are local midwives. The nearest biomedical facility offering obstetric care is five kilometers from the village, in the town of Kancabzonot. Yaxuna women rarely travel to the Kancabzonot clinic to deliver except when emergencies arise during labor. In principle, a Social Security doctor and a Health Department doctor see patients in the village weekly, although their visits are often more irregular than the formal schedule would suggest. Babies are born at home unless complications are severe enough to warrant transferring the mother to the nearest towns. Home births are attended by one of two lay midwives, each in her mid-sixties.[2]

Over the past thirty-five years, Dona Lila, the most popular midwife in the village, has delivered at least one baby in virtually every home. Dona Lila was trained by her father-in-law, a respected shaman. Before becoming a midwife, she assisted other older women who were delivering babies in those days. Gradually she became the only person attending deliveries, and has practiced her specialty in the village and surrounding areas. She is said to have a gift, a special temperament to be a midwife, and she is said to have courage.

Her methodology has been witnessed by almost everyone, is widely shared, and has long since become the standard by which "correct" and "normal" births are judged. Her dynamic personality and the place of her family within the community buttress her authority. In contrast, the other practicing midwife, Dona Flora, is not perceived as having authoritative knowledge; her practices are viewed with skepticism and are not widely regarded as legitimate. Her personality and her family status within the village also contribute to this position.[3] Dona Lila is from a large and prominent family that contains most of the respected village elders to whom others defer in matters of ritual importance. The evident importance of family position in the community for the legitimacy of Dona Lila's views, in contrast to those of Dona Flora, leads us to suggest that control of technology does not necessarily underlie authoritative knowledge. Rather, shared experience—Dona Lila's three decades of visibility as a local midwife—and family status also may generate "knowledge that counts." Status may then become conflated with authority and expertise.

Dona Flora became a midwife about twenty years ago when her niece experienced a difficult labor. Dona Flora grabbed her niece by the hair of her head and pulled hard. The baby was born immediately and the mother quickly recovered. After that Dona Flora had a reputation as a midwife, although even persons who choose her as their birth attendant say she is not skilled. Some who choose her do so because Dona Lila is unavailable, or because Dona Flora is a close relative and kinship ties pose obligations. Dona Flora is from a small, socially isolated family within the village. She and her husband are considered to have difficult and contentious personalities, and her son is seen as scheming and untrustworthy. The rumors and horror stories that circulate about Dona Flora's inability to make appropriate diagnoses or to deliver proper treatment illustrate the links between family status, position in the community, past experience, and perceived authority.

To illustrate the authority displayed by the midwife relative to the laboring woman and other birth attendants, we describe two births in Yaxuna attended by Dona Lila. Each birth clarifies the extent to which control of technology underlies the midwife's authority at the birth and legitimizes her specialized expertise. The first case involves a mother experiencing her sixth delivery; the second case, a primiparous woman. We compare the roles of the participants at the delivery of the more experienced mother with the roles of those participating in the birth of the first-time mother. We focus on how the authoritative position of the midwife varies relative to the experience of the mother and describe the technical procedures employed at each birth.

At one delivery a multiparous woman, Dona Susi, was aided by her husband, the midwife, and the husband's mother, Dona Felicita. It was her sixth delivery; she had not experienced complications in her previous pregnancies or labors, and all the infants had appeared healthy at birth. Dona Susi had labored from morning until early afternoon. The midwife and Bascope were called by Dona Susi at about two o'clock. Two hours later, the baby was born. During this two-hour period, the attending adults did not give any advice to Dona Susi. Rather, those present, including Dona Susi, discussed affairs of the household and village events. They were, however, keenly aware of her body. At the start of a contraction, Dona Susi would assume the position preferred by Dona Lila, the midwife. Without discussion, the mother-in-law wiped her face and blew on her head and the husband supported her in her hammock. At such times, the conversation would turn to verbal encouragement and support. Dona Susi was thus physically surrounded by sympathetic birth attendants, as Jordan ([1978] 1993:36) describes in her portrayal of Maya birth.

Jordan ([1978] 1993:32) notes that for a first birth, when contractions become stronger and more frequent, talk turns to instruction for the inexperienced couple. For Dona Susi and her husband, this was unnecessary. The assumption was that they were knowledgeable about birth and that Dona Susi was competent to assess and comment on the state of her body, if necessary. Very little of the conversation throughout labor had to do with the birth process. At one point, the husband was admonished by Dona Lila for not covering all the holes in the walls to protect against dangerous winds. Other than this, Dona Lila primarily watched Dona Susi, asked her periodically how she felt, and checked her during contractions. At that time, she would stretch the vagina with her fingers, massage the vulva, and offer her opinion concerning the stage of labor. She also massaged the baby's head with olive oil when it crowned. She then received the baby, handed the baby to its grandmother, and waited for the delivery of the placenta, following which she tied and cut the cord. Finally, she bound the mother's abdomen and her forehead with cloth, stretched her on the hammock, and covered her with blankets.

Throughout the birth process, Dona Susi, the mother, remained in charge. None of the other adults chided her or gave her orders. At this birth, the midwife and other adults, including the laboring woman, shared equal knowledge regarding labor and appropriate delivery procedures. All the techniques employed here by Dona Lila may also be practiced by other experienced adult women. In this instance, the midwife's claim to authoritative knowledge is based less on her unique technological expertise (although she is valued for her role in cutting the cord, which others are reluctant to do) than on her reassurance as an observer. She is greatly respected for her participation in previous successful births, as she is held to have delivered half the population of the village. Her status as a member of the oldest family in the village, known to be trustworthy, discreet, and reliable, is remarked on and also enhances her credibility.

The second case involves Dona Nina, who was delivering her first child. She was in advanced labor by the time her mother, husband, and mother-in-law (also Dona Felicita, the mother-in-law of Dona Susi) called Dona Lila and the anthropologist (Bascope). She labored sitting up in her hammock, supported by her mother or husband who took turns behind her in a chair. From the beginning she was encouraged to bear down as much as possible (see Jordan [1978] 1993:38, for a similar description of early pushing). Dona Lila maintained her position seated on a six-inch-high stool, in front of Nina. During contractions she applied considerable pressure to the uterine fundus with one hand while trying to stretch the cervix with the other. She put warmed olive oil on her fingers to lubricate the baby's head so it could slip out. Nina's father arrived and took turns supporting her. The father or husband held Nina's legs out to the sides; then Dona Lila and the mother both pulled on the cervix and oiled the baby's head. Her father occasionally pulled on the cervix as well. (It is our impression that male intervention of this sort is very rare.) During contractions they told Nina to hold her breath as long as possible to aid in pushing and put their hands over her mouth to force her to hold her breath longer. She often fought them and tried to pull their hands away. Her mother also frequently blew on the top of Dona Nina's head during contractions.

Dona Lila gave Nina two shots of oxytocin, forty minutes apart. During and between contractions everyone chided and cajoled Nina to work harder. They said she was young and ignorant as this was her first baby. Nina remained completely quiet throughout the entire labor and delivery and was seldom consulted verbally. Her husband also remained quiet, only responding to the instructions of the relatives and midwife. For the last twenty minutes of contractions the husband stood behind Nina and bent over her. She was instructed to lock her fingers behind his neck and pull. Nina preferred to pull on a rope that had been tied on a pole over the hammock, but the others preferred that she hold her husband's neck and they prevailed.

When the baby was born Dona Lila blew into its mouth. When satisfied the baby was breathing, she handed it to Nina's mother. Dona Lila turned her attention to the delivery of the placenta. She pressed down on the fundus and exerted pressure on the cord until the placenta was delivered. She then cut the cord and molded the baby's head until she approved of its shape. She gave the new mother twenty drops of Baralgina (an analgesic) "for uterine pain" and told her to nurse the baby in about four hours when it began to cry but first to give it two teaspoons of water, as its lungs were dry.

In contrast to the first birth we described, we see in this case that the laboring woman, Dona Nina, was not consulted regarding her preferences or feelings or asked to assess the progress of her labor. The explanation for her marginalized position and the dominant role of the other adults present was her ignorance as a first-time mother. The value attributed to the laboring woman's sense of her body as a form of knowledge thus is associated with birth experience. At this birth, Dona Lila offered more instruction than at the first birth, but she shared responsibility with Dona Nina's older relatives. The midwife's special expertise appears to lie in the provision of the oxytocin injection.

With regard to the innovative oxytocin injections, it is important to note that any of the helpers attending a birth may work to achieve the same objective as that sought with the oxytocin—to accelerate labor—by pushing on the fundus or stretching the cervix. To date, only Dona Lila gives shots and her social standing as representative of a politically important family and respected midwife appears to justify her claim to this practice. In 1990, Dona Lila, of her own accord, had adopted the use of oxytocin injections to accelerate labor. This intervention was borrowed from a practitioner in a neighboring village who is not a doctor but once was a salesman for a pharmaceutical company. Dona Lila began to use oxytocin after she broke her wrist and felt she no longer had the grip or strength needed in her practice to expedite labor by pushing on the fundus or stretching the cervical os. Oxytocin enabled her to continue with her work by substituting the injection for physical strength.

Through the retired drug salesman, the community has become familiar with a small battery of drugs. Oxytocin appears to have been adopted by the midwife and accepted by local women because its function (as interpreted by the drug salesman) corresponded to widespread notions of how labor should progress and what interventions may be necessary. Oxytocin easily fit into the preexisting understanding that labor may need to be accelerated. This may be accomplished by any experienced adult by pushing on the fundus, stretching the cervix, or by means of oxytocin injections. Local women and midwives share the notion that a rapid delivery is much to be desired as birth is a dangerous time. The sooner it is over, the less time the mother and child are exposed to risk.[4]

While we describe Yaxuna birthing practices as low technology, the local midwives have recently been introduced to biomedical obstetrical procedures recommended by the government public health authorities. In the summer of 1991, both midwives went through a traditional midwife training course given by the Social Security doctor in the next village. Bascope's interviews with the midwives and her observations of eight women during labor and delivery suggest that the midwives have not altered their obstetric practices as a result of the training session. Correspondingly, they have not enhanced their position of authority or augmented the public perception of their authoritative knowledge by means of this training.[5]

To summarize, in Yaxuna, Maya married women share widespread understandings of the process of labor and of possible interventions considered beneficial during delivery. This low-technology birthing system may be categorized as collaborative, a system in which authoritative knowledge is broadly distributed. However, personal experience clearly plays a part in the right to claim competence regarding birth practices. Thus a young, inexperienced mother was subordinated to the authority of more knowledgeable adults, foremost among whom was the midwife. At the delivery of the more experienced mother, all the individuals displayed shared notions of the appropriate procedures to follow. All of them, including the mother, informed the anthropologist of what was happening. Because there is only minimal application of specialized technical procedures during delivery, the midwife's authority does not rest solely or primarily on a monopoly of technological expertise. Rather, Dona Lila's claim to authoritative knowledge derives from the respect resulting from her past successes and her position as a member of a family holding high status in the community.[6]

HOSPITAL BIRTH IN TEXAS

Jordan argues that authoritative knowledge is produced through social interaction. Yet this fails to take into account preexisting patterns of authority—hierarchies that shape the way the interaction takes place. With this Texas example, we show an instance in which women submit to a highly technological way of birth, not through negotiation, but through preexisting, shared assumptions regarding the distribution of authoritative knowledge that are silently reinforced. In this discussion of women's experiences with cesarean delivery in a public hospital in Texas, we explore how authoritative knowledge is sustained and reproduced through the silent interactions among patients and physicians. We also document the devaluation of women's ways of knowing about birth and the reinforcing of biomedical knowledge. Finally, we conclude, as did Jordan, that control of technology is linked to decision-making authority surrounding birth. Hospitalized women acknowledged the authority of physicians and respected their expert grasp of high technology, but they contested their exclusion from any dialogue with doctors and nurses.

In this section, we describe women's highly medicalized birth experiences within a particularly medicalized system. Within the hospital birthing system characteristic of the United States, cesarean section—surgical birth—represents the ultimate technological intervention. Accordingly, cesarean delivery is an event that provides information on the display of authoritative knowledge in a high-technology birthing system. As elsewhere in the United States, childbirth in Texas has become increasingly medicalized (Sargent and Stark 1989) so that reliance on technological intervention during labor and delivery represents the norm rather than the exception. Perhaps the most striking feature of the increasing medicalization of birth nationally is the cesarean section rate, 24.7 percent in 1988, and in general, Texas urban institutions reflect this pattern. Memorial Hospital has in recent years had a cesarean rate of about 17 percent, in contrast to local private hospitals where rates are as high as 30 percent (Sargent and Stark 1987, 1989). Our study at Memorial Hospital, conducted in 1986–1987, focused on women who had undergone cesarean delivery, to explore their experience of this high-technology system.

Structured interview schedules exploring women's knowledge about their cesarean, the nature of their interactions and negotiations with biomedical personnel, and the distribution of decision-making authority during their hospital birth experience were administered in Spanish by one of the authors (Bascope) during the three- to five-day hospitalization of the women in the sample. We interviewed thirty-three Hispanic women, some of whom were born in the United States or in Mexico and a few of whom were newly arrived from other Central American countries. We categorized these women together as "Hispanic" (although we recognize the problematic aspects of classifying women of varying ethnicity as one sample; see Quesada 1976; Schreiber and Homiak 1981) because each of them asked that her interview be conducted in Spanish given that limited English significantly affected her ability to communicate with hospital personnel. Several women cried upon realizing that the interviewer spoke Spanish, expressing their desperation to find someone with whom they could communicate.

Interviews with these women led us to suggest that their birth experiences—for example, their interactions with doctors and nurses and the women's potential for influencing such interactions—were especially structured by their limited English. We also suggest that language limitations particularly constrained these women from participating in decision making during labor and delivery. In addition, most women shared notions of physiology and associated birth hazards that were not accepted in biomedicine. Thus the women's understandings of the birth process and their interpretations of body functioning were devalued by doctors and nurses. Perhaps the most striking feature of our encounters with these women is the lack of information or understanding they possessed concerning their birth experience. Because of their minimal English, most women had almost no interactions with hospital staff that the women perceived as satisfactory and comprehensible. Although the hospital employs interpreters, they may not be available for every patient. When Spanish-speaking personnel are unavailable, bilingual patients are sometimes asked to interpret, with varying degrees of success. As one woman observed, "When I had a roommate who spoke Spanish and English, the doctors and everyone would talk to me through her. Now nobody tries since I have a new roommate."

The problems women experienced as a result of language constraints ranged from discomfort at the inability to convey their needs or concerns to serious misunderstandings. For example: "They [the nurses] do everything fast and a little short because we can't talk to them"; "If you don't speak English they don't treat you well." Most patients had little knowledge of why they delivered by cesarean or were misinformed about the future implications of the cesarean birth. One woman explained that no one told her why she had a cesarean; she assumed it was because her first child was premature, born at seven months. Several women feared they would never really return to normal again, that they would be weakened and debilitated by the surgery, unable to exercise or do routine work.

All women in this sample accepted the authoritative position of doctors and nurses and expressed confidence in their technical expertise. In this regard, Jordan's proposition that authoritative knowledge rests on control of technology (the "artifacts of birth") receives support. However, the women's inability to participate in decision making, to discuss, challenge, or agree with hospital staff, leads us to amend the notion that the hierarchical distribution of knowledge is produced through social interaction. The experiences of these women suggest that the status of the doctors, the respect in which they are held, and the dependency that women experience when taken to surgery with only minimal information all contribute to the authoritative position of biomedical specialists and the devaluation of women's personal experience of their body. Thus the silent participation of these women confirms the preexistent hierarchy of knowledge regarding birth.

These women, although silenced, should not be assumed to acquiesce in their exclusion from social interaction. They accepted the ultimate authority of the hospital and acknowledged without challenge the authoritative expertise of physicians. However, they protested their inability to participate in the events surrounding their birth—to obtain information, to express opinions, or to seek alternative decisions. When able to communicate in Spanish, women immediately had numerous unanswered questions and provided opinions regarding their condition that they would have liked to convey earlier. For instance, one woman thought she might have had a tubal ligation at the time of her cesarean but had never been able to ascertain whether this had occurred. She asked the anthropologist to get this information for her. Another believed her cesarean was due to a fall in her fifth month of pregnancy. She had spent anxious months waiting to deliver after the accident, and as she had never received an explanation for her surgery, she continued to assume the cesarean was the consequence of injuring her abdomen. She was also concerned about having injured the baby as well. The health of the baby was an issue for her because he seemed to avoid light as if his eyes hurt and often vomited when he was fed. She had been unable to question the nurse about the baby's well-being and requested that the interviewer speak to the nurse on her behalf.

A twenty-three-year-old patient reported her situation as follows: "I got an infection in my vagina two days before delivery—blisters that burned very much. Now I have an infection in the scar. It's not related to the one in the vagina, that one has been cured. They gave me no information [about why the cesarean was necessary]. I only found out minutes before delivery."

For some women, the inaccessibility of important information generated serious anxiety. While they had confidence that doctors or nurses possessed the answers to their questions, they had no access to these sources of authority. For example, one mother had been unable to see her baby by the third postpartum day and had not been informed of where or how the baby was. She said, "Only today (third day postpartum) at 2:00 P.M. did I get to see the baby. I don't know why they don't bring the baby to me. I want to feed it and my breasts are getting very hard and painful." She solicited the anthropologist's assistance in translating her questions to the nursing staff. Eventually it became clear that the mother had an infection. Because of this, she had not been able to hold her baby and had not been taken to see the baby for the first time until that afternoon. Another woman, suffering from an infection in her incision, was worried and confused about her slow recovery and distressed about her delivery experience. She explained that no one paid any attention to her in labor. She was especially confused by the atmosphere in the delivery room, where the doctors listened to very loud music (which seemed to her characteristic of a party but inappropriate for a hospital) during her cesarean.

The marginalization of these woman from their birth experience generated a widespread sense of lack of knowledge. While the physician's right to authoritative knowledge was assumed, the women felt unable to access or to communicate pertinent information. Every patient interviewed desired more information about the reasons for cesarean delivery, the process of surgery, or the course of recovery. Those women who had previous births outside the United States were particularly unprepared for birth in a large, complex teaching hospital, where their interactions with those attending the birth were so limited. One woman from El Salvador explained on her third postpartum day that she had no idea how long her hospital stay was supposed to last as she spoke no English and could not ask anyone. She had a young child at home whom she needed to care for, and she worried about her own state of health. Like this woman, most of the cesarean patients were disturbed by their inability to understand what had happened to them and its consequences for their health.

Many shared the notion that after a normal birth the vagina was "open," enabling the placenta, blood, and any other retained materials to be expelled. They were concerned that they might be retaining harmful products that should have been discharged. They were unable to convey this anxiety in the absence of receptive, Spanish-speaking medical staff. Thus they were unable to communicate knowledge that they considered valid about their own physiology, to which hospital staff were indifferent.[7] In this regard, our research confirms that of Ellen Lazarus (1988a, 1988b), who documents the impact of language constraints on Puerto Rican women using prenatal services in a major metropolitan area hospital. She observes that "for Puerto Rican women who did not speak English the language barrier contributed to a lack of clinical communication and led to frustration on the part of both the women and clinicians. Important information about perinatal health care and therapeutics was not imparted, and this added considerably to patients' stress" (1988a:41).

The lack of Spanish-speaking doctors and nurses or other interpreters on the labor ward and in the operating room prevented many of these women from even minimal interaction with hospital staff, and certainly prevented them from discussing the course of their labor or their preferences regarding technological interventions at the birth. However, these women were not challenging the authoritative knowledge of the doctors and nurses attending them. Indeed, the major complaint of these women was not the cesarean delivery as technological intervention but the silence surrounding it.[8]

How do the experiences of these women inform our understanding of the decision-making process and of the display of authoritative knowledge at deliveries in a major public hospital? Jordan has said ([1978] 1993:154) that by "authoritative knowledge" she specifically does not mean the knowledge of people in authority positions but rather an "interactionally grounded notion." Based on her argument, we ask to what extent authoritative knowledge about birth in this setting is shared by the participants and produced in the process of social interaction during delivery. Our research suggests that in some cases authoritative knowledge is embedded in positions of authority. Particularly in the case of a surgical birth, patients are dependent on the technological expertise and knowledge of the doctors in attendance (Sargent and Stark 1987, 1989). In cesarean births, control of the technological artifacts of birth, vested in the status of the doctor, most clearly underlie the unique claim to authoritative knowledge.

As Lazarus argues, the "control of medical knowledge, technical procedures, and rules of behavior, as well as control of patients' access to and understanding of information on which treatment decisions are made, creates a world of power for the medical profession" (1988a:45). Patient access to the "technologically- and procedurally-based knowledge" described by Jordan ([1978] 1993:152) as key to authoritative knowledge, is especially problematic where patients do not speak the dominant language and are placed in situations of extreme dependency. The inevitable dependency of the surgical patient is heightened, as their limited English skills prevent them from participation in decision making during labor or even from sustaining dialogue. Women we interviewed were not only unable to assert their preferences concerning the management of their birth or to negotiate decisions regarding technological interventions, they were literally unable to interact at all. The production, possession, and display of knowledge of any sort is a product of the capacity to participate in interactions with doctors and nursing staff. These women accepted that specialized knowledge and expertise are vested in the position of the physician (see also Lazarus 1988b for similar perspectives in a Puerto Rican sample). However, once their silence could be broken in the interview context, they did protest their lack of access to information concerning the causes and consequences of the cesarean and their inability to effectively communicate anxieties associated with cultural concepts of physiology to hospital personnel.

HOSPITAL BIRTH IN JAMAICA

In this section, we explore the linkages between control of technical procedures, authority positions, and the display of authoritative knowledge among those participating in hospital births in Kingston, Jamaica. We show that women have increasingly turned to hospital-based government nurse-midwives for authoritative knowledge regarding birth as lay midwifery has been eliminated. Currently, the lay midwife, or *nana,* previously a significant source of expert knowledge, is rarely an option for birth assistance. However, the public hospital system has experienced problematic budgetary cutbacks related to the decline of the Jamaican economy. In consequence, the hospital labor and delivery service has progressively deteriorated. We suggest that women continue to rely on an increasingly dysfunctional hospital maternity system because they value the authoritative knowledge of biomedical specialists. We discuss the relationship between reliance on the technological expertise of physicians and nurse-midwives and their important role as repositories of knowledge that "counts." We also consider the extent to which alternative ways of knowing, for example, knowledge derived from one's body, which is respected and acknowledged in lay midwifery, are acknowledged in Jamaican biomedicine or by women themselves during labor.

Between 1987 and 1989 we conducted research in Kingston, the capital of Jamaica, regarding the use of prenatal care and delivery services provided at the primary maternity hospital on the island, Victoria Jubilee Hospital. This hospital, like its Texas counterpart, targets an indigent population and handles about fifteen thousand births per year. As part of the research,[9] 225 women who were patients at the hospital and 50 women in a low-income Kingston neighborhood were interviewed for a retrospective analysis of their birth experiences.

Through the birth stories of these women, we examine their participation in decision making during labor and delivery in an urban metropolitan hospital. Birth in Jamaica has become highly medicalized over the past century (Sargent and Rawlins 1992), during which time Jamaica moved from a lay midwife–assisted, home delivery–based birthing system to one characterized by medicalized hospital births where nurse-midwives are the primary caregivers. Doctors serve as resources for particularly complicated deliveries. With the government-sponsored eradication of lay midwifery in urban areas, women have come to view birth as requiring medical supervision in a hospital setting. The nana, once an important authority figure respected for her specialized knowledge, is no longer an urban resource. Rather, low-income urban women turn to the public hospital in search of competent assistance during labor and delivery.

Based on extensive discussions with neighborhood women together with structured interviews with women in the prenatal clinics and postpartum ward at Victoria Jubilee Hospital, we have elicited a widely shared construction of birth as a condition requiring expert medical supervision. Although pregnancy is not usually considered a pathological state and many women do not follow the schedule for prenatal visits, women do seek a knowledgeable assistant at delivery, preferably in a hospital context. The "expert" is usually the certified midwife.

Women interviewed at the hospital and at home who delivered at Victoria Jubilee Hospital expressed strong dissatisfaction with their birth experiences resulting from limited and negative interactions with the nurse-midwives. Approximately 65 percent of women who delivered at Jubilee in 1987 were unattended at the time of the birth (Sargent and Rawlins 1991:184). They labored and delivered alone in their rooms. No relatives or friends were allowed to stay with the mothers during labor, and nurse-midwives were often unavailable. Unattended births at the hospital have been associated with increasing maternal morbidity and mortality from "avoidable factors," for example, delays in response to complications such as bleeding and seizures (Samuels 1987:59). Neighborhood women are increasingly aware of the hazards of unattended births; knowledge of complications occurring among friends and acquaintances is supplemented by periodic newspaper accounts of especially dramatic maternal or infant mortality cases at Jubilee.

A combination of factors, including staff and supply shortages and hospital budget shortages, are implicated in the frequency of unattended births. Fundamentally, the crisis is both a consequence of the current decline in the Jamaican economy (Sargent and Harris 1992) and the product of a century of efforts to eradicate lay midwifery, with no concomitant priority placed on developing a viable hospital birth system for women in urban areas of Jamaica. The deterioration of the Jamaican economy, which has accompanied World Bank–supported structural adjustment policies, has led to cutbacks in health services, in salaries of health professionals, and in provisioning of hospitals. This budgetary retrenchment has generated many of the problems experienced by patients delivering at Jubilee.

During one visit to the Jubilee labor and delivery ward, we observed laboring women lined up in the hall, waiting to be examined by the nurse-midwife and the doctor in a central examining room. Women sat or reclined on wooden benches, waiting for their turn. They were seen by place in line rather than stage of labor. The relative assertion of authority was evident in the tone and volume of the doctor's voice, which overrode the woman's speech during her examination. The twenty-eight-bed wards were often crowded, with one nurse for as many as sixteen patients. In spite of the limited contact with a nurse-midwife or doctor, women report that they do not usually turn to each other for assistance during labor or when unattended at the moment of delivery, although they did establish conversations and help one another with infant care in the postpartum ward.

In addition to staff shortages and lack of supplies and medicines, women perceived that the nurse-midwives with whom they did have contact mistreated them, or "handled them rough." In the opinion of these women, their ill-treatment resulted from their unfavorable status as low-income or indigent patients. Retrospective birth histories obtained from neighborhood women gave a sense of the experience of interacting with nurse-midwives at this hospital. Numerous mothers in the neighborhood described hostile encounters with nurses who disputed their assessment that they needed help or were ready to deliver. The women's interpretations of the course of their labor and their needs were consistently ignored or mocked by the nurse-midwives on duty. This devaluation of the women's knowledge about their bodies was clearly disturbing to them. But while women criticized the behavior and attitudes of the nurse-midwives at Jubilee, they also felt dependent on them in case of an "emergency," when medical expertise would be required to "save" them.

The devaluation of women's knowledge about their bodies by nurse-midwives signifies the distribution of authority at hospital births. The nurse-midwife, rather than the laboring woman, has knowledge that counts. This may be problematic for women who draw on ethnophysiology to inform their understanding of the birth process. For example, in our fieldwork and that of Sheila Kitzinger conducted in the 1960s in Jamaica, we found that humoral theory and the concept of movable organs located in the torso influenced women's notions of body functioning (see also

MacCormack and Draper 1987:159–160). Women may fear that the uterus can come up out of the belly into the mother's chest and choke her. Kitzinger (1982) points out that when women feel the expulsive urge at the end of the first stage of labor, this may be experienced as a catch in the throat and an involuntarily held breath, interpreted by many women as an indication of dangerous organ movement. Women delivering in the hospital find that they do not receive reassurance from the nurse-midwife that the baby is not coming up. In contrast, during a home birth, the lay midwife would reassure the laboring woman that her uterus was not working up to her chest (Kitzinger 1982:199).

Given the likelihood of an unattended delivery or at best the brief attendance of a midwife, we questioned why women would deliver at the hospital at all. Conditions described by mothers suggested to us that women would avoid the hospital at all costs. Many mothers described lying unattended in the hospital, yelling for the nurse-midwife, who would finally arrive, only to say "Shut your mouth, mother, you're not ready yet" (field notes 1987). Others complained of being ignored, criticized, or slapped by staff. One woman, Nadia, whose three children were born at Jubilee, said the nurses tell you not to call until you push the baby out. She complained that she had no sheets, although her bed had previously been occupied by a madwoman with skin sores. It is significant that no one complained of excessive (or any) interventions during the birth. Because of the deteriorating hospital budget and consequent shortages of personnel and supplies, none of the women experienced episiotomies, pain medication, forceps delivery, or other impositions of technology that have been available in previous years. Correspondingly, the hospital had under a 3 percent cesarean rate. Thus it would seem unlikely that women seek to deliver in the hospital because of reliance on technological procedures that are only accessible in a medical setting.

However, neighborhood women interviewed on this subject as well as those interviewed at the hospital prenatal clinic and postpartum wards expressed strong feelings of doubt and anxiety regarding their safety and survival should they attempt a home birth. As a consequence of the explicit health policy generated by British officials and dating from the early colonial period, home deliveries assisted by lay midwives are now almost unknown in Kingston (Sargent and Rawlins 1992), although lay midwives still function in some rural parishes. Thus young women interviewed in Kingston possessed little knowledge about the practices of the nana or about means to enhance reproductive health more generally. However, urban home deliveries attended by nurse-midwives were not uncommon until the 1970s, and women in their fifties and sixties reported in detail on their own experiences with the nana who attended them or whose practice they had observed. The nana had clearly been a source of specialized and authoritative knowledge for the women she served.

Miss Dottie, whose grandmother was a nana, described how the nana would stay with the new mother for nine days following the delivery. In addition to assisting at the delivery, the nana advised the mother on important matters such as how to avoid postpartum complications. "Baby cold," a postpartum affliction caused by humoral imbalance, was a particular concern of newly delivered women, who relied on the knowledge of the nana for its prevention. One older woman, Miss Mac, said that young women no longer fear baby cold, thinking that they've "dried up" following the delivery. These mothers will have problems later, due to the absence of an authority to remind them of appropriate behavior in the month following the birth. Miss Mac recalled how on the ninth day following birth the nana would dress the baby and then take the mother and baby out the door and around the yard, saying, "Now you free, you can wash clothes and care for the baby."

In this way, the nana was responsible for (re)introducing the mother to everyday life and for making the transition from the dangerous period of the birth and postpartum to daily routine. Kitzinger describes a similar role for the nana based on her 1965 fieldwork. She states that "the nana has a central and vitally important role in shepherding those involved through the drama of what is essentially the re-birth of a woman as a mother" (1982:194). Thus for those in urban areas the absence of the nana represents the loss of an authoritative figure with specialized knowledge to take responsibility for decision making at birth and during the postpartum period.

The perspective of women currently of reproductive age regarding home delivery is encapsulated in the remarks of one woman to whom hospital delivery seemed a necessity: "You could die if you stayed home," she said. The sense of dependency on the hospital is evident in the following description of how neighborhood women responded to an unexpected home birth. When one woman in the research neighborhood delivered at home after a precipitous labor, she and other women involved were distraught at the idea that the delivery would occur at home, without "help." In this incident, Anne was unable to find transportation to the hospital before she was ready to deliver. The neighbors reported that they heard cries (some thought a man was beating his wife) and they came to gawk at the door. No one knew what to do. On the advice of the neighbor across the street, Anne's mother sent for the community clinic nurse, who arrived shortly after the delivery (field notes July 1987).

The new mother, her mother, and their neighbors concurred that no one today knows how to manage a delivery; the knowledge of the nana has been lost altogether. As one woman said, "You need to deliver in hospital to have the nurse push out the afterbirth and cut the navel string." The consensus was that only doctors and nurse-midwives "know" about birth. Thus biomedicine retains a monopoly on authoritative knowledge, and the maternity hospital, even in the absence of doctors, nurse-midwives, and technology, is the place for delivery.

Recent efforts by the government of Jamaica to decentralize the over-burdened maternity care system by encouraging women to deliver at neighborhood clinics and to return home within a few hours have met with hesitation and wariness among local women. Most urban women are convinced of the legitimacy of knowledge thought to be monopolized by doctors and nurse-midwives (Wedderburn and Moore 1990). However, although authoritative knowledge and associated decision making are held to be the purview of hospital staff, neighborhood women expressed a desire for a more collaborative role for themselves, in which they would participate more fully in decisions during labor, indicating to medical staff their own sense of the course of labor (such as readiness to push) and their needs for assistance.

CONCLUSION

In our examination of the concept of authoritative knowledge elaborated by Jordan, we suggest that in a collaborative and low-technology birthing system such as that in Yaxuna the midwife and other adult women share general knowledge about birth. The midwife demonstrates minimal technical expertise that distinguishes her from other women, such as her cord-cutting technique and the recent adoption of oxytocin injections. However, her authority resides primarily in her history as an observer and participant at many successful births and in her family status. Given that birth technology is broadly shared among village adults, family status is especially relevant in defining the midwife's claim to influence decision making. In this regard, the midwife is the repository of cultural authority, a greater among equals. The credibility of her family and their reputation in the community enhance her own position as a reliable midwife. Thus she is operating from a position that "compels trust or obedience" (Starr 1982:9).

Jordan ([1978] 1993:152) states that equally legitimate, parallel knowledge systems may exist, where people move easily between them, although frequently one kind of knowledge gains ascendance. In this birthing system, the technical expertise of the midwife, that of other adult women, and the laboring mother's knowledge of her body are all valued. However, it is the experienced mother whose sense of her body is credited while the first-time mother is expected to follow the advice of more experienced women.

Women delivering in public hospitals in Texas and Jamaica demonstrate similarities in the hierarchical distribution of knowledge and in the devaluation of authoritative knowledge based on women's experience of their bodies. In both instances, knowledge that "counts" was that of physicians, nurses, and nurse-midwives. The Spanish-speaking women interviewed in Texas did not dispute this prioritizing of biomedical expertise or the value of technological interventions. They were not critical of the dominant role played by their physician in decision making during labor: they did not complain about their failure to negotiate the use of technological procedures during labor or display skepticism about the need for surgery. The concerns they expressed following their cesarean deliveries dealt with their marginalization from any social interaction surrounding the birth and their lack of information regarding the decision to perform a cesarean.

The inability to speak English and the lack of translators prevented them from obtaining information necessary to understand the basis for the cesarean. Following the surgery, they were unable to communicate with hospital staff concerning their state of health and the baby's well-being. Their interpretation of labor or understanding of the implications of the cesarean were unsolicited, and they were effectively marginalized from any meaningful interaction with medical personnel. Silenced throughout their hospitalization, they submitted to a high-technology system in which they shared preexisting assumptions with physicians regarding the distribution of authoritative knowledge.

The Jamaican case involves a formerly high-technology birthing system that is increasingly dysfunctional. This case suggests that while technological intervention is much less frequent than in the highly medicalized system in Texas, knowledge derived from bodily experience is equally suppressed. In Jamaica, as in Texas, authoritative knowledge resides in positions of power. However, in the Jamaican hospital, although nurse-midwives and doctors monopolize knowledge and decision making, they are unable to operationalize their technological expertise or to follow hospital procedures routinized prior to the current budget crisis. Nevertheless, authoritative knowledge remains embedded in certain statuses even in the absence of technological intervention. In urban Jamaica, the elimination of a once-flourishing tradition of lay midwifery and home delivery has generated the widespread belief that hospital births are obligatory. Nurse-midwives and doctors are believed to be the repositories of knowledge necessary to ensure safe births. While women recognize that many hospital births are unattended and technology unavailable, they nonetheless defer to the superior competence of hospital personnel and the symbolic safety of the hospital itself. Nurse-midwives and doctors retain a monopoly on authoritative knowledge, even in the absence of supplies, equipment, and medicines—the "artifacts" of birth.

The cross-cultural comparisons presented above constitute a response to Jordan's call for a rethinking of authoritative knowledge and a reassessment of the social factors shaping it. These cases validate Jordan's earlier argument by illustrating the demeaning of alternative forms of knowledge in biomedical systems in the United States and in Jamaica. In the Maya birthing system, in contrast, the authoritative knowledge generated by a woman's accumulated experiences of birth is highly valued. While Jordan has specified that by authoritative knowledge she does not mean "the knowledge of people in authority positions" ([1978] 1993:154), in this chapter we extend her argument to suggest that the constitution of authoritative knowledge also reflects the distribution of power within a social group.

The authoritative knowledge of the physicians and nurse-midwives in these examples derives from the social position of the practitioner and has its basis in the legitimacy of the profession and in its claim to generate and control authoritative knowledge. While it is important to document the production of authoritative knowledge in a given encounter, as Jordan has done, we see in the preceding cases that authoritative knowledge is not only re-created through discourse but also is embedded in the status of physicians and midwives and in the cultural authority of medicine—or midwifery—prior to the specific medical event.

The important issue Jordan raises regarding the extent to which control of technology lays claim to authoritative knowledge is elaborated in the example of Maya midwifery, where we see that technological knowledge is not highly differentiated; in the Texas case, where control of technology and authoritative knowledge are congruent; and most significantly, in the Jamaican case, which serves as a reminder that the cultural authority of biomedicine may persist even without the technology that once defined it.

NOTES

1. This research formed part of the multifaceted Yaxuna Archaeological Project, financed by the Selz Foundation, the National Endowment for the Humanities, and the National Geographic Society.

2. In Jordan's (1993) description of Maya midwifery, she also observes that the Yucatecan system relies on formal instruction only during the actual birth. Even so, this instruction is delivered collaboratively by all participants to the new mother and father, not by a single authoritative expert. Like Dona Lila in Yaxuna, the midwife whose work Jordan describes is from a large family and is the daughter of a midwife, suggesting that family status may also be a factor in the achievement of

a successful practice. The midwife Jordan (1993:31) discusses employs more objects and equipment than does Dona Lila. However, Jordan notes that "the midwife's opinion carries considerable weight but even such 'professional' decisions as giving the woman an injection to speed up labor emerge through a process of joint weighing of the evidence of the course of labor so far" ([1978] 1993:87).

3. Similarly, Browner shows that in a Chinantec community in Oaxaca, knowledge about birth is broadly distributed throughout the population. The status of local midwives appears to depend more on personal characteristics than on specialized skills.

4. The drug salesman, a trusted member of the community for many years, is valued as an accessible source of oxytocin. He has been able to provide the midwives with this product in spite of the fact that the Social Security doctor is strongly opposed to its use. However, the doctor commented that while the training he conducted had not altered the performance of the midwives, infants and mothers were not dying of birth complications. The midwives were competently attending uncomplicated deliveries.

5. In the larger Maya village where Jordan conducted research, with a small hospital and resident biomedical personnel, the midwife appears to have had greater access to biomedical knowledge and techniques. She had also undergone a more sophisticated training session and had modified her practice accordingly (Jordan [1978] 1993:31, 1989).

6. See Faust 1993 for similar conclusions with respect to midwives in Campeche.

7. Browner (1985:105) describes similar beliefs regarding the danger of undischarged menstrual blood, which can lead to serious illness; and Hahn and Muecke (1987:153) note the concern of Mexican-American women that improper disposal of the afterbirth could endanger the newborn.

8. Since this research was conducted, the hospital has expanded its interpreting services to better address communication problems (Hospital Chaplain pers. com. 1993).

9. This research was financed by National Science Foundation grant BNS-8703627 and by the International Center for Research on Women through Cooperative Agreement DAN-1010-A-00-7061-00 with the Offices of Nutrition and Health of the U.S. Agency for International Development. The research addressed parents' strategies for child health, prenatal care and hospital utilization among low-income women, and knowledge and use of medicinal plants for reproductive and child health.

REFERENCES

Browner, Carole
  1985   "Traditional Techniques for Diagnosis, Treatment, and Control of Pregnancy in Cali, Colombia." In *Women's Medicine*, ed. Lucille Newman, 99–125. New Brunswick: Rutgers University Press.
  1989   "The Management of Reproduction in an Egalitarian Society." In *Women as Healers*, ed. Carol McClain, 58–73. New Brunswick: Rutgers University Press.

Clifford, James
    1986   "Introduction: Partial Truths." In *Writing Culture: The Poetics and Politics of Ethnography,* ed. James Clifford and George E. Marcus, 1–27. Berkeley: University of California Press.

Davis-Floyd, Robbie
    1992   *Birth as an American Rite of Passage.* Berkeley: University of California Press.
    1994   "The Technocratic Body: American Childbirth as Cultural Expression." *Social Science and Medicine* 38(8):1125–1140.

Faust, Betty, B.
    1993   "When Is a Midwife a Witch? A Case Study from a Modernizing Maya Village." Paper presented at the annual meeting of the American Anthropological Association, Washington, D.C.

Hahn, Robert, and Marjorie A. Muecke
    1987   "The Anthropology of Birth in Five U.S. Ethnic Populations: Implications for Obstetrical Practice." *Current Problems in Obstetrics, Gynecology and Fertility,* no. 4. Chicago: Year Book Medical Publishers.

Jordan, Brigitte
    [1978] 1993   *Birth in Four Cultures: A Cross-Cultural Investigation of Childbirth in Yucatan, Holland, Sweden and the United States.* 4th ed. Prospect Heights, Ill.: Waveland Press.
    1989   "Cosmopolitical Obstetrics: Some Insights from the Training of Traditional Midwives." *Social Science and Medicine* 28(9):925–944.

Jordan, Brigitte, and Susan Irwin
    1989   "The Ultimate Failure: Court-Ordered Cesarean Section." In *New Approaches to Human Reproduction,* ed. Linda Whiteford and Marilyn Poland, 13–24. Boulder, Colo.: Westview Press.

Kaufert, Patricia, and John O'Neil
    1993   "Analysis of a Dialogue on Risks in Childbirth: Clinicians, Epidemiologists, and Inuit Women." In *Knowledge, Power and Practice: The Anthropology of Medicine and Everyday Life,* ed. Shirley Lindenbaum and Margaret Lock, 32–55. Berkeley: University of California Press.

Kitzinger, Sheila
    1982   "The Social Context of Birth: Some Comparisons between Childbirth in Jamaica and Britain." In *Ethnography of Fertility and Birth,* ed. Carol MacCormack, 181–205. London: Academic Press.

Lazarus, Ellen
    1988a   "Theoretical Considerations for the Study of the Doctor-Patient Relationship: Implications of a Perinatal Study." *Medical Anthropology Quarterly* 2(1):34–57.
    1988b   "Poor Women, Poor Outcomes: Social Class and Reproductive Health." In *Childbirth in America,* ed. Karen L. Michaelson, 39–55. South Hadley, Mass.: Bergin and Garvey.

Lindenbaum, Shirley, and Margaret Lock
    1993   Preface. In *Knowledge, Power and Practice: The Anthropology of Medicine and Everyday Life,* ed. Shirley Lindenbaum and Margaret Lock. Berkeley: University of California Press.

Lock, Margaret, and Nancy Scheper-Hughes
  1990   "A Critical-Interpretive Approach in Medical Anthropology: Rituals and Routines of Discipline and Dissent." In *Medical Anthropology: A Handbook of Theory and Method,* ed. Thomas Johnson and Carolyn Sargent, 47–73. Westport, Conn.: Greenwood Press.

MacCormack, Carol, and Alizon Draper
  1987   "Social and Cognitive Aspects of Female Sexuality in Jamaica." In *The Cultural Construction of Sexuality,* ed. Pat Caplan, 143–165. London: Tavistock.

Marcus, George E., and Michael M. J. Fischer
  1986   *Anthropology as Cultural Critique.* Chicago: University of Chicago Press.

Martin, Emily
  1987   *The Woman in the Body: A Cultural Analysis of Reproduction.* Boston: Beacon Press.
  1991   "The Egg and the Sperm: How Science Has Constructed a Romance Based on Stereotypical Male-Female Roles." *Signs: Journal of Women in Culture and Society* 16(3):485–501.

McClain, Carol Shepherd
  1985   "Why Women Choose Trial of Labor or Repeat Cesarean Section." *Journal of Family Practice* 21(3):210–216.

Quesada, Gustavo
  1976   "Language and Communication Barriers for Health Delivery to a Minority Group." *Social Science and Medicine* 10:323–327.

Rapp, Rayna
  1993   "Accounting for Amniocentesis." In *Knowledge, Power and Practice: The Anthropology of Medicine and Everyday Life,* ed. Shirley Lindenbaum and Margaret Lock, 55–79. Berkeley: University of California Press.

Rhodes, Lorna
  1990   "Studying Biomedicine as a Cultural System." In *Medical Anthropology: A Handbook of Theory and Method,* ed. Thomas Johnson and Carolyn Sargent, 159–174. Westport, Conn.: Greenwood Press.

Samuels, Alafia
  1987   *Health Sector Review.* Kingston, Jamaica: Ministry of Health.

Sargent, Carolyn, and Michael Harris
  1992   "Gender Ideology, Childrearing, and Child Health in Jamaica." *American Ethnologist* 19(3):523–537.

Sargent, Carolyn, and Joan Rawlins
  1991   "Factors Influencing Prenatal Care among Low-Income Jamaican Women." *Human Organization* 50(2):179–188.
  1992   "Transformations in Maternity Care in Jamaica." *Social Science and Medicine* 35(10):1225–1233.

Sargent, Carolyn, and Nancy Stark
  1987   "Surgical Birth: Interpretations of Cesarean Delivery among Private Hospital Patients and Nursing Staff." *Social Science and Medicine* 25(12):1269–1276.
  1989   "Childbirth Education and Childbirth Models: Parental Perspectives on Control, Anesthesia, and Technological Intervention in the Birth Process." *Medical Anthropology Quarterly,* n.s., 3:1.

Schreiber, Janet, and John Homiak
   1981   "Mexican Americans." In *Ethnicity and Medical Care,* ed. Alan Harwood,
      264–336. Cambridge, Mass.: Harvard University Press.
Starr, Paul
   1982   *The Social Transformation of American Medicine.* New York: Basic Books.
Wedderburn, Maxine, and Mona Moore
   1990   "Qualitative Assessment of Attitudes Affecting Childbirth Choices of Ja-
      maican Women." Working Paper 5. MotherCare Project Report Prepared for
      the Agency for International Development.
Young, Alan
   1982   "The Anthropologies of Illness and Sickness." *Annual Reviews in Anthro-
      pology* 11:257–285.

EIGHT

Authoritative Touch in Childbirth

A Cross-Cultural Approach

Sheila Kitzinger

Within Western culture great stress is laid on verbal communication. The unspoken elements in discourse tend to be trivialized or ignored. Mary Douglas considers that "speech has been overemphasised as the privileged means of human communication, and the body neglected. It is time to rectify this neglect and to become aware of the body as the physical channel of meaning" (1975:85).

One important element in the interaction of human bodies is touch. Touch conveys messages, either conscious and purposeful or unconscious. Sometimes these messages contradict verbal communication. Sometimes they are mixed or confused. Sometimes touch reinforces messages conveyed in the form of speech. It is not just a way of sending out arbitrary signals. Touch has its own—often intricate—language specific to the culture. In situations that are highly significant for a culture, such as the great transitional experiences of birth and death, the kind of touch given by those attending is often *authoritative.*

Touch is one "way of knowing." Through physical contact—expressed, for example, by stroking and holding but using not only hands but also face, lips, arms, the upper body, feet, legs, or the entire body—powerful messages are communicated and received. Through restriction of touch in situations in which touch is expected or sought, equally strong messages are communicated.

Touch given or withheld by those present during labor and delivery may be a theme central to a social analysis of the culture of birth. In many societies comforting body contact, skin stimulation, massage, and physical support are elements integral to the experience of birth. Through touch a midwife acquires information about the position of the baby, the strength of contractions, and the progress of labor and is able to convey this tactile information to others.

In high-technology birth systems, by contrast, the cumulative knowledge acquired through touch is subordinated to external information provided by electronic equipment and biochemical tests, both of which entail the physical immobilization and penetration of the woman's body with electrodes, intravenous catheters, needles, or other diagnostic tools. The technology constitutes the legitimate basis for decision making. In the absence or breakdown of that technology, or when professionals qualified to interpret the data that it produces are not available, no decisions can be made.

In low-technology birth culture, however, authoritative touch is an expression of a culturally validated system of knowledge and values. Because touch consists of physical contact, it incorporates beliefs about the human body and about relationships between human beings and often, too, relations between the human and the divine. In traditional Balinese culture, for instance, a baby's body does not come in contact with the earth until the ceremony of *oton* when it is six months old. Babies come from the gods and are sacred. They must be held in someone's arms or be carried against the body until this transitional rite celebrates their entry to common humanity (Eiseman 1988:93–95). Within Maoritanga (Maori culture) physical contact (*te tutakitanga*) is one stage in ritual behavior of entry to a *marae*, the community and religious center that represents the identity of the tribe, and the lifting of ceremonial *tapu* (taboo). It consists of an act of welcome that entails grasping the right hand of the other person and pressing noses (*hongi*). Traditionally foreheads may also touch, symbolizing "a sharing of thoughts leading to a sharing of emotions" (Tauroa and Tauroa 1986:65–69). Only after this ritual act are visitors to a marae free to move about. By means of the formal welcome and response, of which touch is one important element, they become "home people" (*tangata whenua*).

Throughout European history, and in widely varied cultures today, those attending a woman in childbirth have used touch in many different ways both to support the physiological birth process and to nurture the mother. Physical contact with hands and body is one expression of women's knowledge of birth. In all societies any individual who touches a childbearing woman has the implied or explicit authority to do so, including touch that is prohibited outside the birth situation. Touch may be generous or constrained. It has been described as used "to support the woman's position, to stimulate contractions, and to relieve pain" (Hedstrom 1986:181–186). Yet the functions of touch go far beyond this. It is employed not only to get the baby out of a woman's body and to reduce pain but is often redolent with meaning for the woman and all those participating, and may be part of a complex ritual.

THE GOD-SIBS

Traditionally, childbirth has been a social rather than a medical act. It takes place in women's space and on territory from which men have often been excluded entirely. Birth is women's work, and every woman is expected to know what to do. Worldwide, the traditional attendants of a woman in childbirth are women themselves. Male experts are few and far between, though men tend to have special status and privileges and are invested with specific authoritative knowledge in situations of acute danger, as shamans, priests, or obstetricians. Even though a man may be present, he is marginal to the community of women who use skills passed on by women, sometimes from mothers to daughters and often by apprenticeship. The period of apprenticeship often involves acquiring knowledge that is "in the hands" (Jordan [1978] 1993:192).

In medieval times a woman called her "god-sibs"—literally, sisters in God—to nurture her during labor and to care for both her and the baby afterward (Kitzinger 1994a:100–103). It was women who formed the birthing circle and women who handed on the skills of nurturing a woman through childbirth. These were an extension of their own mothering skills, for they had all borne children. They came from the surrounding neighborhood to make the birth room ready, to sit with, comfort, and encourage her, to cook sustaining food and prepare herbal drinks, to pray and sing together, and to share in what was essentially an exclusively female process of bonding in love and power. They held and supported her physically, cradled her in their arms, caressed, kissed, and stroked her, and used massage to help her through the birth. For forty days after childbirth the woman was in a transitional ritual state, polluted and vulnerable. Because she endangered men, the new mother could not prepare or cook food and her god-sibs took over her family responsibilities.

The midwife was one of this group of women. She was respected for her specialist knowledge, derived from practical experience, often from apprenticeship to a midwife and sometimes also from more formal learning. Her role was to bring the birth to a safe outcome and, simultaneously, to orchestrate the activities of the helping women. Though a specialist, she was also one of them, sharing her skills and information. The helping women were committed to reciprocal responsibility, not just during the present birth but in the continuity of births in the community and within the female network, which was strengthened with each shared act of participation in pregnancy, birth, and postpartum nurture and celebration.

In Western cultures the social nature of birth was reinforced during the eighteenth and nineteenth centuries as people emigrated from a Europe in turmoil to seek new lands. In pioneer wagons and in rural outposts, North American women felt keenly the isolation from female kin, and helping women traveled over vast distances to be with the woman in child-birth. They gave each other mutual practical assistance and emotional sup-port, which in Canada was called "turnabout help." Each woman came knowing that when she had her next baby, the woman she had helped would in turn come to assist her (Kitzinger 1994b:101–104). In many pre-industrial cultures authoritative touch given to the birthing woman by the helping women and the midwife is expected as an important element in care. It gives reassurance to the woman that all is well.

A survey of maternity care in Jamaica in the 1970s revealed that 47 per-cent of births took place at home, and in 61 percent of these there was no qualified person in attendance. It was estimated that 25 percent of all births were attended by *nanas*. Still today in rural areas of Jamaica childbearing women turn to nanas for help, although because of criminali-zation of the role of the nana, the traditional midwife has to pretend to be a member of the family or a neighbor (as she may in fact be) (Joint Study Group, International Federation of Gynaecology and Obstetrics and Inter-national Confederation of Midwives 1976).

Massage by a Jamaican nana during pregnancy "shapes" the baby and helps it "grow right," and as the birth date approaches corrects any malpo-sition (Kitzinger 1994a:133). During labor it both relieves backache and assists the opening of the woman's pelvis and the swinging wide of the "gate" in her lower spine (Kitzinger 1994b:171–194). When women in any subordinate culture are transported from rural communities to deliver in large, urban, high-technology hospitals, as native American and Inuit women often are in the United States and Canada, the birthing woman feels deprived of the appropriate care that is based on the authoritative knowledge of a midwife and other female helpers who share her system of values, including familiar and expected physical contact. In birth support groups such as these, the meanings encoded in touch are understood by each attendant and by the birthing woman herself. Certain kinds of touch may be restricted to the midwife. Others participating in the birth would not attempt them. It is only the midwife who makes a pelvic examination, for example, or who rotates the baby to a better position for birth.

RESTRICTIONS ON TOUCH

In many human activities touch is a superfluous or prohibited element in communication. Often it is deliberately avoided or severely restricted. Avoidance behavior may be heavily ritualized. It can serve as a marker of social distance, for example. When an Australian prime minister rested his hand on the queen's back as he introduced her to one of her subjects the British press reacted with shock and horror. To touch the sovereign in a casual, friendly way was an insult to the Crown. In an elegant restaurant, the waiter restricts and controls touch so that very limited contact is made with objects, and none at all with the diner. He flips open the napkin and drops it on the diner's lap in a way that avoids touch. While pouring wine, his left arm is held behind his back, so that there is no risk of accidental touch and contamination.

In giving care during the major transitional processes of both birth and death, however, some degree of physical contact is necessary. Who touches, how they touch, who does not touch, and the messages communicated by touch or by physical avoidance, are elements in specific cultural themes. In high-technology birthing systems, touch as a cultural way of knowing has been systematically discredited and devalued, with increasing reliance on the high-technology artifacts of birth. In the nineteenth century delivery chairs, designed to restrict the woman's movement and fix her in a suitable position for manipulation of the baby's head at delivery by the obstetrician, were introduced, thus removing the need to cradle her in human arms or to help her find a more comfortable position. Toward the end of the century metal contraptions were invented which tipped the woman in any position that the obstetrician considered desirable, including the Trendelenburg position in which she was tipped virtually upside down, and metal hoists and pulleys were employed to facilitate delivery of an impacted head. These artifacts of the industrial revolution reduced further the need to touch the laboring woman. The twentieth century saw the introduction of delivery tables with lithotomy stirrups, handcuffs, and shoulder restrainers, which immobilized the woman on her back, and sterile drapes, which isolated the upper part of the woman's body from the obstetrician's working end so that the baby was born through a hole in a sheet.

When physicians first began to take over from midwives in nineteenth-century America they had to negotiate everything they did with the female support group present throughout the birth, and could touch the patient only after permission had been given by the helping woman. Well into the twentieth century experienced neighborhood women continued to assist at home births and to restrict, scrutinize, and direct the physical contact that a doctor had with his patient. An Oklahoma doctor wrote to the *Journal of the American Medical Association* in 1912, explaining that though it was the practice in hospitals of that time to shave off all the woman's pubic hair (in the belief that this would prevent infection), it was impossible for him to do this in home births: "In about 3 seconds after the doctor has made the first rake with his safety (razor), he will find himself on his back out in the yard with the imprint of a woman's bare foot emblazoned on his manly chest, the window sash around his neck and a revolving vision of all the stars in the fermament [*sic*] presented to him" (Landrum 1912:576).

In medicalized childbirth only certain individuals are expected to touch

the laboring woman. In a contemporary North American hospital the baby's father may be encouraged to put his arm around his partner, to hold
her hand, or to massage her back. He is not usually permitted to touch her
perineum, or the crown of the baby's head, and must keep out of the
nurse's/midwife's and the obstetrician's way when they are touching. For
their touch is considered more important than his, and if he is smoothing
her brow, stroking her arm, or embracing her, he must withdraw when it is
indicated that professional assistants are about to examine her or to intervene in the labor by, for example, setting up an intravenous drip or passing
a catheter into her bladder.

Increasingly during the nineteenth century women in childbirth were
isolated from their kin, neighbors, and other women in the community.
With hospital birth that isolation became complete. The reciprocity between women that was an inherent part of traditional birth was lost, and
professional caregivers took over. As doctors took over childbirth in Europe and North America, examination by touch became an essential part
of the physician's expertise.

In the eighteenth century it was considered highly indelicate for a male
accoucheur to see the woman's body, so the examination was conducted
under a sheet. In the early nineteenth century skill in diagnostic touch
was a recognized element in the esteem afforded an accoucheur. But each
examination had to be negotiated with the women attending. If a doctor
did not have "the touch" no amount of book-learning or other abilities
could make up for its absence. The discretion, grace, and, indeed, reassurance with which he employed this touch separated the bumblers from
those with acknowledged flair. In the best hands, it had a magic quality.
There was much debate in medical journals as to how the touch should be
performed and whether the doctor should fix his eyes on his patient's eyes
or gaze into the far corner of the room, so that she could be sure that he
was not looking at her body. One solution was to have the woman standing,
fully clothed, while the doctor crouched on one knee before her, like a
pleading suitor, and slipped a hand under her long skirt, up between her
legs, and into her vagina. Only an experienced and confident man could
find a way between her petticoats, and direct to the goal, with any assurance (Wertz and Wertz 1977:78).

Today diagnostic touch and manipulative touch are the only forms of
physical contact expected from the obstetrician, and in many medicalized
cultures their use is restricted to him. This consists predominantly of vaginal examinations, which may be performed frequently. Every two hours
during active labor is a common protocol, and every ten minutes in the
second stage, with additional examinations when there is concern that labor is not conforming to the norm and that dilation is not progressing at
a constant rate (1 cm every hour).

The nurse touches the patient to examine her, to place her feet in lithotomy stirrups, to restrain, and perhaps also to comfort her, but is not permitted to make the definitive vaginal examination that confirms full dilation of the cervix and that is followed by the command to the birthing woman that she must now push. That is the obstetrician's prerogative. Nor, under normal conditions, is the obstetric nurse expected to catch the baby. Even midwives in hospitals in northern Italy, who otherwise give total care during labor, are not allowed to deliver (Kitzinger pers. obs. 1990–1992). If the baby slips out regardless, it is acceptable for the midwife to pick it up, but she should not actively deliver by supporting the woman's perineum or by controlling the birth of the baby's head. Her role is restricted to physically placing the woman in the correct position for delivery and to keeping her quiet and disciplined, so that the obstetrician is not hindered in his work. In U.S. hospitals, too, the status and authority of the obstetrician is expressed in his right to legitimate the progress of labor by performing the vaginal exam at a critical moment in labor and communicating the information derived from this procedure to subordinate participants in the event (Jordan [1978] 1993:165; see also Jordan, this volume).

THE CLASSIFICATION OF TOUCH IN CHILDBIRTH

Touch in childbirth can be classified in terms of its social function and its implicit value to the actors concerned. It may be instrumental, to perform a task, or expressive, to give affective contact, or both at once. It is often multifunctional and conveys meanings at different levels to the various participants, some of which may be unacknowledged, or interpreted in conflicting ways. The categories I suggest here are not exclusive, and there is much overlap and merging of meanings.

Blessing Touch

In preindustrial cultures birth usually has an element of the sacramental. It links past, present, and future. It unites the world of now with the world of the ancestors and is part of the tree of life or the totem extending in time and eternity. A central religious theme is the emergence of life, often in the form of monsters, serpents, or mystical beings, of birth to male gods, or the splitting of a single animal in two. Sometimes God or the great Mother Goddess breathes life into clay figures or other objects modeled by the divine hands, harnessing the powers of nature to help in this work (Allen 1981; Baring and Cashford 1991; Grace and Kahakiwa 1984; Larrington 1992). Creation myths express wonder and astonishment at life coming out of nothing, the pain of that transformation, and the festive delight of creation. They are an integral part of rebirthing rites in many religions and are celebrated, as Christians do with the birth of Christ, at central points in the religious cycle. In many hunting and agricultural communities human fertility is the powerful force that causes crops to grow, fish and animals to be caught, domesticated animals to bear young, and the whole society to flourish. In these societies, the midwife is not merely a birth attendant with special expertise. She has a spiritual function, and this finds expression in how she touches the woman in childbirth. The physical contact she gives is often accompanied by prayers, invocations, hymns to the ancestors, and sometimes sacred dance. It may be enhanced by the use of ritually significant substances to provide lubrication for massage, and by visual symbols such as charms, lodestones, pottery figures of birthing goddesses (in many South American cultures), paintings of the Virgin, a flower that, opening its petals in the heat of the birth room, represents the dilating cervix (as in parts of India and in rural Greece and Italy), birthing beads representing the birth journey (as among the Navajo), and other objects with ritual meaning (Kitzinger, personal collection of birth sculptures, artifacts, and illustrations).

Massage, hand pressure, and other forms of touch to balance the forces of hot and cold in the body, or to open the way to birth through giving spiritual energy, are examples of the blessing touch and are an expected part of care in many birth cultures. In Jamaica the *nana* describes her work as that of "freeing" the woman's body for birth. To do this, she massages her abdomen and perineum with the oil of the wild castor oil plant, olive oil, or slippery scrapings from the inside of "toona" leaves (Kitzinger 1994a:134). It is a laying-on of hands, and is called *anointing*. The midwife also often works to rotate the baby into the best position for birth, so there is a wide overlap between the spiritual and practical functions of touch. In Malaysia the *bidan* may massage the woman's uterus with coconut oil over which incantations have been recited. She introduces the same oil into the vagina in the second stage of labor to help perineal tissues fan out. Lime juice is also used for abdominal massage, in accordance with the humoral system of healing, since it is a "hot" substance and makes expulsion easier (Laderman 1983:150). In Thailand water that has been sanctified to exorcise evil spirits is used for massage during difficult labors (Rajadhon 1987:49).

Traditionally, the blessing touch confers power from spiritual beings or ancestors. It summons the goddess of birth, calls on companies of angels, and confers *mana* or spiritual power. In Maori tribes a woman might give birth sitting between the thighs of her maternal grandfather or mother's brother, or kneel with her head in his lap, as she pushes the baby out onto a sheepskin or carpet of soft leaves lying on the ground (Kitzinger, unpublished field research 1989, 1992). This close physical contact with her grandfather links her symbolically with the sources of ancestral power.

A modern form of the blessing touch is therapeutic touch. This is incorporated into nursing degree programs in many American universities, though Dolores Krieger, who first used the term in a nursing context, does not associate it with any specific religious belief and suggests that healing occurs by electron resonance (Krieger 1975:784–787; Turton 1986:31–32).

Comfort Touch

Physical contact to give emotional support, ease pain, and help the woman relax and let her body work can be classified as comfort touch. The traditional Japanese word for midwife is *samba*, the massaging elderly woman (Kitzinger, unpublished field research 1991). "I touch the people as soft as I can," a Hispanic *partera* said, "like my grandmother showed me" (Perrone 1989:116). This touch may consist of caresses, deep or superficial massage, or stroking or firm holding, and it may be merely a light brushing of the fingers or entail whole body contact. The range of substances used in massage is wide: vegetable oils of different kinds, animal fat, herbal lotions and juice, or, as in Micronesia, a mixture of grated coconut and ginger root.

The Jamaican nana massages so that the woman does not "hackle" (get worked up, be under stress). She also presses a heated stone against the sacrolumbar spine to counter pain, and if labor is prolonged may wrap the woman in wet towels, which provide yet another skin sensation. Hot compresses and heat in other forms are often used to reduce pain. Among the Kwakiutl of British Columbia heated seaweed was placed over the woman's abdomen or against her back (Boas 1913–1914). The Kiwi of northern Australia press heated leaves in the small of the woman's back, between her legs, and over her lower abdomen (Goodale 1971). A midwifery textbook of the sixteenth century advises the midwife to sit in front of the laboring woman and "diligently observe and wait." She is told to "anoint her hands with the oil of white lilies" and encourage the mother "to patience and tolerance" while "stroking gently with her hands her belly about the navel" (Kitzinger 1994a:111).

In many birth cultures perineal and vaginal massage is given to help the woman relax so that tissues can fan out and to enable her to cope with the stinging sensations as the head distends the vulva and is about to crown. Grace Acton and Letitia Owen, in their *Book of Household Management*, written in the eighteenth century, recommended pork fat for lubricating the perineum (Kitzinger 1994a:116).

The 1797 edition of the *Encyclopaedia Britannica* states that "when there is dryness and constriction of the vagina" in childbirth, and when the cervix is "rigid," "the natural moisture is to be supplied by lubricating with pomatum or butter, or by throwing up injections of warm oil; the parts are

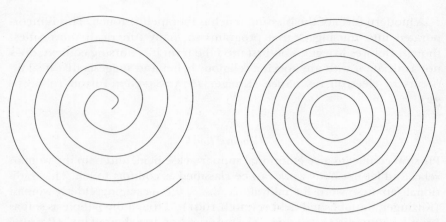

Fig. 8.1.

likewise to be relaxed by . . . warm steams directed to them" (*Encyclopaedia Britannica* 1797).

But comfort touch is not just a question of massage. In many preindustrial cultures birth usually takes place within a circle of women who gather physically close to the laboring woman and to each other. The sense of close contact with others is expressed in the spiral visual symbol drawn for me by an Australian Aboriginal woman. "I am joined. We are part of each other." She contrasted this with a symbol of the disconnectedness she witnessed in "white" society. (See fig. 8.1.)

A British midwife visiting a village in the Yemen remarked how all the women present at birth stroked and embraced the laboring woman, kissing her and giving words of comfort: "Not long, not long, my love." "She was never at a loss of a shoulder to grip, a chest to lean against, or a strong hand to steady an ankle or a knee. If one woman tired or had to return to her children another would quickly take her place" (Dew 1988). Jordan describes how women assisting at a Maya birth encouraged the mother with "birth talk." "With the 'head helper' behind her, not only holding her but physically matching every contraction, the laboring woman is surrounded by intense urging in the touch, sound, and sight of those close to her" ([1978] 1993:36).

There are no barriers of physical contact. As a contraction starts and the laboring woman moves, the whole group stirs, and their watching and waiting or casual conversation changes to a wave of focused activity in order to help her. This may include supporting her head, stroking her brow, grasping her shoulders or the sides of her abdomen, pressing on the fundus, pressing with their knees into the small of her back to ease low backache, swinging or rotating the pelvis, or rocking against her body to encourage her own pelvic mobility. Birthing is like a dance that follows the rhythms of the uterus, in which all are linked by the same music.

With twentieth-century medicalized childbirth touch became much more limited. When psychoprophylaxis was first introduced in the U.S.S.R. in the late 1950s the nurse was instructed to touch patients to "set their bedding right, feed them, put their kerchief in order and sponge their foreheads, arms and shoulders in hot weather" (Velvovsky et al. 1960:274). The woman in childbirth was taught a system of self-massage of her abdomen. But no one was there to hold or to stroke her.

Touch was formalized as massage, and made part of the help given by the *monitrice* in France and of midwifery training in Britain during the 1960s. Comfort stroking was also incorporated into the North American Lamaze and other systems of training for birth, and expectant fathers were instructed in massage techniques.

Yet it was noted that often women could not bear to be massaged in transition between the first and second stages of labor. Systematized touch—touch that is insensitive to what the woman in childbirth wants at that particular time—can be irritating. An anxious partner may convey mounting tension through touch that is given because it is part of a protocol. When massage is rapid—which it tends to be when performed by someone who is anxious or fearful—it has the effect of stimulating the woman's rate of breathing, so that it, too, becomes faster. It thus encourages hyperventilation, with consequent involuntary trembling, disorientation, and feelings of panic.

In the late 1980s the value of female companionship in childbirth began to be rediscovered in the West, and with it the advantages of caring touch, not only for the woman's emotional benefit but also to support the normal physiology of birth. A South African study revealed that female companionship for several hours (but not including the nighttime) had a striking effect on women's experiences of birth. Moreover, six weeks after birth those women who had a companion during part of labor were much more likely to be breastfeeding exclusively (51.4% compared to 29.3%), even though labor companions did not visit the postnatal ward and never discussed breastfeeding with them. The authors of this study suggest that "conventional hospital care may interfere with the development of the confidence needed to breastfeed successfully" (Hofmeyr et al. 1991:756–764).

An American study produced even more impressive results. Following a research project in Guatamala, which revealed that the continuous support of another woman during labor and birth significantly reduced the rate of cesarean section and other obstetric interventions and resulted in shorter labors, less fetal distress, and healthier newborns (Sosa et al. 1980:597–600), a study was undertaken in a high-technology hospital in Texas. In this Texas hospital patients are confined to bed, and have continuous electronic fetal monitoring, intravenous infusions, artificial rupture of the membranes, frequent oxytocin stimulation of the uterus, epidurals, and other forms of pharmacological pain relief. The woman who gave support was known as a *doula* (a Greek word meaning "a woman companion in childbirth"). Each one stayed with the woman from admission until after birth, explained to her what was happening, soothed, touched, and encouraged her, and kept a written record of staff contacts, interactions, and interventions.

The 616 participants in the study were low-risk primigravidas. They were randomly divided into three groups: those who had continuous support from a doula, those who had an observer who sat and watched but did nothing else, and those who were left alone—the control group. Eighteen percent of the control group had cesarean sections, 13 percent in the observed group, and 8 percent of those who were given support. Of the women who had vaginal births, 26 percent in the control group, 21 percent of the observed group, but only 8 percent of those who were supported had forceps deliveries. When spontaneous vaginal births were analyzed, it was found that 55 percent in the control group, 23 percent of those who were observed, and 8 percent of those who had support had epidurals. With spontaneous vaginal births, too, 37 percent in the control group had oxytocin stimulation compared to 13 percent of those who were observed and 14 percent in the supported group. Fewer babies of mothers who had women companions required a prolonged hospital stay. Whereas 24 percent of babies in the control group remained in hospital for medical reasons longer than forty-eight hours, only 17 percent of babies in the observed group and 10 percent in the supported group remained in hospital.

The conclusion is that woman-to-woman companionship reduces rates of interventions and complications and is a simple, cost-effective way of reducing morbidity and of enhancing the health and well-being of both mothers and babies. The authors comment that no randomized study of the presence of a male birth partner has reported any decrease in rates of augmentation of labor, or of forceps and cesarean deliveries, though there are studies that show that his presence reduces the need for drugs for pain relief. They suggest that it may be difficult for a man to give enough support, because he is too focused on his own emotions and lacks personal experience of birth. Touch is highly relevant here, for research comparing the nature of support given by male partners and by doulas reveals that women touch as much as 95 percent of the time they are helping, whereas men touch only 20 percent of the time, and that men often choose to be present for shorter periods (Bertsch 1990:251–260).

To date, there have been eleven methodologically rigorous randomized

controlled trials of companionship in childbirth, carried out in eight different countries, in hospitals affording highly disparate conditions. In a
meta-analysis of these trials Ellen Hodnett (1993; Disk Issue 2) reveals that,
regardless of whether support is given by a companion of the woman's own
choosing or by one provided by the hospital, the presence of a support
person reduces the likelihood of drugs for pain relief, of operative vaginal
delivery, and the baby having a five-minute Apgar score of less than seven,
and increases the likelihood of women rating the birth experience as satisfying. Even when a woman is not allowed to choose her own significant
other, personal companionship by another woman reduces the chances of
her having a cesarean section. The most important elements in support
are continuity of the companion's presence, encouraging language, and
touch. Hodnett concludes that the work of nurses and midwives should be
reorganized so that they spend less time in ineffective activities and more
time in giving support to women in childbirth.

There is a great difference between the way in which these hospital-
based studies were conducted and the historical female tradition. In each
case a single companion was introduced rather than a group of women
friends, neighbors, and family members. Perhaps hospitals would consider
it too disruptive of routine and too challenging to medical authority to
introduce god-sibs. It may be that only when a small group of women interact with each other in giving help during childbirth can the essential elements of authoritative touch be fully explored. This research remains to
be done.

Physically Supportive Touch

In preindustrial cultures, with few exceptions, a woman in childbirth is
given physical support by one or more other women so that she can move
her pelvis and switch between positions with ease. Birth is perceived as
activity. The debate about birth positions in contemporary medical journals is almost exclusively about the advantages and disadvantages of upright or semi-upright positions, compared with the supine position (Hillan
1985:19–23; Kurokawa and Zilkoski 1985:87–90; Lupe and Gross
1986:727–734; Roberts and Wodell 1983:243–249). Yet it is not merely a
matter of "positions" for delivery, but of providing physical support for
movement during contractions, even though this movement may be only
a slight pelvic rock or tilt. Movement is facilitated when a woman has another human body to hold or lean against, or when she is grasped in strong
arms by a helper who is alert to respond at the onset of each contraction,
providing a firm stationary base or moving in unison with her. She may, for
example, sit on a helper's lap, squat or kneel with helpers at either side

supporting her shoulders, or alternately stand and crouch, holding a rope or the branch of a tree, while her helper supports her back.

On each slave plantation in Jamaica, where women were often forced to work until the onset of the second stage, there was a designated "birth tree." When a woman was about to give birth she and two women helpers left the long line of slaves cutting sugar and went to the birth tree, where the mother squatted with her arms around it, a woman holding her at either side (Kitzinger, oral tradition, field notes 1964–1965). In Thailand, as in many other cultures, a female helper uses her own body to cradle the woman in labor (Rajadhon 1987:49). A pre-Columbian pottery jug from Peru shows the mother sitting upright on a woman's lap while the midwife cradles the baby's head in her hands (collection of author). In New Guinea the Usiai woman sits between her sister's thighs, her back supported by her body. Her paternal aunt sits in front of her with her arms around her so that she can massage her back, and the birthing woman rocks between the bodies of these two helpers (Mead 1949). In West Africa the woman kneels with women holding her on either side. When the baby is about to be born she may squat, a woman at either side, their arms crossed with hers, another woman pressing against her back, a fourth massaging her abdomen, and two other women holding her legs (Thompson 1967). A traditional birth position in Japan is for the woman to lean forward over a large sack of rice with each contraction while the midwife or her husband sits behind her grasping her pelvis (Kitzinger, unpublished field research 1989). Still in many traditional cultures, where women are not tethered to electronic fetal monitors and intravenous catheters and are not forced to lie flat on their backs with their legs in the air, they spontaneously crouch, kneel, or squat, thighs abducted, with rounded back and bent knees, clasped in the arms of women who share with them their journey through birth.

By the first decade of the twentieth century, even before the introduction of modern technology, women giving birth in American hospitals had to lie flat on their backs. In Britain, however, midwives continued to encourage women to walk about through the first stage and to get on the bed only when the second stage started. Delivery often took place in the Sim's position—the woman lying on her left side with knees drawn up. Midwifery training included teaching about the value of touch to give physical support when pushing: "Great relief is often given by the nurse supporting the lower part of the back by firm pressure with the hand" (Humphrey 1907:199). The left lateral remained a common birth position in British hospitals into the 1970s, when it was replaced by a supine or semisitting position, often accompanied by instructions to the woman to keep still to avoid interfering with the printout of the electronic fetal monitor. Attendants could, if they wished, concentrate on the machinery, and leave the woman to get on with her labor without personal support—and without being touched.

Diagnostic Touch

The traditional midwife uses her eyes, ears, and, above all, her hands to diagnose. Experience brings skill in abdominal palpation to determine how the baby is lying. She may even feel the fetal heartbeat with her fingers. A Hispanic partera in New Mexico was called to the doctor's office so that he could show her how to use a stethoscope to record the fetal heart. "I don't need that," she said, handing it back to the doctor. Puzzled, he watched her move her hand across the woman's abdomen. "Put your instrument here and listen to the heart," she instructed the obstetrician. "The heartbeat is here" (Perrone, Stockel, and Krueger 1989:118). Midwives traditionally relied on their hands because they had no other diagnostic tools or had simple tools such as Pinard's stethoscope, the use of which entails physical contact with the woman. Ultrasound in the form of the continuous electronic monitor and the Doppler has replaced the midwife's trumpet. After listening to a physician lecturing on fetal heart tones, a midwife who has never owned a Doppler commented that once midwives have them, they use them more and more: "When I just use a fetoscope I not only hear the heartbeat but feel it. I also have been concerned that since the sound range of the Doppler is different from the range picked up with a fetoscope, using it would have a negative effect on my listening skills" (Judy Luce; in letter to Robbie Davis-Floyd, 1994). A modern midwife accustomed to working in hospitals may not trust the evidence of the fingers. She may rely on ultrasound to tell her if the baby is vertex and, at the end of pregnancy, to know whether what she is feeling in the cavity of the pelvis is head or shoulders. In hospitals the ultrasound scan has largely taken the place of skilled hands (see Georges, this volume).

The primary example of diagnostic touch is the vaginal examination, which carries the risk of infection. In the nineteenth century this risk was extremely high. In the main maternity hospital in Budapest some patients were attended by medical students, who performed vaginal examinations without washing their hands between patients and who also did autopsies. Others were tended by midwives. Women on the medical students' wards had a puerperal fever rate 437 percent higher than that of women attended by midwives. Semmelweis met much hostility from doctors when he stated publicly that "puerperal fever is caused by conveyance to the pregnant woman of putrid articles derived from living organisms, through the agency of the examining fingers" (Wertz and Wertz 1977:121).

The risk of infection exists even when vaginal examinations are carried out under apparently sterile conditions in a modern hospital. Following early rupture of the membranes, it is widely accepted as good practice to perform regular vaginal examinations to monitor the progress of labor, because it is known that the longer the labor, the greater the risk of infection. Yet infection is directly related to the number of vaginal examinations performed, not the length of time per se from rupture to delivery (Wagner et al. 1989:93–97).

Custom, cultural familiarity, habit, work protocols, and ceremonial processes impose a sense of inevitability, or blur the edges of the meanings implicit in touch, so that when people are asked about them they stop, surprised, and deny what they do or question the reality of what has occurred, because they do not see it in the same context as the observer. Videotape analysis of the behavior of nurses and obstetricians during the second stage of labor in a contemporary hospital reveals that the nurse raises her gloved hand, making a fist with it so that she does not touch anything that is not sterile, and she says, "You'll feel me touching you, sweetie" (Bergstrom et al. 1992:10–19), then rams her finger through the woman's vagina and into her cervix. The signal of the clenched fist, raised so that it is directly in the laboring woman's line of sight, is one of attack. The words used belie this signal. It is followed by forced entry of the examining hand, which is held in place through two contractions, as the helpless woman writhes in pain. Murray Enkin (1992), an obstetrician and epidemiologist, comments on this analysis in a paper entitled "Do I Do That? Do I Really Do That? Like That?" He states, "Repeated vaginal examinations are an invasive intervention of as yet no proved value. Those who advocate its use have the responsibility to test their belief in an appropriately controlled trial" (Enkin 1992:19–20).

Manipulative Touch

The traditional midwife's hands are her most important tool for healing and manipulation. In South America and the Caribbean women helpers standing at either side of the woman in childbirth may each grasp the end of a long cloth wound around her abdomen at the level of the fundus, pulling on it during contractions to produce pressure. Immediate contact is with cloth, not hands. Yet the helpers' regular action is synchronized with the surge of each contraction, and this involves close physical contact with the woman. If the second stage of labor is prolonged, the Apache midwife stands behind the woman with her arms around her crossing over the front. With each contraction she presses with her hands moving down over the uterus (Opler 1946).

In these societies pressure over the fundus is explained as helping the baby go down and preventing it from coming up out of the uterus. This relates to a body image in which it is believed that there is a single tube between the mouth at one end, branching out into stomach and uterus and dividing into the anus, vagina, and urethra at the other (Kitzinger 1994a:105). The uterus can move out of its place, and even break from its mooring. Many female maladies were ascribed to this, including hysteria (*hystera* is the Greek word for womb). Nineteenth-century doctors considered that only a woman could be hysterical, because only she had a uterus and hysteria was directly attributed to malfunction of this organ.

In traditional cultures it is believed that in difficult labors the baby can come up instead of going down, and may choke the mother. During my field research in Jamaica women often discussed with me the dangers of this occurrence and described preventive action taken by traditional midwives (Kitzinger 1994b:171–194). The nanas themselves did not share the fantasy of the single tube of which the uterus was one part, but were nevertheless concerned to keep the baby on its downward path by massaging it through the mother's abdominal wall, by pressure over the fundus and by advising that a string or cloth be tied at the level of the fundus during pregnancy and in labor.

Traditional midwives in southwestern Mexico and the Zapotec region of Oaxaca employ techniques of massage and pelvic rocking known as *sobada* (abdominal massage) and *manteada* (the sifting), a rocking of the pelvis. These rites of pregnancy and childbirth date back to pre-Columbian times and are designed to "straighten out that which is within the woman," to relieve back pain, to perform external version of the fetus from posterior to anterior, and to rotate and realign the baby into the correct position for birth (Romero 1993).

The partera introduces these techniques from the thirty-second week of pregnancy, employing them every fifteen days from then on, and may also use them in labor. The massage varies in different areas of southern Mexico, but in addition to palpation of the abdomen, light massage with the sides of the hands, abdominal kneading, and "lifting" of the baby so that the mother is more comfortable, it may include heel slapping, back massage, pressure on the sacro-iliac points, and manipulation of the woman's head and neck. A Zapotec partera massages the woman's legs to diagnose tension, for tension in the legs indicates the place against which a baby is pressing into the woman's spine and causing backache and thus reveals how the baby should be repositioned through sobada and manteada. At thirty-seven weeks a partera may use abdominal massage to "separate the baby" so that descent is easier, along with back massage to overcome "coldness" and to transmit energy and heat.

Pelvic rocking, or sobada, is done with the woman lying on her back on the ground, knees drawn up and heels flat. The partera places a long shawl, the *rebozo*, under her back and draws it up at either side so that it cradles her pelvis. Then she pulls alternately with her hands, so that the woman's pelvis is rocked from side to side in the sling of the rebozo. The sobada may also be used in the second stage of labor, with the woman in a standing position, leaning back against the partera, to help her in pushing the baby out.

Thus massage and rocking techniques form a complex system of hands-on touch by traditional midwives in Mexico. These techniques are now being reassessed and incorporated into modern midwifery methods of care (Romero pers. com. 1994).

In medicalized birth manipulative touch includes procedures such as Ritgen's maneuver (pushing a finger or thumb into the woman's anus to lift the baby's chin up over her coccyx), making an episiotomy (surgically incising her perineum), rotating the fetal head (turning it around), and pulling the baby out.

Restraining Touch

In the first decade of the twentieth century various kinds of restraining touch were introduced into hospital obstetrics to keep the patient immobile, to stop her from making a noise, to prevent her touching the "sterile area" of her own body, which became the property of the obstetrician, and to prevent her from interfering with examinations and maneuvers and touching her newborn baby and thus conveying bacteria. The mother's touch is perceived as potentially contaminating for her own body and for her newborn baby. In a Moscow hospital, for example, before a mother can hold her baby her fingers must be painted with iodine or other antiseptic, and prior to putting the baby to the breast iodine is daubed round her nipples and the baby's mouth (Kitzinger pers. obs. 1989).

Early twentieth-century illustrations in obstetric and midwifery books show a midwife or nurse placing the patient in the "correct" position for delivery, holding her arms, and fixing her legs in a position to allow the doctor easy access to her genitals. Illustrations in the 1904 edition of Joseph De Lee's *Obstetrics for Nurses* (p. 104) show a patient prepared for the doctor's internal examination, the nurse holding her leg with one hand and a sheet, with which she hides the woman's face from the obstetrician, in the other. There is a marked contrast between these illustrations, which show how the nurse should touch the patient as part of her service to the obstetrician, and illustrations published in George Engelmann's *Labor among Primitive Peoples* (1882), which depict touch given to help the woman herself do the work of birth.

In North American hospitals sterile drapes were introduced which completely covered the woman's abdomen and legs. These made it impossible for her to touch the lower part of her body even if her hands were free, and the baby was delivered through a small opening in the sheets. Drapes reinforced the territorial divisions of the woman's body, separating them into those she was allowed to touch and those considered to belong to the obstetrician. The positioning of sterile drapes also dictated to a large extent the choreography of the combined posture and movement of each of the professional attendants.

It was often difficult for a single nurse to restrain the patient so that she did not disturb the drapes if she tried to move into a more comfortable position or if she became distressed—especially after she had been injected with scopolamine ("twilight sleep"), which made her disoriented and confused. The physician Michelle Harrison, describing her experience with hospital birth in the 1960s, writes, "When these women thought they were 'out' they were awake and screaming. Made crazy from the drug, they fought; they growled like animals. They had to be restrained, tied by hands and feet to the corners of the bed (with straps padded with lamb's wool so there would be no injury, no telltale marks) or they would run screaming down the halls. Screaming obscenities, they bit, they wept, behaving in ways that would have produced shame and humiliation had they been aware. Doctors and nurses, looking at such behavior induced by the drug they had administered, felt justified in treating the women as crazy wild animals to be tied, ordered, slapped, yelled at, gagged" (1982:87). Scopolamine is still used in some American hospitals.

By the second decade of the century equipment had been manufactured which could take over the task of restraining the patient and free the nurse to be of direct service to the obstetrician. It included lithotomy stirrups, wrist cuffs, shoulder restrainers, and—for women who were out of their minds with scopolamine—special barred and padded cots with canvas covers and a baseball-type helmet to prevent the woman from injuring her head when drugs had made her impossible to control. Thus restraining touch gave way to restraining apparatus.

The first strong protest against this treatment came in letters to the *Ladies' Home Journal* in 1958 (Shultz 1958:44) in which mothers described horrific experiences:

> When my baby was ready the delivery room wasn't. I was strapped to a table, my legs tied together, so I could "wait" until a more convenient and "safer" time to deliver.

> I was strapped to the delivery room table on Saturday morning and lay there until I was delivered on Sunday afternoon.

> I was strapped to a table, hands down, knees up. I remember screaming, "Help me! Help me!" to a nurse who was sitting at a nearby desk. She ignored me.

Since the 1970s electronic equipment to which women are harpooned throughout labor and delivery has made hands-on restraint completely superfluous in the majority of births. Women are physically restrained, immobilized, and isolated and touched only when it is considered necessary for obstetric purposes. Unable to move or change position without interfering with the printout from the continuous electronic fetal monitor, the woman is fixed like a laboratory specimen to be dissected under bright lights, or like an offering on an altar, as gowned and masked acolytes obey the instructions of the senior obstetrician in a delivery room that is at once electronic nerve center and a shrine where the obstetrician is high priest (Pizzini 1987).

Punitive Touch

Anyone who has experience of large inner-city hospitals in a society where there is a wide cultural divide between the patients and overworked staff in a medical system in which harassed nurses or midwives are used as agents of crowd control has probably witnessed punitive touch. A woman's hand is slapped as it reaches out to contaminate the "sterile area." She is slow to turn to the correct position, and the nurse slaps her bottom. A woman screams, and someone puts a pillow over her face. When I was observing births at a large hospital in Kingston, Jamaica, in the sixties this was the only use made of the two pillows available on the delivery ward.

The power of the medical system is such that any handling of the woman in childbirth, especially that which entails physical restraint, may be done in a punitive way, and pregnant women who do not conform often fear that caregivers will punish them when they are in labor. In birth reports women sometimes describe lengthy vaginal examinations and manual stretching of the cervix, which they interpret as being performed punitively to cause maximum pain. An episiotomy is often made without explanation or consent, even when a woman has said that she does not wish to have one. It may be done with inadequate—or no—anesthesia, and is often seen by the woman as intended to punish her because she failed to relax or control herself or because she has made a birth plan. Caregivers may protest that the violence is "all in her mind." Yet it is an indication of the powerlessness many women experience in childbirth. Birth is perceived as violent, not because contractions are painful, but because a woman has no control over what is done to her.

Touch may be experienced as punitive even when this is not the intention of the professionals assisting the birth. They may believe it is necessary for examining or restraining the mother, or for performing acts such as artificial rupture of the membranes, "stretching" or "sweeping" the membranes, passing a catheter into her bladder, setting up an IV, attaching the patient to an electronic fetal monitor, doing vaginal examinations, fixing the legs to lithotomy stirrups, and suturing the perineum.

For some women the way in which they are touched, held, and penetrated in childbirth brings vivid memories, or flashbacks, of previous sexual abuse. In describing their birth experiences they use the language of rape. They feel "violated," "victimized," "invaded." Some say that they were "skewered," "trussed up like an oven-ready turkey," or that they felt like a "slab of meat" or "a heap of old fish." It was "like being sexually abused all over again" (Kitzinger 1992:219–220; J. Kitzinger, 1990a:698–700; 1990b:38–40). In many modern hospitals childbirth has become another form of violence against women.

CONCLUSION

Touch is never neutral. It is emotionally supportive or disabling. It is empowering or disempowering. Authoritative touch by caregivers in pregnancy and childbirth conveys strong messages to the woman concerning her status vis-à-vis her attendants, the reproductive efficiency of her body, the normality or abnormality of this birth, and about her value as a woman.

Though touch is considered the most intimate way of making human contact, when it is restraining or punitive it is an expression of the power that caregivers may exercise over a birthing woman. When it gives comfort, offers physical support, embodies cultural values shared between the giver and the recipient, however, it bridges the social space between them. Diagnostic and manipulative touch—elements of care in traditional as in technocratic cultures—may give contrasting messages, depending on the empathy and skills of the caregiver. It can cause pain, make a woman feel trapped, increase anxiety, and destroy confidence. Or it can help to maintain the spontaneous physiological process, reduce anxiety, and be a means of giving information and emotional support.

For midwives, nurses, and doctors, awareness of the messages implicit in touch enhances reflective practice and leads to deeper understanding of the quality of the relationship created with each birthing woman. Because emotionally supportive touch has a positive effect on physiological outcomes for mothers and babies, it can make birth not only a more satisfying but also a safer experience.

Exploration into the choreography of touch during childbirth is important to the social anthropologist because it reveals culturally significant images of the female body and the process of birth. It may also offer clues to the relative status of all concerned in the birth, their functions vis-à-vis the laboring woman and each other, and the relative power and powerlessness of each of the actors involved. In the comparative sociology of childbirth, it provides the touchstone of a birth culture.

REFERENCES

Allen, M.
  1981   *The Birth Symbol in Traditional Women's Art from Eurasia and the Western Pacific.* Toronto: Museum for Textiles.
Baring, A., and J. Cashford
  1991   *The Myth of the Goddess: Evolution of an Image.* London: Viking/Penguin.
Bergstrom, L., J. Roberts, I. Skillman, and J. Seidel
  1992   "You'll Feel Me Touching You, Sweetie." *Birth* 19(1):10–19.
Bertsch, T. D., L. Nagashima-Whalen, S. Dykeman, J. H. Kennell, and S. McGrath
  1990   "Labor Support by First-Time Fathers: Direct Observations with a Comparison to Experienced Doulas." *Journal of Psychosomatic Obstetrics and Gynecology* 11:251–260.
Boas, Franz
  1913–1914   *Ethnology of the Kwakiutl.* U.S. Bureau of Ethnology, 35th Annual Report. New York: U.S. Bureau of Ethnology.
De Lee, Joseph B.
  1904   *Obstetrics for Nurses.* Philadelphia: W. B. Saunders.
Dew, C. G.
  1988   "A Child Is Born." *She* (December).
Douglas, Mary
  1975   *Implicit Meanings.* London: Routledge and Kegan Paul.
Eiseman, F. B., Jr.
  1988   *BALI Sekala and Niskala.* Vol. 1: *Essays on Religion, Ritual, and Art.* n.p.: Periplus Editions.
Engelmann, George J.
  1882   *Labor among Primitive Peoples.* St. Louis: J. H. Chambers. Reprint New York: AMS Press, 1977.
Enkin, Murray W.
  1992   "Commentary: 'Do I Do That? Do I Really Do That? Like That?' " *Birth* 19(1):19–21.
Fischer, A.
  1963   "Reproduction in Truk." *Ethnology* 12:526–540.
Goodale, Jane C.
  1971   *Tiwi Wives: A Study of the Women of Melville Island, North Australia.* Seattle: University of Washington Press.
Grace, P., and R. Kahakiwa
  1984   *Wahine Toa: Women of Maori Myth.* Auckland: Collins.
Harrison, Michelle
  1982   *A Woman in Residence.* New York: Random House.
Hedstrom, L. W., and Niles Newton
  1986   "Touch in Labor: A Comparison of Cultures and Eras." *Birth* 13(3):181–186.
Hillan, E. M.
  1985   "Posture for Labour and Delivery." *Midwifery* 1:19–23.
Hodnett, E. D.
  1993   "Support from Caregivers during Childbirth." In *Pregnancy and Childbirth*

Module, ed. M. W. Enkin, M. J. Keirse, M. J. Renfrew, and J. P. Neilson. Cochrane Database of Systematic Reviews, Review no. 03871, May. Oxford: Update Software, Disk Issue 2.

Hofmeyr, G. J., V. C. Nikodem, W. L. Wolman, B. E. Chambers, and T. Kramer
1991   "Companionship to Modify the Clinical Birth Environment: Effects on Progress and Perceptions of Labour and Breastfeeding." *British Journal of Obstetrics and Gynaecology* 98 (August):756–764.

Humphrey, L.
1907   *A Manual of Nursing: Medical and Surgical.* London: Griffin.

Jordan, Brigitte
[1978] 1993   *Birth in Four Cultures: A Cross-Cultural Investigation of Childbirth in Yucatan, Holland, Sweden and the United States.* 4th ed. Prospect Heights, Ill.: Waveland Press.

Kennell, J., M. Klaus, S. McGrath, S. Robertson, and C. Hinkley
1991   "Continuous Emotional Support during Labor in a U.S. Hospital." *Journal of the American Medical Association* 265, no. 17 (May):2197–2201.

Kitzinger, Jenny V.
1990a   "Recalling the Pain." *Nursing Times* 86(3):38–40.
1990b   "The Internal Examination." *Practitioner* 234:698–700.
1992   "Counteracting, Not Reenacting, the Violation of Women's Bodies: The Challenge for Prenatal Caregivers." *Birth* 19 (December):219–220.

Kitzinger, Sheila
1991   *The Midwife Challenge.* 2d ed. London: Pandora Press.
1992   "Birth and Violence against Women." In *Women's Health Matters,* ed. H. Roberts, 63–80. London: Routledge.
1994a   *Ourselves as Mothers.* Boston: Addison-Wesley.
1994b   "The Social Context of Birth: Some Comparisons between Childbirth in Jamaica and Britain." In *Ethnography of Fertility and Birth,* ed. C. P. MacCormack, 181–203. Prospect Heights, Ill.: Waveland Press.

Krieger, Dolores
1975   "Therapeutic Touch: The Imprimatur of Nursing." *American Journal of Nursing* 75(5):784–787.

Kurokawa, J., and M. W. Zilkoski
1985   "Adapting Hospital Obstetrics to Birth in the Squatting Position." *Birth* 12(2):87–90.

Laderman, Carol
1983   *Wives and Midwives: Childbirth and Nutrition in Rural Malaysia.* Berkeley: University of California Press.

Landrum, S. H.
1912   Letter to editor. *Journal of the American Medical Association* 58:576.

Larrington, C., ed.
1992   *The Feminist Companion to Mythology.* London: Pandora Press.

Lupe, P. J., and T. L. Gross
1986   "Maternal Upright Posture and Mobility in Labour: A Review." *Obstetrics and Gynecology* 67:727–734.

Mead, Margaret
1949   *Male and Female: A Study of the Sexes.* New York: Morrow.

Opler, Marvin E.
   1946   *Childhood and Youth in Jicarilla Apache Society.* Publications of the Frederick Webb Hodge Society Publication Fund, vol. 5. Los Angeles.
Perrone, B., H. H. Stockel, and V. Krueger
   1989   *Medicine Women, Curanderas, and Women Doctors.* Norman: University of Oklahoma Press.
Pizzini, Franca
   1987   "The Woman Patient in an Obstetrical Situation: Communicative Hierarchies in Humour." Paper presented at the 3d International Interdisciplinary Congress on Women, Dublin, July.
Rajadhon, P. A.
   1987   *Some Traditions of the Thai.* Bangkok: Thai Inter-Religious Commission for Development and Sathirakoses Nagapradipa Foundation.
Roberts, J. E., and D. A. Wodell
   1983   "The Effects of Maternal Position on Uterine Contractility and Efficiency." *Birth* 10(4):243–249.
Romero, Laura C.
   1993   *Sobada and Manteada Obstetrical Techniques Used by Mexican Midwives.* Mexico City: Ticime, PAL. Video.
Shultz, G. D.
   1958   "*Journal* Mothers Report on Cruelty in Maternity Wards." *Ladies' Home Journal* 75(May):44.
Sosa, R., John H. Kennel, Marshall Klaus, S. Roberts, and J. Urrutia
   1980   "The Effects of a Supportive Company on Perinatal Problems, Length of Labor, and Mother-Infant Interaction." *New England Journal of Medicine* 303:597–600.
Tauroa, H., and P. Tauroa
   1986   *Te Marae.* Auckland: Reed.
Thompson, Barbara
   1967   "Infant Feeding and Child Care in a West African Village." *Journal of Tropical Pediatrics* 13(3):113.
Turton, P.
   1986   "Joining Forces." *Nursing Times* (19 November):31–32.
Velvovsky, L., K. Platonov, V. Ploticher, and E. Shugom
   1960   *Painless Childbirth through Psychoprophylaxis.* Moscow: Foreign Languages Publishing House.
Wagner, M. V., V. P. Chin, C. J. Peters, B. Drexler, and L. A. Newman
   1989   "A Comparison of Early and Delayed Induction of Labor with Spontaneous Rupture of Membranes at Term." *Obstetrics and Gynecology* 74(1 July): 93–97.
Wertz, Richard W., and Dorothy C. Wertz
   1977   *Lying-In: A History of Childbirth in America.* New York: Free Press.

NINE

Authority in Translation

Finding, Knowing, Naming, and Training "Traditional Birth Attendants" in Nepal

Stacy Leigh Pigg

We never say or hear words, we say and hear what is true or false, good or bad, important or unimportant, pleasant or unpleasant, and so on. Words are always filled with content and meaning drawn from behavior or ideology. That is the way we understand words, and we can respond only to words that engage us behaviorally or ideologically.

—VOLOSINOV 1973:70

In international health development, "TBA" (traditional birth attendant) is used to refer to the diverse kinds of people who assist women during birth. This chapter examines the hidden process of cross-cultural translation embedded in this generalized notion of the TBA. More broadly, it explores how words organize actions. The language used by the international development establishment for talking about various indigenous healers, including midwives, has practical consequences. It works, I will argue, to position development institutions as the locus of authoritative knowledge while devaluing other, local forms of knowledge. Paradoxically, this devaluation of local practices occurs even as development programs explicitly seek to work with local practitioners. Programs for training TBAs in Nepal offer the basis of a case study that shows how development systematically dismantles different sociocultural realities in the course of taking them into account.

What makes it possible to find TBAs in Nepal? It requires that various Nepalese ideas and practices related to birth be *recognized* as "birth assistance." Training programs are based on a particular way of translating Nepalese frameworks for understanding and managing birth into a generic model of birth assistance. Such translations are always problematic because the categories, values, and practices at work in one cultural context will never map perfectly onto those of another. Health development initiatives face the issue of translation in their very practices: They aim to spread scientific medicine and health knowledge in places where other idioms of care and healing exist.

Training for indigenous healers and birth attendants has been encouraged since the mid-1970s as one means of achieving this goal. These training programs seek, not to replace other medical practices, but to enhance them by improving health service delivery through cooperation with existing indigenous systems. In the course of their implementation, however, many such programs fall short of the ideals of "enhancement" and "cooperation." It is not easy to identify whom to train, or to communicate often-unfamiliar medical principles to trainees, or to introduce new practices into existing routines. Nor is it clear how indigenous practices are to be respected when the explicit goal of these programs is to alter them.

At issue in training programs is how different knowledge systems are to be brought together. Brigitte Jordan ([1978] 1993) has observed that training programs for traditional midwives present cosmopolitan obstetrics as authoritative. They render indigenous knowledge illegitimate and indigenous ways of knowing invisible.[1] What the midwives learn most effectively is how to present themselves to the official health care system and how to legitimate themselves by using its language. Instead of working with indigenous knowledge and ways of knowing, the trainings Jordan observed attempted to override existing knowledge and practices. Trainers worked from the implicit assumption that the midwives' knowledge was wrong or inferior to the medical knowledge being presented. She concludes that by not recognizing indigenous knowledge, "cosmopolitan obstetrics becomes a *cosmopolitical* obstetrics, that is, a system that enforces a particular distribution of power across cultural and social divisions" ([1978] 1993:196; emphasis added).

I want to look more deeply into the ways this power asymmetry is produced. Despite a widespread appreciation of the need to take indigenous knowledge into account, training programs continue to serve the "cosmopolitical" function of establishing medical obstetrics as authoritative. Jordan's insightful analysis shows how this occurs in the classroom where midwives are trained. I look here at how indigenous knowledge is rendered invisible *long before* trainers meet midwives. Training programs are embedded in a wider discourse of health development that systematically produces its authoritative relationship to local cultures.

Three issues of translation arise in training programs for TBAs. First, there is the problem of identifying who—what kinds of lay people and specialists—should be recipients of training. Second, there is the problem of adjusting medical messages to local circumstances. Third, and least apparent to development professionals themselves and virtually unexamined in applied development writing, is the problem of relating a medical model that views physical processes as divorced from social contexts to other conceptualizations of well-being and illness. In this chapter I look closely at how TBA training programs in Nepal grapple with each of these problems of translation. I situate training programs within the larger construction of a globalized vision of "traditional medicine," on the one hand, and within the development-related research that produces specific information about "local ideas and practices," on the other.

"TBA" is a term coined in health development discourse. The abbreviations TBA (traditional birth attendant) and TMP (traditional medical practitioner) stand not simply for more cumbersome generic terms but also for a complex process of translation that produces them. TMP and TBA are especially interesting terms because they refer not to development's internal world, as do abbreviations or acronyms for agency names, but to features of the societies that development aims to change. Both these abbreviations substitute for other words in the languages of specific places. They do not simply abbreviate terms in English; they foreshorten the space separating a local Nepalese world in which people call on certain healing specialists and an international world of health service management.

THE CONCEPT OF TRADITIONAL HEALERS
IN INTERNATIONAL HEALTH POLICY

What happens when local Nepalese practices are rendered as "the traditional"? Looking at what is lost in the translation can be a way of inquiring into the social relations translation produces. My discussion of this process here is based on development agency reports[2] and policy statements connected to the use of "traditional healers" in Nepal and is supplemented by interviews I conducted with foreign and Nepalese development officials. This study forms part of a larger inquiry into the relation between Nepalese villagers' perspectives and the social ideology of development, based on ethnographic research I carried out in the eastern hills of Nepal for two years in the mid-1980s. Though I have not drawn directly on this research here, it informs my understanding of the social context of rural Nepal, and it is the experience that prompted me to look more closely at development rhetoric in the first place. The analysis of discourse in documents that I present here is not a substitute for an analysis of all the social practices taking place in numerous settings. This chapter does not address the interactions and conversations through which programs are actually carried out. I leave what occurs as the training programs actually unfold and what the trainers and trainees make of them as important questions that merit further research. Here I focus on how conceptual categories turn into designs for training programs.

Words are a form of action in development. At every turn concepts take form in institutional structures. Sites are chosen. Offices are established. Jobs are created. Research is conducted. Programs are carried out. Training programs are conducted. Evaluations are commissioned. These are social processes involving actors who view them from particular positions. Thus it is important to consider the processes through which the current concept of traditional birth attendant was formulated.

Training programs for "indigenous healers" emerge at a nexus where particular "problems" that development has identified are being converted into the "solutions" for the next generation of programs. Specifically, the problem of "top-down planning" underlines the need for "community participation" and the importance of "sociocultural information" in appropriately tailoring implementation to local conditions. Thus "the gap," as it is called, between planning agendas and local realities is to be addressed, according to the plan put forth in development writings, by enlisting local people in development efforts. Training programs for "indigenous medical practitioners" are created to "bridge the gap." Greater stress, more generally, is placed on improving the flow of information about local realities to the planning center. Research on "local ideas and practices" is conducted, and numerous reports detailing "knowledge, attitudes, and practices" provide sociocultural information to be used to improve planning. These measures are introduced as solutions to the problematic disjunction between development plans and the communities for which they are intended. Hence the need for TBAs and TMPs. According to the World Health Organization (WHO),

> Traditional medical practitioners and birth attendants are found in most societies. They are often part of the local community, culture and traditions, and continue to have high social standing in many places, exerting considerable influence on local health practices. With the support of the formal health system, these indigenous practitioners can become important allies in organizing efforts to improve the health of the community. Some communities may select them as community health workers. It is therefore well worthwhile exploring the possibilities of engaging them in primary health care and of training them accordingly. (WHO 1978:63)

This concept of the traditional medical practitioner who can be "found in most societies" and "is part of the local community, culture and traditions" came to prominence as part of the World Health Organization's emphasis on primary health care (PHC). Declaring the goal of "health for all in the year 2000" in 1978, WHO proposed the PHC model as a comprehensive strategy for achieving a more equitable provision of health care. This model is the basis for Nepal's national health plans.

This watershed shift in health development policy advocated styles of

community-based education and service delivery that would be closely tailored to the conditions, resources, and culture of particular countries.³

> The Conference considered primary health care to be essential care based
> on practical, scientifically sound and *socially acceptable* methods and technol-
> ogy made universally accessible to individuals and families in the community
> through their *full participation* and at a cost that the community and country
> can afford to maintain at every stage of their development in the spirit of *self-
> reliance and self-determination.* (WHO 1978:16; emphasis added)

In accordance with this vision, the PHC policy supported programs for
training indigenous practitioners to serve as health auxiliaries.⁴ The aim
was to solve the problem of health staffing levels by enlisting already
trusted and experienced traditional medical practitioners in health initiatives. This was seen both as a pragmatic interim solution for countries lacking the resources to establish "modern" health services and as a way to
partially valorize non-Western modes of healing. In broad terms, this was a
shift away from the uniform promotion of a model of modern health care
based on biomedical norms and values to the promotion of what amounts
to the same model, but now achieved through different practical forms
adjusted to the contingencies of place.

Within development circles this shift is understood as a major step in
the advancement of planning expertise, made on the basis of careful assimilation of the lessons of experience. When the World Health Organization
and the United Nations Children's Fund (UNICEF) put their considerable
institutional weight behind the primary health care approach, they endorsed at the level of policy two major reformist trends that emerged in
the 1970s. The first is the swing from a sector-oriented approach to an
integrated approach. Programs focused narrowly on agricultural production, family planning, income generation, or nutrition came to be seen as
ineffective because they failed to take into account the interconnections
between these problems. Second, more locally oriented models of development came to be advocated as solutions to the disappointing results of
earlier "top-down" approaches that emphasized capital-intensive infusions
of technology.⁵ The idea of a flexible, locally sensitive approach to development caught on quickly. Suddenly, this development ethos became attrac-
tive and persuasive, rhetorically at least, to people working in development
all over the world.

It became possible, in this context, to propose working with local healers
in health development schemes, when previously these healers were viewed
as figures who should either be silently replaced or openly fought.⁶ Working with local healers is one very concrete way to "incorporate" local realities in development plans, by literally signing people up as workers in

national health bureaucracies. Proposals to work with local healers offer an inexpensive, immediate solution to the "manpower problem," the shortage of trained personnel to work in rural, often remote areas (e.g., Pillsbury 1979). It is argued that Western medicine will only come to predominate through a strategy of gentle persuasion. Healers who already have the trust of the community are therefore potentially effective health educators and family planning motivators. Further, communication of health messages must be designed, it is asserted, with the existing beliefs and practices of communities in mind. Local healers are part of the reality that must be dealt with by development. The interest in local healers, note, has little to do with their expertise or practice per se, but rather lies in the potential that exists to channel their practice toward health development aims. Working with local healers is proposed as a practical interim strategy.

This heightened focus on TMPs is a function of the distinction made in development discourse between its own role as a catalytic force coming from "outside" and the inner world of closed traditional societies. This picture of global social differences creates by implication a role for mediators and cultural brokers. TMPs are imagined to fit perfectly in this interstitial space. They were discovered to be "like us" as fellow health promoters, but crucially "not like us" in that they are characterized as trusted cultural insiders who can carry development messages into the hidden heart of traditional societies. The shift toward treating traditional healers as a resource is part of the cycle in development through which past mistakes become lessons that continually provide new and improved solutions. It therefore augments the aura of progressive advancement on which development rests.

Members of the international development elite can talk at length, with tremendous conviction, about the "real" medicinal value of folk remedies and the "real" psychological value of traditional healing—without ever having observed or interacted with any actual healers. They *already* know about what these healers do because development lore and literature synthesizes and summarizes data from particular places, molding it into a powerful mythology of traditional healing and its hidden worth. For example, a WHO publication called "The Traditional Birth Attendant in Maternal and Child Health and Family Planning: A Guide to Her Training and Utilization" begins with the following premise:

> Birth practices within a particular culture or sub-cultural group within a larger one, are influenced by the way of living and thinking of the people who share that culture or sub-culture. Although some common elements may be found, these practices, as a rule, vary considerably among societies. (Verderese and Turnbull 1975:8)

It emphasizes "the importance of obtaining information on Traditional Birth Attendants' practices, in each local situation, when planning and conducting training programmes for this type of personnel" (1975:10). It then goes on to sketch food prohibitions, ceremonies, beliefs about pre- and postnatal care, and so on, that are "likely" in a "traditional society." This discussion alternates isolated examples with generalizations about traditional birth practices "in some societies," "as a rule," "often," and "sometimes," using the illusion of attention to cultural particularities to build a coherent model of the traditional. Though this guide was written expressly to provide a structure for incorporating local customs into training programs, its language encourages readers to blur all (non-Western) "beliefs" into an undifferentiated "tradition."[7] Such rhetorical patterns in the presentation of cultural information have an important symbolic dimension. Construing traditional healers as a resource instead of an obstacle ostensibly shows "respect" for "other cultures" while still controlling them.

The idea of working with local healers retains an appeal out of proportion to the number of programs that undertake it. Much to the frustration of advocates, relatively few countries or agencies have taken up WHO's policy initiative to work more closely with indigenous healers (see Pillsbury 1982; UNICEF 1989). When it comes to putting policy into practice, most health planners prefer training community volunteers as health workers to collaborating with local healers. This suggests that pragmatism alone is not the only factor at work, the rationality of planning language notwithstanding.[8] Traditional healers are symbols: for some, moral symbols of a collaborative, culturally appropriate mode of development; for others, symbols of the harmful, backward practices it is development's task to replace.

Although WHO policy does not dictate the design of health services in member countries, it creates an overall policy climate. The wording in its documents must be general enough to fit all nations, cautious enough not to appear dictatorial, yet specific enough to endorse a policy direction. The terms "traditional birth attendant" and "traditional medical practitioner" meet these conditions of linguistic diplomacy. Because they are not the real terms used for any practitioner in any language, they ostensibly allow all societies to come together on equal footing. In the realms of high policy, "traditional birth attendant" stands for a hypothetical person about whom health development planners might usefully know more. While seeming to describe an empirical reality, it operates as a theoretical construction of a role that is believed to exist in those societies labeled traditional. The words "traditional birth attendant" serve as a placeholder, a blank waiting to be filled in at the local level where primary health care is to be carried out.

FINDING AND TRAINING "TRADITIONAL BIRTH ATTENDANTS" IN NEPAL: THE PROBLEMS OF TRANSLATION

In Nepal, efforts to fill in that blank with Nepalese content took the form of initiatives to train local midwives, on the one hand, and the ritual healers known collectively as *dhāmi-jhānkri,* on the other. Though formally the Nepalese health system maintains a small, parallel "Traditional Medicine" division supporting Ayurvedic training and health posts, it was the TBA and TMP training programs begun slowly in the 1970s, and with increasing intensity in the 1980s, that most embodied the ideal of working with local people. Nongovernmental organizations (NGOs), with their smaller projects and flexible planning style, were the first to experiment with training for traditional medical practitioners.

Programs in Nepal follow the trend worldwide: considerably more enthusiasm is shown for training and incorporating midwives into national health schemes than is shown for other kinds of practitioners (Pillsbury 1982). TBA training projects were initiated by a number of NGOs through the 1970s and 1980s. These programs now use a standard curriculum and are coordinated through a central committee. In twenty years the training of TBAs has gone from an experimental program to an institutionalized part of the primary health care delivery strategy.[9]

The standardized TBA training brings together the women selected for ten days of instruction, with a four-day refresher course later that same year. The lessons focus on hygiene and safe birth practices, nutrition, and family planning education. Training for TBAs is intended to teach them to assist only in normal births and to impress on them the need to make referrals in difficult cases. More broadly, the training also links care of mothers and babies to positive attitudes toward family planning. At the end of the training, a TBA receives a kit containing basic supplies.

Identifying TBAs

Trained TBAs are expected to return to their communities, armed with better knowledge, and continue assisting in births as volunteers. Their only compensation is the customary form of ritual payment, if one exists. The training programs are intended to add to a practice that is already taking place; therefore the women are not considered official health workers. In many parts of Nepal, however, women are assisted by other women rather than by a recognized specialist. Training in these areas is for "respected and influential women" who do not have an existing role specifically as birth attendants. It is not uncommon for the women recruited for training to have little or no interest in midwifery. They are there, in some cases, for the prestige that comes from participation in an "official" development activity and the small daily allowance paid for participation. As a result, though the rationale behind the programs is to work with the TBAs who are "out there," the institutional need to have TBAs leads to a program that in many cases is attempting to produce "trained TBAs" out of women who do not identify themselves as any sort of "birth attendant."

The organizers of TBA training are aware of these problems. Arguably, training need not be for recognized specialist-midwives. If most women are likely to assist with childbirth at one time or another in their lives, then training for any woman is worthwhile. If the ultimate goal of training is to enhance local knowledge by introducing new practices, such as ways to prevent neonatal tetanus, then training programs are simply a way to begin to introduce these ideas in local communities. The number of births a particular trained woman attends in a year, some organizers argue, should not be the measure of the effectiveness of the program. These are reasonable arguments. Yet because the training programs are "for TBAs," the impression that there are Nepalese "TBAs" who are midwives—specialists—haunts the program. Though the professionals who have worked with TBAs from the start are well aware of the complexities of the Nepalese reality, they nevertheless face constant criticism of their efforts. Newly arrived foreign advisers repeatedly discover with dismay that TBA training programs are not training "real" TBAs. The women who are trained often do not do what it is assumed that "midwives" in "traditional societies" do. Doubt as to whether TBAs even exist "traditionally" in Nepal has fueled criticism of the TBA programs from the start.

The question of the existence of TBAs arises from the wide variations in Nepal, across regions and ethnic groups, in the role of birth assistance itself and in customs surrounding birth. Some specialized "birth attendants" are untouchables who only perform the polluting task of cutting the cord (for example, in the caste Hindu regions of Nepal bordering on India), while others are specialists called on only to manage difficult births (in regions throughout Nepal, but not necessarily in every village), while still others are highly respected women with religious healing powers who must be called at any birth (e.g., among Newars). In much of Nepal, as I have noted, women deliver with assistance from kinswomen or neighbors with no special expertise.[10] The variation, it must be stressed, lies not only in what these women actually do but also in the stages of pregnancy, labor, and birth during which they are involved. Significantly, the nature of their relationship to the woman they assist also varies. Contrary to Western assumptions about "midwives" who care for women throughout pregnancy and birth, many Nepalese specialists have very limited contact with women and perform only a single role. Care of pregnant women and infants is embedded in myriad customary practices and unspoken assumptions, not entrusted to specialists.

Ambitious attempts to document this variation were made in accordance with the WHO policy guidelines to hone training to "the" culture of a country. Major research was undertaken with the documentation of ethnic and regional variation in mind (Levitt 1987). It illustrates clearly why issues of translation and description are so central to understanding the production of development knowledge. The highly standardized format for presenting and synthesizing sociocultural research for development cannot accommodate the overwhelming fluidity and variability of Nepalese practices. We learn that there are food prohibitions for pregnant women, but different ones at each research site; there are customs for dealing with the delivered placenta, but these vary; there are common notions of birth pollution, but different rules regarding it. Because it is beyond the scope of this type of research to attempt to explain these specific practices within each local context, one is left without a way of understanding the full medical and social significance of the ideas and practices that are detailed in these studies. Does it matter, for instance, that some people in Nepal bury the placenta under a tree while others bury it near the house? From a biomedical definition of safe birth, it does not, while within local frameworks such acts are understood to have repercussions for the infant's future and physical well-being. Identifying the practices relevant to health and to development communication is no easy task, especially when such generalizations are to be made from highly complex and variable local data. For a foreign health planner it may seem enough to know that there are ideas about birth pollution and unnecessary to sort out which ethnic groups do precisely what and why. One of the unresolved difficulties in mounting a national program such as TBA training is what to do with information that a given practice or idea prevails "in many parts of Nepal." There is no mechanism for accommodating the places where the traditional form described as common does *not* exist. Nepal's cultural variation is at odds with the institutional need for a unified, national program for "traditional birth attendants."

The Nepali word chosen as the translation for "traditional birth attendant" is *suḍeni,* whose meanings within the local context itself lead to additional confusion. The word *suḍeni* in Nepali is associated with a woman with *special* skills in assisting with births, particularly, the skill to insert her hand in the birth canal and otherwise intercede in difficult labor. It was found that in areas where TBA training programs have been carried out regularly, people are much more likely to identify their local "suḍeni." Responses in areas where there have been no training programs often fail to identify any local "suḍeni" (Levitt 1987). Many women selected as TBAs for training deny that they are suḍeni, while training programs appear to be actually creating suḍeni by using the word to refer to the TBAs they train (Levitt 1987:60). It seems the word *suḍeni* has come to mean something new as a result of the development interest in birth attendants. Foreign development advisers use the word, thinking it is the Nepali word "for" TBA. It has become the official term used in development offices to refer to the women trained. Ordinary Nepalis, hearing *suḍeni* used in this way, begin to use the term to refer to a role that training programs create.

Extending New Knowledge

The planners, supervisors, and trainers involved in the TBA program in Nepal know that "birth assistance" includes a variety of roles in Nepal. The lesson plan for the training nevertheless sets out a basic medical message about reproductive physiology, cleanliness, and the management of normal labor deemed important *regardless* of local custom. Although planners, many of whom have extensive hands-on nursing experience in rural Nepal, do know that TBA training in different locales will be directed toward women with very different relations to the women they help, the programs provide the same messages in more or less the same way to all of them. Many of the program supervisors I interviewed about TBA training were knowledgeable about practices in the locales where their programs were carried out. Though the trainers are explicitly encouraged to make these adjustments when they carry out training programs, the structure of the training plan restricts them to emphasizing the medical message of the formal curriculum over local ideas, practices, and conditions. Trainers, who are drawn from a comparatively well-educated emergent middle class from both villages and urban areas, vary in their ability to communicate with villagers as well as in the relevance they see in acknowledging local customs. Those who seek to do so must work within the constraints imposed by lesson plans that are at cross-purposes with their efforts. Most health development workers, however, view their job as a task of correcting the "wrong beliefs" of villagers (see Stone 1986). The agenda set in lessons for "TBAs" implicitly confirms the notion that existing practices must be replaced if Nepal is to develop.[11]

In the lesson plans the medical message is clearly primary. The insistence in WHO guidelines (Verderese and Turnbull 1975) on tailoring the messages to local conditions is lost in the Nepalese manual for assistant nurse midwives on the training of TBAs, appearing only as follows:

> The teachings should be presented in simple language and translated into the local dialect as appropriate. The instructor should show respect for the suḍeni [traditional birth attendant]. In running classes, community opinion and customs should be taken into account. If these customs and opinions are not harmful to health then they should be observed and promoted. If these customs do pose a harm then they should be discouraged slowly and gradually. It is important to listen to what the suḍeni have to say. (Ministry of Health, His Majesty's Government of Nepal 1990)

This is the only reference to local practices in the manual. As an official acknowledgment that local birth assistants exist, and that it is worthwhile for representatives of "modern" health services to cooperate with them, it is a significant advance over policies that ignored or condemned local knowledge. Such statements do not come easily to the mainstream medical establishment. As Marsden Wagner (this volume) attests, professional interests are at stake. Formidable battles over authority lie behind the publication of even as cursory a statement as this one. But are formal statements of this sort sufficient to bring about the benevolent cooperation with TBAs that is espoused? Other aspects of the content and context of training programs tend to undermine the ideal, however sincerely put forth, of "listening" to "what the suḍeni have to say." The manual ends up emphasizing what development planners think that trainees need to be taught, not what they assume they already know. It is implicitly assumed that the women trained will *automatically* put their new information to use within locally appropriate forms of practice.[12]

The manual itself is a product of intersecting positions in debates that are at one and the same time about (1) what counts as better health training and (2) what position development should occupy vis-à-vis "tradition." According to at least one of the foreign development workers involved with the preparation of this manual, it was the Nepali nurses who resisted more direct and tolerant references to specific local practices in favor of a generic "modern" health message. For most Nepali development planners, after all, being "developed" means leaving behind those "traditional" ways. They distance themselves from "tradition" to establish both their social status and their institutional authority, while foreign development advisers are able to bolster their authority by talking about "culture" and "tradition." Both positions are based on a logic that distinguishes "tradition" from authoritative development knowledge.

How well do the training programs actually tailor their objectives to local circumstances? It is very difficult to know. Evaluations of the practices of trained TBAs show that while they do gain new knowledge, they also frequently fail to follow to the letter what they have been instructed to do. What appears in program guidelines as simple, basic instruction about hygiene and cleanliness proves enormously complicated to instill correctly in trainees. For example, trainees are taught to boil the razor blade they use to cut the umbilical cord. Program evaluators have observed that many trainees faithfully follow these guidelines but often interpret boiling to mean dipping the instrument in hot water. If dropped on the floor, the "boiled" instrument might simply be picked up and put to use—much to the dismay of the program evaluators. Similarly, program descriptions frequently point to the potentially revolutionary benefits of merely teaching birth attendants to wash their hands. In practice, however, the proper washing of hands is not simple at all, as trainers themselves are quick to point out. Hands must be washed with soap and warm water (already, not always possible in Nepalese households); nails should be cut and clean, and bangles removed; the washed hands should not be dried with a cloth; the hands should be held pointing up to maintain cleanliness; and nothing should be touched. With so many ways to undo the benefits of hand washing, it is no wonder that women fail to observe firsthand the revolutionary improvement that practice alone is supposed to bring. As program evaluators learn more about the ways the trainees frequently misunderstand or mispractice what they are taught, training programs come to emphasize more and more specific points. The rhetoric of development continues to stress the "simple intervention" despite extensive experience with its complexities.

The reason to know about "local ideas and practices" becomes a practical one: identifying ways that training messages are misunderstood. In TBA training, the focus is on distinguishing "harmless" and "harmful" practices in traditional birth assistance. The reason for documenting in detail local techniques for managing birth is to isolate those practices that might be "harmful." This allows health planners to locate precise "points of intervention" where significant health gains could be achieved: for example, in insisting that sterilized instruments be used to cut the umbilical cord. The scientific soundness of these judgments notwithstanding, they are made through a process that reorders definitions of what is most important. (I return to this point below). Women's insistence on "persisting," as the development phrasing puts it, with certain practices is consistently and patronizingly explained as the desire to adhere to the "safety of familiar traditions."

In elevating the medical dimension of birth to such prominence, the so-called beliefs that people in any given place hold are subordinated as secondary factors. "Local ideas and practices" thus enter into development planning as something to be scrutinized and judged, while the medical message is presented as unassailable. There is little scope for dialogue or an exchange of ideas. Information flows from biomedical obstetrics to Nepalese women, but not from Nepalese women to cosmopolitan obstetrics. The training programs reinforce an asymmetry between the ideas and practices of the trainees and medical knowledge, despite calls to listen to the midwives themselves.

Making Midwives

Ways of translating words and concepts take concrete, practical forms in the assumptions made about who and what training programs are for. Governments and development institutions view the training of "TBAs" as an aspect of health service delivery. Accordingly, they define birth assistance as a "medical" act, whether or not the people involved define the practices associated with birth in terms of health and sickness. In Nepal, women who perform a ritual service become defined, for the purposes of trainings, as midwives who perform medical services. A spectrum of birth-related concerns, spanning issues of ritual pollution, the vulnerability of pregnant women and infants to witchcraft, and ritual debt to issues of modesty and embarrassment are reorganized in the framework for training TBAs. The varying social, emotional, protective, or polluting roles the trainees might actually be playing are subsumed under the role of managing birth itself. Within local understanding, for instance, the main role of the woman who cuts the cord may be to carry away the ritual pollution associated with birth. For many Nepalis this pollution is as real as a placenta. But the development perspective regards this role only as a potentially medical one, whose main purpose is to safeguard the health of mother and child. In general, all practices are treated as if they fit a common idealized role of "midwife," even though it is well known in international policy circles that not all "birth attendants" fit the image of the midwife who cares for a woman throughout the pregnancy, birth, and postpartum period. Training programs are nevertheless structured so as to systematically remake the trainees in the image of the traditional midwife. Trained TBAs are fashioned as technicians.

In effect, training programs redefine the practices of the trainees. Birth assistance is particularly malleable. Birth is easier to speak about and speak to than Nepalese notions about spirits that cause illnesses, for instance. Everyone can agree, for example, whether or not the placenta has been delivered, while no such agreement is possible for the chasing away of ghosts. There is a predictability to the known events of pregnancy and childbirth and a concreteness to many of the techniques for dealing with it. Because birth assistance involves many actions externally manipulating parts of the body, it is easier to collect statements from women about "what we do." TBA training programs work with a presumed common and obvious concern with the management of pregnancy, labor, and birth.

The "obviousness" of this common reality is deceptive. Different cultures understand, organize, and manage birth in their own ways (see Jordan 1993). Anthropologists insist that the social aspect of birth can never be separated from its physiological aspect, for the physical events of childbirth are always taking place within a shared understanding of "the best way, the right way, indeed *the* way to bring a child into the world" (Jordan [1978] 1993:4).

TBA training, however, is based on the notion that the "cultural" dimension of childbirth *can* be separated from the "physiological" dimension. While careful not to interfere with beliefs and customs if they are deemed "harmless," they introduce a biomedical understanding of birth through the back door by focusing on a physiological realm divorced from social considerations. Training programs convey a biomedical ideology not simply through the theory of physiology and disease causation they teach but also through the insistence in the format of trainings themselves that the physiological be clearly separated from social, moral, and religious concerns. The medicalization of birth attendants, tacitly enacted through training, requires trainees themselves to fragment their practices, to distinguish between the "medical" and the "social" aspects of what they do.

There are aspects of Nepalese women's practices that are left out or marginalized in training programs, precisely because of the importance placed on techniques and physiology. Nowhere is there a space created for the emotional and social significance of birth. This accounts, I think, for some of the astonishing omissions in discussions of "local ideas and practices." The many ways Nepalis give special care to pregnant women, new mothers, and babies vanish in development accounts. *How* they show care can only be grasped within the framework through which they themselves perceive dangers and problems. The Maithilis of southeastern Nepal, for instance, view the postpartum period as a time of special risk for both mother and infant (Reissland and Burghart 1988). For instance, until the "sore" of the opened birth passage closes (i.e., in the first week postpartum) the mother is especially vulnerable to ghosts who might invade her body, causing madness or sterility. To protect herself, the mother stays in the shuttered birth room for about six days. She avoids eating foods that inhibit the closing of the "wound," a precaution that also protects her baby from the potentially harmful properties that could be transferred to him or her through her breast milk. These customs, then, are not "beliefs" having nothing to do with the "reality" of the body. They are practices through which people care for bodies that are understood in terms other than those of biomedicine.

Cross-cultural research on childbirth has shown just how historically specific the notion of medically managed childbirth is. A medicalized construction of pregnancy and childbirth dictates that these states must be managed and monitored by specialists.[13] In North America, in fact, women who give birth without professional management are accused of negligence (Tsing 1990) and obstetricians tend to treat women in labor as unruly workers who must be monitored lest they damage "the product" (Martin 1987). Emily Martin has shown that the time-management and efficiency approach that breaks the process of childbirth down into stages facilitates the comparison, evaluation, and control of women in labor. Tacitly, childbirth that is not supervised by a trained expert is considered suspect, at least in the United States. Are these deeply ingrained cultural assumptions being transferred to developing countries in notions about how birth is best managed? The fact of expert management itself may be as important to this moralistic sense of what is "best" as the actual techniques that might have positive effects on maternal and infant mortality. TBAs are looked to as the experts who can adopt the role of manager. Their practices, in turn, can be supervised by development institutions.

Last, the structure of training programs itself communicates certain messages to the trainees. For Nepali women, training programs are features of a wider world of "development" and "modernity." They are but one aspect of a larger process in Nepal by which being "modern" becomes associated with a higher social status (see Pigg 1992, 1993). When women attend training programs they learn what "modern" people are supposed to do and say. This knowledge is authoritative for these women not simply because the trainers present it as such but because training comes out of institutions that are creating an authority for "developed" ideas overall. What is learned in training has more relevance in the context of status negotiation, where it matters socially that one appear "developed," than it does in the contexts in which births actually take place. Training programs thus likely widen women's sense of the disparity between "modern" practices and their (now devalued) local realities.

In considering how authoritative knowledge is displayed in interactions, we need to look beyond the rooms where birth takes place to the other sites where authority is produced and reproduced. Training programs are one such site. Development-related research and documentation, to which I turn next, is another.

TECHNIQUES FOR KNOWING ABOUT TRADITIONS

The irony here is that in the attempt to create programs tailored to local conditions, a great deal of what local people think, believe, and do is filtered out. How? Through the circulation of information about the "local" in the apparatuses of development knowledge. The authoritative knowledge about childbirth communicated in trainings is linked to the production of authoritative knowledge about "local ideas and practices." It is therefore important to understand the process that produces the knowledge of "traditional beliefs and practices" on which "culturally appropriate" forms of health development are based. The discursive regulation of what can be said in development begins in the regulation of what can be known.

The research techniques used to gather baseline information and evaluate program effectiveness already screen what is considered relevant and irrelevant information. Questionnaires, surveys, and focus groups are designed with certain ideas about "traditions" already in mind. In this process, a mobile, dislocated concept of tradition comes to be filled with the facts from Nepal.

The authoritative knowledge about local practices that is presented in reports fundamentally alters these practices by inventing new terms in which they can make sense. Facts are selected and rearranged in a way that produces an image of "local tradition" for development observers that not only distorts local practices out of recognition but virtually ensures that local ideas are silenced and shut out of development. In the process of collecting, summarizing, and analyzing data some aspects of local reality pass easily from one stage of reformulation to another, attaining the status of information about local ideas and practices, while other aspects remain unsayable, unreportable, and unknowable. The major study of TBAs in Nepal, for example, candidly admits that a major difference between trained and untrained TBAs was that "we found it much easier to interview the trained TBAs and got far fewer 'don't know' or inappropriate responses from them in comparison to the untrained TBAs" (Levitt 1987:67). As this passage clearly indicates, a response is inappropriate for the purposes of research if it cannot be formulated within development discourse. This observation suggests that what trainings actually teach is how to communicate with development officials. It also raises questions about the interactions that produce "don't know" or "unusable" categories of responses in surveys.

In translating information about "local ideas and practices" into development discourse, "traditions" are systematically rendered as isolated "beliefs" and "customs" with little social basis aside from the fact that they are features of a traditional society. The decontextualization of "tradition" is accomplished through certain habitual procedures embedded in research.

1. *Emphasizing the exotic.* A preconceived notion of what "tradition" looks like guides how data are sorted. Explicit references to rituals, supernatural beings, and pollution beliefs get recorded; the more obviously different from an unmarked "Western norm" (or, in the case of Nepal, an unmarked high-caste Hindu norm), the more likely it is to be noticed. This makes local traditions seem exotic, odd, and arbitrary.

2. *Privileging rules over practice.* The more precise and explicit an informant's statement, the more likely it is to be written down and repeated. Researchers inquire about "rules" and prohibitions (e.g., asking about postpartum taboos on sexual intercourse in a direct way, assuming people can and will articulate "custom"). When explicit rules cannot readily be found, this is often taken as evidence that no

concern or concept exists. For example, if there are no rules about what one "must" feed pregnant women, this is frequently taken as evidence that there isn't concern with the diet of pregnant women. In reports written in English, almost all the Nepali words that appear in reports are nouns—an indication of the emphasis on things over actions. The stress placed on structure and rules reinforces a notion of "tradition" as stagnant, rigid, and passive.

3. *Reifying cultural identity.* Implicitly, "tradition" is understood to inhere in a place or a social identity. For example, if a survey is conducted in a Nepalese village populated by people known as Rais, then respondents' answers are taken to represent what "Rai culture" leads people to do and think.[14] Much that is not necessarily tied to ethnic identity is extrapolated to other people labeled "Rai." Ethnic identity is taken to override all other social factors that might structure opinion, ideologies, and action.

In general, the information gathered is inadequate to account for the connections between the practices reported and the social circumstances that animate these behaviors. The reports compiling this information dutifully allude to local ideas and practices without actually taking them into account. Lacking explanatory anchors, decontextualized references to non-Western practices rhetorically reinforce an impression that "traditional" beliefs are disjointed assertions easily dismantled and replaced with reason.

In one study, focus groups with community women showed "the overwhelming need of women for health information," a conclusion reached on the basis of introductory questions posed to the group on how they would treat common childhood illnesses (JSI 1988). One of the questions is recorded in the report as "What do you do for a child with malnutrition?" The Nepali terms used to talk about malnutrition are given in parentheses: *runche* or *sukenas*. In Nepali, a child who is whiny, uncooperative, and sickly in some vague, indeterminate way is said to be *runche*. *Runche* is a social condition as well as a physical one; it could have any of a number of different causes. So although what the village women heard was "What do you do when your child is *runche*?" their answers were recorded as what they do when their child is malnourished. When the majority of the women responded that they would take the child to a traditional healer rather than increase its food intake, the conclusion was drawn that "knowledge of the relationship of food intake to severe malnutrition is extremely low among village women" (JSI 1988:36).

How was this sweeping conclusion established? The idea that *runche* is "the Nepali word for malnutrition" comes indirectly from a published report of a successful community health program, in which it was noted that nearly all the children that adults identified as *runche* suffered from early stages of malnutrition (Bomgaars 1976). It was sensibly proposed that whenever parents are saying their child is *runche,* they should be taught to make a high-protein porridge for children as a supplemental food. In becoming hoary development lore, however, the lesson that stuck was that *runche* "means" malnutrition. This example shows the interpretive pitfalls of narrowly focused development research. Lost here is attention to the intersecting structures of class, age, and gender inequalities that determine who is well fed and who is not. Lost, too, is a grasp of the ways people actually think about food, nourishment, and health. What this type of development research finds is merely an absence, ignorance.

Reports regarding maternal health show great concern for the possible nutritional deficiencies of new mothers, especially when they include ominous lists of the "prohibited foods." No one seems to ask what happens with regard to such foods in practice, or whether explicit food prohibitions can be taken as a sign of a heightened preoccupation with food instead of a sign of culturally enforced malnutrition. In a culture where food is the outward expression of love, a family's special attention to an individual's diet is a manifestation of care and concern. At the same time, the politics of distribution of food within households reflects patterns of deference and authority that often disadvantage women in their childbearing years. Feeding, being fed, and going hungry are not simply about nutrition.

The first question most development observers ask about a custom or a practice is "Does this do harm?" This is of course an important question to ask. But being too quick to seize on "harmful customs" blinds us to the wider context in which these practices occur. The "prohibition" on feeding colostrum to a newborn is a case in point. The Maithilis studied by Nadja Reissland and Richard Burghart consider colostrum to be so foul "it is only by describing it as pus that one can evoke the kind of repugnance which some mothers felt toward the prospect of feeding it to their babies" (1988:463). Biomedical research shows that colostrum transmits important immunities from mother to infant. Hence this prohibition (common throughout Nepal, and indeed much of South Asia) raises alarm flags for development observers who are screening for "harmful practices." Reissland and Burghart note, however, that we do not know whether or not this practice is actually causing harm. A Maithili woman usually puts her baby to her breast about a day after giving birth. She expresses the colostrum from her breast until she can no longer distinguish it from "real" milk. Babies, it appears, are consuming some colostrum. Perhaps the custom is not as dangerous as it first appears. Scientifically, we just do not know. Reissland and Burghart further note that "this taboo has been isolated from its cultural context largely as a result of bio-medical curiosity" (1988:463). Seen in context, the "prohibition" on feeding colostrum does not seem nearly so ominous as it does at first glance. It is part of a flow of practical and meaningful activities.

Most glaringly, reports on "postpartum" practices do not mention the Nepali word for this special state, *sutkeri,* a word whose very sound evokes for Nepalis the extra care and nurture due to a woman who has just delivered a child. Nor is there recognition of the pain people feel when circumstances limit their ability to treat *sutkeri* women as they should be treated. Responses to research questions are so radically removed from the cultural and economic context that interpretation is reduced to simple tabulation. We are left with a very limited and narrow base for authoritative representations of "local ideas and practices." [15]

There is more than insensitivity or misuse of words at stake here. Translations circulate endlessly through what researchers ask respondents and what researchers hear respondents say. This research occurs, moreover, in situations in which health extension workers whose native language is not English are taught about TBAs, acute respiratory infection (ARI), oral rehydration therapy (ORT), and other English terms specific to development jargon. These workers then use this terminology with villagers who consult them, turning abbreviations such as TBA, ARI, and ORT into words. Even when specific Nepali words such as *suḍeni* are retained, their meaning inevitably changes when interspersed in the English utterances of a foreign official, or institutionalized in the development office jargon of Nepalese staff.

The issue is not one of correctness or authenticity in language use but of social relations, institutional procedures, and power. Discourse has concrete consequences. Villagers find themselves having to interact with development institutions that have structured their programs around these static and distorted representations of "tradition." To get the resources they want they have to frame themselves in the way development has told them traditional people should be. Development induces local realities to conform to development categories, and only those aspects of local reality that can be successfully disguised in these categories can be incorporated in programs and planning.

Ironically, development practices of knowledge production help to perpetuate the "gap" between planning and local realities that so concerns development planners. This gap is the product of systematic techniques for framing and understanding "local ideas and practices." The language used in development work meshes with actual institutional practices, and together they reiterate what Geof Wood (1985) calls the "delinking" of people from their social context.

This "delinking" has effects on several levels. Most obviously, it facilitates bureaucratic administration by narrowing a vision of complex realities. Yet, at the same time, the simplifications that facilitate administrative plans generate problems of program implementation on the ground. When development programs based on decontextualized, distorted notions of "traditional ideas and practices" are set in motion in actual villages, they face numerous practical problems. Messages are not communicated effectively. Even programs explicitly planned with "traditional ideas and practices" and "the local level" in mind fall far short of "bridging the gap" in the way intended. The decontextualization resulting from the practices of translation I have detailed here detracts from the program effectiveness even as it serves bureaucratic purposes. It is difficult for development institutions to really resolve these contradictions, for "delinking" also serves a more far-reaching ideological purpose by positioning development itself as transcendent and authoritative.

CONCLUSION

In sum, both policy and implementation subsume "local tradition" under the universalistic rationality of the development model. Training programs, while aiming to enhance the expertise of those practitioners who are "already out there," require that participants understand that whole areas of their experience and knowledge are irrelevant to the development context. Local practitioners are both portrayed as and made into people whose knowledge has a limited, local importance.

Few development programs ever work as imagined. Our usual response to the looming chasm between the assumptions behind development programs and the realities of local life has been to call for more and better research about local ideas and practices. But even when such information is provided, it is rarely used effectively, as Judith Justice's work (1984, 1986, 1987) on development bureaucracies has shown. The persistent assumption is that a tune-up of the development machine would solve its functional glitches. I suggest we strive to step away from the development paradigm, with its ready-made slot for "cultural beliefs and practices." We should work to formulate other vocabularies for framing concerns about health and culture. In the rush to provide better "sociocultural information," we fail to question how the very definition of "sociocultural" is constrained by development interests. There is a complacent sense that development must proceed if problems of poverty and suffering in the Third World are to be addressed, whatever the flaws an overly zealous anthropologist might find in the fine points of cultural translation. The reaction to my critique is predictable: "We don't have time for those details, there is urgent work to be done"; "We are doing the best we can. No bureaucracy is perfect." These reactions miss the point. I have tried to show that "mere" words are produced by and reproduce a power asymmetry that becomes more entrenched every time development visions turn into policies and policies turn into actual programs. The scale of this activity is immense, global. Instead of joining in development's continual production and marketing of solutions, perhaps it is time to consider that development discourse also produces distinctive *problems,* and in fact these problems are necessary to development power and must be perpetually re-created to sustain it.

Development mediates the circulation of differing medical modes, ensuring that those deemed traditional remain local, limited, and context-specific while modern medicine acquires a global and universal role. This is how cosmopolitan obstetrics becomes, in Jordan's words, a cosmopolitical obstetrics whose authority rests on a certain distribution of power. At present in mainstream international health development other modes of knowledge are recognized as "different" and granted a limited sphere of authority within the bounds of "tradition," but development nevertheless subsumes these other modes of knowledge under the authority development claims for itself.[16] This authority comes not, as development rhetoric implies, from the presumably self-evident superiority of the medical solutions it advocates. Rather, development has authority to the extent that it is able to make its solutions—whatever they might be—appear self-evident. The language practices of development systematically dismantle a socially animated local reality, rendering its pattern as a whole inexpressible within development terms. Development appears as a *naturally* transcendent, *necessarily* global institution juxtaposed against limited, fragmented, decontextualized "local traditions." It is from this constructed position of transcendence that development claims the authority and the obligation to provide solutions for certain societies.

Development discourse presents a certain vision of the way social difference is arranged in the world. In emphasizing the difference between "traditional" and "modern," it effaces differences within and between the societies labeled traditional. On this basis development powerfully channels the circulation of information: It is through development's mediation that the "lessons" from a program in one country are transported and applied in another. When this happens, it is not a pure "Western" framework that is being imposed on a given locale in Asia, Africa, or Latin America. Rather, what is transported and set in place is a model of the relationship between the "modern" and the "traditional," a model created out of everywhere and nowhere.

For the particular answers development offers to be inevitably the right ones, all local problems must be understood as variations of the same problem. The notion of "the traditional" is therefore essential to development discourse, as the common denominator of disparate situations development can bring under control. Development institutions (and by implication, the interests served through their power) must clear the space for their entry into local worlds by establishing as ascendant a specific model of modernity.

These relations are invisible from inside development discourse. As used in development rhetoric, "TMP" and "TBA" appear only to be efficient, quite innocent, terms that allow varieties of the same kind of practitioner to be conveniently grouped together. The authority development (and its experts) has to describe societies, name problems, and propose solutions comes from the aura of truth development creates (Escobar 1988). Planners argue that it is necessary to translate from local terms such as those for the many Nepali forms of "birth assistance" into more general terms; otherwise, it is said, information about local conditions would be impossible to organize and manage. This in fact is exactly my point: without such translations local reality would literally be closed to the power arrangements of development management.

POSTSCRIPT: IF NOT DEVELOPMENT, THEN WHAT?

Is it a mistake to try to work with women and midwives in other countries? I do not think so. My review of the use of a notion of "tradition" in training programs for TBAs and TMPs in Nepal led me to some ideas about what "working with midwives" should be like. Most important, I am convinced that paying lip service to cultural appropriateness is not enough. I agree with other anthropologists that more attention needs to be paid to "local culture," but I would add that we need to think carefully about *how* we pay attention and how we translate between cultural understandings of birth. It is important not to generalize about "tradition" but to talk instead about particular values, situations, and practices as they appear in specific contexts. Yes, this requires much more work and knowledge on the part of anyone who would attempt to be a professional expert on midwives and childbirth in many countries. It also requires a different, more holistic kind of research on childbirth.

Generic plans are of limited use, and they can never be a substitute for place and context-specific birth activism. What would a "training" organized around the understandings of birth in a Nepali community look like? It would have to be a dialogue, a discussion rather than a "training." It would not begin with a biomedical model of managed obstetrical care that is then adapted to certain local idiosyncrasies. It would have to begin with the knowledge, values, and concerns of the women involved instead of with the assumptions that their understandings are inadequate and deficient. It would have to take into account the politics of gender and generation in families in Nepal, and the politics of class, caste, and ethnic relations in specific communities.[17] It would not necessarily begin by targeting birth attendants.

Biomedicine may have some answers that are good for everyone in the world, but it doesn't have all the answers. We have to be more humble about biomedical certainties, just as we have to avoid romanticizing "indigenous knowledge" as unequivocally good. When I lived in a village in Nepal for two years while conducting anthropological research, I met many women in their forties and fifties who told me stories of giving birth in a hospital. They had been stationed in Malaysia in the 1960s with their husbands, who were soldiers in the Gurkha regiments of the British army. These women described to me their silent battle with the hospital nurses over their baby's sleeping position. It is the custom in Nepal to rest a baby on its back. The nurses would come in and turn the baby over on its stomach. The mothers would turn the baby over again, only to have the nurse change the position the next time she saw it. Two decades later, this conflict was one of the most vivid memories these women had of their interaction with Westerners, and with hospitals. When recent research correlating the incidence of sudden infant death syndrome with sleeping position began to be publicized widely in North America, I thought of these women's stories. This research shows that babies sleeping on their backs or sides are much less likely to die suddenly than babies sleeping on their stomachs (e.g., Guntheroth and Spiers 1992; Spiers and Guntheroth 1994). Recommendations to parents on how to care for infants have changed, and these new recommendations are made authoritative on medical grounds, just as the old ones that recommended the prone sleeping position for infants were (see Elders 1994). Biomedical standards change, of course. But the recognition that they do change is often missing when health development efforts take on an evangelical certainty vis-à-vis the practices in non-Western societies. This example makes me think again about all the customary Nepali practices that development experts are making efforts to correct. How certain are we about what is "best"? If Nepalis were in a position to rectify North American childbirth practices, which of our customs would they most want to alter? The one-way flow of information in development may be harmful to us all.

NOTES

This chapter is a revised version of "Acronyms and Effacement: Traditional Medical Practitioners (TMP) in International Health Development," *Social Science and Medicine* 41, no. 1 (1995):47–68.

A grant from the President's Research Fund of Simon Fraser University made it possible for me to spend two months of 1992 in Nepal gathering information on training programs for TBAs and shamans. Many people working in health development in Nepal generously gave their time and shared their knowledge and experiences with me, as informants, colleagues, and friends. Most are as frustrated with the problems of development as I am. I am grateful for their assistance, even though my interpretation of their activities may differ from their own.

1. Jordan observes that training for Mayan midwives has done more to teach these women to speak the authoritative language of biomedicine than to alter their practices.

2. These reports deal explicitly with the perceived need to get accurate information about local conditions and the problematic relation between policy initiatives and community participation. They can offer only a partial perspective. Certainly not every stage of a program is recorded, and much of the knowledge and information fundamental to its formulation, functioning, and revision remains solely within the oral tradition of development experts. Nevertheless, these documents demonstrate quite clearly the highly patterned modes of collecting, processing, and promulgating information and they accurately reflect the language of development.

3. See Stone 1986, 1992 for a critical retrospective discussion of PHC and the models of "culture" and "community participation" implicit in it.

4. World Health Organization statements on traditional birth attendants include Maglacas and Simons 1986; Verderese and Turnbull 1975; and WHO 1975, 1992.

5. For a critical history of development approaches and anthropologists' involvement in them, see Escobar 1991.

6. The administrative question of how to "deal with" traditional medicine predates international development. Jeffery (1982) shows that interest in birth attendants dates from the colonial period. Sargent and Rawlins (1992) show the contemporary effects of the historical British policy toward Jamaican midwives.

7. We can wonder why the "customs" of North American technocratic childbirth (Davis-Floyd 1992) are not included in these inventories of "traditions."

8. On the notion of "planning" see Escobar 1992.

9. The United Mission to Nepal initiated efforts to work with midwives in 1973 through Shanta Bhawan hospital (Pillsbury 1982:1832). Between 1974 and 1987 an estimated 3,500 TBAs were trained by numerous NGOs and government agency programs (Levitt 1987), which eventually merged in a single, integrated training curriculum coordinated from the Division of Nursing. In the mid-1980s the WHO TBA training kit was translated into Nepali. Currently, all training programs use a common set of materials but are carried out independently by government and international agencies. The TBA has been incorporated into the organizational hierarchy of the national health system, and the training of TBAs is one of the duties of assistant nurse midwives, who also are to supervise them. UNICEF now targets training an additional 10,000 in order to provide 1 TBA per 1,000 population (UNICEF 1991).

10. Extensive, though not comprehensive, documentation of this variation can be found in Levitt 1987. Her study, using focus groups from a number of regions, elicited the following terms (from Nepali as well as several local languages) for a person who assists in delivery: *suḍeni, dagrin, chamar, agi, suḍeni amai, bajyai, palaina, gaudarni.*

11. This position is common among Nepali development workers (see Pigg

1992, 1993, 1995) and is rooted in deeper dynamics surrounding social stratification. Yet it is not without contradictions. While elite Nepalis tend to look with disdain at certain village practices, especially when ethnic differences compound social distance, they also have a strong visceral sense that some Nepalese practices are "best," even when foreign development advisers look askance at them. (The practice of rimming an infant's eyes with a mixture of kohl and camphor is one example.) One brief paper written by a Nepali nurse (found gathering dust in the small UNICEF library) discusses the value of customary practices such as massaging infants, oiling the fontanel, and applying kohl (Pradhan 1987; on massage, Pradhan 1981). In stressing the benefits of these practices, Pradhan mixes observations about child development, commonsense rationales offered by informants for these practices, and scientific-sounding reasons that are largely speculative. She also discusses ways that both men and women hold and play with infants, as well as the importance for socialization of rituals such as the first rice-feeding ceremony. Pradhan thus attempts to make visible the customary practices deemed essential by Nepalis yet rarely mentioned in the development literature in its rush to find what is wrong with "traditional" practices. She advocates greater investigation into these practices (e.g., a comparison of infant health in societies that oil and massage babies and those that do not) and more supportive attention in international development to these practices. This is one example of what may become a larger trend. As resentment toward foreign experts and disillusionment with development ideologies builds in Nepal, the disdain evinced by elites toward village practices may turn into a desire for a revalidation of cultural identity.

12. Jordan ([1978] 1993) points out that new information is not necessarily applied. The Mayan midwives she observed did not readily draw the "obvious" practical conclusions from the abstract knowledge presented to them, and they did not always interpret illustrations, drawings, and films in the manner intended.

13. For a radically different view of birth, see Biesele, this volume.

14. The assumption, of course, has a basis: in Nepal many customs, especially those concerning food, marriage, reproduction, and ritual practices, differ by caste and ethnic group, and people themselves use them as markers of identity. Ethnic labels in Nepal are, however, extremely problematic due to the fluidity of identities and the historical politics of ethnic labeling.

15. Jeffery, Jeffery, and Lyon (1989) offer a similar criticism of the narrowly medical focus on maternal and child health. "We believe," they write at the end of their study of women and childbearing in village North India, "that attempts to use medical and public health services to deal with the problems of childbearing are likely to fail because they address only part of the social, political and economic context within which childbearing women live" (1989:221). Women are not individual patients but persons embedded in the hierarchies of family life in which they have limited decision-making power over food, labor, fertility, and so on.

16. The "authoritative knowledge" of international health development therefore *includes* the notion that "TBAs" should be involved in birth in a limited way. It is important to note that, in this case, an "authoritative" cosmopolitan obstetrics is not pitted directly against other forms of knowledge; rather, the authoritative knowledge reproduced in development programs is a knowledge that holds that

"traditional" practices "matter," but only in certain limited ways. The case I discuss here, then, stands in contrast to the situation Wagner (this volume) describes for WHO involvement in Europe through the 1970s and 1980s, where the "truths" of cosmopolitan obstetrics were/are seen as precluding any acknowledgment of the validity of other ways of conducting childbirth. In a sense, the notions about training programs I discuss here represent a second phase in the process of achieving official recognition for midwives, worldwide: I write, after all, about programs in the 1990s that were fought for in the 1970s and 1980s. But the contrast also underscores the role differences race and culture make in the elaboration of authoritative knowledge about birth. When Europeans research and debate practices in Europe, they do so with verbal and political weapons that differ from those used when members of a sophisticated international development elite research and debate practices of the poor and marginalized people of countries targeted for development aid.

17. See Jeffery and Jeffery 1993 on how these factors influence the conduct of childbirth in rural North India. They argue that to focus on the role played by the midwife, or *dai*, is to overlook the fact that "the main sources of maternal and child health problems are not located [in the mismanagement of obstetrical crises] but in the lack of economic and social leverage that childbearing women have over their lives" (1993:27). Though the situation in much of Nepal is somewhat different from what they describe for India, their point is equally relevant.

REFERENCES

Bomgaars, Mona
   1976   "Undernutrition: Cultural Diagnosis and Treatment of 'Runche.' " *Journal of the American Medical Association* 236(22):2513.
Davis-Floyd, Robbie
   1992   *Birth as an American Rite of Passage.* Berkeley: University of California Press.
Elders, Joycelyn M.
   1994   "Reducing the Risk of Sudden Infant Death Syndrome (From the Surgeon General, U.S. Public Health Services)." *Journal of the American Medical Association* 272(21):1646.
Escobar, Arturo
   1988   "Power and Visibility: Development and the Intervention and Management of the Third World." *Cultural Anthropology* 3(4):428–443.
   1991   "Anthropology and the Development Encounter: The Making and Marketing of Development Anthropology." *American Ethnologist* 18(4):658–682.
Guntheroth, Warren G., and Philip S. Spiers
   1992   "Sleeping Prone and the Risk of Sudden Infant Death Syndrome." Review article. *Journal of the American Medical Association* 267(17):2359–2363.
Jeffery, Patricia, Roger Jeffery, and Andrew Lyon
   1989   *Labour Pains and Labour Power: Women and Childbearing in India.* London: Zed Press.

Jeffery, Roger
    1982   "Policies towards Indigenous Healers in Independent India." *Social Science and Medicine* 16:1835–1841.
Jeffery, Roger, and Patricia M. Jeffery
    1993   "Traditional Birth Attendants in Rural North India: The Social Organization of Childbearing." In *Knowledge, Power, and Practice: The Anthropology of Medicine and Everyday Life,* ed. Shirley Lindenbaum and Margaret Lock, 7–31. Berkeley: University of California Press.
Jordan, Brigitte
    [1978] 1993   *Birth in Four Cultures: A Cross-Cultural Investigation of Childbirth in Yucatan, Holland, Sweden and the United States,* 4th ed. Prospect Heights, Ill.: Waveland Press.
JSI (John Snow Inc./Nepal)
    1988   "Community Health Volunteers: Program Review and Recommendations." Submitted to the Public Health Division, Maternal Child Health and USAID, Nepal, March 1988. Kathmandu, Nepal: John Snow Inc.
Justice, Judith
    1984   "Can Socio-Cultural Information Improve Health Planning? A Case Study of Nepal's Assistant Nurse Midwife." *Social Science and Medicine* 19(3):193–198.
    1986   *Policies, Plans, and People: Foreign Aid and Health Development.* Berkeley: University of California Press.
    1987   "The Bureaucratic Context of International Health: A Social Scientist's View." *Social Science and Medicine* 25:1301–1306.
Levitt, Marta
    1987   "A Systematic Study of Birth and Traditional Birth Attendants in Nepal." Kathmandu: John Snow Inc./Nepal. October.
Maglacas, A. M., and J. Simons, eds.
    1986   *The Potential of the Traditional Birth Attendant.* Geneva: World Health Organization.
Martin, Emily
    1987   *The Woman in the Body.* Boston: Beacon Press.
Ministry of Health, His Majesty's Government of Nepal
    1990   "Suḍeni tālīm tathā kārya sanchālan pustikā" (Midwife Training and Supervision Manual). Kathmandu.
Pigg, Stacy Leigh
    1992   "Inventing Social Categories Through Place: Social Representations and Development in Nepal." *Comparative Studies in Society and History* 34(3):491–513.
    1993   "Unintended Consequences: The Ideological Impact of Development in Nepal." *South Asia Bulletin* 8(1-2):45–58.
    1995   "The Credible and the Credulous: The Question of 'Villagers' Beliefs' in Nepal." *Cultural Anthropology* 11(2):160–201.
Pillsbury, Barbara L. K.
    1979   "Reaching the Rural Poor: Indigenous Health Practitioners Are There Already." AID Program Evaluation, Discussion Paper no. 1. The Studies Divi-

sion, Office of Evaluation, Bureau for Program and Policy Coordination, United States Agency for International Development.

1982   "Policy and Evaluation Perspectives on Traditional Health Practitioners in National Health Care Systems." *Social Science and Medicine* 16:1825–1834.

Pradhan, Hari Badan

1981   "Traditional Child Rearing Practices Should Be Maintained." *Journal of the Institute of Medicine* 3, no. 1 (March):71–84.

1987   (B.S. 2043) "The Study of Traditional Baby Care among Selected Ethnic Groups." Mimeograph.

Reissland, Nadja, and Richard Burghart

1988   "The Quality of a Mother's Milk and the Health of Her Child: Beliefs and Practices of the Women of Mithila." *Social Science and Medicine* 27(5):461–469.

Sargent, Carolyn, and Joan Rawlins

1992   "Transformations in Maternity Services in Jamaica." *Social Science and Medicine* 35(10):1225–1232.

Spiers, Philip S., and Warren G. Guntheroth

1994   "Recommendations to Avoid the Prone Sleeping Position and Recent Statistics for Sudden Infant Death Syndrome in the United States." *Journal of the American Medical Association* 271(18):1386.

Stone, Linda

1986   "Primary Health Care for Whom? Village Perspectives from Nepal." *Social Science and Medicine* 22(3):293–302.

1992   "Cultural Influences in Community Participation in Health." *Social Science and Medicine* 34(3-4):409–418.

Tsing, Anna Lowenhaupt

1990   "Monster Stories: Women Charged with Perinatal Endangerment." In *Uncertain Terms: Negotiating Gender in American Culture*, ed. Faye Ginsberg and Anna Lowenhaupt Tsing, 282–299. Boston: Beacon Press.

UNICEF (United Nations Children's Fund)

1989   *All for Health: A Resource Book for Facts for Life*. Geneva: UNICEF.

UNICEF (United Nations Children's Fund) and His Majesty's Government of Nepal

1991   Draft Master Plan of Operations for the HMG–UNICEF Nepal Programme of Cooperation for the Period 1992–1996. Kathmandu: UNICEF-Nepal.

Verderese, Maria de Lourdes, and Lily M. Turnbull

1975   *The Traditional Birth Attendant in Maternal and Child Health and Family Planning: A Guide to Her Training and Utilization*. Geneva: World Health Organization.

Volosinov, V. N.

[1929] 1973   *Marxism and the Philosophy of Language*. Trans. Ladislav Matejka and I. R. Titunik. Cambridge, Mass.: Harvard University Press.

Wood, Geof

1985   "The Politics of Development Policy Labelling." *Development and Change* 16:348–359.

World Health Organization (WHO)

1975   *Traditional Birth Attendants: A Field Guide to Their Training, Evaluation, and Articulation with Health Services.* Geneva: World Health Organization.

1978   *Primary Health Care: Report of the International Conference on Primary Health Care, Alma-Ata, U.S.S.R., 6–12 September.* Jointly sponsored by the World Health Organization and the United Nations Children's Fund. Geneva: World Health Organization.

1986   *Evaluation of the Strategy for Health for All by the Year 2000. Seventh Report on the World Health Situation.* Vol. 4: *South-east Asia Region.* New Delhi: Regional Office for South-east Asia, World Health Organization.

1992   *Traditional Birth Attendants: A Joint WHO/UNFPA/UNICEF Statement.* Geneva: World Health Organization.

TEN

Changing Childbirth in Eastern Europe

Which Systems of Authoritative
Knowledge Should Prevail?

Beverley Chalmers

In the midst of the turmoil that has followed the disintegration of the Soviet Union in 1989, medical systems in Eastern Europe have begun to undergo massive transformation. For maternity care this has meant an opening up to the influx of information regarding prevailing obstetrical practice in North America and Western Europe.

How is change in childbirth effected? What can we learn from the transformations that are taking place in Eastern Europe? What sources of authoritative knowledge in health care are regarded highly in this region? How are these changing? Should representatives from the West seek to influence this process of change, and if so, which Western system of authoritative knowledge should prevail? These are some of the questions addressed in this chapter (see also Pigg, this volume, for a careful consideration of related issues).

METHODS

Information on childbirth in Eastern Europe is drawn primarily from my observations during over forty visits to members of the former Soviet Union—Romania, the Russian Federation, Belarus, Ukraine, Hungary, Czech Republic, Latvia, Estonia, and Poland—on behalf of WHO and UNICEF and the Canadian International Development Agency (CIDA) over the course of the past five years (1991–1996). A health psychologist by training, I began my work in Eastern Europe as a full-time consultant to WHO-Europe (August–December 1991), acting as the coordinator of the Maternal and Child Health Unit, Regional Office for Europe, Copenhagen. Following this period, I remained a short-term adviser for both the Women's and Children's Health Unit (formerly the Maternal and Child

Health Unit; see Wagner, this volume) and the Nutrition Unit of WHO-Europe, as well as for the Baby Friendly Hospital Initiative, UNICEF-Geneva. In these capacities I continued to work in the countries of Central and Eastern Europe, as well as to undertake programs in Eastern Europe on behalf of the Canadian Federal Government and some North American research foundations (see appendix for a full list of the visits made and responsibilities carried out during each of these visits). This work is ongoing: I am currently visiting these countries six to eight times a year.

My activities in Eastern European countries have included leading teams of educators in maternal and child health (in St. Petersburg, Russian Federation) and in breastfeeding (in northwestern parts of the Russian Federation); acting as a consultant on breastfeeding and maternal-child health activities in maternity houses and sick children's hospitals (in the Czech Republic, Hungary, Romania, Belarus, Ukraine, Latvia, Estonia, Moscow, and surrounding regions of the Russian Federation); participating as a team member on consultancies on these topics (in Romania, St. Petersburg, Belarus, and Poland); giving conference presentations (in the Russian Federation, Poland, Romania, Ukraine, Belarus, Latvia, Estonia, Hungary, and the Czech Republic); and participating in and facilitating research programs (in Belarus and St. Petersburg).

At present I am involved in three major programs in Eastern Europe. The first involves leading a multidisciplinary team of Canadian and WHO consultants that is committed to offering twelve workshops on various aspects of maternal-child health (including workshops for maternity hospitals, for prenatal care clinics, and on the training of childbirth educators) in St. Petersburg over the next two years. The program, in association with the Health Committee of St. Petersburg, is funded by the Canadian International Development Agency, Canada. A second major program involves facilitating and contributing to the psychosocial components of a randomized controlled trial of the impact of the Baby Friendly Hospital Initiative on infant outcome. Under the direction of Michael Kramer of McGill University and a multidisciplinary team from both Canada and Belarus, the research is well under way with financial support from UNICEF-Geneva, the National Health Research and Development Foundation of Canada, and the Thrasher Foundation of the United States. My third major involvement, as previously mentioned, is as an active consultant for both the Nutrition Unit of WHO-Europe and UNICEF-Geneva in the capacity of facilitator and hospital assessor for the Baby Friendly Hospital Initiative (BFHI) in Eastern Europe, particularly in the Russian Federation, Belarus, and Ukraine.

Much of my commentary on Eastern European childbirth practices is written, unavoidably, from within the confines of a Western perspective on childbirth (the limitations of this perspective are discussed toward the end of this chapter). Where possible, I refer the reader to English-language literature on childbirth in these countries. Unfortunately, the bulk of the information is not available in English; this chapter is based primarily on my own experiences and observations. Concepts (like "authoritative knowledge") are borrowed freely and without explanation from the childbirth literature, including this present volume, on the assumption that the reader is familiar with them, to save space for presentation of the data. I seek in this chapter not to focus on specific events in any one country but to provide a broad overview of past and present trends in Eastern European childbirth practices.

CHILDBIRTH PRACTICES IN THE COUNTRIES OF CENTRAL AND EASTERN EUROPE

The countries of Central and Eastern Europe are undergoing important political, economic, and social changes as they move toward a mixed ownership, social market economy and multiparty political democracy. Issues such as democratization, individual freedom, consumer choice, and quality are high on the political agenda. In the process of change, however, these countries are experiencing severe economic difficulties resulting from high levels of foreign debt, inflation, and unemployment.

The implications of this major reorientation are many. Health care, including the care of women and children, is undergoing major changes as policies and practices are influenced by reforms in the economic and educational sectors. The practices in place in the various countries share a remarkable similarity. This is not surprising, given that health care systems in all countries forming part of the former Soviet Union have been required, for the past several decades, to follow a set of ordinances established by Moscow and issued as "edicts" governing various aspects of health care. Edict 55, in particular, governed the health care services offered by maternity houses and was (and in many instances still is) most influential regarding childbirth practices. This edict is detailed and extensive; it covers every imaginable activity that occurs in a maternity care unit, from when windows may be opened to the medications and treatments prescribed for babies and mothers. Other edicts governing prenatal care in Women's Consultations, postpartum care in "polyclinics" (community clinics staffed by pediatricians that care for children from infants to teens), and care of preterm and sick children in children's hospitals also defined what care was permitted or forbidden with regard to newborns, their mothers, or other family members.

These edicts were enforced through a system of frequent inspections, with punishments (such as demotions, transfers to outlying hospitals, fines, or worse) meted out to dissidents. Those countries that managed to extricate themselves from Moscow's closest scrutiny were able to obtain some information about Western health care systems during their decades of seclusion; today these countries (which include Hungary, the Czech Republic, and Estonia) appear to be less confined by the edicts of Moscow. Others (such as Belarus) that, subsequent to 1989, have obtained independence have felt free to change these edicts when they are contradicted by current scientific evidence from the West. Some regions, particularly those in the Russian Federation, are still tightly bound by the edicts and fearful of independently changing them when faced with new information. Moscow health authorities themselves are aware of the need to update these edicts; the process of their reform is currently in its infancy.

In general, the countries of Central and Eastern Europe form a group that lags behind the Western countries of Europe on most indicators of health, including those relating to maternal and child health. For instance, almost without exception, these countries (the former U.S.S.R., the former Yugoslavia, the former Czechoslovakia, and Romania, Poland, Bulgaria, and Hungary) are grouped together at the lowest end of the scale on many of the indicators for health utilized by WHO in their assessment of progress toward achieving "Health for all by 2000." This includes measures of life expectancy at birth, incidence of cardiovascular disease, cancer and death from external causes, maternal and infant mortality, tobacco consumption, and inadequate nutrition, among others (WHO 1993).

As is well known, there has been slower overall socioeconomic development in these countries than in Western Europe. Efficient and effective disease prevention and health promotion have not received real priority either as policies or as community actions. Health services have been inefficient and technologically inadequate by Western standards. This disadvantaged health situation is no less evident in the areas of maternal and child health. Accepted primary indicators of maternal and child health care include measures of maternal and infant mortality. While most countries of Europe have reached the WHO target for maternal mortality rates, the Central and Eastern European countries still lag behind their Western European neighbors (fig. 10.1). Infant mortality rates, particularly in Romania, the former U.S.S.R., and the former Yugoslavia, still have not reached WHO target levels (WHO 1993) (fig. 10.2). Perhaps even more compelling than the official statistics is the descriptive view of maternal and child care practices that—with some exceptions—are still fairly common in these countries.

MATERNAL AND CHILD CARE

Under the socialist system, emphasis was placed on birth in maternity houses (the counterpart to the Western hospital–based obstetric unit).

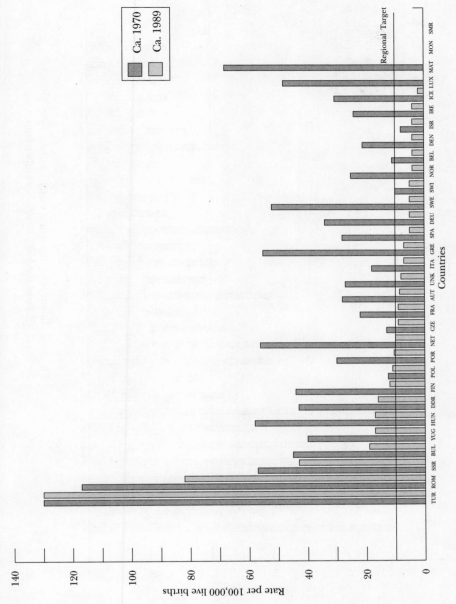

Fig. 10.1. Maternal Mortality Rate ca. 1970 and ca. 1989.
Source: HFA Database ESR/EURO November 1991

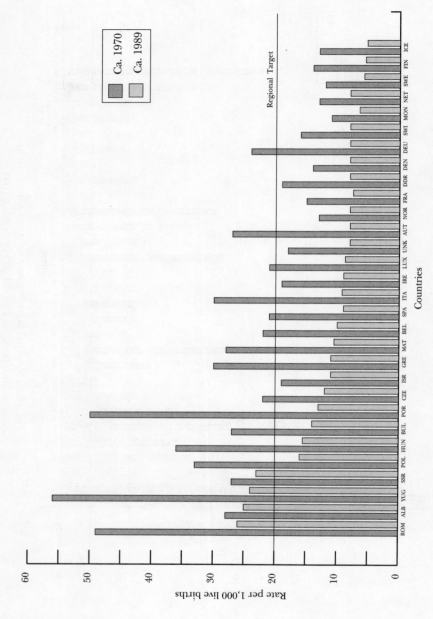

Fig. 10.2. Infant Mortality Rate ca. 1970 and ca. 1989.
Source: HFA Database ESR/EURO November 1991

Corresponding emphasis was placed on strict adherence to a frequent schedule of antenatal visits during pregnancy to Women's Consultations (usually separate institutions in larger centers providing care for women at any stage of life and specifically in pregnancy). Antenatal care was, and still is, provided by trained maternal-child health nurses together with obstetricians. In Hungary, for example—and this is typical of the Eastern European policy—an average of ten antenatal visits is made during pregnancy by women who are also visited at home approximately six times during pregnancy (Tiba 1986). A recent survey of prenatal care in St. Petersburg indicated an average of thirteen antenatal care visits by pregnant women (range 1 to 30) (Dennis 1995), although this report indicated that only half the women surveyed (49%) sought antenatal care before the twelfth week of pregnancy.

Formal preparation for childbirth through hospital/clinic or privately run programs is virtually nonexistent, although in some countries (e.g., Hungary) there has recently been some recognition of the need. At least in Hungary and the Russian Federation, I have noted a recent increase in interest in offering such services during pregnancy and after. Despite the fact that psychoprophylaxis (the forerunner of modern childbirth education) emerged from these countries some decades ago and is still recalled by the older midwives and obstetricians, it is not generally practiced at present.

Under the socialist system it was believed that, as the system was "perfect," there would be no social disasters or psychological problems arising from it. Training of psychologists and social workers was therefore stopped some decades ago, with a consequent current dire shortage in all the Eastern European countries of professionals able to cope with the emotional and social problems that have resulted from the extremely repressive communist system. For example, in Romania and other places even the training of nurses and midwives was halted some decades ago; only doctors were considered necessary to heal the unavoidable physiological illnesses that the system could not prevent. In other countries, such as the Russian Federation itself, midwifery and nursing training was markedly downplayed, with only a specialized high school nursing/midwifery education being offered.

Even more dramatic than its effect on illness care is the impact of decades of emotional repression—a powerful legacy of the Soviet years—on everyday social interaction. In my years of work in these countries, and currently in outlying regions of the Russian Federation, I have frequently observed in the people with whom I interacted an inability to trust one another and an unwillingness to express emotion except most guardedly. Fear of reprisal is still strong, although I do note a growing willingness to confront and challenge both internal and external health authorities in all countries.

Midwifery care and home-based delivery—existing now only in the memories of the older women and practiced by a few isolated "revolution-aries"—was phased out with the growth of a medicalized approach to child-birth, in much the same way as occurred in North America and elsewhere some decades ago. Almost all deliveries take place in state hospitals (private hospitals are a relatively new development in many countries and are not yet well established) and are performed by obstetricians, with midwives in attendance on the doctor rather than the mother. Care is technically ori-ented, within the confines of limited available technology in most places. Striking is the lack of concern for the mother's psychological needs, with little thought given to her possible wishes, for example, for companion-ship, in almost all the numerous maternity houses I have visited in each country. First-stage labor is traditionally, and for the most part currently, spent alone or at best with other laboring women. Small inroads toward changing this custom are beginning to be made in Hungary in particular, but "tradition" still holds strong. Nor is visiting allowed during the postpar-tum hospital stay in most maternity houses, although a few institutions in most countries are beginning to allow restricted visiting.

Technology, if available, is frequently overused, for example, repeated ultrasound during pregnancy and routine fetal heart monitors in labor. Technological intervention is preferred to a noninterventionist approach whenever possible; in this regard, it is sometimes to mothers' advantage that technology is not readily available. Shaving, enemas, and episiotomies are routinely used, as is a supine position for delivery with the aid of stir-rups.

Following delivery the baby is shown to the mother before being sent to the nursery for the remainder of the hospital stay—about one week for normal deliveries and ten days for cesarean sections. Mothers do not tradi-tionally hold or breastfeed their babies after delivery. In most countries, rooming-in is beginning to be considered in some hospitals; small units are experimenting with this method of postpartum care at least during the day. Only a few institutes have introduced twenty-four-hour rooming-in as the preferred care program, although with the recent major impetus being given to the Baby Friendly Hospital Initiative in Eastern Europe by WHO and UNICEF, this practice is beginning to take hold.

Breastfeeding is encouraged, commencing some three to six hours after delivery and concurrently "supported" by bottle feeding, as colostrum, while believed to be good for the newborn, is not regarded as sufficient. Breastfeeding support is often based on inaccurate assumptions about the breastfeeding process. For instance, women are encouraged to empty their breasts "fully" after each feeding, often with the aid of breast pumps or manually to avoid milk remaining in the breast, which, it is believed, will lead to abscesses. At the same time babies are given supplementary feedings. Engorgement is the logical consequence of this practice, which leads to sore breasts and painful breastfeeding. Mastitis is, understandably, not uncommon.

Babies are fed according to schedules. They are usually transported in large multibaby trolleys from the nursery to the mothers in the postnatal wards at feeding times. Between feedings babies are given water or glucose water. Babies may not be undressed, bathed, or changed by their mothers: nurses or midwives ("maternal-child nurses") perform these duties. Mothers are usually required to wear hats, masks, and protective clothing during breastfeeding; in some instances mothers are required to place plastic sheeting between themselves and their babies. Mothers are taught to feed for limited times at each breast in the first few days, increasing these times gradually to accustom the nipples to feeding. Nipple shields are commonly used in some of the countries with greater access to Western technology (such as Hungary), and free samples may be supplied to each mother in postpartum gift packs. The influence of the larger pharmaceutical companies in supplying products for professionals and consumers (including breast milk substitutes) is beginning to be felt. Mothers are often required to spray their breasts and nipples with antiseptic before each feeding or at least to wash them with soap and water. In some hospitals the baby's mouth may be washed out with antiseptic before each feeding "to prevent thrush." The message that mothers are "dangerous" for their babies is consistently conveyed.

Breastfeeding rates are low. Although almost all women breastfeed in hospital after delivery, the rate of breastfeeding drops rapidly in the postpartum period. In Hungary, for example, only 45 percent of mothers breastfeed at all by three months postpartum and approximately 18 percent at six months (Martonne and Kalman 1991). Only in countries where there is no alternative to breastfeeding (because powdered milk is in short supply, cow's milk is not available, and financial resources are scarce, such as in Romania) does the breastfeeding rate (reportedly) stay reasonably high after birth.

In most places, particularly in the Russian Federation and Romania, babies are tightly swaddled, restricting almost all movement of the baby's body, hands, legs, and head. With the encouragement of WHO, a Swedish research team is currently assessing the impact of this on breastfeeding and maternal-child interactions in St. Petersburg. The focus of postpartum care is on the baby in both polyclinics and at home. For example, in Hungary a home visit to check on the condition of the child is prescribed within six days of its leaving the hospital. Regular and frequent clinic visits in the first postnatal year and after are prescribed. During these visits, the child's somatic and psychomotor development is followed in great detail and immunization is carried out. Data are recorded on uniform health care cards, including preventive and curative activities, observations of health care visits, hospitalization reports, and the reports of the caregivers. Children with chronic or special needs receive special care. There is little, if any, form of woman-to-woman or community-based support for the mother after discharge. There are currently few social community centers in the countries of the former Soviet Union.

PSYCHOSOCIAL PERINATAL CARE

Nowhere have I encountered doctors, nurses, or midwives who wished to cause discomfort for mothers: all believe their practices are essential for the most beneficial outcomes for mothers and babies, quoting scientific evidence (usually Soviet in origin) as the grounds for their policies. Nevertheless, it is clear that these practitioners lack awareness and understanding of the woman's point of view, as frequently occurs wherever birth is doctor- rather than woman-centered. For example, in many Russian hospitals delivery beds face the open doorway. In the lithotomy position women are exposed for all passersby with little regard for their privacy and dignity. It is not deliberately done this way. It is unthinkingly done this way. The easy and simple intervention (to turn beds so they face away from the doorway) requires no equipment or expense but does involve a rethinking of birth from the woman's point of view. Intervention from WHO advisers in parts of Eastern Europe is currently being directed toward creating awareness of this need to reconsider the key player in the birth experience. Turning the traditional Doctor-nurse-midwife-mother hierarchy (Capital/lowercase choice is intentional) on its end is one of the current goals of these programs.

In Romania in particular, the systems of care imposed by the Ceaucescu regime were inhuman, to say the least. These systems were implemented by doctors, often reluctantly. Practices included forced, routine, and frequent vaginal examinations of all women to detect pregnancy and thereafter to detect illegal termination of pregnancy; forcing childbirth on women by banning contraception as well as abortion and by expecting five children from each woman during her childbearing years; strict controls over the number of cesarean sections performed (as these were a way to avoid too many pregnancies legitimately) with prosecution of both doctors and mothers who tried to use this escape route. Penalizing and even imprisonment of mothers whose babies died, as well as of the doctors who cared for them, resulted in referral up the medical hierarchy as quickly as possible to avoid blame for fatalities. With inadequate medication, shortages of antibiotics, extremely poor nutrition (also controlled by the government), and inadequate living conditions, doctors and mothers were, in reality, fairly helpless to care for sick children: institutionalization of the child was, understandably, not an uncommon outcome of this health care pattern. It is not surprising that after decades of living with man's inhumanity to woman, it will take time to rethink the values and ideologies that will form the basis for an alternate way of life in these countries and to implement them in practice.

IMPEDIMENTS TO CHANGING CHILDBIRTH IN CENTRAL AND EASTERN EUROPE

In general, as we have seen, maternal and child care in Central and Eastern Europe is lacking in concern for the psychosocial aspects of care, is based on outdated medical knowledge (Chalmers, Enkin, and Keirse 1989), and incorporates care routines during labor, delivery, and the postpartum period that discourage rather than promote breastfeeding. Consequently, changes directed toward improving breastfeeding and maternal care will not only have to include improvements in breastfeeding support, for example, but also will have to involve profound changes in the general principles of maternal and infant care on which obstetricians and pediatricians presently rely. The lack of encouragement of communication and cooperation among people and between disciplines under the former totalitarian system will make such changes difficult to implement until such time as a willingness to trust others and to work in teams rather than as individuals develops. In particular, cross-disciplinary interchange is difficult, as it does not conform to the strict hierarchy found within the traditional medical model. Management training is almost a prerequisite for changes to the health care system. In contrast, however, the enthusiasm and dedication of the current professionals involved in maternal and child health care, and their concern about providing the best possible care, will go a long way toward overcoming the obstacles that lie ahead.

A second challenge to changing childbirth practices arises from conflicting models of childbirth care being offered to Eastern European countries. Their traditional value on technology in childbirth leads them to prefer to modernize in the direction of the Western technomedical approach. This tendency presents a major challenge to health care agencies such as WHO and UNICEF that seek to encourage the adoption of a woman-centered and baby-friendly low-technology approach for the majority of women in childbirth. Consultants for these agencies are regularly confronted during visits to Eastern European hospitals with requests for financial aid to purchase equipment (or for the equipment itself). The priority of the international agencies, as I see it, has been to advise appropriate care for the majority of women rather than to advocate scarce resource allocation for a specialized few. Nevertheless, the call for specialized technical equipment has been heard especially by the industrial sector of Western Europe as well as by those neighboring countries that themselves advocate a high-technology approach to childbirth.

Nowhere is this more evident than in the conflict between the Baby Friendly Hospital Initiative and the formula industry. Just as the UNICEF/WHO BFHI movement takes hold in these countries, the infant formula manufacturers knock on maternity house doors. In some countries the BFHI is dominant. In Poland, Hungary, and the Czech Republic, for example, a number of hospitals are already accredited as Baby Friendly. Belarus, too, has undertaken an active national policy promoting breastfeeding and is participating in a national randomized controlled trial of the Baby Friendly Hospital Initiative conducted by a joint Canadian-Belarussian team with UNICEF, U.S.A., and Canadian funding. As in Norway and Sweden, the formula makers will battle to gain a foothold in these parts of Eastern Europe. Other countries are, however, less far advanced in breastfeeding promotion and the conflict between appropriate health care practices and the formula industries is rife.

AUTHORITATIVE KNOWLEDGE IN EASTERN EUROPE: CHANGING VIEWS

It is apparent that patterns of childbirth care among women and their caregivers in Eastern Europe are even more extremely oriented toward the authority of the medical profession than those of the West. New mothers are subjugated, not allowed to trust themselves or their bodies during childbirth or afterward. The messages they receive are clear: "You cannot give birth without technological assistance; you are not clean enough to feed your baby without washing first and without wearing protective clothing; you are not competent to hold your baby at delivery or in the days after birth; you are not even competent to be able to feed your baby sufficiently—your breast milk requires supplementation; you may not keep your baby with you between feedings or wash and change it, for fear you will infect it." These messages may be more severe than those conveyed to American women during hospital birth (Davis-Floyd 1992); nevertheless, the resemblance is striking.

At present there is little evidence of any opposition to this approach on the part of mothers: even when "permission" is given to mothers from "outside consultants" to unwrap their baby's swaddling or to keep them in their own beds, mothers may express fear and self-doubt at this change in standard practice. There is little support for mothers who wish to defy the existing system: women's movements are few and far between; only a few organizations exist, and these are in their infancy. Authoritative knowledge is clearly vested in the medical professional's hands, and mothers currently accept the situation. This doctor-centered approach extends—albeit unintentionally—to the point of being anti-mother.

In fact, the authoritative knowledge of the medical profession is two-tiered in the former Soviet Union. Mothers have to defer to their physicians in hospitals, and physicians have to defer to other physicians who are based in government. Practicing physicians have little more power or authority than women when it comes to challenging the controls issued from Moscow. The Moscow Edicts rule the day.

Notwithstanding all of the above, it is somewhat false to paint a picture of static childbirth approaches. There are strong movements occurring in the current approaches to appropriate childbirth care worldwide, and these do filter down to those who implement the systems. Poland and Belarus have embraced the Baby Friendly Hospital Initiative, with its enormous implications for postpartum care, with open arms. In Russia and Romania, where the systems have been most repressive by current Western standards, the changes are marked and obvious. Major overhauls of hospital care systems are taking place and within a few months whole hospitals have been converted from nursery care to rooming-in systems. The ripple effects of an intervention such as this, with its concurrent shift from doctor-centered care to infant/mother–centered care, are enormous, and it would be unfair to label all health care services as currently repressive in these countries. Nevertheless, despite the increased shift in the basis of authoritative knowledge from doctor/nurse to mother, it must be remembered that the changes being introduced are being instigated by professionals rather than by mothers.

In their favor is the willingness to change that characterizes many of the professionals in these countries. Rather than assuming that current systems are of a high standard and not requiring improvement, as occurs in many parts of the West, they are acknowledging that change is important and long overdue and that other systems may well offer worthwhile benefits to be added to their own approaches. The result is a rapidly changing knowledge base as well as a changing approach to maternal-child health care. What is happening in these countries is, in effect, authoritative knowledge in transition.

THE PITFALLS OF INTEGRATING DIFFERING CULTURAL APPROACHES TO CHILDBIRTH

There are numerous difficulties involved in working across cultures with regard to childbirth. One of these is the obvious and often difficult-to-avoid problem of seeing things through the eyes of one's own culture and judging all others as inferior instead of as different. The need to question one's own approaches in the light of conflicting ways is forever evident.

A second difficulty emerges when trying to assess which approach is clinically "better." Western standards of judgment call for "facts" in trying to determine which childbirth method is most beneficial. Yet in Eastern Europe, not many accurate facts are available: sophisticated research skills, including the elimination of bias from all stages of the research process, are lacking. Records of mortality and morbidity are extensively collected but are manually recorded: data analysis is largely descriptive rather than inferential. More rigidly screened and assessed information is required by our Western research standards to meet the label "facts." Less hard-core evidence of birth outcome (e.g., patient satisfaction) is also not readily available except in anecdotal form.

I am also acutely aware that many of the so-called safe birth practices that have formed an integral part of the authoritative knowledge base of Western medicine (e.g., shaving, enemas in labor, routine fetal heart monitoring, induction, epidurals, routine multiple ultrasound scanning, C-sections, etc.) have in recent years come under severe fire from objective research assessments (Chalmers, Enkin, and Keirse 1989; Goer 1995). What was regarded as factual and beneficial until recently is being discarded in enlightened Western quarters.

A third difficulty in cross-cultural work arises: new problems can be generated from the partial adoption of Western practices. For example, introducing rooming-in and simultaneously ignoring mothers who have their babies with them ("they are responsible for their babies now") may result in neglect of mothers and babies who need care. A half-baked application of Western approaches can be more harmful than beneficial.

In parts of Eastern Europe such as Hungary, routine ultrasound scanning has been introduced prenatally despite current research questioning its use at all as a routine practice. Scans may be performed at every antenatal visit (see also Georges, this volume). An average of ten to thirteen scans per pregnancy may be done in some centers. Even if this could be of any medical value (and it is not), it is impossible to enter the data obtained from each scan onto the patient's records before the end of the pregnancy. This is yet another example of an inappropriate application of Western technology made in the name of scientific research recommendations. There is little evidence available to indicate what women think of these practices.

Many Eastern European practices offer excellent principles of care: the follow-up support system provided for women after discharge is an Eastern European model that North America would do well to emulate. Although the specific information provided for postpartum mothers needs attention in Eastern Europe, the system of home visits and community-based clinic visits in place at present is to be valued and encouraged as supportive of mothers and babies. In addition, the family-centered postpartum care facility offered in many Estonian maternity houses (where fathers can room-in together with their wives/partners and new babies for the duration of the postpartum stay) is a model for Western hospital consideration.

From a mother- and baby-centered point of view, however, it seems clear that the more widespread practices—such as separation of women from all family support persons from admission in labor until discharge home, routine supplementing of infants with water after birth, and postpartum nursery care—require rethinking and revision. Inadequate breastfeeding practices may well result in morbidity or even mortality. These practices need to be discouraged or alternatives offered in a way that is culturally acceptable. The difficulty lies in finding the right balance between encouraging those practices that are potentially harmless or beneficial and discouraging those that are "known" to be dangerous for the health of mother or baby.

Which practices are regarded as harmful and which as harmless or beneficial also must be judged against the alternatives that are available in any community. For example, is advocating elimination of swaddling of newborns more harmful than maintaining this practice? In a poor community where baby clothes are unavailable or expensive, where heating in winter is essential but not necessarily available, discarding traditional methods of providing warmth for babies (swaddling) may do more harm than good. Unfortunately, ideological criteria based on an ideal (babies should not be so restricted in their ability to move) are often applied in reaching this type of recommendation for birth without reference to individual psychological, social, economic, and cultural issues—all of which are important.

CONCLUSION

In Eastern Europe childbirth practices reminiscent of those prevalent in North America and Europe three decades ago are being modernized, pulled in conflicting directions by the contrasts between the increasing use of technology in many Western nations and the family-centered low-technology approaches advocated by WHO and UNICEF and practiced in northern European countries.

What, then, is the "right" way to "do" birth? Which system of authoritative knowledge should prevail? Until recently (and for most even currently), Eastern European doctors and mothers were convinced that a doctor-centered, highly medicalized approach offered the best deal for mothers and babies. Their northern European counterparts, the WHO and UNICEF consultants active in Eastern Europe, and midwives all over the world believe their woman-centered ways to be superior. Who has the right to say which approach is best, and on what grounds can this be claimed? And if there is a "right way" for birth, is it universal? Does it apply equally in the rural hinterlands and the urbanized home, in the high-technology environment of Western hospitals and their somewhat dilapidated Eastern European counterparts?

My preceding efforts notwithstanding, it is inaccurate to talk of a "country's" approach to birth, even in Eastern Europe. Childbirth practices vary from country to country, from hospital to hospital within the same country, and from doctor to doctor within the same hospital. In many parts of the world (and even in isolated spots in Eastern Europe, such as in Hungary) no doctor is present at birth and it does not take place in a hospital. The mother, in her home setting attended by the midwife or even an obstetrician, is the central focus and it is the variation from mother to mother (and baby to baby) that determines the nature of the birth experience.

Are we even justified to consider that there might be one way to give birth that we could advise other countries to follow? If we accept that there is enormous variability in the world, that people differ widely in knowledge, attitudes, values, expectations, beliefs, societal conditions and economic levels, then is it appropriate to seek a universal childbirth pattern, or less obviously, to seek to influence one culture from the standpoint of another? One mother's experience can vary widely from birth to birth. Why not, then, for different mothers in different settings with different social, cultural, psychological, and biological backgrounds?

Even assuming the desirability of advocating a single approach to birth, what criteria should be used to assess the ideal birth experience? Measures of maternal and infant mortality and morbidity spring readily to mind and are fairly universally acknowledged as crucial indicators. But should we not be developing indicators of successful birthing further than the biological level to include the social, psychological, and cultural implications? Why do we rely on a physiological level of assessment of birth outcome almost to the exclusion of any other level of functioning? Is the medical model still so firmly entrenched that even with years of exposure to a more holistic approach to health and the endorsement of this by such agencies as the World Health Organization, we are still afraid to assess birth outcome in terms of the whole person's experience? Conventional scientific research infrequently suggests that the mother's experience be a central outcome measure in assessing a new intervention for childbirth. Even if such a measure is included, it is frequently relegated to a secondary level of importance, with biological outcomes taking priority.

The very issue of assessing birth outcomes is currently being turned on its head in the Western scientific world. Increased reliance on randomized controlled trials (see Johnson, this volume) as a more objective means of assessment than clinical tradition or inadequately designed research is bringing about a slow revolution in the obstetric community. Meta-analyses of randomized trials of birthing interventions have led to an embarrassing exposé of the inadequacy and even harmfulness of procedures previously considered routinely beneficial for women and babies (Chalmers, Enkin, and Keirse 1989). These authors and others (Northrup 1994; Wagner 1994) within the obstetric circle have leveled indictments against many forms of routine intervention on the basis of solid scientific foundations using accepted "medical" outcome criteria, as have the women's groups who have cried out against the high-technology approach on more humanitarian grounds. The lofty perch occupied by medicalized childbirth is being lowered slowly but surely.

There is yet another revolution taking place which is supportive of the findings of the meta-analyses of randomized trials: the growth of midwifery. Growing in momentum worldwide, midwifery does offer an alternative and a compromise to highly specialized Western obstetrics. Midwives are able to meet the needs of scientific medicine for effective care of the normal pregnancy; they are also, potentially, able to satisfy the universal psychological needs of women as well as the social and cultural expectations of women and their families. At present, and given our available knowledge of childbirth worldwide, the two forces together—the growth of midwifery with its woman-centered approach and the need for effective, evidence-based care in pregnancy and childbirth—seem to indicate a path to follow in future in seeking a way of doing birth that may be universally acceptable. It is these models that are being advocated by international health agencies in Central and Eastern Europe today (see Wagner, this volume).

Where is this revolution likely to be most effective? It is commonly acknowledged that change leads to self-questioning and leaves one open to new learning. This fact has been exploited for years by childbirth educators who recognize the time of pregnancy as a "teachable moment." During times of change, like pregnancy, which leave one uncertain about the future and unsure about the present, one is most open to influences from outside. In Eastern Europe changes of this nature are being experienced on a grand scale. With barriers being thrown wide open, with insecurity and self-doubt rife, with outside influences being readily sought and absorbed, people are open to and actively seeking change. Given the influence of the World Health Organization in Central and Eastern Europe in the field of maternal and child health (among others) and its endorsement of midwifery as well as of the *appropriate* use of childbirth technology, we are more likely to see a change in these parts of the world than anywhere else. The current systems are no longer entrenched: they have to change. If the influences that are introduced there can promote the best of the Western knowledge base and suppress the worst, we can speculate that the future models of effective care in pregnancy and birth will emerge from these countries.

I gratefully acknowledge the assistance of the University of the Witwatersrand Council Research Fellowship, Johannesburg, South Africa; the World Health Organization, Regional Office for Europe, Copenhagen, Denmark; UNICEF-Geneva; and the Canadian International Development Agency in making it possible to work in Hungary, the Czech Republic, Romania, Belarus, Ukraine, Latvia, Estonia, Poland, and the Russian Federation.

Opinions expressed here do not necessarily reflect those of the University of the Witwatersrand, Johannesburg; the World Health Organization, Regional Office for Europe, Copenhagen; UNICEF-Geneva; or the Canadian International Development Agency.

APPENDIX: ACTIVITIES IN CENTRAL AND EASTERN EUROPE (1991–1996)

Fellowship Activities: WHO-Europe, Copenhagen, 1991–1992

Administration of Maternal and Child Health Unit, August 1991–December 1991

Advisory visits to health centers in Hungary and Czechoslovakia, September 1991

Participant in mission to improve neonatal health care services in Romania, September 1991

Development of draft indicators of effective maternal child health care in Europe, October 1991

Proposed development of national policy to improve breastfeeding in Hungary, October 1991

WHO host of Romanian team, 10th International Congress of Psychosomatic Obstetrics and Gynaecology, Stockholm, June 1992

Participant and representative of WHO at conferences:
  Care of Children in Hospital, Tutzing, Germany, September 1991
  13th World Congress of Gynaecology and Obstetrics, Singapore, 1991
  The Ecology of Birth, Italy, November 1991
  Child Protection and Care: Trends and Prospects, Athens, Greece, November 1991
  International Conference on Childbirth, Szeged, Hungary, May 1992
  10th International Congress of Psychosomatic Obstetrics and Gynaecology, Sweden, June 1992

Short-Term Consultancies for WHO-Europe and UNICEF 1992–1996

Exploration of Breastfeeding status in Romania and development of a proposal for a national program for the promotion of breastfeeding in Romania for Nutrition Unit, WHO-Euro, November 1992

Facilitator for update workshop on neonatal health care in Romania for Women's and Children's Health Unit, WHO-Euro, November 1992

Facilitator for workshop promoting the development and upgrading of midwifery in Romania for Women's and Children's Health Unit, WHO-Euro, in Romania, November 1992

Exploration of research activities in Neonatology and Obstetrics in Polizu Hospital, Bucharest, Romania, for Women's and Children's Health Unit, WHO-Euro, November 1992

Facilitator for workshop on the impact of the birth of a child on the family for psychiatry interns in Bucharest, Romania, for Mental Health Unit, WHO-Euro, November 1992

Team member for evaluation of Bucharest UNICEF office 1991–1993, for UNICEF, Bucharest, February 1993

Facilitator for maternal mortality workshop, Vilcea, Romania, June 1993, for Women's and Children's Health Unit, WHO-Euro

Facilitator for midwifery update workshop for Women's and Children's Health Unit, WHO-Euro, Bucharest, June 1993

Consultant on behalf of WHO-Euro Women's and Children's Health Unit to BBC production on birth and family life in Russia, St. Petersburg, July 1993

Consultant on behalf of WHO-Euro Nutrition Unit and Healthy Cities Project–St. Petersburg to the UNICEF Workshops on the Baby Friendly Hospital Initiative and Lactation Management, St. Petersburg, Russia, August 1993

Consultant on behalf of WHO-Euro Healthy Cities Project and Women's and Children's Health Unit on Randomized Controlled Trial of Swaddling and Early Mother-Infant Skin-to-Skin Contact in St. Petersburg, Russia, August 1993

WHO/UNICEF adviser on breastfeeding promotion in Ukraine and Belarus, November 1993

Facilitator for Baby Friendly Hospital Initiative training program, Poland, November 1993 and February 1994, WHO-Euro

WHO/UNICEF adviser on breastfeeding promotion in Estonia and Latvia, February 1994

Baby Friendly Hospital Initiative Assessments in Poland for UNICEF, February 1994

Facilitator for Baby Friendly Hospital Initiative training program, Murmansk, Russian Federation, September 1994, for WHO-Euro

Invited participant in follow-up meeting of Baby Friendly Hospital trainers, Prague, Czech Republic, December 1994, for UNICEF

Facilitator for Baby Friendly Hospital Initiative training program, Belarus, January 1995, for WHO-Euro

Pre-Baby Friendly Hospital Assessment site visit, Elektrostal Maternity House, Russian Federation, June 1995, for WHO-Euro and UNICEF

Facilitator for Baby Friendly Hospital Initiative presentation to Medical Academy of Archangelsk, Russian Federation, July 1995, for WHO-Euro

Team Leader for Baby Friendly Hospital Initiative training program, Murmansk, Russian Federation, September 1995, for WHO-Euro

Team Leader for Baby Friendly Hospital Initiative training program, Archangelsk, Russian Federation, September 1995, for WHO-Euro

Consultant for UNICEF Code of Marketing of Breast Milk Substitutes Conference for CCEE, NIS, and SEAR, December 1995

Facilitator for training of hospital assessors for Baby Friendly Hospital Initiative, St. Petersburg, February 1996, for UNICEF and WHO

Team leader for assessment of Elektrostal Maternity House, Russian Federation, for accreditation as a Baby Friendly Hospital, February 1996

Coordinator for breastfeeding counseling course for the Baby Friendly Hospital Initiative, St. Petersburg, March 1996, for WHO-Geneva, WHO-Euro, and UNICEF

Facilitator for NICU-BFHI course, Belarus, May 1996, for WHO-Euro Nutrition Unit

Course director for breastfeeding counseling course for the Baby Friendly Hospital Initiative, Vilnius, Lithuania, for UNICEF Geneva, July 1996

Conference Presentations

Consensus Conference "Giving Birth to a Healthy Child," St. Petersburg, Russian Federation, December 1992, for Healthy Cities Project and Women's and Children's Health Units, WHO-Euro

"Traditional Medicine and Co-operation for Development: The Experience of Mali: Confrontation between Two Medicines," Perugia, Italy, November 1992, for Women's and Children's Health Unit, WHO-Euro

"Adolescent Gynaecology," St. Petersburg, June 1993, for Women's and Children's Health Unit and Healthy Cities Project, WHO-Euro

"Psycho-Social Aspects of Breastfeeding: The Beginning—Most Important," Warsaw, Poland, November 1993, for Nutrition Unit WHO-Euro and UNICEF, New York

"Psycho-Social Aspects of Childbirth," The Beginning—Most Important. 2d Conference." Warsaw, Poland, February 1994, for Nutrition Unit, WHO-Euro

"Childbearing Practices in Different Cultures." Adaptive Changes to Infant and Child Care in a Rapidly Changing Social-Political-Economic System: Which Models Apply Best? WAIMH Conference on the Mental Health of Infants, Children, and Parents. Riga, Latvia, June 1994, for Nutrition Unit, WHO-Euro

"Breastfeeding Myths." Reproductive Health Seminar. Kiev, Ukraine, October 1994, for Nutrition Unit, WHO-Euro.

"Applying the BFHI in Eastern Europe." Concurrent Reproductive Health Seminar. Kiev, Ukraine, October 1994, for Nutrition Unit, WHO-Euro

"Psychological Aspects of Infant Nutrition in the Countries of Central and Eastern Europe." Nutrition Summer School. Archangelsk, Russian Federation, July 1995, for Nutrition Unit, WHO-Euro

"Childbirth and the BFHI in the Russian Federation." Presentation to the All-Russian Conference of Regional Officers in Maternal and Child Health, Saransk, Russian Federation, June 1995, for Nutrition Unit, WHO-Euro

REFERENCES

Chalmers, Iain, Murray Enkin, and Marc J. N. C. Keirse
    1989   *Effective Care in Pregnancy and Childbirth.* Oxford: Oxford University Press.

Davis-Floyd, Robbie
  1992   *Birth as an American Rite of Passage.* Berkeley: University of California Press.
Dennis, Louise
  1995   "Characteristics of Pregnant Women as Predictors of Utilization of Prenatal Care Services and Satisfaction with Those Services in St. Petersburg, Russia." Ph.D. dissertation preliminary report. Unpublished document.
Goer, Henci
  1995   *Obstetric Myths versus Research Realities: A Guide to the Medical Literature.* Westport, Conn.: Bergin and Garvey.
Jordan, Brigitte
  [1978] 1993   *Birth in Four Cultures: A Cross-Cultural Investigation of Childbirth in Yucatan, Holland, Sweden and the United States.* 4th ed. Prospect Heights, Ill.: Waveland Press.
Martonne, Marianne K., and Frank Kalman
  1991   "Hogy allunk ma a szoptatassal? Egy folmeres tanulsagai—a tovabbi feladatok trategiaja." *Medicus Universalis* 24(6):323–326.
Northrup, Christiane
  1994   *Women's Bodies, Women's Wisdom.* New York: Bantam Books.
Tiba, Janus
  1986   "The State of Childbirth Preparation in Hungary: A Short Review from Hungary." Ministry of Health, Hungary.
Wagner, Marsden
  1994   *Pursuing the Birth Machine: The Search for Appropriate Birth Technology.* Camperdown, Australia: ACE Graphics.
WHO Report
  1993   *The Health of Europe: Summary of the Second "Health for All" Evaluation.* WHO Regional Publication Series, no. 49.

PART FOUR

Fighting the System

Creating and Maintaining Alternative Models
of Authoritative Knowledge

ELEVEN

Resistance to Technology-Enhanced Childbirth in Tuscany

The Political Economy of Italian Birth

Jane Szurek

Who assists women during childbirth, delimits the spaces where the birth may occur, and controls the procedures used by claim to authoritative knowledge? The ways in which a society defines women and values their reproductive capability are reflected and displayed in the cultural treatment of birth. In Italy as elsewhere in Europe, redefinition and revaluation of women are linked to shifts in the aims of the technopolitical economy (Pizzini 1987a:9–28).[1] The State underwrites these aims and definitions, and in turn assumes authority over who will manage childbirth and where it will take place, as part of its responsibility for the safety of women and children. This authority, however, is linked to the politics of access to and control of its female population. In the past, midwives and birth activists who resist this control have had to defend themselves against attacks by representatives of the State to protect their right to practice and the right of women to control childbirth (Ehrenreich and English 1973).

The gradual but inexorable move away from midwife-assisted home birth to physician-assisted institutional birth in Italy was supported by various rationales, at first involving only a few pregnant women. In the early nineteenth century, the purpose of the first maternity wards in Italy was not to provide women with medical care but to sequester and protect unmarried pregnant women from social dishonor (Kertzer 1993:44). But up to the fascist period ending in 1943, most women still gave birth at home assisted by a midwife in the presence of female family members (see Triolo 1994 for an excellent discussion of the role of midwives in the fascist period). Thereafter, the trend from home to institutional birth began to gain momentum, paralleling developments in the technopolitical economy. In 1932, one out of twenty Italian women delivered in a hospital; in 1951, one out of seven; in 1958, one out of three (Livi-Bacci 1977:115). At the time of this research (1992), more than 99 percent of all deliveries in Italy took place in hospitals.

Historically medical professionals in the West have worked to secure control over childbirth and women's bodies by asserting the efficacy of intervention and the superiority of their technomedical knowledge over women's "natural" capabilities (Corea 1985). Their resounding success in this endeavor has resulted in the near-universal acceptance of technomedical birthing; the largely unquestioned, nearly comprehensive, and thoroughly standardized technological perinatal treatment women now receive has become a primary source of concern to birth activists in Italy as elsewhere. Such treatment, they argue, ignores both the normality and the individuality of birth. Psychosocial issues around birth are also a source of concern; some activists reason that when women surrender autonomy over their bodies to the control of the medical system, they lose the possibility of consolidating a strong sense of their own confidence, power, and authority through the act of giving birth.

In Tuscany during the 1970s, female political activists won reproductive choices for women to the extent that the Italian state routinely paid for both hospital births and abortions on request. Initially this contributed to greater safety and control for women over their bodies and the conditions of their daily lives; it also encouraged women to consider the hospital the "natural" and best place in which to give birth. The effects have been paradoxical. In postindustrial Italian hospitals, the centrality of obstetric technology has specific consequences for women and how their children are born: high rates of cesarean section, episiotomies, electronic fetal monitoring, sonography, and labor-inducing drugs. These developments compare negatively with the feminist political visions of the 1970s. Many of the same politicized Italian activists, along with new activists concerned with the general conditions of society and autonomy and health care of women, have come to reevaluate the question of women's reproductive choices within Italy's National Health System (NHS). They argue that urban technocratic hospitals compromise women's rights when it comes to the functioning of their bodies and their sense of self. Thus Italian birth activists now work (1) to define competing cultural representations of birth (to maintain no- or low-technology birth as viable options) and (2) to resist medical control and limitation of reproductive choices that affect the quality of women's lives. The contest over procedures and place of childbirth involves issues of control, assertions of authoritative knowledge, and, significantly, competing "essentialist" definitions of women in the discourses of childbirth.

This chapter concerns birth activists and midwives in Tuscany who question the overuse of technomedical procedures and challenge the authority of the biomedical profession over women and childbirth. The narrative form of this chapter will be mutitiered. I describe, analyze, and contrast the texture of childbirth and the definition of women and of birth in institutional settings that range from high to low utilization of technology (referred to henceforth as high- or low-tech) and reflect on the discourses and practices of birth activists engaged in resistance to technobirth. The practices and beliefs I describe and the interview material I present are framed by my discussion of Italy's political economy. This frame supports a picture of the role women's "choices" play in the high-technology births keyed so neatly into that political economy. Such contextualization of childbirth indicates how pregnant women, defined and courted as a class requiring medical treatment at local levels, have significant economic value in the political economy of Italian health care as well as at the global level in the world marketplace. This perspective begins to explain the complex issues birth activists face as they question and resist the biotechnical definitions of childbirth and of women.

THE RESEARCH

The study is based on anthropological fieldwork carried out in Florence, Italy, in 1992. During four months of research I observed three birth settings: a maternity ward in the large city hospital supported by the Italian state under the National Health System; a small private, "progressive" hospital; and a clinic, Il Marsupio (The Kangaroo), run by midwives (who have legal status in Italy) and volunteers who support its services and ideology. (I was not able to study a much talked about and admired independent birthing clinic known for its range of no-tech birthing choices, located just south of Florence in Poggibonsi.) These institutions span the spectrum from high levels of technical, procedural control over women's bodies to no/low-tech births. I supplement my analyses of the discourse and practices of childbirth activists with brief descriptions of birth in each of these three settings.

In addition to fieldwork in hospitals, I conducted interviews with childbirth workers who practiced within and outside of national health institutions. (A "childbirth worker" is defined here as anyone whose job it is to assist women with some aspect of perinatal care.) These in-depth, unstructured interviews took place in home kitchens, clinics, hospitals, and restaurants. The people who speak in these pages (most of them childbirth activists) have experience with hospital and/or home birth. The interviewees included three pregnant women, three independent midwives, two hospital-employed midwives, one yoga teacher who is concerned with women's political and social autonomy as it relates to their control over childbirth, three doctors, two social welfare workers, a psychologist, four nurses, and a student in her second year at the midwifery school located within the large university hospital mentioned above. Most of these people are known to each other or know of each other's work in the care of women during pregnancy and childbirth. Pseudonyms have been substituted for their real names.

During the interviews I learned how contrasting essentialist definitions of women are integral to both high-tech and no/low-tech childbirth advocates and practitioners in maintaining authoritative knowledge in childbirth (see below). I was interested in the use of technology and the medicalization of perinatal care; these interests guided my questions in interviews and conversations. I wanted to learn how the practices and objectives of childbirth activists came to constitute countervailing alternatives to the State-supported hospital promotion of technological monitoring and intervention during pregnancy and childbirth. I found that the activists involved in the practice of no/low-tech intervention (*interventismo dolce*) strive to provide woman-controlled childbirth as an effective choice in contemporary society. At the same time they demonstrate their scientific knowledge of the processes of human reproduction. Their aim is to make no/low-tech birth appealing and routinely available. They seek to create models and representations of woman-controlled birth showing that it is safe and nonpathological and that the practice of home birth is neither exotic nor risky.

BACKGROUND: THE POLITICAL ECONOMY OF ITALIAN BIRTH

Since the 1970s total health care has been provided to all women by the State as long as it is administered by the region on the site of a State-approved institution by State-licensed medical personnel. It is worth noting that among the fifteen European Economic Community (EEC, now the EU) countries, the Italian state has been the most generous in providing paid pregnancy leave and, in the first year after birth, parental leave from employment. The institution of these rights and provisions accompanied (but did not cause) the dramatic decrease in the Italian birthrate to 1.3 per family, the world's lowest rate in 1993. There are differences in fertility rates, however, between the north and south of Italy. In the industrial, comparatively rich northern and central part of Italy fewer children are born per nuclear family than in the poorer southern regions where the average family size is larger. In Florence the birthrate is less than one child per family. Significantly, Italy's overall low rate compares closely with other industrialized countries with high GNPs, and is an important factor in the competition for women's bodies at childbirth and the application of costly technology, medication, and surgery. This accompanies the popular notion that hospital-managed treatments and interventions are imperative for risk-free, pain-free births and a perfect child.

In 1985 there were 47,497 registered live births in Italy; 99.9 percent of all deliveries occurred in hospitals. The same year "the cesarean section rate was 22.5 per 100 deliveries, comparable to the 1985 rate reported in the USA (22.7%)" (*AJPH* 1987:1554). Coming at a time just after the phenomenon of "Il boom" of the 1950s and 1960s in the Italian economy, based on large-scale industrial development in the north, the generous terms of the National Health Service for women were backed up by the authority of newly developing Euro-American medical science and birth technology. Large sums of money were allocated by the councillors of the Tuscan region for purchases of medical technology, and it became customary for many physicians to be trained in the new biomedical procedures in medical facilities in the United States (Michael Blim, pers. com.). Meanwhile other, older birthing options fell into disuse, especially home births attended by midwives in the cities of northern and central Italy.

Another shift has been taking place. To date, the State is requiring consolidation and centralization of birth sites in large, urban hospitals in Tuscany where heavily capitalized technobirthing equipment and accompanying procedures are concentrated. At the same time the government exerts pressure to shut down small, more autonomous birthing hospitals. (During this research I was asked by a small hospital to give a brief interview in support of its continued operation to a TV news crew sent to cover the story of the State threat to close it.) It is further of note that of all the regions in Italy, Tuscany spent more on health care than any other region; figures from 1983 show the regional government "spent 34 percent more [on health services] than the national average" (Putnam 1993:72). The contradiction is that while expenditures on health are great, women's options for birthing are being spatially narrowed with the closure of hospitals, further limiting their range of choices.

The Economic Context

It is important to contextualize the authoritative knowledge claims of medical professionals within the economy in order to comprehend the scope of power of these professionals. Furthermore, to consider the embeddedness of the medical institutions in the political economy is to begin to appreciate the complexities of any resistance to State-sanctioned childbirth that is part of the medical/industrial/economic complex. Against an economic backdrop we see the increased capitalization of hospitals and health care, the increase in investment in medical real estate and technology, and with this an increase in regulation and standardization of treatment of women's bodies during labor and childbirth. Institutions such as hospitals, once in place, must be utilized to justify their continued existence to the public, or else be threatened with closure. In this instance the state health system appears to have succeeded in "reaching the maximum number of people, through deployment of a unified apparatus linked to the machinery of the state" (Castel 1991:294). One large part of the population that can be counted on to use the hospital are the women who have learned to choose hospitalized birth because they fear risk and damage to the fetus and pain to themselves.

While many childbirth workers outside the State health system earn only a modest livelihood in private practice, they do compete with the State medical establishment for women's bodies and ideas about how women's bodies can be viewed and treated. This competition has the potential to undermine the justification of State tax revenue spent on childbirth. To maintain its position as authoritative manager of women's childbirth, the State responds with emphasis on the "high risks" of childbearing. As Marsden Wagner points out, "Risk is the bludgeon used to scare not only women but also politicians and health care providers" (1986:198–200). For example, while early detection of problems during pregnancy is certainly important, to encourage women to focus on risk, and to impress them with the authoritative evidence of newly identifiable genetic defects in fetuses that can only be detected through technological surveillance, works to ensure that most women will demand high-tech births in hospitals (Rapp 1988). This systemic self-perpetuation both justifies the hospitals' approach to birth and guarantees them the continued business of the childbearing population.

This rhetoric of risk is multivalent; it has a purpose beyond concern with safety. As Mary Douglas notes, "the language of risk is likely to perform a standardizing, centralizing role at the level of public debate in an industrial society as it makes political use of natural dangers" (1992:4). Birth activists, perceiving a larger political purpose in the medical bureaucracy, incorporate this understanding in their efforts to broadcast their messages about the safety of woman-controlled birth.

As Robbie Davis-Floyd (1992:184) observes in her research on women and childbirth, whether midwives assist the body's processes or high-tech physicians ply their trade, tools, and skills, given the resiliency of the female body, births will generally turn out well. She asserts that the real issue is not safety but what aspects of culture are emphasized and perpetuated at birth and what cultural lessons are learned (Davis-Floyd 1994:14). Women living in a culture that values their dependence are encouraged to seek security and safety and to believe that these can only be provided for them by the medical profession. Thus women are increasingly coming to demand from the medical profession assurances of success, efficiency, protection, and perfection for themselves and their newborn children, especially if they plan to have only one child (see, for example, Davis-Floyd's [1994] discussion of women who demand cesarean sections). Indeed, much recent research in social science has clarified women's agency in constructing the medical system and its priorities as they now stand (see Browner and Press, Lazarus, this volume; Arney 1982; Davis-Floyd 1992, 1994; Sargent and Stark 1987).

Several factors operate in gaining the obedience of women to the State-ordered systematicity of childbirth. First, there are the ones that subsist in the popular culture: the media, local myths, popularized science, risk rhetoric, recycled stories and rumors from conversations with friends and relatives. Concerns with danger, safety, fear, pain, blood, and the imperfect child are easily fanned embers. Second, for example, as Antonia, yoga teacher and childbirth activist, emphasizes, "The doctors scare so many women at six or seven months, especially if the baby might be *podalico* [breech]." Fear is quite enough to sweep the majority of women willingly and obediently into a hospital for birth—and the high probability (22.5%) of cesarean surgery. Should a woman voice preference for a home birth, a doctor may accuse her, as one woman reported, "of being a criminal," therefore potentially punishable by the State. The intimation of criminality is a strong threat and moral prod to women to deliver in a hospital. Put another way, the idea of hospitalization as the way to achieve safe, painless, perfect childbirth has been internalized by most urban Italian women. Little information reaches women about alternative birth practices to offset or criticize the authoritative information mass-produced by the major medical/economic interests.

Through the National Health Service the Italian government provides total health care to 57 million people. However, organization, administration, and priority setting in health care are under the jurisdiction of local government officials in the separate regions. (Italy's health system was decentralized to each of twenty regions in the 1970s.) The national government divides up the tax revenues and allocates money to each of the regions. In terms of health care, regional government officials are advised by the medical community and decide specifically on how the money will be spent according to the pressures of professional interest groups in that region. Hence national money is paid out, for example, for purchase of new medical technology, a portion of which is specified for childbirth. The amounts spent on medical care are not insignificant. In 1990, for example, approximately "one-tenth of Italy's gross domestic product was being spent by regional governments, only slightly below the figure for American states" (Putnam 1993:25). Of that sum the regions spent 53.6 percent on health (equivalent to US$37.208 billion). For comparison purposes, overall Italian agricultural expenditures came next at 7.6 percent; 2.9 percent was spent on education (Putnam 1993:25). It is relevant to note that childbirth in Italy is situated in an economy currently defined as in crisis, especially in northern Italy where most manufacturing is located. More-over, Italy is a significant player in the international global economy, which also defines itself as being in crisis.

But how does this connect to women, their bodies, and childbirth? I suggest that as birth technologies are manufactured, bought, and sold and proliferate as profitable trade commodities on the world market, women and their bodies take on a new economic significance in the global market-place. After all, women are the objects and consumers of services in the technobirth market with all its accompaniments: surgical tools, electronic monitoring machines, and pharmaceuticals. When childbearing women are defined as being at risk, their perceived needs additionally justify state taxation and investment in the technomedical system of childbirth. Hence, the stakes can be high for those who command the place and authority to conduct the births of the future.

It appears that an ideology that furthers the use of technology for child-birth works at several levels (though not necessarily conscious ones). As Wagner, a WHO physician, points out, "Although birth is a normal biosocial process, it has been redefined as a medical problem that is either pathological or potentially pathological. . . . The medical profession has thereby created the necessity of its presence at the centre of birth" (1986:196). Authoritative claims of the efficacy of technical-medical expertise on the part of the medical profession to control pain and risk of imperfect babies or death contribute to the functioning of the political economy.

By "political economy," I mean "political" in the sense of institutional structures that have the power to convince (or coerce); "economy" in the sense of the behaviors of buyers and sellers in pursuit of profits in the interconnected local and global marketplaces. (Take for just one example the hundreds of American-made Hewlett-Packard fetal monitors that have been purchased for use on women in Italian hospitals.) I suggest that as the structural economic crisis in Italy deepens in the process of trans-forming an industrial economy controlled by the northern-based commer-cial and industrial interests to an increasingly service-based economy, childbirth has evolved as an important activity in the political economy of Italy. Italy shares this economic state of affairs with other "advanced indus-trial" economies in the West with similar economic concerns, problems, and reliance on technological fixes.[2] Given this situation of political and economic hegemony, the challenge for birth activists is how to secure the survival of the knowledge, legitimacy, and practice of a more lenient, inter-ventismo dolce childbirth, the view of birth as a nonpathological phenome-non, and the mental and physical self-confidence of childbearing women.

International Dimensions of Birth Activists

Although the data in this chapter are based on fieldwork in Florence, it is important to keep in mind that the issues and people involved in this movement have international links, awareness, and experience. One aspect of this internationalism is that many Italian birth activists have worked or been trained in woman-controlled childbirth practices in other countries—Peru, India, England, the United States, Kenya, and Mexico, for example. A second aspect is the international proliferation of the biomedical/technical treatment of childbirth and of women as standardized objects (Ginsburg and Rapp 1995; Jordan [1978] 1993).[3] In Florence regulatory standardization and bureaucratization via the institutional control of women through medicalized childbirth have evolved gradually.

These broad issues underlie the "contested terrain" of pregnancy and childbirth in Florence. The contest between birth activists and the State is illuminated by Brigitte Jordan's notion of "authoritative knowledge." Both the State-supported medical professionals and the independent activists have constructed competing claims to authoritative knowledge. The rationale for each claim is based on complex understandings both of the physiology of childbirth and of what childbirth stands for as it relates to the identity and the place of women and children in the socioeconomic and cultural picture of Italy's future.

Through description and discussion of birth in the three institutional settings that I observed and where I conducted interviews, the next section of this chapter presents the authoritative knowledge of childbirth activists (mothers, midwives, and others)—their analyses of interventive birth and the philosophies and authoritative assertions they have developed from empirical successes in their practice of no or minimally technical intervention for pregnancy and at childbirth.

TECHNOHOSPITAL: BIRTH IN A LARGE DELIVERY ROOM

You step into a hospital. It makes you feel poor and miserable. Why do women ask "Please take me home from the hospital" right after birth? The hospital is a place where you are robbed of your power. They make you take pills you know nothing about and make you do things you don't want to do. Everything is done to make you feel helpless.

—ANTONIA,
yoga teacher and childbirth activist

In the largest hospital complex in Florence stands the four-story OB/GYN building. Approximately 2,500 births take place here each year. The hospital complex, guarded by an electronic gate and uniformed guards, is a campus with buildings, trees, lawns, gift shops, and canteens. The grounds are busy with milling patients dressed in robes and slippers, and with doctors, nurses, students, and staff walking from building to building. Trucks and delivery vans scoot around the grounds to loading docks attached to every edifice. The commerce of running the hospital is much in evidence. Once in the entryway of the OB/GYN building there are patients and visitors socializing near the coffee and chocolate machines and telephones, in the corridors, on the staircase landings. Inside the building, branching off several long, polished corridors are rooms containing between four and eight beds. They have large, curtainless windows. This is where women recover from delivery while their newborns are transported to the nursery. Outside the doorway of each room, fixtures are mounted to hold the garlands of pink or blue bows of ribbons gathered from gifts received by the mothers. (One also sees these bouquets hung on the outer doors of houses and apartments announcing the return of mothers and children from the hospital.)

Discipline and Obedience

Medical professionals expect that women will follow explicit and implicit rules and procedures during pregnancy and childbirth that the profession has deemed medically correct. When a woman enters a hospital for childbirth it is assumed that she is already socialized to obey these rules. Doctors, nurses, and medical personnel are the agents of hospital discipline. A primary expectation is that a woman will come to the hospital in good time to be registered, settled in a bed, and watched internally and externally by the various monitors, staff, and equipment that await women in labor. Industrial-floor sounds of thudding, thumping, and clanging often welcome women in labor as they enter the large hospital maternity ward. Little is done to reduce fear and encourage confidence and relaxation. In *Discipline and Punish* (1977), Michel Foucault discussed the multiple small ways obedience is exacted from human beings by personnel working in institutions. Many of his observations are substantiated by doctors who overtly discipline and in some cases punish women who resist or appear to resist the authority of their expertise and ministrations. I will provide one brief example.

Nicoletta, whose parents pressured her to go to the hospital for her first birth, didn't get there soon enough to satisfy the doctor. She explained that when she started labor at home she was very comfortable, but in the car en route to the hospital with her midwife, sister, and husband, her contractions stopped when they were delayed in cold, rainy weather in rush-hour traffic. Her contractions stopped again when she had to wait to go through repetitive admission procedures at the hospital registration desk. Once she was settled in a room in the maternity ward, the doctor in charge entered and began to ask her questions about her labor "in an angry way. I realized he was accusing me of trying to have the baby at home." Again her contractions stopped. He left the room. Nicoletta continued:

> I piled pillows on the bed so I could rest on them and be on my knees. This was the most comfortable position and my contractions began again. The doctor came into the room again and demanded to know what I was doing. He was angry and ordered me to turn over and lie on my back. He took control over what I did. My contractions stopped again. He intimidated my midwife, my husband, and sister. He told the nurse to give me an injection to start the labor. I didn't want it. My midwife tried to make things easier for me while the doctor was there. She kept saying, "See, she's started," but he didn't pay attention to her or me and gave me the injection. The contractions started with this and they brought me to the *salo parto* [delivery room]. The midwife used her forearm, pressing me in the front to try to help push the baby out. But then the doctor put the suction on the baby's head to pull him out. It was all so different from what I had wanted and planned and the comfortable labor I started at home. I knew it could have been good, the same way I had seen births when I lived in India. For my second child, to keep my parents from interfering and making me go to the hospital, I didn't tell them when I expected to be in labor and just had the baby at home with my midwife and husband.

Rather than inspiring confidence, relaxation, and comfort, the delivery room I observed suggested impending disaster. Nervous energy is displayed by every blue-uniformed maternity attendant. In the room there may be at any one time four to ten or more women near delivery. Lying on their backs on the delivery beds, rendered docile and prepared for birth, they are wheeled into the room. Under grayish sheets they lie on separate metal birthing tables arranged in parallel rows. Suspended above each woman is a high-intensity lamp that bathes the lower half of her body with a circle of light. Some of the sheets and pieces of cloth on the floor are blotched with bloodstains, as are the cover-all smocks of the birth attendants—the doctors, anesthesiologists, nurses, hospital midwives, assistants, and cleanup personnel. The room contains a variety of randomly placed machines, tools, wires, and tubes. A sense of crisis, risk, and emergency hangs in the air. Women are connected to various computers and machines monitoring their biological functions. Other machines are stationed in the room prepared to be called into operation if wanted. Noise and rapid movements make the atmosphere tense and electric with the business of labor, delivery, and birth. There is talking, commanding, yelling, moaning, crying, screaming. Machines are rolled in, out, and around the room. Metallic instruments clank on tables and carts. Water splashes in sinks. Women continue to be wheeled in and out of the room. Birth attendants conducting their tasks flicker in busy traffic patterns between and around the women lying passively on the tables. The delivery room ebbs and flows with waves of loudly articulated crisis. In this hyperactive environment, not only is a woman distracted from her own body's promptings, messages, and knowledge as she progresses toward delivery; what she thinks, knows, and feels is drowned out by the background noise and movement. Under such conditions the possibility of hospital personnel and doctors giving sensitive individual attention to each woman is reduced or totally preempted. Women are excluded as informants about their own bodies. This is a "modern obstetric environment," a central place where technology and its accompanying procedures are authorized. It is the context in which the authoritative knowledge of biomedically trained professionals reigns. In such an environment, accepted as customary by medical personnel, a doctor conveniently need not take notice of the mental/emotional expressions of the woman in labor (Colombo 1987:232–238; Jordan [1978] 1993; Pizzini 1987b:118–143; 1987c:198–231).[4]

ESSENTIALISM TYPE I: WOMAN/MACHINE AND THE DOCTORS

A prominent issue in professional, academic, and public discourses in the 1980s and 1990s has been over sex and gender definitions: What makes a human essentially female or essentially male? Discussions of essentialist definitions, for some, have come to include questions about how technology and machines may be used to enhance these definitions or support beliefs about differences. In the late twentieth century in Italy and elsewhere in the industrialized world, high value is placed on technological artifacts. Donna Haraway (1990) has elaborated for us the notion of cyborgs, our human/machine-extension combinant that lends itself to a greater idealized and enhanced sense of identity. Reinforcing this is the idea that humans are imperfect and in danger or at risk if scientific and technological procedures are not used to enhance physiology. We must ask, however, in terms of gender, whose definition of identity is brought to bear.

Looking at the problem from the physician's point of view, it appears that current medical conceptions of technological use are not consciously gender-biased. Rather, physicians stress the benefits of the technology that the women themselves perceive. As one physician noted,

> Women are afraid not to use technology. Women ask if there is a greater risk without the cesarean cut. They do not accept even a 1 percent risk. More women are having their babies after thirty, so they don't want to risk having a baby with problems.

For a variety of rationales on the part of women who become willing and obedient recipients of technomedical treatment at childbirth (see below), the State/productive sphere and the individual/reproductive sphere are

collapsed together: reproduction is conducted more and more like production. As I mentioned earlier, individual, woman-controlled childbirth
in Florence, possessed as a choice by women just thirty-five years ago, is no
longer an easily available alternative. Nor does it enter the minds of most
women as an option today. Although noninterventionist home birth is perceived by some doctors as ideologically incorrect, in the eyes of most it is
symbolically criminal.[5] In the hands of doctors the reproductive becomes
the productive; that is, children are begun in the bodies of women but can
only be assured perfection through intervention of the machine under the
paternalistic authority of the State.

Medical experts and technicians have aligned their professional aims
with women's fears of danger, pain, and imperfection. Then they proffer
the balms and solutions under their authority: they have the technological
fix. In the medical view, it is not a case of women *versus* machines. Physicians try to redefine and re-create, discursively and in practice, the perfect
birthing machine—a combination of woman and technology, a cyborg
(see Davis-Floyd and Dumit 1997). Their discourse is ever attentive to danger, imperfection, and the implicit incompetence or inefficiency of a woman's body. Such perceptions, paradoxically, make woman-plus-technology,
the cyborg, seem more "feminine" (read incompetent, dependent) in essence than woman alone. Technology reduces women to birthing machines to produce the perfect child, while childbirth is organized and defined by the State as something that can be abstracted from individual
women (Jordan [1978] 1993; Sargent 1989). Thereby a woman is stripped
of most of her freedoms and depersonalized, since her choices and her
knowledge of her own body are of lesser account than the technology that
is used to monitor her (Jordan [1978] 1993). In becoming a cyborg, she
becomes the ideal feminine form as defined by male wants: she becomes
unopposing, renders her body for control and use, and is passive to the desires of doctors and nurses who direct technological procedures. Birth activists argue that the hospital is a prime vehicle by which medical experts divest
women of their power and confidence in themselves and in their unique
sexual capacity to give birth. We will see below how birth activists seek to
reclaim this sexual capacity through their own practice and discourse.

MID-STATION: BETWEEN THE TECHNOHOSPITAL
AND LOW-TECH CLINIC

In a small hospital, which I will call Epifania, rather idyllically located over-
looking Tuscan hillsides and the Duomo of Florence, approximately 600
births and 550 abortions take place annually. Here is a birthplace option that falls between the technohospital and midwife-run clinic, a place
where one finds less regimentation of women. Indeed, women in labor are

encouraged to take greater control over their own deliveries, have a greater choice over how they may deliver (standing up, sitting, or even floating in a cobalt blue birthing pool), and theoretically can easily refuse medicalization. (I was repeatedly told by hospital staff about a woman who went through delivery laughing, standing up, and virtually unassisted.) Yet this hospital has all the needed technology for surgery and cesarean operations. And it has other accoutrements to make women feel more at home. Women and their families, when they wish, can sit in the hospital garden, literally above the clouds, before or after giving birth. On the two floors of the hospital devoted to childbirth are labor and lying-in rooms, most with a two-person capacity, small delivery rooms where one woman at a time will give birth, operating rooms, and a homey lounge. The environment overall is quiet. In 1979, Frederick Leboyer, a French physician advocating nonviolent, natural childbirth, was invited to Florence to give a keynote address at a congress connected to the opening of this hospital committed to "nonviolent" birth.[6] (This same hospital is now under threat of closure.) Guests interested in nonviolent or benign birth came from different parts of the world to celebrate the opening of this model hospital that was dedicated to the social/psychological importance of children being born in a benign, peaceful manner if they are to develop into nonviolent, peaceable adult citizens.

At Epifania Hospital, nine doctors are responsible for officiating at births, but what is special is that midwives hired by the hospital are given more respect by the doctors and have a greater range of responsibilities than at the large OB/GYN hospital in Florence. It was one of the midwives who, in fact, helped design and oversee the installation of the birthing pool. The hospital midwives spoke with affection and gratitude of the director who since 1979 had granted them freedom in their work and who often referred to them proudly as "my midwives." However, even though these women play an enlarged role in childbirth, they are still criticized by midwives who work outside the hospital system. The external midwives claim that the hospital midwives have compromised their principles, have no real power, and are "lackeys" of the doctors, assisting in episiotomies and too many C-sections.

One of the obstetricians at Epifania, Dr. Angelo Scuderi, is the stated favorite of many Florentine women, and even of midwives who work outside the hospital. Scuderi takes a position against rigid regulation of women at childbirth and cautions against unwarranted intervention and overmedicalization. As he states in a paper he wrote in 1990, a doctor's role is to wait attentively should something pathological occur during the delivery process, at which time he can step in and proceed with his medical and technical skills. While a doctor stands by, midwives, because of their knowledge and understanding of birth, are best suited to assist women.

They are the *mediatrice* between the woman and the hospital structure because they understand women and the hospital, and therefore are "best
able to transmit and interpret the needs of the woman to the doctor."
Midwives, he explains, "are halfway between the medical/biological event
and the social/cultural event of labor, while the doctor is primarily interested in the biological aspect." Dr. Scuderi's consistent, progressive work to
keep childbirth alternatives available to women and a 1989 court case
brought against him over an abortion he performed have won him widespread active support among many middle-class women in Florence.[7] Independent midwives value him as a sympathetic collaborator who is receptive
to their ideas. They are also thankful for his help. Yet, given his sympathies
and persuasions, his own work as an obstetrician is not free of contradictions. He himself acknowledges, "When you work among other doctors,
you will have to compromise some of your views and practices. You use
technology partly because you are a member of a team. You have rules and
principles that must be followed, certain rules that everyone must respect.
Otherwise, you would not long remain working there." He continues,

> It is a perversion every time you change nature, intervene in the natural
> process, everything is *rivolta*, upset. Even if you do an amniotomy, then there
> is a particular course of events that follows. So the doctor gives *his* rhythm to
> the women's birth because he controls the oxytocin. Every doctor does a
> birth the way he wants it.

It is no surprise, then, that while many women support and appreciate
Scuderi as a friend and collaborator, they also are critical of him and the
hospital in which he works. One midwife chides him, asking how many
episiotomies he has done in the last month. She also warns me that the
official principles and practices of the hospital, which sound so supportive
of woman-centered birth, hide much of what really happens. Though allegedly Epifania allows more freedoms to women in terms of comfort and self-
control, and the medical staff upholds a principled position against the
overuse of the medical technology available to them, there are subtle ways
in which women note that they are not in full control of their own bodies
at childbirth. Even under what would seem very good conditions, there are
times when they are insulted rather than exalted. I end this section with
an example of such an experience as told by Anna.

> My delivery in the hospital wasn't painful, medicalized, surgical, or confusing.
> Still there was something unsavory that clings to my memory. I had my baby
> comfortably with my husband there, two hospital midwives, and a doctor I
> liked. Everything went well. My labor was calm and overall not very painful.
> But *I* worked and sweated. As soon as I delivered, the first thing that hap-
> pened was the doctor grasped my husband's hand and shook it over me—
> two men in triumph! And here I was. *I* had done all the work and was ex-
> hausted, and they were congratulating each other.

ESSENTIALISM TYPE II: WOMEN, MIDWIVES, AND THEIR PRACTICES

In contrast to the mechanistic essentialist definitions of women mentioned earlier, childbirth activists have another set of beliefs and essentialist definitions of women that guides their practices. In this section I will be referring to the beliefs held by a range of childbirth activists—independent midwives, yoga teachers,[8] women who have given birth with the assistance of a midwife and are volunteers or supporters of the movement, social workers, and those midwives who are part of Il Marsupio (The Kangaroo). Il Marsupio is a midwife-established clinic and training school for alternative-minded midwives who have already been trained by State university hospitals in the "pathology of childbirth" but have sought to work toward woman-controlled birth, and ultimately toward a society in which women control their bodies and the full course of their lives and decisions. I discuss Il Marsupio at greater length below.

As already mentioned, a number of contemporary birth activists in Florence are the same people who struggled politically for comprehensive state medical coverage for women in the 1970s, and now are concerned with the loss of women's physical and mental independence and autonomy under Italy's health system. As one birth activist observed, "While we were working for better health care for women [in the 1970s], they were taking our power in another way." Partly as a consequence of their earlier political activities, their awareness of the intersection of control/authority over women's bodies at birth and the patriarchal political economy and health service of Italy is acute. Given this informed awareness, the discourse surrounding perinatal care and the organization of the midwife-owned clinic and school has become one means through which birth activists can challenge the ideology and hegemony of the State over the bodies of its pregnant female citizens. With a reformulated political acuity in the 1990s, they argue against practices of doctors in State hospitals that submit most women to some kind of standardized, technically assisted childbirth.

Although they take a stand against overuse of technology at childbirth, none of the activists and activist midwives demonize technology. They appreciate it for its help in the small percentage of deliveries where women's lives or that of the fetus are at risk. As one midwife emphasized, "We need technology—women need technology. If it is of help in the situations that need it, it is a good way of birth." Should a woman need the technological procedures available at a large hospital, the midwife will take her client there. Yet modern technology is also a tool in political issues. As an activist gynecologist explains,

> It's not the technology in the hospital used for monitoring pregnant women, the growth of the fetus for detection of fetal problems, that is at the heart of

power over the human body. The seeking of power comes before technology. On the one hand, there is care. If you want to care, if your objective is to work at caring, technology can be used for care. If a doctor's objective is to have power, then the technology will be used to exercise power.

To assert their position against the essentialism of the technomedical establishment, birth activists have developed their own essentialist definitions. These are part of the philosophy that guides their clinical practice and educational program to attract women to a less interventionist approach to childbirth. By taking women's childbirth capacity as the essential core from which women's sense of self, power, and identity derive, they make their argument against the male-doctor essentialist definition of women: that woman-plus-machine approaches the ideal of the feminine, a definition highly congenial to the interests of the State economy. Birth activists, in maintaining an alternate definition of women, strategize to establish control in the area where they have authoritative knowledge, to promote home birth, and to attempt to weaken or break women's reliance on "doctors' masculine knowledge,"[9] which they consider mechanical and disenfranchising for women.

The following illustrates the essentialist tenor of birth activists' philosophy that female biology is basic to women's individuality, although the relationship between female mind and body is also integral. The difference between female and male childbirth techniques and attitudes toward women is taken as axiomatic. As Daniella of Il Marsupio explains, "Technology is male; the doctors who use it substitute it for a relationship with a woman in labor which then leads to unnecessary intervention. This is violent and leads to mutilation of women." They contrast this to feminine, woman-controlled birth as using feminine sensitivities to attend and listen to rather than monitor the female body. "If you listen to the body you can know what is happening. You don't have to reach for the oxytocin if labor stops."

Delivery is often conceived of as a sexual process. One midwife explains it is sexual "because the energy is exercised in the same way, in the same place. Sexual energy is the way of delivery in childbirth." She continues, strongly identifying the consequences of male interference with female sexuality.

A woman has had her sexuality defined by the masculine and has had her power taken away from her—technology interferes in every point where women express their sexuality. Technology stops the body process. To go into another state of consciousness to produce endorphins, a woman becomes excited so the process of the body can take over. An injection prevents the production of endorphins. In the second stage of labor, if a woman is touched, given a local anesthesia, hard massages, these stop a process of sexuality. If she can do it herself, without interference, her vagina will contract itself. This, the "fetus ejection reflex," [10] is physiological. She doesn't even have to push. The midwife says at this moment, "The baby has to come out now. It's time." After the birth, if the baby is taken away, they take away her gratification, her satisfaction. She is left with the pain. . . . [If doctors interfere with the processes of childbirth,] the woman feels the doctor delivers the baby and not her. So she does not feel strong in herself. She does not feel like an adult.

In refutation of the claims and interventions of the doctors at childbirth, one midwife explains,

> Women are used as productive machines. A woman is not a machine to put a baby out. She is human, and she will give her baby good and bad things. There are no perfect babies. In the technomedical thinking of people, of doctors, women are pressured to have the perfect baby. The technology to do this is masculine.

Modern midwives are "technoliterate" (Davis-Floyd, pers. com.; see her chapter, this volume). Many Italian midwives are already highly trained in medicine, having had three years of medical school or having completed nursing school prior to two years of midwifery school. Some have trained in midwifery schools in other countries. Most of the midwives I interviewed had worked abroad with midwives in both underdeveloped and overdeveloped countries where they accumulated hands-on, empirical experience and gained insight into different techniques and alternative ways of birth. One had worked with midwives in California and visited the Farm in Tennessee (see Gaskin 1990).[11] Out of these experiences they came to Florence to work and to challenge the practice of the overuse of birthing technology in deliveries they saw as normal and not requiring invasive procedures.

Midwives and childbirth activists attempt to impart their views not only to pregnant women but also to professionals working in large hospitals. To a certain extent they have succeeded. They have gained respect for the work they do among some medical professionals in hospitals with whom they discuss childbirth practices. Within the medical establishment they have sympathizers who collaborate with them. In part because of their efforts (along with childbirth activists in Milan) during the 1980s the number of drugs urged on women was reduced. Alternative treatments such as massage have been introduced in some hospitals.

IL MARSUPIO AND BIRTH ACTIVISTS

Il Marsupio began in 1979 when five midwives, reacting against Leboyer's philosophy (which emphasizes concern for the child but disregards the woman at childbirth) and its adoption by Epifania Hospital, gathered to discuss and initiate a program with an alternative childbirth ideology. In their philosophy and practice "both" women and children are the focus. They are viewed and treated holistically and are considered key to a potentially benign and peaceful society. In addition, the birth activist midwives noted a lack of training in full perinatal care in doctor-run midwifery schools, which only teach practice for "pathological" childbirth. They considered it their responsibility to provide pre- and postnatal care to women. Their discussions and organizing work resulted six years later in the founding of Il Marsupio, the only childbirth school and clinic in Italy that promotes home births and minimal intervention at childbirth. Il Marsupio midwives and three affiliate doctors have developed a discourse about the power of individual women at childbirth as it relates to control and decision making in other aspects of their lives. They believe in educating a woman about the functioning of her body in the widest possible way so she can participate actively in her pregnancy and remain in charge of her delivery.

At Il Marsupio two intensive eight-day training courses for midwives are taught each year with an enrollment limited to twenty. The course enrolls midwives from all over Italy (there were also a few from France and Switzerland when I was there) who choose to learn practices beyond the ones that center on "pathological" birth in the standard two-year midwifery training program. Il Marsupio's focus is on home delivery. Among the objectives in the course is an introduction to the understanding of procedures of pregnancy and delivery as emotional and psychosomatic moments and a view of "spontaneous delivery" as an expression of women's individuality.

Apart from the courses for midwives are others provided for pregnant women, designed to reinforce confidence and control by teaching them about their bodies and what changes to expect. The objective is to consider the whole woman in the context of her human relationships. The women study the process of physiology, as one midwife explains, in consideration of "the mind/body energy, because it is the mind that governs the body." The course covers pregnancy, childbirth, and postnatal care. Up to the seventh month of pregnancy women who attend Il Marsupio learn about nutrition, especially the importance of eating vegetables and fruits (food supplements are not emphasized); they are introduced to relaxation exercises and stress-reducing techniques (if a woman smokes cigarettes she is taught about the damage it can do to the fetus and is helped to stop, using stress-reducing techniques); they learn about hormonal changes in their bodies during pregnancy and generally about women's physiology; they are taught about the development of the fetus and how it moves. In the last two months of the course the women deal with preparation for birth, how to work with pain, the body, and the baby. Although Il Marsupio advocates home birth during the program, only 25 percent of the women who come to Il Marsupio classes choose it. It must be noted here that Il Marsupio operates outside the NHS and so women who attend the classes and select a midwife must pay for the services. Throughout the pregnancy a midwife will accompany a woman to pregnancy-related events such as physical examinations and at childbirth whether at home or in the hospital. In addition to classes, training sessions, direct care, and attendance at childbirth, Il Marsupio does "cultural work," holding public monthly lectures and discussions. In these meetings, the topics covered are perinatal ecology, pain—its meaning and how to cope—the secret life of the fetus, and the first two hours of a baby's life. These forums both inform women about technical aspects of pregnancy and childbirth and provide them with a social and political context for forming relationships at the point of reproduction. Women are made aware of political connections between women, childbirth, the paternalistic behavior of doctors in hospitals, and the "masculine" birthing technology and technical procedures it supports and enforces. Local awareness of Il Marsupio's practices and beliefs has been spread primarily by word of mouth, and women who have had home births often become advocates and do volunteer work there.

Midwives at Il Marsupio train themselves to be carefully conscious of the many social and psychological factors that form the specific and general context of events taking place in a woman's body at childbirth. One midwife termed this "hyperconsciousness." According to one of the directors of Il Marsupio, "Childbirth is a mirror of social problems. If other things are changing in society and in her life, a pregnant woman can feel them. They will affect whether the birth proceeds easily or not. Birth technology is masculine. For men, the rhythms of the times, the thinking, the way of living, are the masculine rhythms." There are other rhythms, subtler ones that women can sense in their lives and at childbirth, "if they listen."

Midwives at Il Marsupio emphasize and support the physical differences among women. As Teresa, another midwife, explains,

> Everyone has a different physiology because each has a thinking mind—the cerebral cortex—and hormones and emotions—the hypothalamus. You can't separate these things. If you understand this, if you listen to a woman, you can understand why labor stops. Doctors can substitute technology for a relationship with a pregnant woman, because technology works only on the body's physiology. But a midwife will use her relationship with a woman to understand what's happening. I can help her with my being to reestablish her equilibrium. It's the way of the midwife, but not of the doctor.

Doctors focus on the woman's body alone as actor, whereas activists see this body-mechanics approach as undermining women's self-confidence. Il Marsupio midwives take into account the whole woman, her mind acting with the body. This "interpretive control" is at the heart of the contest between the activists and the hospital-based way of birth.

Birth activists deal with women's fears about childbirth, because the activists see these fears as the major reason women seek hospital childbirth. Il Marsupio and activists work to alleviate the fear of pain and the fears of having an imperfect child. Daniella observed,

> If women only knew that pain can be minimal, if they were told what to expect, they wouldn't rush to the doctors. We [midwives] can help them cope by understanding that the pain isn't so unbearable, that if they are confident in themselves and listen to themselves they don't even have to push. There is the fetus ejection reflex that helps get the baby out. There is the relaxation that comes from rhythmic breathing. As long as there is relaxed time, as long as there isn't interference, things can go well.

As Antonia described herself when she attends a birth, "I'm like a tiger when I am at a birth. One wrong word or tone of voice can damage the experience." Another Il Marsupio midwife stated that of the approximately 250 births she last assisted, not one woman required an episiotomy, let alone a cesarean. If, of course, the screening early on in pregnancy indicates a birth will be problematic, the midwife will refer a woman to a doctor. Yet they are aware that many indicators of problems change or disappear over the course of pregnancy.

Activists' political views on childbirth and its social context are not homogeneous. They argue through the issues with each other. But all of them consider the broader social context and quality of life for women and children beyond birth itself. Some of their key concerns are that "doctors are robbing power of women at childbirth." As Antonia explained,

> We need to struggle to get this power back. Men as technicians, men who use tools, should be kept out of the birth room. When we go to them for advice about birth, that's the moment we lose power. I have met women who stay conscious and present at birth, helping their bodies. Afterward they seem stronger, more clear. These women have been able to realize inner wishes. They don't have to ask their doctors and teachers for advice. They have moved from being obedient daughter to adult. They have a sense of power in themselves and will not be victims again. They will step out of the system.

In Italy, as in the United States, women who choose low-tech, no-drug, or home births tend to be well educated, cosmopolitan, middle to upper middle class with the confidence and security that comes with social position. They have confidence that their childbirth will turn out well. They opt not to be part of the NHS administered by the region of Tuscany, and they are able and willing to pay for perinatal care they receive outside of it. While this birth-for-payment by middle-class women makes it possible for Il Marsupio and independent midwives to continue to be financially sound and autonomous, Il Marsupio aspires to reach women of all classes and give them confidence in their own body's capacity for childbirth. As one Il Marsupio proponent states, "Women all make different choices about their ways of life, from women factory workers to professional women. We need to reach them all."

Shoring Up Midwifery Authoritative Knowledge: Support from an Authority

During an interview with a midwife in her kitchen, our discussion had turned to Michel Odent's and Ashley Montagu's views on birth compared to hospitals and the control doctors have over birth. The midwife located her photocopy of Marsden Wagner's 1986 article, "Birth and Power" (see also Wagner, this volume), in her files and gave it to me to copy. The article came from a packet distributed in a training session for midwives at Il Marsupio. She declared that the article explains the beliefs she holds as a midwife and expresses what midwives think and believe about excessive use of high-tech and medical interventions. Wagner's article also affirms the centrality of midwives as providers of alternative birthing services, "an important counterbalance to the previous autocracy of doctors" (Wagner 1986:207). This midwife's statement to me demonstrates the importance to midwives of this authoritative WHO support—a strategic alignment that serves to legitimate their practices and their own authoritative knowledge.

CONCLUSION

In the late twentieth century in Italy and elsewhere in the industrialized world, great value is placed on high-tech machines as they have come to be a regular part of our lives and our bodies. Increasingly the human/machine extension has become integral to the idea that humans are imperfect and in danger or at risk if scientific and technological procedures are not used. To assure order in a society that seeks greater normative perfection through machine aids, humans are seen to need and are encouraged to want upgrading for the purpose of enhancing their identity and control over their lives.

One way to understand both the impetus toward technology-enhanced birth and the opposing attempts to resist that impetus is to view birth technology as a capital investment in the service of the political economy. The medical discourse in Italy feeds into the overarching political economic system, and the State-sanctioned deployment of authoritative knowledge in the domain of medical treatment of childbirth is hegemonic. This contrasts with the purposes of birth activists. Their discourse and practices are intended to empower women and to reduce their dependency on the authority of the medical system. Activists offer the voice of resistance to the State's medical practices of control over women at childbirth. Childbirth activists point out that "doctors with their technology take power away from women at childbirth" by defining them as at risk and fueling their fears of pain and imperfect children. In resistance to State-supported, medical authoritative knowledge and definitions of risk, they educate and support women to allay and cope with their fears about pain and imperfect children. Although birth activists work on a small scale, they are successfully recuperating formerly used birthing methods and alternative practices with technological backup. Through their practices, informed by a synthesis of political insight and medical knowledge, they help a small though increasing number of women to resist use of the state-capitalized medical institutions where medicalized procedures are used in standard ways that treat birth as pathological. In short, birth activists consider a different perspective, overtly seeking to unmask the combination of ideology and instruments of practice that in turn support the political economy. As they resist the biomedical technology and authoritative knowledge of medical professionals, they also resist the institutional conceptualization of women—both the more traditional view of women as primarily producers of children and the modern view of women as defective machines.

Birth activists further challenge the current birth culture that shapes the responses and desires of women, predisposing them to technologically assisted births in hospitals. Indeed, they counter the idea that woman-controlled birth outside a hospital is ideologically incorrect or akin to criminality. They confront the notion that presumes reproduction and production are one and the same act and that medical interventions in childbirth need be conceived in terms of "total quality management."

Clearly one can criticize the essentialism in the idiom "woman in childbirth" for its reductionism and its stereotypical definition which denies a variation of responses among women. What I have referred to in this chapter as Essentialism Type I, deployed by those who would across-the-board treat women mechanistically with drugs, monitors, and tools focused on discrete fractions of a woman's body, severely restricts the range of responses allowed to women. Essentialism Type II, deployed by those who would treat women holistically, with trust in the integral processes of body and mind, honors the body far more than the machine. It does not reduce women to mere facts of biology but accepts variation in biological and mental responses and respects women's personal autonomy. Birth activists use Essentialism Type II strategically to ensure that women need not cede their biological capacities to the Type I definitions on which technoeconomic development depends.

Why do birth activists matter when their number is small? Without the political and practical knowledge of birth activists, the medical establishment could assume full control, claiming a monopoly on authoritative knowledge about birth. Birth activists criticize and ask questions that keep the discourse on technological intervention open to discussion and changes in reasoning. Refusing to allow the ubiquitous presence of high technology and medical control at normal births to be taken for granted, they work to keep available childbirth experiences that can serve as a source for women's independence. As possible results, they see stronger women, more benign births, and the prospect of a better society in which women have a place of autonomy that incorporates the specificities of individual female bodies—a place where self-definition is independent of the technology that serves the bureaucracy and the political economy.

NOTES

I want to express my heartfelt thanks to Robbie Davis-Floyd and Carolyn Sargent for the multiple ways in which they assisted me with this manuscript, and to the childbirth activists in Florence for the time they spent with me and for the work they are doing.

1. Two Italian-made videos provide excellent material on this topic. Mariuccia Giacomini, *From the Hands of Women to the Hands of Men: The Woman in Labor at the Time of the Traditional Midwife, 15th–18th Centuries* (Video system NTSG and PAL, English version 18 min.). Interpreting male-dominated obstetrics as a symptom of the growing domination of men not only over women but also in a wider sense over Nature itself, this video shows the first steps toward the medicalization of childbirth through artistic representations of the woman's body, evolving from the naturalistic images of Italian rural society to the Church's image of the woman as the seat of all evil to the Renaissance scientism that made possible the anatomical exploration of the woman's body and created the basis for medicalizing reproduction. Franca Pizzini, *From the Hands of Women to the Hands of Men: Images from the History of the Medicalization of Childbirth. 18th–20th Centuries* (Video system NTSG and PAL, English version 22 min.). This video shows the medicalization of childbirth as it affected the lives of women in their reproductive and social roles. The relationship between midwives and the science of obstetrics and the beginning of academic learning and the battle between the new and traditional midwives are all presented and discussed. The history of the development of obstetrics is explained and covers the use of forceps, pain relief, and the fight against puerperal fever and the hospitalization of childbirth. Both videos are available from GRIFF (Group Research into the Condition of Women), Via Conservatorio, 7, Milano 20122, Italia.

2. To counter any suggestion of Ludditism on my part, I would like to make known my respect for medical technology. As I write I note that I am the beneficiary of some of the most up-to-date medical engineering and technological treatment for a complicated tibia and fibula fracture. I have become deeply appreciative of the computers, tele X-rays, surgical procedures, precision-made fixators, equipment, expertise, drugs, and "patient management" that make it possible for damaged bones to heal properly. I would only add that, unlike pregnancy, a broken leg is not a normal biosocial experience. Although this chapter is focused on the discourse and practices of Tuscan childbirth activists, it is important for the author to state her own biases: I am in basic agreement with much that the birth activists say and do. My belief is that pregnant women in labor and childbirth do not "need" to resort routinely to multiple technomedical practices and devices housed in hospitals.

3. That biomedical childbirth practices can constitute an arm of imperialism is

shown in my earlier research in Tegucigalpa, Honduras (Szurek, fieldnotes 1977). There, a high-tech hospital, a fifteen-story edifice that towered over the low, dusty buildings and unpaved streets of the city, had just been completed—paid for, I was told, "by the Canadians." Women were being pressured by various international development workers to leave their remote mountain villages to give birth in this new hospital (once there, they were often sterilized if they already had three children). Here we see in a microcosm the process by which control and bureaucratic standardization of women and children are established.

4. As a balancing note, the administration of this hospital has responded to the influence of birth activists by changing some of its policies. If a woman is delivering for the second time, two hospital midwives are allowed to take responsibility for the birth. Also, a doctor observes that in the last fifteen years there is less physical restraint of women in labor. They may amble around and walk into the delivery room when their contractions become closely spaced, and they can assume any position they want until the baby's head is visible. (Some outside midwives claim that this is more principle than practice.)

5. Another woman, Donatella, hired her midwife because she wanted herself and her husband to be "protected from the hospital structure." She attended birth preparation classes and yoga at the Unita Sanitaria Locale housed in the refurbished Innocentti Hospital (the former fifteenth-century orphanage in Florence) where she met the midwife who assisted her with three children, two of whom were born at home. For the second child, because the heat went off in the house just as her contractions began, her midwife, husband, and dog accompanied her in the car to drive to the hospital where, it turned out, she delivered her daughter in the parking lot. Though everything about the birth was calm and under control, since they were already at the hospital they decided to go in anyway. Donatella explained, "The doctor who came out to see me was cross with me because I hadn't come earlier. He just told us to leave. He didn't want to have us there. He said we didn't belong there." She continued, "I would never go to R. [the large urban hospital in Florence]. It's inhuman. They treat you as though you are just another thing."

6. Several Florentine childbirth activists noted Leboyer's neglect or absence of women in his nonviolent birth philosophy. One activist observed, "Leboyer actually disliked women. He was all for the child." Jessica Mitford echoes this in her observations: "his pity [was] for the struggling fetus trying to desperately make its way through the rigid birth canal into an alien environment" (1992:65).

7. According to an Italian weekly news magazine, the case for which he received nationwide notoriety was spearheaded by a European Parliamentarian who is a leader in an incipient European right-to-life movement (*Panorama*, April 1989, 70–71).

8. The yoga teachers with whom I spoke in Florence, although they led classes for women in general, also concentrated on teaching pregnant women a special kind of breathing in preparation for childbirth. This breathing technique, they said, was different from the ones used by Lamaze teachers. One of the yoga teachers expressed that she wished more midwives would learn this breathing technique because it was so effective in dealing with pain. She also explained that she sometimes assists at home births where she coaches the woman in labor. Yoga exercises and breathing have also been incorporated into birth preparation classes at the Unita Sanitaria Locale in Florence.

9. Midwives at Il Marsupio see hospitals and their procedures as male-defined. Indeed, most of the activists I interviewed shared this view and made clear the differences between practices and beliefs held by women and men in the medical profession.

10. "Fetus ejection reflex" is a phrase coined by Niles Newton to describe the instinctive and reflexive nature of mammalian birth. According to Michel Odent, Newton "had imagined as early as the 1960s that one day the phrase might become as relevant to a good understanding of the process of human parturition as the phrase *milk ejection reflex* (or *let-down reflex*) is for a good understanding of lactation" (1992:30). Seeking to reintroduce Newton's insight into the popular and medical discourses on childbirth, Odent emphasizes the fact that while high levels of adrenaline (produced by fear, cold, etc.) make the first stage of labor more difficult, near the end of labor during the pushing phase (second stage), a rush of adrenaline (often visibly manifested by goose bumps) is associated with strong and efficient contractions that quickly bring the baby. He notes that this phenomenon is not noticeable when birth is altered with machines and drugs but can be powerfully present at births that take place in privacy and without interference: "Let us dream of a time when the art of midwifery will be primarily the practice of not hindering the fetus ejection reflex" (1992:37).

11. The Farm in Summertown, Tennessee, is noted in the United States and internationally for its natural childbirth practices and the skills of its midwives—Ina May Gaskin, Pamela Hunt, and Carol Nelson—who attend births at home and in the Farm's birth center.

REFERENCES

American Journal of Public Health (AJPH)
  1987   "Cesarean Section Rates in Italy." *AJPH* 77, no. 12 (December):1554.
Arney, William
  1982   *Power and the Profession of Obstetrics.* Chicago: University of Chicago Press.
Castel, Robert
  1991   "From Dangerousness to Risk." In *The Foucault Effect: Studies in Governmentality,* ed. Braham Burchell, Colin Gordon, and Peter Miller, 281–296. London: Harvester Wheatsheaf.
Colombo, Grazia
  1987   "Dipendenza, accettazione e collusione della donna con l'agire medico." In *Mettere al mondo: La produzione sociale del parto,* 2d ed., ed. G. Colombo, F. Pizzini, and A. Regallia, 232–238. Milan: Franco Angeli.
Colombo, Grazia, Franca Pizzini, and Anita Regalia, eds.
  1987   *Mettere al mondo: La produzione sociale del parto* (Bringing into the World: The Social Production of Childbirth). 2d ed. Milan: Franco Angeli.
Corea, Gena
  1985   *The Mother Machine: Reproductive Technologies from Artificial Insemination to Artificial Wombs.* New York: Harper and Row.
Davis-Floyd, Robbie
  1992   *Birth as an American Rite of Passage.* Berkeley: University of California Press.

1994   "The Technocratic Body: American Childbirth as Cultural Expression."
    Social Science and Medicine 38(8):1125–1140.

Davis-Floyd, Robbie, and Joseph K. Dumit
1997   *Cyborg Babies: From Techno-Sex to Techno-Tots.* New York: Routledge. In press.

Douglas, Mary
1992   *Risk and Blame.* New York: Routledge.

Ehrenreich, Barbara, and Deirdre English
1973   *Witches, Midwives, and Nurses: A History of Women Healers.* Old Westbury,
    N.Y.: Feminist Press.

Foster, Peggy
1991   "Well-Woman Clinics: A Serious Challenge to Mainstream Health Care?"
    In *Women's Issues in Social Policy,* ed. M. Maclean and D. Groves, 79–94. Lon-
    don: Routledge.

Foucault, Michel
1977   *Discipline and Punish: The Birth of the Prison.* New York: Pantheon.

Gaskin, Ina May
1990   *Spiritual Midwifery.* 3d ed. Summertown, Tenn.: Book Publishing Com-
    pany.

Ginsburg, Faye, and Rayna Rapp, eds.
1995   *Conceiving the New World Order: The Global Politics of Reproduction.* Berke-
    ley: University of California Press.

Haraway, Donna
1990   "A Manifesto for Cyborgs: Science, Technology, and Socialist Feminism
    in the 1980s." In *Feminism/Postmodernism,* ed. Linda J. Nicholson, 190–233.
    New York: Routledge.

Horn, David
1994   *Social Bodies: Science, Reproduction, and Italian Modernity.* Princeton:
    Princeton University Press.

Houd, Susanne, and Ann Oakley
1986   "Alternative Perinatal Services." In *Perinatal Health Services in Europe:
    Searching for Better Childbirth,* ed. J. M. L. Phaff, 14–47. Dover, N.H.: Croom
    Helm for WHO, Regional Office for Europe.

Jordan, Brigitte
[1978] 1993   *Birth in Four Cultures: A Cross-Cultural Investigation of Childbirth in
    Yucatan, Holland, Sweden and the United States.* 4th ed. Prospect Heights, Ill.:
    Waveland Press.

Kertzer, David
1993   *Sacrificed for Honor: Italian Infant Abandonment and the Politics of Reproduc-
    tive Control.* Boston: Beacon Press.

Livi-Bacci, Massimo
1977   *A History of Italian Fertility During the Last Two Centuries.* Princeton:
    Princeton University Press.

Mitford, Jessica
1992   *The American Way of Birth.* New York: Dutton (Penguin Books USA).

Odent, Michel
1984   *Birth Reborn: What Birth Can and Should Be.* London: Souvenir Press.
1992   *The Nature of Birth and Breastfeeding.* Westport, Conn.: Bergin and Garvey.

Phaff, J. M. L., ed.
   1986   *Perinatal Health Services in Europe: Searching for Better Childbirth.* Dover, N.H.: Croom Helm for WHO, Regional Office for Europe.
Pizzini, Franca
   1987a   "Introduzione: Il Parto tra biologia e cultura." In *Mettere al mondo: La produzione sociale del parto,* 2d ed., ed. G. Colombo, F. Pizzini, and A. Regalia, 9–28. Milan: Franco Angeli.
   1987b   "La partoriente come paziente." In *Mettere al mondo: La produzione sociale del parto,* 2d ed., ed. G. Colombo, F. Pizzini, and A. Regalia, 118–143. Milan: Franco Angeli.
   1987c   "Note sullo spazio nel reparto di maternita." In *Mettere al mondo: La produzione sociale del parto,* 2d ed., G. Colombo, F. Pizzini, and A. Regalia, 198–231. Milan: Franco Angeli.
Putman, Robert
   1993   *Making Democracy Work: Civic Traditions in Modern Italy.* Princeton: Princeton University Press.
Rapp, Rayna
   1988   "Chromosomes and Communication: The Discourse of Genetic Counseling." *Medical Anthropology Quarterly* 2(2):143–157.
Sargent, Carolyn
   1989   *Maternity, Medicine, and Power: Reproduction Decisions in Urban Benin.* Berkeley: University of California Press.
Sargent, Carolyn, and Nancy Stark
   1987   "Surgical Birth: Interpretations of Cesarean Deliveries among Private Hospital Patients and Nursing Staff." *Social Science and Medicine* 25(12):1269–1276.
Scuderi, Angelo
   1990   "Le culture del parto." Unpublished manuscript.
Shore, Cris
   1992   "Virgin Birth and Sterile Debates: Anthropology and the New Reproductive Technologies." *Current Anthropology* 33(3):295–314.
Signorelli, C., P. Elliott, M. S. Cattaruzza, and J. Osborn
   1991   "Trend of Cesarean Section in Italy: An Examination of National Data 1980–85." *International Journal of Epidemiology* 20(3):712–716.
Stanworth, Michelle, ed.
   1988   *Reproductive Technologies: Gender, Motherhood and Medicine.* Minneapolis: University of Minnesota Press.
Szurek, Jane
   1977   Fieldnotes, Tegucigalpa, Honduras.
Triolo, Nancy
   1994   "Fascist Unionization and the Professionalization of Midwives in Italy: A Sicilian Case Study." *Medical Anthropology Quarterly* 8(3):259–281.
Wagner, Marsden
   1986   "Birth and Power." In *Perinatal Health Services in Europe: Searching for Better Childbirth,* ed. J. M. L. Phaff, 195–208. Dover, N.H.: Croom Helm for WHO, Regional Office for Europe.

TWELVE

Intuition as Authoritative Knowledge in Midwifery and Home Birth

Robbie Davis-Floyd and Elizabeth Davis

> *Diagnostic technologies, from the most mundane and routine ultrasound to the most exotic embryo transplant, have in common that they work toward the construction of the fetus as a separate being—they reify, they make real, the fetus. They make the fetus a visible, audible presence among us, and they do that by doing two other things. They medicalize pregnancy, and they render invisible and inaudible, women.*
>
> *The history of Western obstetrics is the history of technologies of separation. We've separated milk from breasts, mothers from babies, fetuses from pregnancies, sexuality from procreation, pregnancy from motherhood. And finally we're left with the image of the fetus as a free-floating being alone, analogous to man in space, with the umbilical cord tethering the placental ship, and the mother reduced to the empty space that surrounds it.*
>
> *It is very very hard to conceptually put back together that which medicine has rendered asunder. . . . As I speak to different groups, from social scientists to birth practitioners, what I find is that I have a harder and harder time trying to make the meaning of connection, let alone the value of connection, understood.*
>
> —BARBARA KATZ ROTHMAN,
> *Plenary Address, Midwives' Alliance of North America*
> *Conference, New York City, November 1992*

Both of us were in the audience when sociologist Barbara Katz Rothman gave the speech from which the above quote is excerpted. Her words, spoken to an audience of midwives who have no trouble at all understanding the value of connection, crystallized for these midwives their aloneness in the world of medicine—a world in which the subtle rewards of connection are often lost as the value of those technologies of separation is increasingly taken for granted. The warm exchange of breath and sweat, of touch and gaze, of body oils and emotions, that characterizes births in which there is an intimate connection between the mother and her caretaker has given way in the United States to the cool penetration of needles, the distant interpretation of lines on a graph. Building on Rothman's earlier work (1982, 1989), one of us (Davis-Floyd), in *Birth as an American Rite of Passage*

(1992), identifies the "technocratic model" of birth as the core paradigm underlying contemporary obstetric practices, including diagnostic technologies. As Rothman points out, separation is a fundamental tenet of this paradigm, which she calls the "medical model." Other basic tenets include the metaphorization of the female body as a defective machine and the working premise that birth will be "better" when this defective birthing machine is hooked up to other, more perfect diagnostic machines.

Under this model, authoritative knowledge—the knowledge on the basis of which decisions are made and actions taken (Jordan [1978] 1993)—is vested in these machines and in those who know how to manipulate and interpret them. Fascinatingly, this is so despite the fact that the near-universal use of such machines on laboring women in the United States has not resulted in improved birth outcomes, as has been convincingly demonstrated by numerous large-scale studies (Leveno et al. 1986; Prentice and Lind 1987; Sandmire 1990; Shy et al. 1990; see Goer 1995:131–153 for summaries of 39 medical studies of electronic fetal monitor use). These studies have shown that hooking women up to electronic fetal monitors results only in a higher cesarean rate, not in better outcomes. Robbie Davis-Floyd (1992, 1994) discusses these machines as symbols of our culture's "supervaluation" of machines over bodies, technology over nature. She analyzes obstetrical procedures, diagnostic and otherwise, as rituals that not only convey cultural core values to birthing women but also enhance the courage of birth practitioners by deconstructing birth into identifiable and (seemingly) controllable segments, then reconstructing it as a mechanistic process. She found that these ritual procedures enhance courage not only for obstetricians and nurses but also for the women themselves: being hooked up to some of the highest technologies society has invented gives many American women the feeling that they are being well taken care of, that they are safe. A reassuring cultural order is imposed on the otherwise frightening and potentially out-of-control chaos of nature.

But not all women are reassured by the technocratization of birth. There are some women in the United States who supervalue nature and their natural bodies over science and technology, who regard the technocratic deconstruction of birth as harmful and dangerous, who desire to experience the whole of birth—its rhythms, its juiciness, its intense sexuality, fluidity, ecstasy, and pain. Those women who most deeply trust birth usually place themselves quite consciously as far out of the reach of the technocratic model as they can get, choosing to give birth in the sanctity and safety of their own homes and grounding themselves philosophically in a holistic model of birth (Davis-Floyd 1992:154–159; 1995). Like the midwives who attend them, these homebirth[1] women have no trouble understanding the value of connection; indeed, connection is the most fundamental value undergirding their holistic paradigm.

There is increasing evidence that midwife-assisted homebirth is as safe as, and often safer than, hospital birth (see Davis-Floyd 1992:177–184; Goer 1995; Wagner 1994), but this evidence is little known and not at all acknowledged in the wider culture, which still assumes the authority of the technomedical tenet that hospital birth is far superior to birth at home. Thus, as health care practitioners, all midwives, even those who attend women in their homes, are under tremendous cultural pressure to "do birth according to biomedical standards," as one midwife put it. But "doing birth according to biomedical standards" will in many cases mean using interventions and/or transporting the woman to the hospital, despite the midwife's alternative judgment. Midwives must attempt to meet these cultural imperatives. Such attempts place many midwives in conflict with their own holistic paradigm and the patience and trust in birth and the female body that it charters. Contemporary midwives cannot fail to be aware of this dilemma; it is a central defining theme of their practices and their lives, ensuring that for them, every homebirth that is not textbook-perfect will pose ethical, moral, and legal dilemmas that might put them in a courtroom in danger of losing the right to practice. The level of tension between the technocratic and holistic paradigms with which homebirth midwives must constantly cope makes their occasional willingness to rely solely on intuition—sanctioned by the holistic model and condemned by the technocratic model—a strong marker of their commitment to holism and its underlying principle of connection.

The purpose of this chapter is to call attention to midwives' use of intuition as a salient source of authoritative knowledge. Our intention is not to refine the concept of intuition, but simply to utilize Brigitte Jordan's formulation of the notion of authoritative knowledge as a theoretical tool to help us understand the role that intuition plays for contemporary midwives. To begin, we will seek a background understanding through briefly exploring some recent theoretical perspectives on the nature of intuition.

ON THE NATURE OF INTUITION: THEORETICAL PERSPECTIVES

I think, because we're in a culture that doesn't respect intuition, and has a very narrow definition of knowledge, we can get caught into the trap of that narrowness. Intuition is another kind of knowledge—deeply embodied. It's not up there in the stars. It is knowing, just as much as intellectual knowing. It's not fluff, which is what the culture tries to do to it.

—JUDY LUCE,
homebirth midwife

Intuition is defined by the *American Heritage Dictionary* (1993) as "the act or faculty of knowing or sensing without the use of rational processes; immediate cognition." Salient characteristics of intuition as identified by

Tony Bastick (1982) include the suddenness and immediacy of awareness of knowing, the association of affect with insight, the nonanalytic (nonrational, nonlogical) and gestalt nature of the experience, the empathic aspect of intuition, the "preverbal" and frequently ineffable nature of the knowledge, the ineluctable relationship between intuition and creativity, the sense of certainty of the truth of insights, and the contradictory possibility that an insight may prove to be factually incorrect.

The corpus callosum, which plays a major role in conveying information between brain hemispheres, may be significant in the genesis of intuition. In *Women's Intuition* (Davis 1989), one of us postulates that interhemispheric coherence linked to transcendent states and intuitive connections may occur more readily in women than in men, since it appears that the corpus callosum in the female brain is significantly larger. It can be argued, however, that this part of the brain can be deliberately developed in either sex. Davis points out that, regarding the acquisition of information, Western society gives authoritative status only to the highly linear left-brain modes of inductive and deductive reasoning. Yet it is well established that the whole brain is active in all brain functions and that "there is no creativity in science, indeed, in any domain of creative activity, that does not entail intuition" (Laughlin 1997:6; see also Bastick 1982; Hayward 1984:29–33; Jung 1971; Poincaré 1913; Slaate 1983; Vaughn 1979; Weil 1972; Westcott 1968).

Why then is intuition so devalued in the West? As a number of social scientists have pointed out (Martin 1987; Merchant 1983; Rothman 1982), mechanistic metaphors for the earth, the universe, and the body have been gaining increasing cultural prominence since the time of Descartes. Conscious deductive reasoning, which can be logically explained and replicated, is the most machinelike form of human thought. Thus ratiocinative ("to ratiocinate" means "to reason methodically and logically") processes are reified in the West and often couched in terms of normative rules (Beth and Piaget 1966; Rubenstein, Laughlin, and McManus 1984:34). Intuition, in contrast, refers to our experience of the results of deep cognitive processes that occur without conscious awareness and cannot be logically explained or reproduced. Charles Laughlin (1992, 1997) postulates that intuition is *neurognostic*—inherent in the basic structure of the human central nervous system—which would account for the panhuman attributes of the experience of intuitive insight. He suggests that language and its concomitant ratiocinative conceptual structures did not evolve to express the *entire* human cognitive system and its operations but only those relevant to social adaptation, noting that the kind of knowledge that can be expressed by the human brain's linguistic and conceptual structures is superficial in relation to the "deeper neurocognitive processes upon which knowledge in its broader creative sense depends" (Laughlin 1997:16).

As noted above, science, for all its supervaluation of left-brained deductive reasoning, could never have proceeded without the creativity of intuition; concomitantly, no intuition-oriented culture or group could survive without heavy reliance on ratiocination. Likewise, even the most technocratic of physicians can find themselves following their intuition instead of their reason (Fox 1975, 1980), and even the most holistic of midwives, in this postmodern era, is likely to have attained a high level of competence in using the technocratic tools of birth and to be able to explain and defend her actions in scientific, linear, and logical terms. The praxis of postmodern midwifery entails, in many ways, the careful exercise of inductive and deductive reasoning even as it continues to rely for its primary ethos on the enactment of bodily and psychic connection.

BACKGROUND AND CONTEXT:
INTRODUCING THE POSTMODERN MIDWIFE

In the postmodern era in the Western world, we have gone beyond the anesthetized births of the 1940s and 1950s, the near-total demise of lay midwifery by the 1960s, and even the "natural childbirth" movement of the 1970s to a hegemonic focus on technology-assisted reproduction and technobirth, the basic principles and tenets of which have become formally encoded as the "standards of practice" regarded as authoritative in courts of law. Resistance to this technocratic hegemony in birth is strong and has spawned multiple movements and options that offer true alternatives, including the Bradley method of childbirth education (McCutcheon-Rosegg 1984); freestanding birth centers (Rooks et al. 1989); the home-birth movement (Kitzinger 1979; Sullivan and Weitz 1988); and the midwifery renaissance (Davis 1987; Gaskin [1977] 1990; Schlinger 1992). The fact that the legal system so completely supports the praxis of technobirth has forced those midwifery practitioners who take the risk of opposing it to become almost hypereducated in the science of obstetrics so that they can both defend themselves against legal persecution by the medical establishment and work to change the laws that keep them legally marginal.

In response to such pressures, and in service to the increasing numbers of urban middle- and working-class women who request their services, "lay" midwives[2] in the United States have expanded from their original base of traditional practitioners serving specific ethnic groups in bounded communities (see, e.g., Susie 1988) to full participation in the postmodern world. In the Third World, as the viability of indigenous systems of birth knowledge is everywhere challenged by imported biomedical systems (Jordan [1978] 1993; Sargent 1989; Sesia, Georges, Sargent and Bascope, this volume), midwives are emerging as articulate defenders of traditional ways as well as creative inventors of systems of mutual accommodation (see

Jambai and MacCormack, this volume). This phenomenon, which we have labeled "postmodern midwifery"—midwives who are educated, articulate, organized, political, and highly conscious of both their cultural uniqueness and their global importance—is not limited to the United States but is increasingly emergent all over the world (see, e.g., Kitzinger 1990).[3]

Our juxtaposition of "postmodern" (a charged word in the anthropological lexicon) with "midwifery" is far from casual. With this juxtaposition, we are trying to make salient the qualities emergent in the praxis, the discourse, and the political engagement of a certain kind of contemporary midwife. George Marcus has stressed that the power of the postmodern intervention in anthropology has inhered in its "radical critique" (1993:6) of unexamined conventions and monological assumptions, both ethnographic and cultural. As Linda Singer points out in "Feminism and Postmodernism," in feminist writings this radical critique "recurs with variations" as

> an explicit discursive strategy of challenging the terms, conventions, and symbols of hegemonic authority in ways that foreground the explicitly transgressive character of this enterprise. . . . [P]ostmodern discourse disrupt[s] the project of closure by consensus, by insisting on exposing how differences inscribe themselves, even when they are explicitly refused or denied. The voice of rationality is shown to be riddled with contradictions it cannot exclude. (1992:469–470)

This surely is an apt and accurate description of midwifery practice as described in the body of this chapter, during the course of which we will see how midwives, in their intentionally transgressive reliance on intuition, quite regularly expose the contradictions that the voice of rationality proves, in the domain of birth, to be unable to exclude. As we shall see, the transgressive nature of postmodern midwifery is further displayed in the fluidity with which the midwives interviewed for this study move between the biomedical and midwifery domains, appropriating the authoritative lexicon and the whiz-bang technologies of biomedicine to the holistic philosophy and "of service to women" ethos of homebirth midwifery. These same midwives, and others like them, have become adept at challenging the terms, conventions, and symbols of hegemonic authority in the courts, in the press, in their state legislatures, and through the politics generated by the actions and interactions of their national organizations. Through such ongoing activities, as well as in countless aspects of the daily discourse and praxis of midwifery, these midwives self-consciously engage in the most radical of cultural critiques.

In the United States, the two organizations most instrumental in facilitating the advent and transgressive activities of the postmodern midwife have been the Midwives' Alliance of North America (MANA),[4] to which almost all of the midwives interviewed for this study belong, and the American College of Nurse-Midwives (ACNM). Although MANA was conceived and created (in 1982) as an umbrella organization that would unite all North American midwives, to date it has primarily served as a vehicle for the collective voice of homebirth midwives; most members of MANA actively attend births at home or in freestanding birth centers. The ACNM (founded in 1955) limits its membership to certified nurse-midwives (CNMs). Most CNMs must first become registered nurses, after which they undertake an additional year or more of intensive academic and medical midwifery training. Most of the six thousand CNMs currently practicing in the United States work in hospitals; some work in freestanding birth centers; and a few attend births at home.

In spite of the polarization between these two organizations, MANA members have not lost sight of their original charter; in keeping with that vision, from its inception MANA has insisted on inclusivity. It welcomes all midwives as members—including CNMs (who constitute one-third of its membership) and direct-entry midwives, who are trained in midwifery schools, college midwifery programs, or through hands-on apprenticeship. The apprenticeship route to midwifery, not considered legitimate by the ACNM, is highly valued by the members of MANA for the connective and embodied experiential learning it provides.[5]

MANA as an organization operates by consensus, a process that requires a high degree of agreement on basic issues and values. MANA's explicitly stated philosophy of birth, arrived at through the consensus process, is holistic, and its 1,400 members have made it clear that they generally share in that holistic philosophy and approach, as expressed in the following excerpts from the 1992 final draft of MANA's "Statement of Values and Ethics" (MANA 1992).

We value:

Women and their creative, life-affirming and life-giving powers which find expression in a diversity of ways.

The oneness of the pregnant mother and her unborn child—an inseparable and interdependent whole.

The integrity of life's experiences; the physical, emotional, mental, psychological, and spiritual components of a process are inseparable.

Pregnancy and birth as natural processes that technology will never supplant.

Pregnancy and birth as personal, intimate, internal, sexual, and social events to be shared in the environment and with the attendants a woman chooses.

A mother's intuitive knowledge of herself and her baby before, during, and after birth.

A woman's innate ability to nurture her pregnancy and birth her baby; the
power and beauty of her body as it grows and the awesome strength
summoned in labor.

The essential mystery of birth.

Our relationship to a process larger than ourselves, recognizing that birth is
something we can seek to learn from and know, but never control.

Expertise which incorporates academic knowledge, clinical skill, intuitive
judgment, and spiritual awareness.

Relationship. The quality, integrity, equality, and uniqueness of our interactions inform and critique our choices and decisions.

Various versions of this "Statement of Values and Ethics" were developed, reviewed by the membership, revised, and revised again over the
past five years until full consensus was reached on the final draft, from
which the above excerpts are taken.[6] This set of values constitutes a direct
challenge to the technomedical approach to birth; its high degree of reflexivity is thoroughly postmodern. The enormous value that MANA midwives place on relationship and connection is evident throughout. Here
we present these excerpts as a clear illustration of MANA's working philosophy—the context within which the high regard our midwife-interviewees
have for intuition must be understood. The full conceptual and practical
ramifications of this philosophy are complex and far-reaching, and will be
addressed in future works. Here we will only point out the conflicts that
will inevitably arise between this holistic (inclusive, egalitarian) philosophy
and the exclusive, hierarchical demands of the technocracy, which up until
now has consistently devalued "lay" midwifery and has given status and
credibility only to CNMs, who took pains many years ago to constitute
themselves as a profession associated with—and structurally subordinate
to—the medical establishment.[7]

One of the most pressing issues facing postmodern midwives in the
United States and Canada is this question of professionalization. This has
been a divisive issue within MANA for some years, as professionalization
involves more organization, regulation, bureaucracy, and limits on practice than some independent midwives have been willing to accept (see
Schlinger 1992). Part of the fear has been that with the encoding of independent midwifery into a profession with specific certification and practice
requirements will come—as has happened in so many other professions—
a decrease in respect for "softer," situationally responsive elements of practice such as reliance on intuition. In this light, the interest of one of us
(Elizabeth Davis) and some of her midwifery colleagues in writing, speaking, and offering workshops about the use of intuition at birth can be seen
as an attempt to formalize midwives' understanding of intuition in order
to heighten its status as a viable and valid source of authoritative knowledge—an endeavor in which this present study may also play a role.

METHODS

This chapter is based on interview data obtained from twenty-two white middle-class American midwives about the role that intuition plays in their behavior at births. Seventeen of these midwives are empirically trained and primarily attend homebirths; five are CNMs. Most interviewees are experienced midwives with three to sixteen years in practice; three have been in practice less than a year. Three of the CNMs attend births both at home and in the hospital; the other two are hospital-based. Most of the midwives were attendees at the 1992 MANA conference in New York or the 1993 MANA conference in San Francisco; the interviews were conducted at these two conferences and at the Seattle Midwifery School. While we can make no definitive claims as to the representative nature of our interview sample, we can affirm from many years of interaction with midwives that the attitudes, beliefs, and experiences of our interviewees are typical for MANA members.

Our interviews, which were tape-recorded, were generally from one-half to one hour in length; most of them were conducted by Davis-Floyd, who began by interviewing midwives who were recommended to her as having "good stories" to tell. Some of the interviews ended up taking the form of storytelling sessions, as midwives walking by felt moved to join the session and recount their own experiences. Each one was asked to tell us as much as she wished about incidents surrounding birth in which intuition had played a role. Our goal was to elicit as many "intuition stories" from the midwives as we could, so that we could begin to gain a sense of if and how much these midwives relied on intuition, of the results in actual births of their acceptance or rejection of intuitive messages, and of their feelings about the value and usefulness of intuition as a diagnostic tool and guide to action—in other words, as a form of authoritative knowledge.

An additional twenty stories were gathered at a workshop on intuition called "Spinning Tales, Weaving Hope," led by Elizabeth Davis at the 1993 MANA conference, during which all the midwives present were asked to share any experiences with intuition they felt were important. While we cannot be sure what role this workshop and the interviews we conducted played in these midwives' opinions and ideas about intuition, the mere fact that we, as authoritative figures, were particularly focused on intuition no doubt helped to validate or to enhance the idea of intuition as a legitimate source of authoritative knowledge in the minds of our interviewees. Throughout this research, our central organizing question has been: to what extent and under what circumstances do midwives use intuition as a source of authoritative knowledge for decision making during birth?

Our collaboration emerged gradually. In 1992, Davis was one of Davis-Floyd's (no relation) first interviewees for this study. One year later, we agreed to coauthor this chapter. We merge in this endeavor our unique perspectives. Robbie Davis-Floyd is a cultural anthropologist who has applied symbolic, cognitive, and feminist perspectives to the study of American childbirth. For more than fourteen years she has been conducting research on women's experiences of pregnancy and childbirth (1987a, 1992, 1994), on the beliefs, attitudes, and training of obstetricians (1987), and on the ritual and symbolic dimensions of hospital and home birth (1990, 1992, 1995); she has recently become interested in the emergent phenomenon of what she has been calling "postmodern midwifery." Elizabeth Davis is an independent midwife who has been in private practice for sixteen years. She has attended more than three hundred births as primary caregiver; 90 percent of them have taken place at home. Internationally known for her work in women's sexuality and reproductive rights, she is the author of a number of books on birth and related topics (1988, 1994, 1995), most notably the midwifery textbook *Heart and Hands* (1987), *Women's Intuition* (1989), and the coauthored *Women's Wheel of Life* (Davis and Leonard 1996), and is a frequent lecturer at childbirth conferences around the world. She is the director of Heart and Hands Midwifery Intensives, an educational program for direct-entry midwives that she founded in 1982. She initiated the development of midwifery certification in California and was instrumental in getting legislation passed to decriminalize direct-entry midwifery in that state. She served as chair of MANA's Education Committee and as the first president of the Midwifery Education Accreditation Council, a national accrediting body for direct-entry midwifery education.

MIDWIVES AND INTUITION

Connection as a Prerequisite

The first fact that jumped out at us from our interview data was the enormous value midwives place on "connection." Connection as these midwives experience it in homebirth means not only physical but also emotional, intellectual, and psychic links. It is not merely two-way, as with the connectedness of midwife to mother, or mother to child.[8] A diagram might show something like a web, with direct strands connecting mother, child, father, and midwives, each to the other.[9] If, further, we were to look inside each individual, we might see other strands of the web connecting each individual to the deepest essence of herself. Our interviewees insisted that the degree of connection they are able to maintain with mother and child depends on the degree of connection they maintain to the flow of their own thoughts and feelings. So basic is the importance of this internal connectedness that many of them actively seek it during and even before birth. As Elizabeth Davis explained in her interview with Davis-Floyd,

Sometimes, especially when I've been doing a lot, it's really hard for me to clear myself and arrive at the birth open. So before I leave, I lie down and just try to unwind and unfold my concerns of the day and open to myself, so that I can also be open to the woman and her birth.

This effort to "be open" to oneself and to the woman and her birth is a common theme among homebirth midwives. The connectedness it facilitates extends not only to the psyche and emotions but also to physical sensation and experience. Consider the following quote from a Canadian midwife.

In our collective practice, one of the things that we became really aware of over time was that if one of the midwives at a birth had diarrhea, [it was a message that we should] look at things a lot closer. Inevitably in those births something came up. . . .
Q: How would you explain that? Why would a midwife get diarrhea if something's wrong with the birth—what's the connection?
I think you're intuitively picking up that something isn't quite right here. It's coming out in the body—it hasn't gone into the head yet.

The physicality of this knowing of which she speaks is reinforced in this description by a California midwife.

My scientific self believes that everything happens inside my skull, in my brain. [And I have intellectually learned many skills, many techniques for handling emergencies.] But my physical experience is that [in dangerous situations in which my mind isn't sure what to do, which technique would be the very best at that moment]—say, the baby's head comes out, but it won't rotate, and the shoulders are stuck—a cone of power comes straight down the width of my head, through my body, and out through my hands. And my hands begin to do a maneuver, and my mouth begins to speak and I tell the woman to turn over [on her hands and knees], or I reach up and grab hold of the baby's butt and draw the baby down, or I do whatever I do—but I didn't know what I was going to do before that moment—and that's midwife intuition. [Maggie Bennett] [10]

Whence does this "cone of power" originate? While both Maggie and the Canadian midwife quoted above describe intuition as intensely physical, Maggie's "cone of power" adds a spiritual dimension as well. Asking many of our interviewees where intuition is located, we received the following responses: "All through the body"; "It's cellular"; "It's in my stomach"; "It's inner knowledge—you don't know where it comes from"; "Your heart, your dreams"; "Your connection to the universe"; "My higher self"; "My heart, my chest, my throat"; "I'm very auditory—I hear it as a voice coming from deep inside." We can conclude that for our interviewees, intuition seems to involve the body, psyche, and spirit, but not the rational mind.

The midwives say that they experience the kind of openness described by

Maggie Bennett and Elizabeth Davis, and the connectedness it facilitates, as essential to receiving intuitive messages. If they are closed—"shut down," "disconnected"—they cannot hear that inner voice, and must rely on their extensive intellectual knowledge and accumulated expertise. While they see nothing wrong with this, they do seem to regard it as a qualitatively different type of care, as will be evidenced in the following section.

Learning to Trust

In both formal interviews and casual conversations we heard midwives express strong familiarity with biomedical diagnostic technologies. Their in-group jargon is filled with technomedical terms, their midwifery bags bulge with technologies,[11] and their homebirth charts look quite hospital-like, with maternal temperature and blood pressure and fetal heart tones duly recorded at proper intervals. Yet these same midwives who are so competent at using the jargon and the diagnostic tools of technocratic medicine often perceive the information thus obtained as an adulterated blessing, perhaps a source of as many problems as it solves. As Elizabeth Davis explained,

> What I see going on in a lot of midwifery training programs is the idea that here's this body of knowledge, and one needs to be schooled, and one needs to be tested—the idea that the student is empty and waiting to be filled, and the knowledge is there, and after you stuff it in, then the student is "qualified." But in midwifery, no amount of that is ever going to compensate for a lack of self-confidence or an ability to blend critical thinking with personal responsibility. What makes a really good midwife, I think, are those inner-based qualities of analysis and discernment, the emotions that she stays in touch with because she does not divorce her *self* from the process of learning, so that the feelings of self-respect, and self-love, and self-trust blend to make her humane and to keep her connected. I think in birth, if you're not part of the process, you're a threat to the process.

The other midwives we interviewed were in complete agreement with her. For all of them, being part of the process of birth, being connected, constituted the primary ingredient of their success—an ingredient far and away more significant than their (albeit considerable) technical diagnostic skills. One of them even went so far as to say,

> Assisting women at birth—that's all it is, is intuition. I listen to the baby's heartbeat, because, you know, I listen to the baby's heartbeat, but I don't really care about it, because I have this inner knowing that everything's fine.
>
> Q: Do you also know when everything isn't fine?
>
> Sure you know, there's an energy there.
>
> Q: Has there ever been a time when the stethoscope told you one thing but your intuition another?

No. If I detect a problem with the baby's heartbeat, there have already been signs that I'm suspecting there may be a problem. The heartbeat almost never tells me anything, except it looks nice on a piece of paper to document it. I do that for the lawyers. [Jeannette Breen]

It is a working hypothesis of ours that the more intensely midwives are trained in didactic models of medical care based on ratiocinative processes, the less they will trust in and rely on their intuition. Since our interviews to date have focused on midwives who demonstrate their commitment to holism by attending MANA conferences, we have been unable to investigate the truth of this hypothesis. To do so, we would have to interview equal numbers of more medically oriented CNMs. All our interviewees report that learning to trust their intuition is an ongoing process. Our data to date do indicate some differences, however, between the way that process is experienced by medically trained CNMs and empirically trained direct-entry midwives, who learn their skills through the one-on-one interaction of apprenticeship. The CNMs seem to begin by regarding intuition with mistrust, then move into trust through lived experience, whereas the empirically trained midwives seem to begin by trusting intuition and move into confirmation of that trust through lived experience. Consider the following story told to Davis-Floyd by a hospital-based CNM from the Midwest about her first salient experience with intuition at birth.

Last year I [was] seeing a Laotian Hmong woman. She came when she was about four months pregnant from a refugee camp. The very first time I met her I felt like there was something that was not right, but, although I kept looking, I couldn't find anything, ever. . . . Well I happened to be on call the night she was in labor, and her interpreter called me and told me she was going into the hospital and I asked the interpreter if she was coming and the interpreter said no, and—I had had this feeling all along, this voice that was telling me something bad was going to happen, and I thought, it's a mistake for the interpreter not to come, but I didn't say anything—I respected their plan.

And the woman got to the hospital and she was complete with a bag of water that was bulging and a high presenting part. And the nurse said to me, "I think she should go to the high-risk birth center," and I knew that this woman would not be protected—I knew there'd be residents—and so I pushed aside the part that had been telling me something was wrong, and admitted her to the alternative birth center. And when I got there, about five minutes after she arrived up there, she was pushing already, and I [started to check her] and the bag of water broke with her next contraction, and my whole hand filled with umbilical cord.

She'd been in labor all day at home, and I don't know how long the cord was prolapsed, but as soon as I found it we tried to get her to push through, but she wouldn't push, so I pushed the baby's head up and we did a cesarean section, and we got the baby out pretty fast but the baby has only lower brain stem function. Even though we did things right, we did things fast, it was a terrible outcome. And I think, had I listened to that voice, [the translator would have been there and could have convinced her to push] or she would at least have been admitted to a unit where things could have been done faster, and I don't know if there would have been a better outcome or not, but it's the strongest message of intuition I've ever had and from it I learned a lot about listening. I had never been raised to believe in the inner voice, but now I listen, when I slow down enough to hear those things. [Donna Hartmann]

Donna Hartmann's difficulties with learning to listen to her inner voice are echoed in Fran's story.

I went to nursing school, and before I finished my CNM I attended a number of homebirths with a midwife who was not a nurse and watched her make decisions based on intuition and just connection with the client. The nurse-midwifery education that I had didn't teach us that—it was very linear and very objective and taught us to make decisions based on very objective and very specific criteria. In the last few years I've had some very high risk births, very scary outcomes, and have felt in my heart, in my chest, in my throat that things were going to be okay, and have gone against my physician backup and said "Let's keep going for just a little while," and ended up with lovely babies, even with lots of meconium[12] and with strong decelerations.[13] And quite recently I was in a situation where I had all the objective criteria for a really nice birth. The strip [electronic fetal monitor printout] didn't look very bad and we had no meconium. But the whole time my heart and chest were telling me "Things are not going right." And I was trying to get my physician backup to intervene and he was saying, "Based on these objective criteria, things are going to be okay" and they were not. The baby was born with Apgars of 2 and 2.[14] I think we need to listen to our intuition and we need to keep apprenticeships so that we can watch each other and talk to each other during these decisions. If you can say to other midwives you're working with "I'm having a bad feeling about this," even though everything else—all the objective criteria—looks good, you need to trust those feelings. That's what I've learned.

Recounting her early years of homebirth midwifery practice, Elizabeth Davis, who was apprenticeship-trained, introduced the following story by saying, "This is the experience that first got me interested in the role of intuition in birth." In contrast to the CNM quoted above, Davis's first reaction to a strong intuitive experience was not to resist or ignore it but to act on it.

I had received a call that someone was in labor and [I laid down to unwind and open myself], and I heard this voice—I'm pretty auditory, and that's one of the ways my intuition shows up—and the voice said, "She's going to have a partial separation." I immediately fought back the voice. I think a lot of us, when we get intuitive messages, will argue back with our rational minds and refute them—we're schizo enough to do that—and that's what I did. I went over her history in my mind, and there was nothing that would indicate any risk for postpartum bleeding. And the voice said, "No, sorry, this is going to happen." Then I responded with great confidence and said, "Well that's okay, because I've handled this before—I've done manual removals." But after that it came back, "No, you've never done this. You've never had to go this far up and you've never had this much bleeding." I was really scared, but I thought, "Well, this is my fear, and I'm just projecting, God only knows why."

But I told my partner about it, and at the birth I drew up a syringe of pitocin in advance, and pushed fluids by mouth, and the kinds of things that I would do if I anticipated a potential problem with bleeding.

So she gives birth to this gorgeous little girl, the labor was uneventful, nothing strange, and she's holding her baby, and this bleeding starts. I follow up the cord to see where the placenta is and suddenly there's so much blood, and my hand is continuing from that point of exploration on up inside the uterus—I'm on automatic pilot, doing this manual removal as it was fore- shown. And my partner is injecting the syringe of pitocin, and everything worked out great, I think because of the immediacy of the response and the complete lack of double guessing myself. Just going ahead and doing what was necessary without wasting time really kept her blood loss to a minimum, even though it was considerable. We didn't have to transport, she didn't have to be transfused, she didn't go into shock, and that was amazing to me.

Reason versus Intuition: Accuracy and Source

Bastick's (1982) comprehensive list of the qualities of intuition (see above) includes the possibility that an intuition may be incorrect. With this most of the midwives in our study would disagree, as they tend to define intu- ition per se as inherently accurate (see also Vaughn 1979). Many of them told us that the trick, each time the inner voice speaks, is how to know whether or not it is a "real" intuition, and the struggle is to learn the differ- ence between the inner doubt and debate that accompanies ratiocinative thinking and the true voice of intuition. Their unwillingness to assume that an intuition can be wrong, we find, comes from their consensual belief that intuition finds its source in the spiritual realm or their own "higher selves," which by definition cannot be wrong, or from the deepest recesses of their bodies, which, according to the holistic model, are essentially en- ergy fields operating in connection with all other energy fields and there- fore cannot be wrong either.

In contrast, reason/ratiocination, which is site-specific to the neocortex, *can* be wrong, and often is. Thus if a midwife has what she thinks may be an intuition, but it turns out to be wrong, she is likely to conclude that it must not have been an intuition in the first place but a product of her "rational mind." This is not to say that midwives devalue reason and ratioci- nation. They tend to be comfortable with their ratiocinative abilities *and* keenly aware that these are culturally privileged. The voice of reason is loud and aggressive; the harder task, as the midwives see it, is to identify and heed the truths spoken by the still, small, and culturally devalued inner voice. The worth of this enterprise is attested by the outstanding safety record that contemporary homebirth midwives are achieving—a record that compares most favorably with the interventionist, expensive, and often iatrogenic "active management" of labor and birth in many hospitals (see Johnson, this volume).

The midwives we interviewed for this study reported that they averaged a 90 percent or higher success rate for the home or birth center births they have attended, the vast majority of which took place without drugs or other technological interventions. They transferred 8 to 10 percent of their clients to the hospital during labor; fewer than 4 percent ended up with cesareans; and their perinatal mortality rates average 2 to 4 per 1,000. These statistics contrast with the extremely high percentage of women in the hospital who receive drugs during labor (over 90%), the near-universal technological interventions in hospital birth, and the national cesarean rate of 21 percent, and match hospital perinatal mortality rates for low-risk women (2 to 4 per 1,000). (For excellent reviews of studies on midwifery birth outcomes, see Goer 1995:297–347, Rooks 1997; see also Johnson, this volume.)

Maggie's Story: A Case Study in Reliance on Intuition

Although all these midwives know "the rules," the protocols of standard midwifery practice, they often circumvent or ignore them completely in the actual doing of birth. Clearly they do not consider such protocols authoritative per se. Jordan ([1978] 1993) has said that authoritative knowledge is interactionally displayed knowledge on the basis of which decisions are made and actions taken. How far into action and interaction can intuition take a midwife? Given the external diagnostic technologies at her command, including those of the hospital to which she can transport her client, how authoritative can she consider that inner voice to be? What happens when what that voice tells her conflicts with more culturally accepted external parameters of normal, with "standard protocol"? We will take as a case study here a birth that Maggie Bennett, a midwife and past president of the California Midwives' Association, attended which took her far beyond medically accepted standards, right out onto the ragged edge of intuition and trust.

> [Once I had a client named Jane.] It was her third pregnancy and she was thirty-nine. Her first pregnancy . . . was complicated, and that child had some physiological problems. Her second labor began prematurely, and she was delivered by cesarean section—the baby was six weeks premature and had cerebral palsy. Her father is an obstetrician. So she came to me feeling that

hospitals and doctors offered her nothing as far as safety. She was also a VBAC [vaginal birth after cesarean] at a time when VBACs were new to me, and she also had a vertical scar, exterior and interior—a no-no.

Maggie has so far listed no less than five factors that, from a medical point of view, would define this woman as far too high-risk for any midwife to take on for a homebirth: two previous problematic births, both with pathological outcomes, a father who is an obstetrician (a strong indicator for a medically oriented daughter and a potential threat to the midwife's ability to continue to practice), and a woman who wants to give birth vaginally at home but who happens to have the kind of scar, on both her abdomen and her uterus, that is most likely to rupture during a subsequent labor. But, Maggie continues,

what she did have going for her was God. She was a born-again Christian and believed that this was of God's design, and so she had a lot of power from that source. So the first thing that happened was that we got close to term— 37, 38 weeks, and her baby was breech. And we kept waiting for it to turn on its own, and we did crawling and slant boarding [15] and all sorts of things, but the baby didn't turn. So we decided that the baby had to be turned. And the baby was really hard to turn, and it didn't go easily, and at one point I felt that we should stop, because it was just too difficult. But then I had this intuition that the baby could go head down but that *I* was blocking the process.

One of the things that was happening was that the woman wanted to have a beer [to help her relax] and I wouldn't let her do that because I wanted her 100 percent present and in her body, and I wasn't willing to let her check out while I did this procedure on her. I just wouldn't allow it. [But then she began making these statements that semiequated me with the devil, and finally I realized that my refusal was causing a lot of unpleasant tension between us.]

And so I let go of my beliefs about the alcohol, and I called her husband and said, "You need to pray." I had to let go of my being righteous about my own belief system—I am not a Christian—and about religion and about alcohol and let this woman be in her body the way she had to be in her body, and be in her beliefs the way she had to be in her beliefs. And if that meant that I had to bow my head and pray, then that's what I had to do—so it was as much about me as it was about her.

So she had a glass of wine and half a beer, and I had half a beer, and my partner had half a beer, and we mellowed out a whole bunch, and she laid down on the slant board again, and the baby just went around. So again, it was the intuition about knowing that the baby *wanted* to turn around, and looking at what everybody had been doing that was stopping that from happening.

In her willingness to compromise her own religious and health beliefs to facilitate the turning of the baby and to maintain connectedness with the mother, Maggie demonstrates the malleability of the midwife, her willingness to go the distance with the mother on the mother's terms. Maggie as practitioner-in-charge could have retained her authority to deny the woman alcohol by insisting on the authority of her "knowledge" that alcohol would be harmful. Instead, she gave up that claim altogether, gladly surrendering authority to what she saw as the higher good of connectedness and trust.

Yet another opportunity to give up authority quickly arose: hospital guidelines and many midwifery protocols state that babies must be born within twenty-four hours of the rupture of the membranes, as the danger of infection of the baby rises significantly thereafter. This rule of thumb has sent many would-be homebirth mothers to the hospital and has resulted in many cesareans, as it is very common for labor and birth to take far longer than twenty-four hours (indeed, as midwives know, normal labors can take up to five or six days; during that time, if left unpenetrated, ruptured amniotic sacs will often reseal). But a cesarean was not to be Jane's fate. Maggie continues,

> So she goes into labor four days later, but she doesn't just do it normally— She has premature rupture of the membranes for twenty-four hours, seventy-two hours, four days she has premature rupture of the membranes, and you better believe that intuition played a role every single day, because I had to reexamine where we were going with it all the way along. But the answer was always the same—her waters were clear, she had no temperature, and she still had God. She was filled with her faith in God that that baby was safe. And I was able to participate in that faith. . . .
>
> So on the fourth day [after her membranes ruptured], after she is finally in labor, her backup doctor called to check on her, and someone told him that she was in labor and was out walking with her husband. . . . So now the *doctor* knows that she's in labor. And remember that I told you that her father was an obstetrician in a town about four hours away? Well *he* calls up and finds out that she's in labor, and then he starts calling every three hours. And he starts to say, "What's going on there? That baby should have been born by now."
>
> So I have a woman who's four days with ruptured membranes, who's been in labor for about eighteen hours with contractions about five minutes apart. . . . And while I was out for a few minutes picking up food for everybody,[16] I ran into her backup doctor at the restaurant and he said to me, "I just want to know is the baby coming out above or below?" and I said—this was an intuition, come to think of it—"The baby's coming out normally."[17]

The pressure builds. Maggie is attending a woman with significant risk factors from a past birth and now this present birth; two physicians are aware that she is in labor and are trying to monitor the situation from afar. Every midwife knows how fraught with personal peril such a situation is, and that there is also peril for the mother, as the tension induced by such pressure can easily stop or slow labor. Maggie's response at this point to "all this energy, this highly political birth," is that of guardian and protector of the natural process: she pulls the plug on the telephone. She said,

> I think that every time a midwife goes to the edge, it is the intuition that everything is all right that takes her there. I had to keep examining with this woman whether or not it was all right for us to continue, and every single time was an internal process about—we have these signs, and this is not "the rules," but I *know* the baby's all right, and I *know* that the mother is all right, so we can go on from this point.
>
> So eventually, she begins to push the baby out, and the waters broke [again—the bag had resealed] just as she began to push and there was slight meconium staining. And she begins to have a slight temperature, like maybe 99, but this is all right [according to protocols] because she has begun to push.
>
> Guess what? She doesn't push the baby out in one hour, she doesn't push the baby out in two hours, not even in three hours. She takes a rest at four hours.[18] She finally gets that baby out in five hours . . . squatting . . . little by little by little by little. . . . And the baby actually breathes spontaneously and has Apgars of 7 and 8.
>
> So in the end, in retrospect, it was just a challenged birth—a challenged pregnancy, a problem in late pregnancy, a challenged labor all the way along. And I couldn't have done that birth if I had followed *my own* protocols.[19] And there was a point where I had to say, "I am called midwife, and I am in here for whatever happens, because I have to let go. I have to absolutely let go of my desire to control this, because I can't."

Some perspective on the value Maggie places here on letting go of control is provided by an earlier study carried out by Davis-Floyd (1994) on differences between home- and hospital birthers. She found that the hospital birthers placed high value on control, whereas the homebirthers felt that giving up control was far more valuable in birth and in life than trying to maintain it—a philosophical position they arrived at through lived experience.

Maggie reinforces this philosophical position at the same time that she indicates how difficult it is to maintain this view in a society that supervalues control in most aspects of life.

> You know, I would never have the audacity to go to a birth and think that I could control everything that happened, for either the safety or the outcome. Sooner or later, I, along with the mother, have to give up the control. You would think after seventeen years [of attending births] I would know that, but I have to relearn that at almost every birth, over and over again.

We asked Maggie, "How do you feel about staying the course with that birth?" and she responded,

I feel that it was a great gift, a great learning, and I am so incredibly inspired by the woman, and the Goddess that she is (she would hate me for saying that)—that I was able to witness that miracle.

In calling this woman a "Goddess," Maggie expresses an attitude toward women that is held by many midwives who tend to see the birthing woman as a powerful creatrix—a birth- and life-giver. Such midwives espouse the principles of ecofeminism, which links the fate of the planet, metaphorized as Gaia, the Mother Goddess, to the cultural treatment of the female body (see, e.g., Diamond 1994; Diamond and Orenstein 1990; Starhawk 1988, 1989, 1993). Much as they interpret intuition as both spiritual and embodied, they honor the Goddess as a spiritual reality embodied in the earth and as a metaphor of and for women's creative power, of which birth is but one expression. As Maggie points out above, to serve the Goddess is to learn to give up one's desire for control, to surrender to the ebb and flow of Her inscrutable rhythms.

Spirituality is a strong component of independent midwifery, but there is a great deal of variation in spiritual orientation. While most midwives in MANA either actively celebrate the Goddess or are quite comfortable with the Goddess-as-metaphor, some have a strongly Christian orientation toward birth. Christian midwives tend to interpret birth not so much as a manifestation of the woman's own personal power but of God's power flowing through the birthing woman. This is the view held by Maggie's client Jane, and the reason Jane would not appreciate Maggie's calling her a Goddess, which for Maggie is the highest compliment she can give to express her appreciation for Jane's profound inner connectedness and strength.

At this point in Maggie's recounting of this birth, the question of protocols and external diagnostic technologies again came up. The high authority that Maggie placed on her inner knowing during this birth was clearly demonstrated when she said that she never made a decision based on anything that was written on Jane's chart—her blood pressure, urinalysis, information about rate of dilation and progression of labor, and so on—because, as she put it, "it wouldn't be neat, it wouldn't add up, it wouldn't follow any kind of progression that was any kind of normal anything." We asked, "So why didn't you make an effort to make this labor conform to normal by transporting her?" and Maggie answered,

Because every time I checked with Jane, she would tell me that she was fine and that she knew the baby was fine. And every time I looked at her, and every time I looked inside myself, and every time I saw that—whatever it is—the place where the baby was—the baby was safe. . . . Inside my head I saw the baby safe—and this is my own metaphor, I realize, but I saw the baby surrounded by sparkling light, kind of like glittery flecks of amniotic fluid.

Q: So your inner vision of the baby corresponded with the mother's?

Yes.

This correspondence of Maggie's inner vision with the mother's is a prime example of the kind of connectedness that midwives see as essential for the emergence and the credibility of intuition. Our other interviewees generally agreed on the persuasive power of such correspondence of intuitions.[20]

We explored with Maggie in further conversation the mystery of why, in some cases, she will urge a woman to transport in the face of a minimum of indicators while in a case like Jane's she would stay home in the face of a maximum of indicators for transport. We asked her, "Is that a matter of intuition for you every time?" She replied,

> Yes. You see, I don't know about where it all goes together, because I keep charts, and I do signs, and I check dilation, I look at the color of the amniotic fluid, I take blood pressure—I do those kinds of clinical things. . . . But one month I realized that I had been to five births, and only one of them fit within protocols. And I had to look at myself and say, I think of myself as a conservative midwife, but what's wrong here if four out of five births are out of protocol, am I a radical midwife, am I a dangerous midwife—what's going on here?
>
> And I really had to evaluate, and look at my charts with somebody else, before I could come up with a picture of me as a midwife, and what I resolved for *me* is that *where birth is not normal, part of a midwife's job is to return it to normal.* For example, in the case of a VBAC, which is regarded medically as high risk and almost universally by midwives as not high risk, what we're doing in that case is returning birth to normal. And when we go four, five, six hours of pushing, we are also returning birth to normal, a normal that says if the woman pushes for three hours and she's exhausted, then she can take a rest, and maybe in a couple of hours, she'll get her strength up, and then she'll be able to push again—she *will* get her baby out. When we do things like that, we're returning birth to normal.

Rather than deconstructing and reconstructing labor to fit abstract and narrowly drawn technocratic parameters of normal—a process that often results in major surgery as the final reconstructive step—what Maggie and her sister midwives do is to continually redraw the parameters, processually expanding their definitions of normal to encompass the range of behaviors and signs actually exhibited by pregnant women as they labor and birth. In short, these midwives are willing to expand protocol parameters to reflect the realities of individual labors rather than reshape labor to fit protocol parameters. They see a labor that is unlike other labors, not as a dysfunction to be mechanistically normalized according to the standardized technomedical system of authoritative knowledge, but as a meaningful expression of the birthing woman's uniqueness, to be understood on its own terms.[21]

Normalizing Uniqueness: The Connective Dance

The midwifery normalization of uniqueness must be understood in the context of the technomedical pathologization of uniqueness. The techno-cratic model of birth defines as "normal" only those births that fall within specific parameters—twelve hours for labor, cervical dilation of one centi-meter per hour, steady fetal heart tones, and so on. Labors that take too little or too much time, cervixes that remain "stuck" at four centimeters for hours on end, heart tones that speed up or slow down, meconium in the amniotic fluid—all are defined as dysfunctional "deviations from the norm." Aware of technomedical parameters, midwives must constantly weigh their trust in and acceptance of women's individual rhythms against the consequences of straying too far outside of the medical protocols that are regarded as authoritative in the courts.

In a recent paper, Brigitte Jordan, whom we honor in this collection, speaks of authoritative knowledge as grounded in a community of practice, adding that within that community, "authoritative knowledge is persuasive because it seems natural, reasonable, and consensually constructed. For the same reason, it also carries the possibility of powerful sanctions, rang-ing from exclusions from the social group to physical coerciveness" (1992:3). Certainly this is true of the authoritative knowledge of the tech-nomedical community. But midwives who act on intuition do so in *opposi-tion* to the cultural consensus on what constitutes authoritative knowledge in birth. Their protocols are their link to that larger biomedical system of authoritative knowledge; like physicians in the hospital, the farther they stray from those parameters, the more they place themselves at risk of the powerful sanctions of which Jordan speaks.

Yet within the midwifery community, intuition does count as authorita-tive knowledge—"the knowledge that *participants agree* counts in a given situation, that they see as consequential, on the basis of which they make decisions and provide justifications for courses of action" (Jordan 1992:3; emphasis in original). When Maggie shared her records with other mid-wives for peer review and evaluation, she was greeted with reassurance and acceptance; in spite of its devaluation, or simply nonrecognition by the larger culture, these midwives too valued intuition as authoritative.

Jordan points out that "to legitimize one kind of knowing devalues, of-ten totally dismisses, all other ways of knowing, [so that] those who espouse alternative knowledge systems are often seen as backward, ignorant, or na-ive troublemakers" (1992:2). Her words capture in a nutshell what the larger technomedical culture has done, in this country and many others, to the alternative knowledge systems of midwifery. Hanging out on the ragged edge, far outside of the safety net of cultural consensus, these women of tremendous hearts find their courage not in the normalizing performance of standardized routines but in their connectedness to the women and babies they attend. As Maggie put it,

> Mothers and midwives mirror one another. I know that I get all of my courage from the mother. And I bounce it back to her, and she gets her courage from me. . . . It's a dance—the woman has to trust her midwife, and the midwife has to trust her woman for that bouncing back.

In the eyes of midwives, birth has been made abnormal by technocratic medicine. As Maggie's story illustrates, the give-and-take of this "dance" is instrumental in midwives' ongoing efforts to normalize uniqueness in birth.[22]

SANCTIONING INTUITION AS AUTHORITATIVE KNOWLEDGE

> *The midwife provides care according to the following principles:*
> *Midwives work as autonomous practitioners, collaborating with other health and social service providers when necessary.*
> *Midwives understand that physical, emotional, psycho-social, and spiritual factors synergistically comprise the health of individuals and affect the childbearing process.*
> *Midwives recognize that a woman is the only direct care provider for herself and her unborn baby; thus the most important determinant of a healthy pregnancy is the mother herself.*
> *Midwives synthesize clinical observations, theoretical knowledge, intuitive assessment, and spiritual awareness as components of a competent decision-making process.*
> —FROM THE "MANA CORE COMPETENCIES FOR MIDWIFERY PRACTICE,"
> *a five-page document approved in final form by the board of the Midwives' Alliance of North America, October 3, 1994*[23]

Until recently, homebirth midwives' use of intuition as authoritative knowledge at births has been entirely informal, experienced in the uniqueness of the situation, talked about in wonder and awe among themselves and with the mothers[24] they attend, but not formally encoded as an official source of authoritative knowledge. With the finalization and approval by consensus of the "MANA Statement of Values and Ethics" (quoted earlier) in 1993 and the 1994 approval of the "MANA Core Competencies" quoted above, intuition has now received formal recognition from midwives themselves as an integral aspect of competent midwifery practice. Some new challenges thereby arise.

Two of the most pressing issues facing homebirth midwives in the postmodern era are those of certification and licensure. Midwives in many states have been lobbying for legalization and licensing for years, and increasingly are achieving these goals. Members of MANA are well aware that if they do not establish their own testing and certification process, others—

state governments, the American College of Nurse-Midwives, medical boards—will establish one for them. So MANA has created NARM—the North American Registry of Midwives—as a separate, nonprofit corporation and empowered the NARM board to develop and implement a national certification process, guided by a Certification Task Force of approximately forty state representatives.

This in itself is an oxymoronic situation. MANA prides itself on its inclusivity, yet the essence of certification is some degree of exclusivity. When tests and standards are created which all midwives must meet, some will pass and some will fail, and, quite possibly, midwives who are competent at births will remain uncertified simply because they do not test well. In an effort to minimize this type of exclusionary outcome, which would limit homebirth midwifery to those who excel at ratiocinative thinking, the members of the NARM board are trying very hard to create testing and evaluation systems that will be fair to all. Agreeing that written (ratiocinative) tests, although the easiest to administer, cannot provide the whole picture, board members considered the idea of multiple options for demonstrating skill, including a simulated skills exam, in which the aspiring licensee could come to a central site and demonstrate her skills on plastic models of a birthing woman and child. When this idea was presented to the general membership of MANA, a common response was exemplified by one midwife who exclaimed in dismay, "My spiritual guides are the ones who tell me what to do at births, but they will not be there if I am working on plastic dummies!" Another midwife emphasizes intuition's central role.

> Let's decide how a midwife should be tested, and let's test her that way. Let's not kiss up to the standards of the medical profession in order to satisfy them that we are competent. Let's satisfy *ourselves* that we are competent—and we'll know that competency if our hearts are true, and if we're honest about our intuitive skills. Intuition is often what makes us smart, what makes us do the work best, what makes us able to pick up problems earlier than anyone else and therefore deal with them more effectively. (Jill Breen, community midwife, quoted in Chester 1997:3)

In response to such appeals, the NARM board has developed a certification process for the Certified Professional Midwife (CPM) that is balanced between the ratiocinative and the hands-on: besides verification of experience it requires (1) that the applicant be checked off on a long list of skills by her midwifery mentor, who will have many opportunities to see her demonstrate those skills during her training in a connective context in which she can indeed listen to her guides; (2) passing a challenging day-long written exam that tests the extent and depth of her knowledge; (3) passing a hands-on skills assessment exam administered by an experienced midwife.[25] The proposal's balance, as well as MANA's "Statement of Values and Ethics" and "Core Competencies," indicates the increasing determination of these midwives to honor both ratiocination and intuition as communally sanctioned and respected sources of authoritative knowledge.

CONCLUSION

In this chapter we have sought to examine the phenomenon of midwives' occasional willingness to rely on intuition as a primary source of authoritative knowledge in a society that grants conceptual and legal legitimacy only to ratiocination. We have seen that the trust these midwives place in inner knowing is a seamless part of their overall philosophy, as expressed in the "MANA Statement of Values and Ethics" and as exemplified in the stories they tell about their individual experiences with intuition and birth. In contrast to the technocratic model, which charters an ever-expanding plethora of separation-based diagnostic and remedial technologies, this holistic midwifery philosophy supervalues inter- and intrapersonal connection and charters a range of behaviors expressive of that connective "dance."

Intuition, in these midwives' view, emerges out of their own inner connectedness to the deepest bodily and spiritual aspects of their being as well as out of their physical and psychic connections to the mother and the child. The trustworthiness of intuition is intrinsically related to its emergence from that matrix of physical, emotional, and spiritual connection—a matrix that gives intuition more power and credibility, in these midwives' eyes, than the information that arises from the technologies of separation. That midwives nevertheless carry with them and freely utilize such technologies demonstrates not only that they also value ratiocination but that they are becoming experts at balancing the protocols and demands of technologically obtained information with their intuitive acceptance of women's uniqueness during labor and birth. We submit that midwives' deep, connective, woman-to-woman webs, woven so lovingly in a society that grants those connections no authority of knowledge and precious little conceptual reality, hold rich potential for restoring the balance of intimacy to the multiple alienations of technocratic life.

NOTES

We wish to thank Carolyn Sargent, Ann Millard, Gay Becker, and midwives Judy Luce, Karen Erlich, Penfield Chester, Anne Fry, Marimikel Penn, and Sharon Wells for their excellent editorial assistance, four anonymous reviewers for their useful suggestions, and our midwife-interviewees for giving so generously of their time and experience.

1. It is common usage among mothers and midwives in the alternative birth movement to refer to birth at home as "homebirth"—especially when used as an adjective, as in "homebirth mothers." We follow that usage here.

2. Non-nurse midwives in the United States used to be known as "lay midwives." But in recent years, such midwives, including those who are apprentice trained, have developed an extensive array of skills including the ability to use various high technologies (see note 11), have banded together in professional associations, and have organized politically to create a national certification program and to fight for state licensure. Thus many of them have come to think of themselves as professionals and to resent the appellation "lay," which we do not use in this chapter.

3. The global scope of postmodern midwifery was evidenced by the attendance of over 3,000 midwives from 44 countries at the 1993 convention of the International Confederation of Midwives (ICM) in Vancouver, Canada. Members of the ICM share in common a commitment to the midwifery ("with woman") approach to prenatal, natal, and postnatal care and a growing concern for an increasingly compromised scope of practice. In Germany, for example, midwives may assist delivery but can do no prenatal care; in France they may do prenatal care but are greatly restricted in deliveries; and, as we have seen elsewhere in this volume, in the Third World the midwife's role is increasingly constrained by biomedicine. Generally, the ICM represents midwives with professional academic preparation, but its membership is increasingly beginning to reflect a determination on the part of midwives in both developed and developing countries to ensure the continued viability of the independent midwife able to assist birth in any setting, particularly the home.

4. In Hawaiian, "mana" means "an underlying, vital energy that infuses, creates, and sustains the physical body" (*MANA News* 8, no. 3 [1990]:1). And as one of our anonymous reviewers aptly pointed out, *mana* in Greek is the affectionate term for "mother." And, of course, in Hebrew and Greek *manna* means divinely supplied spiritual nourishment.

5. This issue of apprenticeship is a source of profound division and disagreement between MANA and the ACNM, which honors only formal training as an appropriate route to midwifery. (See Jordan [1978] 1993:chap. 7 for a description of midwifery apprenticeship and a detailed discussion of the differences between experiential and didactic learning.) Thus these two organizations are setting up divergent routes to what might seem to be a common goal—a national certification process for non-nurse midwives. Since 1993, MANA members have been actively establishing verification and testing procedures for certification of the Certified Professional Midwife; these procedures honor both formal training programs and apprenticeship as valid educational routes. In 1994–1995, the ACNM voted to accredit qualified direct-entry midwifery programs and certify their graduates as Certified Midwives (CMs); the only such programs ACNM's Division of Accreditation plans to accredit, as of this writing, are medically oriented and university-based postbaccalaureate programs.

6. Copies of the "MANA Statement of Values and Ethics" can be obtained from Signe Rogers, Editor, *MANA News*, P. O. Box 175, Newton, KS 67114; or from MANAinfo@aol.com.

7. Contemporary CNMs, many of whom are or wish to be in independent prac-

tice, are engaged in serious questioning of the limitations imposed by their structural subordination to physicians. Some members and officials of the American College of Nurse-Midwives are currently contemplating a focused effort to re-create nurse-midwifery as an independent primary health care profession, subject not to nursing or medicine but to autonomous midwifery boards.

8. Breastfeeding constitutes a good example of the pragmatic ramifications of insisting on the value of connection: 98 percent of American women give birth in hospitals; less than 50 percent of them breastfeed their babies during the early months of life. Of the 2 percent of women who give birth at home or in freestanding birth centers—in other words, in accordance with the connection-based holistic model of birth—close to 100 percent choose to breastfeed (Arms 1994:201). That connectedness also facilitates birth itself has been amply demonstrated by the doula (labor assistant) studies, which show beyond a doubt that the nurturing presence of a woman companion during labor reduces length of labor, lessens perceptions of pain, and improves birth outcomes, both physical and emotional (Kennell et al. 1988; Sosa et al. 1980).

9. The importance of the web metaphor to the members of MANA as an expression of their lived experience was demonstrated during the closing ceremonies of the 1993 San Francisco conference. Four hundred fifty midwives formed a giant circle around the edges of an otherwise-empty ballroom. They passed balls of yarn in many colors around the circle; each participant looped each color of yarn that came to her around her wrist, until all were physically connected. Then they tossed many more balls of yarn across the floor to each other, tying those around their wrists also, until all that yarn formed a giant rainbow-hued web that filled the ballroom floor, linking everyone to everyone through myriad connections. Spontaneously lifting the giant web into the air by lifting their arms, the midwives quickly discovered that, if one person moved her arm, the whole web would move in response. And if a ball of yarn got stuck in the middle of the floor, at least thirty people had to move in synchrony for one person to retrieve it. This of course was a perfect ritual and symbolic enactment of the high value these midwives place on human interconnectedness.

10. Interviewees Maggie Bennett, Jeannette Breen, Elizabeth Davis, and Judy Luce insisted on being identified by their own names, in keeping with their strong beliefs in the value of their work and their intuitive experiences. All other names following quotations are pseudonyms.

11. Items that a typical postmodern midwife carries with her to a home birth include a pager and/or a cellular phone; a blood pressure cuff; a stethoscope; a fetoscope and a Doppler electronic amplifier for the baby's heartbeat (for monitoring fetal heart tones); sterile gauze; antiseptics such as alcohol, peroxide, betadine, or hibiclens; alcohol prep pads and swabs; Q-tips and cotton balls; flashlights; urinalysis strips (to test for glucose, ketones, pH, blood, and protein); Fleet enema (rarely used); nitrazen paper (to test for leaks in the amniotic sac); culture tubes (for taking a baseline culture of the amniotic fluid); equipment for drawing blood to send to a lab for a white count (to check for infection); urinary catheter kits; sterile KY jelly; a variety of herbs, tinctures, and homeopathic remedies, including rescue remedy (for severe stress), goldenseal (for drying the cord stump after it is cleaned with alcohol), arnica salve (for skin swelling and trauma), black and blue

cohosh and colophyllum (for enhancing contractions), evening primrose oil (for assisting cervical dilation), spirits of peppermint (for assisting bladder function; often can be used instead of a catheter), angelica (for assisting placental expulsion), shepherd's purse (for preventing postpartum hemorrhage), Crampease (a mixture of herbs) for afterpains, black haw (for postpartum cramps), and valerian (for relaxation); olive oil for perineal massage; a birthing stool; an amni-hook for breaking the waters if they are still intact when the baby crowns (so that they won't break all over the midwife—HIV can be transmitted through the amniotic fluid); waterproof pads and sheets; an oxygen tank, mask for the mother, and infant resuscitation bag and mask (rarely used); special scissors for cutting an episiotomy (rarely used); syringes and drugs (injectable pitocin, injectable methergine, and oral methergine) to stop a postpartum hemorrhage; IV lines and fluids; instruments and sutures for repairing vaginal tears; sheets to create a sterile barrier field while suturing; a tensor or desk lamp (for visibility during suturing); a local anesthetic (xylocaine or 1 or 2% lidocaine) for pain relief during suturing; a heating pad to assist in warming the baby; a bulb syringe (for suctioning the baby's airways) and DeLee suction catheters (for sucking amniotic fluid out of the deeper respiratory passages of the newborn; rarely used); assorted hemostats and clamps; special scissors for cutting the cord; scales for weighing the baby and a tape measure; oral vitamin K; erythromycin ointment (to place in the baby's eyes to prevent blindness from venereal disease—a requirement in most states); multicolor footprint pads (for taking the baby's footprint for the birth certificate); sitz bath herbs (for soothing the woman's vaginal area postpartum); red-top sterile vacuum tubes (for collecting umbilical cord blood for testing); and a file full of papers for charting, preparing the birth certificate, and so on. Most midwives carry enough supplies with them at any one time to attend three births in a row without repacking.

Some midwives also carry physician-prescribed antibiotics and Phenergan suppositories for stopping violent vomiting; a laryngoscope (for looking into the baby's trachea and larynges if there is reason to believe the baby may have aspirated meconium) and sterile saline (to wash the baby's vocal cords if necessary), which are very rarely used; breast shields (for cracked nipples) and breast shells (to help nipples become more prominent so the baby can more easily attach to the breast); and a newborn screening kit (this kit consists of a syringe and a specially treated piece of paper, on which the midwife places samples of the baby's blood to be sent to the health department and checked for metabolic disorders). (The above information was gleaned from a questionnaire handed out in January 1995 to 30 and returned by 25 homebirth midwives, all of whom are members of MANA and most of whom serve on the CPM Certification Task Force [see note 4].)

12. Meconium is the baby's first bowel movement. If present in the amniotic fluid, it is sometimes associated with fetal distress, which is usually also indicated by fetal heart patterns. It is generally recognized, even in most hospitals, that thin or light meconium staining during birth is not problematic, especially when the heart rate patterns fall within a normal range. Heavy, thick, and chunky meconium in the amniotic fluid is usually indicative of fetal distress.

13. Decelerations of the fetal heart rate, as recorded on the electronic fetal monitor, are sometimes indicative of fetal distress.

14. The Apgar score provides a standardized means by which birth attendants

can assess the baby's condition at birth. Signs rated at two points each on a pre-printed chart are skin color, muscle tone, breathing attempts, heartbeat, and response to stimulus, such as a touch or pin prick. Babies are rated twice, at one minute after birth and again at five minutes, because many babies, especially anesthetized ones, take some time to turn pink and begin full breathing on their own. Ten is the highest obtainable score. Babies with Apgars of 2 and 2 (2 at one minute and still 2 at five minutes) are severely distressed.

15. "Slant boarding" is a midwifery technique that often proves effective in getting breech babies to turn before delivery. The mother must get her head lower than her pelvis. A bean bag chair can be used, or an ironing board (or door) can be placed against a sofa or heavy chair at a 45-degree angle; the pregnant woman lies on her back, head down on the board with her feet pointing upward for fifteen to twenty minutes two or three times a day. During this time she is encouraged to relax and to visualize the baby turning. (For other such techniques, see Kitzinger 1991:98 or ask a midwife!)

16. Hospital labors are usually artificially speeded up with drugs, episiotomies, forceps, or cesarean section, so homebirth labors, which are allowed to take their natural course, tend to take far more time than hospital births do. During a long labor, it is essential for a mother (and indeed, her birth attendants) to keep up her strength by eating and drinking plenty of nutritious food and fluids. Homebirth midwives recognize that contractions that have been going on for 18 hours and are still 5 minutes apart mean that the mother is still in "early labor"—"active labor" has not yet kicked in—and there is plenty of time for the midwife to go out for food.

17. Note Maggie's refusal to adopt the physician's technomedical discourse here—a discourse that reduces the differences between cesarean and vaginal birth to a matter of geography, at the same time as it subtly expresses the value this culture consistently places on "above" in relation to "below."

18. Hospital practitioners generally allow one hour, and a maximum of two hours, for pushing, after which a cesarean will usually be performed. Homebirth midwives accept a wide range of pushing stages, but more than four hours of pushing is rather unusual, even at home.

19. Following is a summary of Maggie Bennett's personal protocols for qualifying a mother and baby for homebirth.

Mother

Blood pressure has to be no more than 20 pts. diastolic above her baseline.

Dilation should take place at the general rate of 1/2 cm/hr after 4 cm; one 3-hour plateau (in which no dilation takes place) is acceptable. [Authors' note: *Hospital protocols usually call for birth to take place within 24 hours of entry into the hospital, period. For many women, it can take days of "early labor" to reach 4 cm. If such women enter the hospital, they end up with cesareans.*]

Good labor should be established within 24 hours after rupture of membranes.

Birth should take place within 72 hours after rupture of membranes.

[*Hospital protocols call for birth to take place within 24 hours of rupture of membranes, due to the danger of infection, which is increased by the frequent vaginal examinations performed in the hospital. Midwives at home avoid performing such exams as much as possible in cases of prematurely ruptured membranes.*]

Birth should take place within 4 hours from the time the mother learns to push. [*As noted above, hospital protocols generally allow a maximum of two hours for pushing and do not mention the mother's "learning to push." Here again, we see the midwife's woman-centered focus, her respect for the mother as active birth giver.*]

No temperature. Not too fatigued.

Baby

Fetal heart between 124 and 160 and in accordance with baby's baseline.

Good beat-to-beat variability. No heavy meconium—light OK.

20. Our interviewees also agreed that in the rare instances in which the mother and the midwife had conflicting intuitions about a potential problem during labor, clearly they were *not* connected. In such a situation, they felt that transport would be essential, as this "total lack of synergy" would seriously impede their ability to provide good, empathic (i.e., connected) care.

21. It is important to note that this appreciation of women's uniqueness can extend even to crises and complications that midwives cannot handle at home, as is evidenced in the following story from Elizabeth Davis.

Sometimes if a woman has had a difficult birth, part of the reason why it's been difficult is that things have come up for her that she has not worked through. . . . I think of a Japanese woman with a Chinese husband who was culturally supposed to have a son, and it was a girl, and you can bet that nothing I said or did stopped her trickle bleeding from a partially separated placenta that finally took us to the hospital. When she felt safe enough in the hospital, she staged this massive hemorrhage, and rallied her husband to her side, where he had not been since he saw the sex of the baby.

So you know, the choreography of the woman's expression of need is something that's really beyond the practitioner—it's really none of your business. But it *is* your business to maintain the parameters of safety, as we say, so some part of your attention has to turn to doing as much as you can *in advance* to raise those issues and help a woman cope with them. It's a fine line—permission to have your birth be whatever it is going to be and the midwife's skill and also her need to have a safe outcome. I think really most of us struggle with that.

22. As one anonymous reviewer aptly pointed out, the words "normal" and "abnormal" may not even be appropriate when talking about birth from the standpoint of intuitive knowing, as the concept "normal" "has long been grounded in a worldview that is based on a ratiocinative means of reasoning and the averaging of all experiences into one standardized experience. . . . Foucault's concept of 'normalization' might be an interesting springboard here." Space does not allow us to further address the issue of midwives' efforts to normalize uniqueness versus medicine's efforts to pathologize it as "deviance," but it is an issue deserving of scholarly probing, and we call attention to it here in the hope of stimulating further research and analysis.

23. Copies of the "MANA Core Competencies" can be obtained from Signe Rogers, Editor, *MANA News*, P. O. Box 175, Newton, KS 67114; or from MANAinfo@aol.com.

24. Homebirth mothers themselves often have rich intuitive experiences worthy of anthropological study in their own right, as do mothers in general, about birth, about child raising, and so on. We call attention to this understudied subject in

the hope of generating more academic research into women's perceptions of and experiences with intuition. Additionally, we call for more research into how midwives negotiate childbirth with their clients and the role that intuition plays in these negotiations. What difference does it make, for example, when women hire midwives to save money rather than because of a shared worldview?

25. This national certification process is now in place and functioning, making national certification for direct-entry and independent midwives a reality for the first time in U.S. history. Several hundred midwives have taken the NARM exam; the first to successfully pass through the complete evaluation process was Abby J. Kinne, who was formally certified as a CPM on November 11, 1994. As of December 12, 1996, 124 midwives had become CPMs. This first group to pass through the first phase of the certification process consisted primarily of experienced midwives who have been in practice for at least five years. NARM began accepting applications from entry-level midwives in spring 1996. One year later, the number of CPMs had grown to about 300.

REFERENCES

Arms, Suzanne
　1994　*Immaculate Deception II: A Fresh Look at Childbirth.* Berkeley: Celestial Arts.
Bastick, Tony
　1982　*Intuition: How We Think and Act.* New York: Wiley.
Beth, Easton, and Jean Piaget
　1966　*Mathematical Epistemology and Psychology.* Dordrecht: D. Reidel.
Chalmers, Iain, Murray Enkin, and Marc J. Keirse
　1989　*Effective Care in Pregnancy and Childbirth.* Oxford: Oxford University Press.
Chester, Penfield
　1997　*Sisters on a Journey: Portraits of North American Midwives.* New Brunswick: Rutgers University Press.
Csordas, Thomas
　1993　"Somatic Modes of Attention." *Cultural Anthropology* 8(2):135–156.
Davis, Elizabeth
　1987　*Heart and Hands: A Guide to Midwifery.* New York: Bantam Books.
　1988　*Energetic Pregnancy.* Berkeley: Celestial Arts.
　1989　*Women's Intuition.* Berkeley: Celestial Arts.
　1994　*Women's Sexual Cycles.* London: Little, Brown.
　1995　*Woman, Sex, and Desire: Exploring Your Sexuality at Every Phase of Life.* Alameda, Calif.: Hunter House.
Davis, Elizabeth, and Carol Leonard
　1996　*The Women's Wheel of Life: Thirteen Archetypes of Woman at Her Fullest Power.* New York: Viking.
Davis-Floyd, Robbie
　1987a　"Pregnancy and Cultural Confusion: Contradictions in Socialization." In *Cultural Constructions of Woman,* ed. Pauline Kolenda, 9–71. Salem, Wis.: Sheffield Press.

1987b   "Obstetric Training as a Rite of Passage." *Medical Anthropology Quarterly* 1(3):288–318.

1990   "The Role of Obstetrical Rituals in the Resolution of Cultural Anomaly." *Social Science and Medicine* 31(2):175–189.

1992   *Birth as an American Rite of Passage.* Berkeley: University of California Press.

1994   "The Technocratic Body: American Childbirth as Cultural Expression." *Social Science and Medicine* 38(8):1125–1140.

1995   Introduction. In *Holistic Midwifery: A Comprehensive Textbook for Midwives in Home Birth Practice.* Vol. 1: *Care During Pregnancy,* by Anne Frye. Portland, Ore.: Labyrs Press.

Diamond, Irene
1994   *Fertile Ground: Women, Earth, and the Limits of Control.* Boston: Beacon Press.

Diamond, Irene, and Gloria Feman Orenstein
1990   *Reweaving the World: The Emergence of Ecofeminism,* San Francisco: Sierra Club Books.

Eisler, Rianne
1988   *The Chalice and the Blade.* New York: HarperCollins.

Fox, Renée C.
1975   "Training for Uncertainty." In *The Student Physician,* ed. R. Merton, G. Reader, and P. L. Kendall, 122–157. Cambridge, Mass.: Harvard University Press.

1980   "The Evolution of Medical Uncertainty." *Millbank Quarterly* 58:1–49.

Gaskin, Ina May
[1977] 1990   *Spiritual Midwifery.* 3d ed. Summertown, Tenn.: Book Publishing Company.

Goer, Henci
1995   *Obstetric Myths versus Research Realities.* New Haven, Conn.: Bergin and Garvey.

Goldberg, Phillip
1983   *The Intuitive Edge.* Los Angeles: Jeremy P. Tarcher.

Harper, Barbara
1994   *Gentle Birth Choices.* Rochester, Vt.: Healing Arts Press.

Hayward, John
1984   *Perceiving Ordinary Magic.* Boston: Shambala.

Jordan, Brigitte
[1978] 1993   *Birth in Four Cultures: A Cross-Cultural Investigation of Childbirth in Yucatan, Holland, Sweden and the United States.* 4th ed. Prospect Heights, Ill.: Waveland Press.

1992   "Technology and Social Interaction: Notes on the Achievement of Authoritative Knowledge." IRL Technical Report #92-0027. Palo Alto, Calif.: Institute for Research on Learning.

Jung, Carl G.
1971   *Psychological Types.* Princeton: Princeton University Press.

Kennell, John, Marshall Klaus, Susan McGrath, Steven Robertson, and Clark Hinckley

1988 "Medical Intervention: The Effect of Social Support During Labor." *Pediatric Research* (April):211 (Abstract no. 61).

Kitzinger, Sheila
1979 *Birth at Home.* New York: Penguin.
1990 *The Midwife Challenge.* London: Pandora Press.
1991 *Homebirth: The Essential Guide to Giving Birth Outside the Hospital.* New York: Dorling Kindersley.

Laughlin, Charles D.
1992 *Brain, Symbol, and Experience: A Neurophenomenology of Human Consciousness.* New York: Columbia University Press.
1993 "Fuzziness and Phenomenology in Ethnological Research: Insights from Fuzzy-Set Theory." *Journal of Anthropological Research* 49:17–37.
1997 "The Nature of Intuition: A Neuropsychological Approach." In *Intuition: The Inside Story,* ed. Robbie Davis-Floyd and Sven Arvidson, 19–37. New York: Routledge. In press.

Lee, Peter R.
1976 *Symposium on Consciousness.* New York: Penguin.

Leveno, K. J., et al.
1986 "A Prospective Comparison of Selective and Universal Electronic Fetal Monitoring in 34,995 Pregnancies." *New England Journal of Medicine* 315:615.

Marcus, George E.
1993 "What Comes (Just) After 'Post'? The Case of Ethnography." In *The Handbook of Qualitative Social Science,* ed. Norman Denzin and Yvonne Lincoln. Beverly Hills, Calif.: Sage.

Marcus, George E., and Michael J. Fischer
1986 *Anthropology as Cultural Critique: An Experimental Moment in the Human Sciences.* Chicago: University of Chicago Press.

Martin, Emily
1987 *The Woman in the Body.* Boston: Beacon Press.

McCutcheon-Rosegg, Sue
1984 *Natural Childbirth the Bradley Way.* New York: E. P. Dutton.

Merchant, Carolyn
1983 *The Death of Nature: Women, Ecology, and the Scientific Revolution.* San Francisco: Harper and Row.

Midwives' Alliance of North America (MANA)
1992 "MANA Statement of Core Values and Ethics." *MANA News* 10(4):10–12.
1994 "MANA Core Competencies." *MANA News* 12(1):24–27.

Poincaré, Howard
1913 *The Foundations of Science.* New York: Science Press.

Prentice, A., and T. Lind
1987 "Fetal Heart Rate Monitoring During Labor: Too Much Intervention, Too Little Benefit." *Lancet* 2:1375–1377.

Quinn, Daniel
1993 *Ishmael.* New York: Bantam and Turner.

Rooks, Judith Pence
1997 *Childbirth in America: The Past, Present, and Potential Role of Midwives.* Philadelphia: Temple University Press.

Rooks, Judith P., Norman L. Weatherby, Eunice K. M. Ernst, Susan Stapleton, David
Rosen, and Allan Rosenfield
    1989   "Outcomes of Care in Birth Centers: The National Birth Center Study."
        New England Journal of Medicine 321:1804–1811.
Rothman, Barbara Katz
    1982   *In Labor: Women and Power in the Birthplace.* New York: W. W. Norton.
    1989   *Recreating Motherhood: Ideology and Technology in a Patriarchal Society.* New
        York: W. W. Norton.
Rubinstein, Robert A., Charles D. Laughlin, Jr., and John McManus
    1984   *Science as Cognitive Process: Toward an Empirical Philosophy of Science.* Phila-
        delphia: University of Pennsylvania Press.
Sandmire, H. F.
    1990   "Whither Electronic Fetal Monitoring?" *Obstetrics and Gynecology*
        76(6):1130–1134.
Sargent, Carolyn
    1989   *Maternity, Medicine, and Power: Reproductive Decisions in Urban Benin.*
        Berkeley: University of California Press.
Schlinger, Hillary
    1992   *Circle of Midwives: Organized Midwifery in North America.* Independently
        published by Hillary Schlinger.
Shy, Kirkwood, et al.
    1990   "Effects of Electronic Fetal Heart Rate Monitoring, as Compared with
        Periodic Auscultation, on the Neurological Development of Premature In-
        fants." *New England Journal of Medicine* 322(9):588–593.
Singer, Linda
    1992   "Feminism and Postmodernism." In *Feminists Theorize the Political,* ed.
        Judy Butler and Joan W. Scott, 464–474. New York: Routledge.
Slaatte, Harold A.
    1983   *The Creativity of Consciousness: An Empirico-Phenomenonological Psychology.*
        New York: University Press of America.
Sorokin, Pitirim A.
    1941   *The Crisis of Our Age.* New York: E. P. Dutton.
Sosa, R., J. Kennell, S. Robertson, and J. Urrutia
    1980   "The Effect of a Supportive Companion on Perinatal Problems, Length
        of Labor, and Mother-Infant Interaction." *New England Journal of Medicine*
        303:597–600.
Sprenger, Jally, and George Deutsch
    1981   *Left Brain Right Brain.* San Francisco: W. H. Freeman.
Star, Rima Beth
    1986   *The Healing Power of Birth.* Austin: Star Publishing.
Starhawk
    1988   *Dreaming the Dark: Magic, Sex, and Politics.* Boston: Beacon Press.
    1989   *The Spiral Dance: A Rebirth of the Ancient Religion of the Great Goddess.* San
        Francisco: HarperSanFrancisco.
    1993   *The Fifth Sacred Thing.* New York: Bantam Books.
Sullivan, Deborah, and Rose Weitz

1988   *Labor Pains: Modern Midwives and Home Birth.* New Haven: Yale University Press.

Susie, Debra Ann

1988   *In the Way of Our Grandmothers: A Cultural View of Twentieth-Century Midwifery in Florida.* Athens: University of Georgia Press.

TenHouten, Warren

1978–1979   "Hemispheric Interaction in the Brain and the Propositional, Compositional, and Dialectical Modes of Thought." *Journal of Altered States of Consciousness* 4(2):129–140.

Vaughn, Francis E.

1979   *Awakening Intuition.* Garden City, N.Y.: Anchor Books.

Wagner, Marsden

1994   *Pursuing the Birth Machine.* Camperdown, Australia: ACE Graphics.

Weil, Andrew

1972   *The Natural Mind.* Boston: Houghton Mifflin.

Westcott, Alan

1968   *Toward a Contemporary Psychology of Intuition.* New York: Holt, Rinehart, and Winston.

THIRTEEN

Randomized Controlled Trials as Authoritative Knowledge

Keeping an Ally from Becoming a Threat to North American Midwifery Practice

Kenneth C. Johnson

A welcome movement away from belief- and tradition-based "current medical opinion" toward evidence-based care and intervention is occurring in obstetrics. Central to this development have been the increased use of and respect for the randomized controlled trial (RCT) as a research method and the use of meta-analysis as a tool for systematic quantitative summarization of existing RCT research. While RCTs in many instances have provided strong support for the midwifery model of woman-centered care, there are important limitations on their ability to assess certain aspects of midwifery care. This chapter discusses the strengths and limitations of the RCT as a tool for evaluating alternative birth practices and presents an example of an observational epidemiologic study of midwifery care that can address issues not amenable to RCT evaluation.

In 1989 a watershed in the development of evidence-based care in obstetrics was reached with the publication of *Effective Care in Pregnancy and Childbirth* (Chalmers, Enkin, and Keirse 1989), which presented systematic, scientific summaries (meta-analyses) focusing on the available RCT-based epidemiologic research concerning almost three hundred care issues in obstetrics. This scientific approach to evaluating care has proven strongly supportive of many aspects of the woman-centered, low-intervention type of midwifery care that has developed in North America over the last quarter century. Highly interventive approaches to the care of high-risk pregnant women and infants have a place. Intensive care of low birth weight infants, in particular, has contributed to substantial reductions in neonatal mortality (deaths in live-born infants in the first twenty-eight days of life) over the last few decades (Paneth 1990). However, it is less clear that this high-intervention approach is optimal for pregnant women without special medical risks or for infants in the normal birth weight range.

Although the RCT-based research has proven generally supportive of midwifery care, there is a danger in depending almost exclusively on RCT-based evidence. The limitations of RCTs need to be understood: there can be scientific, clinical, ethical, and political problems that make it difficult, if not impossible, to use RCTs to evaluate some important components of midwifery practice, particularly practices that are outside the pharmacologic interventionist medical paradigm. Other epidemiologic methods, in particular prospective observational studies, have different strengths than the RCT. They have played and will continue to play an important role in understanding what constitutes effective care.

In this chapter I first describe the important work that has been done using RCTs and meta-analysis to study perinatal management. Then I address various limitations of the RCT for evaluating effective birthing practice. Finally, a Midwives' Alliance of North America (MANA) research project that involves collecting detailed information on midwife-attended births is discussed as an example of a non-RCT epidemiologic study. The research is anticipated to be a valuable complement to the RCT work, particularly for addressing issues beyond the RCT's scope.

THE OXFORD ACCOMPLISHMENT: STRENGTHS OF THE RCT

Effective Care in Pregnancy and Childbirth was a landmark in the development of an authoritative knowledge of birthing practice. The 1,500-page two-volume tome was the culmination of a vision and a decade of work by three obstetricians, Marc Keirse from the Netherlands, Iain Chalmers from England, and Canadian Murray Enkin, in collaboration with a large number of dedicated colleagues. For the first time in any field of medicine, a thorough, systematic review of available research evidence on the effects of care was assembled. The medical literature was systematically and exhaustively searched from 1950 onward, and more than forty thousand obstetricians and pediatricians worldwide were contacted to locate unpublished research. More than one hundred epidemiologists, obstetricians, midwives, and other birth researchers were recruited to evaluate the more than 275 birthing practice issues for which research, in particular, RCTs, had been undertaken.

The overall results of the analyses were the identification of 99 currently used forms of care that reduce negative outcomes of pregnancy; 38 forms of care that appear promising but require further evaluation; 88 forms of care with unknown effects that require further evaluation; and 61 forms of care that should be abandoned in light of available evidence. An inexpensive paperback presenting only the main conclusions of the analyses was also published to allow access to the information by pregnant women, midwives, physicians, and other clinicians (Enkin, Keirse, and Chalmers

1989). The analyses were extended to include care of the newborn and culminated in the publication of *Effective Care of the Newborn Infant* (Sinclair and Bracken 1992).

Science-based evaluation of care has proven strongly supportive of many aspects of the woman-centered, low-intervention midwifery care that has developed in North America over the last quarter century. These evaluations have provided support for midwifery practices such as allowing women to birth in the position of their choice, promoting vaginal birth after cesarean, restricted use of episiotomy, not automatically inducing labor in women who have gone past their due dates, avoiding arbitrary time limits in the second stage of labor, and placing importance on the woman's input to medical decisions.

Associated with this initial evaluation is another innovation, the Cochrane Database, an electronic database that provides a mechanism for regular updating of the existing evaluations as new research is completed. For each meta-analysis, the database contains a concise, consistently formatted summary of the key issues, including limitations, findings, conclusions, graphic presentations summarizing the results of the individual studies, and references for all studies included in the meta-analysis. As well, addresses and telephone numbers are listed for the individual researchers responsible for the review and for keeping it current. The Cochrane Database runs on IBM personal computers or clones, is updated twice yearly, and is available on diskette by subscription.[1]

Remarkably, to date this remains the only field of medicine that has received a systematic scientific evaluation of existing research. Recently, the Cochrane Collaboration was formed by Iain Chalmers, who was a driving force in the original effective care collaboration, with the express intent of facilitating similar reviews of research in other clinical medicine fields. The importance of this new authoritative knowledge, based for the first time on the available scientific research and evaluated using the procedures of meta-analysis (a systematic search of the literature, setting criteria for individual study quality that must be met for inclusion, numerical summarization of results, and statistical evaluation of effect), should not be underestimated. The use of meta-analysis has gone a long way toward alleviating the subjectivity of conclusion and lack of quantification associated with the traditional literature review that it replaces. Meta-analysis is particularly useful when the available research suffers from any of the following limitations: (1) the number of individuals enrolled in the individual studies is small, so that the conclusions of individual studies have large statistical uncertainty associated with them; (2) individual studies vary in research quality, so that conclusions from poor research may dilute the conclusions of more carefully undertaken studies; (3) numerous studies have been completed, so that systematic summarization is necessary to see the bigger picture.

The Oxford accomplishment has helped raise the profile of the RCT in birth issues. The RCT provides an extremely valuable framework for careful evaluation of much clinical practice. First, by randomly allocating subjects to the standard treatment or the experimental treatment, a new treatment can usually be compared to an existing one "without bias that can result from people at different prior risk selectively receiving one of the alternative forms of care being compared" (Enkin, Keirse, and Chalmers 1989). The idea of randomization in a clinical trial is that it will make it likely that the subjects in each group are so similar overall that the observed effects (or lack of them) are the result only of the treatment(s) or lack of them. Second, by carefully controlling who will be allowed into the trial to make sure they are appropriate candidates for the planned interventions, by describing carefully the procedures for how and when interventions will be carried out, and by making explicit the outcome measures that will be used to evaluate the relative success of a new intervention, a well-designed trial provides an opportunity for concise evaluation of a specific treatment question.

LIMITATIONS OF THE RCT

Although the RCT is an extremely useful clinical research tool for evaluating many specific obstetric practices, like all research methods, it has its limitations. David Grimes (1991) has commented on the need to perform and report RCTs properly, Judith Lumley (1987) describes the many stumbling blocks to performing perinatal RCTs, and Samuel Helman and Deborah Helman (1991) address various ethical dilemmas that can arise. Here I focus on a number of important technical and logistic issues that need to be considered in the debate about appropriate birthing practice, particularly in the context of evaluating several central components of woman-centered midwifery care.

Scientific Method

The gold standard in RCTs is the double blind trial, where both the patient and the practitioner are unaware (i.e., blinded) of whether the patient is receiving the standard or experimental intervention. This ideal is most readily attained in a drug trial in which individuals in a study are randomly allocated to receive a drug or an identical-looking placebo and neither patient nor prescriber knows who gets which. This is rarely possible with regard to birth intervention issues; for example, both the practitioner and the patient know when a woman has been induced or a fetal monitor is being used.

Furthermore, just because a study employs randomization does not mean that the research is good. The question asked may be inappropriate or irrelevant. The study may be unethical (e.g., the use of placebo controls when an effective treatment is proven and available). The advantages of randomization may be undermined by unblinding of allocation or outcome assessment, cointervention(s), biased dropouts or losses to follow-up, or subjective responses. Although the RCT generally minimizes the chance of problems with bias, there are no guarantees—just as is the case in non-RCT research.

Clinical Judgment

When RCTs are used to evaluate birth practices, the criteria for judging outcomes or the need for intervention often depend on practitioners' perception or judgment: Is there fetal distress? Is there a need for intervention in a long second stage of labor? Is there failure to progress? What is the amount of blood loss? What is the newborn infant's physical status? When combined with a lack of blinding, it is possible that the systematic bias that the RCTs have labored to eliminate may creep in. If practitioners participating in the trial are overly optimistic about the new treatment or, conversely, disagree or are uncomfortable with it, it is possible that the observation of the outcome or the pressure to intervene may be skewed. For example, one of the first RCTs in Britain to evaluate active versus physiologic management of the third stage of labor instructed accoucheurs to try to leave the cord attached to the baby until the placenta was delivered. They were unable to comply with this directive in 51 percent of cases, probably because they were unaccustomed to and thus uncomfortable with this procedure. In a recent trial of restricted use of episiotomy (Klein et al. 1992), physicians in the study, when told to do episiotomies only when "absolutely necessary," still perceived a need for them in 25 to 90 percent of the births. In contrast, North American midwives find episiotomies necessary less than 5 percent of the time (Johnson, Daviss, and the Midwives' Alliance of North America Research and Statistics Group 1994).

Evaluating Emotional/Social Issues

The RCT is best suited to study very specific, technical issues with specific, easily measured outcomes (e.g., which type of suture material results in the lowest infection rate). The RCT is much more difficult to undertake for broader and less specific interventions and outcomes such as "satisfaction with care." Ann Oakley (1989) describes in detail the trials, tribulations, and ethical dilemmas for researchers and care providers alike of undertaking an RCT involving randomized allocation of emotional/social support during pregnancy. Furthermore, it is not always clear that evaluating one aspect of care in isolation, removed from the larger context, will provide generalizable or appropriate answers. For example, trying to isolate exactly which components of supportive, personalized, and woman-centered care create a feeling of safety is unlikely to be amenable to RCT evaluation.

Finding Willing Subjects and Practitioners

The RCT can only be used to answer questions when one can get a group of pregnant women and practitioners to agree to choice of intervention based solely on random selection. Important issues like the safety of home versus hospital birth and the short- and long-term benefits of breastfeeding versus formula feeding are not amenable to RCTs.

Efficacy versus Effectiveness

The RCT answers the question, Does a new treatment work better than the existing treatment in an experimental setting? Thus it attempts to answer the question, *Can* it work? This is referred to as the efficacy of the treatment. Equally important is the question, When a new treatment is actually used in the real world, does it result in the expected improvement in outcome—that is, *Does* it work? This is referred to as the treatment's effectiveness. Just because a treatment has been shown to be efficacious does not guarantee that it will necessarily be particularly effective. Evaluations of effectiveness require observational epidemiologic studies, not RCTs. In observational studies data are collected on a specific population—for example, all communities in a certain geographic region, or all infants with a specific birth defect in a state and a comparable sample of healthy babies—and then comparisons of health outcomes within subsets of the study population are made.

RCTs generally involve well-trained and interested practitioners, often in research-oriented progressive teaching hospitals. The subjects eligible for receiving the treatment are carefully selected and are willing to participate, the interventions are performed according to a strict set of rules, and the whole process is carefully documented. In the real world the interventions may be applied incorrectly or by practitioners without the requisite skills, in settings where there is resistance to or undue confidence in the intervention, and thus the interventions may be applied to subjects for which the interventions were never intended or overlooked for subjects who might benefit. Furthermore, the cost of the intervention may not be justified by the derived benefits.

Expense and Funding

RCTs tend to be expensive and therefore can often only be done where significant research resources are available and the question to be resolved would justify the effort to the funding body. Research resources are rarely made available for any therapy not within the Western medical paradigm. If medical research funding is more readily obtained for studies addressing questions considered important within the highly technical, highly interventive approach to childbirth, research into midwifery care will not be readily funded. The situation parallels that of research funding for alternative cancer therapies. Almost all of the extensive resources committed to finding effective cancer therapies continue to be spent on the radiation/ chemotherapy/surgery medical model of cancer therapy. Research into alternative therapies has rarely received funding. As a result there is usually no track record of research, proper studies are not undertaken, and the alternatives remain unevaluated and unaccepted.

"The Gold Standard"

Perhaps of more concern is that when RCTs are considered the gold standard of epidemiologic research, other well-respected types of epidemiologic research may be inappropriately devalued. Applied dogmatically, this notion will undermine established research methods that often are the only methods available to address basic, important issues. Furthermore, RCTs always require that prior descriptive epidemiology studies have been performed. It is from these that the RCT study questions often arise. Why are cesarean section rates going up? The postsection infection rate is too high; what interventions are effective in reducing risk? The framing of the study questions, sample size calculations, estimation of potential recruitment, duration and costs of studies, and ultimate feasibility often depend on such data.

Authority

The idea that the RCT is a "medical" technology should be dispelled. Although it has been popularized recently in a medical context, it is a general study design strategy developed in agricultural research and applicable to many fields, including midwifery. It is one of the most powerful designs but has distinct limitations. A much more rational approach to choice of designs is required. One should start with a clearly stated question, examine the literature and anecdotal experience, and then choose the most powerful and feasible design available. This might be a qualitative study, a case-control analysis, a cohort study, a clinical audit, a utilization study, a quality of life assessment, or an RCT.[2]

When authoritative knowledge becomes based almost exclusively on RCT research, then only techniques or approaches that have been subjected to RCT may be taken as authoritative. Alternative approaches (ones that do not depend on medical technology or prescription drugs) are far less likely to be well studied. For example, there have been a large number of studies evaluating the effectiveness of fetal monitoring (Thacker and Banta 1983) the benefits of which have been shown to be questionable (Leveno et al. 1986; Prentice and Lind 1987; Shy et al. 1990), whereas there have only been five studies reporting on the effectiveness of the "doula" (a woman who provides labor support), whose presence has been shown in the populations studied to result in shortened length of labor, reduced number of medical interventions, and increased maternal satisfaction (Klaus et al. 1992). Furthermore, because of the expense of RCTs and the limited amount of public research money available, more research is likely to become corporately funded, with the likely consequence that funding will be increasingly directed toward marketable, profitable technical interventions such as RCTs of drug interventions funded by drug companies.

AN EXAMPLE OF NON-RCT EPIDEMIOLOGIC RESEARCH: THE MIDWIVES' ALLIANCE OF NORTH AMERICA STUDY

The Midwives' Alliance of North America[3] is currently undertaking a large epidemiologic study that could prove useful for furthering knowledge about the details and outcomes of low-intervention midwifery practices in North America. In 1992, MANA adopted a dataform that elicits detailed information about an individual mother's pregnancy, labor, and birth and the midwifery care she receives through pregnancy, birth, and follow-up of mother and baby to six weeks postpartum (see fig. 13.1 at end of this chapter). The form is being used to collect data in a consistent way from more than two hundred midwives from across North America. In the main part of the study, midwives send a registration form listing births they expect to attend in the following three months and then provide complete dataforms for those births as they occur. As of the summer of 1996, midwifery associations in over a dozen states and provinces including California, Oregon, Alaska, and Quebec had adopted the form; more than six thousand midwife-attended home and birth center births have been reported on the dataform and entered into a database for evaluation.

MANA is uniquely placed to carry out such research. First, a number of midwifery practices differ from those found in the regulated and restricted technomedical system. Home birth midwifery practice has evolved over the last quarter century outside of the control of medical authorities, because until recently midwifery has enjoyed an alegal status in much of the United

States and Canada. Second, MANA provides a neutral forum for data collection because it is an organization that has no disciplinary function. Midwives can feel safe about reporting the truth about their management of birth without fear of repercussions or disciplinary action. With a greater respect for and patience with variations in women's laboring, an expanded view of what is normal during birth has developed. Thus this forum also provides an opportunity to document the range of what "normal birth" may actually be.

The care provided by these midwives is focused on being "with women." It includes continuity of a caregiver or caregivers through pregnancy, labor, and the postpartum period, an emphasis on the development of a caring and trusting relationship between mother and midwife, patience during labor, and the use of modern low-tech intervention tools such as sterile gloves, uristicks, and Pinard horns.[4] Labor and delivery take place in an environment in which a woman feels safe and are attended by midwives who believe in a woman's ability to deal with pain and successfully labor with little intervention. High-quality high-tech obstetrical backup care is available when required.

As an observational study, this research project provides an opportunity to efficiently investigate many different aspects of care and their effects on outcome. Whereas an RCT can be used only to study the practice that has been randomized, an observational study can be used to evaluate many aspects of care. Midwives practice independently and in a variety of ways (e.g., differing methods of perineal support, of using water during labor and birth, of management of second-stage labor, of dealing with delivery of the placenta, of use of herbs during pregnancy, labor, and postpartum, etc.). It should be possible to examine midwifery practices and their relation to pregnancy outcome for issues including the following: the overall approach of woman-centered midwifery care and perinatal mortality rates; not setting arbitrary time limits on the various stages of labor; differing approaches to delivery of the placenta and complications; differing approaches to perineal stretching during the third trimester and perineal tear rates; home versus hospital vaginal birth after cesarean; differing approaches to shoulder dystocia; and restricted use of episiotomy in relation to third- and fourth-degree perineal tear rates. With a database representing several thousand births, a variety of situations that occur rarely such as shoulder dystocia, long second-stage labor, and retained placenta, as well as practices that are not required often such as episiotomy, external cephalic version,[5] and emergency transport can be evaluated in a systematic way not possible through individual or informal observation.

Because the subjects are not randomized to different forms of care, one can never be positive that results do not reflect a bias introduced by some unmeasured factor that is associated with both the choice of practice and the outcome. Cautious evaluation is required as biased information might result because the caregiver is also the observer. However, as with a formally randomized sample, characteristics of mothers (age, parity, prenatal problems, socioeconomic status, ethnicity, etc.) can be compared (and controlled for in analysis if necessary) to increase the likelihood of unbiased evaluation. Furthermore, the development of epidemiologic knowledge, theory, and tools over recent decades has provided a strong backdrop for careful evaluation, and it is likely that considerable useful information can be obtained from observation of the outcomes of different forms of care used by different midwives. As with any study, suitable caution in the interpretation of results will be exercised.

Although no one study is conclusive, this work should be helpful in describing the outcomes of variations of care based on an approach dominated by a belief in women's ability to give birth with little or no intervention. The study analyses should provide a number of leads as to which forms of care may be effective, which may not be useful, and which may be detrimental. Some results may suggest areas in which RCTs would clarify or validate observational data. Because a number of states will be collecting data with the same form (reproduced at the end of this chapter), it should be possible to compare outcomes in different parts of North America, and in different settings, for consistency and reproducibility.

CONCLUSION

Epidemiology, in the form of both the RCT and the observational study, is an important ally for supporting and further developing low-intervention woman-centered midwifery care. The recent meta-analysis work done in the field of obstetrics is giving a new profile to evidence-based care, particularly that gained through RCTs, and is beginning to change obstetrics. The movement of authoritative knowledge away from "current medical opinion" toward evidence-based care has proven strongly supportive of many aspects of the woman-centered low-intervention type of midwifery that has developed in North America over the last quarter century. Armed with a balanced understanding of the strengths and limitations of RCTs and other types of epidemiological studies, we will be better able to assess the efficacy of alternative birth practices.

NOTES

I would like to thank Betty-Anne Daviss, Dr. Donald Sutherland, Sally Inch, Dr. Patrick Mohide, Dr. Nigel Paneth, and Claudia Brann for insightful comments on earlier drafts of this manuscript.

1. The address of the Cochrane Pregnancy and Childbirth Database is Manor Cottage, Little Milton, Oxford OX44 7QB, U.K. In the United States and Canada, contact Canadian Perinatal Clinical Trials Network, Local Do-705, Hospital St.-François d'Assise, 10 rue de l'Espinay, Quebec, Canada G1L 3L5 (418-525-4455; fax 418-525-4481; e-mail 3028wfra@vmi.ulaval.ca). The database is available on disk and CD-ROM for IBM and Apple Macintosh computers.

2. *Case-control studies* involve comparing a set of subjects with a disease or health outcome of concern (cases) with a sample of healthy subjects from the same population (controls) to look for factors that may have contributed to the disease condition. *Cohort studies* involve following large groups of individuals (cohorts) until disease outcomes of interest occur and then examining how the rates of disease differ within subgroups with and without factors of interest.

3. For a description of MANA, see Davis-Floyd and Davis, this volume.

4. The uristick is a small plastic strip with a number of small chemically reactive blotters used to evaluate the constituents of urine. A pregnant women tests her urine on the stick, and color changes of the chemical blotters will indicate normal or abnormal levels indicating the need for more detailed investigation of potential problems. The Pinard horn, a hollow cone about 8 inches long and generally made of wood, was invented in the nineteenth century by the French physician Pinard. When placed against the pregnant woman's belly, it assists the midwife in monitoring the baby's heartbeat by amplifying the heart tones. Its use requires a high degree of tactile and sensory closeness between mother, baby, and midwife.

5. Most babies adopt a head-down position a number of weeks before delivery; this is the safest positioning for delivery. External cephalic version is the procedure of gently moving a baby who is in the breech position (bottom or feet down) to a head-down position in the uterus through positioning of the mother and by the practitioner pushing gently with the hands on the woman's belly in a specific way (see Jordan [1978] 1993).

REFERENCES

Chalmers, Iain, Murray Enkin, and Marc J. N. C. Keirse, eds.
   1989   *Effective Care in Pregnancy and Childbirth.* 2 vols. Oxford: Oxford University Press.
Enkin, Murray, Marc J. N. C. Keirse, and Iain Chalmers, eds.
   1989   *A Guide to Effective Care in Pregnancy and Childbirth.* Oxford: Oxford University Press.
Grimes, David A.
   1991   "Randomized Controlled Trials: 'It Ain't Necessarily So.' " *Obstetrics and Gynecology* 78(4):703–704.
Hellman, Samuel, and Deborah S. Hellman
   1991   "Of Mice but Not Men: Problems of the Randomized Clinical Trial." *New England Journal of Medicine* 324(22):1585–1589.
Johnson, Kenneth C., Betty-Anne Daviss, and the Midwives Alliance of North America Research and Statistics Group
   1994   "Descriptive Analysis of the Midwives Alliance of North America Birth Database." Manuscript.

Jordan, Brigitte

[1978] 1993   *Birth in Four Cultures: A Cross-Cultural Investigation of Childbirth in Yucatan, Holland, Sweden and the United States.* 4th ed. Prospect Heights, Ill.: Waveland Press.

Klaus, Marshall, et al.

1992   "Maternal Assistance and Support in Labor: Father, Nurse, Midwife, or Doula?" *Clinical Consultations in Obstetrics and Gynaecology* 4(4):1–7.

Klein, Michael C., et al.

1992   "Does Episiotomy Prevent Perineal Trauma and Pelvic Floor Relaxation?" *Online Journal of Current Clinical Trials* 1, doc. 10.

Leveno, K. J., et al.

1986   "A Prospective Comparison of Selective and Universal Electronic Fetal Monitoring in 34,995 Pregnancies." *New England Journal of Medicine* 315:615.

Lumley, Judith

1987   "Does This Work?" *Pediatrics* 79(6):1040–1044.

Oakley, Ann

1989   "Who's Afraid of the Randomized Controlled Trial? Some Dilemmas of the Scientific Method and 'Good' Research Practice." *Women and Health* 15(4):25–59.

Paneth, Nigel

1990   "Technology at Birth." *American Journal of Public Health* 80(7):791–792.

Prentice, A., and T. Lind

1987   "Fetal Heart Rate Monitoring During Labor—Too Frequent Intervention, Too Little Benefit." *Lancet* 2:1375–1377.

Shy, Kirkwood, et al.

1990   "Effects of Electronic Fetal Heart Rate Monitoring as Compared with Periodic Auscultation, on the Neurological Development of Premature Infants." *New England Journal of Medicine* (March 1):588–593.

Sinclair, John C., and Michael B. Bracken, eds.

1992   *Effective Care of the Newborn Infant.* Oxford: Oxford University Press.

Thacker, S. B., and H. D. Banta

1983   "Benefits and Risks of Episiotomy: An Interpretive Review of the English-Language Literature, 1860–1980." *Obstetrics and Gynaecology Survey* 38:322–338.

Fig. 13.1 appears on the following four pages.

Revision: APRIL 1993

Please note: in general code: 1=yes, 0=no, ?=don't know; blank=does not apply

DEMOGRAPHIC

Midwife Code   1 **

Midwife's Code for
        Identifying This Birth   1

Client's Municipality _____

Population (1=city >1,000,000, 2=city >250,000,   2
        3=town >10,000, 4=small town (<10,000), 5=rural)

Postal (ZIP) Code

Mother's: Age

        Last grade of high school completed

        Post secondary education (years)

        Occupation _____   * 3

        Ethnic Origin (1=Caucasian, 2=African
            or Caribbean, 3=Native American, 4=Asian,
            5=Other_____)

        Special group (1=Hispanic, 2=Amish,
            3=Francophone, 4=other_____)

        Natural hair colour (1=brown, 2=black, 3=red,
            4=blond)

Partner status at time of birth (1=married couple,
        2=unmarried couple, 3=female partner,
        4=separated/divorced, 5=single, 6=couple,
        marital status not known, 7=other_____)

Partner's: Age

        Last grade of high school completed

        Post Secondary education (years)

        Occupation _____   *

Family socio/economic level (midwife's evaluation)
        (1=low, 2=medium, 3=upper)

PREVIOUS PREGNANCY AND DELIVERY HISTORY

Number of previous :   pregnancies

                            miscarriages   4

                            induced abortions

                            stillbirths   4

                            live births

Number of previous :   home births

                            caesarean sections

                            VBAC's

                            episiotomies

                            postpartum hemorrhages

Other previous pregnancy or delivery concern(s)
        (1=gest <37 wks, 2=gest>42 wks, 3=hypertension,
        4=breech, 5=pre/eclampsia, 6=IUGR, 7=birth defect,
        8=shoulder dys, 9=other_____)

PRESENT PREGNANCY CONCERNS

Maternal problems: (1=pregnancy–induced
        hypertension,2=chronic hypertension,3=pre–eclampsia,   5
        4=eclampsia, 5=gestational diabetes, 6=diabetes
        mellitus, 7=persistent anemia (Hct<30 or Hb<10 g/dl),
        8=Rh sensitized,9=other_____)

Infection (1=genital herpes,
        2=chlamydia, 3=urinary tract infection, 4=yeast,
        5=gonorrhea, 6=other_____)

                                                    1st 2nd 3rd

Bleeding in trimester: (1=light, 2=heavy)

Fetal problems: (1=suspected IUGR, 2= birth

        defect diagnosed in utero(_____),

        3=intrauterine death, 4=other_____)

Midwife perceives emotional/social problems   6
        <---- (specify and describe in margin of form)

BREECH AFTER 28 WEEKS GESTATION

1st time breech noticed (week of gest. from LMP)

Last time breech (week of gest. from LMP)

Breech turning exercises (# of times)

External cephalic version   by midwife   :
(attempts: successes)   by physician   :

Other procedures (1=_____)

PRENATAL CARE

Week (from LMP) any prenatal care began

Week (from LMP) midwife prenatal care began

Prenatal classes (1=this preg, 2=other preg, 3=both)

Two most important reasons for choosing intended
        place of birth (as stated by mother)
        (1=desire for natural birth, 2=effect on baby, 3=control,
        4=social pressure, 5=cost, 6=safety, 7=family unity,
        8=atmosphere, P=partner preference, H= "high risk",
        9=other_____)

Number of prenatal visits: with a midwife

                            estimated with G.P.

                            estimated with obstetrician

Payment (1=client paid, 2=Blue Cross/Shield,
        3=commercial insurance, 4=HMO (other prepay),
        5=Champus,6=Medicaid,7=universal government health
        insurance, 8=other_____)

PRENATAL DETAILS

Mother's height (or estimate)   feet   inches

Mother's prepregnancy weight (pounds)

Weight gain during pregnancy (pounds)

Method of conception (1=coitus, 2=artificial
        insemination, 3=in vitro, 4=other)   1st 2nd 3rd

Ultrasound (# of times each trimester)

Other prenatal testing (1=triple screen,
        2= chorionic villus sampling, 3=AFP, 4=amniocentesis,
        5=biophysical profile, 6=non stress test, 7=GTT,
        8=random glucose, 9=other_____)

Tobacco, Alcohol or Recreational Drugs

Mother smoked cigarettes during pregnancy

        Number of months

        Average # of cigarettes per day

Alcohol during pregnancy

        Average number of drinks per month

Marijuana/THC/hashish   (1=occasional, 2=regular)

Other illegal drugs   (1=occasional, 2=regular)

Drug type (1=cocaine, 2=other_____)

Prescription drugs in pregnancy (1=antibiotics,
        2=antifungals, 3=antiemetics, 4=antihypertensives,
        5=other (specify)_____)

Mother's overall nutrition in pregnancy (midwife's
        assessment)(1=excellent, 2=good, 3=fair, 4=poor)

Diet during pregnancy (1='meat & potatoes',   Primary
        2=whole foods and meat, 3=junkfood,   Secondary
        4=ovo–lacto vegetarian, 5=vegan vegetarian,
        6=macrobiotic, 7=other_____)

Mother restricted calorie intake to limit weight gain

Herbs to ease labour(last 6 wks)(1=daily, 2=less often)

Activity level during majority of pregnancy (1=very
        active, 2=active, 3=sometimes active, 4=sedentary)

Perineal Massage or Stretching

        Estimated # of times during 3rd trimester

Mother reports a history of sexual abuse
        (1=yes before puberty, 2=yes after puberty,
        3=before and after puberty, 4=mother prefers
        not to answer, 5=midwife did not ask)

Risk Factors Why a Home Birth Was Not or Could Not Have Been Initiated, Or Was Outside of Home Birth Protocol (Answer for All clients)

Reasons: (1=preterm/post–term,
        2=breech or malpresentation, 3=multiple birth,
        4=hypertension, 5=anemia, 6=diabetes,
        7=pre–eclampsia/eclampsia, 8=placenta previa/
        abruptio, 9=other(specify)_____)

Woman Stopped Using This Midwife For Primary Care Before Labour Began

Reasons:(1=miscarriage, 2=referral for
        complications, 3=client moved, 4=client chose birth
        centre, 5=client chose hospital, 6=changed midwives,
        7=cost, 8=stillbirth, 9=other_____)

Gestation when midwife primary care stopped

** 1,2,3 etc. are footnotes; see page 4 for clarifications   * Code will be added later

Please note: in general code: 1=yes, 0=no, ?=don't know; blank=does not apply

INTENDED BIRTH PLACE, GESTATION, ATTENDANTS

Midwife Code

Birth Number

Planned during pregnancy to have: (1=home birth, 2=birth centre birth, 3=hospital birth)   10

Began labour intending to deliver: (1=at home, 2=in birthing centre, 3=in hospital)

Referral after first assessment in labour

Gestation – midwife's best estimate before   Weeks   Days
    birth based on all available information

Mother certain about dates (1=yes ,2=fairly, 3=not)

Attendants at labour and birth

Attendants during labour

Attendants at birth
    (1=mother's partner, 2=midwife, 3=2nd midwife,
    4=midwife apprentice, 5=friends, 6=children age 1–4,
    7=children 5+, 8=other family members, 9=FP or GP,
    N=nurse, B=obstetrician, S=other_____)

LABOUR SUMMARY

	Day	Month	Year
Date of birth			

Place of birth (1=home, 2=freestanding birth centre, 3=hosp birth room, centre or "LDR", 4=hosp separate lab/del/rec, 5=hosp OR, 6=other_____)

Midwife's role in hospital (if applicable) (1=primary care giver, 2=doctor's assistant, 3=labour coach, 4=midwife's assistant, 6=not present, 7=_____)

Length of Labour:

Total time:	Days	Hours	Minutes
Early Labour	:	:	
1st stage	:	:	
2nd stage (full dilation)			
3rd stage			

Approximate total time the woman in labour had a:

midwife present before birth	:	
apprentice only before birth	:	
midwife present after birth	:	

Amount of time before birth	:		
membranes ruptured	Hour	Minute	AM/PM
Actual time of birth	:		

11
12

Plateaus, Reversals, Anterior Lip or Pushing Before Full Dilation

	Dilation	Hours	Minutes
1st stage plateaus	cm	:	
(stayed at same centimetre	cm	:	
assessment for > 2 hours)	cm	:	
	cm	:	

Cervical reversal (from what cm to what cm)		to	

	Hours	Minutes
Anterior lip longer than 1 1/2 hours	:	
Pushing before full dilation	:	
2nd stage plateau(full dilation & no pushing)	:	

13
14

Positions and Mobility

Positions of potential concern   Stage 1
    occurring during active labour   Stage 2
    (1=posterior, 2=breech, 3=head deep transverse, 4=tranverse lie, 5=acynclitism, 6=face & brow)

Baby's position at delivery (1=anterior, 2=posterior, 3=frank breech, 4=footling breech,5=complete breech, 6=head deep trans, 7=transverse lie, 8=face, 9=brow)

Mother's mobility during labour   Stage 1
    (1=mother changed positions frequently,   Stage 2
    2=mother didn't choose to take many positions
    3= movement restricted by anaesthetic or attachments,
    4=movement restricted by staff)

Mother's final delivery position (1=semi–sitting, 2=hands & knees, 3=squatting, 4=standing,5=on side, 6=on back, 7=stirrups, 8=birthing stool, 9=deBy birth stool, M=McRoberts(thigh hyperflexion), 0=other_____)

Underwater birth

LABOUR AND BIRTH PROCEDURES

Induction, Augmentation or IV

Induction (1=pitocin, 2=prostag, 3=nipple stimulation, 4=castor oil, 5=art rupture of memb < 5 cm, 6=art rupture of mem >= 5cm, 7=stripping of membranes, 8=intercourse,   By midwife
9=other_____)   By physician

Time until labour started (hours)

Augmentation   By midwife
    (use induction codes)   By physician

I.V. initiated (stage)

Other Procedures During Labour

Number of vaginal examinations

Doppler use (1=1st stage, 2=2nd stage, 3=1st and 2nd)

Use of water (0=none,1=bath, 2=shower,   Stage 1
    3=jacuzzi, 4=other_____)   Stage 2

Drugs (1=analgesics, 2=tranquillizers, 3=sedatives, 4=alcohol, 5=other_____)

Medicinal herbs (specify) (1=_____)

Other procedures (1=body massage, 2=enema, 3=catheterization,4=other_____)

Nourishment during active labour (0=nothing, 2=only clear fluids or jello, 3=other fluids, 4=solid food)

Perineal Care

Active perineal guidance in 2nd stage (0=midwife remained passive,1=manual support, 2=massage,3=compresses,4=oils/lubricants, 5=verbal guidance,6=other_____)

Episiotomy (1=medio lateral by physician,2=median, physician,3=medio lateral,midwife,4=median,midwife)

Perineal tear & degree (0=no tear,1=1st, 2=2nd, 3=3rd(into anal sphincter), 4=4th (into rectal mucosa))

Episiotomy or tear repair (0=no repair)

Local anaesthetic for repair

Labial tear(1=slight, 2=required suture)

Clitoral/urethral tear (1=slight, 2=required suture)

Cervical laceration (2=required suture, 3=extensive)

Hospital or Birth Centre Procedures

Electronic fetal monitoring:(1=internal,2=ext,3=both)

Fetal scalp sample

Cord blood gases

Anaesthesia (1=epidural,2=general,3=pudendal, block,4=entonox,5=other_____)

Forceps (1=outlet,2=low,3=mid,4=rotation,5=other)

Vacuum extraction

Caesarean section

Reason(s) for C–section (1=failure to progress, 2=fetal distress, 3=meconium, 4=not vertex lie, 5=maternal exhaustion, 6=other_____)

Midwife considers C–Section necessary (0=no, 1=yes, 2=possibly, 3=probably)

Apgars (hospital staff assessment)   1 minute
                                       5 minute

TRANSPORT FROM PLANNED HOME BIRTH OR PLANNED BIRTH CENTRE BIRTH

Did the midwife consider transport an emergency?

Transport by– (1=car, 2=ambulance, 3=other)

Labour stage at transport (1=first, 2= second, 3=third, 4=postpartum)

Length of time before or after birth that decision to transport was made (hrs/mins)

Minutes from decision to arrival at hospital

Reason(s) for transport   Primary reason
                           Secondary reason
    (1=failure to progress,
    2=sustained fetal distress, 3=malpresentation,
    4=thick meconium, 5=abruptio/praevia, 6=hemorrhage,
    7=retained placenta, 8=maternal exhaustion, B=baby's
    condition, 9=other_____)

Midwife and clients reception at hospital (1=supportive,2=indifferent,3=unsupportive,4=hostile)

Please note: in general code: 1=yes, 0=no, ?=don't know; blank=does not apply

LABOUR AND DELIVERY FACTORS

Midwife

Birth Number

Delivery Factors

Preterm labour (< 37 weeks)

Compound presentation

Shoulder dystocia (1=minor, 2=moderate, 3=severe)
 # of resolution techniques tried
 Most effective tech(_____)

Fetal bradycardia (prolonged FHT < 110)

Fetal tachycardia (prolonged FHT > 160)

Late or deep decels (1=1st stage,2=2nd,3=1 & 2)

Midwife thinks emotional or social factors may have
 affected course of labour(<----write details in margin)

Cord problems (1=only 1 or 2 vessels, 2=very short,
 3=around neck tightly, 4=around neck 2+ times,
 5=cord prolapse, 6=other_____)

Other complications (1=shock, 2=uterine
 prolapse, 3=placenta previa, 4=abruptio placenta,
 5=hematoma, 6=embolism, 7=ruptured uterus,
 8=anaesthesia complications, 9=other_____)

Meconium

Stage when meconium noticed

Density (1=thin, 2=moderate, 3=thick)

Consistency (1=particulate, 2=well dissolved)

Colour (1=yellow,2=light green,3=dark green,
 4=brown, 5=colour darkened during labour)

Blood Loss

Prophylatic to avoid hemorrhage (1=oxytocin,
 2=sheperd's purse, 3=other_____)

Estimated blood loss _____ milliliters
 or cups (use 2 decimals – e.g. 1.00, 2.25)

Postpartum hemorrhage (> 500 ml or 2 1/4 cups)

Action(s) taken for blood loss
 (1=fundal massage, 2=nipple stimulation,
 3=external bimanual compression, 4=internal
 bimanual comp, 5=IV fluids, 6=blood transfusion,
 7=other_____)

Drugs (1=pitocin,2=methergine(ergotrate),3=_____)

Herbs:(1=_____)

D & C

NEWBORN DATA (first 4 hours)

Number of babies (complete this page for each baby)

Sex (1=girl, 2=boy)

Birthweight _____ grams
 OR _____ lbs. _____ ozs

Apgar (midwife's assessment) 1 minute
 5 minute

Any clinical evidence that baby is preterm

Any clinical evidence that baby is postterm

Stillbirth(1=death before labour, 2=during labour)

Birth defects(1=minor,2=serious,3=life threatening)
 Specify_____

Procedures

Resuscitation: (1=suction on the
 perineum, 2=DeLee, 3=bulb suctioning, 4=tactile stim,
 5=oxygen, 6=ambubag, 7=mouth to mouth, 8=chest
 compressions, 9=intubation, R=respirator, W=wall)

Eye prophylaxis (1=silver nitrate, 2=erythromycin
 (ilotycin), 3=sterile water, 4=other_____)

Vitamin K given (1=oral, 2=IM)

Immediate neonatal complications

Complications: (1=respiratory distress,
 2=meconium aspiration, 3=IUGR, 4=metabolic
 (hypoglycemia,hypocalcemia), 5=prematurity,
 6=seizures, 7=birth injuries_____,
 8=other_____)

Transfer to neonatal intensive care unit

DELIVERY OF PLACENTA AND MEMBRANES

Cord clamped (1=immediately (before pulsing stopped),
 2=after pulsing stopped, 3=after placenta delivered,
 4=other_____)

Cord clamped –# of minutes after birth

Mother's postion waiting to deliver placenta
 (1=lying down, 2=standing, 3=squatting,
 4=sitting, 5=hands & knees, 6=several positions)

Method: (1=maternal effort, 2=controlled
 cord traction,3= manual removal, 4=D&C)

Membranes appear: (1=complete, 2=incomplete)

Placenta appears: (1=complete, 2=incomplete)

Anatomical variations of placenta (1=infarcts,
 2=calcium deposits, 3=succenturiate, 4=accreta,
 5=other_____)

POSTPARTUM CARE AND BREASTFEEDING

Number of postpartum visits with midwives

Estimated postpartum visits: other caregivers

Final midwife postnatal visit or contact (week)

Number of weeks breastfed in first 6 weeks

Number of weeks before any supplement (7= >6 weeks)

Circumcision in first 6 weeks

INFANT'S HEALTH IN FIRST 6 WEEKS

Newborn health problems in first 6 weeks
 (1=jaundice beyond normal physiologic level,
 2=sepsis/infection, 3=respiratory distress, 4=failure to
 thrive,5=premature/immature,6=seizures,7=birth trauma,
 8=other (specify)_____)

Jaundice level if measured (mmol/litre)

Newborn hospitalized in first 6 weeks

Number of days in neonatal intensive care unit

Number of days newborn hospitalized in first 6 weeks

Reason(1=born there,2=baby's cond,3=mother's cond)

Baby's problem(s) (use newborn health problems)

Newborn died in first 6 weeks of life

No. of days after birth that death occurred

Underlying cause of death (1=birth defects,
 2=prematurity, 3=other(specify)_____)
 (Provide details about death in margin ------->)

MOTHER'S HEALTH IN FIRST 6 WEEKS

Postpartum Infections
 (1=yeast, 2=delayed perineal healing/infection,
 3=breast, 4=urinary tract, 5=uterine,
 6=febrile episode(>100.4 after first 24 hours))

Other Postpartum Complications
 (1= late hemorrhage(after 24 hrs), 2=hypertension,
 3=cervical/uterine prolapse, 4=hematoma,
 5=pulmonary embolism, 6= thrombophlebitis,
 7=eclampsia, 8=anemia (<10 mg), 9=other
 (Specify)_____)

Postpartum depression (1=moderate, 2=severe)

# of days mother hospitalized in first 6 weeks

Maternal Death
 Underlying cause _____
 (Please provide details about death in margin ---->)

INFANT'S & MOTHER'S HEALTH at 6 WEEKS

Infant (1=good,no problems, 2=residual problems)

Mother (1=good,no problems, 2=residual problems)

FORM COMPLETION

Form filled out by: (initials)

Date majority of | Day | Month | Year
form filled out

MANA thanks you for spending the time to contribute
to its data collection by carefully filling out this form.

Form developed by Kenneth C. Johnson, PhD and Betty~Anne
Daviss~Putt. Many thanks to 26 midwives, 5 epidemiologists,
2 psychologists and 1 graphic artist who provided invaluable feedback.
Contact: Betty~Anne Daviss~Putt
36 Glen Avenue, Ottawa, Ontario, CANADA K1S 2Z7
Phone (613) 730 0282 or 432 5701, Pager 593~4917

15

16

FOOTNOTES (Further Information About Specific Data Items)
(The numbers refer to footnotes as specified to the right of certain boxes on the form.)

1.   If you haven't yet been assigned a code, use your initials here. Some midwives have a number for each birth. What we need here is an identifying code so that should those analyzing the data have questions about the way in which the form was filled out they can feed back the code to you and you can dig up that particular file. The important thing is that you have a different code for each birth that you have attended.

2.   The client's municipality, population and postal code are used for demographic comparison to other birth datasets.

3.   Please indicate which professions, vocations, or trades the mother has engaged in besides motherhood.

4.   Miscarriage:WHO: Death before 20 weeks of gestation from LMP.
Stillbirth: Death at 20 weeks or more. Baby did not take a breath.

5.   Chronic hypertension (1) is defined by Williams Obstetrics as "A diastolic blood pressure of at least 90 mm Hg. or systolic pressure of at least 140 mm Hg, or a rise in the former of at least 15 mm Hg or in the latter of 30 mm Hg. The blood pressure cited must be manifest on at least two occasions six or more hours apart...Before the 20th week of gestation in the absence of hydatiform mole or extensive molar change, or persistent hypertension beyond six weeks postpartum."
Pregnancy-induced hypertension (2) is defined by Williams Obstetrics as "The development of hypertension in pregnancy after the 20th week of gestation and sometimes earlier when there are extensive hydatidiform changes in the chorionic villi...It may also occur during the first 24 hours after delivery."

6.   Describe serious personal, emotional or family problems that may be adversely affecting the woman during pregnancy.

7.   You must ask the mother about these or put a ?. Do not prompt with categorized answers.

8.   One of the purposes of this form is to study outcomes of low risk women in all settings. This question, therefore, needs to be answered even for the births that were not planned at home to develop a comparison group of low risk women in hospital and birthing centre settings who could have had their babies at home.

9.   Time when care was transferred to other provider even if you continued to provide support.

10.   If this client at any time during her pregnancy planned to have a home birth please respond positively.

11.   Latent or early labour is the beginning of contractions that are regular or irregular up to the point where dilation begins to progress. It is the period in which there is no dilation of the cervix beyond 3-4 cm. Most midwives do not feel that if a woman has had contractions for several hours or days, that this should be dismissed or be unaccounted for merely because the midwife has not been able to recognise any change in the cervix or lower uterine segment. We therefore think that the presence of contractions should be acknowledged no matter how long it has been going on and whether or not there has been cervical change, and it should be included under the title "early labour."

12.   First stage of labour begins when contractions are of sufficient frequency, intensity, and duration to bring about progressive dilatation of the cervix (greater than 3 cm.), and ends when the cervix is sufficiently dilated to allow passage of the presenting fetal part (complete dilation).

13.   Anterior lip sometimes persists when the rest of the cervix has been "taken up". It may be caused by pushing or continue when the woman begins to push before she is completely dilated. A woman may begin to push but if the pushing is not effective because she is not fully dilated and the anterior lip is still there, second stage has not begun.

14.   Some women do not experience the plateau phase of 2nd stage. Others experience this break in which they are neither dilating nor pushing. Although this plateau stage of 2nd stage usually begins at complete dilatation of the cervix and ends at the point at which the mother begins to actively push her baby out, some women have already begun to push when they suddenly stop or fall asleep before they resume pushing. This would be considered plateau phase as well.

15.   In a compound presentation, an extremity prolapses alongside the presenting part with both entering the pelvis simultaneously.

16.   Birth defects are often difficult to categorize. Give enough detail, in the margin, of the nature of the defect and the need for treatment, etc. so we can evaluate severity if in doubt.

Questions or comments contact: Betty-Anne Daviss-Putt, Co-chair of MANA Research and Statistics Committee, 36 Glen Avenue, Ottawa, Ontario, CANADA K1S 2Z7; Phone (613) 730 0282 or 432 5701.

Midwives' Alliance of North America

FOURTEEN

Confessions of a Dissident

Marsden Wagner

One evening in the mid-1980s I found myself, a medical doctor, sitting in a small bar at a Swiss resort with three other speakers for a conference to begin the next morning: Rick Carlson, a lawyer, John McKnight, a sociologist, and Ivan Illich, a sociologist. Although we came from different professions, we had in common that our recent writings challenged the authoritative knowledge (AK) in medical care. Recognizing this, we began to chat about how we came to challenge that AK and what the roots of such behavior might be. Although we found no common denominator in childhood, we came to see that by the time we reached graduate school, each of us was disenchanted with the system and looking for ways to avoid getting sucked too deeply into it. We found that after finishing graduate school, all four of us went through some kind of gestation period during which we quietly worked our way up through the system. Only after we had some experience in our field and had achieved some measure of professional success did we begin to challenge medical AK.

Challenging an established body of authoritative knowledge—especially one that, as in medicine, is perpetrated by "the authorities"—involves at least two steps: recognizing its deficiencies and then wanting to correct those deficiencies strongly enough to be willing to speak out against the authority of the group. Here my father taught me well. He was a Protestant preacher who questioned from the pulpit the validity of literal translations of biblical passages and challenged conventional wisdom by, for example, placing a bench at the bus stop in front of his small church saying "Millions for armaments, how much for peace?" He put up that bench in early 1941 when everyone was preparing for war.

After medical school I marched through an orthodox specialty training in pediatrics and neonatology and eventually served as chief resident in pediatrics at the hospital of the University of California, Los Angeles. Following several years of active pediatric and neonatology practice, I was dissatisfied and restless, feeling that I was just practicing rescue medicine, not solving the child health problems of the community. So I returned to UCLA for two years of postgraduate study in the science of medicine and public health. The single most important thing that happened to me during those two years was being exposed to a different paradigm. While the medical paradigm focuses on the individual who comes for help, on sickness, on curing, and for the most part uses the biological approach, the public health paradigm focuses on populations, on health, on prevention, and uses a biopsychosocial approach. Once that paradigm shift happens, there is no turning back (see, e.g., Konner 1987:40).[1]

Taking a job as assistant professor of pediatrics and public health at UCLA, I found myself in two schools with two different paradigms. My attempts to merge the two were naive and ineffective. I was quickly marginalized in the Department of Pediatrics and the medical school. The only reason I was tolerated was because of my credentials as a clinician.

During this period I had an important experience. I went on a medical anthropology expedition to a settlement of preliterate Indians living in the Sierra Madre of Mexico. The group consisted of a faculty person from the medical school (me), a faculty person from the Department of Anthropology, several medical students, and several anthropology graduate students. At that time, medical anthropology was a relatively new discipline having difficulty bridging the gap between biomedicine and the healing systems of indigenous cultures. The idea behind the expedition was to teach students, before they were too ingrained in their discipline, true cross-disciplinary collaboration. In our camp one day there appeared a young Indian family—mother, father, daughter about six years old, and a baby of perhaps six months. The family had walked for several days to come to where we were camped and where an Indian healer also camped, because the baby was sick. They presented themselves first to us, and I got out my stethoscope and found a severe bilateral pneumonia. But before I could prepare the syringe of long-acting penicillin, the family left and went to the healer. After seeing the healer, they prepared to leave the camp and return home. Through an interpreter we learned that they thought that my use of the stethoscope was in fact our treatment. When we explained that we were not finished, they were adamant that they wanted no more treatment, as the healing was finished.

What to do? The students asked my opinion on what would happen if the baby did not receive the shot of penicillin. I honestly replied that the baby would almost surely die. An argument ensued as to our course of action, sadly split along disciplinary lines. The medical students said that we must save the baby's life with the shot, even against the parents' wishes.

The anthropology students said that such a course of action would be yet another step in destroying this culture and this family, without which neither this baby nor any other baby could survive. The clash of the paradigms, even at graduate student level, did not bode well for our original idea of influencing students while they were still young.

Our solution was a compromise that left no one happy. As the baby was being carried on the back of the six-year-old sister, we seduced her into our camp with candy and while her attention was diverted by a student, I sneaked up behind and quickly injected the baby without the sister's—or the parents'—knowledge. This whole experience pushed me farther along toward a fuller understanding of the limits of the medical model and its inability, in its headlong pursuit of curing and saving lives, to solve the health problems of the community.

During this time, my work in academic public health was not going where I wanted it to. While using what was for me the better paradigm, my public health colleagues were for the most part unwilling to confront real issues that might bring them into conflict with the medical world they both admired and feared. Furthermore, public health academia was removed from the real world of health policy and public health practice, and academicians had little wish to bridge the gaps between research, policy, and practice. So after eight years on the faculty, I elected to stay in public health rather than pediatrics, but to get out of the university setting and into public health practice.

My years in the Department of Maternal and Child Health of the California State Department of Public Health provided me with a whole different set of frustrations. My colleagues now feared both doctors and politicians. The politicians used the public health services as a sop to the poor and as a way of keeping the poor in their place. The doctors saw to it that our public health services used the one-on-one (doctor-patient) clinical model and blamed the victims, poor families, who failed to "comply" with us. Public health practice turned out to be a confusing mix of the medical model and the public health model with no room to maneuver, and no possibility for innovation.

It was when I started working as Responsible Officer for Maternal and Child Health for the World Health Organization (WHO) that, at last, I felt I had the right job. I was working in the European Regional Office, which meant that I worked with health systems in industrialized countries—my real interest. I still had the right paradigm, and although I was still surrounded by colleagues who were mostly afraid of change, at least now I did have the opportunity to develop my own program, which I quickly set about doing.

Shortly after I started at WHO in 1979, at an annual meeting the thirty-two countries in the European region complained that their perinatal services were costing more and more with not much evidence of improved benefits and little evaluation of efficacy. They suggested that our regional office evaluate birth services and report back to them. Since perinatal services were part of my responsibility, I was told to do such an evaluation.

I was less than enthusiastic because I had not been involved previously in maternity services. I had been imbued with obstetrical AK during my years of medical training, and never had any reason to doubt its validity. However, when I worked in the United States I had not been blind to some of the evils of the system: nurses doing most of the work and obstetricians getting most of the glory and the money; a double standard of care, one for private and another for publicly funded hospitals. While in California I had heard of an amazing experiment in a rural town that recruited two midwives (at that time such midwifery was illegal in California) to work in the public hospital. During the three years in which they handled most of the births, the incidence of prematurity dropped almost by half, and neonatal mortality dropped from 23.9 per thousand to 10.3 per thousand— less than half of what it had been before the midwives arrived. This success was followed, nonetheless, by a medical backlash. The program was discontinued, and the perinatal mortality rate returned to its previously high levels (Levy, Wilkinson, and Marine 1971). But, as an American, I knew essentially nothing about midwifery and, while curious about this experiment, I had failed to see its importance.

I had also experienced the births of my own four children. The obstetricians were so nice to me that it was not until the fourth birth that I realized that I had been patronized and denied the opportunity to be present at the births. So I asked the obstetrician at the UCLA hospital where I was on staff to allow me to be present, and he said no. To my everlasting chagrin, I complied. While I had questioned some of the workings of the maternity system, I had not questioned its fundamental authority.

Since I had no experience with maternity care systems, I decided to form a perinatal study group to work with me in evaluating maternity and neonatal services in Europe. In retrospect, the fact that I did not personally identify with obstetrics may have made me more open to what the group was soon to uncover. I started by including only obstetrics and neonatology in the study group, but as we worked I realized we needed other viewpoints, and so I gradually added nursing, midwifery, social science, and finally consumers. We started by reviewing the scientific literature and soon came across the gap between science and practice. To confirm this observation, we recruited a scientist not in the group to survey routine obstetrical procedures. We were shocked when the report from this scientist concluded that only approximately 10 percent of all routine obstetrical procedures had an adequate scientific basis (Fraser 1983).

The group decided to do cross-national surveys of present maternity care practices. We found that not only had this never been done cross-nationally, it also had never been done at a national or local level in many countries. In other words, there was little or no monitoring of maternity services. Our surveys showed great variation in obstetrical practices with little or no relationship to perinatal outcome (Bergsjo, Schmidt, and Pusch 1983). The variation was among countries, within countries, within districts, between hospitals. In other words, obstetrics reflected the opinions and wishes of the chief of obstetrics in a given hospital. The variations also reflected custom: every continental European country preferred the vacuum extractor; Britain and every former British colony preferred forceps. Such findings went a long way to disenchant me not only with "authoritative" knowledge but with authoritative practice (AP) as well.

At this time I began to make acquaintances and connections in the Danish midwifery community. Primary among them was a midwife, Susanne Houd. She played an instrumental role in exposing me to a system of knowledge radically different from obstetrical AK. These two systems in many ways complemented each other, but what was noteworthy was that I had never heard about midwifery knowledge from the obstetrical literature or from obstetricians. I began to study midwifery, and learned how it was a key profession in birthing in every country in the world outside of North America. I visited midwives in many settings in many countries to learn more about their work.

Susanne worked in a hospital (as do most European midwives) but also did some home birth. She asked me if I would like to accompany her to a home birth and I agreed. After asking the pregnant woman for permission, she took me along to a prenatal visit so I would not be a stranger at the time of birth. Already I was beginning to see that this was very different from the obstetrical approach, that the medical and social models of birth were completely distinct. It would be impossible for me to exaggerate the influence of my experience with home birth on my opinion of obstetrical authoritative knowledge and practice. Home birth is as different from hospital birth as night is from day. Trying to describe home birth is like trying to describe sexual intercourse—you can give the outlines, but you can never adequately describe the personal dynamics, feelings, ambience.

I went to home births in a number of countries to try to learn what I could about this way of birthing. I began to look at the scientific literature on home birth, and soon discovered that home birth had been a pivotal issue in the formation of obstetrical AK. It became clear that obstetrics had taken a completely irrational approach to home birth, which was most curious. The scientific data showed it to be as safe as hospital birth for a woman with an uncomplicated pregnancy, and yet obstetricians roundly condemned it. For example, Dr. Keith Russell, former president of the

American College of Obstetrics and Gynecology (ACOG), publicly declared in the *Los Angeles Times* (1992) that "home birth is child abuse in its earliest form." The fact that the Netherlands has never had a home birth rate under 30 percent and has birth outcomes equivalent to or better than neighboring countries is a huge thorn in the side of obstetrical AK. In my travels, I began to bring up the subject of home birth with obstetricians, inevitably getting only angry reactions. When speaking to roomfuls of obstetricians, I began to ask all those who had ever been present at a home birth to raise their hands. No one ever did.

Eventually it became clear to the group that there were two central issues in the debate over maternity services. The first issue concerned who was to control maternity services. Home birth was a subissue, since the hospital is doctor territory, where physicians have control, whereas they are not in control in the family territory of the home. A much larger and more central issue of control was the place of midwifery in maternity care. We gradually realized that the midwife-obstetrician controversy had been going on for at least two centuries. All over Europe, the obstetricians were succeeding in marginalizing midwives and gaining rather complete control of maternity services, in spite of clear evidence of benefit from midwifery.

The second issue was appropriate use of technology. The group soon uncovered the large gap between the scientific evidence and the widespread use of obstetrical technology. Generally speaking, governments were willing to go along with the "expert" opinions of the obstetricians regarding the use of technology, even in the face of scientific evidence to the contrary. Consequently, the group saw this issue as absolutely key to the evolution of maternity care, and it eventually became the focus of the activities that followed on the work of the group. We soon learned that when it came to questions about control (including home birth and midwifery) and technology, obstetricians were adamant and unwilling to consider change, even in the face of compelling evidence.

I became aware that our Perinatal Study Group had forgotten alternative services. Wherever I went, I sought out alternative birth practitioners and observed alternative birth practices, including such unorthodox innovations as underwater birth at the Black Sea in the former Soviet Union and the training of native Inuit women in the northern part of Quebec in Canada to be midwives in their own village (Stonier 1988; Daviss, this volume). I observed a cesarean section birth in China with one acupuncture needle in an earlobe as the only anesthesia and the woman wide awake throughout. (After the operation was concluded, the Western doctors present studied an acupuncture chart and said that since the lines on the chart did not follow nerve pathways, they could not accept what they had just seen with their own eyes—a paradigm clash.) The study group decided to do a cross-national survey of these alternative services, and recruited a mid-wife and a medical sociologist to do the study. The midwife, although fully accredited after orthodox training and practice, had also been involved in some alternative practices, and the sociologist had extensive experience with research in reproductive health. To our knowledge, such a survey of alternative birth had never been done, and the findings made it apparent that there was a vast knowledge completely outside of obstetrical AK. The findings became a chapter in the report of the study group (WHO 1985a).

From 1979 to 1985, our Perinatal Study Group met regularly to look at all of our literature summaries and research results and to debate, argue, and—yes—fight over what it all meant. There were too many unanswered questions regarding obstetrical knowledge and practice: why did it reject home birth out of hand? why did practices vary so widely? why did it not incorporate midwifery knowledge? why did it reject alternative knowledge? All of us in the group went through a long and painful process of confronting ourselves and each other and reevaluating our thinking.

We agreed at the beginning that scientific evidence would be the basis on which we must work. We met once a year for five days. The first day, some group members presented scientific reviews of agreed-upon subjects, and others presented surveys of services the group had asked them to conduct. The rest of the week was open discussion and debate, in an attempt to reach consensus on the issues the group had agreed to address. Ultimately, we did reach consensus on all these issues. We became friends and came more and more to respect each other, and this made it more and more difficult to hang on to our old beliefs. We were, of course, going through a paradigm shift of considerable magnitude that, in most cases, would affect our daily professional lives. No one in the group, most especially myself, was left unmoved or unchanged.

At the end of the Perinatal Study Group's five years of work, it was my responsibility to pull it all together into a report. I decided to write it without the usual WHO jargon, and to write it so that anybody could understand it. The result was a WHO book, *Having a Baby in Europe* (1985). I had many insights as I wrote because the process of writing forced me to organize all of the scientific literature, surveys, discussions, and experiences of the group. The result was a body of knowledge about maternity care very different from obstetrical AK, as the former is based on the public health paradigm while the latter is based on the medical paradigm. And this body of knowledge based on the public health paradigm would be hard to discredit, as it carried the heavy authority of WHO.

One example from the book will illustrate the nature of this public health–based maternity knowledge and how it departs from the orthodox medical paradigm.

By medicalizing birth, i.e., separating a woman from her own environment and surrounding her with strange people using strange machines to do strange things to her in an effort to assist her (and much or all of this may sometimes be necessary), the woman's state of mind and body is so altered that her way of carrying through this intimate act must equally be altered. The result is that it is no longer possible to know what births must have been like before these manipulations. Most health care providers no longer know what non-medicalized birth is. This is an overwhelmingly important issue. Almost all women in most developed countries in Europe give birth in hospital, leaving the providers of the birth services with no genuine yardstick against which to measure their care. What is the range for length of safe labor? What is the true [i.e., noniatrogenic] incidence of respiratory distress syndrome in newborn babies? What is the incidence of tears of the tissues surrounding the vaginal opening if the tissues are not first cut? What is the incidence of depression in women after "non-medicalized" birth? The answer to all these, and many more, questions is the same: no one knows. The entire modern obstetric and neonatological literature is essentially based on observations of medicalized birth. (WHO 1985a:85)

During a WHO visit to China, I realized that the developing world was—and is—in serious jeopardy of unquestioningly importing the orthodox obstetrical model. So I decided to try to export something else—the experience and newfound knowledge of the European Perinatal Study Group. Through WHO we organized a meeting in Beijing so that the group could spend a week in discussion with perinatal experts from all over China.

The meeting was such a success that I, together with the deputy director of the WHO Regional Office of the Americas, who was also at the meeting, was able to convince the European Regional Office of WHO to organize a series of three Consensus Conferences in collaboration with the Regional Office of the Americas. The purpose of the conferences would be to use the experience and knowledge of the Perinatal Study Group, together with thorough review of the scientific literature, as a basis for formulating recommendations for the appropriate use of technology before, during, and following birth. The way in which these meetings were organized, the recommendations generated, and their impact has been described in detail in a book, *Pursuing the Birth Machine* (Wagner 1994). In each Consensus Conference, we again lived through the clash of the orthodox obstetrical and neonatal AKs with the new AK emergent from the Perinatal Study Group and from the scientific literature and the painful struggle of the participants to resolve the differences and reach consensus. The result was an extraordinary set of consensus recommendations for appropriate perinatal technology (see table 14.1) which, when published in the *Lancet* (WHO 1985b, 1986a), started a deluge of angry protest from the obstetrical establishment.

Important lessons can be learned from the way in which the medical

TABLE 14.1 Birth Is Not an Illness: 15 Recommendations from the
World Health Organization, April 1985, Fortaleza, Brazil

These 15 recommendations are based on the principle that each woman has a fundamental right to receive proper prenatal care; that the woman has a central role in all aspects of this care; and that social, emotional, and psychological factors are decisive in the understanding and implementation of proper prenatal care.

- The whole community should be informed about various procedures in birth care, to enable each woman to choose the type of birth care she prefers.
- The training of professional midwives or birth attendants should be promoted. Care during normal pregnancy and birth, and following birth, should be the duty of this profession.
- There is no justification in any specific geographic region to have more than 10 to 15% cesarean section births.
- There is no evidence that a cesarean section is required after a previous transverse low segment cesarean section birth. Vaginal deliveries after cesarean should normally be encouraged wherever emergency surgical capacity is available.
- There is no evidence that routine electronic fetal monitoring during labor has a positive effect on the outcome of pregnancy.
- There is no indication for pubic shaving or a pre-delivery enema.
- Pregnant women should not be put in a lithotomy position [flat on the back] during labor or delivery. They should be encouraged to walk during labor and each woman must freely decide which position to adopt during delivery.
- The systematic use of episiotomy [incision to enlarge the vaginal opening] is not justified.
- Birth should not be induced [started artificially] for convenience, and the induction of labor should be reserved for specific medical indications. No geographic region should have rates of induced labor over 10%.
- During labor, the routine administration of analgesic or anesthetic drugs, that are not specifically required to correct or prevent a complication in delivery, should be avoided.
- Artificial early rupture of the membranes as a routine process is not scientifically justified.
- The healthy newborn must remain with the mother, whenever both their conditions permit it. No process of observation of the healthy newborn justifies a separation from the mother.
- The immediate beginning of breastfeeding should be promoted, even before the mother leaves the delivery room.
- Obstetric care services that have critical attitudes toward technology and that have adopted an attitude of respect for the emotional, psychological, and social aspects of birth should be identified. Such services should be encouraged and the processes that have led them to their position must be studied so that they can be used as models to foster similar attitudes in other centers and to influence obstetrical views nationwide.
- Governments should consider developing regulations to permit the use of new birth technology only after adequate evaluation.

establishment has attempted to discredit *Having a Baby in Europe* and the consensus recommendations. With regard to the knowledge in these publications, I do not know of any attempt to directly challenge their validity or "truth": there are no articles that take on specific recommendations to show why they were not scientifically justified, no requests to debate the specifics. Rather, other strategies were employed. One was to say that the recommendations were relevant only to the Third Word (i.e., maybe the knowledge is valid but it doesn't apply to us). But by far the most common approach has been to attack the authority rather than the knowledge.

Many times, I have witnessed how if a midwife, nurse, or layperson (including social scientists) makes statements supporting the public health model of maternity services, the advocates of obstetrical AK assume a condescending posture and dismiss this person as ignorant, not worthy of attention. But because of my credentials as medical specialty practitioner, my earlier academic appointments, and my position with WHO (and also perhaps the fact that I am a man), this approach was obviously not appropriate for me. Something different was required. So the strategy in my case was to attempt to isolate me from the study group and from WHO and take away my authority by discrediting me. Most of the attempts at discrediting were carried out behind my back, so that I would have no chance to respond.

The one chance I was given to confront my critics in public was a most interesting experience. I had begun to collaborate with Patricia St. Clair, a health service researcher interested in women's health issues, and we had been writing and speaking about the low efficacy, high risk, and high cost of in vitro fertilization (IVF) (Wagner and St. Clair 1989). To my surprise, I was invited to debate IVF at the next international meeting of IVF clinicians. On arriving at the conference hall, I accidentally stumbled into the small room where all those involved in the debate except me had been invited for briefing. The organizers were embarrassed and pretended to have invited me. The debate was held in a large hall. Present were more than one thousand IVF clinicians from many countries. Following the debate, members from the audience could ask questions. When I was asked if it was not true that everything I said was my personal opinion and had nothing to do with WHO, the audience cheered. It was clear that I had been set up. Fortunately, we had already held an official WHO meeting in Copenhagen on IVF and had generated WHO consensus recommendations (WHO 1990). So I replied that everything I had said was included in an official WHO report and pointed to a large pile of WHO reports in several languages lying at the front edge of the stage, suggesting that the audience was welcome to take copies. Most of the audience immediately queued up to get a copy of the WHO report. Their attempt to disassociate me from WHO in public (there were many journalists in the audience) had backfired. Such an experience might discourage direct confrontation.

Similar skepticism was evident in the orthodox obstetric establishment in Germany. When the German Obstetrical Association wrote to their Ministry of Health demanding that home birth be outlawed, I wrote to the same Ministry of Health suggesting that we organize a meeting in Germany to discuss the scientific information on home birth. The association replied that they would never meet with me because I was "subjective and incapable of rational discussion on home birth."

In the opening speech to over two thousand obstetricians at a recent annual meeting of the European Congress of Perinatal Medicine (at which I was not present), Professor Saling, an obstetrician from Berlin, spent several minutes attacking me by name. I was "against the health of mother and child," I was "against modern obstetrics," and I did not understand that the negative effects of obstetrics that I was pointing out were due to the few individual doctors who do not follow modern obstetrics: "As an epidemiologist and nonobstetrician he doesn't understand the difference between good and bad obstetricians." And of course, "he cannot be taken seriously as a scientist."

Attempts to personally discredit me are usually of three types. First, I am not an obstetrician, and only obstetricians have the necessary expertise. My answer to this is to use an analogy that is easily understood by my (sports-oriented) critics. Maternity care is a football game and the obstetricians are the players running up and down the field. But every good team has a coach (reproductive scientist) who does not play but is on the sideline carefully watching the overall patterns of play. The best play is the result of combining the observations of players and coach (Wagner 1989). It is extraordinary how the use of the analogy quickly neutralizes this objection.

The second common accusation is that I am not objective. Doctors have been saying this to women, patients, and politicians for a long time. Such a strategy backfires, however, when it is identified as part of a discredited paradigm—the classical Cartesian model (Wagner 1982). It is extraordinary that medical education still fails to teach the scientific realities that there is no such thing as objectivity and that every doctor is as subjective as his or her patient.

How often I have heard that I am against progress. To criticize technology is tantamount to criticizing science and progress. The misunderstanding that technology = science = progress is widespread in medicine. A strange dichotomy exists in which if I am not in favor of all technology, I am against all technology—you are with us or against us. I find it necessary to repeat often that the technology is not bad but can be misused, that doctors are not bad but can make mistakes.

Attempts to discredit me have sometimes gone to extremes. A group of Australian doctors wrote to the general director of WHO demanding that I be fired. A group of doctors in England started a rumor that I had indeed been fired and reported this to a journalist who, fortunately, checked the story first by calling me before he printed it. Such attempts are more understandable when one realizes that if a doctor steps out of line, his colleagues are usually able to reel in the dissident through local sanctions.

The first sanction usually applied to a local physician is to take away hospital privileges. This is easy, since the decision to do so rests in the hands of other local doctors who can do this in secret. But there are usually other hospitals in the community that the dissident doctor can use. A much tougher sanction is to bring the doctor before some medical tribunal that may decide to suspend or take away a license to practice. While the overt purpose of such tribunals is to protect the community from doctors clearly unable to practice due to alcohol, drug abuse, and so on, they can and have been used to discredit doctors who do not follow the rules of the "club" (see below) and of orthodox medical AK.

Wendy Savage is an obstetrician practicing in London who refused to follow all the edicts of the local old boys' obstetrical network. She consistently offered her patients unconventional choices and options and worked to train residents to treat patients humanistically as well. Displeased with her innovations, her department chairman took the opportunity of a baby's death to suspend Savage's license to practice and institute a formal inquiry. The mother, a Bangladeshi, had requested a trial of labor after a previous cesarean, which Savage allowed but which was not standard practice at the time. The baby was ultimately delivered by cesarean and seemed healthy at birth, but died two days later. Because she went public with the case and received extensive media coverage and popular support, and because her lawyer was able to force the tribunal to open its sessions to the public, she was acquitted (Savage 1986). (It is noteworthy that the old rule "once a cesarean, always a cesarean" is gradually being thrown out of obstetrical AK and a "trial of labor" is now standard practice in some countries, although not, for example, in Australia.)

Peter Lucas, a general practitioner in Melbourne, Australia, was not so lucky. Because he attends some home births and backs up home birth midwives, he was brought before a closed-door tribunal and suspended for four months. His case typifies many others. It is important to remember that only medical doctors sit on these tribunals, so such "peer review" can all too easily become a mechanism for protecting orthodoxy. In the United States, a typical means of forestalling physicians who try to back up home birth midwives is that they are denied insurance by the physicians who sit on the boards of the insurance companies in their communities.

As a WHO staff person, not a practicing M.D., I was immune from the usual sanctions, and new avenues of attack had to be found. Getting me fired would accomplish two purposes—discrediting me and separating me from WHO. Having WHO's name on the books and recommendations that I helped to write gives such authority to the knowledge that it obviously has made problems. So there have been many attempts at this kind of separation. In his speech, Saling said, "These are *his* opinions and have no relation to the official policies of WHO."

Many similar experiences over the past few years have forced me once again to reconsider my assumptions about the medical profession. When I speak in public, as I often do, about the gaps between science and medical practice, I am always met with the reasonable question, But why? Why would intelligent doctors continue practices that science has shown to be wrong? The public finds this difficult to believe, much less accept, and in the beginning so did I. But as the power of the profession was turned against me I came gradually to realize that I had misconstrued the medical profession. Doctors are not bad individuals, but they are human and members of their community and have all the biases and motivations that entails. Furthermore, as a group they often focus on concerns irrelevant to people's health. I remember being somewhat taken aback when I first realized as a young doctor that the American Academy of Pediatrics, of which I was a member, had two goals: to advance the health of children and to advance the well-being of pediatricians. In this second role, the academy functioned like a labor union, and if the two goals came into conflict, as sometimes happened, the second goal almost always took precedence. It became more and more clear that there were many determinants of medical practice, some having nothing at all to do with health. This realization about the nature of doctors and what makes them tick was another revelation for me that became part of the paradigm shift I was making. Eventually my insights into the nature of doctors led to another paper, "Birth and Power" (Wagner 1986).

The list of nonhealth determinants of medical practice is long; a few illustrations from maternity care will suffice to show where my thinking and observations were leading me. I saw that commercial pressures are ever-present. For example, the International Federation of Obstetrics and Gynecology organized a meeting to make recommendations for the use of the electronic fetal monitor. The travel and local costs of the participants were paid for by the industries making the monitors, and to get into the room, it was necessary to pass through a large commercial display of monitors. When I wrote to the obstetrician who had organized the meeting, expressing my concern for possible conflict of interest, he wrote back, indignantly assuring me that he was at all times "objective." My concern remained, since the meeting recommended routine electronic monitoring of all births, although the scientific literature did not and does not justify such a recommendation (Leveno et al. 1986; Prentice and Lind 1987; see Goer 1995:131–153 for summaries of 39 medical studies relevant to electronic fetal monitoring).

Custom and habits are determinants of practice; how else to explain that for operative vaginal birth, forceps are used in Britain and its former colonies while the rest of the world uses the vacuum extractor? Convenience is the best explanation for the fact that induction of labor is so common in many countries that there are statistically significantly fewer births on weekends and at night. Willingness to change involves willingness to admit that you have been doing it wrong. This may help to explain why most obstetricians still prefer the woman to deliver on her back with her legs up during birth even though we have known for decades that, scientifically speaking, that is the worst possible position. Territory, power, and control are certainly involved in the way obstetrics has tried for a long time to suppress midwifery practice (see Arney 1982). Most recently, studies by medical anthropologists have shown me how many obstetrical routines have cultural rather than medical determinants (Kitzinger 1978; Konner 1987; Martin 1987; Rothman 1982, 1989). Robbie Davis-Floyd (1992;104–111), for example, notes that the routine use of the electronic monitor conveys to birthing women the message that their bodies are defective machines dependent on these man-made machines and the authoritative knowledge vested in the technical experts who can manipulate and interpret them. She suggests that these and other routine obstetric practices make not scientific but ritual and symbolic sense as transmitters of technocratic core values. From my perspective, such insights are valid and useful, but they would be rejected out of hand by orthodox adherents.

When I speak about such nonmedical determinants of practice, I am told I am "doctor-bashing." Any criticism whatsoever of physicians is called "doctor-bashing." Whence comes this term? I can criticize my auto mechanic and I am not "bashing." I can tell a joke about lawyers and I am not accused of lawyer-bashing. (Note the paucity of doctor jokes, most of which are about how godlike doctors are.) As part of my paradigm shift, I came to realize that the medical profession has a set of mechanisms meant to set them apart from the rest of society, to protect them from any outside interference and make their AK and AP sacrosanct. To not be able to say something negative about doctors without being labeled a doctor-basher is just such a mechanism. Another is obvious—to insist that one cannot possibly understand the obstetrical paradigm unless one is an obstetrician.

The trappings of doctors are another mechanism to set us apart. Why do doctors wear white coats? There are certainly no hygienic reasons for it: white material is no cleaner than any other color of material, and darker colors would certainly be more practical. Yet I can go to any country in the world, visit any hospital, and there, without fail, are the white coats. When

I was an intern at the UCLA hospital there was even a strict hierarchy of white coats—one type for interns, another for residents, another for attending physicians. Of course, white is on top of the color scale in many countries, especially Western ones. It symbolizes refinement and purity, as in white flour, white rice, and white sugar (all of which have had their nutrients stripped away). It is the color of priestly vestments—as Robert Mendelsohn so aptly pointed out in *Confessions of a Medical Heretic* (1979), the hospital has become the cathedral of the twentieth century.

Why do we put "Doctor" in front of physicians' names in everyday conversation? We don't say "Lawyer Jones." The only other profession with such an honorary title in everyday language, not surprisingly, is the clergy. So often I have heard a doctor who is addressed as "Mister Brown" correct the speaker and say "It is Doctor Brown." From long personal experience I can assure the reader that being called "Doctor" morning, noon, and night has a profound effect on one's self-image. For some years now I have carried out an interesting experiment. I have tried to excise "Doctor" from my name—from everyday conversation, from letters, from participant labels at meetings, and so on. It is difficult to do so. If I say to someone, "Please don't call me Doctor, as that is not what my mother named me," they are confused and embarrassed, and often I get the impression they think I am a crackpot. But the most difficult problem, sad to say, has been with myself. Normally I find it a relief not to be called Doctor, but from time to time I am sorely tempted. When I am trying to get action from someone, all I have to do is use "Doctor" and things happen. This is especially true if I am dealing with a hospital or physician's office where the use of "Doctor" immediately creates an atmosphere of subservience around me. Small wonder that "Doctors" soon come to believe that they and their AK and AP are beyond reproach.

Why do doctors have "patients"? Other professionals have "clients," something very different. Clients hire professionals to perform services for them—they call the shots. But turning a person into a "patient" redefines that person as someone who is sick and under a doctor's supervision—automatically a dependent position. Because pregnancy and birth are not illnesses, I have worked hard the past ten years not to use the word "patient" in maternity care. For example, in *Having a Baby in Europe,* the word "patient" never appears. When speaking or writing about maternity care, health professionals often use "mother," again an unfortunate term since it refers only to the woman in her role as a mother and not to the whole person. So I try to use "woman." Several years ago I finally convinced WHO in Europe to change "Maternal and Child Health" (used everywhere in the world) to "Women's and Children's Health."

Another mechanism to protect medical authoritative knowledge and practice is, as we have seen, for all doctors to join together into an extremely powerful private club known as the medical profession. I have been a member of this club since I took the Hippocratic oath on the day of my graduation from medical school. One central rule of this club is never to criticize other doctors or medical AK or AP in public. As early as medical school, we were told that the doctor who does so is a traitor to the profession.

One day about ten years ago I received a call from a criminal lawyer in Toronto, Canada. She was desperate because for the first time in her career she had a case involving health professionals and was having great difficulty finding any doctor willing to testify in court. Her clients were two midwives who had attended a home birth after which the baby died. Midwifery had been illegal for the last one hundred years in every Canadian province and, with this death, the local obstetricians went to the coroner demanding an inquest. Several obstetricians had agreed to testify for the prosecution at the inquest, but although the lawyer had found several doctors who told her "off the record" that the midwives had done nothing wrong and were not culpable, they would not testify to this in a courtroom open to the public. I went to Toronto and in my testimony at the coroner's inquest talked about midwifery. The members of the jury knew nothing about midwifery but listened as I talked about the central role of midwives in maternity care in the rest of the world. I was simply giving the midwifery AK, as well as the AK developed by our WHO study group. At the end of the trial the jury wrote a ten-page report demanding that the government investigate making midwifery legal. The government eventually did so, and in 1992, midwifery became legal in the province of Ontario.

Shortly thereafter, I testified in another case involving two midwives in Vancouver. Again a leading obstetrician testified for the prosecution. In this case, there was no jury, only a judge. It should not have surprised me that the judge decided against the midwives. Judges, of course, are like doctors—members of the power elite in the community and much more likely to believe in the authority of the local doctor, whom they most likely know socially. Since then I have testified in court in a number of countries, and in every case involving a jury the midwife (or doctor practicing an alternative approach) has won while in every case involving only a judge she has lost (Wagner 1995).

As noted above, doctors are quite willing to see litigation against midwives or dissident doctors but strongly object to the use of the public courts for litigation against doctors. But as long as the complaint system (for those feeling they have been poorly treated by doctors) is physician controlled, the public has no choice but to use the public courts if they are to prevent the possibility of conspiratorial cover-up and get a fair hearing of their complaint. The medical profession believes that systems of knowledge and practice differing in any respect from orthodox medical AK should be judged only by themselves, behind closed doors.

The paradigm shift that helped me to better understand the medical profession also helped me to better understand the public health profession. Public health practitioners are also human, and the determinants of their practice often have little to do with the health of the public. Many public health practitioners are also doctors and members of the club, and not about to go against the rules. But even those who are not have two problems that seriously interfere with their job. In general, they have less power than the medical profession and live in fear for their jobs. And they are confronted by the dilemma that to carry out their primary role—protect the health of the public—they may be called on to take actions that will not make the doctors happy. I have had countless arguments with public health practitioners who insist that the best strategy is always to keep the doctors happy and quietly bring them along. But sooner or later, a case will come along in which they must take a stand to support either the public or the doctors. Their allegiance to the medical club is so strong that most often they cannot go against the club, and the public is the loser.

A simple example will illustrate how public health practitioners acquiesce to the power of medical practitioners. In many countries, fortunately, it is becoming more common to collect data on the practices of hospitals and clinics. These data are collated at the central level by public health authorities who feed them back to the practitioners. So far so good. But how about giving these data to the public so they can make informed choices about which hospital, clinic, or physician to choose? Needless to say, the doctors are against this: they do not want information about their individual practices available to the public ("who can't understand it anyway"), as they are concerned about unfavorable comparisons with other doctors. The result is that in many places these data are still not available to the general public, or, if they are, they do not identify the hospital, clinic, or doctor. I have argued without success against this latter strategy with public health practitioners in Denmark, France, Luxembourg, Australia, and the United States.

Several years ago I went to Leipzig for an annual meeting of a European perinatal organization attended by hundreds of obstetricians. A leading obstetrician gave a lecture on the history of maternity care that covered all the outstanding medical breakthroughs and advances of the past century and the high level of current obstetrical knowledge. The presentation was so unbalanced that during the ensuing discussion I (naively) tried to bring some better balance by noting that some important history was left out, such as the DES (diethylstilbestrol) and thalidomide disasters. Immediately the speaker and audience became quite hostile to me. Gradually, I have come to realize that the central purpose of medical meetings is not the presentation of balanced reports but rather to provide a reconfirmation of the correctness of the obstetrical AK.

Such medical meetings, of course, also serve to confirm the correctness of current obstetrical AP. The most common type of paper at such meetings is a case series from a doctor or clinic demonstrating the efficacy of a particular procedure (a scientific methodology with low validity). Several times in discussions at meetings I have pointed out that our practice and judgment are not infallible. Death is the great enemy, and, according to the medical club, we must carefully hide our failures. Maternal mortality audits and perinatal audits, in which the deaths of women and babies are analyzed, are always done in secret committee. The fact that these committees find a significant proportion of deaths to have been preventable and to have resulted from mistakes in clinical judgment does not usually reach public awareness. In *Pursuing the Birth Machine* I wrote,

> The fact that caesarean section carries serious risks for both woman and baby seems to be one of modern civilization's best-kept secrets. Why is it that an article in a leading American obstetrical journal proving that elective repeat caesarean section has a 6 times higher maternal mortality than vaginal birth (Pettiti et al. 1982) had no apparent effect on the rapidly rising caesarean section rate in that country? Why can a leading medical journal, in all apparent seriousness, publish an article suggesting that all births be caesarean sections (Feldman and Freidman 1985)? Why is it that when the possibility of caesarean section arises, women are *not* told as part of their informed consent that the procedure increases the chance of their dying and increases the chance that their baby will have a life-threatening illness? [1994:185–186]

Orthodox obstetrical AK does not allow sufficient attention to death or to public discussions of deficiencies in knowledge and practice.

After learning that medical meetings are not good forums for balanced debate, I gradually turned more and more to the scientific journals as better places to discuss critical issues. At least in the journals one can argue substance and in a few of the best journals, hope to get a balanced approach. In the *Lancet*, for example, it was even possible to get a paper published which discusses the pros and cons of medical AK versus public health AK (Stephenson and Wagner 1993a).

I gradually learned also to turn to the public for debate on maternity care. Not only is this the appropriate audience (it is they who are having babies, not us), but strategically it is much more effective because, although doctors may have vast expertise behind closed doors, they usually flounder when addressing the public—a result of their condescending attitudes and patronizing approach. I started by accepting requests for interviews for newspapers, television, and popular magazines. Later, I became more proactive about publicity, and would call a journalist myself if something important came along.

I also collaborated more and more with consumer groups such as Foraeldre og Foedsel (Parents and Birth) in Denmark, the Active Birth Movement in Italy, the Association for the Improvement of Maternity Services in Britain, Femme–Sage-Femme (Women and Midwives) in France. These groups and many others have played key roles in opening up the debate and providing more options in maternity services. My knowledge base has been broadened greatly by my association with such groups. Whenever there have been real confrontations between consumer groups and the medical club over maternity services, the consumer groups prevail (see Szurek, this volume). The most effective collaboration seems to combine three elements: a few doctors and scientists who are knowledgeable about obstetrical AK, midwifery AK, public health AK, and the current scientific literature and who are willing to go public; interested journalists not intimidated by doctors; and consumer groups not controlled by health professionals and not afraid to aggressively go public.

Just after the publication of *Having a Baby in Europe*, a Danish midwife and I were discussing how to promote this new knowledge. She suggested we start with Denmark and organize a "birth conference." We approached the Danish consumer group Foraeldre og Foedsel and they were enthusiastic about collaborating. The Danish organization of obstetricians and gynecologists and the Danish organization of midwives also agreed to participate. The conference was held in the WHO building in Copenhagen and was a big success.

The Birth Conference was an idea whose time had come. In the past eight years there have been over fifty similar conferences in over twenty countries. They have varied from country to country; for example, in Eastern Europe there are no consumer groups as yet and the local organizer is usually a public health authority; while in Western Europe the initial local organizer often is a consumer group or a midwife organization. But they all have WHO input and involve bringing together what we call "all interested parties," by which we mean any groups or disciplines or individuals in the community with interest in or responsibility for maternity services. While we at WHO initiated most of the conferences in the beginning, by now they are all locally initiated and continue to pop up everywhere. The central purpose of the birth conferences is to legitimate and confirm the midwifery AK and public health AK found in the WHO publications and to use this knowledge to stimulate change in maternity services. As such, these conferences are the mirror opposite of obstetrical meetings whose central purpose is to reaffirm the obstetrical AK and the status quo.

The atmosphere of the two types of conference is equally different. It is not unfair to describe the ambience of obstetrical meetings as serious self-importance. The participants are mostly men who have exchanged their white coats for dark suits and ties. The ambience of the birth conferences is earnest joyfulness. Participants are mostly women, and it is difficult to get too serious and stuffy with crying babies and breastfeeding mothers everywhere to remind us what this work is really all about.

The methodology of the birth conferences is also different from medical meetings. They are open to the public, and every attempt is made to involve all interested parties, including midwives, physicians, epidemiologists, social scientists, health administrators, consumer groups, and, very important, the media. Presentations on the present status of local birth services are followed by presentations on WHO recommendations and the latest scientific findings. The discussions that follow focus on bringing the local services closer to what WHO and the science suggest. These discussions constitute confrontations between obstetrical AK and midwife and public health AK, or, put another way, a struggle between the medical paradigm and the public health/midwifery paradigms. Finally, an attempt is made to generate consensus recommendations for changes in local maternity services. There is usually considerable media coverage afterward.

The birth conferences can bring surprises to some of the participants, especially physicians only familiar with medical meetings. I remember that during the first birth conference in Denmark, the doctor who was head of the ultrasound department at the university hospital gave a glowing account of the wonders of obstetrical ultrasound. There followed a discussion in which participants brought forward the lack of scientific documentation for his assertions and the fact that not one experimental trial had yet shown efficacy for routine scanning during pregnancy. The physician in question was most dismayed with what for him was clearly an unusual reaction to his standard speech. Similarly, at one of the most recent birth conferences, organized by the Midwives' Association of Luxembourg in 1993, I presented data on how the use of obstetrical interventions in Luxembourg far exceeds WHO recommendations, following which there was a heated debate between the obstetricians and the midwives over these practices. At the end of the conference a local obstetrician told me he was shocked, as the doctors had agreed to come because "we expected to have a friendly chat with the girls."

The birth conferences have had a variety of impacts, some planned and some not. There is no question that they have served to raise the awareness of the public health paradigm's approach to maternity care and to legitimize it. They have also raised awareness about the gap between science and obstetrical AK and about the need for change. And the birth conferences have started a process of building in midwives and consumers the capacity to read, understand, and use the scientific literature. These conferences serve as opportunities to identify those in the community really interested in changing maternity services. Here there may also be surprises. While it is common to invite the more liberal doctors in a given community, they are often exposed during the discussions as being interested only in minor changes around the edges of obstetrical AK, but not at all in giving up the core obstetrical AK and the power that goes with it. Such physicians are often upset during the conference because they are used to being seen as progressive and being attacked from the right, but they are not used to attacks from the left. Surprisingly, however, allies for the public health approach may be found among conservatives. Conservative politicians may see choice at birth as a way to promote conservative values such as individuality and a strong family. Conservative older physicians, trained before the high-technology takeover of obstetrics, may prefer a more cautious and humanistic approach to health care.

Birth conferences have also served to jump-start or accelerate the process of change in maternity care. One of the reasons we pushed ahead with promoting these conferences was because of what happened after the first birth conference in Denmark. Shortly before the conference, the Danish minister of the interior (responsible for health), a woman and a conservative politician, had decided that the present guidelines for maternity services, more than ten years old, needed revision. She asked the National Board of Health to carry this out. The National Board of Health, in turn, asked a leading professor of obstetrics to revise the guidelines, which he was happy to do. The revised guidelines were passed on to the minister, who did not like what she saw but was not sure why, and felt insecure about criticizing a physician and professor.

Then the next morning in the daily newspaper the minister read a long article about the just-finished birth conference. She recognized that many of her concerns about the revised guidelines paralleled the issues discussed at the conference. She wrote to WHO, enclosing a copy of the revised guidelines and asking that we meet with her. The Danish midwife and I wrote a short critique of the guidelines and met with the minister, urging her to get opinions from all interested parties in Denmark. She did just that, and the result was a new set of guidelines completely different from the first revision. Instead of being based only on obstetrical AK, they were based much more on midwifery and public health knowledge. This was an easily visible direct impact of the birth conference. Usually the impact is slower, less direct, and less visible, although from time to time, such as in Italy, Austria, Britain, and Russia, the impact has been clear.

The reaction of the higher-ups at the World Health Organization has been quite ambivalent. The good news is that when *Having a Baby in Europe* became the best-seller among WHO publications, the management in the

European Regional Office was most pleased and proud. The usual standard operating procedure in WHO is to organize "expert" meetings, publish a report, and move on to something else. There was no precedent for going out into the real world to promote the reports or recommendations through collaboration with professional and lay groups. Nevertheless, our efforts to promote appropriate perinatal technology were well received by a small but critical mass within the European office. There were a few key WHO staff people who understood the public health paradigm and let us know that they believed in our work, most important, the director general in Geneva and the regional director in Copenhagen in the early 1980s. Without their support we could never have succeeded in our tradition-breaking efforts.

The bad news is that the great majority of WHO staff have come to the organization straight from the medical world and brought with them the medical AK and allegiance to the medical club. These staff people truly did not understand my efforts, except that I was breaking the rules of the club and making doctors angry. I was seen as a real troublemaker, and could cite countless examples of their efforts to stop me. For one, my immediate director in Copenhagen blocked my plans for the three Consensus Conferences until I went over his head to the regional director and the general director. When another director told me to stop and I refused, he said that if it were up to him, he would fire me, but for some reason, the regional director would not allow him to do it (see below). This same director threatened to take away the funding for my program if I didn't conform to his notion of what I should be doing. When I refused, he took away most of my funding, leaving the Women's and Children's Health Program with, for example, fewer funds than a very medically oriented program for the management of diabetes. But because of all the support I had generated in the countries in my region, I was able to proceed with my program. Financial sanctions are a typical way for the medical club to force conformity to the obstetrical AK. In Germany, many insurance companies will not reimburse a family for a birth if it takes place in an alternative birth clinic. In Australia and other countries, government health insurance will not reimburse midwives for a home birth.

Many attempts were made to stop or change my writings. When I began to publish scientific articles running counter to the medical AK, I was told that all of my writings must be approved by management before I could submit them to journals. I told them this was scientific censorship and I would quit first, and they backed off. The management in the European Office in Copenhagen originally was in favor of my writing a sequel to *Having a Baby in Europe*. However, by this time there was a new regional director in Copenhagen and a new director general in Geneva, and when this new management saw the drafts of *Pursuing the Birth Machine,* they wanted to make such substantial changes that the result would be a watered-down and confusing compromise between the medical and public health paradigms. It was necessary to have this second book published outside WHO. When my article appeared comparing the medical approach used at WHO headquarters in Geneva with the public health approach used in the WHO European Regional Office in Copenhagen (Stephenson and Wagner 1993a), the response of the relevant director in Geneva was not to debate the issue but to attack me for going public.

WHO has an extraordinary means of operation. As I mentioned earlier, a great deal of time and resources go into organizing "expert committee" meetings to consider particular issues in health services. When the committee's final report is published, it contains the disclaimer, "The views expressed in this publication are those of the participants and do not necessarily represent the decisions or stated policy of WHO." When our recommendations on in vitro fertilization were published in a leading medical journal, WHO headquarters in Geneva was angry and wrote a letter to the editor (never published) with the above disclaimer. When the recommendations from *Having a Baby in Europe* or the three Consensus Conferences (all can be found in official WHO publications) are included in my speeches or interviews, and a reader or listener writes to WHO with a complaint, they are sent the disclaimer instead of an explanation that I am making recommendations from a WHO report. The paradox that WHO makes recommendations and then refuses to take responsibility for them must be the result of wanting to be involved in improving the health of the world while, at the same time, never making doctors angry.

Some of WHO's work, for example, the reports "Primary Health Care" from Alma-Ata (WHO 1978a) and *Regional Targets for Health for All* (WHO 1986b) from Copenhagen are based on the public health approach and are outstanding, but the organization has not been able to promote these publications aggressively enough because they contain ideas counter to medical orthodoxy and therefore might displease ministries of health and/or physicians. Both of these WHO documents emphasize the important role of nonphysician health workers such as the midwife and the traditional birth attendant (TBA). Yet for many years there was no midwife on the regular staff in WHO headquarters in Geneva or WHO's European Regional Office in Copenhagen. There is very little possibility for WHO headquarters to influence the regional offices or vice versa. The WHO headquarters' programs for TBAs always tended to emphasize how *we* might train *them,* never honoring their indigenous knowledge or trying to empower them in an egalitarian way as primary health care workers (see Pigg, this volume). Attempts by the European Perinatal Study Group and the subsequent WHO Consensus Conference recommendations to empower midwives and bring back their central role in maternity care in the industrialized countries met with resistance from doctors both within and outside of WHO.

The considerable media coverage I have received makes WHO management nervous. They must agree with me that our primary responsibility is to the people, but they say, again and again, that our credibility depends on our being seen as a serious, scientific organization. Similarly, when the Danish midwife and I received a prize from the Danish consumer organization Foraeldre og Foedsel for our contribution to improving birth care in Denmark, WHO didn't know how to react. No WHO staff person had ever received a prize from consumers—was this good or bad?

Three strategies evolved in my attempt to coexist with WHO. First, whatever I say or write must have a solid scientific basis. This has saved me countless times. For one example, in a speech in Edinburgh I said that birth in Scotland was at least in part based on the convenience of doctors, since there were fewer births at night and on weekends. This comment made the front page of the Sunday paper there and precipitated an angry phone call from the director of health for Scotland to my regional director. I suspect the regional director heaved a sigh as he picked up the phone to call me yet again and ask what this was all about. I was able to give him the exact reference from the scientific literature for a Scottish study showing that the excessive use of artificial induction resulted in a statistically significant decrease in births at night and on the weekends. My regional director was able to call Scotland back with scientific justification for my remarks and thus support me in my work.

Second, whenever possible, I made sure that recommendations were made by a "group of experts" rather than by me personally. Recently I made a mistake that shows the value of the group approach. I had done a survey of the scientific literature on in vitro fertilization and drafted a paper that was highly critical of present services. I sent a copy of the draft to someone in WHO headquarters asking for a personal critique. To my shock and without asking me, he sent the draft to a number of IVF clinicians all over the world. A deluge of angry letters to WHO followed. Learning about this, my regional director suggested that I bring together a group of "experts" to consider the issue. I did just that (although the "experts" included all interested parties), and the result was a WHO report saying pretty much what my first draft had said. Now, however, it has the authority to go along with the knowledge.

Third, perhaps the most important strategy was an unwitting one. From the beginning of my tenure at WHO I spent a good deal of my time "in the field" and developed good relationships with my official public health and medical counterparts in governmental and nongovernmental organizations in many countries. Then, when I began to promote the new birth recommendations, I came into frequent contact with many unofficial counterparts including midwifery organizations, consumer groups, social scientists, and health service researchers in many countries. Later, when efforts to have me fired were under way, my regional director mentioned my "broad power base in many countries" and I suddenly realized that there were a lot of people "out there" who would support me. This was the reason, as mentioned earlier, that one of the directors told me that he couldn't fire me because the regional director found it politically impossible. It is important to point out that when all was said and done, WHO did support my work and all the recommendations in their publications based on the public health paradigm.

Brigitte Jordan ([1978] 1993) defines authoritative knowledge as legitimate, consequential, and worthy of discussion, as the knowledge on the basis of which, in a given community, decisions are made and actions taken. In effect, all my efforts at WHO, as well as the efforts of many dedicated individuals, have been directed at expanding the body of knowledge recognized as authoritative in obstetrics, at opening it up to include the authority of birthing women, midwives, scientific researchers, and public health advocates and professionals. These efforts are part of the global struggle for control of maternity services, which in turn is part of the much larger struggles for (1) control of women in patriarchal cultures and (2) control of all health services. In another paper, Patricia Stephenson, a health service researcher, and I describe how the medical profession is used by society to control women's reproductive health (Stephenson and Wagner 1993b). And in *Pursuing the Birth Machine,* I describe in much more detail how the struggle for maternity services as part of all health services plays itself out in different parts of the world. I also point out a number of outstanding examples of people, including doctors, midwives, and scientists, who have broken out of the obstetrical orthodoxy and made important contributions to broadening both the authority and the knowledge on the basis of which decisions about birth can be made and actions taken.

At the present time there seems to be a cross-disciplinary coming together of understandings about the paradigms influencing contemporary maternity care. In *Pursuing the Birth Machine,* I compare the "medical" model of birth with the "social" model of birth. In *In Labor* (1982), Rothman describes the "medical" and the "midwifery" models of birth, which Robbie Davis-Floyd (1992) renames "technocratic" and "holistic." In another paper, Stephenson and I (1993a) contrast the "medical" and the "public health" approaches to determining the proper management of infertility services. An economist compares a "professional" with "societal" or "state" models of health care systems (Light 1993). There is, not surprisingly, considerable overlap among the alternative (social, midwifery, holistic, public health, and societal) paradigms, indicating a convergence of insights from a variety of viewpoints and disciplines. In other words, the limitations of orthodox medical authoritative knowledge are being challenged from many quarters. This convergence is sure to facilitate the ongoing struggle to transcend these limitations in the interests of improving health care.

NOTES

1. In *Becoming a Doctor,* Melvin Konner describes a conversation with a physician who was an expert on public health that casts light on my own experience. This physician had held an important administrative position in internal medicine and had a strong reputation in research, but had given all that up to take a leadership role in public health.

> People were puzzled, and I, like many others before, gave voice to that puzzlement. He was forthright, even adamant. Public health measures, not medical care, were responsible for all the important reductions of morbidity and mortality in modern times, he said. This was not news to me and I had little trouble with it, but [his] vehemence was surprising. Another physician who joined in the conversation was the designer and implementer of a program for screening newborn infants for hypothyroidism, which if undetected can easily cause profound mental retardation. The two of them insisted not only that public health measures were much more important than medicine, but that medicine had accomplished nothing at all. I protested. Coronary artery bypass surgery? Appendectomy? Antibiotics? Nothing I mentioned impressed them in the least. The treatments were overrated, the numbers of people saved were trivial compared with the numbers, past and future, saved by preventive measures. I felt like an idiot. Here I was, taking my first steps in clinical work, defending the whole enterprise of clinical medicine in an argument with two men who had spent decades practicing medicine at its best and who had abandoned it and insisted that it was useless. There was no getting around the irony of this exchange, nor its implications for the journey on which I had embarked. (1987:40)

REFERENCES

Arney, William R.
   1982   *Power and the Profession of Obstetrics.* Chicago: University of Chicago Press.
Bergsjo, Per, Eberhart Schmidt, and Detlef Pusch
   1983   "Differences in the Reported Frequencies of Some Obstetrical Interventions in Europe." *British Journal of Obstetrics and Gynaecology* 90:628–632.
Capra, Fritjof
   1977   *The Tao of Physics.* New York: Bantam Books.
Davis-Floyd, Robbie
   1992   *Birth as an American Rite of Passage.* Berkeley: University of California Press.
Feldman, G., and J. Freidman
   1985   "Prophylactic Caesarean Section at Term?" *New England Journal of Medicine* 312(19):1264–1267.

Fraser, Cynthia
  1983   "Selected Perinatal Procedures." *Acta Obstetrica et Gynecologica Scandinavica,* Suppl. 117.
Goer, Henci
  1995   *Obstetric Myths versus Research Realities.* New Haven, Conn.: Bergin and Garvey.
Jordan, Brigitte
  [1978] 1993   *Birth in Four Cultures: A Cross-Cultural Investigation of Childbirth in Yucatan, Holland, Sweden and the United States,* 4th ed. Prospect Heights, Ill.: Waveland Press.
Kitzinger, Sheila
  1978   *Giving Birth: The Parents' Emotions in Childbirth.* New York: Schocken Books.
Konner, Melvin
  1987   *Becoming a Doctor: A Journey of Initiation in Medical School.* New York: Penguin Books.
Leveno, K. J., F. G. Cunningham, S. Nelson, M. Roark, M. L. Williams, D. Guzick, S. Dowling, C. R. Rosenfeld, and A. Buckley
  1986   "A Prospective Comparison of Selective and Universal Electronic Fetal Monitoring in 34,995 Pregnancies." *New England Journal of Medicine* 315: 615.
Levy, Barry S., Frederic S. Wilkinson, and William M. Marine
  1971   "Reducing Neonatal Mortality Rate with Nurse-Midwives." *American Journal of Obstetrics and Gynecology* 109:50–58.
Light, Donald
  1993   "Escaping the Traps of Postwar Western Medicine: How to Maximize Health and Minimize Expenses." *European Journal of Public Health* 3(4):281–289.
Martin, Emily
  1987   *The Woman in the Body.* Boston: Beacon Press.
Mendelsohn, Robert
  1979   *Confessions of a Medical Heretic.* New York: Warner Books.
Petitti, D., R. Cefalo, S. Shapiro, and P. Walley
  1982   "In-Hospital Maternal Mortality in the United States: Time Trends and Relation to Method of Delivery." *Obstet Gynecol Val* 59:6–11.
Pirsig, R.
  1975   *Zen and the Art of Motorcycle Maintenance.* New York: Bantam Books.
Prentice, A., and T. Lind
  1987   "Fetal Heart Rate Monitoring during Labor: Too Much Intervention, Too Little Benefit." *Lancet* 2:1375–1377.
Rothman, Barbara Katz
  1982   *In Labor: Women and Power in the Birthplace.* New York: W. W. Norton.
  1989   *Recreating Motherhood: Ideology and Technology in Patriarchal Society.* New York: W. W. Norton.
Savage, Wendy
  1986   *A Savage Inquiry: Who Controls Childbirth?* London: Virago Press.

Stephenson, Patricia, and Marsden Wagner

1993a   "WHO Recommendations for IVF: Do They Fit with 'Health for All'?" *Lancet* 341:1648–1649.

1993b   "Reproductive Rights and the Medical Care System: A Plea for Rational Health Policy." *Journal of Public Health Policy* 14(2):174–182.

Stonier, Jennifer

1988   "The Innultsivik Maternity." Paper presented at the Northern Obstetrical Conference, Churchill, Manitoba, Canada.

Wagner, Marsden

1982   "Getting the Health Out of People's Daily Lives." *Lancet* 2:1207–1208.

1986   "Birth and Power." In *Perinatal Health Services in Europe: Searching for a Better Childbirth,* ed. J. M. L. Phaff. Dover, N.H.: Croom Helm for WHO Regional Office for Europe.

1989   "Playing Football." *Pediatric and Perinatal Epidemiology* 3:4–10.

1994   *Pursuing the Birth Machine: The Search for Appropriate Perinatal Technology.* London and Sydney: ACE Graphics (U.S. distributor: ICEA Bookcenter, P.O. Box 20048, Minneapolis, MN 55420).

1995   "Global Witch Hunt." *Lancet* 346(8981):1020–1023.

Wagner, Marsden, and Patricia St. Clair

1989   "Are In-Vitro Fertilization and Embryo Transfer a Benefit to All?" *Lancet* 2:1027–1038.

World Health Organization (WHO)

1978a   "Primary Health Care." International Conference on Primary Health Care, Alma-Ata, U.S.S.R., September 6–12.

1978b   *Primary Health Care.* A Joint Report by the Director General of the World Health Organization and the Executive Director of UNICEF. Geneva: WHO.

1979   "Formulating Strategies for Health for All by the Year 2000." Document of the Executive Board of the World Health Organization. Geneva: WHO.

1981   "Global Strategy for Health for All by the Year 2000." "Health for All" Series, no. 3. Geneva: WHO.

1985a   *Having a Baby in Europe.* Copenhagen: WHO Regional Office for Europe (Public Health in Europe no. 26).

1985b   "Appropriate Technology for Birth." *Lancet* 2:436–437.

1986a   "Appropriate Technology Following Birth." *Lancet* 2:1387–1388.

1986b   *Regional Targets for Health for All.* Copenhagen: WHO Regional Office for Europe.

1990   "Consultation on the Place of In-Vitro Fertilization in Infertility Care." Copenhagen: WHO Regional Office for Europe.

Viable Indigenous Systems of Authoritative Knowledge

Continuity in the Face of Change

FIFTEEN

"Women come here on their own when they need to"

Prenatal Care, Authoritative Knowledge, and Maternal Health in Oaxaca

Paola M. Sesia

In the state of Oaxaca, as in many other Mesoamerican regions, traditional and empirical *parteras* (midwives) continue to attend the great majority of births (Buekens, Hernández, and Infante 1990:680; Cosminsky 1986:79; Population Information Program 1980:35; Zolla 1983:25–26)—especially those that occur in peasant and indigenous rural areas. In many Oaxacan rural communities, the kind of perinatal care these midwives provide—referred to in this chapter as ethno-obstetrics (McClain 1975)—is usually deeply embedded within its own explanatory model; here obstetric knowledge is collectively valued as the result of long years of practice and accrued hands-on experience.

This chapter addresses the interplay between the hands-on authoritative knowledge of traditional midwives and the biomedical system, through a focus on prenatal care as taught in certification training courses and as actually practiced by the midwives in their communities. After describing the reasons behind national health authorities' increasing interest in traditional midwifery over the last two decades, I turn to the results of that interest—institutional training courses for traditional midwives—and examine their explicit and implicit rationales, objectives, and methodology. Through ethno-obstetric data gathered in southeastern Oaxaca between 1986 and 1988, I show the substantial conceptual differences, as midwives experience them, between the biomedical prenatal care taught during "training" and the kind of care midwives provide to pregnant women, linking these different realities to Brigitte Jordan's ([1978] 1993) concept of authoritative knowledge in distinct settings. Finally, I discuss the relevance of these ethnographic findings for maternal health care policy.

NATIONAL HEALTH POLICIES TOWARD TRADITIONAL MIDWIFERY

In Mexico, health policy makers ignored or blatantly condemned all traditional medical practices, including midwifery,[1] well into the mid-1970s; their concern was the rapid and widespread "modernization" of the health care system through a systematic introduction of, and exclusive reliance on, biomedicine and modern technology.[2] This strategy was pursued in spite of the government's inability to provide coverage to large sectors of the population (COPLAMAR 1985; López Acuña 1984).

Since the late 1970s, in response to a more favorable climate for the recognition of traditional medicine at both the national and the international levels, the official attitude of Mexican health authorities has moved from denial and rejection to partial acknowledgment and acceptance (IMSS 1983a, 1983b, 1983c, 1983d, 1983e). However, efforts toward legitimization and utilization of traditional medical resources within the national health system have proceeded in a very selective manner. Since the conceptual foundation of the biomedical model has undergone no substantial changes and its hegemonic role in the provision of care has continued undisputed, the only areas of traditional medicine that could logically receive attention and recognition are precisely those that show a greater "potential" for being successfully "incorporated" within the national health system as well as "justified" within biomedical thinking: herbalism (Zolla 1983:27) and midwifery. To a great extent, their acceptance has had to do with what Eduardo Menéndez (1983:42) calls the primarily empirical and technical nature of their practices, which health authorities believe can be easily reduced to the scientific rationale supporting the biomedical model without representing any substantial ideological threat to the hegemonic care system.

From a practical viewpoint, the recognition of traditional midwifery in particular by national health authorities has been dictated by the magnitude of the phenomenon within Mexico. In the 1970s parteras attended well over two-thirds of all births occurring in the country (Zolla 1983:26); according to more recent estimates by the national health sector, up to 80 percent of all births in rural Mexico are managed by traditional and certified empirical midwives (IMSS 1987, cited in Mellado, Zolla, and Castañeda 1989:21). This percentage maintains very high levels in southern Mexico, especially in those states—like Oaxaca—characterized by a predominantly rural peasant population and a low socioeconomic standard of living. In Oaxaca at the end of the 1980s less than 20 percent of deliveries were attended by biomedical practitioners (INEGI 1991).[3]

The declared necessity to improve maternal and child health (MCH) services and coverage—one of the highest priorities of the primary health care (PCH) approach adopted by Mexico since the late seventies—has also made empirical midwives the natural target of institutional interest. In the mid-seventies, moreover, the reduction of the high Mexican natality rate through massive population control campaigns became a national priority; immediately midwives were identified as potential intermediaries for the implementation of family planning services in their communities. They were already there, and they did not represent any additional cost to an already very strained governmental health budget (Urbina Fuentes 1986).

TRAINING COURSES

Mexican health officers therefore embarked on a large-scale effort directed at the incorporation of midwives into institutional health care services through training courses. More than 15,000 parteras underwent training between 1974 and the beginning of the 1980s (Martínez Manautou 1986:74; Population Information Program 1980:35). In Oaxaca, training began at the same time; between 1979 and 1985, 779 midwives were certified by the Mexican Institute for Social Security alone (IMSS 1986). Training continues today, although in a more sporadic manner. The main objectives of certification courses have been to "upgrade" midwives' skills in perinatal care, teach them to identify and refer high-risk pregnancies and deliveries, and enroll them in family planning campaigns (Castañeda et al. 1992:268). As Jordan (1989) convincingly explained when she first addressed the issue of authoritative knowledge, these trainings are the settings in which the transmission of knowledge and skills becomes, additionally, a powerful instrument for imposing, extending, and further legitimizing biomedical obstetrics; this process parallels and is reinforced by the concurrent devaluation of ethno-obstetrics.

With few exceptions—such as the recent attempt to introduce a "dialogue methodology" whereby trainers make an initial effort to take into account the previous knowledge of the partera attending the course by asking her a series of questions about her practice—the rationale behind courses continues to be the same today. Parteras are there to "learn"; course content, teaching methodology, and interactional attitudes repeatedly stress the appropriateness and implicit superiority of biomedical obstetrical care and family planning. In the eyes of most medical officers and trainers, traditional midwives continue to represent a subordinate system of care, toward which health personnel feel "an absolute certainty about the ignorance and ineffectiveness of [their] ideas and practices" (Aguirre Beltrán 1986:234).

My observations of institutional training courses for Oaxacan midwives during the late 1980s and again in the early 1990s confirm that an unequal power relationship continues to characterize training. The lack of information on midwives' conceptual views, accrued knowledge, and practices is still accompanied by not always subtle undertones of contempt toward parteras' alleged ignorance, backwardness, and superstition.

THE RESEARCH SETTING

The Isthmus of Tehuantepec is located in the southeastern portion of the state of Oaxaca in southern Mexico. Because of its strategic location—it is the narrowest land tract that unifies the Pacific and the Atlantic oceans in North America—this region became the center of national as well as transnational economic interests in the late nineteenth and early twentieth centuries when the first transoceanic railroad was built. The isthmus was the target of agricultural development during the same period; with alternating periods of economic growth and recession throughout this century, this region continues to be, relatively speaking, one of the wealthiest and most developed of Oaxaca. Since the nineteenth century, the region has experienced the consolidation of an already existing urban-based Zapotec Indian dominant elite, composed mostly of merchants or commercial farmers. Their relationship with the neighboring Huave Indians and other peasant villages has been historically characterized by economic exploitation and, at times, political dominance, leading to the periodic surge of interethnic conflicts (Frey 1989).

The four isthmus villages in which we conducted our research—San Francisco del Mar Pueblo Viejo, Coyul, Cabestrada, and Santo Domingo Coyotera—are, to different degrees, all linked to a regional market economy dominated by the mostly Zapotec urban centers. Ethnic identity is strong among the Huaves; San Francisco del Mar Pueblo Viejo maintains very distinctive cultural features that set it apart from the other communities under study. It is a settlement of approximately two hundred fifty families located in a secluded part of the Lower Lagoon of the isthmus. The Huaves are primarily shrimp fishers, a product they sell in the Zapotec urban markets of the region. The organization of labor follows gender lines: men fish and women sell at markets.

Language, dress, and forms of social organization are important historical markers of both change and continuity. Although the Huave language has been supplanted by Spanish in the last generation, several older people in the village still speak it. Although men have abandoned the traditional dress, women commonly wear the *huipil* (traditional Indian blouse) and *enagua* (traditional Indian skirt) they adopted long ago from the neighboring Zapotecs. San Francisco maintains a traditional form of local government through the communal assembly and the system of *cargos*;[4]

traditional customs, such as patronal feasts and ritual celebrations, are carried out throughout the year.

Coyul is a small coastal town of approximately twelve hundred inhabitants, mostly dedicated to farming and fishing for self-consumption as well as for the market. Recently, with the completion of a major highway that divides the town in two halves, the pull to fully enter the market economy has greatly increased. Fruit cash crops are increasingly common, and a growing number of adult males have found temporary employment in the construction sites of nearby tourist complexes or in the oil refineries of a nearby town. Women help in the fields during the peak season; otherwise they attend their homes, make food for sale, or are in charge of petty stores. Coyul is a recent settlement, mostly populated by second- and third-generation migrants from the Chontal highlands, one of the indigenous areas of the isthmus. Although local government is officially incorporated into the national political party system, it maintains the indigenous system of cargos on a rotating basis. Visible manifestations of ethnic identity, though, are minimal, and Spanish has been the only language spoken for at least twenty years.

Cabestrada and Santo Domingo Coyotera are two rural communities in proximity to each other; they are located almost at the border between the states of Oaxaca and Chiapas. Forty-two mestizo families constitute the entire population of Cabestrada; Coyotera consists of approximately fifty households. The villagers are first- and second-generation migrants from nearby Zapotec localities, from other areas of the region, or from the state of Chiapas. Like Coyul, these two villages are increasingly switching from subsistence farming and fishing to cash crops and cattle raising. Disparity in size and quality of land parcels creates social stratification and considerable land conflicts among the communities' campesinos (peasants).

Of the four communities, only Coyul boasts a government clinic, established by the Mexican Institute for Social Security in 1979 and staffed with a *pasante* (a young doctor recently graduated from medical school) and a resident nurse. The pasante usually serves in the facility for a period of one year, but the same nurse has been working in the clinic since it was first established. Although the clinic offers all basic PHC services at no cost, including prenatal and delivery care, almost no pregnant women take advantage of them. San Francisco del Mar falls under the jurisdiction of a government clinic located at a distance of approximately two hours (11.3 miles); Cabestrada and Coyotera are served by a public clinic an hour away (8.1 miles). As in Coyul, these villagers may resort to health facilities for different medical complaints; women, nevertheless, almost never utilize them for prenatal and delivery services. Midwives are present in each of the four villages and attend most births.

RESEARCH METHODS AND UNITS OF ANALYSIS

This study is part of a larger research project on conceptions and management of childbirth and other reproductive practices as they took place in the late 1980s in rural and indigenous areas of the isthmus region. Some of the midwives were first contacted during attendance at a twenty-five-day institutional training course. Most of the eighteen midwives attending this training came from Indian villages of the region. After visiting most of these communities, we selected four for study, taking into consideration the willingness on the part of the certified midwife to participate and distinctive intervillage characteristics such as ethnicity, natural environment, and the availability of institutional health services. Once in the communities, we contacted all midwives, certified and uncertified, who were providing perinatal care. The data presented in this chapter are derived from fieldwork with eight parteras; at the time of this study they were the only midwives practicing in these four communities, where they were managing more than 90 percent of the local births. In each locality, we carried out extensive open-ended interviews with the midwives, observed their practices, and interviewed several of their women clients. We also interviewed institutional and private medical personnel practicing in the areas or with whom parteras were maintaining professional interaction. The actual amount of time spent in each of the four communities during fieldwork was more than six months.

Because of the synchronic character of the study, which focused on contemporary midwifery, we did not directly examine the dimension of change in the management and conception of pregnancy and birth. Nevertheless, we did consider several diachronic variables, such as parteras' age, ethnicity, initial learning process and modality, participation in training courses, and extent of interaction with the biomedical health sector.

RESULTS

The Midwives

Five of the eight parteras in these villages had undergone training recently; of these, three were certified in a course that we were able to attend. Prior to training, one of them, forty-year-old Yolanda, had acquired her obstetrical skills with a physician; for that reason, but also with a few interesting adaptations, her provision of care fell closer to the realm of biomedical obstetrics. The other three midwives had not received any formal training; and all three expressed lack of interest in institutional courses.[5]

Faustina, a thirty-nine-year-old Huave certified partera, and Estela, a forty-five-year-old mestizo uncertified midwife, began their profession through a magical or religious calling. Four of the other midwives acquired their skills as apprentices to senior parteras; one began to practice on the spot by assisting another woman giving birth. At the time of the study, one midwife was under forty years of age; three were between forty and forty-five; and four were over sixty. All of them had at least ten years of midwifery experience and, with the exception of sixty-seven-year-old Sabino, a *partero* (male midwife), all had experienced motherhood by giving birth to four to ten children.

All midwives were charging a fee for their services; attending a birth and providing postnatal care to the mother and the newborn entailed the highest fees. In 1988, these ranged from US$3 to $35, depending on the services provided and the midwife. Yolanda was the only midwife who charged over US$15 for attending a childbirth. Those women who could not raise the requested amount could usually pay the midwife in several smaller payments or give her gifts in exchange.

Early on in the research it became apparent that the actual conception and management of pregnancy, childbirth, and the postpartum period were very similar in the four villages, regardless of midwives' age, ethnicity, or previous participation in a training course. Most salient of all was the tremendous gap between ethno-obstetric care and biomedical obstetrics as taught in training courses. The entire rationale supporting prenatal, childbirth, and postnatal care in these communities was strikingly different from its biomedical correspondent; anatomical and physiological concepts mostly worked within a separate reference framework. Likewise, high-risk categories, diagnostic tools, and treatment of gyneco-obstetrical complications differed remarkably between the two models of care (Sesia 1992).

Three major remarks are pertinent here. First, this conceptual gap was never (and still is not) taken into account in training courses. The devaluation of ethno-obstetrics during training involves disregard for midwives' practices as well as for their underlying rationales. Assuming the authority of biomedicine, training personnel never showed any interest in finding out what parteras do or why. Attending midwives were never asked about their physiological or anatomical conceptualizations around reproduction. Second, once back in their villages, none of the certified midwives substantially changed their conceptual ways or the type of care they provide. With very few exceptions, obstetrical practices of these trained parteras were strikingly similar to those of uncertified ones, even in those aspects of care that trainings overtly attempt to change.[6] Contrary to the government health sector's expectations, certification courses seem to be one of the variables that have had the least impact on changing local midwives' views and practices. In accordance with other studies (Franzoni Lobo 1993; Mellado, Zolla, and Castañeda 1989), our results suggest that the initial experience of becoming a partera and the extent and quality of interaction with the formal health sector after training may in fact have a much greater impact on local midwives' ways of conceiving and managing the birthing process than certification courses (Sesia-Lewis 1987). Third, through our interviews and extensive interaction with women villagers, it soon became apparent that the great majority of them widely shared and supported ethno-obstetric rationales and activities, regarding them as authoritative.

Prenatal Care: The Sobada and the Detection of High-Risk Pregnancies

In this section I focus on prenatal care—specifically, on the *sobada* (massage) and on the definition and the detection of complications during gestation as they usually took place in these villages during our fieldwork. Through this specific example, I seek to demonstrate the full extent and the long-range implications of the conceptual and practical differences between ethno-obstetrics and biomedicine as systems of authoritative knowledge.

After missing a period, women usually wait for two or three months before they pay their first visit to the midwife. The purpose of this visit is not so much to have their pregnancy confirmed (most women, especially those who have already had children, have few doubts about their own diagnostic abilities) as to have their first sobada with the person who will attend them. All midwives reported that most women initially call on them between the third and fifth month of gestation. Some wait until the last trimester; a few will not see the partera, or anyone else, until the onset of labor.

Regardless of age, experience, certification, or community origin, all the midwives participating in the study—with the partial exception of Yolanda, who was medically trained—offer a very similar type of care to the pregnant woman. The visit is very different from the equivalent one in a medical office or clinic, both in its activities and in its rationale. Usually it takes place inside the one bedroom in the midwife's house; sometimes the partera goes to the woman's home. Yolanda is the only one who has a special, fully equipped room where she receives her clients and attends deliveries—a very powerful statement of professionalism that she does not share with anyone else in these communities.

The locus of activity in the prenatal visit is the sobada, the external massage. The woman lies down on the bed completely dressed, her gown only raised enough so that the abdomen is visible. To detect a pregnancy the midwife feels the uterus by gentle external manipulation, looking for the *bolita* (little ball), a common euphemism for an engrossed and hardened uterus. On locating and palpating it, the partera gives an estimate of the month of gestation by the size of the uterus. (According to the mothers, parteras are usually correct in their estimates with a variance of one or two weeks.) She then moves the uterus from side to side and from bottom to top for several minutes. Meanwhile, she explains to her client that it is necessary to pull the bolita up and toward the center so that it becomes accustomed to its correct position and will not hurt the mother by excessive pressure on her bones or other organs.

After the woman positions herself on the side, the partera will apply some gentle pressure through similar movements on her lower back. If she complains of pain or ache in any specific place, the midwife will massage her patiently on the indicated point. It is important to stress that the entire examination is external; the partera never comes into contact with the woman's pubic area or with her internal reproductive organs.[7] During the sobada she checks to see if the baby is in correct head-down position. If it is not and the mother is at least five to six months pregnant, she will attempt an external version, a maneuver that most midwives claim they can easily do (see Jordan 1984). Parteras agree that they usually have to repeat the version at least three to four times in subsequent sessions before the baby adopts the head-down position. In such a case, they recommend that the woman come back at specific times for more sobadas. Otherwise, most parteras do not set any time for the woman's next visit because, as María, a sixty-two-year-old certified midwife from Coyul, says, "Women come here on their own when they need to."[8]

During training, teaching personnel usually place no importance on the sobada, at times neglecting to mention it at all. When they do, it is in negative terms since the sobada is associated with the external version, a maneuver they strongly discourage. Midwives are repeatedly told that they should not attempt external version because it allegedly can cause harm to the fetus.[9] Despite these warnings, trained parteras continue to give sobadas and perform external versions. Even Yolanda, the medically trained midwife, resorts to it:

> Many older women prefer not to come with me because I am not used to assisting in the old ways. But with all the women I provide care to, regardless of their age, I have not been able to refuse sobadas because they request it; this is so even if the doctor did prohibit me from doing it.[10]

Throughout certification courses, trainers stress the importance of regular and periodic prenatal visits to control the healthy progression of pregnancies, identify possible risk factors, and detect complications as soon as they arise. Certified and uncertified alike, though, midwives do not actively encourage their expectant clients to see them on a regular basis. Although they all agree that it is desirable for the woman to come at least three or four times during pregnancy—every two or three months at first, more regularly after the fifth or sixth month—their reasoning differs from that in the biomedical model. Faustina, the Huave certified midwife, expresses it clearly:

It is not good when they come for a massage when their belly is already big. If the baby is positioned too far up or on the side and you do not give a massage, it becomes more difficult to put him or her in the right head-down position. On the contrary, when you have been giving massages, it is much easier for the child to come out properly. One knows that this is the case because by giving massages in the last months of pregnancy, one feels that everything is working out right.[11]

The desirability of some continuity in the provision of care during gestation, then, is once again associated with the sobada; it has little or nothing to do with regular biomedical prenatal care. The prenatal sobada is undoubtedly the most important diagnostic tool, as well as the most significant preventive and curative prenatal strategy, that midwives have. It has, in fact, several different functions: to estimate gestation time, identify fetal position (especially in the last trimester), relocate the baby in the head-down position, relieve and soothe pain and ache in the expectant mother, establish physical and emotional contact between the midwife and the woman, and detect when the time of labor and childbirth approaches.

Although parteras and women coincide in their appreciation of the sobada's multiple functions, they each tend to stress some meanings over others according to their differential identity location vis-à-vis the experience of pregnancy. Gestating women privilege in their narratives the physical relief and the sensation of well-being that the massage provides.

When I was pregnant, I felt really heavy and I had much nausea. . . . I went to see my midwife and she massaged me. After the sobada one feels much better, much lighter. (Alba, 29 years old, San Francisco del Mar)[12]

I liked the way in which the midwife assisted me because she gave me warm baths and she massaged my waist and belly. With sobadas I felt good. (Romelia, 20 years old, Cabestrada)[13]

Some explicitly point to the sobada as the factor that most clearly distinguishes midwifery from biomedical prenatal care and to the sensation of well-being it provides as the main reason they prefer the former to the latter.

I prefer the midwife to the doctor during pregnancy because she massages me and he does not. I go for at least three sobadas, once at four months of pregnancy, another time at six months, and a third time when I am eight months pregnant. Then, once more during labor. . . . The sobada makes me feel well. (Josefina, 26 years old, Coyotera)[14]

Midwives tend instead to stress the sobada's potential as a diagnostic and corrective tool in case of a transverse or breech fetal position.

When they come [for a sobada] I probe with my hand to find out how the baby is located. The best is when the baby comes right, but if it is positioned wrongly I have to relocate it. Sometimes one has to relocate [the baby] just once and there it stays. Other times, though, one has to continue massaging because certain babies are stubborn. If I did not massage, the baby could come in the wrong position and then who can bring it out? It is more difficult and one suffers more. (Josefa, 61 years old, uncertified midwife, Coyotera) [15]

The importance parteras place on the relocation of the baby needs to be understood within the context of their acquired knowledge and long-term experience. The delivery of a breech or transverse infant is the major complication they recognize as such, face from time to time, and try to resolve with the tools and knowledge they have at their disposal. Unlike other anomalous or pathological conditions during pregnancy and childbirth, a breech or transverse baby is an obvious physical phenomenon that the midwife can easily and immediately detect. As the previous narrative points out, during the sobada the partera purposely uses the external version as a preventive measure to avoid later the potential difficulty and risk of attending a breech or transverse delivery. Thus this maneuver becomes a sensible, rational, coherent, and effective strategy among the limited technical resources that are available to these midwives.

Besides a breech or transverse baby, the only other pregnancies that midwives (sometimes) recognize as potentially difficult are those of older mothers, usually in their forties, who have already had several children and had previously experienced complications, or when the pregnant woman experiences bleeding and hemorrhage prior to labor. Signs of hypertension, edema, toxemia, or other preexisting conditions in the mother that could adversely affect the pregnancy (such as tuberculosis, diabetes, or any STDs) are usually neither detected nor recognized as potentially harmful. Even if a partera recognizes anemia as a condition that requires intervention (e.g., a vitamin shot) during pregnancy, an anemic pregnant woman is not considered at any particular risk for childbirth.

The notion of "risk" is, in fact, a biomedical one, mostly unknown to local midwives. As in Yucatán (Jordan [1978] 1993), in southeastern Oaxaca pregnancies are also considered normal events; for that reason, signs of abnormalities are not sought. When a biomedically defined pathological condition arises, parteras usually do not recognize it. In the few cases in which they face what they consider a worrisome situation, midwives will do whatever they can, usually attempting to bring the condition back to normal through the sobada. Even when a midwife concurs with biomedical practice in the identification of a risk factor, she will not usually refer the case to a doctor or a clinic; she will instead mostly follow traditional normative patterns in the management of the problem. For example, Eugenia, a forty-four-year-old certified partera from Coyul, was the only one besides Yolanda to ever mention "swelling" as a potential problem. She then added that she could easily "fix" it through a sobada of the expectant mother's entire body.

Within each of these communities, the ability and willingness to attend any woman who seeks her regardless of any specific adverse conditions is considered a desirable quality because it is interpreted as a sign of courage, strength, and expertise on the part of the midwife. Although trained parteras are more likely to seek external help when a very difficult situation arises, none of these midwives, not even Yolanda, will refuse to attend a pregnant woman when called on.[16] To refuse is socially unacceptable; a midwife who would do so would be the target of community criticism as a *partera sin valor* (midwife without courage); her reputation would suffer and she would lose clientele and prestige.

Courage, strength, and expertise are precisely the three qualities that confer local authority and prestige on a midwife. They also mark what distinguishes her from any other woman. Most women share with parteras experientially based obstetrical knowledge, multiple motherhood, and even the experience of having assisted a daughter, a daughter-in-law, a granddaughter, a niece, or a neighbor when giving birth. Most could become midwives themselves; what makes the midwife stand out is precisely the authority she has acquired in her community through cumulative experience and display of courage (Galante 1988).

When a skilled partera faces a complication she has learned to fear— such as profuse bleeding during gestation or after delivery—there are ways by which she can seek outside help without losing her reputation. According to Faustina, one such way is never to abandon her client but instead to escort her to the nearest private or governmental physician, clinic, or hospital, to keep her company during the medical consultation or visit her during a clinic stay, and then to bring her back home. Interesting enough, Faustina and Yolanda—the two parteras who have referred particularly difficult cases—are the only ones who throughout their years of practice have been able to establish a good rapport with physicians whom they trust in nearby towns. These doctors have learned to respect them, and do acknowledge their midwifery skills in multiple ways, including in front of their women clients. These two parteras can protect their reputations because in the eyes of their communities they continue to successfully maintain full responsibility for their clients' well-being. At the same time, their authority and expertise are not questioned by the medical personnel to whom they resort; during these interactions, they actually get reinforced vis-à-vis their women clients and any other accompanying family members. Unfortunately, these circumstances are quite exceptional.

DISCUSSION

Three aspects deserve further consideration: the failure of certification courses to replace ethno-obstetrics with biomedicine as the primary source of authoritative knowledge; the construction and meaning of authoritative knowledge within midwives' own social milieu; and the relevance for maternal health policy of the prevalence of the ethno-obstetric model of care at the local level. All three are addressed below.

Authoritative Knowledge

Brigitte Jordan's (1992) analysis of the construction of knowledge in very complex technological settings illuminated the relationship between the processes of teaching and learning, on the one hand, and the reproduction of power and authority, on the other. She convincingly argued that in technologically sophisticated social settings, such as the delivery room in an American hospital, differential access to information and to technology works to the exclusion of laboring women in the generation of knowledge that "counts." This produces or reproduces a hierarchical distribution of knowledge in which the privileged party—the physician and his medical staff—establishes its knowledge system as the only authoritative and legitimate one, to the devaluation of all alternative sources of information and practice (Jordan 1992:2–4, 27–29). In such a situation, the social order that authoritative knowledge builds and reflects is perceived by all parties as natural, since it is socially and consensually constructed (1992:2; 1993:209–210). Conversely, in a situation in which access to complex technology and to the production of information is evenly distributed, authoritative knowledge is collectively and horizontally shared (1992:18–29).

In her discussion of knowledge production and transmission in training courses for traditional midwives, Jordan ([1978] 1993:chap. 7) analyzed the unequal power relationships established between the authoritative and imposing biomedical model of care and midwives' devalued concepts and practices. She came to the significant conclusion that by forcefully promoting bio-obstetrics as the only legitimate and authoritative model of care, trainings "not only devalue indigenous ethno-obstetric wisdom and skills, they disallow the very methods of indigenous knowledge and skill acquisition" (1989:935).

Jordan's insights into the unequal power relationship established between the biomedical and the ethno-obstetric system, and between those with authoritative access to high technology and those who lack such access, become particularly relevant when we examine the contradictory situation that Oaxacan parteras have faced, first in certification courses and again back in their communities. During training, these parteras did experience a situation in which knowledge was produced and transmitted hierarchically and in which they were placed in the subordinate and passive role. Similarly, the superiority of a technologically sophisticated model of care was implicitly or, at times, explicitly stressed in multiple ways. Yet after their subordination to biomedicine was effected, parteras were encouraged to assume a more authoritative role vis-à-vis their women clients in pregnancy and childbirth management.

If they had followed trainers' suggestions, the parteras would themselves have become actively engaged in the reproduction and expansion of the bio-obstetric model of care. But this hegemonic project has mostly failed to win midwives' consent[17] for several reasons, including the structural weaknesses of the project itself as well as the relative strength at the community level of ethno-obstetrics. The ineffectiveness of training methodology is paralleled by the inability of the state health sector to either "follow up" on parteras after courses or offer further training to "reinforce" what they allegedly learned during certification.

Once back in their villages, certified midwives usually revert to a more horizontally distributed knowledge modality—characterized by the greater and more equal participation of women clients in obstetric decision making—and to their own ethno-obstetric model of care. In prenatal care, all continue with external versions and very rarely refer difficult cases despite persistent warnings during biomedical training. The sobada maintains its central role to the exclusion of other preventive diagnostic measures taught in certification courses. As a technical fix, it even takes over new spaces for intervention opened up by biomedical training. It also continues to serve as the privileged locus of interaction between midwives and gestating women despite biomedical efforts to displace it: a space managed as much according to women's expectations as to parteras' skills.

As probably the best example of a relationship marked by a much more egalitarian ethos than in bio-obstetrics, parteras do not attempt to impose a regular schedule of prenatal visits on their clients, although they were encouraged to do so repeatedly in certification courses. In most cases, their behavior is consequential to their midwifery knowledge and values, which they began to internalize during their own apprenticeship, which have continued to accrue during several years of practice, and which are not likely to be displaced by a single biomedical training course. These midwives sustain the ethno-obstetric model of care and actively participate in its modality of knowledge production precisely because this model is still widely shared—and reinforced in the process—by the great majority of the villagers with whom midwives live and work. It tends to be consensually constructed and socially reproduced at the community level. Perhaps the best statement about the collective strength of ethno-obstetrics at the moment of our research comes from Yolanda, who is particularly cognizant of and moderately sympathetic to the biomedical hegemonic project in training courses. Reflecting on her own client-induced use of the sobada, she expresses an implicit notion of cultural struggle in which local ways have successfully—albeit for the time being—fended off biomedical assaults.

I have not been able to refuse sobadas because the women request it; this is so even if the doctor did prohibit me from doing it. Doctors have attempted to change local ways, but they have not succeeded because here people's ways are stronger.[18]

The nature of the power relationship between the midwife and her clients is perhaps the most appropriate site for exploring how ethno-obstetric knowledge is constructed and distributed. In these villages, the partera with several years of experience is the one who enjoys her community's recognition as "expert" in the management of pregnancy and birth. Whether or not she is certified does not influence villagers' perceptions of the quality of her work. Trained parteras are very much aware of this and, although some of them use their certification diploma as a symbol of higher status vis-à-vis untrained colleagues, they do not attempt to do the same with their clients or their families. At the community level, recognition for their work is linked to their acquisition and mastery of specific manual skills such as sobada, to their knowledge of how to support and encourage the laboring woman, to their successful management of multiple and difficult births, to their willingness to take care of the mother and the newborn according to local norms, values, and expectations, and to their cumulative show of strength and courage in the performance of their duties.

Despite the public recognition of their expertise and authority and regardless of certification, midwives' relationships with gestating or laboring women tend to be much more egalitarian in gestures, words, actions, and even in the process of decision making than the medical provider-patient relationships of bio-obstetrics. This becomes especially true with older and multiparous clients, whose experiences with multiple pregnancies and births are highly regarded and valued by parteras. Midwifery expertise does not bring with it the imposition of vertical authority. Within the ethno-obstetric model of care, the woman, not the midwife, is still the active subject. As we have seen, pregnant women decide when and how many times to visit their parteras. During birth the nature of this power relationship becomes even more explicit: the partera helps, advises, supports, and even facilitates the process; what she never does is turn the woman into a passive subject whom she delivers.

We can thus argue that while midwives do enjoy special consideration for their expertise, their empirical knowledge tends to be much more evenly distributed than in bio-obstetrics. Insofar as this knowledge is considered "important, relevant, and consequential for decision-making" (Jordan 1989:925), it is authoritative at the local level. Perhaps this collective sharing of ethno-obstetric knowledge does not threaten the role of the partera as the expert because knowledge is not everything that counts at the local birth scene. Other qualities are what single her out from other women; these are personal qualities that slowly build up a reputation, bring about authority and recognition, and, at the same time, offer the observer a glimpse of the profound metamedical components of the local management of pregnancy and childbirth.

Relevance for Maternal Health

Widely recognized advantages of bio- over ethno-obstetrics include the identification of relevant risk factors during pregnancy and the ability to resolve complications and emergencies successfully whenever they arise. The timely identification of risk during gestation and the successful resolution of obstetrical problems can significantly reduce maternal and perinatal morbidity and mortality. This holds great relevance for Oaxaca, a state where maternal mortality is the highest in Mexico, more than double the national average (120 per 100,000 versus 54 per 100,000) (SSA 1992). To ameliorate this situation, maternal health services need to be readily available and reach an adequate level of quality in the management of obstetrical complications.

In Oaxaca, as we have seen, training courses have been largely unsuccessful in teaching parteras to identify risk factors or arising obstetrical emergencies or to promptly refer affected women to institutional care. Institutional maternal health care (MHC), moreover, has faced serious limitations in the provision of services that could effectively reduce maternal morbidity and mortality. The problem of an insufficient number of primary care facilities in many rural regions of the state is exacerbated by the existence of services truly unprepared to manage serious obstetrical complications. In short, many Oaxacan mothers have very limited access— geographically and financially—to specialized obstetrical care; should their midwives wish to transport, in many places there is simply nowhere to go.

Considering Mexico's recurrent economic crises from the early 1980s to the present and the severe budgetary restrictions that the public sector currently (1995) faces, it is unlikely that government health services will make major headway in extending or improving formal MHC coverage for rural Oaxaca in the near future. Attempts to extend coverage or improve the quality of existing services are hampered twofold. First, the ministry of health and other public health institutions involved in primary care face increasing problems of understaffing, funding cuts, decreasing wages, shortages in medical supplies, and inexperienced personnel. Second, despite a formal discourse to the contrary, institutional MHC policies and services at the primary care level, as we have seen, continue to be largely directed by an ideology that strives for modernization, sophisticated technology, and the medicalization of pregnancy and childbirth. It is completely unrealistic to attempt to implement this "cosmopolitical" (Jordan [1978] 1993:chap. 8) model in a state like Oaxaca; it cannot and should not be promoted at the primary care level. Among other drawbacks, this model is unsustainable economically and is not well accepted culturally in many peasant and indigenous areas of the state. An extension of formal MHC coverage could well result in the establishment of additional services of questionable quality and unjustifiable expense that many rural populations would likely underutilize.

Under present circumstances, then, reliance on traditional midwifery in poor and isolated regions of the state is likely to continue—if not to increase—in years to come. The strategy of implementing training courses for practicing parteras is appropriate; what needs to change is the content, methodology, and underlying ideology of these courses. This strategy, moreover, should be complemented by other interventions directed at the other social actors who, in multiple ways, operate within and make decisions about the management of pregnancy and birth.

Training courses have been the focus of much critique in the anthropological literature; suggestions for change have been put forward repeatedly (Castañeda et al. 1992; Jordan 1989, 1993). Here I will add that in a climate of profound respect and with the employment of a culturally and educationally appropriate methodology, parteras should be taught not only the detection and referral of gestating women at risk but also specific techniques of intervention when complications arise. When done appropriately, midwives have shown a tremendous interest in learning new techniques aimed at improving the type of care they provide. Parteras could, for instance, learn how to detect high blood pressure during gestation with the use of the stethoscope, an instrument that should be made available to each of them after training. The detection of this condition should be accompanied by training in its management with effective herbal and drug therapy and other strategies, such as bed rest for the severely affected person. The appropriateness of teaching midwives how to use pharmaceuticals correctly is indicated by the fact that several parteras have already incorporated certain drug therapies in their pharmacopeia and that drugs are freely available in the market.

Besides midwives, medical personnel operating at the primary and secondary level of care should also receive training. They should learn about ethno-obstetric practices, benefits, and underlying rationales. At the same time, they should be made aware of the limitations not only of ethno-obstetrics but also of the bio-obstetric model, especially when the latter is applied in rural regions. Courses for medical staff should aim at teaching trainees respect for parteras' ways and skills and should stress the necessity of establishing effective communication with all empirical providers of care. The relevance for maternal health of establishing a good rapport with traditional midwives is well illustrated in our case study: the only two parteras who did refer women with severe complications were the ones who were successful in finding physicians willing to back them up and stand up for them in emergencies. To be effective, such training should start early in medical or nursing school.

Finally, it is important to stress that both the women who receive midwives' care and some of their family members—especially husbands and mothers or mothers-in-law—are active decision makers in the management of reproduction. In ethno-obstetrics, pregnancy and birth are complex phenomena in which social control mechanisms, cultural values, and locally prevailing norms play important roles. In a context in which obstetric knowledge is, to a large extent, collectively shared and socially normed, any intervention to improve maternal health that is directed at parteras to the exclusion of other participating social actors is likely to fail.

The need to involve mothers *and* their families becomes even more crucial when we consider that many of the obstetrical complications that peasant and indigenous women face transcend the immediate context of midwifery care to include personal and socioeconomic issues such as poor maternal nutrition. Efforts should be made to increase awareness of the importance of the gestation period not only among parteras and their women clients but also—and especially—among their husbands, mothers, and mothers-in-law. Such efforts should be interdisciplinary in nature, should include medical as well as nonmedical aspects of care, and should provide simple instruments to ameliorate families' life conditions—such as, for instance, agricultural techniques and products to improve and diversify the local diet. Among these social actors, awareness of the need for adequate prenatal care as well as of the importance of detecting and treating specific risk factors should be complemented—minimally—by awareness of the need for adequate maternal nutrition and rest during pregnancy and after birth.

In *Birth in Four Cultures* ([1978] 1993:135–139), Jordan calls for a "mutual accommodation of the biomedical and indigenous systems." Such an accommodation could be accomplished in Oaxaca by the national health sector through relinquishing its exclusively biomedical focus, changing the philosophy and content of certification courses to address ethno-obstetric realities and needs, and including in intervention programs all actors involved in the cultural management of parturition. These strategies have great potential to effectively reduce maternal morbidity and mortality in Oaxaca; moreover, they offer the advantage of striving to accomplish such important goals in full respect for local cultures and their vital and consensually constructed systems of authoritative knowledge.

NOTES

The research on which this chapter is based was supported by a community grant from the Inter-American Foundation (no. MEX-249) from June 1986 to December 1988. It also benefited from a 1986–1987 master's thesis fellowship from the Inter-American Foundation (no. F2-081); a supplemental 1986 summer stipend made available from funds of the Public Health Service Traineeship and awarded to me by the School of Public Health at the University of California, Berkeley; and a 1987 travel grant from the Program in Mexican Studies (Center for Latin American Studies) and the Cowell Foundation of the University of California, Berkeley. To all, my deepest thanks. I want to express my gratitude to Cristina Galante and Virginia Alejandre, my research colleagues in Oaxaca, for their support, friendship, and help. Above all, I want to thank all the women and midwives whom we interviewed extensively and with whom we spent long and gratifying times. I am thankful to Robbie Davis-Floyd for inviting me to participate in the panel "Birth in Twelve Cultures: Papers in Honor of Brigitte Jordan," which she organized and chaired in 1992 during the 91st annual meeting of the American Anthropological Association. An earlier version of this chapter was presented at that meeting. To Ana Ortíz at the University of Arizona, Tucson, and to Robbie Davis-Floyd go my thanks for commenting on this chapter and giving me important editing suggestions.

1. In Mexico "traditional medicine" refers to all medical views and modalities of care that peasant and indigenous communities, among other sectors, have dynamically and historically developed to explain and cope with illness. Specifically, traditional medicine in Indian regions has been characterized by (a) a collectively shared and socially constructed knowledge of the local environment's biological resources, which includes those identified and used for healing purposes; (b) an organizationally structured medical system composed of several different medical specialties; (c) the valued social role that healers play within the group for their recognized knowledge and skills; (d) the presence of "antimedical" specialists who have powers to wishfully cause harm to individuals; and (e) the integration of biological, sociopsychological, and religious components in disease etiologies, diagnoses, and treatments, with the inclusion of supernatural as well as natural illness categories (Anzures y Bolaños 1983). This typology can be safely extended to many Mesoamerican agrarian localities that may have lost a specific Indian identity— such as expressed by language—but still maintain sociocultural and economic characteristics that resemble those of Indian communities.

2. Biomedical medicine is the hegemonic model of care in contemporary Mexico; from an ideological and practical viewpoint, all other medical practices and conceptions are considered by national health authorities as subordinate (Menéndez 1984). See note 17.

3. According to the most recently available statistics (INEGI 1991), slightly over 10,000 births were registered in government medical facilities out of a total of approximately 108,000 births that occurred that same year in the state of Oaxaca. Registration of births in government medical establishments includes all facilities that belong to the Ministry of Health (SSA), the Mexican Institute of Social Security (IMSS), and the Institute for Social Security at the Service of Federal Workers

(ISSSTE), among others. Unfortunately, there are no official data recorded on private medical care; according to SSA estimates, though, the private medical sector accounts for approximately 7 to 10 percent of all provision of formal care in the state. This would bring the total figure of births occurring within the formal health sector up to 17 to 20 percent. Due to the prevailing rural composition of the Oaxacan population, though, the presence of the private medical sector is minimal outside of the state capital and a few other smaller cities.

4. The cargo system is an administrative and religious organizational structure that was originally imposed by the Spaniards during colonial times. It survived the demise of colonial rule to become an important distinctive marker of Mesoamerican Indian organization and identity. It consists of the community civil and religious duties that all males have to fulfill periodically, beginning in early adulthood. Duties are assigned by the community assembly on a rotating basis according to age, experience, and previous performances on lower-status and less demanding assignments. Duties follow an ascending hierarchy that involves greater involvement, responsibility, prestige, and financial burden on each following step.

5. Mellado, Zolla, and Castañeda (1989:29, 42) identify three different categories of rural midwives according to training received, type of care provided, and medical resources utilized: the traditional, the empirical with certification, and the empirical without certification. They postulate a continuum along which certified empirical midwives' care most closely resembles biomedical obstetrics, while traditional midwives' concepts and practices fall within (what here I refer to as) ethno-obstetrics. With the full exception of one certified empirical midwife—Yolanda, the medically trained partera—and the partial exception of another, the other six midwives participating in the study fall within the category of "traditional" for the care they provide and the way they learned their obstetrical skills. I want to emphasize that all my observations concerning the strength of ethno-obstetrics are pertinent to the fact that the majority of the midwives in these communities fall into the category of "traditional"; in other words, their practice is at the end of the continuum farthest away from the biomedical.

6. Trainings have had an impact on the type of care that certified midwives provide in unforeseen ways. A good example is the length of postpartum care: trained midwives provide an average of two to four days of care after delivery, whereas untrained ones follow up on their women clients during the next three to seven days. With the usual exception of Yolanda, whose standard length of care to the mother and the newborn has been of one to two days' duration since she began to practice and has not changed, the other four certified midwives did overall decrease the time of postpartum care after attending training. During courses, teaching personnel do not explicitly remark on the "ideal" length of postpartum care. Nevertheless, midwives are compelled to assist in mandatory teaching sessions devoted to observing obstetrical hospital procedures as the "ideal" model of obstetrical care. Here, they are exposed to the hospital time frame, where efficiency and medical technology rule over natural birthing time and most women are dismissed from the hospital within twenty-four hours after delivery. Indirectly, midwives perceive the message that swiftness and efficiency are the ideal model toward which they need to strive and that there is no need to provide care for more than a couple of days.

7. Internal examinations are performed routinely in biomedical perinatal care. Nakedness in general and the exposure of the pubic area and internal examinations in particular are major sources of concern, anxiety, and disapproval for village women; it becomes one of the sites of greatest rejection and fiercest resistance toward bio-obstetrics: "Cuando llegamos [al hospital] me desvistieron y me acostaron. ¡Me dió muchísima pena! Después me razuraron el parto [pubis]; los dejé hacer pero mi verguenza creció más. Me dieron una bata blanca que no se podía cerrar, me hicieron acostar y cuando los médicos empezaron a poner sus dedos adentro y a lastimarme mucho, ¡mi verguenza ya no tuvo límite! ¡Nunca más voy a regresar! [When we arrived (at the hospital) they undressed me and made me lie down. I felt so ashamed! Afterward they shaved my pubis; I let them do it but my shame grew. They gave me a white gown that could not be closed, they made me lie down and when the doctors came and started to put their fingers inside it really hurt a lot, and I was overwhelmed by shame! I will never go back!] (Olga, 37 years old, San Francisco del Mar)

8. "Las señoras vienen solitarias cuando necesitan."

9. According to many biomedical practitioners in the United States and Mexico, the external version carries the risk of detaching the placenta from the uterine walls, provoking a premature birth. Nevertheless, it is noteworthy that U.S. biomedical obstetricians interested in lowering their cesarean rates are beginning to obtain training—often from midwives—in the performance of external versions (Bethany Hays, M.D., and Robbie Davis-Floyd, pers. com.).

10. "Muchas mujeres más grandes prefieren no venir conmigo porque yo no estoy acostumbrada a atender como antes. Pero con todas las mujeres que atiendo, con las más jóvenes y con las más viejas, no he podido negarme a dar sobadas porque me lo piden, aun si el médico, sí, él me lo prohibió."

11. "Es malo que vengan a sobarse cuando ya tienen la panza grande. La razón es que si el niño viene muy arriba o de lado cuando no se soba es difícil ponerlo bien para dar a luz. En cambio si el niño se ha ido sobando es más fácil que salga bien. Uno se da cuenta porque en los últimos meses uno soba y se siente que todo está bien."

12. "Cuando estaba embarazada, me sentía muy pesada y tenía mucho mareo. . . . Me fui con mi partera y ella me sobó. Después de la sobada una se siente mucho mejor, mucho más ligera."

13. "A mí me gustó cómo me asistió la partera porque me dió baños tibios y me sobaba la cintura y la panza. Con las sobadas me sentía bien."

14. "Prefiero ir con la partera durante el embarazo porque ella me soba y el médico no. Yo voy porlomenos a tres sobadas, una a los cuatro meses, una a los seis y otra a los ocho. Después, otra más durante el parto. . . . La sobada me hace sentir bien."

15. "Cuando vienen [para sobarse] yo la tiento para buscar cómo viene el niño. Lo mejor es cuando el niño viene bien, pero si está mal puesto lo tengo que acomodar. A veces hay que acomodarlo nomás una vez y ya se queda. Pero a veces hay que seguir sobando porque hay niños necios. Si no sobará, el niño podría venir mal acomodado y después quién lo saca, es más difícil y se sufre más."

16. None of the midwives ever admitted the occurrence of a maternal death while they were attending; some did state, though, that they had to deliver a

stillborn once or twice during their years of practice. Commenting privately about each other, nevertheless, parteras do make assertions about others' inability to save the life of a baby during a serious childbirth crisis. Unfortunately, these declarations could not be properly cross-checked, for reliable data on neonatal and perinatal infant mortality are not available for any of these communities. Infant mortality rates in rural Oaxaca suffer from chronic underreporting, mostly as a result of the widespread practice of registering babies only after they are over six months old. Extensive interviews with the mothers suggest that infant mortality rates have decreased in the last ten years; most of the references, though, were made in relation to babies after their first two or three months of life.

17. Hegemony refers to the process of social formation by which ruling classes (re)produce their power not just through coercive means but also by winning the active consent of subordinate social groups. Hegemony, then, involves the acceptance of the existing social order by those it subordinates. For Gramsci (1971:52–54), the institutions of civil society—education, medicine, mass media, religion, etc.—are the ones specifically involved in creating consent.

18. "No he podido negarme a dar sobadas porque me lo piden, aun si el médico, sí, él me lo prohibió. Los médicos han tratado de cambiar las costumbres pero no han podido porque las costumbres de la gente aquí son más fuertes."

REFERENCES

Aguirre Beltrán, Gonzalo
    1986   *Antropología médica.* Mexico City: CIESAS.

Anzures y Bolaños, María del Carmen
    1983   *La medicina tradicional en México: Proceso histórico, sincretismo y conflictos.* Mexico City: Universidad Nacional Autónoma de México.

Buekens, Pierre, Patricia Hernández, and Claudia Infante
    1990   "La atención prenatal en América Latina." *Salud Pública de México* 32(6):673–682.

Castañeda, Martha, Cristina Galante, Paola Sesia, and Ruth Piedrasanta
    1992   "Metodología de los talleres de aprendizaje materno-infantil para regiones indígenas." In *Medicina tradicional, herbolaria y salud comunitaria en Oaxaca,* ed. Paola Sesia, 265–291. Oaxaca: CIESAS and the State Government of Oaxaca.

COPLAMAR
    1985   *Necesidades esenciales en México.* Vol. 4: *Salud.* 3d ed. Mexico City: Siglo XXI Editores.

Cosminsky, Sheila
    1986   "Traditional Birth Practices and Pregnancy Avoidance in the Americas." In *The Potential of the Traditional Birth Attendant,* ed. Mangay A. Maglacas and John Simons, 75–89. Geneva: WHO Offset Publication no. 95.

Franzoni Lobo, Josefína
    1993   "El programa de atención materna en Oaxaca: 1980–1992." Master's thesis, Instituto de Investigaciones Sociológicas of the Universidad Autónoma Benito Juárez of Oaxaca, Mexico.

Frey, Hans Rudy
1989 "Economic Integration, Peasant Strategies and Indian Tradition." Unpublished manuscript.
Galante, M. Cristina
1988 "Le ostetriche empiriche: Un esempio di rifiuto e adattamento culturali." Unpublished manuscript.
Gramsci, Antonio
1971 *Selections from the Prison Notebooks*. Ed. and trans. Quintin Hare and Geoffrey Nowell Smith. New York: International Publishers.
IMSS, Coordinación General del Programa IMSS-COPLAMAR
1983a *La medicina tradicional y el médico del IMSS-COPLAMAR*. Documento de trabajo no. 1. Mexico City: IMSS.
1983b *La medicina tradicional y las políticas mundiales desalud*. Documento de trabajo no. 2. Mexico City: IMSS.
1983c *Nosologías de la medicina tradicional mexicana*. Documento de trabajo no. 3. Mexico City: IMSS.
1983d *Curanderos y parteras en la medicina tradicional de México*. Documento de trabajo no. 4. Mexico City: IMSS.
1983e *Importancia de la herbolaria en la medicina tradicional de México*. Documento de trabajo no. 5. Mexico City: IMSS.
IMSS, Delegación Oaxaca, Jefatura de Servicios Médicos y Planificación Familiar
1986 "Lista de las parteras capacitadas 1979–1985." Unpublished document.
Instituto Mexicano del Seguro Social (IMSS)
1987 *Memorias de descentralización de los servicios del programa IMSS-COPLAMAR al Gobierno del Estado de Morelos*. Mexico City: IMSS.
1989 *Guía de enseñanza para los cursos de adiestramento a parteras empíricas: La metodología dialogada*. Mexico City: IMSS.
Instituto Nacional de Estadística, Geografía e Informática (INEGI)
1991 *Información estadística sector salud y seguridad social*. Cuaderno no. 7. Aguascalientes: INEGI.
Jordan, Brigitte
[1978] 1993 *Birth in Four Cultures: A Cross-Cultural Investigation of Childbirth in Yucatan, Holland, Sweden and the United States*. 4th ed. Prospect Heights, Ill.: Waveland Press.
1984 "External Cephalic Version as an Alternative to Breech Delivery and Cesarean Section." *Social Science and Medicine* 18(8):637–651.
1989 "Cosmopolitical Obstetrics: Some Insights from the Training of Traditional Midwives." *Social Science and Medicine* 28(9):925–944.
1992 "Technology and Social Interaction: Notes on the Achievement of Authoritative Knowledge in Complex Settings." Unpublished document.
López Acuña, Daniel
1984 *La salud desigual en México*, 5th ed. Mexico City: Siglo XXI Editores.
Martínez Manautou, J., ed.
1986 *Planificación familiar, población y salud en el México rural*. Mexico City: Instituto Mexicano del Seguro Social.
McClain, Carol S.
1975 "Ethno-Obstetrics in Ajijic." *Anthropological Quarterly* 40(1):38–56.

Mellado, Virginia, Carlos Zolla, and Xochitl Castañeda
    1989   *La atención al embarazo y el parto en el medio rural mexicano.* Mexico City: Centro Interamericano de Estudios de Seguridad Social (CIESS).
Menéndez, Eduardo
    1983   "Recursos y prácticas médicas 'tradicionales.' " In *La medicina invisible,* ed. Xavier Lozoya and Carlos Zolla, 38–61. Mexico City: Folios Ediciones.
    1984   *Hacia una práctica médica alternativa: Hegemonía y autoatención en salud.* Cuadernos de la Casa Chata 86. Mexico City: CIESAS.
Population Information Program
    1980   *Traditional Midwives and Family Planning.* Population Reports, Series J, 22:1–58. Baltimore: Johns Hopkins University.
Secretaría de Salud (SSA)
    1992   *Mortalidad, 1990.* Mexico City: SSA.
Sesia(-Lewis), Paola
    1987   "The Persistence of Traditional Midwifery Practices in Four Mexican Villages of the Isthmus of Tehuantepec, Oaxaca." Master's thesis, School of Public Health, University of California, Berkeley.
    1992   "La obstetricia tradicional en el Istmo de Tehuantepec: Marco conceptual y diferencia con el modelo biomédico." In *Medicina tradicional, herbolaria y salud comunitaria en Oaxaca,* ed. Paola Sesia, 17–49. Oaxaca: CIESAS and the State Government of Oaxaca.
Stavenhagen, Rodolfo
    1976   *Las clases sociales en las sociedades agrarias.* Mexico City: Siglo XXI Editores.
Urbina Fuentes, Manuel
    1986   "Programa nacional de planificación familiar, objetivos, estrategias nacionales y regionales, relación en el bienestar familiar." Paper read at the 3d Reunión sobre investigación demográfica en México, Mexico City, November.
Verderese, María de Lourdes, and Lily M. Turnbull
    1975   *The Traditional Birth Attendant in Maternal and Child Health and Family Planning.* Geneva: WHO Offset Publication no. 18.
World Health Organization (WHO)
    1974   *Report of the Interregional Meeting on the Training and Utilization of the Traditional Birth Attendant in Maternal and Child Health and Family Planning,* Quezon City, Philippines, December 2–6. Geneva: WHO.
    1978   *The Promotion and Development of Traditional Medicine.* Technical Report Series 622. Geneva: WHO.
    1979   *Traditional Birth Attendants.* Geneva: WHO Offset Publication no. 44.
Zolla, Carlos
    1983   "La medicina tradicional mexicana y la noción de recurso para la salud." In *La medicina invisible,* ed. Xavier Lozoya and Carlos Zolla, 14–37. Mexico City: Folios Ediciones.

SIXTEEN

Maternal Health, War, and Religious Tradition

Authoritative Knowledge in Pujehun District, Sierra Leone

Amara Jambai and Carol MacCormack

Yema, heavily pregnant, walked several miles on a bush path from her hamlet to the health center in a larger village. In the health center, a simple building in a community where most houses are made of mud and roofed with thatch or galvanized iron, a maternal and child health aide, working cooperatively with a trained traditional midwife, gave Yema a prenatal examination. As they sat chatting, the war came. Young men, some merely boys of 14, came into the village shooting guns, killing, and looting. They stripped the health center of its few basic pharmaceuticals and simple equipment, as well as its furniture, doors, and window shutters. They set fire to the village. Then they told the women in the health center to come away with them as "wives," and to give nursing care to their sick and wounded. As they began to walk, Yema and the nurses whispered a word or two of a plan. Yema pretended to go into labor. The boys with guns, knowing nothing of this "women's business," told them to stay there until the baby was born, then continue on the path to their camp. When the "war boys" were out of sight, Yema and the health center staff ran off on another path through the forest, not knowing if they would meet war on that path or reach a place to hide. But as they ran, real labor began, Yema gave birth, and continued to safety—until the war came again a few months later.

This chapter is an account of the strength, indeed the heroic strength in adversity, of birthing women and primary health care workers in coastal Pujehun district, Sierra Leone, where tropical and other diseases flourish, and infant, child, and maternal mortality rates have been among the

Medical Anthropology Quarterly 10(2):270–286. Copyright © 1996 American Anthropological Association.

highest in the world. We will consider the risks of childbirth and constraints to ideal care. This is also a case study of a primary health care
approach in which government-trained health workers, if they are wise,
work in respectful alliance with traditional midwives, who are usually important political and religious figures. Health workers and midwives each
have their own type of legitimacy or authoritative knowledge. Traditional
midwives are also key actors in the financing of a primary health care service that is only minimally funded by the central government. This analysis
is located in the real world of the arms trade that heaps another layer of
misery on these heroic people, and ends by considering the resilience of
their culture in a refugee camp.

The narrative revolves around the concepts of authoritative knowledge
and the legitimacy to advise and act. When we consider a range of factors
affecting women's reproductive health we see clearly that authority and
legitimacy are constantly tested by circumstances and renegotiated in practical situations. In Pujehun district of Sierra Leone, as in all regions of the
world, there is never one single system of authoritative knowledge, but
several. In any particular frame of observation the dominant system either
better explains the experienced world to the actors, or is associated with a
stronger power base (see Jordan [1978] 1993:152–154). Systems coexist
with varying degrees of cooperation and conflict. People seeking help often move from one to another, and practitioners borrow techniques from
each other. Indeed, they are even urged to borrow, as in traditional birth
attendant training programs, and syncretistic medical systems evolve.

We especially focus on legitimacy and authority as expressed within the
local women's religious and political domain, and in interaction with the
Western type of health care. A rather constructive postcolonial system of
cooperation has been replacing the colonialist mentality of superiority and
conflict. War disrupted that process, but it recommenced again under Dr.
Jambai's guidance in a refugee camp setting. We hope Pujehun district's
farming villages will soon rise again from the ashes of war, and that constructive progress toward primary health care will go home again to the
countryside, where most people lived and where most productive work was
done.

METHODS

This study combines qualitative and quantitative methods. One author
(Jambai) has been district medical officer (DMO) in the area under investigation for the past five years, actively extending primary health care services to remote villages. He was taken hostage in war, escaped after three
months, was sheltered in one of those remote villages, and was a key actor
in setting up a refugee camp. In all settings he has worked cooperatively

with traditional midwives. He is a native Mende speaker and deeply steeped in his culture. The other author (MacCormack) has worked inter- mittently as an anthropologist in coastal Sierra Leone for 25 years. Both have built up a fund of goodwill and trust that allows gentle enquiry into sensitive or secret matters, such as childbirth.

We have drawn on data collected in several different ways. First, there was routine data gathered through the Sierra Leone national health ser- vice. As DMO, and later as an organizer of a refugee camp, Jambai had access to such information at its grassroots source. For example, he knows the figures for immunization coverage in Pujehun district before war and how coverage has dropped since war began. He knows the incidence of neonatal tetanus seen in public health units in his district, and how inci- dence has been dropping. These are proxy indicators suggesting that im- munization coverage and traditional midwife training were having a health impact. Second, special funds for surveys to support planning, implemen- tation, and evaluation of primary health care in Pujehun district had come from the German aid agency Gesellschaft für Technische Zusammenarbeit (G.T.Z.). The quantitative data from both routine health information sys- tems and special surveys were not published, but were accessible to us. We have used figures and tables only where they advance the narrative of this paper.

Both authors had participated in aspects of G.T.Z.-funded surveys. For example, MacCormack worked with a very senior Mende public health nurse. Together they met with high officials of Sande, the women's reli- gious sodality ("secret society") (MacCormack 1972, 1979). Those officials were also traditional midwives and healers. Working through a network of local chiefs and Sande officials we did group interviews in various villages, meeting within the women's own sacred space. Those were self-selected samples, and groups of Sande officials ranged in size from 6 to 20 women, with a total sample size of about 300. Conversations were guided by a brief memorized list of topics we wished to cover with each group. All relevant comments and observations were recorded in field notebooks and post- coded, and an index was created for data retrieval. We also drew on coded and indexed field notes MacCormack had collected over a quarter century.

The two authors have known each other for many years, and we princi- pally wrote this chapter by telling each other stories. The chapter's validity draws as much on Mende canons of authentic narrative as on Western scientific conventions. When war came, Jambai, as a physician, had to deal with atrocities and other inhumanities that cut to the core of his heart. He also had to deal with moral dilemmas. For example, when insurgents were approaching Pujehun town he put his wife, young children, and others from his household in his vehicle to leave. He went to the hospital com- pound to get petrol and found his staff there, waiting for him to take them to safety. There was only one vehicle. He stepped down, asked that his close family might remain, and invited the rest to either stay with him in the hospital or find a place in the vehicle if they could. Then came the descent into chaos, and the need to make sense of it by telling the narratives. In both the anthropological tradition and the caring tradition in medicine, this study is based primarily on participant-observation.

THE SETTING

By understanding in some detail the national and local setting of this study we begin to understand the very real constraints to ideal maternal health care. The study is focused on Pujehun district, one of the 12 administrative areas of Sierra Leone. The district, located along the Atlantic coast of West Africa, about seven degrees north of the equator, forms part of the national boundary between Sierra Leone and Liberia.

In Sierra Leone the centrally organized national health service reaches only 35 percent of the population. Among the poor in urban areas, and in most rural areas, the majority of health care comes from self-treatment or the traditional sector. Of all the former British colonies, Sierra Leone alone was known as "the white man's grave." Any Sierra Leone medical officer will give you a wry smile and tell you the grave calls to all, not only white men in their prime, but local children, women in the midst of their productive and reproductive years, and others as well. Pujehun district, a remote rural area, had an infant mortality rate of about 308 per 1,000 in 1980 (Kandeh and Dow 1980). Of every 1,000 children born in the previous year, over a quarter were dead by their first birthday, and more than half did not reach their fifth birthday. With government effort, and special assistance from G.T.Z., death rates dropped. Following five years of an integrated agriculture and primary health care project emphasizing appropriate training and appropriate technology at the village level, the infant mortality rate in 1988 had dropped to 127 per 1,000, compared with a national average of 165. Especially in the health sector, the approach was not to provoke a clash of authoritative knowledge systems but to work cooperatively within the indigenous structure of chiefs, and with the indigenous religious structure, notably Sande, in which virtually every woman is socially, emotionally, and conceptually embedded (MacCormack 1979). However, since the civil war in Liberia spilled across the border into Sierra Leone in April 1991 there has been civic chaos, and the infant mortality rate has been rising.

Women between ages 15 and 45 are considered to be in their childbearing years and make up 24 percent of the Sierra Leone population, but the true maternal mortality rate is difficult to know. Only an estimated 34 percent of all births in the country, and far fewer in rural areas, are supervised by people with any medical training, even a few weeks of training (World Development Report 1993). If Yema had died on the path, who in the Central Statistics Office would have known? Had she not walked those miles to the health center, who in the Central Statistics Office would have known she was pregnant? Who, beyond her immediate locality, would even have known her name? The national maternal mortality rate is only an estimate of 7 deaths in childbirth per 1,000 births. Because women have so many pregnancies, the chances of their remaining alive until age 45 become increasingly slender. Nevertheless, the population of the country is growing at 2.3 percent per year, and 20.8 percent of the population is under the age of five. About 85 percent of the nation is illiterate, and the proportion of people who cannot read tends to be higher in rural and remote areas, and among women, than the national average. Traditional midwives, especially the older and much respected ones, are seldom literate.

About 95 percent of the people in Pujehun district speak Mende or the closely related Krim language. The population of 137,000 people covers 1,585 square miles. Sparsely populated, with an average of 86 people per square mile, the coastal part of the district is intersected by unbridged broad tidal rivers and vast areas of swamp and shallow lake. It is an ideal habitat for *Anopheles gambiae* and other malaria mosquito vectors. There are other vector-borne diseases as well. For example, women more than men stand in water to transplant rice, wash clothes, or collect drinking water, and are especially vulnerable to bleeding from Schistosomiasis hematobium (White et al. 1982). Malaria is holoendemic; it is always there, but intensifies as the rainy season, which drops from 160 to 200 inches of rain on the coast, leaves vast areas of wetlands. Pregnant women are especially vulnerable as they lose their acquired immunity to malaria during pregnancy.

There was one medical officer (Jambai) for this district. With only one doctor, a primary health care structure with many paramedical workers is essential. In addition to his hospital staff, the DMO was supported by a district health nurse, a health superintendent, a district pharmacist, an operations officer, a social mobilization and health education officer, two people doing monitoring and evaluation, and a specialist in maintaining a cold room and a cold chain for vaccines. The district also had seven community health officers and four community health nurses in rural health centers, linked with 22 maternal and child health (MCH) aides in satellite villages. There were eight vaccinators, some with enough additional training to man rural health posts.

The district has only a few miles of paved road, and most villages and hamlets are not accessible by motor vehicle. They can only be reached by foot, or a combination of taking a boat along the dangerous margin of the sea, up tidal rivers, and then walking. Given these constraints, the district had done very well in beginning to build a primary health care structure. The proportion of fully immunized children rose to 82 percent in early 1991, but since war began coverage had dropped to 45 percent in 1993 and is still falling. In 1991, 86 percent of women in the district had at least one vaccination for tetanus, a disease that can kill them and their newborn infant. However, with the chaos of war few are receiving booster shots, and risk is rising.

Sierra Leone now allocates less than 1 percent of government expenditure to health, a proportion that has been falling steadily since the colonial period (MacCormack 1984:199). Most of the health programs in the country are vertical programs funded by outside donor agencies, rather than a rationally planned and integrated national primary health care structure. Donors include national bilaterals (e.g., Germany), multilaterals (e.g., UNICEF) and nongovernmental organizations (e.g., Save the Children Fund). The Ministry of Health is caught in a paradox familiar to many African countries: it has lost much control to the donors, but without those special program funds the ministry would have a much-attenuated function. The donors, because they have the money, tend to rank at the top of the hierarchy that decides what constitutes real or useful knowledge. They sometimes, but not always, have pushed ready-made inappropriate programs onto a district. Coordination and rational planning, when it occurred, was often at the district level, as was the case with Pujehun district. However, with war, the donors have withdrawn funds in Pujehun district as they saw the tangible signs of their efforts destroyed. People had to flee their farms, health centers were looted and burned, and authority came out of the barrel of a gun. But the intangibles remain. Training given to local people, which is perceived by them as useful, remains an excellent investment, the skills surfacing again in a refugee camp. In time people may return with their skills to their rural villages.

Much of the country is following the Bamako initiative, attempting to recover the cost of health services by having primary health care workers sell basic pharmaceuticals at a profit. This burden of cost recovery falls heavily on the rural population during the rainy season, the time of hunger, when most diseases peak and people have little cash. Acute cases referred to the 45-bed Pujehun district hospital had fallen to only eight or nine inpatients, most of them obstetric emergencies or dying children. Through the export of diamonds, gold, bauxite, and rutile, Sierra Leone earns foreign exchange for use of such things as importation of basic pharmaceuticals. However, most of the diamonds and gold are smuggled out of the country, and the wealth is therefore not available for building a health infrastructure. Some of the income from bauxite, rutile, and other sources leaks away through financial mismanagement, a problem not unique to

Sierra Leone and somewhat endemic in Africa. The internal economy of Pujehun district is based on subsistence agriculture and fishing with small-scale marketing and barter. These transactions are not taxed and do not yield government income for local and national health services.

Sierra Leone once had a national health service patterned on the same type of service Britain has had since 1947. By degrees the Sierra Leone health service has collapsed into a fee-for-service system, which many of the donors favor for ideological reasons. Hospital patients buy their own drugs and supplies. However, a DMO and his staff, all of them on the most meager salary, function to a large extent in a barter economy. A patient may, for example, bring a five-gallon tin of locally made palm oil to the DMO, who shares it out with his staff. Much emergency work is done without a fee, and the grateful family may, at some time, bring gifts. For example, a mother brought in her severely anemic son, with malaria, hookworm, and other simultaneous infections. Although he was near death on arrival, he survived, and the DMO did not attempt to collect a fee. Some time later the mother appeared at the hospital to tell the DMO she had left a gift at his house. There he found 12 large live chickens. (The magnitude of this gift can be measured against the observation that some whole villages do not have as many as 12 mature chickens!) Another more subtle reciprocity is the many children named for the DMO and other health workers in appreciation of their services.

TRADITIONAL MIDWIVES AND PRIMARY SERVICES

In the 1940s, decades before the World Health Organization began to advocate the training of traditional midwives (traditional birth attendant),[1] a medical officer in Pujehun district began to work with women who were paramount chiefs, and women who were high officials of Sande, the women's religion in the district (MacCormack 1972, 1979). Virtually all women in the district are active members of Sande, a religion that includes much practical knowledge about birth and healing, wisdom evolved over centuries and conferred upon the living by ancestresses. High officials tend to be skilled in midwifery. In the 1940s a young medical officer, Milton Margai, introduced some practical European health and hygiene skills into the curriculum of the puberty initiation ceremonies, and gave additional practical skills in obstetrics to Sande officials already providing childbirth services (Margai 1948). Some of those Mende midwives Margai trained, officially called village maternity assistants, are still alive. They are addressed with great respect and affection as "Mamma Nurse." They may say "I am Margai trained" and the listener falls into a respectful hush. The irony is that Margai was driven out of Pujehun district by officials of Poro, the men's religion, and by male political leaders (see Little 1965, 1966).

They said "this man is playing with our wives," but when that man became Sir Milton Margai, the first prime minister in the newly independent nation of Sierra Leone, those same local leaders went very apologetically to the capital city to make their peace with the great man.

Today a "mamma nurse" is such a politically strong person that in one case, when she opposed the building of a health center in her area, none was built until after she died. She was the authoritative person on childbirth and did not wish to share power with young government-trained workers, and the chiefs were in solidarity with her. She controlled the thinking about health care in the area, and if one were so foolish as to go over her head and post a maternal and child health aide there, the social ostracism would be so great that the aide would not stay. Medical officers know the cases where such young women soon reappear at district headquarters saying, "Doctor, I don't want to stay there." Without any questions asked they are posted elsewhere.

This kind of interplay between aides and traditional midwives illustrates the postcolonial process of conflict and reconciliation between European and Mende systems of legitimacy to heal. Aides are the lowest grade of government health worker. They have completed form three (ninth grade), are 21 or older, and are recruited in their local district and serve communities, especially rural areas, in their district. Because they are relatively young and inexperienced in the praxis of reproductive health, the authoritative knowledge of new MCH aides is not derived from experience and religious respect but from professional qualifications, however minimal. But that rational-legal legitimacy must be negotiated within larger contexts that include the powerful traditional legitimacy of Sande officials (see Weber 1947). In the early days, when government health expenditure was higher, aides had a small salary. Now few have a salary unless it comes out of donor project funds. Economically they are like traditional midwives, relying on gifts from grateful patients. If people do not feel the aide is helping them they will not give gifts for service. However, they have the advantage over traditional midwives of having access to more training programs, and they have a few pharmaceuticals such as antimalarials, oral antibiotics, analgesics, iron for anemia, and injectable ergometrine to control postpartum bleeding. In lieu of salary, they keep 10–20 percent of the sale price as profit. For some, of course, there is a temptation to overcharge and maximize profit, or resort to polypharmacy, taking their percentage off each item. Before the war in Pujehun district, some nurses were working with officials of Sande, negotiating agreement on fair prices for basic drugs, but now with rampant inflation and unstable prices no one knows the true price of anything.

Medically, socially, and economically, the best strategy for an MCH aide is to collaborate with local trained traditional midwives. They can share practical skills; the Mende midwives usually have done far more deliveries than young school-educated aides. From the point of view of a traditional midwife, working with a good MCH aide gives her access to knowledge about the use of pharmaceuticals and other health techniques. Since there are only three qualified pharmacists in government service in all of Sierra Leone, availability of pharmaceuticals is not well regulated, and they can therefore be purchased by anyone who knows what to ask for.

If MCH aides antagonize local traditional midwives, who are usually high officials of Sande, they seldom remain in their post. Where a respectful working relationship is negotiated, the traditional midwives may mobilize local women to make a farm for the aide, provisioning her household and perhaps giving her a surplus to market as well. Those occasions of harmony based on shared traditional and European medical authoritative knowledge result in a win-win situation for both women, and better health for all.

Today, a relative of Sir Margai, a very senior public health nurse, has overall responsibility for training and supervising MCH aides and traditional midwives in Pujehun district and three neighboring districts. Sister Onita Samai is effective because she is steeped in the local religio-political tradition, and she is a skillful nurse. When she enters an area for any purpose she greets the local chief first, pays her respects with a small gift, informs him or her of her intentions, and asks permission to train or supervise. She may wait until the chief and elders, or prominent men in Poro, "hang heads" to talk through her request and reach a consensus agreement on how to respond. For example, if she informs a male chief that there will be a new training cycle for traditional midwives, he will typically have a cursory discussion with his elders. Then, by rather strict rules of cultural convention, he will meet with the religio-political domain of women. These robust conventions of political etiquette help information and scarce resources cross the gender barrier. Sande women then choose the trainees, usually the traditional midwives' younger assistants. Since the traditional midwives, who are also senior women of Sande, are often wives or kin of local chiefs and leaders, lines of communication are further facilitated. But the crucial decisions about this kind of "women's business" are taken in the female domain.

Training in maternal and child health under Sister Samai has gone beyond the mere training of a few traditional midwives. Before war came, 234 traditional midwives in the district had been trained. But Sister Samai was well into the process of extending training to all the *soweisia,* the senior officials of Sande, in each local congregation. Some officials in a local congregation are midwives and the rest are intelligent respected women in other roles. In those training programs local chiefs were consulted first. Then they sent out word to all the villages under their care that the soweisia should come to a village on a particular date. As many as 50 women might come together and go with Sister Samai, a senior woman in Sande herself, to the sacred grove or sacred house of the women, the places where child-birth occurs. No men, not even little boys, go near. Women sit comfortably, hitch up their skirts, fan themselves, put a child to the breast, and talk about the most intimate and powerful things women know. When they discuss avoiding risks in birth a pregnant woman among them serves as demonstration model. When they discuss diagnosis and treatment of malaria, a feverish infant may provide an example. They actually taste antimalarials so as to better distinguish them from aspirin, counterfeit chloriquine, and all those other white tablets swilling around in developing countries. Because their knowledge about birth and health is not overtly shared with men, their secret skills help to underpin the relatively high social status women have in Mende country.

In those training sessions Sister Samai first confirmed what the healers already knew about diagnosis of a range of diseases and conditions. She emphasized such common things as diagnosis of anemia in pregnancy, the correct dosage for antimalarial drugs for pregnant women and young children, and other lifesaving skills. Knowledge about correct dosage, for example, was often composed into songs on the spot, becoming part of future initiation ceremonies and other women's celebrations. Not only the trained Mende midwives, but all women, had become much more aware of the benefits of vaccination and the need for clean hands and a new razor blade to cut the umbilical cord in delivery. In Sande puberty initiation rites, when girls go into the forest to begin the liminal stage of the ritual, they are traditionally "washed" with protective traditional medicine. They are also washed again a few weeks later when they reemerge in the new status of women. Under Sister Samai's culturally sensitive guidance, vaccination with tetanus toxoid had become part of the protective washing upon entering, and the booster was given as part of the concluding cleansing ritual. Neonatal tetanus is now culturally defined in much of Mende country as an offense to the ancestors/ancestresses, and incidence of neonatal tetanus had dropped to only 0.1 percent of diseases seen in public health units in Pujehun district in 1989. Women were also coming to know more about the stages of dilation and therefore not to encourage their laboring kinswomen to push too soon, causing them to become exhausted in the birthing process. They were becoming better at spotting signs of risk in pregnancy, encouraging women who might be at risk to go to a health center or hospital in good time, rather than arriving as a dire emergency. Some groups of women had formed revolving credit associations so that funds for transportation and drugs might be had at short notice. The benefits of a range of basic vaccinations had become widely known, and a trained traditional midwife accompanying a mother and newborn on a visit to the nearest health center for vaccination had become a ritual act. In these ways health improved and the social status of women who have acquired these practical skills improved as well.

Belmont Williams, the former Chief Medical Officer of Sierra Leone, conducted a survey with Sister Samai in the Pujehun area and found that most of the senior women she interviewed did not feel that government trained traditional midwives were any better than the other traditional midwives. The explanation is probably that the two-week government training course is very short compared with a traditional apprenticeship that commonly lasts between one and five years, and may continue as long as ten years. Government training teaches only technical things rather than the holistic Mende approach that sees mind-body-spirit as a socially embedded unity. Perhaps of most importance, Sande puts much emphasis on social unity. Choosing only one traditional midwife from a local congregation or local community splits the group of soweisia, setting one above all the others. Sande women resist this imposition of state bureaucratic thinking. They do not particularly recognize the legitimacy of government or donor attempts to confer status, especially when a not very adept woman has been chosen for traditional birth attendant training for political reasons.

However, should all the soweisia in each district become trained, and if that training is done well, as under Sister Samai's direction, the conflict of authoritative knowledge systems is minimized. In Pujehun district the training language and the conceptual system was Mende. The prior skill and social status of Sande officials was honored, and in the best situation useful skill-enhancing European medical knowledge was shared. In the worst cases, however, trainers do little more than attempt to confirm their uneasy status by trying to teach dependency. They lecture at Sande officials, saying "you must never touch a woman with breech presentation, you must never touch a woman with twins," and so on. However, in the real world of Pujehun district, as Sister Samai well knows, villages are often remote and isolated, and when labor begins twins just appear. There is no one but the Sande officials and their assistants to see the births through. Young government-trained health workers either remember to be respectful to their elders and learn fast, or have little job satisfaction and are an ineffective drag on the health system. The effective ones are like influential chiefs: they are effective leaders because the people love them.

THE SOCIAL POWER OF WOMEN

The health of women is related to their social status. When they are active in production and distribution of goods and services, and have overt political and religious offices, they survive in greater numbers compared with

men than in other societies where they have little social power (MacCormack 1988). Pujehun district has a very labor-intensive economy in which
the work of women is crucial. About 40 percent of the edible palm oil in
Sierra Leone comes from Pujehun district. Men cut the palm fruits from
the tops of trees, but women do the remainder of the laborious tasks which
render the fruits into marketable oil. They plant, weed, and harvest rice,
cassava, and other crops, and prepare them for market. They prepare
parched cassava, which they sell as gari. They dry fish and trade it. Along
the coast they do the heavy hard work of making briny mud into salt, and
sell it. They are the chief actors in fixed markets in larger towns, and in
the seven-day periodic markets that characterize the area.

Women also have some overt political offices. Pujehun district is internally divided into 12 chiefdoms, 3 of them headed by women who are
paramount chiefs. Each chiefdom is subdivided into between six and nine
sections. At least 15 of the sections are headed by women chiefs, and some
towns are headed by women town chiefs. A political candidate cannot
hope to be elected unless he has the endorsement of Sande women. They
meet in local congregations, discuss issues, reach consensus, and block
vote. The high officials of Sande, if secular political leaders in their own
right, tend to also be influential wives or sisters of paramount chiefs and
other leaders. In the religious domain, as in the economic domain, the
roles of men and women are somewhat separate. In Sande women are not
subsumed under a single male religious hierarchy as is common in the
"great" religions (see Sered 1994). Childbirth and much healing also takes
place in this feminine-religious domain; it is literally "women's business."

RISKS AND PREFERENCES

There is a Mende way of thinking about risk, and there is the perspective
of international health planners. Although Mende culture does not define
pregnancy as a disease, women are aware of risk, but few appear in hospital
for obstetric services. To some extent that is as it should be in a country
with considerable economic constraints. A primary health care system is
working well when only high-risk pregnancies and a few women from the
professional and commercial elite appear for hospital deliveries. But of
course many rural women truly at risk do not appear for assistance that
might save their lives because of constraints of distance, transportation,
and mobilization of social support for resort to hospital. There are also
more subtle reasons. Mende women think holistically and do not make the
kind of separations between mind, emotion, spirit, society, and cosmology
that European medicine has made in the past few centuries. For example,
a woman tense and fearful among people she feels hate her will not go to
hospital for help with an obstructed labor. Hospital staff are not trained in

social mediation, which is the cure for witchcraft. Thus Mende women see a wider range of risk than do the medical and nursing professions (MacCormack 1994).

However, attempts to relate professional and Mende perspectives have been made and are sometimes fruitful, as when immunization for tetanus was integrated into the Sande society's puberty rites. Girls are initiated into Sande at puberty and are then legitimately eligible for marriage and pregnancy. But the skeletal development of some is not completed, their pelvis is still narrow, and the first delivery may be difficult if not life threatening. There is the potential in the kind of primary health care system Pujehun district is developing, with a degree of mutual respect between Mende and European systems, to delay the age of marriage. With guidance from someone such as Sister Samai and other wise women and men, chiefs and elders of both the men's and women's religious societies might be approached. Discussion in those separate but linked domains could begin. Since there is a great deal of local autonomy, one at a time a village and/or a local congregation of Sande or Poro might reach consensus on delayed age of marriage. Everyone knows, by looking at girls clad only in the traditional wraparound skirt, if they are biologically mature. Throughout much of the developing world maternal mortality rates would drop dramatically if first pregnancy could be delayed by just one or two years (Liljestrand and Povey 1992). Where women have little social power it is not likely to happen, but in Sierra Leone it is just possible through the process of shared authoritative knowledge we have been describing.

Epidemiologically, maternal mortality risk everywhere takes a U-shaped curve and rises again with high parity. The placenta attaches at a new place in the uterus with each pregnancy. After many pregnancies the "good" places, high in the uterus, are used up. When the placenta attaches low in the uterus it does not attach so firmly, increasing the risk of excessive bleeding, or it may even block the birth canal. A much-used uterus in a woman who may also be generally depleted may simply lose its power to contract sufficiently. Women literally say "I have grown tired of childbearing." Might a range of contraceptives, with enough choice to suit women's different physiologies, be discussed in traditional forums? They are hardly available in rural Pujehun district now.

Anemia is the shadowy specter, always in the background. In 1989, 959 (6.2%) cases of serious anemia were treated in public health units in Pujehun district. Malaria is one cause of anemia in pregnancy. Pregnant women lose their acquired immunity to the disease and plasmodium parasites may destroy large numbers of red cells. Malaria pressure in Pujehun district is intense, and malaria cases accounted for 44 percent of all diseases diagnosed in public health units in Pujehun district in 1989. Because of the sexual division of labor, women are also more likely to lose blood

TABLE 16.1   Risk Factors of Clinic Attenders

Risk	Number	%
Age under 15 or above 35	372	12.5
More than five previous deliveries	728	24.4
Twin delivery	150	5.0
Stillbirths	347	11.7
Miscarriages	476	16.0
Previous cesarean section	26	1.0
Prolonged labor	218	7.3
Postpartum hemorrhage	323	10.9
Retained placenta	89	3.0
Death of child by seventh day	215	7.2
Cough more than four weeks	31	1.0
Total	2,975	100.0

from Schistosomiasis hematobium (White et al. 1982). Hookworm, other infections, and seasonal famine may also reduce hemoglobin and compromise the body of a woman in labor, leaving her with insufficient energy to sustain several hours of uterine contractions or infections that may follow birth. Nor can an anemic woman afford to lose much blood. Another of the many risks is eclampsia, when blood pressure soars and muscles go into spasms. Uncontrolled eclampsia progresses to convulsions, as if the laboring body had been possessed. Then, what began as birth usually ends as death for both the mother and the unborn child.

Table 16.1 shows risk factors among new prenatal clinic attenders at public health units in Pujehun district in 1989. Given these and other risks, and the attribution of risk to physical, social, and cosmological domains, it is not surprising that women prefer to be cared for in childbirth by people they know and trust. Traditional midwives do not work alone but in small teams in the sacred space of the Sande society. A woman facing labor prefers to be cared for by women of the same ethnic and language group who may also be her kin. They trust the midwife who safely delivered their first child, or if that midwife has grown too old, a younger midwife trained by her. In Mende country residence following marriage tends to be patrilocal, and older women often prefer a midwife in their community of marriage residence. But young wives usually prefer to return to their mother's village and the Sande congregation in which they were initiated at puberty. In polygynous families, if the first wife has chosen the second wife, her "little wife," to help her, both women may feel comfortable giving birth in their marriage residence village. But if the husband alone has chosen a second— or sixth—wife there is sometimes mutual distrust among them. Under

those circumstances a young wife would feel vulnerable in labor, and wish
to return to the safety of her mother's village. Similarly, if the first wife had
not yet borne a child there is the possibility of jealousy (witchcraft). This
kind of emotional experience, perceived locally as risk, is foreign to European donors and planners, who often try to impose the place of birth
on women, or advocate training only one traditional birth attendant in a
village.

WAR

On April 4, 1991, the civil war in Liberia spilled across the border into
Sierra Leone. Some local youths, restive under the authority of elders, became recruits and enjoyed the power of a gun. By April 20 this confused
combination of outsiders and insiders overran Pujehun town, taking the
DMO (Jambai) and his staff captive. Houses, the hospital, and all health
centers in the district were looted; some villages and health centers were
burned. Crops were looted or abandoned in the fields. The DMO and his
staff, using the medical supplies left them by their captors, dealt as best
they could with gunshot wounds, bone fractures, and unspeakable war
atrocities. On July 14 Sierra Leone government forces retook Pujehun
town, and by the end of July most of the district was under government
control. By late August people had decided it was safe and drifted back,
but that was nearly the end of the rainy season, too late to start a new crop
cycle. Médecine sans Frontière, Catholic Relief Services, and other donors
reequipped the hospital and provided some temporary mobile clinics. By
March 1992 the hospital and 10 health centers had been restored. There
was peace for about a year, with only a few skirmishes. Not uncommonly
young men would appear in a sleeping village, shoot off their guns, and
demand food stores, women, and other prizes in a kind of "freelance" war.
Then, on January 20, 1993, there was a massive incursion, Pujehun town
fell, and refugees from all over the district fled. Dr. Jambai and others set
up a refugee camp on the banks of the Sewa River, seven miles from Bo,
the old provincial capital in the center of the country. Later, government
forces retook Pujehun district, but there were so many skirmishes, and so
many uncontrolled men with guns about, and so many scores to settle that
people are still afraid to go back.

From the perspective of maternal health this mass migration could not
have come at a worse time. It was the end of the rainy season. Women,
whose bodies had been doing domestic work and the "work" of growing a
fetus, had also expended maximum energy in farming. In the rains most
diseases peak, and food stores are running very low, leaving everyone
malnourished. In January the rice harvest would have begun, and palm
oil making would begin to produce a cash surplus. In addition to these

physical blows, the grief of war deaths and mutilation, and the grief of leaving farms, animals, and homes adversely affect immune system function. All people, especially pregnant women, arrived as refugees in a state of added risk.

SHARED AUTHORITY IN A REFUGEE CAMP

The refugees traveled west, away from the Liberian border, to the banks of the Sewa River. Some walked as far as 60 or 70 miles, deep into the Mende ethnic area. Most of the refugees were ethnically and linguistically Mende; most were women and children. Virtually all women were members of Sande. At first they built simple palm leaf shelters anywhere along the river bank, thinking they would soon be returning home. Instead, more and more people came, until there were more than 40,000 in June 1993. The six-month dry season ended and a new rainy season began, washing way some shelters and pouring through the inadequate roofs of all the rest. There were many child deaths from diarrhea as people used the Sewa River for drinking water at the same time the rains were washing excreta into it. Later a few wells were dug, and people began to build houses of mud if they could. However, almost all the country is now in the chaos of war, and refugees from Sierra Leone are appearing as far away as The Gambia.

Dr. Jambai is ethnically and linguistically Mende, and had been in Pujehun district long enough to build good working relationships with all types of health workers, down to the village level. When a refugee camp was still possible within Sierra Leone, he and senior nurses took stock of health workers who had come as refugees and began to rebuild a primary health care structure in exile. There were three Margai-trained "mamma nurses," with daughters and other junior kin who had been trained by them. Forty government-trained traditional midwives were also in the camp. They usually lived very active lives, farming, marketing, doing domestic work, and healing. However, the forced leisure of refugee camp life was an opportunity to provide additional training for them. They received in-service training, and 80 additional traditional midwives among the refugees were given the standard two-week training course. Eight exiled MCH aides assisted in this training, backed up by other community health nurses in various categories. There were four vaccinators, a dispenser, and sufficient vaccines given by UNICEF and other donors. Areas of the camp were set aside for general clinical work, prenatal care, under-five clinics, vaccination, and dispensing pharmaceuticals.

Politically, the camp replicated the district's 12 chiefdoms. If the actual chiefs were not there, others were chosen to act as substitutes. They met with health workers, and soon there was a primary health care structure in each chiefdom-in-exile. Birthing huts were built where pregnant women,

Sande midwives, and MCH aides congregated. The huts had three rooms: a clean room for deliveries, a room for teams of midwives and aides to rest, and an oral rehydration therapy room for children with diarrhea. A hut sometimes facilitated as many as four deliveries in a single night.

Those flimsy huts offered little privacy from the surrounding crush of refugees, and were not the same for women in labor as going to the Sande house at the interface of village and forest, perceived by them as a safe and spiritually powerful place to give birth. However, if the refugee women did not feel safe in the birthing huts they had few alternatives. If they had a politically secure home area where they might have gone before the onset of labor, there were frequent ambushes along the road. Also, refugee women had to leave their farms before the palm oil and other crop marketing season. They therefore were without cash for transportation if they could even find a vehicle going the right direction. Furthermore, some people in the area around the camp blamed those from Pujehun for "bringing" war into the country, and with this animosity it was often not safe to leave the camp.

In general, though, we see a picture of the adaptability and resilience of culture. A culture, including its political, social, and religious systems, is portable. People carry culture in their heads and can re-create it anywhere. Stressed people may even be very open to re-creation in innovative ways if they see a clear benefit.

AUTHORITATIVE KNOWLEDGE

This case study tells us much about the social uses of authoritative knowledge, especially when two systems of knowledge, Mende and European, come together. We see this coming together in the training of traditional midwives, but also we see it in senior doctors and nurses who wish to be effective in training programs. All health providers in Pujehun district, whether they are in traditional roles or in the government health service, have achieved their status. For all, their status is enhanced if fewer people under their care die. A traditional midwife, for example, has much to gain if she learns new methods for controlling postpartum bleeding.

In Sande, women rise by stages, and a few become much-respected so-weisia. Their intelligence, social concern, and practical adeptness identify them. Some of those wise women are remembered and talked about with respect for many generations after they have died. Similarly, doctors and nurses earn respect, and virtually all in Pujehun district are embedded within Sande or Poro.

People invest legitimacy in the healers to whom they turn, whether they are scientifically trained physicians in state bureaucracies or traditional practitioners. In investing legitimacy in healers, people reassure themselves that the system of healing has meaning, and they can undertake the quest for health with conviction. As Max Weber put it, practitioners with such legitimacy are able to command patients' "uncoerced obedience" (1947). Weber explored three kinds of legitimacy: rational-legal, traditional, and charismatic. Rational-legal legitimacy was linked to his advocacy of bureaucracy in which ideally a society maintained itself through impersonal, efficient procedures. By passing examinations, for example, people earn certificates to practice according to a specific job description. Giving government-trained traditional midwives a certificate, and perhaps a UNICEF kit for deliveries, is the government's way of conferring legal legitimacy upon them. However, their legitimacy may also derive from other sources.

Traditional legitimacy develops through time as qualities of merit, valor, and holiness become associated with a corporate group such as Sande, or a descent line of a famous midwife and the junior kinswomen she has trained. Indeed, all the wisdom associated with ancestral time is of this nature, and uncoerced obedience arises from personal loyalty to those recognized as the heirs and bearers of that legitimacy.

Charismatic legitimacy is analogous to the idea that God and his manifestations cannot be anything other than pure legitimacy. People of exceptional heroism and sanctity present a vision of hope and health. Believers follow in obedience in order to attain those goals. They have personal trust in the extraordinary qualities of the healer.

Paradoxically, a medical system based upon traditional or charismatic legitimacy may have more flexibility to respond to changing conditions than one based upon rational-legal bureaucracy. In the latter, scientists often find difficulty in thinking outside the established paradigm which has rewarded them. In bureaucracies, people should be loyal to the rules. With traditional legitimacy, however, the obligation of obedience to authoritative knowledge is based on personal loyalty, free from cumbersome rules. As long as the actions of traditional healers follow what Weber called principles of substantive ethical common sense, they are quite free to innovate. Change does not come from legislation; rather it is claimed to have always been in force but only recently to have become known through the wisdom of the healer.

Charismatic authority is potentially most flexible, even revolutionary. But it has the drawback of being unorganized and not amenable to replication or to systematic administration over wide geographical areas or through time. When charismatic authority becomes organized the system has transformed into one of the other types of legitimacy. Mende doctors and nurses know these kinds of legitimacy by having lived them in their culture, and are well placed to share authoritative knowledge.

CONCLUSION

Much discourse in industrial countries about primary health care planning in developing countries is a closed loop of Western assumptions about the ignorance and rigidity of "traditional" culture. It speaks authoritatively about the need for "change agents." In the tradition of medical single-cause explanations, it names poverty as *the* cause of poor health while all the while rich countries become richer still on debt interest payments and the arms trade.

In this case study we see dynamic possibilities where there are even a few people of goodwill within the Western-trained medical system who know their cultural roots and are willing to listen, appreciate what traditional midwives already know and do, and work in respectful collaboration with them. Even as arms pour through international trade networks into the free port of Monrovia, spreading chaos in their wake, culture is not obliterated. Constructive relationships can be re-created, or even enhanced, under the dire stimulus of an ad hoc refugee camp awash in its own excrement in the rainy season. Useful concepts and skills travel with people, in their songs, rituals, and redefined symbols about birthing and nurturing.

NOTES

Acknowledgments. German government aid, through G.T.Z., has made much of the innovative program described above possible. We also wish to acknowledge the assistance of two key colleagues. Sister Onita Samai is a wise woman in Sierra Leone's splendid tradition of public health nurses. More than anyone else she has worked for years in great harmony and respect with traditional midwives and other senior officials of Sande. The validity of research and the quality of training owes much to her maturity and vitality. Hilary Lyons, a physician and Holy Rosary Sister, came to Sierra Leone from Ireland more than 30 years ago to build a small rural dispensary into an excellent rural hospital. For the past two decades she has been committed to the primary health care approach based on indigenous social structures. These two women are among the most respected people in Sierra Leone.

Correspondence may be addressed to the second author at 486 Walnut Hill Rd., Millersville, PA 17551.

1. Mende midwives do far more in a health, social, and spiritual sense than attend births. International health bureaucracies, when they designate these women "traditional birth attendants," use a phrase that speaks volumes about who is attempting to authoritatively define whom. Therefore that designation is intentionally not used in this collection. Even the phrase "trained traditional midwife" denies the years of training that apprentices have under the guidance of older women.

REFERENCES

Jordan, Brigitte
    [1978] 1993   *Birth in Four Cultures: A Cross-Cultural Investigation of Childbirth in Yucatan, Holland, Sweden and the United States.* 4th ed. Prospect Heights, Ill.: Waveland Press.

Kandeh, H., and T. Dow
    1980   "Correlates of Infant Mortality in the Chiefdoms of Sierra Leone." Paper, University College, Njala, Sierra Leone.

Liljestrand, J., and W. G. Povey, eds.
    1992   *Maternal Health Care in an International Perspective.* Uppsala: Department of Obstetrics and Gynaecology, Uppsala University, and World Health Organization.

Little, Kenneth
    1965   "The Political Function of the Poro, Part I." *Africa* 35:349–356.
    1966   "The Political Function of the Poro, Part II." *Africa* 36:63–71.

MacCormack, Carol
    1972   "Mende and Sherbro Women in High Office." *Canadian Journal of African Studies* 6:151–164.
    1979   "Sande: The Public Face of a Secret Society." In *The New Religions of Africa,* ed. B. Jules-Rosette, 27–38. Norwood, N.J.: Ablex.
    1984   "Primary Health Care in Sierra Leone." *Social Science and Medicine* 19:199–208.
    1988   "Health and the Social Power of Women." *Social Science and Medicine* 26:677–683.
    1994   "Health, Fertility and Birth in Moyamba District, Sierra Leone." In *Ethnography of Fertility and Birth,* 2d ed, ed. C. MacCormack, 115–139. Prospect Heights, Ill.: Waveland Press.

Margai, Milton
    1948   "Welfare Work in a Secret Society." *African Affairs* 47:227–230.

Sered, Susan Starr
    1994   *Priestess, Mother and Sacred Sister: Religions Dominated by Women.* Oxford: Oxford University Press.

Weber, Max
    1947   *The Theory of Social and Economic Organization.* Trans. and ed. Talcott Parsons. New York: Free Press.

White, P., M. Coleman, and B. Jupp
    1982   "Swamp Rice Development, Schistosomiasis and Onchocerciasis in Southeast Sierra Leone." *American Journal of Medicine and Hygiene* 3:490–498.

World Development Report
    1993   *Investing in Health.* Oxford: Oxford University Press.

SEVENTEEN

Heeding Warnings from the Canary, the Whale, and the Inuit

A Framework for Analyzing Competing Types of Knowledge about Childbirth

Betty-Anne Daviss

Some of the elders leaned closer to the microphones at their table, as if the move might enable them to hear better. One stopped sewing her *kamik* (boot) and looked up. This was going to require more attention than they thought. It was true, then, what I was telling them, that a contingent of white apprentice-trained midwives was "taking birth back home" in the southern Canadian communities and that these midwives were about to become legally accepted. Such news, to this gathering of Inuit elders and young women from regions across the Northwest Territories back in 1985, was revolution. It was as if the Renaissance of Reason had occurred. But there was a silence in the room, as if one still had to be cautious about this sort of news. I wasn't surprised by their skepticism. Just the day before, one of the elders had told me that it may be because of our simple naïveté that television's trick photography has duped us into believing that a man has actually been sent to the moon.

In the years following that 1985 Igloolik meeting, I did whatever I could to spend time with Inuit elders and younger women who were trying to figure out what had happened to birth in their culture. Even before the miles of ethnographic videotape that I took, it had become obvious to me that a kind of culture shock in birth is upon the Inuit. A similar shock is felt by many of us who have discovered birth in the so-called developing world[1] and then returned to North America. When the elders asked me why doctors think that they own birth, I tried to explain to them that some physicians believe, as preposterous as it may seem, that birth is a medical act. The elders regard it as a community, social, and spiritual act. The individual young Inuk[2] woman thinks of it as her own personal act. Many southern Canadian midwives have come to regard birth as the supreme political act. The statistician sees each birth as one act of many. Everyone's focus reflects his or her particular vested interest.

In searching for clues about what is considered to be authoritative knowledge in northern Canada, I have concluded, from the ethnographic literature and my own experience, that the Inuit treat the white people, or Qallunaaq,[3] like children who need to be allowed to have their own way in order for them to learn their lesson and see their folly. The unfortunate problem is that white men, even more than children, usually get their way, the deed done, the lesson not always learned. My perception is that the Inuit see the Qallunaaq (pronounced "ha-loo-nuk") as a people with a lot of attitude, needing to impose it on others; the Qallunaaq see the lack of combative spirit among the Inuit as a sign that they have accepted Qallunaaq authority. It was with apparent passivity that the Inuit stood back in the 1960s to allow white federal medical services to start the evacuation of all pregnant women away from their settlements, separated from their husbands, families, friends, and midwives for the "privilege" of a southern hospital birth under the control of white physicians. But over the ensuing thirty years the almost entire obliteration of their childbirth traditions became for the Inuit a focus of political, community, and personal outrage (O'Neil and Kaufert 1990).

Southern Canadian history tells us that miners used to take a canary with them into the mine shaft as a security measure because the weaker metabolism of the little bird would act as a sign that the buildup of gases was nearing incompatibility with life. The northern symbol of environmental danger is provided by the beluga whales that wash up on shore with highly toxic chemical residues in their systems. It is the purpose of this chapter to demonstrate that just as the canary can serve as a barometer of air quality and the whale of the integrity of the sea, the ability of a community to retain control over its birth culture is a good indicator of the lifeforce of that community. The vulnerability of indigenous childbirth systems everywhere is a warning sign that not only birth but also community life itself are at risk in this overly technologized time. The story of how one Inuit community in northern Québec is reclaiming both birth and community is a strong story of hope for us all.

ARRIVING AT THE ANALYTICAL FRAMEWORK

In 1975 and 1976, while Brigitte Jordan was studying birth in the Yucatan, Sweden, and Holland, I was becoming a midwife with the traditional midwives in Guatemala. Subsequently I worked in rural Alabama among black midwives; with traditional midwives and an obstetric team in Afghan refugee camps in Pakistan; and, like Jordan, with Dutch midwives in Holland. A practicing midwife for twenty years (I have served as primary attendant at over a thousand births and have participated in many more), I have continually experienced firsthand the contradictions and tensions between traditional and medical definitions of reproductive risk and normalcy. So that I could deal with the constraints these tensions placed on being a midwife in various parts of the world, I began to develop, as a "mental survival" strategy, a vocabulary for analyzing what motivated people to manage birth so differently, and why attitudes toward childbirth were so polarized everywhere I went. I came to see that each player in the health care system, from the caregiver to the administrator to the recipient of care, creates and articulates his or her own system of logic and assumes that it is logical. These assumptions affect the individual's perception of what constitutes risk and what constitutes normalcy. Therefore, different types of people using different systems of logic will arrive at differing perceptions of how to manage birth. I came to see regularities in these competing rationales, and to classify them in terms of the types of logic being used. I have found that this system of classification constitutes a useful framework through which one can analyze the dynamics of these systems of logic interacting with each other in each act of birth. The types of logic I have thus far identified are as follows:

1. *Scientific* logic is based on evidence, not only from biology and physics, but from available epidemiologic knowledge—that is, from statistical analysis of health and disease or normalcy and risk patterns in birth.

2. *Clinical* logic is used by health care practitioners to assess the health and determine the treatment of the mother and baby at the office, home, or hospital visit. It varies according to the training, experience, knowledge, philosophy, and peer pressure of the practitioner dealing with the case. Unfortunately, it is sometimes presented by practitioners as, or assumed by their patients to be, scientific logic, even when there are no statistics or trials to back it up.

3. *Personal* logic is used when individuals and families make decisions about what they stand to lose or gain on a personal level from their birth plans and compromises. This also includes the personal logic of practitioners, whose careers may be positively or negatively affected by particular health care decisions.

4. *Cultural* logic is concerned with the development or demise of fundamental beliefs about how a given society should manage birth. This category can include traditional community logic and spiritual logic.

5. *Intuitive* logic is based on information directly apprehended by a person who has the ability to become familiar with and make decisions about a situation without necessarily depending on the other forms of logic. Some people have more of this intuitive ability than others.

I consider cultural logic to be a kind of common sense, and intuition to be a kind of uncommon sense. (See also Davis-Floyd and Davis, this volume.)

6. *Political* logic assesses the projected consequences of what will be said and done about birth plans and birth outcome by family, community, "public opinion," peers, other practitioners, and government policy makers. It is concerned with issues of who has the power to control childbirth and of what cultural institutions and values will be reinforced and perpetuated through that control.

7. *Legal* logic is based on concerns about liability should anything go wrong during the pregnancy or birth. Even though the notion of "informed consent" grew out of legal logic, it tends to undervalue "informed choice," as court battles are usually conducted by legal and professional experts, and lay opinion does not carry much weight. Legal logic—read "fear of liability"—is often the deep underlying basis for decisions made by birth practitioners.

8. *Economic* logic has to do with assessing cost benefits and risks. It is applied differentially, depending on whether one's goal is to save or to make money from a given birth.

While I classify as types of logic the rationales people use to decide what actions to take and to justify those decisions, Jordan uses the term "authoritative knowledge." It is my perception that in our different disciplines, but traveling through similar geography, Jordan and I have developed the two terms "logic" and "authoritative knowledge" to label much the same thing. When I combine our perspectives, I can see that what kind of logic is considered to be authoritative in a given birth situation will depend on many factors. The story of how the Inuit in one village are reclaiming birth is the story of profound shifts in what kinds of logic, what systems of knowledge, they accept as authoritative.

The health care system in North America rarely has the time or desire to consider the implications of either of these terms, let alone to try to balance the eight types of logic described above. Technomedicine tends to look at decisions about birth in terms of *levels of risk,* rather than as decisions about choice of logic or about the conflicting claims to authority of different knowledge systems. Even when the medical system does acknowledge the existence of some of these categories, they are perceived as categories of risk—"the clinical risk," "the legal risk." These are the authoritative categories in technomedicine, whereas cultural and personal factors are rarely acknowledged as being at risk. For example, to send a mother by plane from the Northwest Territories to Montreal is seen as a triumph of decision making based on clinical risk—"the important thing is that the mother and baby are well." What this means is that they both physically made it through the birth. If the mother is emotionally traumatized by the experience, if one of her children was sexually abused by a neighbor while she was away, if the fabric of community life was disrupted by her absence, these are simply less important than the all-important clinical rationale. It was to avoid all the biases of the term "risk" that I came to prefer the term "logic" as an umbrella for our understanding of risk, benefit, and normalcy. To call these various priorities "types of logic" frames them in a nonthreatening way and clarifies the need to recognize their competing claims to validity.

By the time I reached northern Canada in 1985, I had already identified most of the components of this framework. It became useful for helping the elders sort out the various reactions to evacuation without invalidating anyone's perspective, because it allowed those whose logic was being undermined to more clearly state their case. In northern Canada, the decisions about evacuation for birth are made in a highly political milieu; they play their part in an ongoing battle, subtle and overt, over which kind of logic will be authoritative and therefore which parties will control birth. The proponents of keeping birth in the settlements accuse those who advocate evacuation of using clinical reasoning at the expense of personal, cultural, spiritual, and economic logic. Evacuation proponents accuse those who want to stay in the settlements of not being aware of the clinical risks. Ironically, both sides accuse each other of not using scientific logic, as who decides what constitutes "good science" often depends on who has the most political power.

When using this framework, it is important not to operate out of preconceived or stereotypical notions about who will use what kind of logic. A physician rarely uses only clinical logic, or an Inuit elder only cultural logic. Many physicians attracted to the North have more hope and faith in restoring Inuit traditions than the Inuit themselves, and some Inuit leaders have more respect for the medical model than physicians. Such apparent incongruities remind us of the ability of all participants to adjust and change.

THE PRESENT SITUATION: A CASE STUDY OF ONE EVACUEE

In an earlier work (Daviss-Putt 1990:91–114), I described how evacuation was introduced and the social upheaval that it has caused in the Northwest Territories—the breakup of families, the loss of community knowledge about birth, and the health problems of women who must sit for weeks in southern cities waiting to go into labor, with strange food, little exercise, and no family support. The Northern Health Research Unit at the University of Manitoba has been diligent in providing intimate and honest reporting on the problem in Keewatin (Kaufert et al. 1988). In brief, evacuation was implemented in the 1970s with the explanation that it would reduce risks, but without conclusive epidemiological research to back up that assertion. Although evacuation may have benefited high-risk mothers, it has created more problems than it has solved.

Consider the following typical situation. At age seventeen, Elisapee (a pseudonym) is pregnant with her second baby. The only time that she has been out of the settlement was when she was twelve—due to language communication difficulties, she was mistakenly sent out instead of her brother, who needed his tonsils out. She has been told that she has to fly to a southern Canadian city, a five-hour plane trip away, more than a month before her due date because her last pregnancy terminated at thirty-six weeks (clinical logic). She knows that she will be billeted by a white family whom she does not know, or stay in a transient center by herself for this period. With the encouragement of her mother, she had hidden her first pregnancy from the primary health care practitioner in the settlement, the Qallunaaq nurse, because she was afraid to go and because her mother had told her that you couldn't get Arctic char, seal, or caribou to eat while down south, or go fishing (personal logic). Another woman in the settlement had also hidden her pregnancy, and the nurse had attended her birth, so Elisapee knew that the nurse could handle a delivery (clinical logic on Elisapee's part). The nurse, who is sympathetic to the plight of Inuit pregnant women, had obliged with Elisapee's first baby when they couldn't get a plane out on time, and "fortunately, everything went all right." This first baby, who has just begun to walk, is still nursing, and Elisapee's brother, who is three, is living with her because her mother has a heart condition. Elisapee doesn't want to leave the children at home, but neither does she want to take them down South where she will have to care for them in unfamiliar surroundings. When Elisapee's boyfriend is under stress, even though theirs is a dry community he manages to get alcohol and becomes irresponsible and aggressive, and she worries about leaving the children in his care. This time she is unable to hide the pregnancy from the nurse and is flown out.

Five days after she arrives in the city, Elisapee, who is living in the transient center and feeling very lonely, finds out that her baby daughter back in the settlement has been in a skidoo accident. Shortly afterward, she gets a call from the nurse at the doctor's office in the city, who tells her that her hemoglobin is low (110 mg/dL) [4] and that she should be taking iron (incomplete clinical logic; iron causes constipation and may actually be unnecessary, as a lowered hemoglobin may simply represent hemodilution,[5] a normal condition of pregnancy). Elisapee, apart from feeling depressed, shows no symptoms that would indicate a need for iron: she is not lethargic, pale, or feeling tired. She tells the nurse that she is going home where she will get a better diet (community logic, which in this case is supported by scientific logic). The nurse tells the doctor, who instructs the nurse (political logic—he thinks the nurse will be more persuasive) to tell Elisapee that if she goes home she could be risking her life, because she might have a postpartum hemorrhage (political logic to convince her to stay; medical clinical logic that is scientifically questionable).[6]

Elisapee ignores the clinical and political logic of the physician and the nurse and takes the next plane home (intuitive logic). The nurse back home is very understanding but also quite nervous because she is worried about being faced with another premature baby (clinical logic, but the baby at this point will only be a week or so premature—scientifically, not much risk). Elisapee does indeed go into labor two days after arriving home, has the baby with the nurse, does hemorrhage, but feels fine. The nurse sets up an intravenous line and transports Elisapee by air back to the city (clinical, political, and legal logic). Ready to go home the next day, she cannot find a return flight and is forced to stay a week waiting for a plane.

None of this is based on economic logic. And through the entire process, the mother, according to her own report, has felt like a cross between a beached whale and a canary flying to and fro to save herself.

AUTHORITY FIGURES: ANY LOGIC HERE?

Historical Authorities

According to the literature of the explorers, historians, and ethnographers, traditional Inuit society had no formal authority. The elders explain that every person is an individual, and no one should speak for another person or carry great authority over another—an egalitarianism that is characteristic of many hunter-gatherer groups. The Inuit think that everyone's needs should be respected, and I find that the elders see the white need for hierarchical power structures as immature. Historically, it appears that the Inuit did grant authority to entities that were feared, such as shamans. The shaman was the vessel through which one could know what the spirits were thinking and make the right choice to appease them. In fact, a good deal of time was spent appeasing the shamans (Graeburn 1972:355).

With the arrival of the white man, white men of power were incorporated into the same belief system. It is little wonder that the Inuit were reported to have disliked the explorer William Perry and at the same time almost worshiped him. This history helps us to understand why physicians and priests who were overbearing, threatening, or otherwise powerful were treated with respect and obeyed.

In the traditional childbirth of the nomadic hunter-gatherer days, power apparently inhered in the grandmothers and mothers, whose duty it was to remind the pregnant woman about the necessity of following traditional taboos and rituals (Daviss-Putt 1990:92–95). In some areas, when the time came for birth, the laboring woman was taken to an isolation hut made of snow or skins where she gave birth alone, a practice that began to decline in the twentieth century. In Spence Bay, one of the oldest elders told us that in the old days the shaman used to wait near the isolation hut, chanting, while the woman was inside laboring. As Inuit nomadism gave way to larger groups of people clustering at given sites, the community began to share a more developed birth culture. In the 1950s, the government of Canada relocated many such clustering groups into permanent settlements. Traders, missionaries, nurses, and the Royal Canadian Mounted Police at various times influenced childbirth among the Inuit, serving as sources of information and sometimes dictating what choices would be available. The Qallunaaq brought with them their own perceptions of what constituted risk and normalcy, and began to take over decision making in childbirth affairs with little resistance from the Inuit. The colonial attitude of political and religious superiority and authority extended even to birth.

> I have . . . conducted an obstetrical clinic for the benefit of the old women in whose hands all obstetric authority lies. Little impression was made, but the important fact is that some impression, no matter how superficial, was made. Like religion it is true, they will shortly adopt the obedient attitude. (Bildfell 1934:6)

When such authority figures took over decision making in birth, they were not necessarily considered "wise," but it was clear that they had to be appeased. In an interview with another elder in Spence Bay who had given birth during the 1960s, I found an exchange of the shaman of the old days for a new version of power: she had invited the manager from the Bay (the general store) to her birth! As is hinted in the following historical text, it is possible that the impending intrusion of such an authority figure was enough to cause the baby to come: "Two married women attended her but her delivery was long and painful. Her husband was hurriedly sent out to invoke our assistance, but the child was delivered almost as soon as he left the hut" (Jenness 1922:164).

Nurses and Midwives as Authority Figures

When I first arrived up North, I could not understand how a nurse who had worked for years with the Inuit could tolerate women being forced from their homes to give birth. But then I witnessed the stress of isolation and the overwhelming workload borne by the nurses and nurse-midwives who serve as the primary health care practitioners in Inuit settlements. Their specific responsibilities vis-à-vis pregnancy and birth are to do only pre- and postnatal care. It became clear that although the nurses themselves would like to be responsive to what the Inuit desire, they receive no support from the government bureaucracy to do so; in fact, they are under extreme pressure to evacuate women for birth, because of the government's—and their own—fear of lawsuit should something go wrong in the settlement.

At that first Northern meeting I attended, I was introduced to a nurse-midwife who had worked for almost two decades among the Inuit. I asked her to point out to me the elders who were midwives. She said in a definitive way, "There are none." I realized that this ultimatum was for my immediate education. Regardless of the fact that the express intent of the Inuit Women's Association was to introduce me at this meeting to the elders who were midwives, I would have to recognize her authority: by Qallunaaq government standards, the elders who had done births were not really midwives. They were not medically trained, as this nurse-midwife had been in Britain, nor did they fit the international definition of a midwife, which says that you have to be recognized by your government. (The government of Canada did not recognize midwifery at that time, except for the nurse-midwives in the North.) What I refrained from telling her was that I had already worked as a midwife for a decade without formal recognition from a government, and that it was specifically because I had originally been trained by indigenous elders in Central America that I was trusted by the elders and invited to come.

Annie Okalik, one of the elders from Pangnirtung, laughed at me when I told her that I only had two children—to think that I could be any kind of midwife, when I had had so few! When the young, single nurse-midwives first arrived in the settlements, what authority could they have had? My impression is that they must have been accepted as authority figures who fit into the same historical script as the shamans and the white men of power. I doubt that the elders ever relinquished in their hearts their place at the side of the birthgiving woman, because they tell me that they are still willing to assist women during birth. But their credibility is being eroded by the bedazzle of fancy technology. They are not sanctioned by the government to attend births anywhere in the North. They take the responsibility only if they are asked by the woman to attend her. None of the elders I have interviewed has any qualms about doing that; they tell me that if it is the woman's choice, they will do it. I view this willingness to take over where they left off as an indication that they have not been convinced, in the last forty years, of the superiority of medical, clinical logic.

The younger women often possess the same inner defiance that the elders express, but they have no experience of what birth used to be like in Inuit culture—only the impression they get from the elders that it was simpler, with less interference. These young women are products of this era, in which rumor holds that one can be put in jail if one refuses to be evacuated to the South. Such fear augments the split reaction that, I have observed, is common to pregnant women in all countries when faced with the possibility of intervention that they do not want but are afraid that they need. To give an example, one day when I was visiting a woman—I'll call her Nina—in an Inuit settlement, we received news that her sister was going into labor, and Nina asked me to see her sister, even though she was headed to the nursing station. Nina wanted me to take over and do the birth, to save her sister a transport to a hospital, and to stand up for her right to give birth in the settlement. I found out when I got to the nursing station that this was a clear case of prematurity. The woman was only thirty-one weeks into her pregnancy, and I knew that if I were in charge I would set up an intravenous line and transport her to a hospital—the same treatment chosen by the doctor who happened to be in the settlement. Nina was still pressuring me to take over, but before I had time to explain that in this case it would not be good judgment for me to interfere (clinical logic), the doctor entered the room. Nina's personality change was immediate and dramatic. She mentioned nothing more about staying in the settlement, but spoke with the physician in a friendly manner, relinquishing all authority to him and asking few questions about his care. I watched this woman turn from radical to submissive within a few minutes. This phenomenon is not uncommon when I transport white women in the South. Medical authority is a power that paralyzes women, compromising their ability to sort out their own logic.

POVUNGNITUK: REVIVING THE BELUGA

In 1985 when I first started seeing scenarios like Elisapee's, I could not fathom how the Northern communities could remain incapable of rejecting evacuation, nor could I see how the government could overlook a basic requirement of a vital community life: community ownership of birth. Anywhere else in the world that I had been, from Afghan refugee camps in Pakistan to the rural areas of South America and Thailand, at least a token effort is made to utilize and even upgrade the skills of traditional midwives. From speaking with Inuit women, I had learned that many still wanted to give birth at home or at least in their settlements. But after three decades of dependency on the nurse in the nursing station for all aspects of health care, most of the young women had become fearful about leaving the health professionals entirely out of the picture. These young Inuit women feel overwhelmed at the thought of tackling the federal bureaucracy and the mystique of the medical profession. However, unlike the beluga whales who are helpless to clean up the pollution, they are starting to hear that there are solutions.

An Inuit settlement in northern Québec, Povungnituk (glossed by the community as "POV") was the only community with representatives at that 1985 Igloolik meeting who returned home and implemented a concrete plan to bring birth back to their homeland. In 1997, POV is still the only settlement that has been able to generate a viable answer to the loss of Inuit control over birth (see also O'Neil and Kaufert 1995). The rest of this chapter will be devoted to an explanation of the way in which the women of POV have detoxified their beached beluga—in this case, an apt metaphor for their dying traditional childbirth system—by demanding a better balance of the types of logic in our eight-category framework.

Much of the information in the following pages was consolidated during my last two-month visit to POV in February and March of 1994. An earlier visit to POV had been primarily concerned with research and video production; now I was sent on a return visit by the government of Ontario to be trained under new legislation that requires all midwives to be officially trained and certified. The irony was becoming customary to me: I had been "trained" by traditional midwives in Guatemala; later I was sent to Nicaragua to "train" traditional midwives who had forty years more experience than I; and now I was being sent for "training" to a program I had helped to initiate. My role during this training process was primarily that of an observer at prenatal and postpartum exams and during labor and delivery. As it turned out, I also served as a consultant, helping the POV midwives with the adaptation of a data form for clinical statistics.

As in the rest of the North, the pressures in POV to bend toward the Qallunaaq way are steady. The continued viability of the POV Maternity requires constant vigilance on the part of the Inuit midwives, as well as the awareness that the steps their community has taken are part of an important political process of reclaiming both birth and a sense of continuity and identity. It seems likely that the POV midwives will be well equipped to contend with possible future encroachments into birth in the settlements by white administrators. They are trained through an effective combination of apprenticeship and formal classroom teaching, and they are developing systematic knowledge about all the types of logic in our analytical framework and strong convictions about the need for an appropriate balance among them. The discussion below reveals the particular pressures brought to bear on the POV midwives by examining each type of logic in turn.

Political Logic: Taking Back the Power

In 1993 I wrote a paper entitled "Informed Choice in Childbirth: Is It Possible in the North?" with the help and advice of a woman in Cape Dorset, Akalayok Qavavao. Akalayok had been the deputy mayor of her settlement and one of the few women who had the strength to say no to the health care system's plan for her evacuation: she handpicked some elders who assisted her in a traditional birth at home. In the paper we raised the question, "Does introducing the concept of informed choice impose another white construct on an already colonized Inuit populace?" From our review of the history of the Inuit relationship to authority figures, the isolation huts, and the Inuit insistence on strict obedience to taboos, it was not clear to us that such a plan would work in a traditional society in which choice has never been part of the equation. The difficulty in demanding choice, for a people who never knew that they were allowed to have it, cannot be overestimated. You have to learn decision making and, even more basic, realize that it is your prerogative to make decisions. To defend your principles, you must be willing to speak out, to debate, often in a language not your own, often in the face of political uncertainty and the threat that what you say may later be used against you, or that your priorities will be minimized once more.

When I was in POV in 1989 working on the research for a video about the evacuation crisis, I searched for a reason why POV was able to overcome the obstacles that have paralyzed other Inuit communities, rendering them incapable of bringing birth back to Nunavik ("our homeland"). Mina and Harry Tulugak, young leaders in the community, told me at the time that POV has a reputation for not always saying yes to the white man. Harry said that the people of POV do not allow things to get past them: "We ask questions." It was in Povungnituk that one of the first cooperatives was established, a store run by Inuit, bravely tackling the formidable competition of the Hudson's Bay Company monopoly. POV was also one of the three communities that would not sign the James Bay and Northern Québec Agreement, refusing, as Harry Tulugak put it, to "sell for beads the heritage that is rightly ours" (see also O'Neil and Kaufert 1995).[7]

When the women of POV asked to have a maternity unit, which they decided to call "The Maternity," I doubt that the world understood what a marked revolution that represented. Here was a community, eight hours by small plane from any hospital large enough to have cesarean section facilities or a neonatal intensive care unit, making a political decision to reject clinical logic to save the integrity of their cultural, personal, and intuitive logic. In clear words and actions POV was willing to state that the clinical risk of losing a baby was worth the benefit of returning birth to the Inuit community.

POV went even farther than establishing a facility where women could have babies close to home. A decision was made not to duplicate the problem of the past by hiring only white midwives to take care of the births, thereby perpetuating the dependency on the South. (When such practitioners head south and there is no replacement for them, the births follow them south again.) Instead, the people of POV had the foresight and enthusiasm to immediately begin to train community-chosen Inuit women to be more than just aides, to be primary caregivers who would be entirely responsible for a woman's care, consulting with medical practitioners only when necessary. At present there are two to three white midwives (one of whom acts as coordinator) working on the training of the Inuit midwives. There are two fully trained Inuit midwives, two more about to be given that status, and two more about to start training. They are assisted by a dozen part-time "maternity workers," whose job is to stay with the woman postpartum, taking vital signs and informing the midwives of any abnormalities. The POV Maternity is a small wing of a small primary-level hospital, which has a basic laboratory and a staff that includes nurses and three to four general practitioners.

Thirty years before, without any overt policy statement, the Canadian health care system had eliminated Inuit ownership of birth simply by rewarding the nurses for evacuating and criticizing them if they did not, and by the default system of not maintaining nurse-midwives in the settlements. Now POV used similar strategies to bring birth back to the community, step-by-step. Although POV did not hide its undertakings, it also did not broadcast its new policies loudly in circles that might try to stop the repatriation. The Maternity was established after a survey was taken up and down the coast asking women what birth choices they considered ideal. It was decided from the start that the Maternity would operate under a midwifery model—a paradigm of childbirth that values the integrity of the natural process of birth, nurturant emotional and physical support of the laboring woman, mutual connection and respect between patient and practitioner, and non-hierarchical relationships among the practitioners themselves (see Davis-Floyd 1992; Rothman 1982). At the very beginning, the first director general of the Maternity, a white administrator, was replaced by an Inuk woman because of his lack of support for a midwifery model. Since then there have been consistent attempts to ensure that it remains an Inuk-held position, and commitment to the midwifery model has remained strong.

Peer review is done with a "perinatal committee" that reviews all decisions of potential concern, with input from community midwives as well as the nurses and physicians. For example, the last time I was there, a case was called up at the perinatal committee involving a physician attending a woman in a settlement a couple of hours away from POV who had made decisions and performed interventions prior to transporting the woman to the POV Maternity, without consulting the midwives. It became clear at the committee meeting that in the future it would be in the best interests of all involved for consultation to be carried out in advance with the midwives who would be receiving the mother. Povungnituk is one of the few places in the world where physicians have to consult with midwives before imposing an intervention.

It is still sometimes difficult for Inuit midwives to say what they really think during perinatal committee meetings. These meetings have full agendas, move along rapidly in English, and require facing intimidating personalities. By and large, however, the Inuit midwives and student midwives excel in presenting their own cases and making critical suggestions about the cases of others. They have a special role on this committee because they are often the ones who really know what is going on behind the scenes. It is they, for instance, who keep in check the exposure of intimate details of a woman's private life in this small community while still providing enough information not to compromise her care. White practitioners, who may not be aware of the intricacies of community life, do not always share the same sensitivity to issues of confidentiality.

Scientific Logic

The POV Maternity is making contributions to the study of some diseases and effects of contaminants that are more prevalent up North than in other settings, for example, toxoplasmosis[8] and PCBs.[9] The present coordinator of the POV Maternity, Qallunaaq midwife Colleen Crosbie, would like to do some practical randomized controlled trials; only half in jest, she says, "We need to determine the effect of skidoo rides within a week of delivery on a mother's perineum." Although science is taught to the midwives, it would not be true to say that scientific logic is highest on their priority list. When the POV nurses and midwives travel south to give presentations about the Maternity, the white midwives present the graphs and statistics, and the Inuit midwives tell the stories. Their skepticism of scientific logic is understandable; it was claimed to be the rationale for removing birth from the settlements in the first place, since health care officials assumed that statistics on complications and perinatal morbidity and mortality that were too "high" would be corrected by transporting every woman to a hospital. Scientific logic was also invoked to convince people in the early settlement days that raw meat was unhealthy, carried disease, and should always be cooked. Then anemia became a problem, one of the speculations being that the vitamin C in the raw meat was one of the nutrients that not only prevented scurvy but also helped the assimilation of iron. Such history creates warranted misgivings about white man's science as authoritative knowledge. In POV, some of the women now generalize that good food is "country food"—Inuit food such as seal, caribou, walrus meat, and Arctic char—and categorize white man's food as junk food. It is eaten, but not considered to be healthy. Unlike other aboriginal populations of Canada, Inuit women were not convinced by medical practitioners to start their babies on supplemental milk. They still believe breast milk is best, a belief that science has ultimately confirmed (although the scare of contaminants may alter this somewhat). The fact that the Inuit all along had a "hunch" that avoiding evacuation, Qallunaaq food, and neonatal milk supplements would be beneficial suggests why Inuit women feel less need to "prove" things scientifically, and have more affinity for cultural and intuitive logic.

Acquiring accurate perinatal statistics in the North is made difficult by the small numbers of births in each settlement: there can be significant fluctuations in the numbers from year to year and from one settlement to another that make statistical analysis problematic. For example, if a community has two perinatal deaths one year and four the next, it appears that the mortality rate has "doubled"; if no babies die the following year, there appears to have been a dramatic decline when in fact these may be statistically meaningless fluctuations. It took me over a year, involving phone calls to midwives, epidemiologists, statisticians, and various government departments, to finally bring together the closest that we can get to the correct data on perinatal deaths (see tables 17.1, 17.2).

In table 17.1 it appears that the stillborn rate has gone up and the early neonatal death rate has gone down since the Maternity opened, but this may simply be a result of random fluctuation. Also, the information I obtained on deaths for the same years from the Bureau de Statistique du Québec (see table 17.2) shows two fewer early neonatal deaths, for a tally of six rather than eight in the years 1982 to 1986, and one more in the years 1987–1991 (7 deaths rather than the 6 shown above). Also suspect is a stillborn rate of 1.5 per 1,000 for the years 1982–1986 in table 17.1 because it is unusually low compared to other years and to other Northern settlements. Recording systems are far from ideal and highly suspect; should a woman be transported and her baby die, the same number of deaths theoretically should be recorded by the hospital, the settlement from which she comes, and the Bureau de Statistique du Québec, but discrepancies do exist. Thus in table 17.2 note (in round and square brackets) that different agencies report a different number of deaths for the same time period. I had constructed table 17.1 before the information in table 17.2 was put together at my request by Brian Schnarch at the Nunavik Regional Board of Health and Social Services. It compares neonatal death rates in POV and its sister settlement Kuujjuaq, which takes care of women living on the Ungava coast using physicians rather than midwives, but, like POV, without cesarean section facilities or a neonatal intensive care unit. Stillborn rates could not be retrieved for table 17.2.

From the data in tables 17.1 and 17.2, it is not possible to conclude definitively that the perinatal death rate has gone down since the Maternity opened, or that it has gone up significantly when compared to either the pre-Maternity period or to the physician-attended births of Kuujjuaq. I can accurately say that keeping the births in POV results in fewer interventions

TABLE 17.1   Stillborns and Early Neonatal Deaths
on the Hudson Coast Before and After the Maternity
in Povungnituk Commenced Operation

	1982–1986 (the five years prior to the Maternity when 95% of pregnant women were evacuated out of the Hudson Coast)	1987–1991 (the five years after the Maternity started when only high-risk pregnant women were evacuated out of the Hudson Coast)
Number of births	656***	682**
Stillborns (defined as a death of a fetus weighing 500 g or more) rate per thousand	1* 1.5/1,000	5** 7.3/1,000
Early neonatal deaths (deaths between birth and the sixth day of life) rate per thousand	8* 12.2/1,000	6** 8.8/1,000

*Jean-François Proulx, "Towards Healthy Communities on the Hudson Coast, 1982–1986" (Innuulisivik Health Centre, POV, July 1988).

**These figures come from the addition of (a) deaths reported 1989–1991 and published in Susan Chatwood, "Indications for Transfer for Childbirth in Women Served by the Innuu-litsivik Maternity" (Master's thesis, Department of Epidemiology Biostatistics, McGill University 1996), and (b) deaths reported 1987–1988 and quoted in Chatwood's thesis, from F. Meyer and D. Belanger, *Evaluation of Perinatal Care and Services: Hudson Bay and Ungava Bay. Pregnancies and Births in Two Inuit Populations of Northern Quebec* (Department of Community Health, Centre hospitalier de l'Université Laval, April 1991).

***Calculated from the information sent by Proulx on deaths, as it was nowhere to be found in the actual literature.

(although actual statistics are not yet available, the lack of need to transport everybody already affirms that) and happier mothers, apparently without compromise to overall safety. The fact that accurate statistics are so hard to come by reveals a large hole in the original rationale to evacuate; statistics would have been even harder to come by at the time that the evacuation decisions were being made.

Accurate science sometimes demonstrates that what cultures and women do intuitively is what they need the most; in many cases, cultural and scientific authoritative knowledge are congruent. The entire Inuit population could be scientifically considered high-risk because of their high incidence of postpartum hemorrhage, sexually transmitted diseases, and socioeconomic problems. But the midwives believe that, given these

TABLE 17.2 Nunavik Neonatal Mortality
by Days of Life, Coast, and Year*

	Early Neonatal Deaths (<7 days)		Late Neonatal Deaths (7–28 days)	
Year	Hudson	Ungava	Hudson	Ungava
1975	0	1	1	1
1976	2	4	0	1
1977	2	1	0	1
1978	4	1	0	0
1979	2	1	1	1
1980	1[0]	1[1]	1[0]	1[0]
1981	2[1]	0[0]	0[0]	0[0]
1982	0[0]	2[2]	1[0]	0[1]
1983	0[0]	2[2]	0[0]	0[0]
1984	2[2]	0[0]	0[0]	1[1]
1985	4[4]	1[0]	0[0]	0[0]
1986	0[0]	0[0]	0[0]	1[1]
1987	1(0)[0]	1(1)[1]	0(0)[0]	0(0)[0]
1988	0(3)[3]	0(0)[0]	0(1)[1]	0(0)[0]
1989	1(2)[2]	0(1)[1]	0(0)[0]	0(0)[0]
1990	0(0)[0]	0(0)[0]	0(0)[0]	0(0)[0]
1991	0(1)[1]	0(2)[2]	0(1)[1]	1(1)[1]
1992	1(3)[3]	0(1)[1]	0(0)[0]	0(0)[0]
1993	0(2)[2]	0(0)[0]	0(1)[1]	0(0)[0]
1994	0[2]	0[0]	0[0]	0[0]

NOTE: N = Public Health Department, (N) = Ministry of Health and Social Services, or MSSS, [N] = Bureau de la Statistique du Québec, or BSQ.

*Note that there may be missing deaths in any or all years. This is related, in particular, to deaths occurring outside of the region that often do not end up in Northern records.

—Public Health Department data from 1975–1986 were vigorously collected from available sources including the MSSS, nursing stations, the Kuujjuaq, Moose Factory, and Povungnituk hospitals and elsewhere. Nonetheless, particularly for Hudson between 1975 and 1978, the completeness of the data is suspect.

—Public Health Department data from 1987 to 1994 were collected from hospital archives on the two coasts and are likely missing several deaths occurring outside of the region. (See next point.)

—Data in round brackets ( ) from 1987 to 1993 are based on MSSS data and include deaths occurring anywhere in the province. Coding is based on mother's residence. As a result, this source is, since 1988, usually more complete than regionally collected data.

—Data indicated in square brackets [ ] were provided by the Bureau de la Statistique du Québec and are based on the same MSSS data as reported in round brackets. Minor discrepancies between MSSS and BSQ data in 1990 and 1992 are explained by the removal of duplicate records from the BSQ data which remain in the MSSS data.

—We recommend that, for virtually all purposes, the *higher value* from either the BSQ or the Public Health Department records be used as the best estimate. This applies to each cell individually. Do not use multicell totals from just one source. This recommendation is based on the assumption that, in any given year, the BSQ data will include all of the Public Health Department records or vice versa. In other words, for any given year, we assume that there are not records which are exclusive to the Public Health Department *and simultaneously* records exclusive to the BSQ.

SOURCE: Brian Schnarch, Public Health Department, Nunavik RRSSS. Revised May 7, 1996.

risk factors, increased community input on each individual birth works better than blanket evacuation. Colleen Crosbie is attempting to convince the staff to use the Midwives' Alliance of North America (MANA) data form to tally and analyze birth outcomes in a more systematic and detailed way than their statistics are currently collected. (For a detailed explanation of this data form, see Johnson, this volume.) Using the MANA form will enable researchers to compare POV outcomes to those of other provinces and states in North America, including Mexico. We simply modified the form slightly to accommodate such distinctions as a diet that includes walrus flippers and raw caribou.

The POV midwives find it ironic that science, which originally was assumed to provide the logic for evacuation, may turn out instead to show that it is better to avoid evacuation.

Clinical Logic

When the city physician told Elisapee that she might lose her baby if she returned home, he was probably operating out of genuine fear based on his prior clinical experience. He would probably not have taken the time to explain to her exactly how statistically significant his fear was, nor would he necessarily have known.

The elders, meanwhile, have their own clinical biases. They say, for instance, that they did not have as many interventions—inductions, episiotomies, transfers—in the old days, and why are they needed now? One of the unfortunate results of near-total evacuation is that the elders have no opportunity to learn who really could benefit from evacuation and who would benefit more from staying home. The result has been that sometimes those who have refused transfer have been the very ones who most needed to go: those with high blood pressure, or diabetes, or a history of stillbirths. The elders can also be as adamant as physicians about the "right" position for birth: in Dorset it is on your knees, supported in the back and on the sides by three people; in Pangnitung it is lying on your side. Clinical logic is influenced by prior experience.

Thus it seems fortunate that both the Inuit and the Qallunaaq staff at the Maternity in POV give themselves permission to throw out their former sacred cows of maternity management. For example, it has been scientifically shown that smoking increases the risk of postpartum hemorrhage. In the South, the Qallunaaq would most emphatically counsel a pregnant woman to stop smoking. In POV, they proffer that advice, but one of the realities of life is that barely an hour after birth many women are wheeled out to the garage for a smoke. The women consider it to be social therapy, and there is a concern that abrupt nicotine withdrawal in heavy smokers immediately postpartum would be more harmful than continuing to smoke. Those of us who arrive in POV unaccustomed to giving routine oxytocin injections (to avoid postpartum hemorrhage) to low-risk women are rapidly converted to giving the injection with almost every birth.[10] Meanwhile, Inuit midwives diligently accept modern medical training; they learn to draw blood, read lab results, and do clinical reasoning the Southern, Qallunaaq way.

At the POV Maternity, flexibility seems to be the key to clinical success. Job definitions and organizational structures can change according to need in ways that are not always possible in the established pecking orders that entrench themselves in Southern training and clinical settings. For example, while I was there I served as note-taker during some of the births. The coordinator realized how much better it was to have someone other than the student midwives writing notes during a woman's labor. She resolved that thenceforth the maternity workers would take the notes, so that the student midwives would be free to concentrate on being "with woman" during labor and birth. For another example, the "risk factors" that used to be listed on the front page of the mother's chart are now called simply "factors," because the POV Maternity explicitly rejects the medical approach in which every woman is labeled according to her potential risk, with no mention of social factors and special wishes that she may have for her birth.

To date, the Inuit student midwives do not hunger for the theories and details of clinical practice in the same way that the more competitive Southern white midwives do. Inuit midwives do not seek to be "right" about clinical details to prove their expertise, nor do they seek out conferences that focus on such details. (Akinisie Qumaluk says that she prefers gatherings where traditional practices will be discussed.) But in their thoughtful, unpreoccupied way, they are legitimately proud of triumphs demonstrating their clinical skills. Leah Qinuajuak discovered a heart murmur that was missed by a physician in Montreal and a first trimester toxoplasmosis conversion on lab results that had been overlooked by the Qallunaaq midwives. I remember a comment made in 1989 by one of the Inuit women in a nearby settlement after Akinisie had made a presentation to them: "I never knew that Inuit could know so much." This is no longer a "surprise" in the Kativik region of Québec served by the POV midwives.

Cultural Logic

Historically, the Inuit obeyed the laws of nature and of land, community, family, and tradition. This interwoven knowledge system guided their lives to the extent that health and disease were considered the result of abiding by or transgressing the social and spiritual order. Since these factors were interdependent, how a woman's pregnancy and birth transpired would reflect her overall relationship to her cultural and physical environment.

In the 1980s, the obstacles to working with the elders and young women to salvage the former intricate balance and make it congruent with the contemporary Inuit world seemed insurmountable. I also realized that it was going to be difficult to obtain grants to develop programs that would challenge evacuation. In order to get funding, it was politically correct only to collect stories about what birth used to be like, and never hint that we might consider returning birth to the community. We first proposed a study of the history of "traditional midwifery." It became clear that the government was not going to fund something that acknowledged that there had indeed been a functional midwifery system among the Inuit. The letter of response from the federal health minister, Jake Epp, stated, "Birth is safest in the hospital. We cannot fund this project at this time. We wish you every luck in your endeavor." When we used the phrase "traditional childbirth" instead of "traditional midwifery," we got a grant. Even national Inuit organizations find it difficult to receive funding if they threaten the established health administration.

In a similar vein, in the Northwest Territories, where evacuation is still the rule, birth traditions that do not present a threat to the medical system, such as taboos about behavior, eating, and drinking, are not frowned on by health practitioners. In both rural and urban hospitals, even various positions taken in labor and birth can now be negotiable. But the most important cultural factors, such as the Inuit concern about loss of cultural identity from not being born on the land in one's own territory and their concern that the elders have lost to the Southern doctors the prerogative of being proprietors of the authoritative knowledge about birth in their community—these are the areas that the health care system cannot seem to face and act on.

In contrast, Povungnituk not only has confronted the latter two issues, it has also tackled some that are more subtle—for instance, the differences in Qallunaaq and Inuit perceptions of time, the importance of professionalization, and education.

Time.   In a land of long nights and, as the season changes, long days, the nine-to-five job and taking birth control pills—actions that must be performed on schedule, by the clock—become problematic and require vigorous adjustment on the part of the Inuit to a time frame that is irrelevant to their cultural and geographic reality. One of the legends about the Qallunaaq describes them as people who are always in a rush, obsessed, ambitious, boorish, and with an agenda. Such character traits are excused with the explanation that "the boat their mother put them on leaked and they had to frantically bail it out—that is why they are always in a hurry and have too much to do" (Kurelek 1976:88). To a woman in labor it can seem incongruent to accept the authority of a health care practitioner who is always looking at his or her watch. One elder told me that she thought the actual purpose of such behavior was to slow down her labor, that the doctor's diagnosis that her labor was too slow was actually a treatment.

For the midwives and maternity workers at the POV Maternity, the constant focus on work hours and time is a strain on families, as it is anywhere in the world. But the midwives at POV are finding ways of accommodating both Western schedules and their own needs for unscheduled time with friends and family. When Mina and Leah suggested that the midwives have one week off a month, it was put up for discussion and agreed on. The Inuit midwives themselves see their responsibility to make sure that the Maternity runs smoothly and is properly staffed, but they find ways to do this while maintaining their traditional priority on family and friends. This is the Inuit Way.

Professionalization. At a time when the need for "professionalism" is the battle cry in southern Canadian midwifery circles, it is of interest to me that it is not a term I have ever heard used among the elders or young Inuit midwives. Between 1992 and 1994, the introduction of legislation in the provinces of Ontario and Québec required that midwives who had been practicing for many years be "professionally" evaluated. Because most of the white midwives who have been employed at the Maternity in POV are either from Ontario or Québec, the Inuit midwives were able to witness firsthand the problems resulting from the new testing and evaluation process, which was designed under a European model of midwifery care that in some important ways was not responsive to the very real ideological and practical differences between European and Canadian midwifery.[11] As a result, some of the women whom the Inuit midwives considered to be the best Qallunaaq midwives in Québec were found lacking according to the newly introduced criteria.

Additionally, despite the fact that she had been working as a midwife for over five years, Inuit midwife Akinisie's application for licensure was initially turned down in Québec because she did not have a secondary school education. By the time the government got around to reconsidering Akinisie's request, the Maternity had already realized that the evaluation process was inappropriate and had withdrawn Akinisie's application. External validation and the ability to call oneself a licensed professional, so important to the Qallunaaq midwives, seemed to the Inuit to translate into license to consider oneself "above" instead of "with" women. Mina's direct observation of the evaluations was that they rewarded intrusiveness rather than sensitivity to women. As I listened to Akinisie, Mina, and Leah express their concerns, they began to appear to me like three mother beluga whales, riding the tops of the waves with watchful prudence, aware of the dangers of swimming too close to polluted shores.

Midwifery Training: The Inuit Way.   Akinisie says that modeling is the key to training and being a good midwife. This seems to be a part of every aspect of Inuit teaching. Inuit show rather than tell. (I recall watching a team of men who were showing me how to make an igloo in Iqaluit. They went about their work in almost complete silence, stopping once to apologize for the quality of the snow, explaining, "It usually fits together just like Legos," and again to welcome me, once it was done, to the "White House.") The system of midwifery training at the POV Maternity does include class work, but the major method is what Jordan and North American midwives label "apprenticeship" rather than "didactic" learning. It is not apprenticeship as I knew it in Central America—that is, a system by which the apprentice evaluates herself (rather than being tested by the teacher/expert), can see for herself how well she is doing, and takes on new tasks as need and abilities arise. It is not the system of apprenticeship that Jordan describes where "knowledge acquisition occurs, for the most part, without active teacher intervention" ([1978] 1993:194). Each Inuk student is assigned a Qallunaaq midwife teacher, formal classes are given, and written tests are conducted. However, most of the learning is directly acquired through hands-on experience, and the midwives' responsibility to the birthing women and direct sanction or censorship by them is strong. The midwives are embedded in and constantly accountable to their community. For example, Akinisie believes that correct comportment should extend to one's entire life, that midwives have to be models, good mothers, caring, smart. The integrity of the person who is the professional is as important as the instruction they give. Character is the major factor taken into consideration, and the Maternity likes to ask the community: Who do you want as midwives? Who do you consider to have enough integrity to be worthy of the training? Not who had the best marks in high school or who can persuade women to accept interventions. Their apprenticeship takes place not only through their hands-on learning at the Maternity but also in the constant access to the community's broader knowledge base provided by their frequent interactions with the elders and the other women.

Within the Maternity itself, once hired, the talents of each midwife are channeled as they are perceived by the coordinator, the midwife herself, and the other members of the team of midwives. Leah was put in charge of the training and organization of the maternity workers. She is also very capable of standing up to the administrators and physicians; she is being groomed for leadership. Akinisie has a lot of clinical experience and is good at public presentations. Mina is the critic, analyst, and protector of women's confidentiality. Nellie has become particularly adept at dealing with women who need refuge from potentially dangerous family situations. Of course, all of the midwives do all of these things. It is just that some have focused on certain aspects more than others. Professionalism and appearances are not as important to them as strength of purpose and dedication to women and community-centered birth.

Finding one's niche in the evolving culture of the POV Maternity does not just involve the Inuit. Colleen Crosbie, the coordinator, is one of the rare Qallunaaq who has maintained a special intimate relationship with the women of the Maternity, and has stayed there longer than any other southern midwife. They call her "Mom." At perinatal committee meetings, she is able to say the things that need to be said that other people might not want to say; she is forthright and strong-minded but consistently careful to make sure that the Inuit midwives understand that it is their Maternity and they make the rules. Whoever has to fill her shoes in the future will have a difficult task, but one hopes, should she leave, the Inuit midwives will be ready to take over many of the roles that she has played, because of the care she has taken to hand over authority to them whenever possible.

One of the problems the Maternity midwives encounter when they try to relearn lost birth traditions is that the elders conduct no deliveries at the Maternity. In a culture in which demonstration is the key and it is not considered polite to ask an elder a direct question, their expertise is not easily transferable if one cannot watch them in action. Elders are freely invited to the Maternity to act as support for women in labor, and once in a while an elder will be asked to review the traditions and taboos. It is possible that the real key would be to allow elders to conduct births with one of the Inuit midwives present. Still, the Maternity is inside the hospital, and there the elders seem to feel outside of their domain. The answer may be to invite them to work with a trained Inuit midwife in a home birth situation where they would feel less inhibited to share what they know. Mina says that if she has another baby, she would like to have it at home. Memories and storytelling about preevacuation days might flow more easily in such a context.

One of the experiences that most brought home to me how important cultural traditions are to the women happened one day when Mina was in the midst of charting clinical and social health "factors." A young pregnant Qallunaaq woman walked in for her appointment. Mina dropped what she was doing to enthusiastically demonstrate for this white woman the various Inuit taboos: "You shouldn't be standing in that doorway. And don't tie your *kamiks* [boots], tuck them in at the back." [12] Far more interesting than charting, it was a chance to offer something that was hers, from the Inuit store of knowledge, to this Qallunaaq woman.

In sum, the midwives of POV have created their own midwifery culture, which is neither entirely Qallunaaq nor wholly traditional Inuit, but which serves a vibrant group of parents determined to keep birth in their homeland and to benefit from the most appropriate pregnancy and birth care for their community.

Legal Logic

With the appalling Canadian legacy of Inuit and other native land claim disputes, it should not be surprising that Inuit families fear what being born or not being born on their land means to their rights to own it. There are those who believe that evacuation of pregnant women has been a government plot to take away land claims, and that belief has certainly been one of the factors stimulating the return of birth to the community.

While the Inuit communities understand well the land claims issue, other areas of legal logic are less comprehensible to them. Trying to fathom why a physician or nurse would be concerned that an Inuit woman would sue them if something went wrong with a birth merely demonstrates to the Inuit what a different set of rules they live by. What the Qallunaaq fear, as expressed by one administrator at the Northern Obstetric Conference in Churchill in 1988, is that even if the Inuit themselves do not think of it, "some white lawyer" some day is going to convince an Inuk woman to sue a practitioner. Inuit women are always puzzled when I mention this; they tell me that Inuit communities simply do not work that way. Searching for a way to explain to the Qallunaaq how Inuit people maintain law and order, the Inuit Women's Association came forth with a publication that identified the closest Inuit parallel to "legal logic." This publication stated that the traditional method of dealing with unacceptable behavior was "by either ignoring the behavior entirely and withdrawing from the situation, or by mocking, shaming, and gossiping about the person who is acting inappropriately" (Bolt 1990:6).

The settlements are so small (800 to 1,000 people) that if a Qallunaaq acts inappropriately, everyone knows it, and he or she will ultimately be run out of town. Usually the person leaves voluntarily. One can stay if one has the correct attitude; experience is the only teacher. It rarely occurs to anyone to bring legal action, as social sanctions seem sufficient.

When the Inuit settlements were established in the 1950s and 1960s, the Qallunaaq legal system assumed many of the responsibilities of traditional law. Canadian law enforcement agencies like the police and the court system acted as the main mediators in disputes (Bolt 1990:9), and many women came to believe that if they stayed at home or demanded that the nurse do the birth in the nursing station, they might have to face criminal charges. They know better now in POV. Should an attempt ever be made again to remove birth from the community, its people will not be convinced that it is "legal."

Personal Logic

The Inuit midwives, student midwives, and maternity workers hold a special position at the Maternity that is difficult for any Qallunaaq to fill. They have grown up in the community and know the fears and frustrations of the women they serve. They have lived through similar experiences. In this small community that has no halfway house to provide a refuge from family violence, the "family" at the Maternity becomes a haven for pregnant women who need special help. The Inuit midwife's role has naturally evolved to include particular responsibilities of safeguarding informed choice and confidentiality. The following case illustrates the difficulties involved when the Inuit midwives try to preserve a delicate balance between personal logic and clinical and scientific logic.

A woman who had come to the POV Maternity from another settlement had changed her plans about breastfeeding; with the encouragement of the Inuit midwives, she had decided to do it. On the ninth day postpartum the baby had still not gained back its birth weight, and the midwives suggested that the mother try waking the baby up every two hours to nurse. The next day the baby had gained, and the mother's flight home was arranged for two days later. Unfortunately, the following day the baby's weight dropped again and the decision was made to keep her. Both the Qallunaaq and the Inuit midwives involved realized the mother might be feeling as though she were imprisoned in POV, but they were concerned about letting the baby go home because the primary health care practitioner there, a Qallunaaq nurse, had other commitments and would not be immediately available.

> *Qallunaaq midwife (Q.M.) to mother (speaking through a translator):* You're not going to be able to go home because the baby needs to be watched.
>
> [*The grandmother does not agree with this decision and comes to the mother's defense.*]
>
> *Inuk Student Midwife (I.S.M.) to Q.M.:* They'll do the same thing at home as here.
>
> *Q.M.:* But they'll have to do more. It hasn't been enough.
>
> [*The student midwife explains to the mother and grandmother that the problem is probably happening because the mother had a hemorrhage and is not quite strong enough yet to produce all the milk the baby needs. She explains that sometimes they use a feeding tube in such situations. The mother begins to cry.*]
>
> *I.S.M. to Q.M.:* We shouldn't have told the mother she could go, and then take it back.

Q.M. to mother: If you go, you might have to come back. We want the baby finished, ready to be gone.

Grandmother: The baby was born at 36 weeks, and is probably behind in weight because of that, and will gain according to when it was born. Probably in a month it will be OK. . . .

Q.M.: If it was small-for-dates, we are even more concerned. Usually a baby that comes early will be okay in three or four days, with a supplement.

Grandmother: Is the baby going to die?

Q.M.: No, but it could suffer damage, yes. It could become very sick. If it does not grow at all, it will suffer brain damage. We're not worried for today, though.

Grandmother: This is just a baby that was born too soon.

Q.M.: But babies that are born early grow fast, usually, but [turning to student midwife] if that's what she thinks, what can we do?

Grandmother: It's too soon to weigh the baby.

Q.M.: When should we weigh her? We can weigh her on Saturday. Maybe if we see the baby up until Sunday, maybe the nurse-midwife in the community will follow her when she gets home, during the week.

Grandmother: We can get the supplement here?

Q.M.: Yes. If the baby wakes up, we supplement after the next nurse.

Both the Qallunaaq and the Inuk student midwife realized the personal, political, and cultural risks of coercing the mother and grandmother to stay against their will. The decision to go or stay belonged to them. The student midwife recognized that the risk of making the mother feel that a decision not in her or her baby's best interests was being made for her, against her wishes, was greater than the actual risk to the baby, if the baby received special care at home. By the next day, the baby had gained weight but the young mother had stopped breastfeeding. The Inuk student midwife was upset because she felt that the mother had stopped breastfeeding because the midwives had been so adamant about keeping her in POV. To avoid such a problem in the future, at the next Friday meeting of all the midwives and students, it was decided that (a) one should never tell a woman that she can go home until it is known for sure that she can; and (b) the skills of the Inuit maternity worker in the community, where the Qallunaaq nurse may often be unavailable, should be utilized to allow women from that settlement to go home earlier.

Intuitive Logic

Having an intuition about a situation does not necessarily mean that one will act on it. Intuition is a highly personal and fragile phenomenon; when it clashes with the kinds of logic more accepted by the powers that be, the tendency to follow the "more sensible" approach of clinical logic often takes over in decision making. To allow oneself to follow one's intuition requires peace of mind, strength of conviction, and a safe environment (see Davis-Floyd and Davis, this volume).

The elders from the various regions have told me that they have had premonitions of problems regarding certain women, either because they know the woman's family life is problematic or because she has unresolved emotional issues. Transgressions of pregnancy taboos create additional concerns.

Elder Annie Okalik from Pangnirtung told us the following story several years ago. She said she was attending a mother who was unconscious and bleeding terribly after a birth, and the gathering of women realized that the only thing left to do was pray. Annie intuited that it was important that they pray out loud, and the women began to do so in a lilting chant. Annie chuckled as she was telling the story, noting that the mother came around, saying that she felt she was drawn back into the room by a desire to "join in the ruckus."

I have on occasion tried to get the elders and the new midwives to talk about intuitive experiences by sharing with them some of my own. The first time that I remember doing this was with an Inuit elder by the name of Ooksuralik with whom I stayed in Cape Dorset in 1989. I described to her a long labor that I had attended of a first-time mother.

> I got concerned that the mother was holding something back that might be impeding the birth. When I sensed that something was wrong and some obscure thing was holding us up, I asked the mother to tell me about images from the distant past that she might be thinking of, sitting here in her bathtub. Sure enough, she had one—she immediately recounted the memory of a childhood incident involving her favorite doll, which had fallen out of a third-story window. As she watched it fall to the ground, she felt absolutely no compulsion to go down and pick it up. She was feeling the same way now, and so we spent the rest of her labor helping her to become motivated to "go down and pick up her baby, to get it out."

I remember Ooksuralik staring at me intently as I was telling the story. She finally said, "I had no idea that a Qallunaaq could think that way."

The Inuit do not believe that the Qallunaaq can think intuitively because the main types of logic to which whites have demonstrated commitment are clinical expertise and intervention, concern about legal liability, and an arrogant claim to scientific truth. Why share your innermost knowing with someone who may laugh at you or who does not have the psychological maturity to understand you?

The POV Maternity is an environment that creates a feeling of safety, an atmosphere in which intuition can freely flourish. Colleen often asks the midwives and birthing women, "What do you really feel is the right thing to do here?" It's difficult to say whether the Inuit midwives follow their intuition more than the white midwives do, but it seems clear that Inuit women are highly intuitive. I do not see it as my place to go into more depth about intuition and how it is used in the POV Maternity, but I have asked Mina to write down her own experiences with intuition, and we need, together, to address this type of experience in future publications.

In a culture in which a remarkable number of people remember being born, and having dreams about a person who has recently died is one way to know you may name your baby after her or him, it stands to reason that intuition would be respected as a valuable source of authoritative knowledge. It would be encouraging to think that as the Inuit midwives feel increasingly comfortable with clinical and scientific logic, they will also increasingly give themselves permission to cultivate and act on the intuitive. In this effort, they will no doubt be impeded by the Western privileging of other kinds of logic.

Economic Logic

According to one estimate, every time the Maternity midwives do a birth in POV, they save Québec taxpayers approximately $10,000 Canadian (about U.S.$7,000). This figure includes the cost of the plane trip to a southern city, living expenses for a month or more before going into labor, and the often highly technological southern hospital delivery. Because of our Canadian system of comprehensive insurance for health care, individual hospitals and practitioners do not particularly benefit from these high costs. But in the United States, where hospitals and practitioners do profit directly from the high cost of birth, it is questionable whether the savings generated by birth centers such as the POV Maternity would be welcomed.

CONCLUSION

I began by stating that there is a tension between traditional and modern definitions of reproductive risk and normalcy. This chapter has presented an analytical framework that classifies and illuminates the types of logic that compete in most birth settings around the world—a framework useful for showing how some types of logic are given undue authority while others, such as cultural or intuitive logic, are devalued or simply ignored. Traditionally, to the Inuit, birth seemed a natural event, a time for serious reflection and examination of the woman's spiritual and social integration with her community, as upon this hung the success or failure of the birth itself. Today, medical services in most of northern Canada have made birth into an entirely secular affair for which the mother is allowed little responsibility. Traditionally, Inuit women had some small degree of choice about where and with whom to give birth, although those choices were constrained by survival needs and tradition-based customs and taboos. Since the 1960s, their choices have been severely restricted in another way by the medical takeover of Inuit birth. Up until the 1950s, Inuit women had no access to modern medical information and intervention. Today, in most places, they have no choice to refuse it. Traditionally, in many areas, they were put into isolation huts to give birth. With evacuation, they are isolated from their families but exposed to the medical team in the delivery room. Before evacuation, they listened to the elders and the shaman. After, they listened to the doctor. It would be tempting to say that things have not changed much, that evacuation has merely imposed a different authority. But, in fact, evacuation changed things so drastically that it has become one of the greatest affronts to Inuit identity.

The POV Maternity has tried to make a shift in this picture. It is trying to leave behind the pattern of women's victimization in whatever setting, and to balance competing ideologies in a viable way. The women of POV do not buy into the medical myth that more technology equals safer outcome. They balance the clinical risks of harming mothers and babies with the risks of personal trauma and cultural and spiritual assimilation, and find that *when the personal, the spiritual, and the cultural are prioritized, less overall harm occurs*. Thus scientific logic now undergirds their personal and cultural choices. Through the process of reclaiming birth as a part of community life, Inuit women not only have created more choices for themselves but also are coming to learn what choice means. While I realize that anthropologists may have a different perspective on this issue, as a midwife—one who is committed to support women's choices—I can only celebrate such a development.

I have come to see the Inuit experience of evacuation as an example of what can happen when one type of logic gains priority over all the others. The clear need we can observe in Inuit birth for balance among our eight categories of logic sheds light on events elsewhere. As a southern Canadian midwife, I can say that in the South we are not usually brave enough to allow a mother to refuse intervention even if her intuition tells her that the intervention is not needed, because we are so conscious of our legal liabilities. It seems evident that the more fragile types of logic—the cultural, personal, and intuitive forms—are the canaries/beluga whales of our eight-category framework. Even when they are backed up by science, they are undervalued in relation to clinical, legal, and political logic, toward which Southern childbirth is heavily skewed.

There seems to be no system of checks and balances to reconfigure this framework in the South. Yet the Southern system, elsewhere referred to as the "Western" system, dominates worldwide. Our typology of logic could enable policy makers to avoid more mistakes like the evacuation crisis that hit northern Canada. Yet given the current realities and priorities of Western technocratic life, institutionalized respect for the more vulnerable types of logic seems very far away. The World Health Organization has been diligently attempting for more than ten years to propagate public health models "liberating what people already know about health and illness, and legitimizing this knowledge" (North American Working Group on Health 1989; see also Wagner, this volume). Their efforts have been hampered not only by the technomedical establishment but also by the reality that indigenous people have been told for so long that they don't know anything about health care, they often make health care decisions as if they believe it.

Ten years after initiating the Maternity, POV[13] remains the only community in northern Canada to have reclaimed birth, not only geographically but also into the hands of its own midwives.[14] Being made to believe that one's own logic is inferior and unworthy could have sapped the life force of POV, as it has in other communities. Realizing that evacuation was adding to the continuum of dependency on white man's logic and that the Inuit community had been robbed of its own authoritative knowledge over a basic human function was an important step for the people of POV. An equally important step is the realization that as birth returns to the community, "progress" is not synonymous with adopting the logic of the Qallunaaq.

NOTES

Special thanks to the midwives at the Innuulitsivik Maternity in Povungnituk, Québec, Mina Tulugak, Akinisie Qumaluk, Leah Qinuajuak, Nellie Qumaluk, and Colleen Crosbie for their comments on this chapter, and to Robbie Davis-Floyd for her editorial assistance. Thanks also to Brian Schnarch and Steve Hodgins at the Nunavik Regional Board of Health and Social Services (Kuujjuaq), Susan Chatwood, whose statistics appear from her master's thesis in epidemiology at McGill, and Jean-François Proulx, from the Santé/Nunavik/Health in Québec City, who was able to acquire the statistics from le Bureau de la Statistique du Québec, and who was instrumental in initiating the program in Povungnituk to ensure the development of the dream. Finally, thanks to Ken Johnson for epidemiological advice and ongoing support.

1. At a workshop for consultants working in the "developing world" held in Oslo, Norway, prior to the International Confederation of Midwives' Congress in May 1996, I took issue with the term "developing." It is becoming increasingly problematic to apply "developing" to countries that may be heading toward a "goal" that at this point the so-called developed world has supposedly reached, when in fact, parts of the "developed" world should more appropriately be labeled "overdeveloped." A policy maker from Gambia suggested that we're really talking about the "Haves" and the "Have Nots." Perhaps the politically correct term would be "financially challenged." Others used "industrialized" and "nonindustrialized."

But all these commodity and financial terms are found wanting when trying to figure out where the rich oil-producing countries fit; there, in spite of wealth, there is still underdevelopment in meeting basic human needs. The United States, too, while rich in commodity and monetary gain, is sorely lacking in social and health reform. Until we can find more appropriate terms, however, it looks as though "developing" is the word to use here; quotation marks seem to be the operative form of protest.

2. "Inuk" is the singular form of "Inuit," which is the name this group of Arctic people call themselves. They have explicitly rejected the label "Eskimo," which was given to them by other Native American groups and which means "eater of raw meat."

3. In the North, the term Qallunaaq is spelled in various ways depending on the place. Here I use the spelling used in Povungnituk.

4. A hemoglobin level below 110 mg/dL is considered anemia by the World Health Organization.

5. *Hemodilution* refers to the fact that the amount of blood in a pregnant woman's circulation increases as pregnancy advances; it is therefore normal for the hemoglobin to drop.

6. It is true that postpartum hemorrhage can pose greater risk if one has no hemoglobin reserves, but low hemoglobin does not cause postpartum hemorrhage. Whether such a hemorrhage would be life-threatening when the nurse has intravenous equipment is debatable. Postpartum hemorrhage is a frequent occurrence among the Inuit and is tolerated quite well by them. It is managed in home births much the same as in the hospital, with injections of syntocinon (an artificial hormone, a variant of pitocin). There have been a number of postulations about the reason for the high rate of hemorrhage. One is the fact that about 85 percent of the pregnant women are listed as smokers, and there is a known correlation between smoking and postpartum hemorrhage. There has also been an association suggested between the low rate of coronary heart disease and the fact that there is a component of sea mammal meat that acts as a natural anticoagulant. Could it be that this same factor, then, causes women to bleed more easily?

7. In the 1970s the Canadian government tried to expropriate the land in the James Bay Area to build a hydroelectric plant. The people of POV refused to sell their land.

8. Toxoplasmosis is an intracellular parasite transmitted to humans via raw or poorly cooked meat, as well as by cat or bird feces. It is prevalent in sea mammals. If acquired during pregnancy, it can cause serious congenital abnormalities in the fetus.

9. PCBs are organohalides (toxins) that remain stable when ingested in the body, are not metabolized, and accumulate in fat cells.

10. Pitocin is a synthetic form of the natural hormone oxytocin, which stimulates both the frequency and the force of uterine contractions and is often used to stop a hemorrhage. It is given routinely by some practitioners, but many midwives do not give it unless there is a need. The laissez-faire attitude of the Southern midwives was brought into check when they first began realizing how frequently, by Southern definition, Inuit women had hemorrhages (>500 ml and >1,000 ml of

blood loss). More study needs to be done and more precaution taken, however, regarding increased routine use of this "active management" of this stage of labor with medication, not only in the North but also in "developing" countries.

11. See Introduction, note 14, this volume, for more information.

12. How much credibility Inuit women give to these taboos is hard to know and may vary from one person to the next. But they do serve still as important markers of community membership and respect for connection with the past.

13. Editors' note: We have been informed by the author of this chapter that in 1996, Povungnituk changed its name to Puvirnituq.

14. In Rankin Inlet, a project is under way to return birth to the community. However, the births are being attended by nurse-midwives, with no program yet for training Inuit midwives.

REFERENCES

Bildfell, J. A.
 1934 "Medical Reports." National Archives: RG 85/815, files 6954, PP3. Pangnirtung.

Bolt, David
 1990 *The Inuit Way.* Ottawa: Pauktuutit (Inuit Women's Association).

Davis-Floyd, Robbie
 1992 *Birth as an American Rite of Passage.* Berkeley: University of California Press.

Daviss-Putt, Betty Anne
 1990 "Rights of Passage in the North: From Evacuation to the Birth of a Culture." In *Gossip: A Spoken History of Women in the North,* ed. Mary Crnkovich, 91–114. Ottawa: Canadian Arctic Resources Committee.

Daviss-Putt, Betty Anne, and Akalayok Qavavao
 1993 "Informed Choice in Childbirth: Is It Possible in the North?" In *Proceedings of the International Confederation of Midwives 23d International Congress in Vancouver, Canada* 1:518–528. Vancouver, B.C., Canada.

Graeburn, Nelson
 1972 *Eskimos of Northern Canada.* Vol. 2. New Haven, Conn.: HRAFlex Books.

Jenness, D.
 1992 *Part A: The Life of the Copper Eskimos, Canadian Arctic Expedition Report 1913–1918.* Vol. 12. Ottawa: Department of the Naval Service.

Jordan, Brigitte
 [1978] 1993 *Birth in Four Cultures: A Cross-Cultural Investigation of Childbirth in Yucatan, Holland, Sweden and the United States.* 4th ed. Prospect Heights, Ill.: Waveland Press.

Kaufert, Patricia Gilbert, J. D. O'Neil, R. Brown, P. Brown, B. Postl, M. Moffat, B. Binns, and L. Harris
 1988 "Obstetrical Care in Keewatin: Changes in the Place of Birth 1971–1985." In *Circumpolar Health 87,* ed. H. Linderholm, C. Backman, N. Broadbent, and I. Joelsson, 481–484. Oulu, Finland: Nordic Council on Arctic Medical Research.

Kurelek, William
    1988   *The Last of the Arctic.* Toronto: Pagurian Press.

North American and European Consulting Groups (combined consensus)
    1986   "Draft Report on Health Promotion." Unpublished manuscript. Ottawa (November).

O'Neil, John D., and Patricia L. Kaufert
    1990   "The Politics of Obstetric Care: The Inuit Experience." In *Births and Power: Social Change and the Politics of Reproduction,* ed. W. Penn Handwerker, 53–68. Boulder, Colo.: Westview Press.
    1995   " '*Irniktakpunga!*' Sex Determination and the Inuit Struggle for Birthing Rights in Northern Canada." In *Conceiving the New World Order: The Global Politics of Reproduction,* ed. Faye Ginsburg and Rayna Rapp. Berkeley: University of California Press.

Rasmussen, Knud
    1931   *The Netsilik Eskimo: Report of the 5th Thule Expedition 1921–1924.* Vol. 8, nos. 1–2. Copenhagen: Gyldenhal.

Rothman, Barbara Katz
    1982   *In Labor: Women and Power in the Birthplace.* New York: W. W. Norton. (Reprinted in paperback under the title *Giving Birth: Alternatives in Childbirth.* New York: Penguin Books, 1985.)

Weyer, Edward Moffat
    1969   *The Eskimos: Their Environment and Folkways.* New Haven: Yale University Press.

EIGHTEEN

An Ideal of Unassisted Birth

Hunting, Healing, and Transformation among the Kalahari Ju/'hoansi

Megan Biesele

How should I fear childbirth? Isn't it just a thing you do, just quietly give birth alone and then sit up and carry the child in a sling? Doesn't the child just grow up and work for you?

—TKAE//'AE N!A'AN,
/Kae/kae, Botswana, 1 June 1989

CHILDBIRTH, DEATH, AND RITUAL TRANCE

On a spectrum from technologically managed birth (on the left) to personal birthing empowerment privileging the authoritative knowledge of the mother (on the right), Ju/'hoan (San)[1] women of Botswana and Namibia, in southern Africa, stand at the far right end. These women, living until recently as foragers of the Kalahari semidesert, have long pursued a cultural ideal of giving birth outdoors in the bush alone. This ideal is usually achieved after the first birth, which is attended by older female relatives. Lions and other predators make this practice genuinely hazardous, especially as the women also aspire not to make fires to see by if the birth occurs at night. The ecological and historical conditions alone under which Ju/'hoan women have forged their birthing practices provide ample reason for a look at their specific orientations toward authoritative knowledge in childbirth.

I became aware early in my acquaintance with the Ju/'hoansi that childbirth knowledge and the ability to use it in specific ways may have spiritual dimensions for them. The possibility that an ideal of unassisted birth in fact poses a spiritual challenge to Ju/'hoan women, one that is highly valued by their culture, was suggested to me by Melvin Konner. Konner is an anthropologist who studied Ju/'hoan mothers and infants during the 1960s and 1970s, when most of Ju/'hoan subsistence still came from foraging. He also studied the Ju/'hoan healing tradition (itself one of authoritative knowledge for both men and women) as a personal discipline and later went on to obtain his M.D. in the United States. Konner wrote *Becoming a Doctor* (1987) to describe his experience of Western medical education. This chronicle starts from intuitions Konner had early in his anthropological fieldwork about the contrasts between a healing discipline emphasizing accessible authoritative knowledge (though this phrase was not yet in vogue) and one that vests all knowledge in "experts." In particular, he was concerned with the spiritual, transformative aspects of authoritative healing as it existed among the Ju/'hoansi and its possible use as a paradigm in other Ju/'hoan contexts. One of these contexts was birth.

Talking to me and to his wife, Marjorie Shostak, in the early 1970s, when all three of us were doing fieldwork in Botswana, Konner pointed to a possible structural parallel between Ju/'hoan women's birthing practice and the practice of Ju/'hoan men in their culturally valued risking of trance experience. Ju/'hoan men describe going into trance as a kind of death: statements to this effect have been assembled by Richard Katz (1982). Lorna Marshall (1976) wrote that the healers referred to their altered state as "half-death." Daring death seems to be part of cultural maturation for the Ju/'hoansi, as it is in fact for many other groups of people. Both the men's and the women's daring—in trance and in giving birth—seem to function as transformational rites of passage in Ju/'hoan society. Other clues in the symbolism of hunting suggest balanced valuations in Ju/'hoan society between hunting as production and giving birth as reproduction.

Shostak, who later wrote *Nisa: The Life and Words of a !Kung Woman* (1981), and I, in my work on Ju/'hoan women's healing (Biesele 1975b, 1979), often had occasion to return to Konner's original observation. Shostak and Konner collaborated with S. Boyd Eaton on *The Paleolithic Prescription* (Eaton, Shostak, and Konner 1988), which, like Nisa, contains a detailed discussion of Ju/'hoan women's birthing practices. This present work goes one step further to look at the cultural clues linking Ju/'hoan women's display of authoritative knowledge with their transcendent maturational processes. It also assembles symbolic and ritual information to make a case for parallelisms among concepts in domains of hunting and healing with those in the domain of birth. In fact, an evident triad of hunting-healing-birthing ideas in Ju/'hoan society provides a rich matrix for the understanding of this one culture's way of learning to master and live with death and fear.

Keeping in mind my early discussions with Konner and Shostak, I went on to do several years of fieldwork on Ju/'hoan folklore and ritual (Biesele 1978, 1979, 1987). I found many symbolic references to a structural parallelism in ideology between (1) men's daring death in trance and (2) women's braving the challenge of death and transformation in childbirth. These discoveries led me to examine here Ju/'hoan symbolic ideas of

women's altered state healing and reproductive status, using research materials from work I did in the 1970s in Botswana and in the 1980s and
1990s in Namibia (Biesele 1978, 1979, 1987). I also look at the related
ideology of the Ju/'hoan n!ao (or n!ow, or now) complex concerning fate,
which structures childbirth and hunting as symbolic oppositions, using an
idiom of effects on weather and the great meat animals. This symbolic
complex was first described by Lorna Marshall (1957), and I collected further information on it in the 1970s and afterward. Together, the symbolisms of healing, hunting, and childbirth point to a Ju/'hoan preoccupation with the power of altered states. These altered states are viewed as
accessible to all, due to the pervasively available *n/om* (or *n/um,* spiritual
energy) that provides the strength to make change possible in all three
important realms. The democratic dispersal of n/om is ideologically related to the dispersed authority found throughout Ju/'hoan social relations.

The egalitarianism of Ju/'hoan society also joins these symbolisms in a
pervasive insistence on the idea of complementary male and female
strengths. Both men and women, it seems, have ready access in that society
to processes of transformation and self-actualization. What is more, these
processes are integrated by their culture within a gender complementarity
felt to be important to the whole society.

All these factors make it seem appropriate to reexamine Ju/'hoan wom-
en's ways of knowing about birth, their management of fear, and the conceptual space they hold open for themselves in their society by daring this
profound form of creativity. Shostak's work makes possible the use of interview material from the 1970s on the confidence with which Ju/'hoan
women approach birth. "Who told you it was painful?" one woman asked
her. My own more recent experience corroborates her sense of the authority of Ju/'hoan women's knowledge and suggests the symbolic reinforce-
ment that authority receives from many sources in the culture. I propose
in this chapter that the way the Ju/'hoansi honor traditional concepts of
birth's relationships to spiritual initiation and the social maturation process offers vital new cultural perspectives on women's spirituality.

PREVIOUS CROSS-CULTURAL WORK ON WOMEN'S
AUTHORITATIVE KNOWLEDGE IN CHILDBIRTH

During the 1970s and 1980s, a number of anthropologists set out specifically to study birth in non-Western cultures, producing ethnographies that
demonstrate the integrity and viability of indigenous birthing systems (see
Introduction, this volume). Their work generated renewed scholarly interest in the studies of the first Western medical researcher to show apprecia-

tion for the value of non-Western birthways, the physician George J. Engelmann. In 1884 he published *Labor among Primitive Peoples,* showing the physiological benefits of upright birth. He intended to counteract the Western trend toward making women lie down for birth for the convenience of the practitioner.[2] Because he tried to grant authority of knowing to women in other cultures, his work was ignored by his medical contemporaries, who insisted on the sole authority of their own knowledge.

Yet in later years trends in Western women's birthing attitudes have borne Engelmann out. One of several recent proponents of women's authoritative birthing in the United States is Laura Kaplan Shanley. Her *Unassisted Childbirth* (1994) draws together cross-cultural sources, studies and observations of animal birth, and her own experiences of birthing four children alone, to argue for the primacy and sanctity of women's unmediated birth knowing. Shanley's efforts find a powerful single cross-cultural corroboration in Carolyn Sargent's *Maternity, Medicine, and Power* (1989). Sargent makes it clear that rural Bariba people in Benin have long held a preference for solitary delivery and that it is only with pressures for modernization that urban mothers are opting for medically mediated birth. Among the rural Bariba, in contrast, the mother who delivers her child alone in silence is admired.

> Birth represents a rare opportunity for a woman to demonstrate the proverbial virtue of courage and to bring honor to her and her husband's families by her stoic demeanor. The woman who manages to deliver without indicating that she is in labor and without calling for assistance until the child is born is especially esteemed. (Sargent 1989:111)

A similar code of honor regarding pain and courage was observed among the Inuit.

> Managing birth by oneself, or helping other women birth, emerged as a source of pride for women, a public sign of virtue. Competence was linked with the possession of knowledge: "Back then, the women had the knowledge to take care of a woman in labor . . . we were informed by our elders on what to do and what not to do" (Meeting at Rankin Inlet). (O'Neil and Kaufert 1990:56–58)

THE ETHNOGRAPHY OF JU/'HOAN BIRTH

Lorna Marshall wrote that "a woman goes into the bushes apart from the encampment to give birth, either alone or with her own mother. A *n/um k"xau* (*n/omkxao,* medicine man) does not attend her except in the rare instances of a very difficult birth" (1976:166). A more extended discussion of the actual events at birth among the Ju/'hoansi appears in Shostak's oral history, *Nisa.* Supported with lengthy sections of quoted material, Shostak's description of Ju/'hoan birth practices and attitudes is drawn from interviews and from sharing daily life with dozens of women still living mostly from foraging during the late 1960s and early 1970s. In the material below, I quote from the chapter "First Birth," selecting those passages that emphasize cultural beliefs and attitudes toward birthing knowledge and supplementing them with new material from my own work with Ju/'hoan women in 1995. Shostak wrote,

> [The] !Kung ideal of fulfillment can be achieved only after a number of less comfortable stages have been passed. For girls, social recognition and adult status come with motherhood—after a girl has confronted the often frightening events of pregnancy and childbirth. . . . When a second and third moon have passed [without menstruation], probability turns to certainty. Although others may already suspect it, a woman will not speak openly about it until after the next moon passes—in adherence, perhaps, to the general expectation of humility whenever the enviable happens. (1981:177–178)

This "expectation of humility" is an important clue that general Ju-/'hoan attitudes toward correct behavior, very marked (as we see below) in regard to men's hunting, are being applied here to the manner in which pregnancy is socially conducted. Peaceful acceptance of fate meted out by an impersonal providence is also marked, among Ju/'hoansi, as desirable behavior for both men and women. A woman expressed it to me this way during my recent fieldwork: "You 'work' with a man, and if !Xu [God] agrees, you get a child. . . . You don't worry if you feel pain: pain is the sign of the child's existence." Shostak went on, "Pregnant women face childbirth with no medical facilities and with no traditional midwives or other birth specialists to call upon. The prospect of giving birth is frightening, especially for women pregnant for the first time" (1981:179).

My own interviews in 1995 with twenty-one Ju/'hoan women who had given birth revealed that many women still actively desire to give birth alone in the bush. They said that they learned from their mothers what to do during labor and birth and that some of their own women could turn a child if she was presenting wrong. Several women remarked, however, that a few women choose nowadays to go to the clinic "if they are afraid." The Tjum!kui government clinic is between ten and fifty kilometers walking distance from most Nyae Nyae communities. Records are extremely uneven, so it is impossible to know the exact percentage of clinic births that do occur, but I can say with certainty that very few Ju/'hoan women choose to go there to deliver their babies. Distance is not the major deterrent; rather, the high cultural valuation on unassisted birth makes that the ideal to which women themselves aspire. When I asked how experienced birth givers felt about young women who choose to go to the clinic, the answer was, "It is very bad to go and put your crotch in the hands of someone you don't know." The implication was that the woman would lose her control of the process and that her dignity would be compromised. Shostak noted,

> Although solitary childbirth is the stated cultural ideal, other women often help, especially with a first birth. A young woman may prefer to have her mother or other close female relatives with her, but if she is living with her husband's family, she will receive assistance from his female relatives. Even with others present, however, the woman herself is considered responsible— except on the rare occasions when God capriciously intervenes—for the progress of labor and delivery. (1981:179–180)

Acceptance of that responsibility, along with the recognition that labor has its own pace and process that must be honored, marked the comments of all the women I spoke with in 1995. For example, one of them noted, "Our belief is that pushing too hard or too soon can ruin your insides. . . . My own mother didn't push too hard when I was born, and therefore I was fine. . . . Bleeding never fails to stop after a birth; it always stops by itself." Shostak commented,

> An uncomplicated delivery is said to reflect [the woman's] full acceptance of childbearing: she sits quietly, she does not scream or cry out for help, and she stays in control throughout the labor. A difficult delivery, by contrast, shows her ambivalence about the birth, and may even be seen as a rejection of the child. Fear of childbirth is thought to be dangerous, causing tension that makes delivery more difficult. It brings on an even greater danger; however: God, interpreting a woman's apprehension as indicating that the child is not wanted, may kill the child and "take it back to the spirit world." In such cases, the mother may also be taken away. So strong is the !Kung belief in the necessity for facing childbirth bravely that women who prove cowardly may be privately ridiculed, while those who give birth "properly" may be used as models for young girls, who will be encouraged to observe their births. (1981:180)

My interviews in 1995 echoed Shostak's findings. Two women who spoke with me together, collaborating comfortably in the conversation though not always agreeing, told me that "if you give birth alone, you receive praise, and gifts of beads, and cooked food [a special treat]. But if you fear, and surround yourself with people, and give birth inside a house, people will laugh at you and scold you and call you fearful." The anthropologist Patricia Draper (pers. com. 1995) reinforces these comments, affirming that Ju/'hoan women are proud of the achievement of giving birth alone. One woman told Draper that "fear is the worst enemy of childbirth. If you are afraid, the birth will be hard and painful. But if you don't fear the birth will be untroubled."

This emphasis on facing childbirth bravely is part and parcel of a general Ju/'hoan stoicism with regard to pain and death. Shostak described it thus:

> A fifteen-year-old girl who had not yet begun to menstruate responded to my question about childbirth this way: "People tell me that I am female and that I will marry and give birth to a child one day. They also say that giving birth is like something that kills. Those who fear, die and are buried. Those who don't fear, live. A woman who isn't afraid sits quietly; she doesn't walk around or even brush the flies off her face. If she does, others will say that she is afraid and will laugh at her. Her husband will yell at her, too; he will search for a wife who isn't afraid, and their marriage will die. When I look at everything people have told me, I say that childbirth is about death—and that makes me afraid. Am I not afraid of dying?" (1981:180)

Daring death is thus an important part of attaining a Ju/'hoan woman's cultural ideal in regard to birthing.

> A !Kung woman will have, on average, four or five live births during her reproductive life. With each successive birth, she is more likely to attain the ideal of delivering alone. Without telling anyone, she walks a few hundred yards from the village, prepares a cushion of leaves, and gives birth to her child. Accompanied or not, most births occur close enough to the village so that others can hear the baby's first cries. This signals the woman's female relatives and friends that the child has been born and that the mother may welcome assistance in delivering the afterbirth, cutting the umbilical cord, and wiping the baby clean. Perhaps carrying the baby for her, other women will accompany her back to the village. Only the most experienced and determined women insist on being alone during these last stages.
>
>   Although most !Kung women aspire to this ideal, those who actually meet it may be admonished by their closest relatives. One woman was criticized for having exposed herself to danger when she came back with her baby after giving birth alone and at night. She had not asked anyone for help, even after the baby was born. When scolded, she merely said, "Am I not a woman who had a job to do? I went and did it, that's all." (Shostak 1981:181)

Not everyone agreed on just how to fulfill the ideal. In this and other Ju/'hoan instances, the way individuals, male or female, participate in debate about cultural ideals is itself an important act of creating those ideals. Each woman with whom I spoke in 1995 had her own version of how best to live up to cultural expectations. The wide sharing of authoritative knowledge is thus, paradoxically perhaps to Westerners, also highly individualized. Every person gets to tell her own story of childbirth, and though the stories differ, each is in a sense "the same": each is the story of personal authority. Maturing means becoming "the same"—adult, powerful, responsible, productive—in one's own unique way. Shostak continued,

The birth of her first child marks a woman's full entry into adulthood. . . . [W]ith this entrance into the adult world, the young woman becomes the focus of loving attention from family, friends, and in-laws. She may feel that she has proved herself by having faced the ordeal of childbirth and, in most cases, by having produced a healthy child. (1981:182)

The first-birth story recorded by Shostak in *Nisa* affirms the theme of creative interaction between cultural expectation and personal experience in giving birth.

I watched as my mother gave birth to my younger brother. She didn't fear or cry out; she had courage. . . . I wasn't afraid when I saw my mother give birth, and because of that, I went alone. I just sat there until the birth was over; only then did people come to me. . . . While I was pregnant, I'd think, "Here I am, just a child. The old people tell me that childbirth is something that hurts. . . . I know what I'll do—I'll go to the white people and give myself to them. They'll open the mouth of my stomach and take the baby out. That way it won't hurt." Then I thought, "No, even if the pain feels as though I will surely die, I'll just sit there and feel it. Then my child will be born."

. . . We spent the day digging *sha* roots and walking about. My stomach was huge and stood far out. The pains in my lower back came again. I thought, "Am I going to give birth today? I'm only a child. Will I be afraid?" When the pains came again, they hurt for a while and then they were quiet. They came and they went. I thought, "This really hurts. Hey, hey everyone, how come my stomach hurts so much?" But I didn't say anything. Later that night, the pains came again. I thought, "Why should this hurt so much? If only I were here with my mother, then I would be able to cry. But I'm living with other people and I won't cry. If I do, they'll laugh at me and say, 'How come you're already a young woman, yet when you feel the labor, you start to cry?' Later they'll laugh and say I cried during childbirth."

. . . Then I felt something wet, the beginning of the birth. . . . I thought, "Eh, hey, maybe it is the child." I got up, took a blanket, and covered my husband with it; he was still sleeping. Then I took another blanket and my smaller duiker skin covering and I left. . . . I walked a short distance from the village and sat down beside a tree. I sat there and waited; she wasn't ready to be born. I lay down, but still she didn't come out. I sat up again. I leaned against the tree and began to feel the labor. The pains came over and over, again and again. It felt as though the baby was trying to jump right out! . . . I cried out, but only to myself. I thought, "Oh, I almost cried out in my in-laws' village." After she was born . . . I thought, "Is this my child? Who gave birth to this child? . . . A big thing like that? How could it possibly have come out from my genitals?" (Shostak 1981:chap. 8 passim)

The same value on "proving oneself" by meeting cultural expectations through one's personal authority and capability are also expressed in the following birth story (which is highly representative of the other birth

stories I heard) told to me by a young Namibian Ju/'hoan woman, a
mother of three little girls and a boy.

> The first time I gave birth my mother and N/haokxa [her aunt] were with
> me. I felt pain until after the birth, and then I felt fine. I was unhappy while
> in labor, but happy after the child was born. Pain tells you the child is being
> born. Mother told me to cut the cord, and I did. My womb hurt a little
> afterward, so Mother cooked a tea of *makaka* twigs and I felt better.
>
> [The other three times I gave birth alone.] . . . With my last child, I knew
> I was pregnant when I didn't "see the moon" for two or three months and
> then began to feel movement in my womb. I didn't feel any pain because the
> child was all right—I just felt the weight of the child. During the pregnancy
> I ate things that my heart wanted [like *g//uia*, a succulent salad plant], not
> things that smelled bad to me [like meat]. An unborn child really has the say
> over what you will like to eat. Toward the time of birth my nipples got black,
> but I felt no urgency until a clear liquid started coming out of my breasts.
> Then I went to the bush. My husband stayed at the village. I just waited until
> the baby was ready to come out. Her body coming out didn't hurt me; I was
> just a little irritated by the hairs of her head. She came out just fine. I didn't
> push too much, and the child was born easily.
>
> We call the afterbirth the "older sister." It is blood, but we call it the older
> sister of the child. If it refuses to come out, you may die. We don't have any
> medicine to make it come out if it doesn't want to. I breastfed all my babies;
> all of us do. Babies need breast milk. If the milk doesn't come down, we tie
> a string around our breasts until it does.

The value placed in this and Shostak's account on authoritative fearless-
ness and self-confidence is echoed in John Marshall's extraordinary film,
A Curing Ceremony (1973). The film is about a stillbirth and the community's efforts to provide spiritual healing to the laboring woman. Following
are some comments on this event from another of Marshall's films, *N!ai:
The Story of a !Kung Woman.*[3]

> We're scared. Many of us are scared about sleeping with men and having
> babies. Because of the pain and danger. My friend Seg//ae was afraid of
> childbirth. Her stomach was lying there. I didn't know what the matter was.
> But I thought, "That woman is terrified of the childbirth." . . . It was as if she
> was dying. My mother said, "Don't go there. A woman who's going to have
> her very first child shouldn't be afraid of the childbirth. Girls like you, who
> haven't given birth, mustn't watch a woman who fears." But I went and I
> watched. . . . Mother told me I mustn't fear. Because when a woman fears
> childbirth, her baby dies. Her own blood kills it. I thought and thought about
> that. But I didn't become brave right away.

These sentiments are similar to those expressed to Sargent by the Bariba. In fact, both male and female constructs of courage, honor, and pain
are similar for both the Ju/'hoansi and the Bariba. For the Bariba, "pain

. . . relates to a paradigm of male power, expressed in the social realm through warfare and hunting, and of female power, expressed in birthing, an equally dangerous endeavor and one necessary to the survival of the Bariba as a people" (Sargent 1989:178). For the Ju/'hoansi, the gender complementarity with birth is expressed in the realms of hunting and of altered state healing, as we will see in detail below. All these pursuits have in common danger and the necessity to develop courage to face that danger.

THE JU/'HOAN MALE MODEL: EDUCATION FOR TRANSCENDENCE

Becoming brave is the main preoccupation of young Ju/'hoan men in several initiatory contexts. Those aspiring to become healers struggle to gain control of their fear of the spiritual curing journey, which involves an altered state of consciousness. Boys and men learning hunting must brave real dangers from fierce carnivores, poisonous snakes, and cornered prey alike. There are many clues in Ju/'hoan folklore and ritual practice that announce that hunting is an activity for which special power must be cultivated through supernatural disciplines.

Ju/'hoan women, too, become healers and perform cures when they are in an altered state, but most of them aspire to this and achieve it only after their reproductive years have passed. Many (but not all) believe that the "arrows" of the healing power, shot into their bellies by older, experienced healers, are dangerous to unborn children. Thus there is a distinction made by some Ju/'hoansi between men, who may heal at any age, and women, who may "receive the arrows of healing" quite early in life but often have them ritually "removed" for the duration of their childbearing years and do not usually "ask for them again" until quite late in life.

I say "most" and "usually" advisedly. Not all Ju/'hoan women say that their reproductive status is key in whether they ask for n/om (healing energy) and maintain it or not. In 1989 an elderly woman at /Kae/kae told Verna St. Denis and me that she had not had her n/om arrows "removed" while she was in her childbearing years. "I didn't do that," she said. "I wasn't afraid, and gave birth just fine." When we asked her why some other women were afraid to leave the n/om arrows in their stomachs when they gave birth, she replied, "Well, they just did it their own way. I myself didn't do it that way. Some people may fear childbirth, so that's why."

It seems that Ju/'hoan women express in this way an active, energetic, and individual relationship to cultural ideas such as the effect that cultivating altered state healing may have on birth. In both realms, there is creative interaction between cultural expectation and what is actually experienced. As Katz put it in relation to altered state healing, "During the experience itself, cultural concepts and descriptions are not available. So, while there is conceptual clarity, there is experiential mystery" (1976:290). This variability and tolerance make for flexibility in approaches to life career and give scope for each woman to experience her own truth as participating in the cultural ideal.

Similarly, hunting as a realm mainly of male endeavor is entered by some women by choice in a most authoritative way when they begin to help their husbands track animals (see Barclay and Biesele 1998). This often occurs after their children are grown but sometimes even when children are still young. Many young women put their babies in a kaross, or sling, on their backs and accompany their husbands on long forays into the bush to assess and follow promising tracks. Married couples take advantage of the complementarity they have developed in other areas of life to communicate without words in the potentially dangerous and difficult world of hunting.

Complementarity and collaboration are valued throughout the society and its activities. They can be seen as another way in which the society underscores its valuation on individual differences—precisely because difference increases the varied strengths available to all. One context in which the value of working together is especially vivid is that of altered state healing. Men and women healers alike work collaboratively both to heal the ill and to encourage the development of healing power in younger people. Different healers are known for the different strengths they possess, and the sum of their strengths is felt to be greater than the mere addition of what each can do individually.

The initiation and apprenticeship of young healers, mostly men, has been thoroughly described by Katz (1976, 1979, 1982). He and I collaborated on works in which we compared the experiences of Ju/'hoan men and women as healers (Katz and Biesele 1980, 1986); with Verna St. Denis, we have recently completed a book on Ju/'hoan men's and women's healing as practiced under rapidly changing circumstances today (Katz, Biesele, and St. Denis 1997).

In all these publications, the religious and spiritual nature of the dance—which is the most usual site of healing—is unmistakably clear. Its religious orientation has also been fully discussed by Lorna Marshall (1962, 1969, n.d.). These works, like those of other colleagues who have done research with the !Kung-Ju/'hoansi, emphasize the long, highly social nature of the search for courage to dare death in order to heal.

The word for trance, *!aia,* is a derivative of the word *!ai,* which means death or to die. Interviewing men repeatedly about this connection, Richard Katz was finally assured, "Yes, the death we mean is the death that kills us all." Daring an altered or enhanced state that is equated with death requires real dedication. People who do not succeed in becoming healers are said to have feared too much. Facing death for the Ju/'hoansi is also to face n/om, their extremely powerful spiritual energy. N/om is activated at the healing dances, boiling up out of the bellies of the healers into their spines and eventually into their fingers, where it can be used to cure the sick by laying on of hands. The "education for transcendence" referred to in Katz's 1976 article consists in confronting and learning to manage the power of n/om. Going with the flow of energy, rather than opposing it, is an important part of being able to accept and use the energy of n/om.

In his analysis of n/om, Katz draws on Huston Smith's discussion of "transcendence" as a particularly powerful altered state of consciousness, one in which great learning and personal growth are possible: "Transcendence should be defined neither quantitatively as 'more of the same' nor qualitatively as 'better than anything previously experienced' but in terms of the *kind* of value it designates. The effect of its appearance is to counter predicaments that are ingrained in the human situation" (1969:43). Abraham Maslow offered a similar description of "peak experiences," during which "many dichotomies, polarities and conflicts are fused, transcended or resolved." Transcendence, he says, has a "special flavor of . . . surrender before something great" (1962:135).

Education for transcendence, writes Katz, "deals directly with an experiential threshold. It must teach how one can cross the threshold of fear into the state of transcendence. This education must also bring transcendence into ordinary life" (1976:284). Ju/'hoan men regard the social apprenticeship of young men in their sometimes lifelong learning about the ways of n/om as of supreme importance for their society. Often people ask themselves how else they would keep their people alive, were it not for this arduous learning of the healers. Women and men alike thank and praise those who dare n/om's strength to heal others. Experientially, n/om's power is awesome.

> N/om lifts you in your belly and it lifts you in your back, and then you start to shiver. N/om makes you tremble; it's hot. Your eyes are open but you don't look around; you hold your eyes still and look straight ahead. But when you get into !kia (!aia), you're looking around because you see everything, because you see what's troubling everybody. . . . Rapid shallow breathing, that's what draws n/om up, . . . then n/om enters every part of your body, right to the tip of your feet and even your hair. (Quoted in Katz 1976:286)

THE N!AO COMPLEX: MEN'S AND WOMEN'S SYMBOLIC STRENGTH

Menstrual blood and the blood of childbirth also have n/om. The afterbirth and the ground where a child has been born are so full of n/om that a man must not step there: if he did, his power to hunt would be affected.

The n/om of birth and of birthing women is not thought of as unclean but as having a strength equal and opposite to that of men in their hunting power. Both kinds of n/om are necessary to the continuation of society.

Elizabeth Marshall Thomas wrote of this complementarity in her well-known *The Harmless People* ([1959] 1988), written after she and her mother, Lorna Marshall, had spent many months living with Ju/'hoan families. Marshall first wrote about power concepts in hunting and childbirth that involve a supernatural essence called "n!ow" (*n!ao*) in a classic 1957 paper, and has expanded her account for another book, *Beliefs and Rites of the Nyae Nyae !Kung*. Because Thomas's narrative account of the events of birth is presented in a way that flows directly into an account of the symbolic relationship between birth and hunting, I quote extensively from it with her permission.

> We were at her werf at the time, sitting in the shade. That day the young woman had not gone out for veld food, but was lying propped up on her elbow in front of her scherm when suddenly, without telling anyone what was happening, she stood up and walked into the bushes, only to come back some time later with her baby in the fold of her kaross. We might not have known what had happened except that she was smiling a sure, sweet smile because she was pleased with herself. Her belly was flatter, and a tiny foot with a pink sole and curled toes stuck out from her kaross. . . .
>
> When labour starts, the woman does not say what is happening, but lies down quietly in the werf, her face arranged to show nothing, and waits until the pains are very strong and very close together, though not so strong that she will be unable to walk, and then she goes by herself to the veld, to a place she may have chosen ahead of time and perhaps prepared with a bed of grass. If she has not prepared a place, she gathers what grass she can find and, making a little mound of it, crouches above it so that the baby is born onto something soft. Unless the birth is very arduous and someone else is with the woman, the baby is not helped out or pulled, and when it comes the woman saws its cord off with a stick and wipes it clean with grass. Then the mother collects the stained grass, the placenta, and the bloody sand and covers them all with stones or branches, marking the spot with a tuft of grass stuck up in a bush so that no man will step on or over the place. . . . The woman does not bury the placenta, for if she did she would lose her ability to bear more children.
>
> The moment of birth is a very important one for the child and for the mother; it is at this moment that the child acquires a power . . . a supernatural essence that forever after connects the person born with certain forces in the world around him: with weather, with childbearing, with the great game antelope, and with death, and this essence is called the *now* [n!ow, n!ao].
>
> . . . There are two kinds of *now*, a rainy or cold one and a hot or dry one. . . . The effect of *now* is (sometimes) simple. . . . With childbearing for women and with killing the great antelope for men (as the great antelope also have *now*, although the small ones do not) the *now* has a larger, more

complex effect. In these cases the *now* of the hunter interacts with the *now* of the child newly born, and when the blood of the antelope falls upon the ground as the antelope is killed, when the fluid of the womb falls upon the ground at the child's birth, the interaction of *now*s takes place, and this brings a change in the weather. In this way a mother may bring rain or drought when she bears a child, a hunter may bring rain or drought when he kills an animal. . . .

    Now is intangible, mystic, and diffuse, and Bushmen themselves do not fully understand its workings. . . . When the fluid from a mother's womb falls upon the ground the child's *now* is determined, and it is partly for this reason that birth is such a mighty thing. (Thomas [1959] 1988:148–150)

The many rituals surrounding hunting in Ju/'hoan society, especially those connected with hunting the huge, fleshy eland, point to this activity as a supremely important and transcendent one for men. Though the topic is too long to go into deeply here, a few examples of hunting ritual can suggest the depth of the association of hunting with initiations and passages in life (see also Lewis-Williams and Biesele 1978). Young men receive ritual scarifications on their right and left arms for the first time they kill a male and a female, respectively, of each species of the great meat animals. Each of these scarifications is a kind of initiation. They celebrate the young man's entry into fuller and fuller productivity for the society.

Traditionally, obtaining a bride required that a young man hunt down an eland on foot until the antelope tired of running, at which point, ideally, it should be killed not far from where his prospective in-laws were watching. This enormous feat of strength and skill required the equivalent of an altered state, with the prospective husband at the very peak of his powers as a male.

The eland is associated by the Ju/'hoansi with family and fertility and is used as the central symbol in the women's dance of first menstruation, in which both men and women participate. The menstruating girl is sequestered inside a hut, and all the other women dance around the hut for her for some days. They decorate themselves in imitation of eland cows. Men participate from time to time, playing the part of eland bulls. The transformation the girl undergoes at this time has many ramifications for the rain and the health of the land, the ripening bush vegetables, and the hunting powers of young men. As later when she bears a child, creativity and triumph over death are celebrated in her menstrual initiation.

"CHILDBIRTH IS ABOUT DEATH": SPIRITUALITY AND MATURATION

There are very many clues linking the observation of male and female rites of passage in Ju/'hoan society to spiritual triumph over death. Some of these imply enhanced states of consciousness and overcoming fear. Others imply helping to harmonize with the bounteous productivity of nature. Both men and women are encouraged to observe ritual circumspection during these times of passage: not speaking or showing emotion is a common injunction for men in hunting and in learning to heal, and for women in first menstruation and in childbirth. "Not even brushing away flies" is an often-repeated description of the self-control desired in these contexts. One is also not supposed to "brush away flies" or otherwise compromise quiet circumspection when visiting sacred sites like the Tsodilo Hills in Botswana, which have ancient rock paintings and may have been used for initiation.

When men have put an arrow into an animal and are waiting for the poison to do its work, they must never draw attention to this hopeful fact. They invariably say they "have not seen anything" and must comport themselves quietly until they leave their fires again to track the animal to where it will die. Above all, they must not draw attention to themselves in a self-aggrandizing way, or the success of the hunt will be jeopardized. They must emphasize in their demeanor the social nature of their obligation to hunt. Practices of arrow sharing and of meat sharing reinforce their symbolism of egalitarianism and of the leveling of individuals.

Like the women when they leave to give birth quietly and alone, men brave considerable danger and hardship alone in hunting. Though comradeship and cooperation are valued, as is also true of women helping each other in menstruation and birth, there is that moment of solitary truth to be faced by each individual. This is true for each person, man or woman, who aspires to become a healer. "The death that kills us all" must be confronted in everyday life. For the Ju/'hoansi, social contexts like childbirth, hunting, and healing are, in Rayna Rapp's words, "spiritually isomorphic as they grapple with fear and death" (pers. com. 1995).

It is clear, from both archaeological evidence and oral tradition, that Ju/'hoan society has sustained itself through ritual mechanisms like those described above for many thousands of years. It is a society that has institutionalized and celebrated chances for transcendence for each and every person, by idealizing such opportunities for maturation. This emphasis on each individual's experience is of a piece with the society's egalitarianism, which effectively disperses both authority and responsibility. In supporting individuals' processes of maturation, their society nurtures them, but does not shelter them from fearful realities that have the power to transform. As the young girl told Marjorie Shostak, "Childbirth is about death." Perhaps a mature society is one that encourages those who give birth not to hide from pain and ecstasy but squarely to confront them—and death—in that moment of maturation.

NOTES

In some important ways, this chapter is a product of the work of many colleagues. I wish to acknowledge that fact here. My own pre-1995 research work with bearing on this study was not done directly with birthing women; I worked in the areas of altered state healing by both men and women and general cultural symbolism of subsistence, crisis, and transformation (Biesele 1975, 1993). In 1995, however, I began to work with Ju/'hoan women through interviews and through hearing the stories of their birthing experiences. Along with Steve Barclay, an experienced hunter, I also worked with Ju/'hoan husband-and-wife tracking/hunting teams. From these work sources I have presented here a contextualization of Ju/'hoan birth concepts within a matrix of symbolism referring to hunting, healing, and transformation.

For direct observations of women around the time of birth and for historical testimony from birthing Ju/'hoan women spanning a forty-year period, I draw substantially on the work of my female colleagues Lorna Marshall, Elizabeth Marshall Thomas, Patricia Draper, and Marjorie Shostak. This chapter is in a sense a group effort of colleagues who have long been in collaboration with each other, though it has been most expedient to have the information drawn together here by one author. I would further like to acknowledge the excellent work bearing on birth by several of my male colleagues, Melvin Konner, Richard Katz, and John Marshall, who also provided material and insights.

I was brought into contact with the above and other field-workers by being part of the Harvard Kalahari Research Group (HKRG), which worked continuously in northwestern Botswana and northeastern Namibia between 1963 and 1972 under the leadership of Irven DeVore and Richard Lee. Many HKRG members have since maintained contact with me over the years, and I wish to acknowledge here the value to me of our long-term collaboration and reflection processes.

1. Ju/'hoan is the name the people previously referred to as !Kung are opting to call themselves now. The spelling is that of their own new orthography, endorsed by the Ju/'hoan people's movement and accepted by the Namibian government as the official literacy orthography for Ju/'hoan education. An English approximation for the pronunciation of Ju/'hoan (without the clicks) is "ju-twa." In October 1996 the peoples formerly known as "Bushmen" (of whom the Ju/'hoan make up one group) met and decided to accept the general appellation "San."

2. For a summary of Engelmann's work, see Ashford 1988.

3. These films are available from Documentary Educational Resources, 101 Morse St., Watertown, MA 02142.

REFERENCES

Armstrong, Penny, and Sheryl Feldman
    1990   *A Wise Birth.* New York: William Morrow.
Ashford, Janet Isaacs, ed.
    1988   *George Engelmann and "Primitive" Birth.* Solana Beach, Calif.: Janet Isaacs Ashford.

Barclay, Steve, and Megan Biesele
    1998   "Ju/'hoan Women's Knowledge of Tracking and Its Contribution to
        Their Husbands' Hunting Success." Paper prepared for the Eighth Interna-
        tional Conference on Hunting and Gathering Societies, Osaka, Japan.

Biesele, Megan
    1975a   "Song Texts by the Master of Tricks: Kalahari San Thumb Piano Music."
        Botswana Notes and Records, 7:171–188. Gaborone, Botswana: Government
        Printer.
    1975b   "Folklore and Ritual of !Kung Hunter-Gatherers." Ph.D. dissertation,
        Department of Anthropology, Harvard University.
    1976   "Aspects of !Kung Folklore." In *Kalahari Hunter-Gatherers,* ed. Rich-
        ard Lee and Irven DeVore, 24–49. Cambridge, Mass.: Harvard University
        Press.
    1978   "Religion and Folklore." In *The Bushmen,* ed. P. V. Tobias, 162–172. Cape
        Town, South Africa: Human and Rousseau.
    1979   "Old K"xau." In *Shamanic Voices,* ed. Joan Halifax, 54–62. New York:
        Dutton.
    1993   *"Women Like Meat": The Folklore and Foraging Ideology of the Kalahari Ju-
        /'hoan.* Bloomington: Indiana University Press/Johannesburg: Witwaters-
        rand University Press.

Biesele, Megan, ed.
    1987   *The Past and Future of !Kung Ethnography: Critical Reflections and Symbolic
        Perspectives: Essays in Honour of Lorna Marshall.* Hamburg: Helmut Buske
        Verlag.

Chalmers, Beverley
    1990   *African Birth: Childbirth in Cultural Transition.* Johannesburg, South Af-
        rica: Berev Publications.

Davis-Floyd, Robbie
    1992   *Birth as an American Rite of Passage.* Berkeley: University of California
        Press.

Dick-Read, Grantly
    [1944] 1972   *Childbirth Without Fear.* 4th ed. New York: Harper and Row.

Draper, Patricia
    1976   "Social and Economic Constraints on Child Life among the !Kung." In
        Kalahari Hunter-Gatherers, ed. Richard B. Lee and Irven DeVore, 199–217.
        Cambridge, Mass.: Harvard University Press.

Eaton, S. Boyd, Marjorie Shostak, and Melvin Konner
    1988   *The Paleolithic Prescription.* New York: Harper and Row.

Engelmann, George Julius
    1884   *Labor among Primitive Peoples.* St. Louis: J. H. Chambers.

Goldsmith, Judith
    1990   *Childbirth Wisdom from the World's Oldest Societies.* Brookline, Mass.: East
        West Health Books.

Katz, Richard
    1976   "Education for Transcendence: !Kia-Healing with the Kalahari !Kung."
        In *Kalahari Hunter-Gatherers,* ed. Richard Lee and Irven DeVore, 281–301.
        Cambridge, Mass.: Harvard University Press.

1979   "The Painful Ecstasy of Healing." In *Consciousness, Brain, States of Aware-ness, and Mysticism,* ed. D. Goleman and R. Davidson. New York: Harper and Row.

1982   *Boiling Energy: Community Healing among the Kalahari !Kung.* Cambridge, Mass.: Harvard University Press.

Katz, Richard, and Megan Biesele

1980   "Male and Female Approaches to Healing among the Kalahari !Kung." Paper delivered at the workshop "Male/Female Relationships: Ideology and Politics," at the 2d International Conference on Hunting and Gathering So-cieties, Quebec, Canada, 19–24 September.

1986   "!Kung Healing: The Symbolism of Sex Roles and Culture Change." In *The Past and Future of !Kung Ethnography,* ed. Megan Biesele, 195–230. Ham-burg: Helmut Buske Verlag.

Katz, Richard, Megan Biesele, and Verna St. Denis

1997   *"Healing Makes Our Hearts Happy": Spirituality and Transformation among the Ju/'hoansi of the Kalahari.* Rochester, Vt.: Inner Traditions International.

Konner, Melvin

1987   *Becoming a Doctor: A Journey of Initiation in Medical School.* New York: Viking.

Konner, Melvin, and Marjorie Shostak

1987   "Timing and Management of Birth among the !Kung: Biocultural Inter-action in Reproductive Adaptation." *Cultural Anthropology* 2:11–28.

Lewis-Williams, J. David, and Megan Biesele

1978   "Eland Hunting Rituals among Northern and Southern San Groups: Striking Similarities." *Africa* 48(2):117–134.

Marshall, John

1973   *A Curing Ceremony* (video, 8 minutes). Watertown, Mass.: Documentary Educational Resources.

1983   *N!ai: The Story of a !Kung Woman* (film). Watertown, Mass.: Documentary Educational Resources.

Marshall, Lorna

1957   "N!ow." *Africa* 27(3):232–240.

1962   "!Kung Bushman Religious Beliefs." *Africa* 32:221–252.

1969   "The Medicine Dance of the !Kung Bushmen." *Africa* 39:347–381.

1976   *The !Kung of Nyae Nyae.* Cambridge, Mass.: Harvard University Press.

n.d.   *Beliefs and Rites of the Nyae Nyae !Kung.*

Maslow, Abraham

1962   *Toward a Psychology of Being.* Princeton: Van Nostrand.

Moran, Marilyn A.

1981   *Birth and the Dialogue of Love.* Leawood, Kan.: New Nativity Press.

1992   "Attachment and Loss within Marriage: The Effect of the Medical Model of Birthing on the Marital Bond of Love." *Pre- and Perinatal Psychology Journal* 6(4):265–279.

1993   "The Effect of Lovemaking on the Progress of Labor." *Pre- and Perinatal Psychology Journal* 7(3):231–241.

O'Neil, John, and Patricia A. Kaufert

1990   "The Politics of Obstetric Care: The Inuit Experience." In *Births and*

Power: Social Change and the Politics of Reproduction, ed. Penn Handwerker, 53–68. Boulder, Colo.: Westview Press.

Sargent, Carolyn F.

1989   *Maternity, Medicine, and Power: Reproductive Decisions in Urban Benin.* Berkeley: University of California Press.

Shanley, Laura Kaplan

1994   *Unassisted Childbirth.* Westport, Conn.: Bergin and Garvey.

Shostak, Marjorie

1981   *Nisa: The Life and Words of a !Kung Woman.* Cambridge, Mass.: Harvard University Press.

1984   "The Creative Individual in the World of the !Kung San." Paper delivered at the annual meeting of the American Anthropological Association, 15 November.

Smith, Huston

1969   "The Reach and the Grasp: Transcendence Today." In *Transcendence,* ed. H. W. Richardson and D. R. Cutler, 43. Boston: Beacon Press.

Thomas, Elizabeth Marshall

[1959] 1988   *The Harmless People.* Cape Town: AfricaSouth Paperbacks, David Philip.

NOTES ON CONTRIBUTORS

Grace Bascope is a Ph.D. candidate in Medical Anthropology at Southern Methodist University. Formerly she was an assistant professor and deputy director of Family Planning and Maternal Health Clinics in the Department of Obstetrics and Gynecology at the University of Texas Southwestern Medical School. She has administered immunization and tuberculosis control programs in Honduras and Bolivia and most recently has conducted ethnographic fieldwork in Dallas, Texas, Yucatan, Mexico, and Kingston, Jamaica.

Megan Biesele is a social anthropologist who has spent most of her twenty-five-year career involved in development and land rights work with the Ju/'hoan Bushmen of Botswana and Namibia. The research in Ju/'hoan folklore, beliefs, and ritual she carried out for her Ph.D. from Harvard University is now being put to practical use to develop academic curricula in the Ju/'hoan language. She is a member of several ongoing research groups and development teams, each of which involves the close participation of Ju/'hoan women and men.

Carole H. Browner is Professor in the Department of Psychiatry and Biobehavioral Sciences and the Department of Anthropology at the University of California, Los Angeles. She is a medical anthropologist with more than twenty years of research experience in Colombia, Mexico, and the United States on various aspects of the politics of reproduction; she has published widely in this area. Her current work focuses on the considerations Mexican-origin couples take into account when deciding whether to agree to prenatal diagnosis, specifically, how power differences between women and men shape women's decisions about fetal testing.

Beverley Chalmers is a social psychologist involved in research on cross-cultural pregnancy and childbirth and is Associate Professor in the Departments of Obstetrics and Gynaecology and Nursing at the University of Toronto. Formerly she held a professorship in the Department of Psychology, University of the Witwatersrand, Johannesburg, South Africa, and an honorary professorship in the Department of Obstetrics and Gynaecology. She is author of *Pregnancy and Parenthood: Heaven or Hell* and *African Birth: Childbirth in Cultural Transition,* thirteen book chapters, and eighty-six articles, and has given more than two hundred presentations on reproduction in various parts of the world. Since 1991 she has served as a short-term consultant to WHO and UNICEF in Central and Eastern Europe on maternal and infant health and the Baby Friendly Hospital Initiative. She coordinates the Canada–WHO–St. Petersburg Maternal and Child Health Program in St. Petersburg, Russian Federation, supported by the Canadian Department of External Affairs. Since 1993 she has been a core investigator at the University of Toronto Maternal, Infant and Reproductive Health Unit at Women's College, Toronto.

Elizabeth Davis, CPM, has been a midwife, women's health care specialist, educator, and consultant for the past twenty years. She is internationally active in women's rights and is widely sought after for her ability to apply principles of openness and humanism to specific problems. She has served as a representative to the Midwives Alliance of North America and as president of the Midwifery Education and Accreditation Council for the United States. She holds a degree in holistic maternity care from Antioch University and is certified by the North American Registry of Midwives. She lives in Windsor, California, and is the mother of three children. Her books include the classic midwifery text *Heart and Hands: A Midwife's Guide to Pregnancy and Birth; Energetic Pregnancy; Women's Intuition;* and *Women, Sex, and Desire: Exploring Your Sexuality at Every Stage of Life.* Her latest book (with Carol Leonard) is *The Women's Wheel of Life: Thirteen Archetypes of Woman at Her Fullest Power.*

Robbie E. Davis-Floyd is a cultural anthropologist specializing in medical anthropology, ritual and gender studies, and the anthropology of science and technology, and is nationally known as a lecturer in these fields. She is author of *Birth as an American Rite of Passage* and *The Technocratic Body and The Organic Body: Hegemony and Heresy in Women's Birth Choices* (in press); coauthor of *From Doctor to Healer: The Paradigm Shift of Holistic Physicians* (in press); editor of *Birth in Four Cultures,* by Brigitte Jordan (1993), and coeditor of *Intuition: Interdisciplinary Perspectives* and *Cyborg Babies: From Techno-Sex to Techno-Tots.* She is Research Fellow in the Department of Anthropology, University of Texas, Austin, and a Research Associate at Rice University; her current research projects address the politics and professionalization of direct-entry midwives in North America and the oral histories of pioneers of the American space program.

Betty-Anne Daviss has worked as a midwife on five continents over a twenty-year span. Intimately involved with the establishment of midwifery as a profession in Quebec and Ontario, today she is a registered practicing midwife in both provinces. Her experience in studying the dynamics of decision making between health caregivers and clients stems from her original training by traditional midwives in 1975–1978 in Guatemala and her work experience with physicians, government bureaucracies, fundamentalist religions (in the United States and among Afghan refugees in Pakistan), and European midwives. Because of her respect for the traditional midwives with whom she has worked—in Thailand, Afghanistan, Alabama, Nicaragua, and the Canadian North—she has integrated traditional knowledge into modern midwifery practice. She has been involved with the Midwives' Alliance of North America since its inception, and is currently a member of the Midwives Alliance of North America Board and chair of the Statistics and Research Committee.

Deborah Cordero Fiedler has worked in women's health care as a registered nurse and childbirth educator, including three years as a clinical instructor in labor and delivery at Magee Women's Hospital in Pittsburgh. Her research interests in Japanese childbirth practices stem from that work experience. She completed her doctoral work in cultural anthropology at the University of Pittsburgh and is Assistant Professor in Japanese Studies and Women's Studies at Gettysburg College.

Eugenia Georges is Associate Professor of Anthropology at Rice University. Since 1990, she has been conducting research on Greek women's experiences with a variety of new reproductive technologies, and is currently working on a manuscript based on her fieldwork. In addition to her work on health, gender, and the politics of reproduction, she has written on the relationship between health and development in Mexico and on transnational labor migration from the Dominican Republic to New York City. She is the author of *The Making of a Transnational Community: Migration, Development, and Cultural Change in the Dominican Republic.*

Amara Jambai graduated from the Bo Government School in Sierra Leone and qualified in medicine in Craova, Romania. Returning to Sierra Leone, he became a District Medical Officer in the National Health Service. After the civil chaos in Sierra Leone, he was sent by UNICEF to do a short course in maternal and child health at Emory University, then took his M.Sc. in Public Health in Developing Countries at the University of London (London School of Hygiene and Tropical Medicine). He has won a poetry prize and speaks eight languages.

Kenneth C. Johnson, Ph.D., has worked as an epidemiologist in Canada's national health department for the last fifteen years. He directed the national birth defects registry in the late 1980s; since then he has been involved in cancer epidemiology with the National Cancer Institute of Canada. He is currently running a national cancer case-control study with the federal government. For the past seven years he has pursued an interest in perinatal epidemiology, spending three months at the National Perinatal Epidemiology Unit in Oxford in 1991 and providing epidemiologic support to midwives. Since 1991 he has collaborated with the Midwives' Alliance of North America to develop a birth data collection form and run an ongoing data collection project.

Brigitte Jordan, author of *Birth in Four Cultures,* is an anthropologist who studies learning in the workplace and the participatory design of productive, culturally appropriate working and learning environments. She has conducted ethnographic research in industrial and preindustrial communities in this country and abroad, looking at the effectiveness of different modes of learning and the impact of social and technological innovations on work practice. She was Professor of Anthropology and Adjunct Professor of Pediatrics at Michigan State University, where for many years she carried out research and taught in the field of cross-cultural obstetrics and midwifery. During her long tenure as a consultant to WHO in Geneva, she focused on such questions as how to overcome cultural obstacles to the dissemination of information on AIDS and the development of culturally and ecologically appropriate learning materials for maternal and child health. She now does research and consulting at Xerox PARC, an industrial research laboratory in Silicon Valley, California, and at the Institute for Research on Learning, a nonprofit institute devoted to better understanding learning, innovation, and change in all human settings. Her current research and consulting interests revolve around the globally changing nature of work and leisure under the impact of new communication and information technologies and the consequent transformation of ways of life, societal institutions, and global economics. She is at work on *Midwifing the Organization,* a book that applies the principles of midwifery work to the work of corporations.

Sheila Kitzinger is a social anthropologist who studies birth, breastfeeding, and motherhood in different cultures. After reading social anthropology at Oxford, she did research and taught at the University of Edinburgh; her Oxford M.Litt. thesis was on race relations in Britain. Her studies in the culture of childbirth include research on pregnancy and birth among Jamaican women and the induction of labor, episiotomy, epidurals, and women's experiences of hospital care. She has authored more than twenty-five books, some of which have been translated into as many as 19 languages, and is known worldwide as a writer and lecturer. She has inspired three generations of birth activists around the world with her profound understanding of the ways the Western obstetrical system has denied women a satisfying psychosexual experience of birth. In her native England, she has for many years led the national movement for radical improvement in services for childbearing women. She is currently researching the pregnancy and childbirth experiences of women prisoners, asylum seekers, and detainees, and continues to strive for better conditions for women who have no voice. Awarded the MBE for her services to education for birth, she is Honorary Professor at Thames Valley University. Her recent books include *The Year after Childbirth, Ourselves as Mothers, The Complete Book of Pregnancy and Childbirth,* and *Becoming a Grandmother.*

Ellen Lazarus is a social/cultural anthropologist. Her research focuses on human reproduction, women's health issues, and the political economy of medical care; she has published widely on these issues. Having taught at Oberlin College and Cleveland State University, she is currently Adjunct Assistant Professor in the School of Medicine at Case Western Reserve University. Her present projects examine gender and stress in residency training and decision making for hysterectomy.

Carol MacCormack has worked intermittently for over a quarter of a century in West Africa and has also worked in East Africa, Asia, and the Caribbean. She taught anthropology at Cambridge University, the University of London, and Bryn Mawr College. Her work with international agencies such as WHO has included both detailed fieldwork in the interface between anthropology and tropical public health and policy formulation. Her publications include *Ethnography of Fertility and Birth.*

Stacy Leigh Pigg is Assistant Professor of Anthropology at Simon Fraser University in Burnaby, British Columbia. Her fieldwork in the eastern hills of Nepal focused on the cultural politics of national development and on shifting frames of medical knowledge in everyday life. Recent publications include "The Credible and the Credulous: The Question of 'Villagers' Beliefs' in Nepal," *Cultural Anthropology;* "The Social Symbolism of Healing in Nepal," *Ethnology;* and "Inventing Social Categories through Place: Social Representations and Development in Nepal," *Comparative Studies in Society and History.*

Nancy Press is Associate Research Anthropologist in the Department of Psychiatry and Biobehavioral Sciences at the University of California, Los Angeles. Her research focuses on women's health and genetics and the cultural construction of risk. She has published on issues in prenatal diagnosis in the context of a California state-sponsored screening program and is currently investigating attitudes toward genetic susceptibility testing for breast cancer. She is the sole social scientist on the Task Force on Genetic Testing of the NIH Working Group on Ethical, Legal, and Social Implications of the Human Genome Project.

Rayna Rapp teaches anthropology at the Graduate Faculty, New School for Social Research, New York City, where she also chairs a graduate program in gender studies and feminist theory. She has edited *Toward an Anthropology of Women* and has coedited *Promissory Notes, Articulating Hidden Histories,* and *Conceiving the New World Order: The Global Politics of Reproduction.* Her current research on the social impact and cultural meaning of amniocentesis is forthcoming in *Moral Pioneers: Women, Men, and Fetuses on a Frontier of Reproductive Technology.*

Carolyn F. Sargent is Professor of Anthropology and Director of Women's Studies at Southern Methodist University. She received an M.A. from the University of Manchester, England, where she studied as a Marshall Scholar, and a Ph.D. in anthropology from Michigan State University. She has conducted fieldwork in West Africa, Jamaica, and Dallas. She is author of *The Cultural Context of Therapeutic Choice* and *Maternity, Medicine, and Power: Reproductive Decision-Making in Urban Benin.* Her research interests include women's reproductive health, child survival, and bioethics.

Paola Sesia is a Ph.D. candidate in cultural and medical anthropology at the University of Arizona, Tucson. She holds a master's degree in public health from the University of California, Berkeley and is Associate Professor at the Center for Research and Advanced Studies in Social Anthropology (CIESAS) in Oaxaca, Mexico. Her research in Oaxaca has focused on reproductive health, child survival, and medical ethnobotany; she has also collaborated on numerous grass-roots, nongovernmental, and governmental health, nutrition, and development projects.

Jane Szurek holds a Ph.D. in anthropology from Brown University and teaches at the Rhode Island School of Design. She has conducted research on childbirth rituals and differential medical treatment of women in Latin America, on change in the social roles of women in a coal-mining town in northern England, and on shifts in the work roles of urban women in China. Her recent research in Italy and England investigates the social and economic contexts of new birth technologies and women's acceptance or refusal of different ways of birth. She is currently writing a book on birth activists and changes in birthing practices in England, the United States, and Italy.

Wenda R. Trevathan received her Ph.D. in anthropology from the University of Colorado in 1980 and is Professor of Anthropology at New Mexico State

University. Her major research interests are the evolution of human female reproductive behavior, including sexuality, pregnancy, childbirth, and menopause. Her major publications include *Human Birth: An Evolutionary Perspective* and articles on menstrual synchrony, sexuality, and evolutionary medicine. She received the Margaret Mead Award from the American Anthropological Association and the Society for Applied Anthropology in 1990 for her research and publications on childbirth.

Marsden Wagner is an American-born physician, neonatologist, perinatal epidemiologist, and reproductive scientist who, following some years on the faculty at the University of California, Los Angeles, in the Schools of Medicine and Public Health and as co-director of Maternal-Child Health for the California State Department of Public Health, spent fifteen years as director of Women's and Children's Health in the World Health Organization. His special interest is in reproductive health services, including maternity care in industrialized countries. The author of over eighty articles, he has also written five books that have been published in nine languages. He has lectured in over thirty countries and testified before legislators in six countries on issues of reproductive health, as well as before twenty tribunals involving midwives in ten countries. A single father, he raised four children by himself, which, he points out, was a far greater challenge than all of the above.

INDEX

Compositor:	Maple-Vail Book Mfg. Group
Text:	10/12 New Baskerville
Display:	New Baskerville
Printer:	Maple-Vail Book Mfg. Group
Binder:	Maple-Vail Book Mfg. Group